# AMERICAN NOTES

CHARLES DICKENS: Born 1812—Died 1870

## Editor's Note

Americans quickly became enthusiastic admirers of Dickens's works. It was one of the reasons which urged him to make his first visit to the United States—the other (and usual) reason being the search for copy. He went, he saw, he criticised. It is an old story now how the Americans were chagrined by his criticisms, and how resentment softened and died away in the general appreciation of the man and his genius. That the temporary ill-feeling was so soon forgotten is a tribute alike to the hosts and to the guest—who had "no desire to court, by any adventitious means, the popular applause." The visit that resulted in American Notes was made in 1842; and the book was published the same year. Frankly written as are these Notes, it will be seen from the following Life that Dickens was much more critical and outspoken of Americans, their habits and institutions, in his letters to Forster. But when he visited America for the second and last time, he noted "amazing changes"—as he acknowledged in the 1868 postscript to the Notes. By then, resentment had given way to "unsurpassable politeness, delicacy, sweet temper, hospitality," etc., on the part of the criticised Americans. Since 1868 there have been many more amazing changes in the United States : but there has been no change in the affection for Charles Dickens and his works. This edition is printed from the one carefully corrected by the author in 1867–68.

# AMERICAN NOTES

BY

CHARLES DICKENS

LONDON:
HAZELL, WATSON & VINEY, LTD.

# PREFACE

My readers have opportunities of judging for themselves whether the influences and tendencies which I distrusted in America had, at that time, any existence but in my imagination. They can examine for themselves whether there has been anything in the public career of that country since, at home or abroad, which suggests that those influences and tendencies really did exist. As they find the fact, they will judge me. If they discern any evidences of wrong-going, in any direction that I have indicated, they will acknowledge that I had reason in what I wrote. If they discern no such indications, they will consider me altogether mistaken—but not wilfully.

Prejudiced, I am not, and never have been, otherwise than in favour of the United States. I have many friends in America, I feel a grateful interest in the country, I hope and believe it will successfully work out a problem of the highest importance to the whole human race. To represent me as viewing AMERICA with ill-nature, coldness, or animosity, is merely to do a very foolish thing : which is always a very easy one.

# AMERICAN NOTES

## CHAPTER I

### GOING AWAY

I SHALL never forget the one-fourth serious and three-fourths comical astonishment, with which, on the morning of the third of January eighteen-hundred-and-forty-two, I opened the door of, and put my head into, a "state-room" on board the Britannia steam-packet, twelve hundred tons burthen per register, bound for Halifax and Boston, and carrying Her Majesty's mails.

That this state-room had been specially engaged for "Charles Dickens, Esquire, and Lady," was rendered sufficiently clear even to my scared intellect by a very small manuscript, announcing the fact, which was pinned on a very flat quilt, covering a very thin mattress, spread like a surgical plaster on a most inaccessible shelf. But that this was the state-room concerning which Charles Dickens, Esquire, and Lady, had held daily and nightly conferences for at least four months preceding: that this could by any possibility be that small snug chamber of the imagination, which Charles Dickens, Esquire, with the spirit of prophecy strong upon him, had always foretold would contain at least one little sofa, and which his lady, with a modest yet most magnificent sense of its limited dimensions, had from the first opined would not hold more than two enormous portmanteaus in some odd corner out of sight (portmanteaus which could now no more be got in at the door, not to say stowed away, than a giraffe could be persuaded or forced into a flower-pot): that this utterly impracticable, thoroughly hopeless, and profoundly preposterous box, had the remotest reference to, or connection with, those chaste and pretty, not to say gorgeous little bowers, sketched by a masterly hand, in the highly varnished lithographic plan hanging up in the agent's counting-house in the city of London : that this room of state, in short, could be anything but a pleasant fiction and cheerful jest of the captain's, invented and put in practice for the better relish and enjoyment of the real state-room presently to be disclosed:—these were truths which I really could not, for the moment, bring my mind at all to bear upon or comprehend. And I sat down upon a kind of horsehair slab, or perch, of which there were two within; and looked, without any expression of countenance whatever, at some friends who had come on board with us, and who were crushing their faces into all manner of shapes by endeavouring to squeeze them through the small doorway.

We had experienced a pretty smart shock before coming below, which, but that we were the most sanguine people living, might have prepared us for the worst. The imaginative artist to whom I have already made allusion, has depicted in the same great work, a chamber of almost interminable perspective, furnished, as Mr. Robins would say, in a style of more than Eastern splendour, and filled (but not inconveniently so) with groups of ladies and gentlemen, in the very highest state of enjoyment and vivacity. Before descending into the bowels of the ship, we had passed from the deck into a long narrow apartment, not unlike a gigantic hearse with windows in the sides; having at the upper end a melancholy stove, at which three or four chilly stewards were warming their hands; while on either side, extending down its whole dreary length, was a long, long table, over each of which a rack, fixed to the low roof, and stuck full of drinking-glasses and cruet-stands, hinted dismally at rolling seas and heavy weather. I had not at that time seen the ideal presentment of this chamber which has since gratified me so much, but I observed that one of our friends who had made the arrangements for our voyage, turned pale on entering, retreated on the friend behind him, smote his forehead involuntarily, and said below his breath, "Impossible! it cannot be!" or words to that effect. He recovered himself however by a great effort, and after a preparatory cough or two, cried, with a ghastly smile which is still before me, looking at the same time round the walls, "Ha! the breakfast-room, steward—eh?" We all foresaw what the answer must be: we knew the agony he suffered. He had often spoken of *the saloon;* had taken in and lived upon the pictorial idea; had usually given us to understand, at home, that to form a just conception of it, it would be necessary to multiply the size and furniture of an ordinary drawing-room by seven, and then fall short of the reality. When the man in reply avowed the truth; the blunt, remorseless, naked truth; "This is the saloon, sir"—he actually reeled beneath the blow.

In persons who were so soon to part, and interpose between their else daily communication the formidable barrier of many thousand miles of stormy space, and who were for that reason anxious to cast no other cloud, not even the passing shadow of a moment's disappointment or discomfiture, upon the short interval of happy companionship that yet remained to them—in persons so situated, the natural transition from these first surprises was obviously into peals of hearty laughter, and I can report that I, for one, being still seated upon the slab or perch before mentioned, roared outright until the vessel rang again. Thus, in less than two minutes after coming upon it for the first time, we all by common consent agreed that this state-room was the pleasantest and most facetious and capital contrivance possible; and that to have had it one inch larger, would have been quite a disagreeable and deplorable state of things. And with this; and with showing how,—by very nearly closing the door, and twining in and out like serpents, and by counting the little washing slab as standing-room,—we could manage to insinuate four people into it, all at one time; and entreating each other to observe how very airy it was (in dock), and how there was a beautiful port-hole which could be kept open all day (weather permitting), and how there was quite a large bull's-eye just over the looking-glass which would render shaving a perfectly easy and delightful process (when the ship didn't roll too much); we arrived, at last, at the unanimous conclusion that it was rather spacious than otherwise: though I do verily believe that, deducting the two berths, one above the other, than which nothing smaller for sleeping in was ever made except coffins, it was no bigger than one of those hackney cabriolets which have the door behind, and shoot their fares out, like sacks of coals upon the pavement.

Having settled this point to the perfect satisfaction of all parties, concerned and unconcerned, we sat down round the fire in the ladies' cabin—just to try the effect. It was rather dark, certainly; but somebody said, "of course it would be light, at sea," a proposition to which we all assented; echoing "of course, of course;" though it would be exceedingly difficult to say why we thought so. I remember, too, when we had discovered and exhausted another topic of consolation in the circumstance of this ladies' cabin adjoining our state-room, and the consequently immense feasibility of sitting there at all times and seasons, and had fallen into a momentary silence, leaning our faces on our hands and looking at the fire, one of our party said, with the solemn air of a man who had made a discovery, "What a relish mulled claret will have down here!" which appeared to strike us all most forcibly; as though there were something spicy and high-flavoured in cabins, which essentially improved that composition, and rendered it quite incapable of perfection anywhere else.

There was a stewardess, too, actively engaged in producing clean sheets and table-cloths from the very entrails of the sofas, and from unexpected lockers, of such artful mechanism, that it made one's head ache to see them opened one after another, and rendered it quite a distracting circumstance to follow her proceedings, and to find that every nook and corner and individual piece of furniture was something else besides what it pretended to be, and was a mere trap and deception and place of secret stowage, whose ostensible purpose was its least useful one.

God bless that stewardess for her piously fraudulent account of January voyages! God bless her for her clear recollection of the companion passage of last year, when nobody was ill, and everybody dancing from morning to night, and it was "a run" of twelve days, and a piece of the purest frolic, and delight, and jollity! All happiness be with her for her bright face and her pleasant Scotch tongue, which had sounds of old Home in it for my fellow-traveller; and for her predictions of fair winds and fine weather (all wrong, or I shouldn't be half so fond of her); and for the ten thousand small fragments of genuine womanly tact, by which, without piecing them elaborately together, and patching them up into shape and form and case and pointed application, she nevertheless did plainly show that all young mothers on one side of the Atlantic were near and close at hand to their little children left upon the other; and that what seemed to the uninitiated a serious journey, was, to those who were in the secret, a mere frolic, to be sung about and whistled at! Light be her heart, and gay her merry eyes, for years!

The state-room had grown pretty fast; but by this time it had expanded into something quite bulky, and almost boasted a bay-window to view the sea from. So we went upon deck again in high spirits; and there, everything was in such a state of bustle and active preparation, that the blood quickened its pace, and whirled through one's veins on that clear frosty morning with involuntary mirthfulness. For every gallant ship was riding slowly up and down, and every little boat was splashing noisily in the water; and knots of people stood upon the wharf, gazing with a kind of "dread delight" on the far-famed fast American steamer; and one party of men were "taking in the milk," or, in other words, getting the cow on board; and another were filling the icehouses to the very throat with fresh provisions; with butchers'-meat and garden-stuff, pale sucking-pigs, calves' heads in scores, beef, veal, and pork, and poultry out of all proportion; and others were coiling ropes and busy with oakum yarns; and others were lowering heavy packages into the hold; and the purser's head was barely visible as it loomed in a state of exquisite perplexity from the midst of a vast pile of passengers' luggage; and there seemed to be nothing going on anywhere, or uppermost in the mind of anybody, but preparations for this mighty voyage. This, with the bright cold sun, the bracing air, the crisply-curling water, the thin white crust of morning ice upon the decks which crackled with a sharp and cheerful sound beneath the lightest tread, was irresistible. And when, again upon the shore, we turned and saw from the vessel's mast her name signalled in flags of joyous colours, and fluttering by their side the beautiful American banner with its stars and stripes,—the long three thousand miles and more, and, longer still, the six whole months of absence, so dwindled and faded, that the ship had gone out and come home again, and it was broad spring already in the Coburg Dock at Liverpool.

I have not inquired among my medical acquaintance, whether Turtle, and cold Punch, with Hock, Champagne, and Claret, and all the slight et cetera usually included in an unlimited order for a good dinner—especially when it is left to the liberal construction of my faultless friend, Mr. Radley, of the Adelphi Hotel—are peculiarly calculated to suffer a sea-change; or whether a plain mutton-chop, and a glass or two of sherry, would be less likely of conversion into foreign and disconcerting material. My own opinion is, that whether one is discreet or indiscreet in these particulars, on the eve of a sea-voyage, is a matter of little consequence; and that, to use a common phrase, "it comes to very much the same thing in the end." Be this as it may, I know that the dinner of that day was undeniably perfect; that it comprehended all these items, and a great many more; and that we all did ample justice to it. And I know too, that, bating a certain tacit avoidance of any allusion to to-morrow; such as may be supposed to prevail between delicate-minded turnkeys, and a sensitive prisoner who is to be hanged next morning; we got on very well, and, all things considered, were merry enough.

When the morning—*the* morning—came, and we met at breakfast, it was curious to see how eager we all were to prevent a moment's pause in the conversation, and how astoundingly gay everybody was: the forced spirits of each member of the little party having as much likeness to his natural mirth, as hot-house peas at five guineas the quart, resemble in flavour the growth of the dews, and air, and rain of Heaven. But as one o'clock, the hour for going aboard, drew near, this volubility dwindled away by little and little, despite the most persevering efforts to the contrary, until at last, the matter being now quite desperate, we threw off all disguise; openly speculated upon where we should be this time to-morrow, this time next day, and so forth; and entrusted a vast number of messages to those who intended returning to town that night, which were to be delivered at home and elsewhere without fail, within the very shortest possible space of time after the arrival of the railway train at Euston Square. And commissions and remembrances do so crowd upon one at such a time, that we were still busied with this employment when we found ourselves fused, as it were, into a dense conglomeration of passengers and passengers' friends and passengers' luggage, all jumbled together on the deck of a small steamboat, and panting and snorting off to the packet, which had worked out of dock yesterday afternoon and was now lying at her moorings in the river.

And there she is! all eyes are turned to where she lies, dimly discernible through the gathering fog of the early winter afternoon; every finger is pointed in the same direction; and murmurs of interest and admiration—as "How beautiful she looks!" "How trim she is!" —are heard on every side. Even the lazy gentleman with his hat on one side and his hands in his pockets, who has dispensed so much consolation by inquiring with a yawn of another gentleman whether he is "going across"—as if it were a ferry—even he condescends to look that way, and nod his head, as who should say, "No mistake about *that*:" and not even the sage Lord Burleigh in his nod, included half so much as this lazy gentleman of might who has made the passage (as everybody on board has found out already; it's impossible to say how) thirteen times without a single accident! There is another passenger very much wrapped-up, who has been frowned down by the rest, and morally trampled upon and crushed, for presuming to inquire with a timid interest how long it is since the poor President went down. He is standing close to the lazy gentleman, and says

American Notes

with a faint smile that he believes She is a very strong Ship; to which the lazy gentleman, looking first in his questioner's eye and then very hard in the wind's, answers unexpectedly and ominously, that She need be. Upon this the lazy gentleman instantly falls very low in the popular estimation, and the passengers, with looks of defiance, whisper to each other that he is an ass, and an impostor, and clearly don't know anything at all about it.

But we are made fast alongside the packet, whose huge red funnel is smoking bravely, giving rich promise of serious intentions. Packing-cases, portmanteaus, carpet-bags, and boxes, are already passed from hand to hand, and hauled on board with breathless rapidity. The officers, smartly dressed, are at the gangway handing the passengers up the side, and hurrying the men. In five minutes' time, the little steamer is utterly deserted, and the packet is beset and over-run by its late freight, who instantly pervade the whole ship, and are to be met with by the dozen in every nook and corner: swarming down below with their own baggage, and stumbling over other people's; disposing themselves comfortably in wrong cabins, and creating a most horrible confusion by having to turn out again; madly bent upon opening locked doors, and on forcing a passage into all kinds of out-of-the-way places where there is no thoroughfare; sending wild stewards, with elfin hair, to and fro upon the breezy decks on un-intelligible errands, impossible of execution: and in short, creating the most extraordinary and bewildering tumult. In the midst of all this, the lazy gentleman, who seems to have no luggage of any kind—not so much as a friend, even—lounges up and down the hurricane deck, coolly puffing a cigar; and, as this unconcerned demeanour again exalts him in the opinion of those who have leisure to observe his proceedings, every time he looks up at the masts, or down at the decks, or over the side, they look there too, as wondering whether he sees anything wrong anywhere, and hoping that, in case he should, he will have the goodness to mention it.

What have we here? The captain's boat! and yonder the captain himself. Now, by all our hopes and wishes, the very man he ought to be! A well-made, tight-built, dapper little fellow; with a ruddy face, which is a letter of invitation to shake him by both hands at once; and with a clear, blue honest eye, that it does one good to see one's sparkling image in. "Ring the bell!" "Ding, ding, ding!" the very bell is in a hurry. "Now for the shore—who's for the shore?"—"These gentlemen, I am sorry to say." They are away, and never said, Good b'ye. Ah! now they wave it from the little boat. "Good b'ye! Good b'ye!" Three cheers from them; three more from us; three more from them: and they are gone.

To and fro, to and fro, to and fro again a hundred times! This waiting for the latest mail-bags is worse than all. If we could have gone off in the midst of that last burst, we should have started triumphantly: but to lie here, two hours and more in the damp fog, neither staying at home nor going abroad, is letting one gradually down into the very depths of dulness and low spirits. A speck in the mist, at last! That's something. It is the boat we wait for! That's more to the purpose. The captain appears on the paddle-box with his speaking trumpet; the officers take their stations; all hands are on the alert; the flagging hopes of the passengers revive; the cooks pause in their savoury work, and look out with faces full of interest. The boat comes alongside; the bags are dragged in anyhow, and flung down for the moment anywhere. Three cheers more: and as the first one rings upon our ears, the vessel throbs like a strong giant that has just received the breath of life; the two great wheels turn fiercely round for the first time; and the noble ship, with wind and tide astern, breaks proudly through the lashed and foaming water.

## CHAPTER II

### THE PASSAGE OUT

WE all dined together that day; and a rather formidable party we were: no fewer than eighty-six strong. The vessel being pretty deep in the water, with all her coals on board and so many passengers, and the weather being calm and quiet, there was but little motion; so that before the dinner was half over, even those passengers who were most distrustful of themselves plucked up amazingly; and those who in the morning had returned to the universal question, "Are you a good sailor?" a very decided negative, now either parried the inquiry with the evasive reply, "Oh! I suppose I'm no worse than anybody else;" or, reckless of all moral obligations, answered boldly "Yes:" and with some irritation too, as though they would add, "I should like to know what you see in *me*, sir, particularly, to justify suspicion!"

Notwithstanding this high tone of courage and confidence, I could not but observe that very few remained long over their wine; and that everybody had an unusual love of the open air; and that the favourite and most coveted seats were invariably those nearest to the door. The tea-table, too, was by no means as well attended as the dinner-table; and there was less whist-playing than might have been expected. Still, with the exception of one lady, who had retired with some precipitation at dinner-time, immediately after being assisted to the finest cut of a very yellow boiled leg of mutton with very green capers, there were no invalids as yet; and walking, and smoking, and drinking of brandy-and-water (but always in the open air), went on with unabated spirit, until eleven o'clock or thereabouts, when "turning in"—no sailor of seven hours' experience talks of going to bed—became the order of the night. The perpetual tramp of boot-heels on the decks gave place to a heavy silence, and the whole human freight was stowed away below, excepting a very few stragglers, like myself, who were probably, like me, afraid to go there.

To one unaccustomed to such scenes, this is a very striking time on shipboard. Afterwards, and when its novelty had long worn off, it never ceased to have a peculiar interest and charm for me. The gloom through which the great black mass holds its direct and certain course; the rushing water, plainly heard, but dimly seen; the broad, white, glistening track, that follows in the vessel's wake; the men on the lookout forward, who would be scarcely visible against the dark sky, but for their blotting out some score of glistening stars; the helmsman at the wheel, with the illuminated card before him, shining, a speck of light amidst the darkness, like something sentient and of Divine intelligence; the melancholy sighing of the wind through block, and rope, and chain; the gleaming forth of light from every crevice, nook, and tiny piece of glass about the decks, as though the ship were filled with fire in hiding, ready to burst through any outlet, wild with its resistless power of death and ruin. At first, too, and even when the hour, and all the objects it exalts, have come to be familiar, it is difficult, alone and thoughtful, to hold them to their proper shapes and forms. They change with the wandering fancy; assume the semblance of things left far away; put on the well-remembered aspect of favourite places dearly loved; and even people them with shadows. Streets, houses, rooms; figures so like their usual occupants, that they have startled me by their reality, which far exceeded, as it seemed to me, all power of mine to conjure up the absent; have, many and many a time, at such an hour, grown suddenly out of objects with whose real look, and use, and purpose, I was as well acquainted as with my own two hands.

My own two hands, and feet likewise, being very cold, however, on this particular occasion, I crept below at midnight. It was not exactly comfortable below. It was decidedly close; and it was impossible to be unconscious of the presence of that extraordinary compound of strange smells, which is to be found nowhere but on board ship, and which is such a subtle perfume that it seems to enter at every pore of the skin, and whisper of the hold. Two passengers' wives (one of them my own) lay already in silent agonies on the sofa; and one lady's maid (*my* lady's) was a mere bundle on the floor, execrating her destiny, and pounding her curl-papers among the stray boxes. Everything sloped the wrong way: which in itself was an aggravation scarcely to be borne. I had left the door open, a moment before, in the bosom of a gentle declivity, and, when I turned to shut it, it was on the summit of a lofty eminence. Now every plank and timber creaked, as if the ship were made of wicker-work; and now crackled, like an enormous fire of the driest possible twigs. There was nothing for it but bed; so I went to bed.

It was pretty much the same for the next two days, with a tolerably fair wind and dry weather. I read in bed (but to this hour I don't know what) a good deal; and reeled on deck a little; drank cold

brandy-and-water with an unspeakable disgust, and ate hard biscuit
perseveringly: not ill, but going to be.

It is the third morning. I am awakened out of my sleep by a
dismal shriek from my wife, who demands to know whether there's
any danger. I rouse myself, and look out of bed. The water-jug is
plunging and leaping like a lively dolphin; all the smaller articles are
afloat, except my shoes, which are stranded on a carpet-bag, high
and dry, like a couple of coal-barges. Suddenly I see them spring into
the air, and behold the looking-glass, which is nailed to the wall,
sticking fast upon the ceiling. At the same time the door entirely
disappears, and a new one is opened in the floor. Then I begin to
comprehend that the state-room is standing on its head.

Before it is possible to make any arrangement at all compatible
with this novel state of things, the ship rights. Before one can say
"Thank Heaven!" she wrongs again. Before one can cry she *is*
wrong, she seems to have started forward, and to be a creature
actually running of its own accord, with broken knees and failing
legs, through every variety of hole and pitfall, and stumbling constantly. Before one can so much as wonder, she takes a high leap into
the air. Before she has well done that, she takes a deep dive into the
water. Before she has gained the surface, she throws a summerset.
The instant she is on her legs, she rushes backward. And so she goes
on staggering, heaving, wrestling, leaping, diving, jumping, pitching,
throbbing, rolling, and rocking: and going through all these movements, sometimes by turns, and sometimes altogether: until one feels
disposed to roar for mercy.

A steward passes. "Steward!" "Sir?" "What *is* the matter? what
*do* you call this?" "Rather a heavy sea on, sir, and a head-wind."

A head-wind! Imagine a human face upon the vessel's prow, with
fifteen thousand Samsons in one bent upon driving her back, and
hitting her exactly between the eyes whenever she attempts to
advance an inch. Imagine the ship herself, with every pulse and
artery of her huge body swollen and bursting under this maltreatment, sworn to go on or die. Imagine the wind howling, the sea
roaring, the rain beating: all in furious array against her. Picture the
sky both dark and wild, and the clouds, in fearful sympathy with the
waves, making another ocean in the air. Add to all this, the clattering
on deck and down below; the tread of hurried feet; the loud hoarse
shouts of seamen; the gurgling in and out of water through the
scuppers; with, every now and then, the striking of a heavy sea upon
the planks above, with the deep, dead, heavy sound of thunder heard
within a vault;—and there is the head-wind of that January morning.

I say nothing of what may be called the domestic noises of the
ship: such as the breaking of glass and crockery, the tumbling down
of stewards, the gambols, overhead, of loose casks and truant dozens
of bottled porter, and the very remarkable and far from exhilarating
sounds raised in their various state-rooms by the seventy passengers
who were too ill to get up to breakfast. I say nothing of them: for

although I lay listening to this concert for three or four days, I don't think I heard it for more than a quarter of a minute, at the expiration of which term, I lay down again, excessively sea-sick.

Not sea-sick, be it understood, in the ordinary acceptation of the term: I wish I had been: but in a form which I have never seen or heard described, though I have no doubt it is very common. I lay there, all the day long, quite coolly and contentedly; with no sense of weariness, with no desire to get up, or get better, or take the air; with no curiosity, or care, or regret, of any sort or degree, saving that I think I can remember, in this universal indifference, having a kind of lazy joy—of fiendish delight, if anything so lethargic can be dignified with the title—in the fact of my wife being too ill to talk to me. If I may be allowed to illustrate my state of mind by such an example, I should say that I was exactly in the condition of the elder Mr. Willet, after the incursion of the rioters into his bar at Chigwell. Nothing would have surprised me. If, in the momentary illumination of any ray of intelligence that may have come upon me in the way of thoughts of Home, a goblin postman, with a scarlet coat and bell, had come into that little kennel before me, broad awake in broad day, and, apologising for being damp through walking in the sea, had handed me a letter directed to myself, in familiar characters, I am certain I should not have felt one atom of astonishment: I should have been perfectly satisfied. If Neptune himself had walked in, with a toasted shark on his trident, I should have looked upon the event as one of the very commonest everyday occurrences.

Once—once—I found myself on deck. I don't know how I got there, or what possessed me to go there, but there I was; and completely dressed too, with a huge pea-coat on, and a pair of boots such as no weak man in his senses could ever have got into. I found myself standing, when a gleam of consciousness came upon me, holding on to something. I don't know what. I think it was the boatswain: or it may have been the pump: or possibly the cow. I can't say how long I had been there; whether a day or a minute. I recollect trying to think about something (about anything in the whole wide world, I was not particular) without the smallest effect. I could not even make out which was the sea, and which the sky, for the horizon seemed drunk, and was flying wildly about in all directions. Even in that incapable state, however, I recognised the lazy gentleman standing before me: nautically clad in a suit of shaggy blue, with an oilskin hat. But I was too imbecile, although I knew it to be he, to separate him from his dress; and tried to call him, I remember, *Pilot*. After another interval of total unconsciousness, I found he had gone, and recognised another figure in its place. It seemed to wave and fluctuate before me as though I saw it reflected in an unsteady looking-glass; but I knew it for the captain; and such was the cheerful influence of his face, that I tried to smile: yes, even then I tried to smile. I saw by his gestures that he addressed me; but it was a long time before I could make out that he remonstrated against my standing up to my knees in water—as I was; of course I don't know why. I tried to thank him, but couldn't. I could only point to my boots—or wherever I supposed my boots to be—and say in a plaintive voice, "Cork soles:" at the same time endeavouring, I am told, to sit down in the pool. Finding that I was quite insensible, and for the time a maniac, he humanely conducted me below.

There I remained until I got better: suffering, whenever I was recommended to eat anything, an amount of anguish only second to that which is said to be endured by the apparently drowned, in the process of restoration to life. One gentleman on board had a letter of introduction to me from a mutual friend in London. He sent it below with his card, on the morning of the head-wind; and I was long troubled with the idea that he might be up, and well, and a hundred times a day expecting me to call upon him in the saloon. I imagined him one of those cast-iron images—I will not call them men—who ask, with red faces, and lusty voices, what sea-sickness means, and whether it really is as bad as it is represented to be. This was very torturing indeed; and I don't think I ever felt such perfect gratification and gratitude of heart, as I did when I heard from the ship's doctor that he had been obliged to put a large mustard poultice on this very gentleman's stomach. I date my recovery from the receipt of that intelligence.

It was materially assisted though, I have no doubt, by a heavy gale of wind, which came slowly up at sunset, when we were about ten days out, and raged with gradually increasing fury until morning, saving that it lulled for an hour a little before midnight. There was something in the unnatural repose of that hour, and in the after gathering of the storm, so inconceivably awful and tremendous, that its bursting into full violence was almost a relief.

The labouring of the ship in the troubled sea on this night I shall never forget. "Will it ever be worse than this?" was a question I had often heard asked, when everything was sliding and bumping about, and when it certainly did seem difficult to comprehend the possibility of anything afloat being more disturbed, without toppling over and going down. But what the agitation of a steam-vessel is, on a bad winter's night in the wild Atlantic, it is impossible for the most vivid imagination to conceive. To say that she is flung down on her side in the waves, with her masts dipping into them, and that, springing up again, she rolls over on the other side, until a heavy sea strikes her with the noise of a hundred great guns, and hurls her back—that she stops, and staggers, and shivers, as though stunned, and then, with a violent throbbing at her heart, darts onward like a monster goaded into madness, to be beaten down, and battered, and crushed, and leaped on by the angry sea—that thunder, lightning, hail, and rain, and wind, are all in fierce contention for the mastery—that every plank has its groan, every nail its shriek, and every drop of water in the great ocean its howling voice—is nothing. To say that all is grand, and all appalling and horrible in the last degree, is nothing. Words

cannot express it. Thoughts cannot convey it. Only a dream can call
it up again, in all its fury, rage, and passion.

And yet, in the very midst of these terrors, I was placed in a situation so exquisitely ridiculous, that even then I had as strong a sense
of its absurdity as I have now, and could no more help laughing than
I can at any other comical incident, happening under circumstances
the most favourable to its enjoyment. About midnight we shipped a
sea, which forced its way through the skylights, burst open the doors
above, and came raging and roaring down into the ladies' cabin, to
the unspeakable consternation of my wife and a little Scotch lady—
who, by the way, had previously sent a message to the captain by the
stewardess, requesting him, with her compliments, to have a steel
conductor immediately attached to the top of every mast, and to the
chimney, in order that the ship might not be struck by lightning.
They and the handmaid before mentioned, being in such ecstasies of
fear that I scarcely knew what to do with them, I naturally bethought
myself of some restorative or comfortable cordial; and nothing better
occurring to me, at the moment, than hot brandy-and-water, I procured a tumbler full without delay. It being impossible to stand or sit
without holding on, they were all heaped together in one corner of a
long sofa—a fixture extending entirely across the cabin—where they
clung to each other in momentary expectation of being drowned.
When I approached this place with my specific, and was about to
administer it with many consolatory expressions to the nearest
sufferer, what was my dismay to see them all roll slowly down to the
other end! And when I staggered to that end, and held out the glass
once more, how immensely baffled were my good intentions by the
ship giving another lurch, and their all rolling back again! I suppose
I dodged them up and down this sofa for at least a quarter of an
hour, without reaching them once; and by the time I did catch them,
the brandy-and-water was diminished, by constant spilling, to a
teaspoonful. To complete the group, it is necessary to recognise in
this disconcerted dodger, an individual very pale from sea-sickness,
who had shaved his beard and brushed his hair last, at Liverpool: and
whose only article of dress (linen not included) were a pair of dread-
nought trousers; a blue jacket, formerly admired upon the Thames at
Richmond; no stockings; and one slipper.

Of the outrageous antics performed by that ship next morning;
which made bed a practical joke, and getting up, by any process short
of falling out, an impossibility; I say nothing. But anything like the
utter dreariness and desolation that met my eyes when I literally
"tumbled up" on deck at noon, I never saw. Ocean and sky were all
of one dull, heavy, uniform, lead colour. There was no extent of prospect even over the dreary waste that lay around us, for the sea ran
high, and the horizon encompassed us like a large black hoop. Viewed
from the air, or some tall bluff on shore, it would have been imposing
and stupendous, no doubt; but seen from the wet and rolling decks, it
only impressed one giddily and painfully. In the gale of last night the

life-boat had been crushed by one blow of the sea like a walnut-shell;
and there it hung dangling in the air: a mere faggot of crazy boards.
The planking of the paddle-boxes had been torn sheer away. The
wheels were exposed and bare; and they whirled and dashed their
spray about the decks at random. Chimney, white with crusted salt;
topmasts struck; storm-sails set; rigging all knotted, tangled, wet,
and drooping: a gloomier picture it would be hard to look upon.

I was now comfortably established by courtesy in the ladies' cabin,
where, besides ourselves, there were only four other passengers.
First, the little Scotch lady before mentioned, on her way to join her
husband at New York, who had settled there three years before.
Secondly and thirdly, an honest young Yorkshireman, connected
with some American house; domiciled in that same city, and carrying
thither his beautiful young wife to whom he had been married but
a fortnight, and who was the fairest specimen of a comely English
country girl I have ever seen. Fourthly, fifthly, and lastly, another
couple: newly married too, if one might judge from the endearments
they frequently interchanged: of whom I know no more than that
they were rather a mysterious run-away kind of couple; that the lady
had great personal attractions also; and that the gentleman carried
more guns with him than Robinson Crusoe, wore a shooting-coat,
and had two great dogs on board. On further consideration, I remember that he tried hot roast pig and bottled ale as a cure for sea-sickness; and that he took these remedies (usually in bed) day after day,
with astonishing perseverance. I may add, for the information of the
curious, that they decidedly failed.

The weather continuing obstinately and almost unprecedentedly
bad, we usually straggled into this cabin, more or less faint and miserable, about an hour before noon, and lay down on the sofas to recover;
during which interval, the captain would look in to communicate the
state of the wind, the moral certainty of its changing to-morrow (the
weather is always going to improve to-morrow, at sea), the vessel's
rate of sailing, and so forth. Observations there were none to tell us
of, for there was no sun to take them by. But a description of one day
will serve for all the rest.   Here it is.

The captain being gone, we compose ourselves to read, if the place
be light enough; and if not, we doze and talk alternately. At one, a
bell rings, and the stewardess comes down with a steaming dish of
baked potatoes, and another of roasted apples; and plates of pig's
face, cold ham, salt beef; or perhaps a smoking mess of rare hot
collops. We fall to upon these dainties; eat as much as we can (we
have great appetites now); and are as long as possible about it. If the
fire will burn (it *will* sometimes) we are pretty cheerful. If it won't,
we all remark to each other that it's very cold, rub our hands, cover
ourselves with coats and cloaks, and lie down again to doze, talk,
and read (provided as aforesaid), until dinner-time. At five, another
bell rings, and the stewardess reappears with another dish of potatoes
—boiled this time—and store of hot meat of various kinds: not for-

getting the roast pig, to be taken medicinally. We sit down at table again (rather more cheerfully than before); prolong the meal with a rather mouldy dessert of apples, grapes, and oranges; and drink our wine and brandy-and-water. The bottles and glasses are still upon the table, and the oranges and so forth are rolling about according to their fancy and the ship's way, when the doctor comes down, by special nightly invitation, to join our evening rubber: immediately on whose arrival we make a party at whist, and as it is a rough night and the cards will not lie on the cloth, we put the tricks in our pockets as we take them. At whist we remain with exemplary gravity (deducting a short time for tea and toast) until eleven o'clock, or thereabouts; when the captain comes down again, in a sou'-wester hat tied under his chin, and a pilot-coat: making the ground wet where he stands. By this time the card-playing is over, and the bottles and glasses are again upon the table; and after an hour's pleasant conversation about the ship, the passengers, and things in general, the captain (who never goes to bed, and is never out of humour) turns up his coat collar for the deck again; shakes hands all round; and goes laughing out into the weather as merrily as to a birthday party.

As to daily news, there is no dearth of that commodity. This passenger is reported to have lost fourteen pounds at Vingt-et-un in the saloon yesterday; and that passenger drinks his bottle of champagne every day, and how he does it (being only a clerk), nobody knows. The head engineer has distinctly said that there never was such times—meaning weather—and four good hands are ill, and have given in, dead beat. Several berths are full of water, and all the cabins are leaky. The ship's cook, secretly swigging damaged whisky, has been found drunk; and has been played upon by the fire-engine until quite sober. All the stewards have fallen down-stairs at various dinner-times, and go about with plasters in various places. The baker is ill, and so is the pastry-cook. A new man, horribly indisposed, has been required to fill the place of the latter officer; and has been propped and jammed up with empty casks in a little house upon deck, and commanded to roll out pie-crust, which he protests (being highly bilious) it is death to him to look at. News! A dozen murders on shore would lack the interest of these slight incidents at sea.

Divided between our rubber and such topics as these, we were running (as we thought) into Halifax Harbour, on the fifteenth night, with little wind and a bright moon—indeed, we had made the Light at its outer entrance, and put the pilot in charge—when suddenly the ship struck upon a bank of mud. An immediate rush on deck took place of course; the sides were crowded in an instant; and for a few minutes we were in as lively a state of confusion as the greatest lover of disorder would desire to see. The passengers, and guns, and water-casks, and other heavy matters, being all huddled together aft, however, to lighten her in the head, she was soon got off; and after some driving on towards an uncomfortable line of objects (whose vicinity had been announced very early in the disaster by a loud cry

of "Breakers a-head!") and much backing of paddles, and heaving of
the lead into a constantly decreasing depth of water, we dropped
anchor in a strange outlandish-looking nook which nobody on board
could recognise, although there was land all about us, and so close
that we could plainly see the waving branches of the trees.

It was strange enough, in the silence of midnight, and the dead
stillness that seemed to be created by the sudden and unexpected
stoppage of the engine which had been clanking and blasting in our
ears incessantly for so many days, to watch the look of blank
astonishment expressed in every face: beginning with the officers,
tracing it through all the passengers, and descending to the very
stokers and furnacemen, who emerged from below, one by one, and
clustered together in a smoky group about the hatchway of the
engine-room, comparing notes in whispers. After throwing up a few
rockets and firing signal guns in the hope of being hailed from the
land, or at least of seeing a light—but without any other sight or
sound presenting itself—it was determined to send a boat on shore.
It was amusing to observe how very kind some of the passengers
were, in volunteering to go ashore in this same boat: for the general
good, of course: not by any means because they thought the ship
in an unsafe position, or contemplated the possibility of her heeling
over in case the tide were running out. Nor was it less amusing
to remark how desperately unpopular the poor pilot became in
one short minute. He had had his passage out from Liverpool, and
during the whole voyage had been quite a notorious character, as a
teller of anecdotes and cracker of jokes. Yet here were the very men
who had laughed the loudest at his jests, now flourishing their fists in
his face, loading him with imprecations, and defying him to his teeth
as a villain!

The boat soon shoved off, with a lantern and sundry blue lights on
board; and in less than an hour returned; the officer in command
bringing with him a tolerably tall young tree, which he had plucked
up by the roots, to satisfy certain distrustful passengers whose minds
misgave them that they were to be imposed upon and shipwrecked,
and who would on no other terms believe that he had been ashore, or
had done anything but fraudulently row a little way into the mist,
specially to deceive them and compass their deaths. Our captain had
foreseen from the first that we must be in a place called the Eastern
passage; and so we were. It was about the last place in the world in
which we had any business or reason to be, but a sudden fog, and
some error on the pilot's part, were the cause. We were surrounded by
banks, and rocks, and shoals of all kinds, but had happily drifted, it
seemed, upon the only safe speck that was to be found thereabouts.
Eased by this report, and by the assurance that the tide was past the
ebb, we turned in at three o'clock in the morning.

I was dressing about half-past nine next day, when the noise above
hurried me on deck. When I had left it overnight, it was dark, foggy,
and damp, and there were bleak hills all round us. Now, we were

gliding down a smooth, broad stream, at the rate of eleven miles an hour: our colours flying gaily; our crew rigged out in their smartest clothes; our officers in uniform again; the sun shining as on a brilliant April day in England; the land stretched out on either side, streaked with light patches of snow; white wooden houses; people at their doors; telegraphs working; flags hoisted; wharfs appearing; ships; quays crowded with people; distant noises; shouts; men and boys running down steep places towards the pier: all more bright and gay and fresh to our unused eyes than words can paint them. We came to a wharf, paved with uplifted faces; got alongside, and were made fast, after some shouting and straining of cables; darted, a score of us along the gangway, almost as soon as it was thrust out to meet us, and before it had reached the ship—and leaped upon the firm glad earth again!

I suppose this Halifax would have appeared an Elysium, though it had been a curiosity of ugly dulness. But I carried away with me a most pleasant impression of the town and its inhabitants, and have preserved it to this hour. Nor was it without regret that I came home, without having found an opportunity of returning thither, and once more shaking hands with the friends I made that day.

It happened to be the opening of the Legislative Council and General Assembly, at which ceremonial the forms observed on the commencement of a new Session of Parliament in England were so closely copied, and so gravely presented on a small scale, that it was like looking at Westminster through the wrong end of a telescope. The governor, as her Majesty's representative, delivered what may be called the Speech from the Throne. He said what he had to say manfully and well. The military band outside the building struck up "God save the Queen " with great vigour before his Excellency had quite finished; the people shouted; the in's rubbed their hands; the out's shook their heads; the Government party said there never was such a good speech; the Opposition declared there never was such a bad one; the Speaker and members of the House of Assembly withdrew from the bar to say a great deal among themselves and do a little: and, in short, everything went on, and promised to go on, just as it does at home upon the like occasions.

The town is built on the side of a hill, the highest point being commanded by a strong fortress, not yet quite finished. Several streets of good breadth and appearance extend from its summit to the water-side, and are intersected by cross streets running parallel with the river. The houses are chiefly of wood. The market is abundantly supplied; and provisions are exceedingly cheap. The weather being unusually mild at that time for the season of the year, there was no sleighing: but there were plenty of those vehicles in yards and by-places, and some of them, from the gorgeous quality of their decorations, might have " gone on" without alteration as triumphal cars in a melodrama at Astley's. The day was uncommonly fine; the air bracing and healthful; the whole aspect of the town cheerful, thriving, and industrious.

We lay there seven hours, to deliver and exchange the mails. At length, having collected all our bags and all our passengers (including two or three choice spirits, who, having indulged too freely in oysters and champagne, were found lying insensible on their backs in unfrequented streets), the engines were again put in motion, and we stood off for Boston.

Encountering squally weather again in the Bay of Fundy, we tumbled and rolled about as usual all that night and all next day. On the next afternoon, that is to say, on Saturday, the twenty-second of January, an American pilot-boat came alongside, and soon afterwards the Britannia steam-packet, from Liverpool, eighteen days out, was telegraphed at Boston.

The indescribable interest with which I strained my eyes, as the first patches of American soil peeped like molehills from the green sea, and followed them, as they swelled, by slow and almost imperceptible degrees, into a continuous line of coast, can hardly be exaggerated. A sharp keen wind blew dead against us; a hard frost prevailed on shore; and the cold was most severe. Yet the air was so intensely clear, and dry, and bright, that the temperature was not only endurable, but delicious.

How I remained on deck, staring about me, until we came alongside the dock, and how, though I had had as many eyes as Argus, I should have had them all wide open, and all employed on new objects —are topics which I will not prolong this chapter to discuss. Neither will I more than hint at my foreigner-like mistake in supposing that a party of most active persons, who scrambled on board at the peril of their lives as we approached the wharf, were newsmen, answering to that industrious class at home; whereas, despite the leathern wallets of news slung about the necks of some, and the broad sheets in the hands of all, they were Editors, who boarded ships in person (as one gentleman in a worsted comforter informed me), "because they liked the excitement of it." Suffice it in this place to say, that one of these invaders, with a ready courtesy for which I thank him here most gratefully, went on before to order rooms at the hotel; and that when I followed, as I soon did, I found myself rolling through the long passages with an involuntary imitation of the gait of Mr. T. P. Cooke, in a new nautical melodrama.

"Dinner, if you please," said I to the waiter.

"When?" said the waiter.

"As quick as possible," said I.

"Right away?" said the waiter.

After a moment's hesitation, I answered " No," at hazard.

"*Not* right away?" cried the waiter, with an amount of surprise that made me start.

I looked at him doubtfully, and returned, "No; I would rather have it in this private room. I like it very much."

At this, I really thought the waiter must have gone out of his mind:

as I believe he would have done, but for the interposition of another man, who whispered in his ear, "Directly."

"Well! and that's a fact!" said the waiter, looking helplessly at me: "Right away."

I saw now that "Right away" and "Directly" were one and the same thing. So I reversed my previous answer, and sat down to dinner in ten minutes afterwards; and a capital dinner it was.

The hotel (a very excellent one) is called the Tremont House. It has more galleries, colonnades, piazzas, and passages than I can remember, or the reader would believe.

# CHAPTER III

## BOSTON

IN all the public establishments of America, the utmost courtesy prevails. Most of our Departments are susceptible of considerable improvement in this respect, but the Custom-house above all others would do well to take example from the United States and render itself somewhat less odious and offensive to foreigners. The servile rapacity of the French officials is sufficiently contemptible; but there is a surly boorish incivility about our men, alike disgusting to all persons who fall into their hands, and discreditable to the nation that keeps such ill-conditioned curs snarling about its gates.

When I landed in America, I could not help being strongly impressed with the contrast their Custom-house presented, and the attention, politeness and good humour with which its officers discharged their duty.

As we did not land at Boston, in consequence of some detention at the wharf, until after dark, I received my first impressions of the city in walking down to the Custom-house on the morning after our arrival, which was Sunday. I am afraid to say, by the way, how many offers of pews and seats in church for that morning were made to us, by formal note of invitation, before we had half finished our first dinner in America, but if I may be allowed to make a moderate guess, without going into nicer calculation, I should say that at least as many sittings were proffered us, as would have accommodated a score or two of grown-up families. The number of creeds and forms of religion to which the pleasure of our company was requested, was in very fair proportion.

Not being able, in the absence of any change of clothes, to go to church that day, we were compelled to decline these kindnesses, one and all; and I was reluctantly obliged to forego the delight of hearing Dr. Channing, who happened to preach that morning for the first time in a very long interval. I mention the name of this distinguished and accomplished man (with whom I soon afterwards had the pleasure of becoming personally acquainted), that I may have the gratification of recording my humble tribute of admiration and respect for his high abilities and character; and for the bold philanthropy with which he has ever opposed himself to that most hideous blot and foul disgrace—Slavery.

To return to Boston. When I got into the streets upon this Sunday morning, the air was so clear, the houses were so bright and gay; the signboards were painted in such gaudy colours; the gilded letters were so very golden; the bricks were so very red, the stone was so very white, the blinds and area railings were so very green, the knobs and plates upon the street doors so marvellously bright and twinkling; and all so slight and unsubstantial in appearance— that every thoroughfare in the city looked exactly like a scene in a pantomime. It rarely happens in the business streets that a tradesman, if I may venture to call anybody a tradesman, where everybody is a merchant, resides above his store; so that many occupations are often carried on in one house, and the whole front is covered with boards and inscriptions. As I walked along, I kept glancing up at these boards, confidently expecting to see a few of them change into something; and I never turned a corner suddenly without looking out for the clown and pantaloon, who, I had no doubt, were hiding in a doorway or behind some pillar close at hand. As to Harlequin and Columbine, I discovered immediately that they lodged (they are always looking after lodgings in a pantomime) at a very small clockmaker's one story high, near the hotel; which, in addition to various symbols and devices, almost covering the whole front, had a great dial hanging out—to be jumped through, of course.

The suburbs are, if possible, even more unsubstantial-looking than the city. The white wooden houses (so white that it makes one wink to look at them), with their green jalousie blinds, are so sprinkled and dropped about in all directions, without seeming to have any root at all in the ground; and the small churches and chapels are so prim, and bright, and highly varnished; that I almost believed the whole affair could be taken up piecemeal like a child's toy, and crammed into a little box.

The city is a beautiful one, and cannot fail, I should imagine, to impress all strangers very favourably. The private dwelling-houses are, for the most part, large and elegant; the shops extremely good; and the public buildings handsome. The State House is built upon the summit of a hill, which rises gradually at first, and afterwards by a steep ascent, almost from the water's edge. In front is a green enclosure, called the Common. The site is beautiful: and from the top there is a charming panoramic view of the whole town and neighbourhood. In addition to a variety of commodious offices, it contains two handsome chambers; in one the House of Representatives of the State hold their meetings: in the other, the Senate. Such proceedings as I saw here, were conducted with perfect gravity and decorum;

and were certainly calculated to inspire attention and respect.

There is no doubt that much of the intellectual refinement and superiority of Boston, is referable to the quiet influence of the University of Cambridge, which is within three or four miles of the city. The resident professors at that university are gentlemen of learning and varied attainments; and are, without one exception that I can call to mind, men who would shed a grace upon, and do honour to, any society in the civilised world. Many of the resident gentry in Boston and its neighbourhood, and I think I am not mistaken in adding, a large majority of those who are attached to the liberal professions there, have been educated at this same school. Whatever the defects of American universities may be, they disseminate no prejudices; rear no bigots; dig up the buried ashes of no old superstitions; never interpose between the people and their improvement; exclude no man because of his religious opinions; above all, in their whole course of study and instruction, recognise a world, and a broad one too, lying beyond the college walls.

It was a source of inexpressible pleasure to me to observe the almost imperceptible, but not less certain effect, wrought by this institution among the small community of Boston; and to note at every turn the humanising tastes and desires it has engendered; the affectionate friendships to which it has given rise; the amount of vanity and prejudice it has dispelled. The golden calf they worship at Boston is a pigmy compared with the giant effigies set up in other parts of that vast counting-house which lies beyond the Atlantic; and the almighty dollar sinks into something comparatively insignificant, amidst a whole Pantheon of better gods.

Above all, I sincerely believe that the public institutions and charities of this capital of Massachusetts are as nearly perfect, as the most considerate wisdom, benevolence, and humanity, can make them. I never in my life was more affected by the contemplation of happiness, under circumstances of privation and bereavement, than in my visits to these establishments.

It is a great and pleasant feature of all such institutions in America, that they are either supported by the State or assisted by the State; or (in the event of their not needing its helping hand) that they act in concert with it, and are emphatically the people's. I cannot but think, with a view to the principle and its tendency to elevate or depress the character of the industrious classes, that a Public Charity is immeasurably better than a Private Foundation, no matter how munificently the latter may be endowed. In our own country, where it has not, until within these later days, been a very popular fashion with governments to display any extraordinary regard for the great mass of the people or to recognise their existence as improvable creatures, private charities, unexampled in the history of the earth, have arisen, to do an incalculable amount of good among the destitute and afflicted. But the government of the country, having neither act nor part in them, is not in the receipt of any portion of the gratitude they inspire; and, offering very little shelter or relief beyond that which is to be found in the workhouse and the jail, has come, not unnaturally, to be looked upon by the poor rather as a stern master, quick to correct and punish, than a kind protector, merciful and vigilant in their hour of need.

The maxim that out of evil cometh good, is strongly illustrated by these establishments at home; as the records of the Prerogative Office in Doctors' Commons can abundantly prove. Some immensely rich old gentleman or lady, surrounded by needy relatives, makes, upon a low average, a will a-week. The old gentleman or lady, never very remarkable in the best of times for good temper, is full of aches and pains from head to foot; full of fancies and caprices; full of spleen, distrust, suspicion, and dislike. To cancel old wills, and invent new ones, is at last the sole business of such a testator's existence; and relations and friends (some of whom have been bred up distinctly to inherit a large share of the property, and have been, from their cradles, specially disqualified from devoting themselves to any useful pursuit, on that account) are so often and so unexpectedly and summarily cut off, and re-instated, and cut off again, that the whole family, down to the remotest cousin, is kept in a perpetual fever. At length it becomes plain that the old lady or gentleman has not long to live; and the plainer this becomes, the more clearly the old lady or gentleman perceives that everybody is in a conspiracy against their poor old dying relative; wherefore the old lady or gentleman makes another last will—positively the last this time—conceals the same in a china teapot, and expires next day. Then it turns out, that the whole of the real and personal estate is divided between half-a-dozen charities; and that the dead and gone testator has in pure spite helped to do a great deal of good, at the cost of an immense amount of evil passion and misery.

The Perkins Institution and Massachusetts Asylum for the Blind, at Boston, is superintended by a body of trustees who make an annual report to the corporation. The indigent blind of that state are admitted gratuitously. Those from the adjoining state of Connecticut, or from the states of Maine, Vermont, or New Hampshire, are admitted by a warrant from the state to which they respectively belong; or, failing that, must find security among their friends, for the payment of about twenty pounds English for their first year's board and instruction, and ten for the second. "After the first year," say the trustees, "an account current will be opened with each pupil; he will be charged with the actual cost of his board, which will not exceed two dollars per week;" a trifle more than eight shillings English; "and he will be credited with the amount paid for him by the state, or by his friends; also with his earnings over and above the cost of the stock which he uses; so that all his earnings over one dollar per week will be his own. By the third year it will be known whether his earnings will more than pay the actual cost of his board; if they should, he will have it at his option to remain and receive his earnings, or not. Those who prove unable to earn their own livelihood will not be retained; as it is not desirable to convert the establishment into an almshouse, or to retain any but working bees in the hive. Those who by physical or mental imbecility are disqualified from work, are thereby disqualified from being members of an industrious community; and they can be better provided for in establishments fitted for the infirm."

I went to see this place one very fine winter morning: an Italian sky above, and the air so clear and bright on every side, that even my eyes, which are none of the best, could follow the minute lines and scraps of tracery in distant buildings. Like most other public institutions in America, of the same class, it stands a mile or two without the town, in a cheerful healthy spot; and is an airy, spacious, handsome edifice. It is built upon a height, commanding the harbour. When I paused for a moment at the door, and marked how fresh and free the whole scene was—what sparkling bubbles glanced upon the waves, and welled up every moment to the surface, as though the world below, like that above, were radiant with the bright day, and gushing over in its fulness of light: when I gazed from sail to sail away upon a ship at sea, a tiny speck of shining white, the only cloud upon the still, deep, distant blue—and, turning, saw a blind boy with his sightless face addressed that way, as though he too had some sense within him of the glorious distance: I felt a kind of sorrow that the place should be so very light, and a strange wish that for his sake it were darker. It was but momentary, of course, and a mere fancy, but I felt it keenly for all that.

The children were at their daily tasks in different rooms, except a few who were already dismissed, and were at play. Here, as in many institutions, no uniform is worn; and I was very glad of it, for two reasons. Firstly, because I am sure that nothing but senseless custom and want of thought would reconcile us to the liveries and badges we are so fond of at home. Secondly, because the absence of these things presents each child to the visitor in his or her own proper character, with its individuality unimpaired; not lost in a dull, ugly, monotonous repetition of the same unmeaning garb: which is really an important consideration. The wisdom of encouraging a little harmless pride in personal appearance even among the blind, or the whimsical absurdity of considering charity and leather breeches inseparable companions, as we do, requires no comment.

Good order, cleanliness, and comfort, pervaded every corner of the building. The various classes, who were gathered round their teachers, answered the questions put to them with readiness and intelligence, and in a spirit of cheerful contest for precedence which pleased me very much. Those who were at play, were gleesome and noisy as other children. More spiritual and affectionate friendships appeared to exist among them, than would be found among other young persons suffering under no deprivation; but this I expected and was prepared to find. It is a part of the great scheme of Heaven's merciful consideration for the afflicted.

In a portion of the building, set apart for that purpose, are work-shops for blind persons whose education is finished, and who have acquired a trade, but who cannot pursue it in an ordinary manu-factory because of their deprivation. Several people were at work here; making brushes, mattresses, and so forth; and the cheerfulness, industry, and good order discernible in every other part of the build-ing, extended to this department also.

On the ringing of a bell, the pupils all repaired, without any guide or leader, to a spacious music-hall, where they took their seats in an orchestra erected for that purpose, and listened with manifest delight to a voluntary on the organ, played by one of themselves. At its con-clusion, the performer, a boy of nineteen or twenty, gave place to a girl; and to her accompaniment they all sang a hymn, and afterwards a sort of chorus. It was very sad to look upon and hear them, happy though their condition unquestionably was; and I saw that one blind girl, who (being for the time deprived of the use of her limbs, by illness) sat close beside me with her face towards them, wept silently the while she listened.

It is strange to watch the faces of the blind, and see how free they are from all concealment of what is passing in their thoughts; observ-ing which, a man with eyes may blush to contemplate the mask he wears. Allowing for one shade of anxious expression which is never absent from their countenances, and the like of which we may readily detect in our own faces if we try to feel our way in the dark, every idea, as it rises within them, is expressed with the lightning's speed and nature's truth. If the company at a rout, or drawing-room at court, could only for one time be as unconscious of the eyes upon them as blind men and women are, what secrets would come out, and what a worker of hypocrisy this sight, the loss of which we so much pity, would appear to be!

The thought occurred to me as I sat down in another room, before a girl, blind, deaf, and dumb; destitute of smell; and nearly so of taste: before a fair young creature with every human faculty, and hope, and power of goodness and affection, inclosed within her deli-cate frame, and but one outward sense—the sense of touch. There she was, before me; built up, as it were, in a marble cell, impervious to any ray of light, or particle of sound; with her poor white hand peeping through a chink in the wall, beckoning to some good man for help, that an Immortal soul might be awakened.

Long before I looked upon her, the help had come. Her face was radiant with intelligence and pleasure. Her hair, braided by her own hands, was bound about a head, whose intellectual capacity and development were beautifully expressed in its graceful outline, and its broad open brow; her dress, arranged by herself, was a pattern of neatness and simplicity; the work she had knitted, lay beside her; her writing-book was on the desk she leaned upon.—From the mournful ruin of such bereavement, there had slowly risen up this gentle, tender, guileless, grateful-hearted being.

Like other inmates of that house, she had a green ribbon bound round her eyelids. A doll she had dressed lay near upon the ground. I took it up, and saw that she had made a green fillet such as she wore herself, and fastened it about its mimic eyes.

She was seated in a little enclosure, made by school-desks and forms, writing her daily journal. But soon finishing this pursuit, she engaged in an animated communication with a teacher who sat beside her. This was a favourite mistress with the poor pupil. If she could see the face of her fair instructress, she would not love her less, I am sure.

I have extracted a few disjointed fragments of her history, from an account, written by that one man who has made her what she is. It is a very beautiful and touching narrative; and I wish I could present it entire.

Her name is Laura Bridgman. "She was born in Hanover, New Hampshire, on the twenty-first of December, 1829. She is described as having been a very sprightly and pretty infant, with bright blue eyes. She was, however, so puny and feeble until she was a year and a half old, that her parents hardly hoped to rear her. She was subject to severe fits, which seemed to rack her frame almost beyond her power of endurance: and life was held by the feeblest tenure: but when a year and a half old, she seemed to rally; the dangerous symptoms subsided; and at twenty months old, she was perfectly well.

"Then her mental powers, hitherto stinted in their growth, rapidly developed themselves; and during the four months of health which she enjoyed, she appears (making due allowance for a fond mother's account) to have displayed a considerable degree of intelligence.

"But suddenly she sickened again; her disease raged with great violence during five weeks, when her eyes and ears were inflamed, suppurated, and their contents were discharged. But though sight and hearing were gone for ever, the poor child's sufferings were not ended. The fever raged during seven weeks; for five months she was kept in bed in a darkened room; it was a year before she could walk unsupported, and two years before she could sit up all day. It was now observed that her sense of smell was almost entirely destroyed; and, consequently, that her taste was much blunted.

"It was not until four years of age that the poor child's bodily health seemed restored, and she was able to enter upon her apprenticeship of life and the world.

"But what a situation was hers! The darkness and the silence of the tomb were around her: no mother's smile called forth her answering smile, no father's voice taught her to imitate his sounds:—they, brothers and sisters, were but forms of matter which resisted her touch, but which differed not from the furniture of the house, save in warmth, and in the power of locomotion; and not even in these respects from the dog and the cat.

"But the immortal spirit which had been implanted within her could not die, nor be maimed nor mutilated; and though most of its avenues of communication with the world were cut off, it began to manifest itself through the others. As soon as she could walk, she began to explore the room, and then the house; she became familiar with the form, density, weight, and heat, of every article she could lay her hands upon. She followed her mother, and felt her hands and arms, as she was occupied about the house; and her disposition to imitate, led her to repeat everything herself. She even learned to sew a little, and to knit."

The reader will scarcely need to be told, however, that the opportunities of communicating with her, were very, very limited; and that the moral effects of her wretched state soon began to appear. Those who cannot be enlightened by reason, can only be controlled by force; and this, coupled with her great privations, must soon have reduced her to a worse condition than that of the beasts that perish, but for timely and unhoped-for aid.

"At this time, I was so fortunate as to hear of the child, and immediately hastened to Hanover to see her. I found her with a well-formed figure; a strongly-marked, nervous-sanguine temperament; a large and beautifully-shaped head; and the whole system in healthy action. The parents were easily induced to consent to her coming to Boston, and on the 4th of October, 1837, they brought her to the Institution.

"For a while, she was much bewildered; and after waiting about two weeks, until she became acquainted with her new locality, and somewhat familiar with the inmates, the attempt was made to give her knowledge of arbitrary signs, by which she could interchange thoughts with others.

"There was one of two ways to be adopted: either to go on to build up a language of signs on the basis of the natural language which she had already commenced herself, or to teach her the purely arbitrary language in common use: that is, to give her a sign for every individual thing, or to give her a knowledge of letters by combination of which she might express her idea of the existence, and the mode and condition of existence, of any thing. The former would have been easy, but very ineffectual; the latter seemed very difficult, but, if accomplished, very effectual. I determined therefore to try the latter.

"The first experiments were made by taking articles in common use, such as knives, forks, spoons, keys, &c., and pasting upon them labels with their names printed in raised letters. These she felt very carefully, and soon, of course, distinguished that the crooked lines *s p o o n*, differed as much from the crooked lines *k e y*, as the spoon differed from the key in form.

"Then small detached labels, with the same words printed upon them, were put into her hands; and she soon observed that they were similar to the ones pasted on the articles. She showed her perception of this similarity by laying the label *k e y* upon the key, and the label *s p o o n* upon the spoon. She was encouraged here by the natural sign of approbation, patting on the head.

"The same process was then repeated with all the articles which she could handle; and she very easily learned to place the proper labels upon them. It was evident, however, that the only intellectual exercise was that of imitation and memory. She recollected that the label *b o o k* was placed upon a book, and she repeated the process first from imitation, next from memory, with only the motive of love of approbation, but apparently without the intellectual perception of any relation between the things.

"After a while, instead of labels, the individual letters were given to her on detached bits of paper: they were arranged side by side so as to spell *b o o k, k e y*, &c.; then they were mixed up in a heap and a sign was made for her to arrange them herself so as to express the words *b o o k, k e y*, &c.; and she did so.

"Hitherto, the process had been mechanical, and the success about as great as teaching a very knowing dog a variety of tricks. The poor child had sat in mute amazement, and patiently imitated everything her teacher did; but now the truth began to flash upon her: her intellect began to work: she perceived that here was a way by which she could herself make up a sign of anything that was in her own mind, and show it to another mind; and at once her countenance lighted up with a human expression: it was no longer a dog, or parrot: it was an immortal spirit, eagerly seizing upon a new link of union with other spirits! I could almost fix upon the moment when this truth dawned upon her mind, and spread its light to her countenance; I saw that the great obstacle was overcome; and that henceforward nothing but patient and persevering, but plain and straightforward, efforts were to be used.

"The result thus far, is quickly related, and easily conceived; but not so was the process; for many weeks of apparently unprofitable labour were passed before it was effected.

"When it was said above, that a sign was made, it was intended to say, that the action was performed by her teacher, she feeling his hands, and then imitating the motion.

"The next step was to procure a set of metal types, with the different letters of the alphabet cast upon their ends; also a board, in which were square holes, into which holes she could set the types; so that the letters on their ends could alone be felt above the surface.

"Then, on any article being handed to her, for instance, a pencil or a watch, she would select the component letters, and arrange them on her board, and read them with apparent pleasure.

"She was exercised for several weeks in this way, until her vocabulary became extensive; and then the important step was taken of teaching her how to represent the different letters by the position of her fingers, instead of the cumbrous apparatus of the board and types. She accomplished this speedily and easily, for her intellect had begun to work in aid of her teacher, and her progress was rapid.

"This was the period, about three months after she had commenced, that the first report of her case was made, in which it was stated that 'she has just learned the manual alphabet, as used by the deaf mutes, and it is a subject of delight and wonder to see how rapidly, correctly, and eagerly, she goes on with her labours. Her teacher gives her a new object, for instance, a pencil, first lets her examine it, and get an idea of its use, then teaches her how to spell it by making the signs for the letters with her own fingers: the child grasps her hand, and feels her fingers, as the different letters are formed; she turns her head a little on one side like a person listening closely; her lips are apart; she seems scarcely to breathe; and her countenance, at first anxious, gradually changes to a smile, as she comprehends the lesson. She then holds up her tiny fingers, and spells the word in the manual alphabet; next, she takes her types and arranges her letters; and last, to make sure that she is right, she takes the whole of the types composing the word, and places them upon or in contact with the pencil, or whatever the object may be.

"The whole of the succeeding year was passed in gratifying her eager inquiries for the names of every object which she could possibly handle; in exercising her in the use of the manual alphabet; in extending in every possible way her knowledge of the physical relations of things; and in proper care of her health.

"At the end of the year a report of her case was made, from which the following is an extract.

" 'It has been ascertained beyond the possibility of doubt, that she cannot see a ray of light, cannot hear the least sound, and never exercises her sense of smell, if she have any. Thus her mind dwells in darkness and stillness, as profound as that of a closed tomb at midnight. Of beautiful sights, and sweet sounds, and pleasant odours, she had no conception ; nevertheless, she seems as happy and playful as a bird or a lamb; and the employment of her intellectual faculties, or the acquirement of a new idea, gives her a vivid pleasure, which is plainly marked in her expressive features. She never seems to repine, but has all the buoyancy and gaiety of childhood. She is fond of fun and frolic, and when playing with the rest of the children, her shrill laugh sounds loudest of the group.

" 'When left alone, she seems very happy if she have her knitting or sewing, and will busy herself for hours; if she have no occupation, she evidently amuses herself by imaginary dialogues, or by recalling past impressions; she counts with her fingers, or spells out names of things which she has recently learned, in the manual alphabet of the deaf mutes. In this lonely self-communion she seems to reason, reflect, and argue; if she spell a word wrong with the fingers of her right hand, she instantly strikes it with her left, as her teacher does, in sign of disapprobation; if right, then she pats herself upon the head, and looks pleased. She sometimes purposely spells a word wrong with the left hand, looks roguish for a moment and laughs, and then with the right hand strikes the left, as if to correct it.

" 'During the year she has attained great dexterity in the use of the manual alphabet of the deaf mutes; and she spells out the words and sentences which she knows, so fast and so deftly, that only those accustomed to this language can follow with the eye the rapid motions of her fingers.

" 'But wonderful as is the rapidity with which she writes her thoughts upon the air, still more so is the ease and accuracy with which she reads the words thus written by another; grasping their hands in hers, and following every movement of their fingers, as letter after letter conveys their meaning to her mind. It is in this way that she converses with her blind playmates, and nothing can more forcibly show the power of mind in forcing matter to its purpose than a meeting between them. For if great talent and skill are necessary for two pantomimes to paint their thoughts and feelings by the movements of the body, and the expression of the countenance, how much greater the difficulty when darkness shrouds them both, and the one can hear no sound.

" 'When Laura is walking through a passage-way, with her hands spread before her, she knows instantly every one she meets, and passes them with a sign of recognition: but if it be a girl of her own age, and especially if it be one of her favourites, there is instantly a bright smile of recognition, a twining of arms, a grasping of hands, and a swift telegraphing upon the tiny fingers; whose rapid evolutions convey the thoughts and feelings from the outposts of one mind to those of the other. There are questions and answers, exchanges of joy or sorrow, there are kissings and partings, just as between little children with all their senses.'

"During this year, and six months after she had left home, her mother came to visit her, and the scene of their meeting was an interesting one.

"The mother stood some time, gazing with overflowing eyes upon her unfortunate child, who, all unconscious of her presence, was playing about the room. Presently Laura ran against her, and at once began feeling her hands, examining her dress, and trying to find out if she knew her; but not succeeding in this, she turned away as from a stranger, and the poor woman could not conceal the pang she felt, at finding that her beloved child did not know her.

"She then gave Laura a string of beads which she used to wear at home, which were recognised by the child at once, who, with much joy, put them around her neck, and sought me eagerly to say she understood the string was from her home.

"The mother now sought to caress her, but poor Laura repelled her, preferring to be with her acquaintances.

"Another article from home was now given her, and she began to look much interested; she examined the stranger much closer, and gave me to understand that she knew she came from Hanover; she even endured her caresses, but would leave her with indifference at the slightest signal. The distress of the mother was now painful

to behold; for, although she had feared that she should not be
recognised, the painful reality of being treated with cold indifference
by a darling child, was too much for woman's nature to bear.

"After a while, on the mother taking hold of her again, a vague
idea seemed to flit across Laura's mind, that this could not be a
stranger; she therefore felt her hands very eagerly, while her countenance assumed an expression of intense interest; she became very
pale; and then suddenly red; hope seemed struggling with doubt and
anxiety, and never were contending emotions more strongly painted
upon the human face: at this moment of painful uncertainty, the
mother drew her close to her side, and kissed her fondly, when at
once the truth flashed upon the child, and all mistrust and anxiety
disappeared from her face, as with an expression of exceeding joy
she eagerly nestled to the bosom of her parent, and yielded herself
to her fond embraces.

"After this, the beads were all unheeded; the playthings which
were offered to her were utterly disregarded; her playmates, for
whom but a moment before she gladly left the stranger, now vainly
strove to pull her from her mother; and though she yielded her usual
instantaneous obedience to my signal to follow me, it was evidently
with painful reluctance. She clung close to me, as if bewildered and
fearful; and when, after a moment, I took her to her mother, she
sprang to her arms, and clung to her with eager joy.

"The subsequent parting between them, showed alike the affection,
the intelligence, and the resolution of the child.

"Laura accompanied her mother to the door, clinging close to her
all the way, until they arrived at the threshold, where she paused,
and felt around, to ascertain who was near her. Perceiving the
matron, of whom she is very fond, she grasped her with one hand,
holding on convulsively to her mother with the other; and thus she
stood for a moment; then she dropped her mother's hand; put her
handkerchief to her eyes; and turning round, clung sobbing to the
matron; while her mother departed, with emotions as deep as those
of her child.

.        .        .        .        .        .

"It has been remarked in former reports, that she can distinguish
different degrees of intellect in others, and that she soon regarded,
almost with contempt, a new-comer, when, after a few days, she
discovered her weakness of mind. This unamiable part of her
character has been more strongly developed during the past year.

"She chooses for her friends and companions, those children who
are intelligent, and can talk best with her; and she evidently dislikes
to be with those who are deficient in intellect, unless, indeed, she
can make them serve her purposes, which she is evidently inclined
to do. She takes advantage of them, and makes them wait upon her,
in a manner that she knows she could not exact of others; and in
various ways shows her Saxon blood.

"She is fond of having other children noticed and caressed by the teachers, and those whom she respects; but this must not be carried too far, or she becomes jealous. She wants to have her share, which, if not the lion's, is the greater part; and if she does not get it, she says, '*My mother will love me.*'

"Her tendency to imitation is so strong, that it leads her to actions which must be entirely incomprehensible to her, and which can give her no other pleasure than the gratification of an internal faculty. She has been known to sit for half an hour, holding a book before her sightless eyes, and moving her lips, as she has observed seeing people do when reading.

"She one day pretended that her doll was sick; and went through all the motions of tending it, and giving it medicine; she then put it carefully to bed, and placed a bottle of hot water to its feet, laughing all the time most heartily. When I came home, she insisted upon my going to see it, and feel its pulse; and when I told her to put a blister on its back, she seemed to enjoy it amazingly, and almost screamed with delight.

"Her social feelings, and her affections, are very strong; and when she is sitting at work, or at her studies, by the side of one of her little friends, she will break off from her task every few moments, to hug and kiss them with an earnestness and warmth that is touching to behold.

"When left alone, she occupies and apparently amuses herself, and seems quite contented; and so strong seems to be the natural tendency of thought to put on the garb of language, that she often soliloquizes in the *finger language*, slow and tedious as it is. But it is only when alone, that she is quiet: for if she becomes sensible of the presence of any one near her, she is restless until she can sit close beside them, hold their hand, and converse with them by signs.

"In her intellectual character it is pleasing to observe an insatiable thirst for knowledge, and a quick perception of the relations of things. In her moral character, it is beautiful to behold her continual gladness, her keen enjoyment of existence, her expansive love, her unhesitating confidence, her sympathy with suffering, her conscientiousness, truthfulness, and hopefulness."

Such are a few fragments from the simple but most interesting and instructive history of Laura Bridgman. The name of her great benefactor and friend, who writes it, is Dr. Howe. There are not many persons, I hope and believe, who, after reading these passages, can ever hear that name with indifference.

A further account has been published by Dr. Howe, since the report from which I have just quoted. It describes her rapid mental growth and improvement during twelve months more, and brings her little history down to the end of last year. It is very remarkable, that as we dream in words, and carry on imaginary conversations, in which we speak both for ourselves and for the shadows who appear to us in those visions of the night, so she, having no words, uses her finger alphabet in her sleep. And it has been ascertained that when her slumber is broken, and is much disturbed by dreams, she expresses her thoughts in an irregular and confused manner on her fingers: just as we should murmur and mutter them indistinctly, in the like circumstances.

I turned over the leaves of her Diary, and found it written in a fair legible square hand, and expressed in terms which were quite intelligible without any explanation. On my saying that I should like to see her write again, the teacher who sat beside her, bade her, in their language, sign her name upon a slip of paper, twice or thrice. In doing so, I observed that she kept her left hand always touching, and following up, her right, in which, of course, she held the pen. No line was indicated by any contrivance, but she wrote straight and freely.

She had, until now, been quite unconscious of the presence of visitors; but, having her hand placed in that of the gentleman who accompanied me, she immediately expressed his name upon her teacher's palm. Indeed her sense of touch is now so exquisite, that having been acquainted with a person once, she can recognise him or her after almost any interval. This gentleman had been in her company, I believe, but very seldom, and certainly had not seen her for many months. My hand she rejected at once, as she does that of any man who is a stranger to her. But she retained my wife's with evident pleasure, kissed her, and examined her dress with a girl's curiosity and interest.

She was merry and cheerful, and showed much innocent playfulness in her intercourse with her teacher. Her delight on recognising a favourite playfellow and companion—herself a blind girl—who silently, and with an equal enjoyment of the coming surprise, took a seat beside her, was beautiful to witness. It elicited from her at first, as other slight circumstances did twice or thrice during my visit, an uncouth noise which was rather painful to hear. But on her teacher touching her lips, she immediately desisted, and embraced her laughingly and affectionately.

I had previously been into another chamber, where a number of blind boys were swinging, and climbing, and engaged in various sports. They all clamoured, as we entered, to the assistant-master, who accompanied us, "Look at me, Mr. Hart! Please, Mr. Hart, look at me!" evincing, I thought, even in this, an anxiety peculiar to their condition, that their little feats of agility should be *seen*. Among them was a small laughing fellow, who stood aloof, entertaining himself with a gymnastic exercise for bringing the arms and chest into play; which he enjoyed mightily; especially when, in thrusting out his right arm, he brought it into contact with another boy. Like Laura Bridgman, this young child was deaf, and dumb, and blind.

Dr. Howe's account of this pupil's first instruction is so very striking, and so intimately connected with Laura herself, that I cannot refrain from a short extract. I may premise that the poor boy's name is Oliver Caswell; that he is thirteen years of age; and that he was in full possession of all his faculties, until three years and four months old. He was then attacked by scarlet fever; in four weeks became deaf; in a few weeks more, blind; in six months, dumb. He showed his anxious sense of this last deprivation, by often feeling the lips of other persons when they were talking, and then putting his hand upon his own, as if to assure himself that he had them in the right position.

"His thirst for knowledge," says Dr. Howe, "proclaimed itself as soon as he entered the house, by his eager examination of everything he could feel or smell in his new location. For instance, treading upon the register of a furnace, he instantly stooped down, and began to feel it, and soon discovered the way in which the upper plate moved upon the lower one; but this was not enough for him, so lying down upon his face, he applied his tongue first to one, then to the other, and seemed to discover that they were of different kinds of metal.

"His signs were expressive: and the strictly natural language, laughing, crying, sighing, kissing, embracing, &c., was perfect.

"Some of the analogical signs which (guided by his faculty of imitation) he had contrived, were comprehensible; such as the waving motion of his hand for the motion of a boat, the circular one for a wheel, &c.

"The first object was to break up the use of these signs and to substitute for them the use of purely arbitrary ones.

"Profiting by the experience I had gained in the other cases, I omitted several steps of the process before employed, and commenced at once with the finger language. Taking, therefore, several articles having short names, such as key, cup, mug, &c., and with Laura for an auxiliary, I sat down, and taking his hand, placed it upon one of them, and then with my own, made the letters *k e y*. He felt my hands eagerly with both of his, and on my repeating the process, he evidently tried to imitate the motions of my fingers, In a few minutes he contrived to feel the motions of my fingers with one hand, and holding out the other he tried to imitate them, laughing most heartily when he succeeded. Laura was by, interested even to agitation; and the two presented a singular sight: her face was flushed and anxious, and her fingers twining in among ours so closely as to follow every motion, but so lightly as not to embarrass them; while Oliver stood attentive, his head a little aside, his face turned up, his left hand grasping mine, and his right held out: at every motion of my fingers his countenance betokened keen attention; there was an expression of anxiety as he tried to imitate the motions; then a smile came stealing out as he thought he could do so, and spread into a joyous laugh the moment he succeeded, and felt me pat his head, and Laura clap him heartily upon the back, and jump up and down in her joy.

"He learned more than a half-dozen letters in half an hour, and seemed delighted with his success, at least in gaining approbation. His attention then began to flag, and I commenced playing with

# American Notes

him. It was evident that in all this he had merely been imitating the motions of my fingers, and placing his hand upon the key, cup, &c., as part of the process, without any perception of the relation between the sign and the object.

"When he was tired with play I took him back to the table, and he was quite ready to begin again his process of imitation. He soon learned to make the letters for *key*, *pen*, *pin* ; and by having the object repeatedly placed in his hand, he at last perceived the relation I wished to establish between them. This was evident, because, when I made the letters *p i n*, or *p e n*, or *c u p*, he would select the article.

"The perception of this relation was not accompanied by that radiant flash of intelligence, and that glow of joy, which marked the delightful moment when Laura first perceived it. I then placed all the articles on the table, and going away a little distance with the children, placed Oliver's fingers in the positions to spell *key*, on which Laura went and brought the article: the little fellow seemed much amused by this, and looked very attentive and smiling. I then caused him to make the letters *b r e a d*, and in an instant Laura went and brought him a piece: he smelled at it; put it to his lips; cocked up his head with a most knowing look; seemed to reflect a moment; and then laughed outright, as much as to say, 'Aha! I understand now how something may be made out of this.'

"It was now clear that he had the capacity and inclination to learn, that he was a proper subject for instruction, and needed only persevering attention. I therefore put him in the hands of an intelligent teacher, nothing doubting of his rapid progress."

Well may this gentleman call that a delightful moment, in which some distant promise of her present state first gleamed upon the darkened mind of Laura Bridgman. Throughout his life, the recollection of that moment will be to him a source of pure, unfading happiness; nor will it shine less brightly on the evening of his days of Noble Usefulness.

The affection which exists between these two—the master and the pupil—is as far removed from all ordinary care and regard, as the circumstances in which it has had its growth, are apart from the common occurrences of life. He is occupied now, in devising means of imparting to her, higher knowledge; and of conveying to her some adequate idea of the Great Creator of that universe in which, dark and silent and scentless though it be to her, she has such deep delight and glad enjoyment.

Ye who have eyes and see not, and have ears and hear not; ye who are as the hypocrites of sad countenances, and disfigure your faces that ye may seem unto men to fast; learn healthy cheerfulness, and mild contentment, from the deaf, and dumb, and blind! Self-elected saints with gloomy brows, this sightless, earless, voiceless child may teach you lessons you will do well to follow. Let that poor hand of hers lie gently on your hearts; for there may be something in its healing touch akin to that of the Great Master whose precepts you mis-

construe, whose lessons you pervert, of whose charity and sympathy
with all the world, not one among you in his daily practice knows
as much as many of the worst among those fallen sinners, to whom
you are liberal in nothing but the preachment of perdition!

As I rose to quit the room, a pretty little child of one of the
attendants came running in to greet its father. For the moment, a
child with eyes, among the sightless crowd, impressed me almost as
painfully as the blind boy in the porch had done, two hours ago.
Ah! how much brighter and more deeply blue, glowing and rich
though it had been before, was the scene without, contrasting with
the darkness of so many youthful lives within!

---

At SOUTH BOSTON, as it is called, in a situation excellently adapted
for the purpose, several charitable institutions are clustered together.
One of these, is the State Hospital for the insane; admirably conducted on those enlightened principles of conciliation and kindness,
which twenty years ago would have been worse than heretical, and
which have been acted upon with so much success in our own pauper
Asylum at Hanwell. "Evince a desire to show some confidence, and
repose some trust, even in mad people," said the resident physician,
as we walked along the galleries, his patients flocking round us un-
restrained. Of those who deny or doubt the wisdom of this maxim
after witnessing its effects, if there be such people still alive, I can
only say that I hope I may never be summoned as a Juryman on a
Commission of Lunacy whereof they are the subjects; for I should
certainly find them out of their senses, on such evidence alone.

Each ward in this institution is shaped like a long gallery or hall,
with the dormitories of the patients opening from it on either hand.
Here they work, read, play at skittles, and other games; and when
the weather does not admit of their taking exercise out of doors, pass
the day together. In one of these rooms, seated, calmly, and quite
as a matter of course, among a throng of mad-women, black and
white, were the physician's wife and another lady, with a couple of
children. These ladies were graceful and handsome; and it was not
difficult to perceive at a glance that even their presence there, had
a highly beneficial influence on the patients who were grouped about
them.

Leaning her head against the chimney-piece, with a great assumption of dignity and refinement of manner, sat an elderly female, in
as many scraps of finery as Madge Wildfire herself. Her head in
particular was so strewn with scraps of gauze and cotton and bits
of paper, and had so many queer odds and ends stuck all about it,
that it looked like a bird's-nest. She was radiant with imaginary
jewels; wore a rich pair of undoubted gold spectacles; and gracefully
dropped upon her lap, as we approached, a very old greasy newspaper, in which I dare say she had been reading an account of her
own presentation at some Foreign Court.

I have been thus particular in describing her, because she will serve to exemplify the physician's manner of acquiring and retaining the confidence of his patients.

"This," he said aloud, taking me by the hand, and advancing to the fantastic figure with great politeness—not raising her suspicions by the slightest look or whisper, or any kind of aside, to me: "This lady is the hostess of this mansion, sir. It belongs to her. Nobody else has anything whatever to do with it. It is a large establishment, as you see, and requires a great number of attendants. She lives, you observe, in the very first style. She is kind enough to receive my visits, and to permit my wife and family to reside here; for which it is hardly necessary to say, we are much indebted to her. She is exceedingly courteous, you perceive," on this hint she bowed condescendingly, "and will permit me to have the pleasure of introducing you: a gentleman from England, Ma'am: newly arrived from England, after a very tempestuous passage: Mr. Dickens,—the lady of the house!"

We exchanged the most dignified salutations with profound gravity and respect, and so went on. The rest of the mad-women seemed to understand the joke perfectly (not only in this case, but in all the others, except their own), and be highly amused by it. The nature of their several kinds of insanity was made known to me in the same way, and we left each of them in high good humour. Not only is a thorough confidence established, by those means, between the physician and patient, in respect of the nature and extent of their hallucinations, but it is easy to understand that opportunities are afforded for seizing any moment of reason, to startle them by placing their own delusion before them in its most incongruous and ridiculous light.

Every patient in this asylum sits down to dinner every day with a knife and fork; and in the midst of them sits the gentleman, whose manner of dealing with his charges, I have just described. At every meal, moral influence alone restrains the more violent among them from cutting the throats of the rest; but the effect of that influence is reduced to an absolute certainty, and is found, even as a means of restraint, to say nothing of it as a means of cure, a hundred times more efficacious than all the strait-waistcoats, fetters, and handcuffs, that ignorance, prejudice, and cruelty have manufactured since the creation of the world.

In the labour department, every patient is as freely trusted with the tools of his trade as if he were a sane man. In the garden, and on the farm, they work with spades, rakes, and hoes. For amusement, they walk, run, fish, paint, read, and ride out to take the air in carriages provided for the purpose. They have among themselves a sewing society to make clothes for the poor, which holds meetings, passes resolutions, never comes to fisty-cuffs or bowie-knives as sane assemblies have been known to do elsewhere; and conducts all its proceedings with the greatest decorum. The irritability, which would otherwise be expended on their own flesh, clothes, and furniture, is dissipated in these pursuits. They are cheerful, tranquil, and healthy.

Once a week they have a ball, in which the Doctor and his family, with all the nurses and attendants, take an active part. Dances and marches are performed alternately, to the enlivening strains of a piano; and now and then some gentleman or lady (whose proficiency has been previously ascertained) obliges the company with a song: nor does it ever degenerate, at a tender crisis, into a screech or howl; wherein, I must confess, I should have thought the danger lay. At an early hour they all meet together for these festive purposes; at eight o'clock refreshments are served; and at nine they separate.

Immense politeness and good breeding are observed throughout. They all take their tone from the Doctor; and he moves a very Chesterfield among the company. Like other assemblies, these entertainments afford a fruitful topic of conversation among the ladies for some days; and the gentlemen are so anxious to shine on these occasions, that they have been sometimes found "practising their steps" in private, to cut a more distinguished figure in the dance.

It is obvious that one great feature of this system, is the inculcation and encouragement, even among such unhappy persons, of a decent self-respect. Something of the same spirit pervades all the Institutions at South Boston.

There is the House of Industry. In that branch of it, which is devoted to the reception of old or otherwise helpless paupers, these words are painted on the walls: "WORTHY OF NOTICE. SELF-GOVERNMENT, QUIETUDE, AND PEACE, ARE BLESSINGS." It is not assumed and taken for granted that being there they must be evil-disposed and wicked people, before whose vicious eyes it is necessary to flourish threats and harsh restraints. They are met at the very threshold with this mild appeal. All within-doors is very plain and simple, as it ought to be, but arranged with a view to peace and comfort. It costs no more than any other plan of arrangement, but it speaks an amount of consideration for those who are reduced to seek a shelter there, which puts them at once upon their gratitude and good behaviour. Instead of being parcelled out in great, long, rambling wards, where a certain amount of weazen life may mope, and pine, and shiver, all day long, the building is divided into separate rooms, each with its share of light and air. In these, the better kind of paupers live. They have a motive for exertion and becoming pride, in the desire to make these little chambers comfortable and decent.

I do not remember one but it was clean and neat, and had its plant or two upon the window-sill, or row of crockery upon the shelf, or small display of coloured prints upon the whitewashed wall, or, perhaps, its wooden clock behind the door.

The orphans and young children are in an adjoining building; separate from this, but a part of the same Institution. Some are such little creatures, that the stairs are of Lilliputian measurement, fitted to their tiny strides. The same consideration for their years and weakness is expressed in their very seats, which are perfect curiosities, and look like articles of furniture for a pauper doll's-house. I can imagine the glee of our Poor Law Commissioners at the notion of these seats having arms and backs; but small spines being of older date than their occupation of the Board-room at Somerset House, I thought even this provision very merciful and kind.

Here again, I was greatly pleased with the inscriptions on the wall, which were scraps of plain morality, easily remembered and understood : such as "Love one another"—"God remembers the smallest creature in his creation:" and straightforward advice of that nature. The books and tasks of these smallest of scholars, were adapted, in the same judicious manner, to their childish powers. When we had examined these lessons, four morsels of girls (of whom one was blind) sang a little song, about the merry month of May, which I thought (being extremely dismal) would have suited an English November better. That done, we went to see their sleeping-rooms on the floor above, in which the arrangements were no less excellent and gentle than those we had seen below. And after observing that the teachers were of a class and character well suited to the spirit of the place, I took leave of the infants with a lighter heart than ever I have taken leave of pauper infants yet.

Connected with the House of Industry, there is also an Hospital, which was in the best order, and had, I am glad to say, many beds unoccupied. It had one fault, however, which is common to all American interiors : the presence of the eternal, accursed, suffocating, red-hot demon of a stove, whose breath would blight the purest air under Heaven.

There are two establishments for boys in this same neighbourhood. One is called the Boylston school, and is an asylum for neglected and indigent boys who have committed no crime, but who in the ordinary course of things would very soon be purged of that distinction if they were not taken from the hungry streets and sent here. The other is a House of Reformation for Juvenile Offenders. They are both under the same roof, but the two classes of boys never come in contact.

The Boylston boys, as may be readily supposed, have very much the advantage of the others in point of personal appearance. They were in their school-room when I came upon them, and answered correctly, without book, such questions as where was England; how far was it; what was its population; its capital city; its form of government; and so forth. They sang a song too, about a farmer sowing his seed: with corresponding action at such parts as "'tis thus he sows," "he turns him round," "he claps his hands;" which gave it greater interest for them, and accustomed them to act together, in an orderly manner. They appeared exceedingly well-taught, and not better taught than fed; for a more chubby-looking full-waistcoated set of boys, I never saw.

The juvenile offenders had not such pleasant faces by a great deal, and in this establishment there were many boys of colour. I saw them first at their work (basket-making, and the manufacture of palm-leaf hats), afterwards in their school, where they sang a chorus in praise of Liberty: an odd, and, one would think rather aggravating, theme for prisoners. These boys are divided into four classes, each denoted by a numeral, worn on a badge upon the arm. On the arrival of a new-comer, he is put into the fourth or lowest class, and left, by good behaviour, to work his way up into the first. The design and object of this Institution is to reclaim the youthful criminal by firm but kind and judicious treatment; to make his prison a place of purification and improvement, not of demoralisation and corruption; to impress upon him that there is but one path, and that one sober industry, which can ever lead him to happiness; to teach him how it may be trodden, if his footsteps have never yet been led that way; and to lure him back to it if they have strayed: in a word, to snatch him from destruction, and restore him to society a penitent and useful member. The importance of such an establishment, in every point of view, and with reference to every consideration of humanity and social policy, requires no comment.

One other establishment closes the catalogue. It is the House of Correction for the State, in which silence is strictly maintained, but where the prisoners have the comfort and mental relief of seeing each other, and of working together. This is the improved system of Prison Discipline which we have imported into England, and which has been in successful operation among us for some years past.

America, as a new and not over-populated country, has in all her prisons, the one great advantage, of being enabled to find useful and profitable work for the inmates; whereas, with us, the prejudice against prison labour is naturally very strong, and almost insurmountable, when honest men who have not offended against the laws are frequently doomed to seek employment in vain. Even in the United States, the principle of bringing convict labour and free labour into a competition which must obviously be to the disadvantage of the latter, has already found many opponents, whose number is not likely to diminish with access of years.

For this very reason though, our best prisons would seem at the first glance to be better conducted than those of America. The treadmill is conducted with little or no noise; five hundred men may pick oakum in the same room, without a sound; and both kinds of labour admit of such keen and vigilant superintendence, as will render even a word of personal communication amongst the prisoners almost impossible. On the other hand, the noise of the loom, the forge, the carpenter's hammer, or the stonemason's saw, greatly favour those opportunities of intercourse—hurried and brief no doubt, but opportunities still—which these several kinds of work, by rendering it necessary for men to be employed very near to each other, and often side by side, without any barrier or partition between them, in their very nature present. A visitor, too, requires to reason and reflect a little, before the sight of a number of men engaged in ordinary

labour, such as he is accustomed to out of doors, will impress him
half as strongly as the contemplation of the same persons in the same
place and garb would, if they were occupied in some task, marked and
degraded everywhere as belonging only to felons in jails. In an
American state prison or house of correction, I found it difficult at
first to persuade myself that I was really in a jail: a place of
ignominious punishment and endurance. And to this hour I very
much question whether the humane boast that it is not like one, has
its root in the true wisdom or philosophy of the matter.

I hope I may not be misunderstood on this subject, for it is one
in which I take a strong and deep interest. I incline as little to the
sickly feeling which makes every canting lie or maudlin speech of a
notorious criminal a subject of newspaper report and general
sympathy, as I do to those good old customs of the good old times
which made England, even so recently as in the reign of the Third
King George, in respect of her criminal code and her prison regulations, one of the most bloody-minded and barbarous countries on the
earth. If I thought it would do any good to the rising generation, I
would cheerfully give my consent to the disinterment of the bones of
any genteel highwayman (the more genteel, the more cheerfully),
and to their exposure, piecemeal, on any sign-post, gate, or gibbet,
that might be deemed a good elevation for the purpose. My reason is
as well convinced that these gentry were as utterly worthless and
debauched villains, as it is that the laws and jails hardened them in
their evil courses, or that their wonderful escapes were effected by the
prison-turnkeys who, in those admirable days, had always been felons
themselves, and were, to the last, their bosom-friends and pot-
companions. At the same time I know, as all men do or should, that
the subject of Prison Discipline is one of the highest importance to
any community; and that in her sweeping reform and bright example
to other countries on this head, America has shown great wisdom,
great benevolence, and exalted policy. In contrasting her system with
that which we have modelled upon it, I merely seek to show that with
all its drawbacks, ours has some advantages of its own.

The House of Correction which has led to these remarks, is not
walled, like other prisons, but is palisaded round about with tall
rough stakes, something after the manner of an enclosure for keeping
elephants in, as we see it represented in Eastern prints and pictures.
The prisoners wear a parti-coloured dress; and those who are sentenced
to hard labour, work at nail-making, or stone-cutting. When I was
there, the latter class of labourers were employed upon the stone for
a new custom-house in course of erection at Boston. They appeared
to shape it skilfully and with expedition, though there were very few
among them (if any) who had not acquired the art within the prison
gates.

The women, all in one large room, were employed in making light
clothing, for New Orleans and the Southern States. They did their
work in silence like the men; and like them were overlooked by the

person contracting for their labour, or by some agent of his appointment. In addition to this, they are every moment liable to be visited by the prison officers appointed for that purpose.

The arrangements for cooking, washing of clothes, and so forth, are much upon the plan of those I have seen at home. Their mode of bestowing the prisoners at night (which is of general adoption) differs from ours, and is both simple and effective. In the centre of a lofty area, lighted by windows in the four walls, are five tiers of cells, one above the other; each tier having before it a light iron gallery, attainable by stairs of the same construction and material: excepting the lower one, which is on the ground. Behind these, back to back with them and facing the opposite wall, are five corresponding rows of cells, accessible by similar means: so that supposing the prisoners locked up in their cells, an officer stationed on the ground, with his back to the wall, has half their number under his eye at once; the remaining half being equally under the observation of another officer on the opposite side; and all in one great apartment. Unless this watch be corrupted or sleeping on his post, it is impossible for a man to escape; for even in the event of his forcing the iron door of his cell without noise (which is exceedingly improbable), the moment he appears outside, and steps into that one of the five galleries on which it is situated, he must be plainly and fully visible to the officer below. Each of these cells holds a small truckle bed, in which one prisoner sleeps; never more. It is small, of course; and the door being not solid, but grated, and without blind or curtain, the prisoner within is at all times exposed to the observation and inspection of any guard who may pass along that tier at any hour or minute of the night. Every day, the prisoners receive their dinner, singly, through a trap in the kitchen wall; and each man carries his to his sleeping cell to eat it, where he is locked up, alone, for that purpose, one hour. The whole of this arrangement struck me as being admirable; and I hope that the next new prison we erect in England may be built on this plan.

I was given to understand that in this prison no swords or fire-arms, or even cudgels, are kept; nor is it probable that, so long as its present excellent management continues, any weapon, offensive or defensive, will ever be required within its bounds.

Such are the Institutions at South Boston! In all of them, the unfortunate or degenerate citizens of the State are carefully instructed in their duties both to God and man; are surrounded by all reasonable means of comfort and happiness that their condition will admit of; are appealed to, as members of the great human family, however afflicted, indigent, or fallen; are ruled by the strong Heart, and not by the strong (though immeasurably weaker) Hand. I have described them at some length; firstly, because their worth demanded it; and secondly, because I mean to take them for a model, and to content myself with saying of others we may come to, whose design and purpose are the same, that in this or that respect they practically fail, or differ.

I wish by this account of them, imperfect in its execution, but in its just intention, honest, I could hope to convey to my readers one-hundredth part of the gratification, the sights I have described, afforded me.

---

To an Englishman, accustomed to the paraphernalia of Westminster Hall, an American Court of Law is as odd a sight as, I suppose, an English Court of Law would be to an American. Except in the Supreme Court at Washington (where the judges wear a plain black robe), there is no such thing as a wig or gown connected with the administration of justice. The gentlemen of the bar being barristers and attorneys too (for there is no division of those functions as in England) are no more removed from their clients than attorneys in our Court for the Relief of Insolvent Debtors are, from theirs. The jury are quite at home, and make themselves as comfortable as circumstances will permit. The witness is so little elevated above, or put aloof from, the crowd in the court, that a stranger entering during a pause in the proceedings would find it difficult to pick him out from the rest. And if it chanced to be a criminal trial, his eyes, in nine cases out of ten, would wander to the dock in search of the prisoner, in vain; for that gentleman would most likely be lounging among the most distinguished ornaments of the legal profession, whispering suggestions in his counsel's ear, or making a toothpick out of an old quill with his penknife.

I could not but notice these differences, when I visited the courts at Boston. I was much surprised at first, too, to observe that the counsel who interrogated the witness under examination at the time, did so *sitting*. But seeing that he was also occupied in writing down the answers, and remembering that he was alone and had no "junior," I quickly consoled myself with the reflection that law was not quite so expensive an article here, as at home; and that the absence of sundry formalities which we regard as indispensable, had doubtless a very favourable influence upon the bill of costs.

In every Court, ample and commodious provision is made for the accommodation of the citizens. This is the case all through America. In every Public Institution, the right of the people to attend, and to have an interest in the proceedings, is most fully and distinctly recognised. There are no grim door-keepers to dole out their tardy civility by the sixpenny-worth; nor is there, I sincerely believe, any insolence of office of any kind. Nothing national is exhibited for money; and no public officer is a showman. We have begun of late years to imitate this good example. I hope we shall continue to do so; and that in the fulness of time, even deans and chapters may be converted.

In the civil court an action was trying, for damages sustained in some accident upon a railway. The witnesses had been examined, and counsel was addressing the jury. The learned gentleman (like a few of his English brethren) was desperately long-winded, and had a remarkable capacity of saying the same thing over and over again. His great theme was "Warren the ĕn*gine* driver," whom he pressed into the service of every sentence he uttered. I listened to him for about a quarter of an hour; and, coming out of court at the expiration of that time, without the faintest ray of enlightenment as to the merits of the case, felt as if I were at home again.

In the prisoner's cell, waiting to be examined by the magistrate on a charge of theft, was a boy. This lad, instead of being committed to a common jail, would be sent to the asylum at South Boston, and there taught a trade; and in the course of time he would be bound apprentice to some respectable master. Thus, his detection in this offence, instead of being the prelude to a life of infamy and a miserable death, would lead, there was a reasonable hope, to his being reclaimed from vice, and becoming a worthy member of society.

I am by no means a wholesale admirer of our legal solemnities, many of which impress me as being exceedingly ludicrous. Strange as it may seem too, there is undoubtedly a degree of protection in the wig and gown—a dismissal of individual responsibility in dressing for the part—which encourages that insolent bearing and language, and that gross perversion of the office of a pleader for The Truth, so frequent in our courts of law. Still, I cannot help doubting whether America, in her desire to shake off the absurdities and abuses of the old system, may not have gone too far into the opposite extreme; and whether it is not desirable, especially in the small community of a city like this, where each man knows the other, to surround the administration of justice with some artificial barriers against the "Hail fellow, well met" deportment of everyday life. All the aid it can have in the very high character and ability of the Bench, not only here but elsewhere, it has, and well deserves to have; but it may need something more: not to impress the thoughtful and the well-informed, but the ignorant and heedless; a class which includes some prisoners and many witnesses. These institutions were established, no doubt, upon the principle that those who had so large a share in making the laws, would certainly respect them. But experience has proved this hope to be fallacious; for no men know better than the Judges of America, that on the occasion of any great popular excitement the law is powerless, and cannot, for the time, assert its own supremacy.

The tone of society in Boston is one of perfect politeness, courtesy, and good breeding. The ladies are unquestionably very beautiful—in face: but there I am compelled to stop. Their education is much as with us; neither better nor worse. I had heard some very marvellous stories in this respect; but not believing them, was not disappointed. Blue ladies there are, in Boston; but like philosophers of that colour and sex in most other latitudes, they rather desire to be thought superior than to be so. Evangelical ladies there are, likewise, whose attachment to the forms of religion, and horror of theatrical entertainments, are most exemplary. Ladies who have a passion for attending lectures are to be found among all classes and all conditions. In the kind of provincial life which prevails in cities such as this, the Pulpit has great influence. The peculiar province of the Pulpit in New England (always excepting the Unitarian Ministry) would appear to be the denouncement of all innocent and rational amusements. The church, the chapel, and the lecture-room, are the only means of excitement excepted; and to the church, the chapel, and the lecture-room, the ladies resort in crowds.

Wherever religion is resorted to, as a strong drink, and as an escape from the dull monotonous round of home, those of its ministers who pepper the highest will be the surest to please. They who strew the Eternal Path with the greatest amount of brimstone, and who most ruthlessly tread down the flowers and leaves that grow by the wayside, will be voted the most righteous; and they who enlarge with the greatest pertinacity on the difficulty of getting into heaven, will be considered by all true believers certain of going there: though it would be hard to say by what process of reasoning this conclusion is arrived at. It is so at home, and it is so abroad. With regard to the other means of excitement, the Lecture, it has at least the merit of being always new. One lecture treads so quickly on the heels of another, that none are remembered; and the course of this month may be safely repeated next, with its charm of novelty unbroken, and its interest unabated.

The fruits of the earth have their growth in corruption. Out of the rottenness of these things, there has sprung up in Boston a sect of philosophers known as Transcendentalists. On inquiring what this appellation might be supposed to signify, I was given to understand that whatever was unintelligible, would be certainly transcendental. Not deriving much comfort from this elucidation, I pursued the inquiry still further, and found that the Transcendentalists are followers of my friend Mr. Carlyle, or I should rather say, of a follower of his, Mr. Ralph Waldo Emerson. This gentleman has written a volume of Essays, in which, among much that is dreamy and fanciful (if he will pardon me for saying so), there is much more that is true and manly, honest and bold. Transcendentalism has its occasional vagaries (what school has not?), but it has good healthful qualities in spite of them; not least among the number a hearty disgust of Cant, and an aptitude to detect her in all the million varieties of her everlasting wardrobe. And therefore if I were a Bostonian, I think I would be a Transcendentalist.

The only preacher I heard in Boston was Mr. Taylor, who addresses himself peculiarly to seamen, and who was once a mariner himself. I found his chapel down among the shipping, in one of the narrow, old, water-side streets, with a gay blue flag waving freely from its roof. In the gallery opposite to the pulpit were a little choir of male and female singers, a violoncello, and a violin. The preacher already sat in the pulpit, which was raised on pillars, and ornamented behind him with painted drapery of a lively and somewhat theatrical appearance.

He looked a weather-beaten hard-featured man, of about six or eight and fifty; with deep lines graven as it were into his face, dark hair, and a stern, keen eye. Yet the general character of his countenance was pleasant and agreeable. The service commenced with a hymn, to which succeeded an extemporary prayer. It had the fault of frequent repetition, incidental to all such prayers; but it was plain and comprehensive in its doctrines, and breathed a tone of general sympathy and charity, which is not so commonly a characteristic of this form of address to the Deity as it might be. That done he opened his discourse, taking for his text a passage from the Song of Solomon, laid upon the desk before the commencement of the service by some unknown member of the congregation: "Who is this coming up from the wilderness, leaning on the arm of her beloved!"

He handled his text in all kinds of ways, and twisted it into all manner of shapes; but always ingeniously, and with a rude eloquence, well adapted to the comprehension of his hearers. Indeed if I be not mistaken, he studied their sympathies and understandings much more than the display of his own powers. His imagery was all drawn from the sea, and from the incidents of a seaman's life; and was often remarkably good. He spoke to them of "that glorious man, Lord Nelson," and of Collingwood; and drew nothing in, as the saying is, by the head and shoulders, but brought it to bear upon his purpose, naturally, and with a sharp mind to its effect. Sometimes, when much excited with his subject, he had an odd way—compounded of John Bunyan, and Balfour of Burley—of taking his great quarto Bible under his arm and pacing up and down the pulpit with it; looking steadily down, meantime, into the midst of the congregation. Thus, when he applied his text to the first assemblage of his hearers, and pictured the wonder of the church at their presumption in forming a congregation among themselves, he stopped short with his Bible under his arm in the manner I have described, and pursued his discourse after this manner:

"Who are these—who are they—who are these fellows? where do they come from? Where are they going to?—Come from! What's the answer?"—leaning out of the pulpit, and pointing downward with his right hand: "From below!"—starting back again, and looking at the sailors before him: "From below, my brethren. From under the hatches of sin, battened down above you by the evil one. That's where you came from!"—a walk up and down the pulpit: "and where are you going"—stopping abruptly: "where are you going? Aloft!"—very softly, and pointing upward: "Aloft!"—louder: "aloft!"—louder still: "That's where you are going—with a fair wind,—all taunt and trim, steering direct for Heaven in its glory, where there are no storms or foul weather, and where the wicked cease from troubling, and the weary are at rest."—Another walk: "That's where you're going to, my friends. That's it. That's the place. That's the port. That's the haven. It's a blessed harbour—still water there, in all changes of the winds and tides; no driving ashore upon

the rocks, or slipping your cables and running out to sea, there:
Peace—Peace—Peace—all peace!"—Another walk, and patting the
Bible under his left arm: "What! These fellows are coming from the
wilderness, are they? Yes. From the dreary, blighted wilderness of
Iniquity, whose only crop is Death. But do they lean upon anything
—do they lean upon nothing, these poor seamen?"—Three raps upon
the Bible: "Oh yes.—Yes.—They lean upon the arm of their Beloved"
—three more raps: "upon the arm of their Beloved"—three more, and
a walk: "Pilot, guiding-star, and compass, all in one, to all hands—
here it is"—three more: "Here it is. They can do their seaman's duty
manfully, and be easy in their minds in the utmost peril and danger,
with this"—two more: "They can come, even these poor fellows can
come, from the wilderness leaning on the arm of their Beloved, and
go up—up—up!"—raising his hand higher, and higher, and higher,
at every repetition of the word, so that he stood with it at last
stretched above his head, regarding them in a strange, rapt manner,
and pressing the book triumphantly to his breast, until he gradually
subsided into some other portion of his discourse.

I have cited this, rather as an instance of the preacher's eccentricities than his merits, though taken in connection with his look and
manner, and the character of his audience, even this was striking.
It is possible, however, that my favourable impression of him may
have been greatly influenced and strengthened, firstly, by his impressing upon his hearers that the true observance of religion was not
inconsistent with a cheerful deportment and an exact discharge of
the duties of their station, which, indeed, it scrupulously required of
them; and secondly, by his cautioning them not to set up any
monopoly in Paradise and its mercies. I never heard these two points
so wisely touched (if indeed I have ever heard them touched at all),
by any preacher of that kind before.

Having passed the time I spent in Boston, in making myself
acquainted with these things, in settling the course I should take in
my future travels, and in mixing constantly with its society, I am
not aware that I have any occasion to prolong this chapter. Such of
its social customs as I have not mentioned, however, may be told in
a very few words.

The usual dinner-hour is two o'clock. A dinner party takes place at
five; and at an evening party, they seldom sup later than eleven;
so that it goes hard but one gets home, even from a rout, by midnight.
I never could find out any difference between a party at Boston and
a party in London, saving that at the former place all assemblies are
held at more rational hours; that the conversation may possibly be a
little louder and more cheerful; and a guest is usually expected to
ascend to the very top of the house to take his cloak off; that he is
certain to see, at every dinner, an unusual amount of poultry on the
table; and at every supper, at least two mighty bowls of hot stewed
oysters, in any one of which a half-grown Duke of Clarence might be
smothered easily.

There are two theatres in Boston, of good size and construction, but sadly in want of patronage. The few ladies who resort to them, sit, as of right, in the front rows of the boxes.

The bar is a large room with a stone floor, and there people stand and smoke, and lounge about, all the evening: dropping in and out as the humour takes them. There too the stranger is initiated into the mysteries of Gin-sling, Cocktail, Sangaree, Mint Julep, Sherry-cobbler, Timber Doodle, and other rare drinks. The house is full of boarders, both married and single, many of whom sleep upon the premises, and contract by the week for their board and lodging: the charge for which diminishes as they go nearer the sky to roost. A public table is laid in a very handsome hall for breakfast, and for dinner, and for supper. The party sitting down together to these meals will vary in number from one to two hundred: sometimes more. The advent of each of these epochs in the day is proclaimed by an awful gong, which shakes the very window-frames as it reverberates through the house, and horribly disturbs nervous foreigners. There is an ordinary for ladies, and an ordinary for gentlemen.

In our private room the cloth could not, for any earthly consideration, have been laid for dinner without a huge glass dish of cranberries in the middle of the table; and breakfast would have been no breakfast unless the principal dish were a deformed beef-steak with a great flat bone in the centre, swimming in hot butter, and sprinkled with the very blackest of all possible pepper. Our bedroom was spacious and airy, but (like every bedroom on this side of the Atlantic) very bare of furniture, having no curtains to the French bedstead or to the window. It had one unusual luxury, however, in the shape of a wardrobe of painted wood, something smaller than an English watch-box; or if this comparison should be insufficient to convey a just idea of its dimensions, they may be estimated from the fact of my having lived for fourteen days and nights in the firm belief that it was a shower-bath.


## CHAPTER IV

### AN AMERICAN RAILROAD.  LOWELL AND ITS FACTORY SYSTEM

BEFORE leaving Boston, I devoted one day to an excursion to Lowell. I assign a separate chapter to this visit; not because I am about to describe it at any great length, but because I remember it as a thing by itself, and am desirous that my readers should do the same.

I made acquaintance with an American railroad, on this occasion, for the first time. As these works are pretty much alike all through the States, their general characteristics are easily described.

There are no first and second class carriages as with us; but there is a gentlemen's car and a ladies' car: the main distinction between which is that in the first, everybody smokes; and in the second, nobody does. As a black man never travels with a white one, there is also a negro car; which is a great, blundering, clumsy chest, such as Gulliver put to sea in, from the kingdom of Brobdingnag. There is a great deal of jolting, a great deal of noise, a great deal of wall, not much window, a locomotive engine, a shriek, and a bell.

The cars are like shabby omnibuses, but larger: holding thirty, forty, fifty, people. The seats, instead of stretching from end to end, are placed crosswise. Each seat holds two persons. There is a long row of them on each side of the caravan, a narrow passage up the middle, and a door at both ends. In the centre of the carriage there is usually a stove, fed with charcoal or anthracite coal; which is for the most part red-hot. It is insufferably close; and you see the hot air fluttering between yourself and any other object you may happen to look at, like the ghost of smoke.

In the ladies' car, there are a great many gentlemen who have ladies with them. There are also a great many ladies who have nobody with them: for any lady may travel alone, from one end of the United States to the other, and be certain of the most courteous and considerate treatment everywhere. The conductor or check-taker, or guard, or whatever he may be, wears no uniform. He walks up and down the car, and in and out of it, as his fancy dictates; leans against the door with his hands in his pockets and stares at you, if you chance to be a stranger; or enters into conversation with the passengers about him. A great many newspapers are pulled out, and a few of them are read. Everybody talks to you, or to anybody else who hits his fancy. If you are an Englishman, he expects that that railroad is pretty much like an English railroad. If you say "No," he says "Yes?" (interrogatively), and asks in what respect they differ. You enumerate the heads of difference, one by one, and he says "Yes?" (still interrogatively) to each. Then he guesses that you don't travel faster in England; and on your replying that you do, says, "Yes?" again (still interrogatively), and it is quite evident, don't believe it. After a long pause he remarks, partly to you, and partly to the knob on the top of his stick, that "Yankees are reckoned to be considerable of a go-ahead people too;" upon which *you* say "Yes," and then *he* says "Yes" again (affirmatively this time); and upon your looking out of window, tells you that behind that hill, and some three miles from the next station, there is a clever town in a smart lo-ca-tion, where he expects you have concluded to stop. Your answer in the negative naturally leads to more questions in reference to your intended route (always pronounced rout); and wherever you are going, you invariably learn that you can't get there without immense difficulty and danger, and that all the great sights are somewhere else.

If a lady take a fancy to any male passenger's seat, the gentleman who accompanies her gives him notice of the fact, and he immediately vacates it with great politeness. Politics are much discussed, so are banks, so is cotton. Quiet people avoid the question of the Presidency, for there will be a new election in three years and a half, and party feeling runs very high: the great constitutional feature of this institution being, that directly the acrimony of the last election is over, the acrimony of the next one begins; which is an unspeakable comfort to all strong politicians and true lovers of their country: that is to say, to ninety-nine men and boys out of every ninety-nine and a quarter.

Except when a branch road joins the main one, there is seldom more than one track of rails; so that the road is very narrow, and the view, where there is a deep cutting, by no means extensive. When there is not, the character of the scenery is always the same. Mile after mile of stunted trees: some hewn down by the axe, some blown down by the wind, some half fallen and resting on their neighbours, many mere logs half hidden in the swamp, others mouldered away to spongy chips. The very soil of the earth is made up of minute fragments such as these; each pool of stagnant water has its crust of vegetable rottenness; on every side there are the boughs, and trunks, and stumps of trees, in every possible stage of decay, decomposition, and neglect. Now you emerge for a few brief minutes on an open country, glittering with some bright lake or pool, broad as many an English river, but so small here that it scarcely has a name; now catch hasty glimpses of a distant town, with its clean white houses and their cool piazzas, its prim New England church and school-house; when whir-r-r-r! almost before you have seen them, comes the same dark screen: the stunted trees, the stumps, the logs, the stagnant water—all so like the last that you seem to have been transported back again by magic.

The train calls at stations in the woods, where the wild impossibility of anybody having the smallest reason to get out, is only to be equalled by the apparently desperate hopelessness of there being anybody to get in. It rushes across the turnpike road, where there is no gate, no policeman, no signal: nothing but a rough wooden arch, on which is painted "WHEN THE BELL RINGS, LOOK OUT FOR THE LOCOMOTIVE." On it whirls headlong, dives through the woods again, emerges in the light, clatters over frail arches, rumbles upon the heavy ground, shoots beneath a wooden bridge which intercepts the light for a second like a wink, suddenly awakens all the slumbering echoes in the main street of a large town, and dashes on haphazard, pell-mell, neck-or-nothing, down the middle of the road. There— with mechanics working at their trades, and people leaning from their doors and windows, and boys flying kites and playing marbles, and men smoking, and women talking, and children crawling, and pigs burrowing, and unaccustomed horses plunging and rearing, close to the very rails—there—on, on, on—tears the mad dragon of an engine with its train of cars; scattering in all directions a shower of burning sparks from its wood fire; screeching, hissing, yelling, panting; until at last the thirsty monster stops beneath a covered way to drink, the people cluster round, and you have time to breathe again.

I was met at the station at Lowell by a gentleman intimately connected with the management of the factories there; and gladly putting
myself under his guidance, drove off at once to that quarter of the
town in which the works, the object of my visit, were situated.
Although only just of age—for if my recollection serve me, it has been
a manufacturing town barely one-and-twenty years—Lowell is a
large, populous, thriving place. Those indications of its youth which
first attract the eye, give it a quaintness and oddity of character
which, to a visitor from the old country, is amusing enough. It was a
very dirty winter's day, and nothing in the whole town looked old to
me, except the mud, which in some parts was almost knee-deep, and
might have been deposited there, on the subsiding of the waters after
the Deluge. In one place, there was a new wooden church, which,
having no steeple, and being yet unpainted, looked like an enormous
packing-case without any direction upon it. In another there was a
large hotel, whose walls and colonnades were so crisp, and thin, and
slight, that it had exactly the appearance of being built with cards.
I was careful not to draw my breath as we passed, and trembled when
I saw a workman come out upon the roof, lest with one thoughtless
stamp of his foot he should crush the structure beneath him, and
bring it rattling down. The very river that moves the machinery in
the mills (for they are all worked by water power), seems to acquire a
new character from the fresh building of bright red brick and painted
wood among which it takes its course; and to be as light-headed,
thoughtless, and brisk a young river, in its murmurings and tum-
blings, as one would desire to see. One would swear that every
"Bakery," "Grocery," and "Bookbindery," and other kind of store,
took its shutters down for the first time, and started in business
yesterday. The golden pestles and mortars fixed as signs upon the
sun-blind frames outside the Druggists', appear to have been just
turned out of the United States' Mint; and when I saw a baby of
some week or ten days old in a woman's arms at a street corner, I
found myself unconsciously wondering where it came from: never
supposing for an instant that it could have been born in such a
young town as that.

There are several factories in Lowell, each of which belongs to
what we should term a Company of Proprietors, but what they call
in America a Corporation. I went over several of these; such as a
woollen factory, a carpet factory, and a cotton factory: examined
them in every part; and saw them in their ordinary working aspect,
with no preparation of any kind, or departure from their ordinary
everyday proceedings. I may add that I am well acquainted with our
manufacturing towns in England, and have visited many mills in
Manchester and elsewhere in the same manner.

I happened to arrive at the first factory just as the dinner hour was
over, and the girls were returning to their work; indeed the stairs of
the mill were thronged with them as I ascended. They were all well

dressed, but not to my thinking above their condition; for I like to
see the humbler classes of society careful of their dress and appearance, and even, if they please, decorated with such little trinkets as
come within the compass of their means. Supposing it confined within reasonable limits, I would always encourage this kind of pride, as a
worthy element of self-respect, in any person I employed; and should
no more be deterred from doing so, because some wretched female
referred her fall to a love of dress, than I would allow my construction
of the real intent and meaning of the Sabbath to be influenced by any
warning to the well-disposed, founded on his backslidings on that
particular day, which might emanate from the rather doubtful
authority of a murderer in Newgate.

These girls, as I have said, were all well dressed: and that phrase
necessarily includes extreme cleanliness. They had serviceable
bonnets, good warm cloaks, and shawls; and were not above clogs
and pattens. Moreover, there were places in the mill in which they
could deposit these things without injury; and there were conveniences for washing. They were healthy in appearance, many of
them remarkably so, and had the manners and deportment of young
women: not of degraded brutes of burden. If I had seen in one of
those mills (but I did not, though I looked for something of this
kind with a sharp eye), the most lisping, mincing, affected, and ridiculous young creature that my imagination could suggest, I should
have thought of the careless, moping, slatternly, degraded, dull
reverse (I *have* seen that), and should have been still well pleased to
look upon her.

The rooms in which they worked, were as well ordered as themselves. In the windows of some, there were green plants, which were
trained to shade the glass; in all, there was as much fresh air, cleanliness, and comfort, as the nature of the occupation would possibly
admit of. Out of so large a number of females, many of whom were
only then just verging upon womanhood, it may be reasonably supposed that some were delicate and fragile in appearance: no doubt
there were. But I solemnly declare, that from all the crowd I saw in
the different factories that day, I cannot recall or separate one young
face that gave me a painful impression; not one young girl whom,
assuming it to be matter of necessity that she should gain her daily
bread by the labour of her hands, I would have removed from those
works if I had had the power.

They reside in various boarding-houses near at hand. The owners
of the mills are particularly careful to allow no persons to enter upon
the possession of these houses, whose characters have not undergone
the most searching and thorough inquiry. And complaint that is
made against them, by the boarders, or by any one else, is fully inves-
tigated; and if good ground of complaint be shown to exist against
them, they are removed, and their occupation is handed over to some
more deserving person. There are a few children employed in these
factories, but not many. The laws of the State forbid their working

more than nine months in the year, and require that they be educated during the other three. For this purpose there are schools in Lowell; and there are churches and chapels of various persuasions, in which the young women may observe that form of worship in which they have been educated.

At some distance from the factories, and on the highest and pleasantest ground in the neighbourhood, stands their hospital, or boarding-house for the sick; it is the best house in those parts, and was built by an eminent merchant for his own residence. Like that institute at Boston, which I have before described, it is not parcelled out into wards, but is divided into convenient chambers, each of which has all the comforts of a very comfortable home. The principal medical attendant resides under the same roof; and were the patients members of his own family, they could not be better cared for, or attended with greater gentleness and consideration. The weekly charge in this establishment for each female patient is three dollars, or twelve shillings English; but no girl employed by any of the corporations is ever excluded for want of the means of payment. That they do not very often want the means, may be gathered from the fact, that in July, 1841, no fewer than nine hundred and seventy-eight of these girls were depositors in the Lowell Savings Bank: the amount of whose joint savings was estimated at one hundred thousand dollars, or twenty thousand English pounds.

I am now going to state three facts, which will startle a large class of readers on this side of the Atlantic, very much.

Firstly, there is a joint-stock piano in a great many of the boarding-houses. Secondly, nearly all these young ladies subscribe to circulating libraries. Thirdly, they have got up among themselves a periodical called THE LOWELL OFFERING, "A repository of original articles, written exclusively by females actively employed in the mills,"—which is duly printed, published, and sold; and whereof I brought away from Lowell four hundred good solid pages, which I have read from beginning to end.

The large class of readers, startled by these facts, will exclaim, with one voice, "How very preposterous!" On my deferentially inquiring why, they will answer, "These things are above their station." In reply to that objection, I would beg to ask what their station is.

It is their station to work. And they *do* work. They labour in these mills, upon an average, twelve hours a day, which is unquestionably work, and pretty tight work too. Perhaps it is above their station to indulge in such amusements, on any terms. Are we quite sure that we in England have not formed our ideas of the "station" of working people, from accustoming ourselves to the contemplation of that class as they are, and not as they might be? I think that if we examine our own feelings, we shall find that the pianos, and the circulating libraries, and even the Lowell Offering, startle us by their novelty, and not by their bearing upon any abstract question of right or wrong.

For myself, I know no station in which, the occupation of to-day cheerfully done and the occupation of to-morrow cheerfully looked to, any one of these pursuits is not most humanising and laudable. I know no station which is rendered more endurable to the person in it, or more safe to the person out of it, by having ignorance for its associate. I know no station which has a right to monopolise the means of mutual instruction, improvement, and rational entertainment; or which has ever continued to be a station very long, after seeking to do so.

Of the merits of the Lowell Offering as a literary production, I will only observe, putting entirely out of sight the fact of the articles having been written by these girls after the arduous labours of the day, that it will compare advantageously with a great many English Annuals. It is pleasant to find that many of its Tales are of the Mills and of those who work in them; that they inculcate habits of self-denial and contentment, and teach good doctrines of enlarged benevolence. A strong feeling for the beauties of nature, as displayed in the solitudes the writers have left at home, breathes through its pages like wholesome village air; and though a circulating library is a favourable school for the study of such topics, it has very scant allusion to fine clothes, fine marriages, fine houses, or fine life. Some persons might object to the papers being signed occasionally with rather fine names, but this is an American fashion. One of the provinces of the state legislature of Massachusetts is to alter ugly names into pretty ones, as the children improve upon the tastes of their parents. These changes costing little or nothing, scores of Mary Annes are solemnly converted into Bevelinas every session.

It is said that on the occasion of a visit from General Jackson or General Harrison to this town (I forget which, but it is not to the purpose), he walked through three miles and a half of these young ladies all dressed out with parasols and silk stockings. But as I am not aware that any worse consequence ensued, than a sudden looking-up of all the parasols and silk stockings in the market; and perhaps the bankruptcy of some speculative New Englander who bought them all up at any price, in expectation of a demand that never came; I set no great store by the circumstance.

In this brief account of Lowell, and inadequate expression of the gratification it yielded me, and cannot fail to afford to any foreigner to whom the condition of such people at home is a subject of interest and anxious speculation, I have carefully abstained from drawing a comparison between these factories and those of our own land. Many of the circumstances whose strong influence has been at work for years in our manufacturing towns have not arisen here; and there is no manufacturing population in Lowell, so to speak: for these girls (often the daughters of small farmers) come from other States, remain a few years in the mills, and then go home for good.

The contrast would be a strong one, for it would be between the Good and Evil, the living light and deepest shadow. I abstain from it, because I deem it just to do so. But I only the more earnestly adjure all those whose eyes may rest on these pages, to pause and reflect upon the difference between this town and those great haunts of desperate misery: to call to mind, if they can in the midst of party strife and squabble, the efforts that must be made to purge them of their suffering and danger: and last, and foremost, to remember how the precious Time is rushing by.

I returned at night by the same railroad and in the same kind of car. One of the passengers being exceedingly anxious to expound at great length to my companion (not to me, of course) the true principles on which books of travel in America should be written by Englishmen, I feigned to fall asleep. But glancing all the way out at window from the corners of my eyes, I found abundance of entertainment for the rest of the ride in watching the effects of the wood fire, which had been invisible in the morning but were now brought out in full relief by the darkness: for we were travelling in a whirlwind of bright sparks, which showered about us like a storm of fiery snow.

## CHAPTER V

### WORCESTER. THE CONNECTICUT RIVER. HARTFORD. NEW HAVEN. TO NEW YORK

LEAVING Boston on the afternoon of Saturday the fifth of February, we proceeded by another railroad to Worcester: a pretty New England town, where we had arranged to remain under the hospitable roof of the Governor of the State, until Monday morning.

These towns and cities of New England (many of which would be villages in Old England), are as favourable specimens of rural America, as their people are of rural Americans. The well-trimmed lawns and green meadows of home are not there; and the grass, compared with our ornamental plots and pastures, is rank, and rough, and wild: but delicate slopes of land, gently-swelling hills, wooded valleys and slender streams, abound. Every little colony of houses has its church and school-house peeping from among the white roofs and shady trees; every house is the whitest of the white; every Venetian blind the greenest of the green; every fine day's sky the bluest of the blue. A sharp dry wind and a slight frost had so hardened the roads when we alighted at Worcester, that their furrowed tracks were like ridges of granite. There was the usual aspect of newness on every object, of course. All the buildings looked as if they had been built and painted that morning, and could be taken down on Monday with very little trouble. In the keen evening air, every sharp outline looked a hundred times sharper than ever. The clean cardboard colonnades had no more perspective than a Chinese bridge on a teacup, and appeared equally well calculated for use. The razor-like edges of the detached cottages seemed to cut the very wind as it whistled against them, and to send it smarting on its way with a shriller cry than before. Those slightly-built wooden dwellings behind which the sun was setting with a brilliant lustre, could be so looked through and through, that the idea of any inhabitant being able to hide himself from the public gaze, or to have any secrets from the public eye, was not entertainable for a moment. Even where a blazing fire shone through the uncurtained windows of some distant house, it had the air of being newly lighted, and of lacking warmth; and instead of awakening thoughts of a snug chamber, bright with faces that first saw the light round that same hearth, and ruddy with warm hangings, it came upon one suggestive of the smell of new mortar and damp walls.

So I thought, at least, that evening. Next morning when the sun was shining brightly, and the clear church bells were ringing, and sedate people in their best clothes enlivened the pathway near at hand and dotted the distant thread of road, there was a pleasant Sabbath peacefulness on everything, which it was good to feel. It would have been the better for an old church; better still for some old graves; but as it was, a wholesome repose and tranquillity pervaded the scene, which after the restless ocean and the hurried city, had a doubly grateful influence on the spirits.

We went on next morning, still by railroad, to Springfield. From that place to Hartford, whither we were bound, is a distance of only five-and-twenty miles, but at that time of the year the roads were so bad that the journey would probably have occupied ten or twelve hours. Fortunately, however, the winter having been unusually mild, the Connecticut River was "open," or, in other words, not frozen. The captain of a small steamboat was going to make his first trip for the season that day (the second February trip, I believe, within the memory of man), and only waited for us to go on board. Accordingly, we went on board, with as little delay as might be. He was as good as his word, and started directly.

It certainly was not called a small steamboat without reason. I omitted to ask the question, but I should think it must have been of about half a pony power. Mr. Paap, the celebrated Dwarf, might have lived and died happily in the cabin, which was fitted with common sash-windows like an ordinary dwelling-house. These windows had bright-red curtains, too, hung on slack strings across the lower panes; so that it looked like a parlour of a Lilliputian public-house, which had got afloat in a flood or some other water accident, and was drifting nobody knew where. But even in this chamber there was a rocking-chair. It would be impossible to get on anywhere, in America, without a rocking-chair.

I am afraid to tell how many feet short this vessel was, or how many feet narrow: to apply the words length and width to such measurement would be a contradiction in terms. But I may state that we all kept the middle of the deck, lest the boat should un-expectedly tip over; and that the machinery, by some surprising process of condensation, worked between it and the keel; the whole forming a warm sandwich, about three feet thick.

It rained all day as I once thought it never did rain anywhere, but in the Highlands of Scotland. The river was full of floating blocks of ice, which were constantly crunching and cracking under us; and the depth of water, in the course we took to avoid the larger masses, carried down the middle of the river by the current, did not exceed a few inches. Nevertheless, we moved onward dexterously; and being well wrapped up, bade defiance to the weather, and enjoyed the journey. The Connecticut River is a fine stream; and the banks in summer-time are, I have no doubt, beautiful: at all events, I was told so by a young lady in the cabin; and she should be a judge of beauty, if the possession of a quality include the appreciation of it, for a more beautiful creature I never looked upon.

After two hours and a half of this odd travelling (including a stoppage at a small town, where we were saluted by a gun con-siderably bigger than our own chimney), we reached Hartford, and straightway repaired to an extremely comfortable hotel: except, as usual, in the article of bedrooms, which, in almost every place we visited, were very conducive to early rising.

We tarried here, four days. The town is beautifully situated in a basin of green hills; the soil is rich, well-wooded, and carefully improved. It is the seat of the local legislature of Connecticut, which sage body enacted, in bygone times, the renowned code of "Blue Laws," in virtue whereof, among other enlightened provisions, any citizen who could be proved to have kissed his wife on Sunday, was punishable, I believe, with the stocks. Too much of the old Puritan spirit exists in these parts to the present hour; but its influence has not tended, that I know, to make the people less hard in their bar-gains, or more equal in their dealings. As I never heard of its working that effect anywhere else, I infer that it never will, here. Indeed, I am accustomed, with reference to great professions and severe faces, to judge of the goods of the other world pretty much as I judge the goods of this; and whenever I see a dealer in such com-modities with too great a display of them in his window, I doubt the quality of the article within.

In Hartford stands the famous oak in which the charter of King Charles was hidden. It is now inclosed in a gentleman's garden. In the State House is the charter itself. I found the courts of law here, just the same as at Boston; the public institutions almost as good. The Insane Asylum is admirably conducted, and so is the Institution for the Deaf and Dumb.

I very much questioned within myself, as I walked through the Insane Asylum, whether I should have known the attendants from the patients, but for the few words which passed between the former, and the Doctor, in reference to the persons under their charge. Of course I limit this remark merely to their looks; for the conversation of the mad people was mad enough.

There was one little, prim old lady, of very smiling and good-humoured appearance, who came sidling up to me from the end of a long passage, and with a curtsey of inexpressible condescension, propounded this unaccountable inquiry:

"Does Pontefract still flourish sir, upon the soil of England?"

"He does, ma'am," I rejoined.

"When you last saw him, sir, he was——"

"Well, ma'am," said I, "extremely well. He begged me to present his compliments. I never saw him looking better."

At this, the old lady was very much delighted. After glancing at me for a moment, as if to be quite sure that I was serious in my respectful air, she sidled back some paces; sidled forward again; made a sudden skip (at which I precipitately retreated a step or two); and said:

"*I* am an antediluvian, sir."

I thought the best thing to say was, that I had suspected as much from the first. Therefore I said so.

"It is an extremely proud and pleasant thing, sir, to be an antediluvian," said the old lady.

"I should think it was, ma'am," I rejoined.

The old lady kissed her hand, gave another skip, smirked and sidled down the gallery in a most extraordinary manner, and ambled gracefully into her own bed-chamber.

In another part of the building, there was a male patient in bed; very much flushed and heated.

"Well," said he, starting up, and pulling off his night-cap: "It's all settled at last. I have arranged it with Queen Victoria."

"Arranged what?" asked the Doctor.

"Why, that business," passing his hand wearily across his forehead, "about the siege of New York."

"Oh!" said I, like a man suddenly enlightened. For he looked at me for an answer.

"Yes. Every house without a signal will be fired upon by the British troops. No harm will be done to the others. No harm at all. Those that want to be safe, must hoist flags. That's all they'll have to do. They must hoist flags."

Even while he was speaking he seemed, I thought, to have some faint idea that his talk was incoherent. Directly he had said these words, he lay down again; gave a kind of a groan; and covered his hot head with the blankets.

There was another: a young man, whose madness was love and music. After playing on the accordion a march he had composed, he was very anxious that I should walk into his chamber, which I immediately did.

By way of being very knowing, and humouring him to the top of his bent, I went to the window, which commanded a beautiful prospect, and remarked, with an address upon which I greatly plumed myself:

"What a delicious country you have about these lodgings of yours!"

"Poh!" said he, moving his fingers carelessly over the notes of his instrument: *"Well enough for such an Institution as this!"*

I don't think I was ever so taken aback in all my life.

"I come here just for a whim," he said coolly. "That's all."

"Oh! That's all!" said I.

"Yes. That's all. The Doctor's a smart man. He quite enters into it. It's a joke of mine. I like it for a time. You needn't mention it, but I think I shall go out next Tuesday!"

I assured him that I would consider our interview perfectly confidential; and rejoined the Doctor. As we were passing through a gallery on our way out, a well-dressed lady, of quiet and composed manners, came up, and proffering a slip of paper and a pen, begged that I would oblige her with an autograph. I complied, and we parted.

"I think I remember having had a few interviews like that, with ladies out of doors. I hope *she* is not mad?"

"Yes."

"On what subject? Autographs?"

"No. She hears voices in the air."

"Well!" thought I, "it would be well if we could shut up a few false prophets of these later times, who have professed to do the same; and I should like to try the experiment on a Mormonist or two to begin with."

In this place, there is the best Jail for untried offenders in the world. There is also a very well-ordered State prison, arranged upon the same plan as that at Boston, except that here, there is always a sentry on the wall with a loaded gun. It contained at that time about two hundred prisoners. A spot was shown me in the sleeping ward, where a watchman was murdered some years since in the dead of night, in a desperate attempt to escape, made by a prisoner who had broken from his cell. A woman, too, was pointed out to me, who, for the murder of her husband, had been a close prisoner for sixteen years.

"Do you think," I asked of my conductor, "that after so very long an imprisonment, she has any thought or hope of ever regaining her liberty?"

"Oh dear yes," he answered. "To be sure she has."

"She has no chance of obtaining it, I suppose?"

"Well, I don't know:" which, by-the-bye, is a national answer. "Her friends mistrust her."

"What have *they* to do with it?" I naturally inquired.

"Well, they won't petition."

"But if they did, they couldn't get her out, I suppose?"

"Well, not the first time, perhaps, nor yet the second, but tiring and wearying for a few years might do it."

"Does that ever do it?"

"Why yes, that'll do it sometimes. Political friends'll do it sometimes. It's pretty often done, one way or another."

I shall always entertain a very pleasant and grateful recollection of Hartford. It is a lovely place, and I had many friends there, whom I can never remember with indifference. We left it with no little regret on the evening of Friday the 11th, and travelled that night by railroad to New Haven. Upon the way, the guard and I were formally introduced to each other (as we usually were on such occasions), and exchanged a variety of small-talk. We reached New Haven at about eight o'clock, after a journey of three hours, and put up for the night at the best inn.

New Haven, known also as the City of Elms, is a fine town. Many of its streets (as its *alias* sufficiently imports) are planted with rows of grand old elm-trees; and the same natural ornaments surround Yale College, an establishment of considerable eminence and reputation. The various departments of this Institution are erected in a kind of park or common in the middle of the town, where they are dimly visible among the shadowing trees. The effect is very like that of an old cathedral yard in England; and when their branches are in full leaf, must be extremely picturesque. Even in the winter time, these groups of well-grown trees, clustering among the busy streets and houses of a thriving city, have a very quaint appearance: seeming to bring about a kind of compromise between town and country; as if each had met the other half-way, and shaken hands upon it; which is at once novel and pleasant.

After a night's rest we rose early, and in good time went down to the wharf, and on board the packet New York *for* New York. This was the first American steamboat of any size that I had seen; and certainly to an English eye it was infinitely less like a steamboat than a huge floating bath. I could hardly persuade myself, indeed, but that the bathing establishment off Westminster Bridge, which I left a baby, had suddenly grown to an enormous size; run away from home; and set up in foreign parts as a steamer. Being in America, too, which our vagabonds do so particularly favour, it seemed the more probable.

The great difference in appearance between these packets and ours, is, there is so much of them out of the water: the main-deck being enclosed on all sides, and filled with casks and goods, like any second or third floor in a stack of warehouses; and the promenade or hurricane-deck being a-top of that again. A part of the machinery is always above this deck; where the connecting-rod, in a strong and lofty frame, is seen working away like an iron top-sawyer. There is seldom any mast or tackle: nothing aloft but two tall black chimneys. The man at the helm is shut up in a little house in the fore part of the boat (the wheel being connected with the rudder by iron chains, working the whole length of the deck); and the passengers, unless

# American Notes

and there, in that one instance (look while it passes, or it will be too late), in suits of livery. Some southern republican that, who puts his blacks in uniform, and swells with Sultan pomp and power. Yonder where that phaeton with the well-clipped pair of grays has stopped—standing at their heads now—is a Yorkshire groom, who has not been very long in these parts, and looks sorrowfully round for a companion pair of top-boots, which he may traverse the city half a year without meeting. Heaven save the ladies, how they dress! We have seen more colours in these ten minutes, than we should have seen elsewhere, in as many days. What various parasols! what rainbow silks and satins! what pinking of thin stockings, and pinching of thin shoes, and fluttering of ribbons and silk tassels, and display of rich cloaks with gaudy hoods and linings! The young gentlemen are fond, you see, of turning down their shirt-collars and cultivating their whiskers, especially under the chin; but they cannot approach the ladies in their dress or bearing, being, to say the truth, humanity of quite another sort. Byrons of the desk and counter, pass on, and let us see what kind of men those are behind ye: those two labourers in holiday clothes, of whom one carries in his hand a crumpled scrap of paper from which he tries to spell out a hard name, while the other looks about for it on all the doors and windows.

Irishmen both! You might know them, if they were masked, by their long-tailed blue coats and bright buttons, and their drab trousers, which they wear like men well used to working dresses, who are easy in no others. It would be hard to keep your model republics going, without the countrymen and countrywomen of those two labourers. For who else would dig, and delve, and drudge, and do domestic work, and make canals and roads, and execute great lines of Internal Improvement! Irishmen both, and sorely puzzled too, to find out what they seek. Let us go down, and help them, for the love of home, and that spirit of liberty which admits of honest service to honest men, and honest work for honest bread, no matter what it be.

That's well! We have got at the right address at last, though it is written in strange characters truly, and might have been scrawled with the blunt handle of the spade the writer better knows the use of, than a pen. Their way lies yonder, but what business takes them there? They carry savings: to hoard up? No. They are brothers, those men. One crossed the sea alone, and working very hard for one half year, and living harder, saved funds enough to bring the other out. That done, they worked together side by side, contentedly sharing hard labour and hard living for another term, and then their sisters came, and then another brother, and lastly, their old mother. And what now? Why, the poor old crone is restless in a strange land, and yearns to lay her bones, she says, among her people in the old graveyard at home: and so they go to pay her passage back: and God help her and them, and every simple heart, and all who turn to the Jerusalem of their younger days, and have an altar-fire upon the cold hearth of their fathers.

This narrow thoroughfare, baking and blistering in the sun, is Wall Street: the Stock Exchange and Lombard Street of New York. Many a rapid fortune has been made in this street, and many a no less rapid ruin. Some of these very merchants whom you see hanging about here now, have locked up money in their strong-boxes, like the man in the Arabian Nights, and opening them again, have found but withered leaves. Below, here by the water-side, where the bowsprits of ships stretch across the footway, and almost thrust themselves into the windows, lie the noble American vessels which have made their Packet Service the finest in the world. They have brought hither the foreigners who abound in all the streets: not, perhaps, that there are more here, than in other commercial cities; but elsewhere, they have particular haunts, and you must find them out; here, they pervade the town.

We must cross Broadway again; gaining some refreshment from the heat, in the sight of the great blocks of clean ice which are being carried into shops and bar-rooms; and the pine-apples and water melons profusely displayed for sale. Fine streets of spacious houses here, you see!—Wall Street has furnished and dismantled many of them very often—and here a deep green leafy square. Be sure that it is a hospitable house with inmates to be affectionately remembered always, where they have the open door and pretty show of plants within, and where the child with laughing eyes is peeping out of window at the little dog below. You wonder what may be the use of this tall flagstaff in the by-street, with something like Liberty's head-dress on its top: so do I. But there is a passion for tall flagstaffs hereabout, and you may see its twin brother in five minutes, if you have a mind.

Again across Broadway, and so—passing from the many-coloured crowd and glittering shops—into another long main street, the Bowery. A railroad yonder, see, where two stout horses trot along, drawing a score or two of people and a great wooden ark, with ease. The stores are poorer here; the passengers less gay. Clothes ready-made, and meat ready-cooked, are to be bought in these parts; and the lively whirl of carriages is exchanged for the deep rumble of carts and waggons. These signs which are so plentiful, in shape like river buoys, or small balloons, hoisted by cords to poles, and dangling there, announce, as you may see by looking up, "OYSTERS IN EVERY STYLE." They tempt the hungry most at night, for then dull candles glimmering inside, illuminate these dainty words, and make the mouths of idlers water, as they read and linger.

What is this dismal-fronted pile of bastard Egyptian, like an enchanter's palace in a melodrama!—a famous prison, called The Tombs. Shall we go in?

So. A long, narrow, lofty building, stove-heated as usual, with four galleries, one above the other, going round it, and communicating by stairs. Between the two sides of each gallery, and in its centre, a bridge, for the greater convenience of crossing. On each of these bridges sits a man: dozing or reading, or talking to an idle companion. On each tier, are two opposite rows of small iron doors. They look like furnace-doors, but are cold and black, as though the fires within had all gone out. Some two or three are open, and women, with drooping heads bent down, are talking to the inmates. The whole is lighted by a skylight, but it is fast closed; and from the roof there dangle, limp and drooping, two useless windsails.

A man with keys appears, to show us round. A good-looking fellow, and, in his way, civil and obliging.

"Are those black doors the cells?"

"Yes."

"Are they all full?"

"Well, they're pretty nigh full, and that's a fact, and no two ways about it."

"Those at the bottom are unwholesome, surely?"

"Why, we *do* only put coloured people in 'em. That's the truth."

"When do the prisoners take exercise?"

"Well, they do without it pretty much."

"Do they never walk in the yard?"

"Considerable seldom."

"Sometimes, I suppose?"

"Well, it's rare they do. They keep pretty bright without it."

"But suppose a man were here for a twelvemonth. I know this is only a prison for criminals who are charged with grave offences, while they are awaiting their trial, or under remand, but the law here affords criminals many means of delay. What with motions for new trials, and in arrest of judgment, and what not, a prisoner might be here for twelve months, I take it, might he not?"

"Well, I guess he might."

"Do you mean to say that in all that time he would never come out at that little iron door, for exercise?"

"He might walk some, perhaps—not much."

"Will you open one of the doors?"

"All, if you like."

The fastenings jar and rattle, and one of the doors turns slowly on its hinges. Let us look in. A small bare cell, into which the light enters through a high chink in the wall. There is a rude means of washing, a table, and a bedstead. Upon the latter, sits a man of sixty; reading. He looks up for a moment; gives an impatient dogged shake; and fixes his eyes upon his book again. As we withdraw our heads, the door closes on him, and is fastened as before. This man has murdered his wife, and will probably be hanged.

"How long has he been here?"

"A month."

"When will he be tried?"

"Next term."

"When is that?"

"Next month."

"In England, if a man be under sentence of death, even he has air and exercise at certain periods of the day."

"Possible?"

With what stupendous and untranslatable coolness he says this, and how loungingly he leads on to the women's side: making, as he goes, a kind of iron castanet of the key and the stair-rail!

Each cell door on this side has a square aperture in it. Some of the women peep anxiously through it at the sound of footsteps; others shrink away in shame.—For what offence can that lonely child, of ten or twelve years old, be shut up here? Oh! that boy? He is the son of the prisoner we saw just now; is a witness against his father; and is detained here for safe keeping, until the trial; that's all.

But it is a dreadful place for the child to pass the long days and nights in. This is rather hard treatment for a young witness, is it not?—What says our conductor?

"Well, it an't a very rowdy life, and *that's* a fact!"

Again he clinks his metal castanet, and leads us leisurely away. I have a question to ask him as we go.

"Pray why do they call this place The Tombs?"

"Well, it's the cant name."

"I know it is. Why?"

"Some suicides happened here, when it was first built. I expect it come about from that."

"I saw just now, that that man's clothes were scattered about the floor of his cell. Don't you oblige the prisoners to be orderly, and put such things away?"

"Where should they put 'em?"

"Not on the ground surely. What do you say to hanging them up?"

He stops and looks round to emphasise his answer:

"Why, I say that's just it. When they had hooks they *would* hang themselves, so they're taken out of every cell, and there's only the marks left where they used to be!"

The prison-yard in which he pauses now, has been the scene of terrible performances. Into this narrow, grave-like place, men are brought out to die. The wretched creature stands beneath the gibbet on the ground; the rope about his neck; and when the sign is given, a weight at its other end comes running down, and swings him up into the air—a corpse.

The law requires that there be present at this dismal spectacle, the judge, the jury, and citizens to the amount of twenty-five. From the community it is hidden. To the dissolute and bad, the thing remains a frightful mystery. Between the criminal and them, the prison-wall is interposed as a thick gloomy veil. It is the curtain to his bed of death, his winding-sheet, and grave. From him it shuts out life, and all the motives to unrepenting hardihood in that last hour, which its mere sight and presence is often all-sufficient to sustain. There are no bold eyes to make him bold; no ruffians to uphold a ruffian's name before. All beyond the pitiless stone wall, is unknown space.

Let us go forth again into the cheerful streets.

Once more in Broadway! Here are the same ladies in bright colours, walking to and fro, in pairs and singly; yonder the very same light blue parasol which passed and repassed the hotel-window twenty times while we were sitting there. We are going to cross here. Take care of the pigs. Two portly sows are trotting up behind this carriage, and a select party of half-a-dozen gentlemen hogs have just now turned the corner.

Here is a solitary swine lounging homeward by himself. He has only one ear; having parted with the other to vagrant-dogs in the course of his city rambles. But he gets on very well without it; and leads a roving, gentlemanly, vagabond kind of life, somewhat answering to that of our club-men at home. He leaves his lodgings every morning at a certain hour, throws himself upon the town, gets through his day in some manner quite satisfactory to himself, and regularly appears at the door of his own house again at night, like the mysterious master of Gil Blas. He is a free-and-easy, careless, indifferent kind of pig, having a very large acquaintance among other pigs of the same character, whom he rather knows by sight than conversation, as he seldom troubles himself to stop and exchange civilities, but goes grunting down the kennel, turning up the news and small-talk of the city in the shape of cabbage-stalks and offal, and bearing no tails but his own: which is a very short one, for his old enemies, the dogs, have been at that too, and have left him hardly enough to swear by. He is in every respect a republican pig, going wherever he pleases, and mingling with the best society, on an equal if not superior footing, for every one makes way when he appears, and the haughtiest give him the wall, if he prefer it. He is a great philosopher, and seldom moved, unless by the dogs before mentioned. Sometimes, indeed, you may see his small eye twinkling on a slaughtered friend, whose carcase garnishes a butcher's doorpost, but he grunts out "Such is life: all flesh is pork!" buries his nose in the mire again, and waddles down the gutter: comforting himself with the reflection that there is one snout the less to anticipate stray cabbage-stalks, at any rate.

They are the city scavengers, these pigs. Ugly brutes they are; having, for the most part, scanty brown backs, like the lids of old horsehair trunks: spotted with unwholesome black blotches. They have long gaunt legs, too, and such peaked snouts, that if one of them could be persuaded to sit for his profile, nobody would recognise it for a pig's likeness. They are never attended upon, or fed, or driven, or caught, but are thrown upon their own resources in early life, and become preternaturally knowing in consequence. Every pig knows where he lives, much better than anybody could tell him. At this hour, just as evening is closing in, you will see them roaming towards bed by scores, eating their way to the last. Occasionally, some youth among them who has over-eaten himself, or has been worried by dogs, trots shrinkingly homeward, like a prodigal son: but this is a rare case: perfect self-possession and self-reliance, and immovable composure, being their foremost attributes.

The streets and shops are lighted now; and as the eye travels down the long thoroughfare, dotted with bright jets of gas, it is reminded of Oxford Street, or Piccadilly. Here and there a flight of broad stone cellar-steps appears, and a painted lamp directs you to the Bowling Saloon, or Ten-Pin alley; Ten-Pins being a game of mingled chance and skill, invented when the legislature passed an act forbidding Nine-Pins. At other downward flight of steps, are other lamps, marking the whereabouts of oyster-cellars—pleasant retreats, say I: not only by reason of their wonderful cookery of oysters, pretty nigh as large as cheese-plates (or for thy dear sake, heartiest of Greek Professors!), but because of all kinds of eaters of fish, or flesh, or fowl, in these latitudes, the swallowers of oysters alone are not gregarious; but subduing themselves, as it were, to the nature of what they work in, and copying the coyness of the thing they eat, do sit apart in curtained boxes, and consort by twos, not by two hundreds.

But how quiet the streets are! Are there not itinerant bands; no wind or stringed instruments? No, not one. By day, are there no Punches, Fantoccini, Dancing-dogs, Jugglers, Conjurers, Orchestrinas, or even Barrel-organs? No, not one. Yes, I remember one. One barrel-organ and a dancing-monkey—sportive by nature, but fast fading into a dull, lumpish monkey, of the Utilitarian school. Beyond that, nothing lively; no, not so much as a white mouse in a twirling cage.

Are there no amusements? Yes. There is a lecture-room across the way, from which that glare of light proceeds, and there may be evening service for the ladies thrice a week, or oftener. For the young gentlemen, there is the counting-house, the store, the bar-room: the latter, as you may see through these windows, pretty full. Hark! to the clinking sound of hammers breaking lumps of ice, and to the cool gurgling of the pounded bits, as, in the process of mixing, they are poured from glass to glass! No amusements? What are these suckers of cigars and swallowers of strong drinks, whose hats and legs we see in every possible variety of twist, doing, but amusing themselves? What are the fifty newspapers, which those precocious urchins are bawling down the street, and which are kept filed within, what are they but amusements? Not vapid, waterish amusements, but good strong stuff; dealing in round abuse and blackguard names; pulling off the roofs of private houses, as the Halting Devil did in Spain; pimping and pandering for all degrees of vicious taste, and gorging with coined lies the most voracious maw; imputing to every man in public life the coarsest and the vilest motives; scaring away from the stabbed and prostrate body-politic, every Samaritan of clear conscience and good deeds; and setting on, with yell and whistle and the clapping of foul hands, the vilest vermin and worst birds of prey.—No amusements!

Let us go on again; and passing this wilderness of an hotel with stores about its base, like some Continental theatre, or the London Opera House shorn of its colonnade, plunge into the Five Points. But it is needful, first, that we take as our escort these two heads of the police, whom you would know for sharp and well-trained officers if you met them in the Great Desert. So true it is, that certain pursuits, wherever carried on, will stamp men with the same character. These two might have been begotten, born, and bred, in Bow Street.

We have seen no beggars in the streets by night or day; but of other kinds of strollers, plenty. Poverty, wretchedness, and vice, are rife enough where we are going now.

This is the place: these narrow ways, diverging to the right and left, and reeking everywhere with dirt and filth. Such lives as are led here bear the same fruits here as elsewhere. The coarse and bloated faces at the doors, have counterparts at home, and all the wide world over. Debauchery has made the very houses prematurely old. See how the rotten beams are tumbling down, and how the patched and broken windows seem to scowl dimly, like eyes that have been hurt in drunken frays. Many of those pigs live here. Do they ever wonder why their masters walk upright in lieu of going on all-fours? and why they talk instead of grunting?

So far, nearly every house is a low tavern; and on the bar-room walls, are coloured prints of Washington, and Queen Victoria of England, and the American Eagle. Among the pigeon-holes that hold the bottles, are pieces of plate-glass and coloured paper, for there is, in some sort, a taste for decoration, even here. And as seamen frequent these haunts, there are maritime pictures by the dozen: of partings between sailors and their lady-loves, portraits of William, of the ballad, and his Black-Eyed Susan; of Will Watch, the Bold Smuggler; of Paul Jones the Pirate, and the like: on which the painted eyes of Queen Victoria, and of Washington to boot, rest in as strange companionship, as on most of the scenes that are enacted in their wondering presence.

What place is this, to which the squalid street conducts us? A kind of square of leprous houses, some of which are attainable only by crazy wooden stairs without. What lies beyond this tottering flight of steps, that creak beneath our tread?—a miserable room, lighted by one dim candle, and destitute of all comfort, save that which may be hidden in a wretched bed. Beside it, sits a man: his elbows on his knees: his forehead hidden in his hands. "What ails that man?" asks the foremost officer. "Fever," he sullenly replies, without looking up. Conceive the fancies of a feverish brain in such a place as this!

Ascend these pitch-dark stairs, heedful of a false footing on the trembling boards, and grope your way with me into this wolfish den, where neither ray of light nor breath of air, appears to come. A negro lad, startled from his sleep by the officer's voice—he knows it well—but comforted by his assurance that he has not come on business, officiously bestirs himself to light a candle. The match flickers for a moment, and shows great mounds of dusty rags upon the ground; then dies away and leaves a denser darkness than before, if there can be degrees in such extremes. He stumbles down the stairs and presently comes back, shading a flaring taper with his hand. Then the mounds of rags are seen to be astir, and rise slowly up, and the floor is covered with heaps of negro women, waking from their sleep: their white teeth chattering, and their bright eyes glistening and winking on all sides with surprise and fear, like the countless repetition of one astonished African face in some strange mirror.

Mount up these other stairs with no less caution (there are traps, and pitfalls here, for those who are not so well escorted as ourselves) into the housetop; where the bare beams and rafters meet overhead, and calm night looks down through the crevices in the roof. Open the door of one of these cramped hutches full of sleeping negroes. Pah! They have a charcoal fire within; there is a smell of singeing clothes, or flesh, so close they gather round the brazier; and vapours issue forth that blind and suffocate. From every corner, as you glance about you in these dark retreats, some figure crawls half-awakened, as if the judgment-hour were near at hand, and every obscene grave were giving up its dead. Where dogs would howl to lie, women, and men, and boys slink off to sleep, forcing the dislodged rats to move away in quest of better lodgings.

Here too are lanes and alleys, paved with mud knee-deep, underground chambers, where they dance and game; the walls bedecked with rough designs of ships, and forts, and flags, and American eagles out of number: ruined houses, open to the street, whence, through wide gaps in the walls, other ruins loom upon the eye, as though the world of vice and misery had nothing else to show: hideous tenements which take their name from robbery and murder: all that is loathsome, drooping, and decayed is here.

Our leader has his hand upon the latch of "Almack's," and calls to us from the bottom of the steps; for the assembly-room of the Five Point fashionables is approached by a descent. Shall we go in? It is but a moment.

Heyday! the landlady of Almack's thrives! A buxom fat mulatto woman, with sparkling eyes, whose head is daintily ornamented with a handkerchief of many colours. Nor is the landlord much behind her in his finery, being attired in a smart blue jacket, like a ship's steward, with a thick gold ring upon his little finger, and round his neck a gleaming golden watch-guard. How glad he is to see us! What will we please to call for? A dance? It shall be done directly, sir: "a regular break-down."

The corpulent black fiddler, and his friend who plays the tambourine, stamp upon the boarding of the small raised orchestra in which they sit, and play a lively measure. Five or six couple come upon the floor, marshalled by a lively young negro, who is the wit of the assembly, and the greatest dancer known. He never leaves off making queer faces, and is the delight of all the rest, who grin from ear to ear incessantly. Among the dancers are two young mulatto girls, with large, black, drooping eyes, and head-gear after the fashion of the hostess, who are as shy, or feign to be, as though they never danced before, and so look down before the visitors, that their partners can see nothing but the long fringed lashes.

But the dance commences. Every gentleman sets as long as he likes to the opposite lady, and the opposite lady to him, and all are so long about it that the sport begins to languish, when suddenly the lively hero dashes in to the rescue. Instantly the fiddler grins, and goes at it tooth and nail; there is new energy in the tambourine; new laughter in the dancers; new smiles in the landlady: new confidence in the landlord; new brightness in the very candles. Single shuffle, double shuffle, cut and cross-cut; snapping his fingers, rolling his eyes, turning in his knees, presenting the backs of his legs in front, spinning about on his toes and heels like nothing but the man's fingers on the tambourine; dancing with two left legs, two right legs, two wooden legs, two wire legs, two spring legs—all sorts of legs and no legs—what is this to him? And in what walk of life, or dance of life, does man ever get such stimulating applause as thunders about him, when, having danced his partner off her feet, and himself too, he finishes by leaping gloriously on the bar-counter, and calling for something to drink, with the chuckle of a million of counterfeit Jim Crows, in one inimitable sound!

The air, even in these distempered parts, is fresh after the stifling atmosphere of the houses; and now, as we emerge into a broader street, it blows upon us with a purer breath, and the stars look bright again. Here are The Tombs once more. The city watch-house is a part of the building. It follows naturally on the sights we have just left. Let us see that, and then to bed.

What! do you thrust your common offenders against the police discipline of the town, into such holes as these? Do men and women, against whom no crime is proved, lie here all night in perfect darkness, surrounded by the noisome vapours which encircle that flagging lamp you light us with, and breathing this filthy and offensive stench! Why, such indecent and disgusting dungeons as these cells, would bring disgrace upon the most despotic empire in the world! Look at them, man—you, who see them every night, and keep the keys. Do you see what they are? Do you know how drains are made below the streets, and wherein these human sewers differ, except in being always stagnant?

Well, he don't know. He has had five-and-twenty young women locked up in this very cell at one time, and you'd hardly realise what handsome faces there were among 'em.

In God's name! shut the door upon the wretched creature who is in it now, and put its screen before a place, quite unsurpassed in all the vice, neglect, and devilry, of the worst old town in Europe.

Are people really left all night, untried, in those black sties?—Every night. The watch is set at seven in the evening. The magistrate opens his court at five in the morning. That is the earliest hour at which the first prisoner can be released; and if an officer appear against him, he is not taken out till nine o'clock or ten.—But if any one among them die in the interval, as one man did, not long ago? Then he is half-eaten by the rats in an hour's time; as that man was; and there an end.

What is this intolerable tolling of great bells, and crashing of wheels, and shouting in the distance? A fire. And what that deep red light in the opposite direction? Another fire. And what these charred and blackened walls we stand before? A dwelling where a fire has been. It was more than hinted, in an official report, not long ago, that some of these conflagrations were not wholly accidental, and that speculation and enterprise found a field of exertion, even in flames: but be this as it may, there was a fire last night, there are two to-night, and you may lay an even wager there will be at least one, to-morrow. So, carrying that with us for our comfort, let us say, Good night, and climb up-stairs to bed.

---

One day, during my stay in New York, I paid a visit to the different public institutions on Long Island, or Rhode Island: I forget which. One of them is a Lunatic Asylum. The building is handsome; and is remarkable for a spacious and elegant staircase. The whole structure is not yet finished, but it is already one of considerable size and extent, and is capable of accommodating a very large number of patients.

I cannot say that I derived much comfort from the inspection of this charity. The different wards might have been cleaner and better ordered; I saw nothing of that salutary system which had impressed me so favourably elsewhere; and everything had a lounging, listless, madhouse air, which was very painful. The moping idiot, cowering down with long dishevelled hair; the gibbering maniac, with his hideous laugh and pointed finger; the vacant eye, the fierce wild face, the gloomy picking of the hands and lips, and munching of the nails: there they were all, without disguise, in naked ugliness and horror. In the dining-room, a bare, dull, dreary place, with nothing for the eye to rest on but the empty walls, a woman was locked up alone. She was bent, they told me, on committing suicide. If anything could have strengthened her in her resolution, it would certainly have been the insupportable monotony of such an existence.

The terrible crowd with which these halls and galleries were filled, so shocked me, that I abridged my stay within the shortest limits, and declined to see that portion of the building in which the re-fractory and violent were under closer restraint. I have no doubt that the gentleman who presided over this establishment at the time

I write of, was competent to manage it, and had done all in his power to promote its usefulness: but will it be believed that the miserable strife of Party feeling is carried even into this sad refuge of afflicted and degraded humanity? Will it be believed that the eyes which are to watch over and control the wanderings of minds on which the most dreadful visitation to which our nature is exposed has fallen, must wear the glasses of some wretched side in Politics? Will it be believed that the governor of such a house as this, is appointed, and deposed, and changed perpetually, as Parties fluctuate and vary, and as their despicable weathercocks are blown this way or that? A hundred times in every week, some new most paltry exhibition of that narrow-minded and injurious Party Spirit, which is the Simoom of America, sickening and blighting everything of wholesome life within its reach, was forced upon my notice; but I never turned my back upon it with feelings of such deep disgust and measureless contempt, as when I crossed the threshold of this mad-house.

At a short distance from this building is another called the Alms House, that is to say, the workhouse of New York. This is a large Institution also: lodging, I believe, when I was there, nearly a thousand poor. It was badly ventilated, and badly lighted; was not too clean; and impressed me, on the whole, very uncomfortably. But it must be remembered that New York, as a great emporium of commerce, and as a place of general resort, not only from all parts of the States, but from most parts of the world, has always a larger pauper population to provide for; and labours, therefore, under peculiar difficulties in this respect. Nor must it be forgotten that New York is a large town, and that in all large towns a vast amount of good and evil is intermixed and jumbled up together.

In the same neighbourhood is the Farm, where young orphans are nursed and bred. I did not see it, but I believe it is well conducted; and I can the more easily credit it, from knowing how mindful they usually are, in America, of that beautiful passage in the Litany which remembers all sick persons and young children.

I was taken to these Institutions by water, in a boat belonging to the Island Jail, and rowed by a crew of prisoners, who were dressed in a striped uniform of black and buff, in which they looked like faded tigers. They took me, by the same conveyance, to the Jail itself.

It is an old prison, and quite a pioneer establishment, on the plan I have already described. I was glad to hear this, for it is unquestionably a very indifferent one. The most is made, however, of the means it possesses, and it is as well regulated as such a place can be.

The women work in covered sheds, erected for that purpose. If I remember right, there are no shops for the men, but be that as it may, the greater part of them labour in certain stone-quarries near at hand. The day being very wet indeed, this labour was suspended, and the prisoners were in their cells. Imagine these cells, some two or three hundred in number, and in every one a man locked up; this one at his door for air, with his hands thrust through the grate; this one in bed (in the middle of the day, remember); and this one flung down in a heap upon the ground, with his head against the bars, like a wild beast. Make the rain pour down, outside, in torrents. Put the ever-lasting stove in the midst; hot, and suffocating, and vaporous, as a witch's cauldron. Add a collection of gentle odours, such as would arise from a thousand mildewed umbrellas, wet through, and a thousand buck-baskets, full of half-washed linen—and there is the prison, as it was that day.

The prison for the State at Sing Sing, is, on the other hand, a model jail. That, and Auburn, are, I believe, the largest and best examples of the silent system.

In another part of the city, is the Refuge for the Destitute: an Institution whose object is to reclaim youthful offenders, male and female, black and white, without distinction; to teach them useful trades, apprentice them to respectable masters, and make them worthy members of society. Its design, it will be seen, is similar to that at Boston; and it is a no less meritorious and admirable estab-lishment. A suspicion crossed my mind during my inspection of this noble charity, whether the superintendent had quite sufficient know-ledge of the world and worldly characters; and whether he did not commit a great mistake in treating some young girls, who were to all intents and purposes, by their years and their past lives, women, as though they were little children; which certainly had a ludicrous effect in my eyes, and, or I am much mistaken, in theirs also. As the Institution, however, is always under a vigilant examination of a body of gentlemen of great intelligence and experience, it cannot fail to be well conducted; and whether I am right or wrong in this slight particular, is unimportant to its deserts and character, which it would be difficult to estimate too highly.

In addition to these establishments, there are in New York, excellent hospitals and schools, literary institutions and libraries; an admirable fire department (as indeed it should be, having constant practice), and charities of every sort and kind. In the suburbs there is a spacious cemetery: unfinished yet, but every day improving. The saddest tomb I saw there was "The Strangers' Grave. Dedicated to the different hotels in this city."

There are three principal theatres. Two of them, the Park and the Bowery, are large, elegant, and handsome buildings, and are, I grieve to write it, generally deserted. The third, the Olympic, is a tiny show-box for vaudevilles and burlesques. It is singularly well conducted by Mr. Mitchell, a comic actor of great quiet humour and originality, who is well remembered and esteemed by London playgoers. I am happy to report of this deserving gentleman, that his benches are usually well filled, and that his theatre rings with merriment every night. I had almost forgotten a small summer theatre, called Niblo's, with gardens and open air amusements attached; but I believe it is not exempt from the general depression under which Theatrical

Property, or what is humorously called by that name, unfortunately labours.

The country round New York is surpassingly and exquisitely picturesque. The climate, as I have already intimated, is somewhat of the warmest. What it would be, without the sea breezes which come from its beautiful Bay in the evening time, I will not throw myself or my readers into a fever by inquiring.

The tone of the best society in this city, is like that of Boston; here and there, it may be, with a greater infusion of the mercantile spirit, but generally polished and refined, and always most hospitable. The houses and tables are elegant; the hours later and more rakish; and there is, perhaps, a greater spirit of contention in reference to appearances, and the display of wealth and costly living. The ladies are singularly beautiful.

Before I left New York I made arrangements for securing a passage home in the George Washington packet ship, which was advertised to sail in June: that being the month in which I had determined, if prevented by no accident in the course of my ramblings, to leave America.

I never thought that going back to England, returning to all who are dear to me, and to pursuits that have insensibly grown to be a part of my nature, I could have felt so much sorrow as I endured, when I parted at last, on board this ship, with the friends who had accompanied me from this city. I never thought the name of any place, so far away and so lately known, could ever associate itself in my mind with the crowd of affectionate remembrances that now cluster about it. There are those in this city who would brighten, to me, the darkest winter-day that ever glimmered and went out in Lapland; and before whose presence even Home grew dim, when they and I exchanged that painful word which mingles with our every thought and deed; which haunts our cradle-heads in infancy, and closes up the vista of our lives in age.

## CHAPTER VII

### PHILADELPHIA, AND ITS SOLITARY PRISON

THE journey from New York to Philadelphia, is made by railroad, and two ferries; and usually occupies between five and six hours. It was a fine evening when we were passengers in the train: and watching the bright sunset from a little window near the door by which we sat, my attention was attracted to a remarkable appearance issuing from the windows of the gentleman's car immediately in front of us, which I supposed for some time was occasioned by a number of industrious persons inside, ripping open feather beds, and giving the feathers to the wind. At length it occurred to me that they were only spitting, which was indeed the case; though how any number of passengers which it was possible for that car to contain, could have maintained such a playful and incessant shower of expectoration, I am still at a loss to understand: notwithstanding the experience in all salivatory phenomena which I afterwards acquired.

I made acquaintance, on this journey, with a mild and modest young quaker, who opened the discourse by informing me, in a grave whisper, that his grandfather was the inventor of cold-drawn castor oil. I mention the circumstance here, thinking it probable that this is the first occasion on which the valuable medicine in question was ever used as a conversational aperient.

We reached the city, late that night. Looking out of my chamber-window, before going to bed, I saw, on the opposite side of the way, a handsome building of white marble, which had a mournful ghost-like aspect, dreary to behold. I attributed this to the sombre influence of the night, and on rising in the morning looked out again, expecting to see its steps and portico thronged with groups of people passing in and out. The door was still tight shut, however; the same cold cheerless air prevailed; and the building looked as if the marble statue of Don Guzman could alone have any business to transact within its gloomy walls. I hastened to inquire its name and purpose, and then my surprise vanished. It was the tomb of many fortunes; the Great Catacomb of investment; the Memorable United States Bank.

The stoppage of this Bank, with all its ruinous consequences, had cast (as I was told on every side) a gloom on Philadelphia, under the depressing effect of which it yet laboured. It certainly did seem rather dull and out of spirits.

It is a handsome city, but distractingly regular. After walking about it for an hour or two, I felt that I would have given the world for a crooked street. The collar of my coat appeared to stiffen, and the brim of my hat to expand, beneath its quakery influence. My hair shrunk in a sleek short crop, my hands folded themselves upon my breast of their own calm accord, and thoughts of taking lodgings in Mark Lane over against the Market Place, and of making a large fortune by speculations in corn, came over me involuntarily.

Philadelphia is most bountifully provided with fresh water, which is showered and jerked about, and turned on, and poured off, every-where. The Waterworks, which are on a height near the city, are no less ornamental than useful, being tastefully laid out as a public garden, and kept in the best and neatest order. The river is dammed at this point, and forced by its own power into certain high tanks or reservoirs, whence the whole city, to the top stories of the houses, is supplied at a very trifling expense.

There are various public institutions. Among them a most excellent Hospital—a quaker establishment, but not sectarian in the great benefits it confers; a quiet, quaint old library, named after Franklin;

a handsome Exchange and Post Office; and so forth. In connection with the quaker Hospital, there is a picture by West, which is exhibited for the benefit of the funds of the institution. The subject is, our Saviour healing the sick, and it is, perhaps, as favourable a specimen of the master as can be seen anywhere. Whether this be high or low praise, depends upon the reader's taste.

In the same room, there is a very characteristic and life-like portrait of Mr. Sully, a distinguished American artist.

My stay in Philadelphia was very short, but what I saw of its society, I greatly liked. Treating of its general characteristics, I should be disposed to say that it is more provincial than Boston or New York, and that there is afloat in the fair city, an assumption of taste and criticism, savouring rather of those genteel discussions upon the same themes, in connection with Shakespeare and the Musical Glasses, of which we read in the Vicar of Wakefield. Near the city, is a most splendid unfinished marble structure for the Girard College, founded by a deceased gentleman of that name and of enormous wealth, which, if completed according to the original design, will be perhaps the richest edifice of modern times. But the bequest is involved in legal disputes, and pending them the work has stopped; so that like many other great undertakings in America, even this is rather going to be done one of these days, than doing now.

In the outskirts, stands a great prison, called the Eastern Penitentiary: conducted on a plan peculiar to the state of Pennsylvania. The system here, is rigid, strict, and hopeless solitary confinement. I believe it, in its effects, to be cruel and wrong.

In its intention, I am well convinced that it is kind, humane, and meant for reformation; but I am persuaded that those who devised this system of Prison Discipline, and those benevolent gentlemen who carry it into execution, do not know what it is that they are doing. I believe that very few men are capable of estimating the immense amount of torture and agony which this dreadful punishment, prolonged for years, inflicts upon the sufferers; and in guessing at it myself, and in reasoning from what I have seen written upon their faces, and what to my certain knowledge they feel within, I am only the more convinced that there is a depth of terrible endurance in it which none but the sufferers themselves can fathom, and which no man has a right to inflict upon his fellow-creature. I hold this slow and daily tampering with the mysteries of the brain, to be immeasurably worse than any torture of the body: and because its ghastly signs and tokens are not so palpable to the eye and sense of touch as scars upon the flesh; because its wounds are not upon the surface, and it extorts few cries that human ears can hear; therefore I the more denounce it, as a secret punishment which slumbering humanity is not roused up to stay. I hesitated once, debating with myself, whether, if I had the power of saying "Yes" or "No," I would allow it to be tried in certain cases, where the terms of imprisonment were short; but now, I solemnly declare, that with no rewards or honours could I walk a happy man beneath the open sky by day, or lie me down upon my bed at night, with the consciousness that one human creature, for any length of time, no matter what, lay suffering this unknown punishment in his silent cell, and I the cause, or I consenting to it in the least degree.

I was accompanied to this prison by two gentlemen officially connected with its management, and passed the day in going from cell to cell, and talking with the inmates. Every facility was afforded me, that the utmost courtesy could suggest. Nothing was concealed or hidden from my view, and every piece of information that I sought, was openly and frankly given. The perfect order of the building cannot be praised too highly, and of the excellent motives of all who are immediately concerned in the administration of the system, there can be no kind of question.

Between the body of the prison and the outer wall, there is a spacious garden. Entering it, by a wicket in the massive gate, we pursued the path before us to its other termination, and passed into a large chamber, from which seven long passages radiate. On either side of each is a long, long row of low cell doors, with a certain number over every one. Above, a gallery of cells, like those below, except that they have no narrow yard attached (as those in the ground tier have), and are somewhat smaller. The possession of two of these, is supposed to compensate for the absence of so much air and exercise as can be had in the dull strip attached to each of the others, in an hour's time every day; and therefore every prisoner in this upper story has two cells, adjoining and communicating with, each other.

Standing at the central point, and looking down these dreary passages, the dull repose and quiet that prevails, is awful. Occasionally, there is a drowsy sound from some lone weaver's shuttle, or shoemaker's last, but it is stifled by the thick walls and heavy dungeon-door, and only serves to make the general stillness more profound. Over the head and face of every prisoner who comes into this melancholy house, a black hood is drawn; and in this dark shroud, an emblem of the curtain dropped between him and the living world, he is led to the cell from which he never again comes forth, until his whole term of imprisonment has expired. He never hears of wife and children; home or friends; the life or death of any single creature. He sees the prison officers, but with that exception he never looks upon a human countenance, or hears a human voice. He is a man buried alive; to be dug out in the slow round of years; and in the mean time dead to everything but torturing anxieties and horrible despair.

His name, and crime, and term of suffering, are unknown, even to the officer who delivers him his daily food. There is a number over his cell-door, and in a book of which the governor of the prison has one copy, and the moral instructor another: this is the index of his history. Beyond these pages the prison has no record of his existence: and though he live to be in the same cell ten weary years, he has no means of knowing, down to the very last hour, in what part of the building it is situated; what kind of men there are about him; whether in the long winter nights there are living people near, or he is in some lonely corner of the great jail, with walls, and passages, and iron doors between him and the nearest sharer in its solitary horrors.

Every cell has double doors: the outer one of sturdy oak, the other of grated iron, wherein there is a trap through which his food is handed. He has a Bible, and a slate and pencil, and, under certain restrictions, has sometimes other books, provided for the purpose, and pen and ink and paper. His razor, plate, and can, and basin, hang upon the wall, or shine upon the little shelf. Fresh water is laid on in every cell, and he can draw it at his pleasure. During the day, his bedstead turns up against the wall, and leaves more space for him to work in. His loom, or bench, or wheel, is there; and there he labours, sleeps and wakes, and counts the seasons as they change, and grows old.

The first man I saw, was seated at his loom, at work. He had been there six years, and was to remain, I think, three more. He had been convicted as a receiver of stolen goods, but even after his long imprisonment, denied his guilt, and said he had been hardly dealt by. It was his second offence.

He stopped his work when we went in, took off his spectacles, and answered freely to everything that was said to him, but always with a strange kind of pause first, and in a low, thoughtful voice. He wore a paper hat of his own making, and was pleased to have it noticed and commended. He had very ingeniously manufactured a sort of Dutch clock from some disregarded odds and ends; and his vinegar-bottle served for the pendulum. Seeing me interested in this contrivance, he looked up at it with a great deal of pride, and said that he had been thinking of improving it, and that he hoped the hammer and a little piece of broken glass beside it "would play music before long." He had extracted some colours from the yarn with which he worked, and painted a few poor figures on the wall. One, of a female, over the door, he called, "The Lady of the Lake."

He smiled as I looked at these contrivances to while away the time; but when I looked from them to him, I saw that his lip trembled and could have counted the beating of this heart. I forget how it came about, but some allusion was made to his having a wife. He shook his head at the word, turned aside, and covered his face with his hands.

"But you are resigned now!" said one of the gentlemen after a short pause, during which he had resumed his former manner. He answered with a sigh that seemed quite reckless in its hopelessness, "Oh yes, oh yes! I am resigned to it." "And are a better man, you think?" "Well, I hope so: I'm sure I hope I may be." "And time goes pretty quickly?" "Time is very long, gentlemen, within these four walls!"

He gazed about him—Heaven only knows how wearily!—as he

said these words; and in the act of doing so, fell into a strange stare as if he had forgotten something. A moment afterwards he sighed heavily, put on his spectacles, and went about his work again.

In another cell, there was a German, sentenced to five years imprisonment for larceny, two of which had just expired. With colours procured in the same manner, he had painted every inch of the walls and ceiling quite beautifully. He had laid out the few feet of ground, behind, with exquisite neatness, and had made a little bed in' the centre, that looked by-the-bye, like a grave. The taste and ingenuity he had displayed in everything were most extraordinary; and yet a more dejected, heart-broken, wretched creature, it would be difficult to imagine. I never saw such a picture of forlorn affliction and distress of mind. My heart bled for him; and when the tears ran down his cheeks, and he took one of the visitors aside, to ask, with his trembling hands nervously clutching at his coat to detain him, whether there was no hope of his dismal sentence being commuted, the spectacle was really too painful to witness. I never saw or heard of any kind of misery that impressed me more than the wretchedness of this man.

In a third cell, was a tall, strong black, a burglar, working at his proper trade of making screws and the like. His time was nearly out. He was not only a very dexterous thief, but was notorious for his boldness and hardihood, and for the number of his previous convictions. He entertained us with a long account of his achievements, which he narrated with such infinite relish, that he actually seemed to lick his lips as he told us racy anecdotes of stolen plate, and of old ladies whom he had watched as they sat at windows in silver spectacles (he had plainly had an eye to their metal even from the other side of the street) and had afterwards robbed. This fellow, upon the slightest encouragement, would have mingled with his professional recollections the most detestable cant; but I am very much mistaken if he could have surpassed the unmitigated hypocrisy with which he declared that he blessed the day on which he came into that prison, and that he never would commit another robbery as long as he lived.

There was one man who was allowed, as an indulgence, to keep rabbits. His room having rather a close smell in consequence, they called to him at the door to come out into the passage. He complied of course, and stood shading his haggard face in the unwonted sunlight of the great window, looking as wan and unearthly as if he had been summoned from the grave. He had a white rabbit in his breast; and when the little creature, getting down upon the ground, stole back into the cell, and he, being dismissed, crept timidly after it, I thought it would have been very hard to say in what respect the man was the nobler animal of the two.

There was an English thief who had been there but a few days out of seven years: a villainous, low-browed, thin-lipped fellow, with a white face; who had as yet no relish for visitors, and who, but for the additional penalty, would have gladly stabbed me with his shoemaker's knife. There was another German who had entered the jail but yesterday, and who started from his bed when we looked in, and pleaded, in his broken English, very hard for work. There was a poet, who after doing two days' work in every four-and-twenty hours, one for himself and one for the prison, wrote verses about ships (he was by trade a mariner), and "the maddening wine-cup," and his friends at home. There were very many of them. Some reddened at the sight of visitors, and some turned very pale. Some two or three had prisoner nurses with them, for they were very sick; and one, a fat old negro whose leg had been taken off within the jail, had for his attendant a classical scholar and an accomplished surgeon, himself a prisoner likewise. Sitting upon the stairs, engaged in some slight work, was a pretty coloured boy. "Is there no refuge for young criminals in Philadelphia, then?" said I. "Yes, but only for white children." Noble aristocracy in crime!

There was a sailor who had been there upwards of eleven years, and who in a few months' time would be free. Eleven years of solitary confinement!

"I am very glad to hear your time is nearly out." What does he say? Nothing. Why does he stare at his hands, and pick the flesh upon his fingers, and raise his eyes for an instant, every now and then, to those bare walls which have seen his head turn grey? It is a way he has sometimes.

Does he never look men in the face, and does he always pluck at those hands of his, as though he were bent on parting skin and bone? It is his humour: nothing more.

It is his humour too, to say that he does not look forward to going out; that he is not glad the time is drawing near; that he did look forward to it once, but that was very long ago; that he has lost all care for everything. It is his humour to be a helpless, crushed, and broken man. And, Heaven be his witness that he has his humour thoroughly gratified!

There were three young women in adjoining cells, all convicted at the same time of a conspiracy to rob their prosecutor. In the silence and solitude of their lives they had grown to be quite beautiful. Their looks were very sad, and might have moved the sternest visitor to tears, but not to that kind of sorrow which the contemplation of the men awakens. One was a young girl; not twenty, as I recollect; whose snow-white room was hung with the work of some former prisoner, and upon whose downcast face the sun in all its splendour shone down through the high chink in the wall, where one narrow strip of bright blue sky was visible. She was very penitent and quiet; had come to be resigned, she said (and I believe her); and had a mind at peace. "In a word, you are happy here?" said one of my companions. She struggled—she did struggle very hard—to answer, Yes; but raising her eyes, and meeting that glimpse of freedom overhead, she burst into tears, and said, "She tried to be; she uttered no complaint; but it was natural that she should sometimes long to go out of that one cell: she could not help *that*," she sobbed, poor thing!

I went from cell to cell that day; and every face I saw, or word I heard, or incident I noted, is present to my mind in all its painfulness. But let me pass them by, for one, more pleasant, glance of a prison on the same plan which I afterwards saw at Pittsburg.

When I had gone over that, in the same manner, I asked the governor if he had any person in his charge who was shortly going out. He had one, he said, whose time was up next day; but he had only been a prisoner two years.

Two years! I looked back through two years of my own life—out of jail, prosperous, happy, surrounded by blessings, comforts, good fortune—and thought how wide a gap it was, and how long those two years passed in solitary captivity would have been. I have the face of this man, who was going to be released next day, before me now. It is almost more memorable in its happiness than the other faces in their misery. How easy and how natural it was for him to say that the system was a good one; and that the time went "pretty quick—considering;" and that when a man once felt that he had offended the law, and must satisfy it, "he got along, somehow:" and so forth!

"What did he call you back to say to you, in that strange flutter?" I asked of my conductor, when he had locked the door and joined me in the passage.

"Oh! That he was afraid the soles of his boots were not fit for walking, as they were a good deal worn when he came in; and that he would thank me very much to have them mended, ready."

Those boots had been taken off his feet, and put away with the rest of his clothes, two years before!

I took the opportunity of inquiring how they conducted themselves immediately before going out; adding that I presumed they trembled very much.

"Well, it's not so much a trembling," was the answer—"though they do quiver—as a complete derangement of the nervous system. They can't sign their names to the book; sometimes can't even hold the pen; look about 'em without appearing to know why, or where they are; and sometimes get up and sit down again, twenty times in a minute. This is when they're in the office, where they are taken with the hood on, as they were brought in. When they get outside the gate, they stop, and look first one way and then the other; not knowing which to take. Sometimes they stagger as if they were drunk, and sometimes are forced to lean against the fence, they're so bad:—but they clear off in course of time."

As I walked among these solitary cells, and looked at the faces of the men within them, I tried to picture to myself the thoughts and feelings natural to their condition. I imagined the hood just taken off, and the scene of their captivity disclosed to them in all its dismal monotony.

At first, the man is stunned. His confinement is a hideous vision;

and his old life a reality. He throws himself upon his bed, and lies there abandoned to despair. By degrees the insupportable solitude and barrenness of the place rouses him from this stupor, and when the trap in his grated door is opened, he humbly begs and prays for work. "Give me some work to do, or I shall go raving mad!"

He has it; and by fits and starts applies himself to labour; but every now and then there comes upon him a burning sense of the years that must be wasted in that stone coffin, and an agony so piercing in the recollection of those who are hidden from his view and knowledge, that he starts from his seat, and striding up and down the narrow room with both hands clasped on his uplifted head, hears spirits tempting him to beat his brains out on the wall.

Again he falls upon his bed, and lies there, moaning. Suddenly he starts up, wondering whether any other man is near; whether there is another cell like that on either side of him: and listens keenly.

There is no sound, but other prisoners may be near for all that. He remembers to have heard once, when he little thought of coming here himself, that the cells were so constructed that the prisoners could not hear each other, though the officers could hear them. Where is the nearest man—upon the right, or on the left? or is there one in both directions? Where is he sitting now—with his face to the light? or is he walking to and fro? How is he dressed? Has he been here long? Is he much worn away? Is he very white and spectre-like? Does *he* think of his neighbour too?

Scarcely venturing to breathe, and listening while he thinks, he conjures up a figure with his back towards him, and imagines it moving about in this next cell. He has no idea of the face, but he is certain of the dark form of a stooping man. In the cell upon the other side, he puts another figure, whose face is hidden from him also. Day after day, and often when he wakes up in the middle of the night, he thinks of these two men until he is almost distracted. He never changes them. There they are always as he first imagined them—an old man on the right; a younger man upon the left—whose hidden features torture him to death, and have a mystery that makes him tremble.

The weary days pass on with solemn pace, like mourners at a funeral; and slowly he begins to feel that the white walls of the cell have something dreadful in them: that their colour is horrible: that their smooth surface chills his blood: that there is one hateful corner which torments him. Every morning when he wakes, he hides his head beneath the coverlet, and shudders to see the ghastly ceiling looking down upon him. The blessed light of day itself peeps in, an ugly phantom face, through the unchangeable crevice which is his prison window.

By slow but sure degrees, the terrors of that hateful corner swell until they beset him at all times; invade his rest, make his dreams hideous, and his nights dreadful. At first, he took a strange dislike to it; feeling as though it gave birth in his brain to something of corresponding shape, which ought not to be there, and racked his head with pains. Then he began to fear it, then to dream of it, and of men whispering its name and pointing to it. Then he could not bear to look at it, nor yet to turn his back upon it. Now, it is every night the lurking-place of a ghost: a shadow:—a silent something, horrible to see, but whether bird, or beast, or muffled human shape, he cannot tell.

When he is in his cell by day, he fears the little yard without. When he is in the yard, he dreads to re-enter the cell. When night comes, there stands the phantom in the corner. If he have the courage to stand in its place, and drive it out (he had once: being desperate), it broods upon his bed. In the twilight, and always at the same hour, a voice calls to him by name; as the darkness thickens, his Loom begins to live; and even that, his comfort, is a hideous figure, watching him till daybreak.

Again, by slow degrees, these horrible fancies depart from him one by one: returning sometimes, unexpectedly, but at longer intervals, and in less alarming shapes. He has talked upon religious matters with the gentleman who visits him, and has read his Bible, and has written a prayer upon his slate, and hung it up as a kind of protection, and an assurance of Heavenly companionship. He dreams now, sometimes, of his children or his wife, but is sure that they are dead, or have deserted him. He is easily moved to tears; is gentle, submissive, and broken-spirited. Occasionally, the old agony comes back: a very little thing will revive it; even a familiar sound, or the scent of summer flowers in the air; but it does not last long, now: for the world without, has come to be the vision, and this solitary life, the sad reality.

If his term of imprisonment be short—I mean comparatively, for short it cannot be—the last half year is almost worse than all; for then he thinks the prison will take fire and he be burnt in the ruins, or that he is doomed to die within the walls, or that he will be detained on some false charge and sentenced for another term: or that something, no matter what, must happen to prevent his going at large. And this is natural, and impossible to be reasoned against, because, after his long separation from human life, and his great suffering, any event will appear to him more probable in the contemplation, than the being restored to liberty and his fellow-creatures.

If his period of confinement have been very long, the prospect of release bewilders and confuses him. His broken heart may flutter for a moment, when he thinks of the world outside, and what it might have been to him in all those lonely years, but that is all. The cell-door has been closed too long on all his hopes and cares. Better to have hanged him in the beginning than bring him to this pass, and send him forth to mingle with his kind, who are his kind no more.

On the haggard face of every man among these prisoners, the same expression sat. I know not what to liken it to. It had something of that strained attention which we see upon the faces of the blind and deaf, mingled with a kind of horror, as though they had all been secretly terrified. In every little chamber that I entered, and at every grate through which I looked, I seemed to see the same appalling countenance. It lives in my memory, with the fascination of a remarkable picture. Parade before my eyes, a hundred men, with one among them newly released from this solitary suffering, and I would point him out.

The faces of the women, as I have said, it humanises and refines. Whether this be because of their better nature, which is elicited in solitude, or because of their being gentler creatures, of greater patience and longer suffering, I do not know; but so it is. That the punishment is nevertheless, to my thinking, fully as cruel and as wrong in their case, as in that of the men, I need scarcely add.

My firm conviction is that, independent of the mental anguish it occasions—an anguish so acute and so tremendous, that all imagination of it must fall far short of the reality—it wears the mind into a morbid state, which renders it unfit for the rough contact and busy action of the world. It is my fixed opinion that those who have undergone this punishment, MUST pass into society again morally unhealthy and diseased. There are many instances on record, of men who have chosen, or have been condemned, to lives of perfect solitude, but I scarcely remember one, even among sages of strong and vigorous intellect, where its effect has not become apparent, in some disordered train of thought, or some gloomy hallucination. What monstrous phantoms, bred of despondency and doubt, and born and reared in solitude, have stalked upon the earth, making creation ugly, and darkening the face of Heaven!

Suicides are rare among these prisoners: are almost, indeed, unknown. But no argument in favour of the system, can reasonably be deduced from this circumstance, although it is very often urged. All men who have made diseases of the mind their study, know perfectly well that such extreme depression and despair as will change the whole character, and beat down all its powers of elasticity and self-resistance, may be at work within a man, and yet stop short of self-destruction. This is a common case.

That it makes the senses dull, and by degrees impairs the bodily faculties, I am quite sure. I remarked to those who were with me in this very establishment at Philadelphia, that the criminals who had been there long, were deaf. They, who were in the habit of seeing these men constantly, were perfectly amazed at the idea, which they regarded as groundless and fanciful. And yet the very first prisoner to whom they appealed—one of their own selection—confirmed my impression (which was unknown to him) instantly, and said, with a genuine air it was impossible to doubt, that he couldn't think how it happened, but he *was* growing very dull of hearing.

That it is a singularly unequal punishment, and affects the worst man least, there is no doubt. In its superior efficiency as a means of reformation, compared with that other code of regulations which allows the prisoners to work in company without communicating together, I have not the smallest faith. All the instances of reformation that were mentioned to me, were of a kind that might have been—and I have no doubt whatever, in my own mind, would have been—equally well brought about by the Silent System. With regard to such men as the negro burglar and the English thief, even the most enthusiastic have scarcely any hope of their conversion.

It seems to me that the objection that nothing wholesome or good has ever had its growth in such unnatural solitude, and that even a dog or any of the more intelligent among beasts, would pine, and mope, and rust away, beneath its influence, would be in itself a sufficient argument against this system. But when we recollect, in addition, how very cruel and severe it is, and that a solitary life is always liable to peculiar and distinct objections of a most deplorable nature, which have arisen here, and call to mind, moreover, that the choice is not between this system, and a bad or ill-considered one, but between it and another which has worked well, and is, in its whole design and practice, excellent; there is surely more than sufficient reason for abandoning a mode of punishment attended by so little hope or promise, and fraught, beyond dispute, with such a host of evils.

As a relief to its contemplation, I will close this chapter with a curious story arising out of the same theme, which was related to me, on the occasion of this visit, by some of the gentlemen concerned.

At one of the periodical meetings of the inspectors of this prison, a working man of Philadelphia presented himself before the Board, and earnestly requested to be placed in solitary confinement. On being asked what motive could possibly prompt him to make this strange demand, he answered that he had an irresistible propensity to get drunk; that he was constantly indulging it, to his great misery and ruin; that he had no power of resistance; that he wished to be put beyond the reach of temptation; and that he could think of no better way than this. It was pointed out to him, in reply, that the prison was for criminals who had been tried and sentenced by the law, and could not be made available for any such fanciful purposes; he was exhorted to abstain from intoxicating drinks, as he surely might if he would; and received other very good advice, with which he retired, exceedingly dissatisfied with the result of his application.

He came again, and again, and again, and was so very earnest and importunate, that at last they took counsel together, and said, "He will certainly qualify himself for admission, if we reject him any more. Let us shut him up. He will soon be glad to go away, and then we shall get rid of him." So they made him sign a statement which would prevent his ever sustaining an action for false imprisonment, to the effect that his incarceration was voluntary, and of his own seeking; they requested him to take notice that the officer in attendance had orders to release him at any hour of the day or night, when he might knock upon his door for that purpose; but desired him to understand, that once going out, he would not be admitted any more. These conditions agreed upon, and he still remaining in the same mind, he was conducted to the prison, and shut up in one of the cells.

In this cell, the man, who had not the firmness to leave a glass of liquor standing untasted on a table before him—in this cell, in solitary confinement, and working every day at his trade of shoemaking, this man remained nearly two years. His health beginning to fail at the expiration of that time, the surgeon recommended that he should work occasionally in the garden; and as he liked the notion very much, he went about this new occupation with great cheerfulness.

He was digging here, one summer day, very industriously, when the wicket in the outer gate chanced to be left open: showing, beyond, the well-remembered dusty road and sun-burnt fields. The way was as free to him as any man living, but he no sooner raised his head and caught sight of it, all shining in the light, than, with the involuntary instinct of a prisoner, he cast away his spade, scampered off as fast as his legs would carry him, and never once looked back.

## CHAPTER VIII

### WASHINGTON. THE LEGISLATURE. AND THE PRESIDENT'S HOUSE

WE left Philadelphia by steamboat, at six o'clock one very cold morning, and turned our faces towards Washington.

In the course of this day's journey, as on subsequent occasions, we encountered some Englishmen (small farmers, perhaps, or country publicans at home) who were settled in America, and were travelling on their own affairs. Of all grades and kinds of men that jostle one in the public conveyances of the States, these are often the most intolerable and the most insufferable companions. United to every disagreeable characteristic that the worst kind of American travellers possess, these countrymen of ours display an amount of insolent conceit and cool assumption of superiority, quite monstrous to behold. In the coarse familiarity of their approach, and the effrontery of their inquisitiveness (which they are in great haste to assert, as if they panted to revenge themselves upon the decent old restraints of home), they surpass any native specimens that came within my range of observation: and I often grew so patriotic when I saw and heard them, that I would cheerfully have submitted to a reasonable fine, if I could have given any other country in the whole world, the honour of claiming them for its children.

As Washington may be called the headquarters of tobacco-tinctured saliva, the time is come when I must confess, without any disguise, that the prevalence of those two odious practices of chewing and expectorating began about this time to be anything but agreeable, and soon became most offensive and sickening. In all the public places of America, this filthy custom is recognised. In the courts of law, the judge has his spittoon, the crier his, the witness his, and the prisoner his; while the jurymen and spectators are provided for, as so many men who in the course of nature must desire to spit incessantly. In the hospitals, the students of medicine are requested, by notices upon the wall, to eject their tobacco juice into the boxes provided for that purpose, and not to discolour the stairs. In public buildings, visitors are implored, through the same agency, to squirt the essence of their quids, or "plugs," as I have heard them called by gentlemen learned in this kind of sweetmeat, into the national spittoons, and not about the bases of the marble columns. But in some parts, this custom is inseparably mixed up with every meal and morning call, and with all the transactions of social life. The stranger, who follows in the track I took myself, will find it in its full bloom and glory, luxuriant in all its alarming recklessness, at Washington. And let him not persuade himself (as I once did, to my shame) that previous tourists have exaggerated its extent. The thing itself is an exaggeration of nastiness, which cannot be outdone.

On board this steamboat, there were two young gentlemen, with shirt-collars reversed as usual, and armed with very big walking-sticks; who planted two seats in the middle of the deck, at a distance of some four paces apart; took out their tobacco-boxes; and sat down opposite each other to chew. In less than a quarter of an hour's time, these hopeful youths had shed about them on the clean boards, a copious shower of yellow rain; clearing, by that means, a kind of magic circle, within whose limits no intruders dared to come, and which they never failed to refresh and re-refresh before a spot was dry. This being before breakfast, rather disposed me, I confess, to nausea; but looking attentively at one of the expectorators, I plainly saw that he was young in chewing, and felt inwardly uneasy, himself. A glow of delight came over me at this discovery; and as I marked his face turn paler and paler, and saw the ball of tobacco in his left cheek, quiver with his suppressed agony, while yet he spat, and chewed, and spat again, in emulation of his older friend, I could have fallen on his neck and implored him to go on for hours.

We all sat down to a comfortable breakfast in the cabin below, where there was no more hurry or confusion than at such a meal in England, and where there was certainly greater politeness exhibited than at most of our stage-coach banquets. At about nine o'clock we arrived at the railroad station, and went on by the cars. At noon we turned out again, to cross a wide river in another steamboat; landed at a continuation of the railroad on the opposite shore: and went on by other cars; in which, in the course of the next hour or so, we crossed by wooden bridges, each a mile in length, two creeks, called respectively Great and Little Gunpowder. The water in both was blackened with flights of canvas-backed ducks, which are most delicious eating, and abound hereabouts at that season of the year.

These bridges are of wood, have no parapet, and are only just wide enough for the passage of the trains; which, in the event of the smallest accident, would inevitably be plunged into the river. They are startling contrivances, and are most agreeable when passed.

We stopped to dine at Baltimore, and being now in Maryland, were waited on, for the first time, by slaves. The sensation of exacting any service from human creatures who are bought and sold, and being, for the time, a party as it were to their condition, is not an enviable one. The institution exists, perhaps, in its least repulsive and most mitigated form in such a town as this; but it *is* slavery; and though I was, with respect to it, an innocent man, its presence filled me with a sense of shame and self-reproach.

After dinner, we went down to the railroad again, and took our seats in the cars for Washington. Being rather early, those men and boys who happened to have nothing particular to do, and were curious in foreigners, came (according to custom) round the carriage in which I sat; let down all the windows; thrust in their heads and shoulders; hooked themselves on conveniently, by their elbows; and fell to comparing notes on the subject of my personal appearance, with as much indifference as if I were a stuffed figure. I never gained so much uncompromising information with reference to my own nose and eyes, and various impressions wrought by my mouth and chin on different minds, and how my head looks when it is viewed from behind, as on these occasions. Some gentlemen were only satisfied by exercising their sense of touch; and the boys (who are surprisingly precocious in America) were seldom satisfied, even by that, but would return to the charge over and over again. Many a budding president has walked into my room with his cap on his head and his hands in his pockets, and stared at me for two whole hours: occasionally refreshing himself with a tweak of his nose, or a draught from the water-jug; or by walking to the windows and inviting other boys in the street below, to come up and do likewise: crying, "Here he is!" "Come on!" "Bring all your Brothers!" with other hospitable entreaties of that nature.

We reached Washington at about half-past six that evening, and had upon the way a beautiful view of the Capitol, which is a fine building of the Corinthian order, placed upon a noble and commanding eminence. Arrived at the hotel; I saw no more of the place that night; being very tired, and glad to get to bed.

Breakfast over next morning, I walk about the streets for an hour or two, and, coming home, throw up the window in the front and back, and look out. Here is Washington, fresh in my mind and under my eye.

Take the worst parts of the City Road and Pentonville, or the straggling outskirts of Paris, where the houses are smallest, preserving all their oddities, but especially the small shops and dwellings, occupied in Pentonville (but not in Washington) by furniture-brokers, keepers of poor eating-houses, and fanciers of birds. Burn the whole down; build it up again in wood and plaster; widen it a little; throw in part of St. John's Wood; put green blinds outside all the private houses, with a red curtain and a white one in every window; plough up all the roads; plant a great deal of coarse turf in every place where it ought *not* to be; erect three handsome buildings in stone and marble, anywhere, but the more entirely out of everybody's way the better; call one the Post Office, one the Patent Office, and one the Treasury; make it scorching hot in the morning, and freezing cold in the afternoon, with an occasional tornado of wind and dust; leave a brick-field without the bricks, in all central places where a street may naturally be expected: and that's Washington.

The hotel in which we live, is a long row of small houses fronting on the street, and opening at the back upon a common yard, in which hangs a great triangle. Whenever a servant is wanted, somebody beats on this triangle from one stroke up to seven, according to the number of the house in which his presence is required; and as all the servants are always being wanted, and none of them ever come, this enlivening engine is in full performance the whole day through. Clothes are drying in the same yard; female slaves, with cotton handkerchiefs twisted round their heads, are running to and fro on the hotel business; black waiters cross and recross with dishes in their hands; two great dogs are playing upon a mound of loose bricks in the centre of the little square; a pig is turning up his stomach to the sun, and grunting "that's comfortable!" and neither the men, nor the women, nor the dogs, nor the pig, nor any created creature, takes the smallest notice of the triangle, which is tingling madly all the time.

I walk to the front window, and look across the road upon a long, straggling row of houses, one story high, terminating, nearly opposite, but a little to the left, in a melancholy piece of waste ground with frowzy grass, which looks like a small piece of country that has taken to drinking, and has quite lost itself. Standing anyhow and all wrong, upon this open space, like something meteoric that has fallen down from the moon, is an odd, lop-sided, one-eyed kind of wooden building, that looks like a church, with a flag-staff as long as itself sticking out of a steeple something larger than a tea-chest. Under the window is a small stand of coaches, whose slave-drivers are sunning themselves on the steps of our door, and talking idly together. The three most obtrusive houses near at hand are the three meanest. On one—a shop, which never has anything in the window, and never has the door open—is painted in large characters, "THE CITY LUNCH." At another, which looks like a backway to somewhere else, but is an independent building in itself, oysters are procurable in every style. At the third, which is a very, very little tailor's shop, pants are fixed to order; or in other words, pantaloons are made to measure. And that is our street in Washington.

It is sometimes called the City of Magnificent Distances, but it might with greater propriety be termed the City of Magnificent Intentions; for it is only on taking a bird's-eye view of it from the top of the Capitol, that one can at all comprehend the vast designs of its projector, an aspiring Frenchman. Spacious avenues, that begin in nothing, and lead nowhere; streets, mile-long, that only want houses, roads and inhabitants; public buildings that need but a public to be complete; and ornaments of great thoroughfares, which only lack great thoroughfares to ornament—are its leading features. One might fancy the season over, and most of the houses gone out of town for ever with their masters. To the admirers of cities it is a Barmecide Feast: a pleasant field for the imagination to rove in; a monument raised to a deceased project, with not even a legible inscription to record its departed greatness.

Such as it is, it is likely to remain. It was originally chosen for the seat of Government, as a means of averting the conflicting jealousies and interests of the different States; and very probably, too, as being remote from mobs: a consideration not to be slighted, even in America. It has no trade or commerce of its own: having little or no population beyond the President and his establishment; the members of the legislature who reside there during the session; the Government clerks and officers employed in the various departments; the keepers of the hotels and boarding-houses; and the tradesmen who supply their tables. It is very unhealthy. Few people would live in Washington, I take it, who were not obliged to reside there; and the tides of emigration and speculation, those rapid and regardless currents, are little likely to flow at any time towards such dull and sluggish water.

The principal features of the Capitol, are, of course, the two houses of Assembly. But there is, besides, in the centre of the building, a fine rotunda, ninety-six feet in diameter, and ninety-six high, whose circular wall is divided into compartments, ornamented by historical pictures. Four of these have for their subjects prominent events in the revolutionary struggle. They were painted by Colonel Trumbull, himself a member of Washington's staff at the time of their occurrence; from which circumstance they derive a peculiar interest of their own. In this same hall Mr. Greenough's large statue of Washington has been lately placed. It has great merits of course, but it struck me as being rather strained and violent for its subject. I could wish, however, to have seen it in a better light than it can ever be viewed in, where it stands.

There is a very pleasant and commodious library in the Capitol; and from a balcony in front, the bird's-eye view, of which I have just spoken, may be had, together with a beautiful prospect of the adjacent country. In one of the ornamented portions of the building, there is a figure of Justice; whereunto the Guide Book says, "the artist at first contemplated giving more of nudity, but he was warned that the public sentiment in this country would not admit of it, and in his caution he has gone, perhaps, into the opposite extreme."

Poor Justice! she has been made to wear much stranger garments in America than those she pines in, in the Capitol. Let us hope that she has changed her dress-maker since they were fashioned, and that the public sentiment of the country did not cut out the clothes she hides her lovely figure in, just now.

The House of Representatives is a beautiful and spacious hall, of semicircular shape, supported by handsome pillars. One part of the gallery is appropriated to the ladies, and there they sit in front rows, and come in, and go out, as at a play or concert. The chair is canopied, and raised considerably above the floor of the House; and every member has an easy chair and a writing desk to himself: which is denounced by some people out of doors as a most unfortunate and injudicious arrangement, tending to long sittings and prosaic speeches. It is an elegant chamber to look at, but a singularly bad one for all purposes of hearing. The Senate, which is smaller, is free from this objection, and is exceedingly well adapted to the uses for which it is designed. The sittings, I need hardly add, take place in the day; and the parliamentary forms are modelled on those of the old country.

I was sometimes asked, in my progress through other places, whether I had not been very much impressed by the *heads* of the law-makers at Washington; meaning not their chiefs and leaders, but literally their individual and personal heads, whereon their hair grew, and whereby the phrenological character of each legislator was expressed: and I almost as often struck my questioner dumb with indignant consternation by answering "No, that I didn't remember being at all overcome." As I must, at whatever hazard, repeat the avowal here, I will follow it up by relating my impressions on this subject in as few words as possible.

In the first place—it may be from some imperfect development of my organ of veneration—I do not remember having ever fainted away, or having even been moved to tears of joyful pride, at sight of any legislative body. I have borne the House of Commons like a man, and have yielded to no weakness, but slumber, in the House of Lords. I have seen elections for borough and county, and have never been impelled (no matter which party won) to damage my hat by throwing it up into the air in triumph, or to crack my voice by shouting forth any reference to our Glorious Constitution, to the noble purity of our independent voters, or, the unimpeachable integrity of our inde-pendent members. Having withstood such strong attacks upon my fortitude, it is possible that I may be of a cold and insensible tempera-ment, amounting to iciness, in such matters; and therefore my impressions of the live pillars of the Capitol at Washington must be received with such grains of allowance as this free confession may seem to demand.

Did I see in this public body an assemblage of men, bound together in the sacred names of Liberty and Freedom, and so asserting the chaste dignity of those twin goddesses, in all their discussions, as to exalt at once the Eternal Principles to which their names are given, and their own character and the character of their countrymen, in the admiring eyes of the whole world?

It was but a week, since an aged, grey-haired man, a lasting honour to the land that gave him birth, who has done good service to his country, as his forefathers did, and who will be remembered scores upon scores of years after the worms bred in its corruption, are but so many grains of dust—it was but a week, since this old man had stood for days upon his trial before this very body, charged with having dared to assert the infamy of that traffic, which has for its accursed merchandise men and women, and their unborn children. Yes. And publicly exhibited in the same city all the while; gilded, framed and glazed; hung up for general admiration, shown to strangers not with shame, but pride; its face not turned towards the wall, itself not taken down and burned; is the Unanimous Declaration of the Thirteen United States of America, which solemnly declares that All Men are created Equal; and are endowed by their Creator with the Inalienable Rights of Life, Liberty, and the Pursuit of Happiness!

It was not a month, since this same body had sat calmly by, and heard a man, one of themselves, with oaths which beggars in their drink reject, threaten to cut another's throat from ear to ear. There he sat, among them; not crushed by the general feeling of the assembly, but as good a man as any.

There was but a week to come, and another of that body, for doing his duty to those who sent him there; for claiming in a Republic the Liberty and Freedom of expressing their sentiments, and making known their prayer; would be tried, found guilty, and have strong censure passed upon him by the rest. His was a grave offence indeed; for years before, he had risen up and said, "A gang of male and female slaves for sale, warranted to breed like cattle, linked to each other by iron fetters, are passing now along the open street beneath the windows of your Temple of Equality! Look!" But there are many kinds of hunters engaged in the Pursuit of Happiness, and they go variously armed. It is the Inalienable Right of some among them, to take the field after *their* Happiness equipped with cat and cartwhip, stocks, and iron collar, and to shout their view halloa! (always in praise of Liberty) to the music of clanking chains and bloody stripes.

Where sat the many legislators of coarse threats; of words and blows such as coalheavers deal upon each other, when they forget their breeding? On every side. Every session had its anecdotes of that kind, and the actors were all there.

Did I recognise in this assembly, a body of men, who, applying themselves in a new world to correct some of the falsehoods and vices of the old, purified the avenues to Public Life, paved the dirty ways to Place and Power, debated and made laws for the Common Good, and had no party but their Country?

I saw in them, the wheels that move the meanest perversion of virtuous Political Machinery that the worst tools ever wrought.

Despicable trickery at elections; under-handed tamperings with public officers; cowardly attacks upon opponents, with scurrilous newspapers for shields, and hired pens for daggers; shameful trucklings to mercenary knaves, whose claim to be considered, is, that every day and week they sow new crops of ruin with their venal types, which are the dragon's teeth of yore, in everything but sharpness; aidings and abettings of every bad inclination in the popular mind, and artful suppressions of all its good influences: such things as these, and in a word, Dishonest Faction in its most depraved and most unblushing form, stared out from every corner of the crowded hall.

Did I see among them, the intelligence and refinement: the true, honest, patriotic heart of America? Here and there, were drops of its blood and life, but they scarcely coloured the stream of desperate adventurers which sets that way for profit and for pay. It is the game of these men, and of their profligate organs, to make the strife of politics so fierce and brutal, and so destructive of all self-respect in worthy men, that sensitive and delicate-minded persons shall be kept aloof, and they, and such as they, be left to battle out their selfish views unchecked. And thus this lowest of all scrambling fights goes on, and they who in other countries would, from their intelligence and station, most aspire to make the laws, do here recoil the farthest from that degradation.

That there are, among the representatives of the people in both Houses, and among all parties, some men of high character and great abilities, I need not say. The foremost among those politicians who are known in Europe, have been already described, and I see no reason to depart from the rule I have laid down for my guidance, of abstaining from all mention of individuals. It will be sufficient to add, that to the most favourable accounts that have been written of them, I more than fully and most heartily subscribe; and that personal intercourse and free communication have bred within me, not the result predicted in the very doubtful proverb, but increased admiration and respect. They are striking men to look at, hard to deceive, prompt to act, lions in energy, Crichtons in varied accomplishments, Indians in fire of eye and gesture, Americans in strong and generous impulse; and they as well represent the honour and wisdom of their country at home, as the distinguished gentleman who is now its Minister at the British Court sustains its highest character abroad.

I visited both houses nearly every day, during my stay in Washington. On my initiatory visit to the House of Representatives, they divided against a decision of the chair; but the chair won. The second time I went, the member who was speaking, being interrupted by a laugh, mimicked it, as one child would in quarrelling with another, and added, "that he would make honourable gentlemen opposite, sing out a little more on the other side of their mouths presently." But interruptions are rare; the speaker being usually heard in silence. There are more quarrels than with us, and more threatenings than gentlemen are accustomed to exchange in any civilised society of which we have record: but farm-yard imitations have not as yet been imported from the Parliament of the United Kingdom. The feature in oratory which appears to be the most practised, and most relished, is the constant repetition of the same idea or shadow of an idea in fresh words; and the inquiry out of doors is not, "What did he say?" but, "How long did he speak?" These, however, are but enlargements of a principle which prevails elsewhere.

The Senate is a dignified and decorous body, and its proceedings are conducted with much gravity and order. Both houses are handsomely carpeted; but the state to which these carpets are reduced by the universal disregard of the spittoon with which every honourable member is accommodated, and the extraordinary improvements on the pattern which are squirted and dabbled upon it in every direction, do not admit of being described. I will merely observe, that I strongly recommend all strangers not to look at the floor; and if they happen to drop anything, though it be their purse, not to pick it up with an ungloved hand on any account.

It is somewhat remarkable too, at first, to say the least, to see so many honourable members with swelled faces; and it is scarcely less remarkable to discover that this appearance is caused by the quantity of tobacco they contrive to stow within the hollow of the cheek. It is strange enough too, to see an honourable gentleman leaning back in his tilted chair with his legs on the desk before him, shaping a convenient "plug" with his penknife, and when it is quite ready for use, shooting the old one from his mouth, as from a popgun, and clapping the new one in its place.

I was surprised to observe that even steady old chewers of great experience, are not always good marksmen, which has rather inclined me to doubt that general proficiency with the rifle, of which we have heard so much in England. Several gentlemen called upon me who, in the course of conversation, frequently missed the spittoon at five paces; and one (but he was certainly short-sighted) mistook the closed sash for the open window, at three. On another occasion when I dined out, and was sitting with two ladies and some gentlemen round a fire before dinner, one of the company fell short of the fireplace, six distinct times. I am disposed to think, however, that this was occasioned by his not aiming at that object; as there was a white marble hearth before the fender which was more convenient, and may have suited his purpose better.

The Patent Office at Washington, furnishes an extraordinary example of American enterprise and ingenuity; for the immense number of models it contains are the accumulated inventions of only five years; the whole of the previous collection having been destroyed by fire. The elegant structure in which they are arranged is one of design rather than execution, for there is but one side erected out of four, though the works are stopped. The Post Office is a very compact and very beautiful building. In one of the departments, among a collection of rare and curious articles, are deposited the presents which have been made from time to time to the American ambassadors at foreign courts by the various potentates to whom they were the accredited agents of the Republic; gifts which by the law they are not permitted to retain. I confess that I looked upon this as a very painful exhibition, and one by no means flattering to the national standard of honesty and honour. That can scarcely be a high state of moral feeling which imagines a gentleman of repute and station, likely to be corrupted, in the discharge of his duty, by the present of a snuff-box, or a richly-mounted sword, or an Eastern shawl; and surely the Nation who reposes confidence in her appointed servants, is likely to be better served, than she who makes them the subject of such very mean and paltry suspicions.

At George Town, in the suburbs, there is a Jesuit College; delightfully situated, and, so far as I had an opportunity of seeing, well managed. Many persons who are not members of the Romish Church, avail themselves, I believe, of these institutions, and of the advantageous opportunities they afford for the education of their children. The heights of this neighbourhood, above the Potomac River, are very picturesque: and are free, I should conceive, from some of the insalubrities of Washington. The air, at that elevation, was quite cool and refreshing, when in the city it was burning hot.

The President's mansion is more like an English club-house, both within and without, than any other kind of establishment with which I can compare it. The ornamental ground about it has been laid out in the garden walks; they are pretty, and agreeable to the eye; though they have that uncomfortable air of having been made yesterday, which is far from favourable to the display of such beauties.

My first visit to this house was on the morning after my arrival, when I was carried thither by an official gentleman, who was so kind as to charge himself with my presentation to the President.

We entered a large hall, and having twice or thrice rung a bell which nobody answered, walked without further ceremony through the rooms on the ground floor, as divers other gentlemen (mostly with their hats on, and their hands in their pockets) were doing very leisurely. Some of these had ladies with them, to whom they were showing the premises; others were lounging on the chairs and sofas; others, in a perfect state of exhaustion from listlessness, were yawning drearily. The greater portion of this assemblage were rather asserting their supremacy than doing anything else, as they had no particular business there, that anybody knew of. A few were closely eyeing the movables, as if to make quite sure that the President (who was far from popular) had not made away with any of the furniture, or sold the fixtures for his private benefit.

After glancing at these loungers; who were scattered over a pretty drawing-room, opening upon a terrace which commanded a beautiful prospect of the river and the adjacent country; and who were sauntering, too, about a larger state-room called the Eastern Drawing-room; we went up-stairs into another chamber, where were certain visitors, waiting for audiences. At sight of my conductor, a black in plain clothes and yellow slippers who was gliding noiselessly about, and whispering messages in the ears of the more impatient, made a sign of recognition, and glided off to announce him.

We had previously looked into another chamber fitted all round with a great, bare, wooden desk or counter, whereon lay files of newspapers, to which sundry gentlemen were referring. But there were no such means of beguiling the time in this apartment, which was as unpromising and tiresome as any waiting-room in one of our public establishments, or any physician's dining-room during his hours of consultation at home.

There were some fifteen or twenty persons in the room. One, a tall, wiry, muscular old man, from the west; sunburnt and swarthy; with a brown white hat on his knees, and a giant umbrella resting between his legs; who sat bolt upright in his chair, frowning steadily at the carpet, and twitching the hard lines about his mouth, as if he had made up his mind "to fix" the President on what he had to say, and wouldn't bate him a grain. Another, a Kentucky farmer, six-feet-six in height, with his hat on, and his hands under his coat-tails, who leaned against the wall and kicked the floor with his heel, as though he had Time's head under his shoe, and were literally "killing" him. A third, an oval-faced, bilious-looking man, with sleek black hair cropped close, and whiskers and beard shaved down to blue dots, who sucked the head of a thick stick, and from time to time took it out of his mouth, to see how it was getting on. A fourth did nothing but whistle. A fifth did nothing but spit. And indeed all these gentlemen were so very persevering and energetic in this latter particular, and bestowed their favours so abundantly upon the carpet, that I take it for granted the Presidential housemaids have high wages, or, to speak more genteelly, an ample amount of "compensation:" which is the American word for salary, in the case of all public servants.

We had not waited in this room many minutes, before the black messenger returned, and conducted us into another of smaller dimensions, where, at a business-like table covered with papers, sat the President himself. He looked somewhat worn and anxious, and well he might; being at war with everybody—but the expression of his face was mild and pleasant, and his manner was remarkably unaffected, gentlemanly, and agreeable. I thought that in his whole carriage and demeanour, he became his station singularly well.

Being advised that the sensible etiquette of the republican court admitted of a traveller, like myself, declining, without any impropriety, an invitation to dinner, which did not reach me until I had concluded my arrangements for leaving Washington some days before that to which it referred, I only returned to this house once. It was on the occasion of one of those general assemblies which are held on certain nights, between the hours of nine and twelve o'clock, and are called, rather oddly, Levees.

I went, with my wife, at about ten. There was a pretty dense crowd of carriages and people in the court-yard, and so far as I could make out, there were no very clear regulations for the taking up or the setting down of company. There were certainly no policemen to soothe startled horses, either by sawing at their bridles or flourishing truncheons in their eyes; and I am ready to make oath that no inoffensive persons were knocked violently on the head, or poked acutely in their backs or stomachs; or brought to a stand-still by any such gentle means, and then taken into custody for not moving on. But there was no confusion or disorder. Our carriage reached the porch in its turn, without any blustering, swearing, shouting, backing, or other disturbance: and we dismounted with as much ease and comfort as though we had been escorted by the whole Metropolitan Force from A to Z inclusive.

The suite of rooms on the ground-floor were lighted up and a military band was playing in the hall. In the smaller drawing-room, the centre of a circle of company, were the President and his daughter-in-law, who acted as the lady of the mansion; and a very interesting, graceful, and accomplished lady too. One gentleman who stood among this group, appeared to take upon himself the functions of a master of the ceremonies. I saw no other officers or attendants, and none were needed.

The great drawing-room, which I have already mentioned, and the other chambers on the ground-floor, were crowded to excess. The company was not, in our sense of the term, select, for it comprehended persons of very many grades and classes; nor was there any great display of costly attire: indeed, some of the costumes may have been, for aught I know, grotesque enough. But the decorum and propriety of behaviour which prevailed, were unbroken by any rude or disagreeable incident; and every man, even among the miscellaneous crowd in the hall who were admitted without any orders or tickets to look on, appeared to feel that he was a part of the Institution, and was responsible for its preserving a becoming character, and appearing to the best advantage.

That these visitors, too, whatever their station, were not without some refinement of taste and appreciation of intellectual gifts, and gratitude to those men who, by the peaceful exercise of great abilities, shed new charms and associations upon the homes of their countrymen, and elevate their character in other lands, was most earnestly testified by their reception of Washington Irving, my dear friend, who had recently been appointed Minister at the court of Spain, and who was among them that night, in his new character, for the first and last time before going abroad. I sincerely believe that in all the madness of American politics, few public men would have been so earnestly, devotedly, and affectionately caressed, as this most charming writer: and I have seldom respected a public assembly more, than I did this eager throng, when I saw them turning with one mind from noisy orators and officers of state, and flocking with a generous and honest impulse round the man of quiet pursuits: proud in his promotion as reflecting back upon their country: and grateful to him with their whole hearts for the store of graceful fancies he had poured out among them. Long may he dispense such treasures with unsparing hand; and long may they remember him as worthily!

----

The term we had assigned for the duration of our stay in Washington was now at an end, and we were to begin to travel; for the railroad distances we had traversed yet, in journeying among these older towns, are on that great continent looked upon as nothing.

I had at first intended going South—to Charleston. But when I came to consider the length of time which this journey would occupy, and the premature heat of the season, which even at Washington had been often very trying; and weighed moreover, in my own mind, the pain of living in the constant contemplation of slavery, against the more than doubtful chances of my ever seeing it, in the time I had to spare, stripped of the disguises in which it would certainly be dressed, and so adding any item to the host of facts already heaped together on the subject; I began to listen to old whisperings which had often been present to me at home in England, when I little thought of ever being here; and to dream again of cities growing up, like palaces in fairy tales, among the wilds and forests of the west.

The advice I received in most quarters when I began to yield to my desire of travelling towards that point of the compass was, according to custom, sufficiently cheerless: my companion being threatened with more perils, dangers, and discomforts, than I can remember or would catalogue if I could; but of which it will be sufficient to remark that blowings-up in steamboats and breakings-down in coaches were among the least. But, having a western route sketched out for me by the best and kindest authority to which I could have resorted, and putting no great faith in these discouragements, I soon determined on my plan of action.

This was to travel south, only to Richmond in Virginia; and then to turn, and shape our course for the Far West; whither I beseech the reader's company, in a new chapter.

# CHAPTER IX

A NIGHT STEAMER ON THE POTOMAC RIVER. VIRGINIA ROAD, AND A BLACK DRIVER. RICHMOND. BALTIMORE. THE HARRISBURG MAIL, AND A GLIMPSE OF THE CITY. A CANAL BOAT.

WE were to proceed in the first instance by steamboat; and as it is usual to sleep on board, in consequence of the starting-hour being four o'clock in the morning, we went down to where she lay, at that very uncomfortable time for such expeditions when slippers are most

322*

valuable, and a familiar bed, in the perspective of an hour or two, looks uncommonly pleasant.

It is ten o'clock at night: say half-past ten: moonlight, warm, and dull enough. The steamer (not unlike a child's Noah's ark in form, with the machinery on the top of the roof) is riding lazily up and down, and bumping clumsily against the wooden pier, as the ripple of the river trifles with its unwieldly carcase. The wharf is some distance from the city. There is nobody down here; and one or two dull lamps upon the steamer's decks are the only signs of life remaining, when our coach has driven away. As soon as our footsteps are heard upon the planks, a fat negress, particularly favoured by nature in respect of bustle, emerges from some dark stairs, and marshals my wife towards the ladies' cabin, to which retreat she goes, followed by a mighty bale of cloaks and great-coats. I valiantly resolve not to go to bed at all, but to walk up and down the pier till morning.

I begin my promenade—thinking of all kinds of distant things and persons, and of nothing near—and pace up and down for half-an-hour. Then I go on board again; and getting into the light of one of the lamps, look at my watch and think it must have stopped; and wonder what has become of the faithful secretary whom I brought along with me from Boston. He is supping with our late landlord (a Field Marshal, at least, no doubt) in honour of our departure, and may be two hours longer. I walk again, but it gets duller and dulier: the moon goes down: next June seems farther off in the dark, and the echoes of my footsteps make me nervous. It has turned cold too; and walking up and down without my companion in such lonely circumstances, is but poor amusement. So I break my staunch resolution, and think it may be, perhaps, as well to go to bed.

I go on board again; open the door of the gentlemen's cabin; and walk in. Somehow or other—from its being so quiet, I suppose—I have taken it into my head that there is nobody there. To my horror and amazement it is full of sleepers in every stage, shape, attitude, and variety of slumber: in the berths, on the chairs, on the floors, on the tables, and particularly round the stove, my detested enemy. I take another step forward, and slip on the shining face of a black steward, who lies rolled in a blanket on the floor. He jumps up, grins half in pain and half in hospitality; whispers my own name in my ear; and groping among the sleepers, leads me to my berth. Standing beside it, I count these slumbering passengers, and get past forty. There is no use in going further, so I begin to undress. As the chairs are all occupied, and there is nothing else to put my clothes on, I deposit them on the ground: not without soiling my hands, for it is in the same condition as the carpets in the Capitol, and from the same cause. Having but partially undressed, I clamber on my shelf, and hold the curtain open for a few minutes while I look round on all my fellow-travellers again. That done, I let it fall on them, and on the world: turn round: and go to sleep.

I wake, of course, when we get under weigh, for there is a good deal of noise. The day is then just breaking. Everybody wakes at the same time. Some are self-possessed directly, and some are much perplexed to make out where they are until they have rubbed their eyes, and leaning on one elbow, looked about them. Some yawn, some groan, nearly all spit, and a few get up. I am among the risers: for it is easy to feel, without going into the fresh air, that the atmosphere of the cabin is vile in the last degree. I huddle on my clothes, go down into the fore-cabin, get shaved by the barber, and wash myself. The washing and dressing apparatus for the passengers generally, consists of two jack-towels, three small wooden basins, a keg of water and a ladle to serve it out with, six square inches of looking-glass, two ditto ditto of yellow soap, a comb and brush for the head, and nothing for the teeth. Everybody uses the comb and brush, except myself. Everybody stares to see me using my own; and two or three gentlemen are strongly disposed to banter me on my prejudices, but don't. When I have made my toilet, I go upon the hurricane-deck, and set in for two hours of hard walking up and down. The sun is rising brilliantly; we are passing Mount Vernon, where Washington lies buried; the river is wide and rapid; and its banks are beautiful. All the glory and splendour of the day are coming on, and growing brighter every minute.

At eight o'clock we breakfast in the cabin where I passed the night, but the windows and doors are all thrown open, and now it is fresh enough. There is no hurry or greediness apparent in the despatch of the meal. It is longer than a travelling breakfast with us; more orderly, and more polite.

Soon after nine o'clock we come to Potomac Creek, where we are to land; and then comes the oddest part of the journey. Seven stage-coaches are preparing to carry us on. Some of them are ready, some of them are not ready. Some of the drivers are blacks, some whites. There are four horses to each coach, and all the horses, harnessed or unharnessed, are there. The passengers are getting out of the steamboat, and into the coaches; the luggage is being transferred in noisy wheelbarrows; the horses are frightened, and impatient to start; the black drivers are chattering to them like so many monkeys; and the white ones whooping like so many drovers: for the main thing to be done in all kinds of hostlering here, is to make as much noise as possible. The coaches are something like the French coaches, but not nearly so good. In lieu of springs, they are hung on bands of the strongest leather. There is very little choice or difference between them; and they may be likened to the car portion of the swings at an English fair, roofed, put upon axle-trees and wheels, and curtained with painted canvas. They are covered with mud from the roof to the wheel-tire, and have never been cleaned since they were first built.

The tickets we have received on board the steamboat are marked No. 1, so we belong to coach No. 1. I throw my coat on the box, and hoist my wife and her maid into the inside. It has only one step, and that being about a yard from the ground, is usually approached by a chair: when there is no chair, ladies trust in Providence. The coach holds nine inside, having a seat across from door to door, where we in England put our legs: so that there is only one feat more difficult in the performance than getting in, and that is, getting out again. There is only one outside passenger, and he sits upon the box. As I am that one, I climb up; and while they are strapping the luggage on the roof, and heaping it into a kind of tray behind, have a good opportunity of looking at the driver.

He is a negro—very black indeed. He is dressed in a coarse pepper-and-salt suit excessively patched and darned (particularly at the knees), grey stockings, enormous unblacked high-low shoes, and very short trousers. He has two odd gloves: one of parti-coloured worsted, and one of leather. He has a very short whip, broken in the middle and bandaged up with string. And yet he wears a low-crowned, broad-brimmed, black hat: faintly shadowing forth a kind of insane imitation of an English coachman! But somebody in authority cries "Go ahead!" as I am making these observations. The mail takes the lead in a four-horse waggon, and all the coaches follow in procession: headed by No. 1.

By the way, whenever an Englishman would cry "All right!" an American cries "Go ahead!" which is somewhat expressive of the national character of the two countries.

The first half-mile of the road is over bridges made of loose planks laid across two parallel poles, which tilt up as the wheels roll over them; and IN the river. The river has a clayey bottom and is full of holes, so that half a horse is constantly disappearing unexpectedly, and can't be found again for some time.

But we get past even this, and come to the road itself, which is a series of alternate swamps and gravel-pits. A tremendous place is close before us, the black driver rolls his eyes, screws his mouth up very round, and looks straight between the two leaders, as if he were saying to himself, "We have done this often before, but now I think we shall have a crash." He takes a rein in each hand; jerks and pulls at both; and dances on the splashboard with both feet (keeping his seat, of course) like the late lamented Ducrow on two of his fiery coursers. We come to the spot, sink down in the mire nearly to the coach windows, tilt on one side at an angle of forty-five degrees, and stick there. The insides scream dismally; the coach stops; the horses flounder; all the other six coaches stop; and their four-and-twenty horses flounder likewise: but merely for company, and in sympathy with ours. Then the following circumstances occur.

BLACK DRIVER (to the horses). "Hi!"

Nothing happens. Insides scream again.

BLACK DRIVER (to the horses). "Ho!"

Horses plunge, and splash the black driver.

GENTLEMAN INSIDE (looking out). "Why, what on airth—"

Gentleman receives a variety of splashes and draws his head in again, without finishing his question or waiting for an answer.

BLACK DRIVER (still to the horses). "Jiddy! Jiddy!"

Horses pull violently, drag the coach out of the hole, and draw it up a bank; so steep, that the black driver's legs fly up into the air, and he goes back among the luggage on the roof. But he immediately recovers himself, and cries (still to the horses),

"Pill!"

No effect. On the contrary, the coach begins to roll back upon No. 2, which rolls back upon No. 3, which rolls back upon No. 4, and so on, until No. 7 is heard to curse and swear, nearly a quarter of a mile behind.

BLACK DRIVER (louder than before). "Pill!"

Horses make another struggle to get up the bank, and again the coach rolls backward.

BLACK DRIVER (louder than before). "Pe-e-e-ill!"

Horses make a desperate struggle.

BLACK DRIVER (recovering spirits). "Hi, Jiddy, Jiddy, Pill!"

Horses make another effort.

BLACK DRIVER (with great vigour). "Ally Loo! Hi. Jiddy, Jiddy. Pill. Ally Loo!"

Horses almost do it.

BLACK DRIVER (with his eyes starting out of his head). "Lee, den. Lee, dere. Hi. Jiddy, Jiddy. Pill. Ally Loo. Lee-e-e-e-e!"

They run up the bank, and go down again on the other side at a fearful pace. It is impossible to stop them, and at the bottom there is a deep hollow, full of water. The coach rolls frightfully. The insides scream. The mud and water fly about us. The black driver dances like a madman. Suddenly we are all right by some extraordinary means, and stop to breathe.

A black friend of the black driver is sitting on a fence. The black driver recognises him by twirling his head round and round like a harlequin, rolling his eyes, shrugging his shoulders, and grinning from ear to ear. He stops short, turns to me, and says:

"We shall get you through sa, like a fiddle, and hope a please you when we get you through sa. Old 'ooman at home sa:" chuckling very much. "Outside gentleman sa, he often remember old 'ooman at home sa," grinning again.

"Ay ay, we'll take care of the old woman. Don't be afraid."

The black driver grins again, but there is another hole, and beyond that, another bank, close before us. So he stops short: cries (to the horses again) "Easy. Easy den. Ease. Steady. Hi. Jiddy. Pill. Ally. Loo," but never "Lee!" until we are reduced to the very last extremity, and are in the midst of difficulties, extrication from which appears to be all but impossible.

And so we do the ten miles or thereabouts in two hours and a half; breaking no bones, though bruising a great many; and in short getting through the distance, "like a fiddle."

This singular kind of coaching terminates at Fredericksburgh, whence there is a railway to Richmond. The tract of country through which it takes its course was once productive; but the soil has been exhausted by the system of employing a great amount of slave labour in forcing crops, without strengthening the land; and it is now little better than a sandy desert overgrown with trees. Dreary and uninteresting as its aspect is, I was glad to the heart to find anything on which one of the curses of this horrible institution has fallen; and had greater pleasure in contemplating the withered ground, than the richest and most thriving cultivation in the same place could possibly have afforded me.

In this district, as in all others where slavery sits brooding, (I have frequently heard this admitted, even by those who are its warmest advocates:) there is an air of ruin and decay abroad, which is inseparable from the system. The barns and outhouses are mouldering away; the sheds are patched and half roofless; the log cabins (built in Virginia with external chimneys made of clay or wood) are squalid in the last degree. There is no look of decent comfort anywhere. The miserable stations by the railway side; the great wild wood-yards, whence the engine is supplied with fuel; the negro children rolling on the ground before the cabin doors, with dogs and pigs; the biped beasts of burden sinking past: gloom and dejection are upon them all.

In the negro car belonging to the train in which we made this journey, were a mother and her children who had just been purchased; the husband and father being left behind with their old owner. The children cried the whole way, and the mother was misery's picture. The champion of Life, Liberty, and the Pursuit of Happiness, who had bought them, rode in the same train; and, every time we stopped, got down to see that they were safe. The black in Sinbad's Travels with one eye in the middle of his forehead which shone like a burning coal, was nature's aristocrat compared with this white gentleman.

It was between six and seven o'clock in the evening, when we drove to the hotel: in front of which, and on the top of the broad flight of steps leading to the door, two or three citizens were balancing themselves on rocking-chairs, and smoking cigars. We found it a very large and elegant establishment, and were as well entertained as travellers need desire to be. The climate being a thirsty one, there was never, at any hour of the day, a scarcity of loungers in the spacious bar, or a cessation of the mixing of cool liquors: but they were a merrier people here, and had musical instruments playing to them o' nights, which it was a treat to hear again.

The next day, and the next, we rode and walked about the town, which is delightfully situated on eight hills, overhanging James River; a sparkling stream, studded here and there with bright islands, or brawling over broken rocks. Although it was yet but the middle of March, the weather in this southern temperature was extremely warm; the peach-trees and magnolias were in full bloom; and the trees were green. In a low ground among the hills, is a valley known as "Bloody Run," from a terrible conflict with the Indians which once occurred there. It is a good place for such a struggle, and, like every other spot I saw associated with any legend of that wild people now so rapidly fading from the earth, interested me very much.

The city is the seat of the local parliament of Virginia; and in its shady legislative halls, some orators were drowsily holding forth to the hot noon day. By dint of constant repetition, however, these constitutional sights had very little more interest for me than so many parochial vestries; and I was glad to exchange this one for a lounge in a well-arranged public library of some ten thousand volumes, and a visit to a tobacco manufactory, where the workmen are all slaves.

I saw in this place the whole process of picking, rolling, pressing, drying, packing in casks, and branding. All the tobacco thus dealt with, was in course of manufacture for chewing; and one would have supposed there was enough in that one storehouse to have filled even the comprehensive jaws of America. In this form, the weed looks like the oil-cake on which we fatten cattle; and even without reference to its consequences, is sufficiently uninviting.

Many of the workmen appeared to be strong men, and it is hardly necessary to add that they were all labouring quietly, then. After two o'clock in the day, they are allowed to sing, a certain number at a time. The hour striking while I was there, some twenty sang a hymn in parts, and sang it by no means ill; pursuing their work meanwhile. A bell rang as I was about to leave, and they all poured forth into a building on the opposite side of the street to dinner. I said several times that I should like to see them at their meal; but as the gentleman to whom I mentioned this desire appeared to be suddenly taken rather deaf, I did not pursue the request. Of their appearance I shall have something to say, presently.

On the following day, I visited a plantation or farm, of about twelve hundred acres, on the opposite bank of the river. Here again, although I went down with the owner of the estate, to "the quarter," as that part of it in which the slaves live is called, I was not invited to enter into any of their huts. All I saw of them, was, that they were very crazy, wretched cabins, near to which groups of half-naked children basked in the sun, or wallowed on the dusty ground. But I believe that this gentleman is a considerate and excellent master, who inherited his fifty slaves, and is neither a buyer nor a seller of human stock; and I am sure, from my own observation and conviction, that he is a kind-hearted, worthy man.

The planter's house was an airy, rustic dwelling, that brought Defoe's description of such places strongly to my recollection. The day was very warm, but the blinds being all closed, and the windows and doors set wide open, a shady coolness rustled through the rooms, which was exquisitely refreshing after the glare and heat without. Before the windows was an open piazza, where, in what they call the hot weather—whatever that may be—they sling hammocks, and drink and doze luxuriously. I do not know how their cool reflections may taste within the hammocks, but having experience, I can report that, out of them, the mounds of ices and the bowls of mint-julep and sherry-cobbler they make in these latitudes, are refreshments never to be thought of afterwards, in summer, by those who would preserve contented minds.

There are two bridges across the river: one belongs to the railroad, and the other, which is a very crazy affair, is the private property of some old lady in the neighbourhood, who levies tolls upon the townspeople. Crossing this bridge, on my way back, I saw a notice painted on the gate, cautioning all persons to drive slowly: under a penalty, if the offender were a white man, of five dollars; if a negro, fifteen stripes.

The same decay and gloom that overhang the way by which it is approached, hover above the town of Richmond. There are pretty villas and cheerful houses in its streets, and Nature smiles upon the country round; but jostling its handsome residences, like slavery itself going hand in hand with many lofty virtues, are deplorable tenements, fences unrepaired, walls crumbling into ruinous heaps. Hinting gloomily at things below the surface, these, and many other tokens of the same description, force themselves upon the notice, and are remembered with depressing influence, when livelier features are forgotten.

To those who are happily unaccustomed to them, the countenances in the streets and labouring-places, too, are shocking. All men who know that there are laws against instructing slaves, of which the pains and penalties greatly exceed in their amount the fines imposed on those who maim and torture them, must be prepared to find their faces very low in the scale of intellectual expression. But the darkness —not of skin, but mind—which meets the stranger's eye at every turn; the brutalizing and blotting out of all fairer characters traced by Nature's hand; immeasurably outdo his worst belief. That travelled creation of the great satirist's brain, who fresh from living among horses, peered from a high casement down upon his own kind with trembling horror, was scarcely more repelled and daunted by the sight, than those who look upon some of these faces for the first time must surely be.

I left the last of them behind me in the person of a wretched drudge, who, after running to and fro all day till midnight, and moping in his stealthy winks of sleep upon the stairs between whiles, was washing the dark passages at four o'clock in the morning; and went upon my way with a grateful heart that I was not doomed to live where slavery was, and had never had my senses blunted to its wrongs and horrors in a slave-rocked cradle.

It had been my intention to proceed by James River and Chesapeake Bay to Baltimore; but one of the steamboats being absent from her station through some accident and the means of conveyance being consequently rendered uncertain, we returned to Washington by the way we had come (there were two constables on board the steamboat, in pursuit of runaway slaves), and halting there again for one night, went on to Baltimore next afternoon.

The most comfortable of all the hotels of which I had any experience in the United States, and they were not a few, is Barnum's, in that city: where the English traveller will find curtains to his bed, for the first and probably the last time in America (this is a disinterested remark, for I never use them); and where he will be likely to have enough water for washing himself, which is not at all a common case.

This capital of the state of Maryland is a bustling, busy town, with a great deal of traffic of various kinds, and in particular of water commerce. That portion of the town which it most favours is none of the cleanest, it is true; but the upper part is of a very different character, and has many agreeable streets and public buildings. The Washington Monument, which is a handsome pillar with a statue on its summit; the Medical College; and the Battle Monument in memory of an engagement with the British at North Point; are the most conspicuous among them.

There is a very good prison in this city, and the State Penitentiary is also among its institutions. In this latter establishment there were two curious cases.

One was that of a young man, who had been tried for the murder of his father. The evidence was entirely circumstantial, and was very conflicting and doubtful; nor was it possible to assign any motive which could have tempted him to the commission of so tremendous a crime. He had been tried twice; and on the second occasion the jury felt so much hesitation in convicting him, that they found a verdict of manslaughter, or murder in the second degree; which it could not possibly be, as there had, beyond all doubt, been no quarrel or provocation, and if he were guilty at all, he was unquestionably guilty of murder in its broadest and worst signification.

The remarkable feature in the case was, that if the unfortunate deceased were not really murdered by this own son of his, he must have been murdered by his own brother. The evidence lay in a most remarkable manner, between those two. On all the suspicious points, the dead man's brother was the witness: all the explanations for the prisoner (some of them extremely plausible) went, by construction and inference, to inculcate him as plotting to fix the guilt upon his nephew. It must have been one of them; and the jury had to decide between two sets of suspicions, almost equally unnatural, unaccountable, and strange.

The other case, was that of a man who once went to a certain distiller's and stole a copper measure containing a quantity of liquor. He was pursued and taken with the property in his possession, and was sentenced to two years' imprisonment. On coming out of the jail, at the expiration of that term, he went back to the same distiller's, and stole the same copper measure containing the same quantity of liquor. There was not the slightest reason to suppose that the man wished to return to prison: indeed everything, but the commission of the offence, made directly against that assumption. There are only two ways of accounting for this extraordinary proceeding. One is, that after undergoing so much for this copper measure he conceived he had established a sort of claim and right to it. The other that, by dint of long thinking about, it had become a monomania with him, and had acquired a fascination which he found it impossible to resist; swelling from an Earthly Copper Gallon into an Ethereal Golden Vat.

After remaining here a couple of days I bound myself to a rigid adherence to the plan I had laid down so recently, and resolved to set forward on our western journey without any more delay. Accordingly, having reduced the luggage within the smallest possible compass (by sending back to New York, to be afterwards forwarded to us in Canada, so much of it as was not absolutely wanted); and having procured the necessary credentials to banking-houses on the way; and having moreover looked for two evenings at the setting sun, with as well-defined an idea of the country before us as if we had been going to travel into the very centre of that planet; we left Baltimore by another railway at half-past eight in the morning, and reached the town of York, some sixty miles off, by the early dinner-time of the Hotel which was the starting-place of the four-horse coach, wherein we were to proceed to Harrisburg.

This conveyance, the box of which I was fortunate enough to secure, had come down to meet us at the railroad station, and was as muddy and cumbersome as usual. As more passengers were waiting for us at the inn-door, the coachman observed under his breath, in the usual self-communicative voice, looking the while at his mouldy harness as if it were to that he was addressing himself,

"I expect we shall want *the big* coach."

I could not help wondering within myself what the size of this big coach might be, and how many persons it might be designed to hold; for the vehicle which was too small for our purpose was something larger than two English heavy night coaches, and might have been the twin-brother of a French Diligence. My speculations were speedily at rest, however, for as soon as we had dined, there came rumbling up the street, shaking its sides like a corpulent giant, a kind of barge on wheels. After much blundering and backing, it stopped at the door: rolling heavily from side to side when its other motion had ceased, as if it had taken cold in its damp stable, and between that, and the having been required in its dropsical old age to move at any faster pace than a walk, were distressed by shortness of wind.

"If here ain't the Harrisburg mail at last, and dreadful bright and smart to look at too," cried an elderly gentleman in some excitement, "darn my mother!"

I don't know what the sensation of being darned may be, or whether a man's mother has a keener relish or disrelish of the process than anybody else; but if the endurance of this mysterious ceremony by the old lady in question had depended on the accuracy of her son's vision in respect to the abstract brightness and smartness of the Harrisburg mail, she would certainly have undergone its infliction. However, they booked twelve people inside; and the luggage (including such trifles as a large rocking-chair, and a good-sized dining-table) being at length made fast upon the roof, we started off in great state.

At the door of another hotel, there was another passenger to be taken up.

"Any room, sir?" cries the new passenger to the coachman.

"Well, there's room enough," replies the coachman, without getting down, or even looking at him.

"There an't no room at all, sir," bawls a gentleman inside. Which another gentleman (also inside) confirms, by predicting that the attempt to introduce any more passengers "won't fit nohow."

The new passenger, without any expression of anxiety, looks into the coach, and then looks up at the coachman: "Now, how do you mean to fix it?" says he, after a pause: "for I *must* go."

The coachman employs himself in twisting the lash of his whip into a knot, and takes no more notice of the question: clearly signifying that it is anybody's business but his, and that the passengers would do well to fix it, among themselves. In this state of things, matters seem to be approximating to a fix of another kind, when another inside passenger in a corner, who is nearly suffocated, cries faintly, "I'll get out."

This is no matter of relief or self-congratulation to the driver, for his immovable philosophy is perfectly undisturbed by anything that happens in the coach. Of all things in the world, the coach would seem to be the very last upon his mind. The exchange is made, however, and then the passenger who has given up his seat makes a third upon the box, seating himself in what he calls the middle; that is, with half his person on my legs, and the other half on the driver's.

"Go a-head, cap'en," cries the colonel, who directs.

"Gŏ-lāng!" cries the cap'en to his company, the horses, and away we go.

We took up at a rural bar-room, after we had gone a few miles, an intoxicated gentleman who climbed upon the roof among the luggage, and subsequently slipping off without hurting himself, was seen in the distant perspective reeling back to the grog-shop where we had found him. We also parted with more of our freight at different times, so that when we came to change horses, I was again alone outside.

The coachmen always change with the horses, and are usually as dirty as the coach. The first was dressed like a very shabby English baker; the second like a Russian peasant: for he wore a loose purple camlet robe, with a fur collar, tied round his waist with a parti-coloured worsted sash; grey trousers; light blue gloves: and a cap of bearskin. It had by this time come on to rain very heavily, and there was a cold damp mist besides, which penetrated to the skin. I was glad to take advantage of a stoppage and get down to stretch my legs, shake the water off my great-coat, and swallow the usual anti-temperance recipe for keeping out the cold.

When I mounted to my seat again, I observed a new parcel lying on the coach roof, which I took to be a rather large fiddle in a brown bag. In the course of a few miles, however, I discovered that it had a glazed cap at one end and a pair of muddy shoes at the other; and further observation demonstrated it to be a small boy in a snuff-coloured coat, with his arms pinioned to his sides, by deep forcing into his pockets. He was, I presume, a relative or friend of the coachman's, as he lay a-top of the luggage with his face towards the rain; and except when a change of position brought his shoes in contact with my hat, he appeared to be asleep. At last, on some occasion of our stopping, this thing slowly upreared itself to the height of three feet six, and fixing its eyes on me, observed in piping accents, with a complaisant yawn, half quenched in an obliging air of friendly patronage, "Well now, stranger, I guess you find this a'most like an English arternoon, hey?"

The scenery which had been tame enough at first, was, for the last ten or twelve miles, beautiful. Our road wound through the pleasant valley of the Susquehanna; the river, dotted with innumerable green islands, lay upon our right; and on the left, a steep ascent, craggy with broken rock, and dark with pine trees. The mist, wreathing itself into a hundred fantastic shapes, moved solemnly upon the water; and the gloom of evening gave to all an air of mystery and silence which greatly enhanced its natural interest.

We crossed this river by a wooden bridge, roofed and covered in on all sides, and nearly a mile in length. It was profoundly dark; perplexed, with great beams, crossing and recrossing it at every possible angle; and through the broad chinks and crevices in the floor, the rapid river gleamed, far down below, like a legion of eyes. We had no lamps; and as the horses stumbled and floundered through this place, towards the distant speck of dying light, it seemed interminable. I really could not at first persuade myself as we rumbled heavily on, filling the bridge with hollow noises, and I held down my head to save it from the rafters above, but that I was in a painful dream; for I have often dreamed of toiling through such places, and as often argued, even at the time, "this cannot be reality."

At length, however, we emerged upon the streets of Harrisburg, whose feeble lights, reflected dismally from the wet ground, did not shine out upon a very cheerful city. We were soon established in a snug hotel, which though smaller and far less splendid than many we put up at, is raised above them all in my remembrance, by having for its landlord the most obliging, considerate, and gentlemanly person I ever had to deal with.

As we were not to proceed upon our journey until the afternoon, I walked out, after breakfast the next morning, to look about me; and was duly shown a model prison on the solitary system, just erected, and as yet without an inmate; the trunk of an old tree to which Harris, the first settler here (afterwards buried under it), was tied by hostile Indians, with his funeral pile about him, when he was saved by the timely appearance of a friendly party on the opposite shore of the river; the local legislature (for there was another of those bodies here again, in full debate); and the other curiosities of the town.

I was very much interested in looking over a number of treaties made from time to time with the poor Indians, signed by the different chiefs at the period of their ratification, and preserved in the office of the Secretary to the Commonwealth. These signatures, traced of course by their own hands, are rough drawings of the creatures or weapons they were called after. Thus, the Great Turtle makes a crooked pen-and-ink outline of a great turtle; the Buffalo sketches a buffalo; the War Hatchet sets a rough image of that weapon for his mark. So with the Arrow, the Fish, the Scalp, the Big Canoe, and all of them.

I could not but think—as I looked at these feeble and tremulous productions of hands which could draw the longest arrow to the head in a stout elk-horn bow, or split a bead or feather with a rifle-ball—of Crabbe's musings over the Parish Register, and the irregular scratches made with a pen, by men who would plough a lengthy furrow straight from end to end. Nor could I help bestowing many sorrowful thoughts upon the simple warriors whose hands and hearts were set there, in all truth and honesty, and who only learned in course of time from white men how to break their faith, and quibble out of forms and bonds. I wonder, too, how many times the credulous Big Turtle, or trusting Little Hatchet, had put his mark to treaties which were falsely read to him; and had signed away, he knew not what, until it went and cast him loose upon the new possessors of the land, a savage indeed.

Our host announced, before our early dinner, that some members of the legislative body proposed to do us the honour of calling. He had kindly yielded up to us his wife's own little parlour, and when I begged that he would show them in, I saw him look with painful apprehension at its pretty carpet; though, being otherwise occupied at the time, the cause of his uneasiness did not occur to me.

It certainly would have been more pleasant to all parties concerned, and would not, I think, have compromised their independence in any material degree, if some of these gentlemen had not only yielded to the prejudice in favour of spittoons, but had abandoned themselves, for the moment, even to the conventional absurdity of pocket-handkerchiefs.

It still continued to rain heavily, and when we went down to the Canal Boat (for that was the mode of conveyance by which we were to proceed) after dinner, the weather was as unpromising and obstinately wet as one would desire to see. Nor was the sight of this canal boat, in which we were to spend three or four days, by any means a cheerful one; as it involved some uneasy speculations concerning the disposal of the passengers at night, and opened a wide field of inquiry touching the other domestic arrangements of the establishment, which was sufficiently disconcerting.

However, there it was—a barge with a little house in it, viewed from the outside; and a caravan at a fair, viewed from within: the gentlemen being accommodated, as the spectators usually are, in one of those locomotive museums of penny wonders; and the ladies being partitioned off by a red curtain, after the manner of the dwarfs and giants in the same establishments, whose private lives are passed in rather close exclusiveness.

We sat here, looking silently at the row of little tables, which extended down both sides of the cabin, and listening to the rain as it dripped and pattered on the boat, and plashed with a dismal merriment in the water, until the arrival of the railway train, for whose final contribution to our stock of passengers, our departure was alone deferred. It brought a great many boxes, which were bumped and tossed upon the roof, almost as painfully as if they had been deposited on one's own head, without the intervention of a porter's knot; and several damp gentlemen, whose clothes, on their drawing round the stove, began to steam again. No doubt it would have been a thought more comfortable if the driving rain, which now poured down more soakingly than ever, had admitted of a window being opened, or if our number had been something less than thirty; but there was scarcely time to think as much, when a train of three horses was attached to the tow-rope, the boy upon the leader smacked his whip, the rudder creaked and groaned complainingly, and we had begun our journey.

## CHAPTER X

SOME FURTHER ACCOUNT OF THE CANAL BOAT, ITS DOMESTIC ECONOMY, AND ITS PASSENGERS. JOURNEY TO PITTSBURG ACROSS THE ALLEGHANY MOUNTAINS. PITTSBURG.

As it continued to rain most perseveringly, we all remained below: the damp gentlemen round the stove, gradually becoming mildewed by the action of the fire; and the dry gentlemen lying at full length upon the seats, or slumbering uneasily with their faces on the tables, or walking up and down the cabin, which it was barely possible for a man of the middle height to do, without making bald places on his head by scraping it against the roof. At about six o'clock, all the small tables were put together to form one long table, and everybody sat down to tea, coffee, bread, butter, salmon, shad, liver, steaks, potatoes, pickles, ham, chops, black-puddings, and sausages.

"Will you try," said my opposite neighbour, handing me a dish of potatoes, broken up in milk and butter, "will you try some of these fixings?"

There are few words which perform such various duties as this word "fix." It is the Caleb Quotem of the American vocabulary. You call upon a gentleman in a country town, and his help informs you that he is "fixing himself" just now, but will be down directly: by which you are to understand that he is dressing. You inquire, on board a steamboat, of a fellow-passenger, whether breakfast will be ready soon, and he tells you he should think so, for when he was last below, they were "fixing the tables:" in other words, laying the cloth. You beg a porter to collect your luggage, and he entreats you not to be uneasy, for he'll "fix it presently:" and if you complain of indisposition, you are advised to have recourse to Doctor So-and-so who will "fix you" in no time.

One night, I ordered a bottle of mulled wine at an hotel where I was staying, and waited a long time for it; at length it was put upon the table with an apology from the landlord that he feared it wasn't "fixed properly." And I recollect once, at a stage-coach dinner, overhearing a very stern gentleman demand of a waiter who presented him with a plate of underdone roast-beef, "whether he called *that*, fixing God A'mighty's vittles?"

There is no doubt that the meal, at which the invitation was tendered to me which has occasioned this digression, was disposed of somewhat ravenously; and that the gentlemen thrust the broad-bladed knives and the two-pronged forks further down their throats than I ever saw the same weapons go before, except in the hands of a skilful juggler: but no man sat down until the ladies were seated; or omitted any little act of politeness which could contribute to their comfort. Nor did I ever once, on any occasion, anywhere, during my rambles in America, see a woman exposed to the slightest act of rudeness, incivility, or even inattention.

By the time the meal was over, the rain, which seemed to have worn itself out by coming down so fast, was nearly over too; and it became feasible to go on deck: which was a great relief, notwithstanding its being a very small deck, and being rendered still smaller by the luggage, which was heaped together in the middle under a tarpaulin covering; leaving, on either side, a path so narrow, that it became a science to walk to and fro without tumbling overboard into the canal. It was somewhat embarrassing at first, too, to have to duck nimbly every five minutes whenever the man at the helm cried "Bridge!" and sometimes, when the cry was "Low Bridge," to lie down nearly flat. But custom familiarises one to anything, and there were so many bridges that it took a very short time to get used to this.

As night came on, and we drew in sight of the first range of hills, which are the outposts of the Alleghany Mountains, the scenery, which had been uninteresting hitherto, became more bold and striking. The wet ground reeked and smoked, after the heavy fall of rain; and the croaking of the frogs (whose noise in these parts is almost incredible) sounded as though a million of fairy teams with bells were travelling through the air, and keeping pace with us. The night was cloudy yet, but moonlight too: and when we crossed the Susquehanna river—over which there is an extraordinary wooden bridge with two galleries, one above the other, so that even there, two boat teams meeting, may pass without confusion—it was wild and grand.

I have mentioned my having been in some uncertainty and doubt, at first, relative to the sleeping arrangements on board this boat. I remained in the same vague state of mind until ten o'clock or thereabouts, when going below, I found suspended on either side of the cabin, three long tiers of hanging book-shelves, designed apparently for volumes of the small octavo size. Looking with greater attention at these contrivances (wondering to find such literary preparations in such a place), I descried on each shelf a sort of microscopic sheet and blanket; then I began dimly to comprehend that the passengers were the library, and that they were to be arranged edge-wise, on these shelves, till morning.

I was assisted to this conclusion by seeing some of them gathered round the master of the boat, at one of the tables, drawing lots with all the anxieties and passions of gamesters depicted in their countenances; while others, with small pieces of cardboard in their hands, were groping among the shelves in search of numbers corresponding with those they had drawn. As soon as any gentleman found his number, he took possession of it by immediately undressing himself and crawling into bed. The rapidity with which an agitated gambler subsided into a snoring slumberer, was one of the most singular effects I have ever witnessed. As to the ladies, they were already abed, behind the red curtain, which was carefully drawn and pinned up the centre; though as every cough, or sneeze, or whisper, behind this curtain, was perfectly audible before it, we had still a lively consciousness of their society.

The politeness of the person in authority had secured to me a shelf in a nook near this red curtain, in some degree removed from the great body of sleepers: to which place I retired, with many acknowledgments to him for his attention. I found it, on after-measurement, just the width of an ordinary sheet of Bath post letter-paper; and I was at first in some uncertainty as to the best means of getting into it. But the shelf being a bottom one, I finally determined on lying upon the floor, rolling gently in, stopping immediately I touched the mattress, and remaining for the night with that side uppermost, whatever it might be. Luckily, I came upon my back at exactly the right moment. I was much alarmed on looking upward, to see, by the shape of his half-yard of sacking (which his weight had bent into an exceedingly tight bag), that there was a very heavy gentleman above me, whom the slender cords seemed quite incapable of holding; and I could not help reflecting upon the grief of my wife and family in the event of his coming down in the night. But as I could not have got up again without a severe bodily struggle, which might have alarmed the ladies; and as I had nowhere to go to, even if I had; I shut my eyes upon the danger, and remained there.

One of two remarkable circumstances is indisputably a fact, with reference to that class of society who travel in these boats. Either they carry their restlessness to such a pitch that they never sleep at all; or they expectorate in dreams, which would be a remarkable mingling of the real and ideal. All night long, and every night, on this canal, there was a perfect storm and tempest of spitting; and once my coat, being in the very centre of the hurricane sustained by five gentlemen (which moved vertically, strictly carrying out Reid's Theory of the Law of Storms), I was fain the next morning to lay it on the deck, and rub it down with fair water before it was in a condition to be worn again.

Between five and six o'clock in the morning we got up, and some of us went on deck, to give them an opportunity of taking the shelves down; while others, the morning being very cold, crowded round the rusty stove, cherishing the newly kindled fire, and filling the grate with those voluntary contributions of which they had been so liberal all night. The washing accommodations were primitive. There was a tin ladle chained to the deck, with which every gentleman who thought it necessary to cleanse himself (many were superior to this weakness), fished the dirty water out of the canal, and poured it into a tin basin, secured in like manner. There was also a jack-towel. And, hanging up before a little looking-glass in the bar, in the immediate vicinity of the bread and cheese and biscuits, were a public comb and hair-brush.

At eight o'clock, the shelves being taken down and put away and the tables joined together, everybody sat down to the tea, coffee, bread, butter, salmon, shad, liver, steak, potatoes, pickles, ham, chops, black-puddings, and sausages, all over again. Some were fond of compounding this variety, and having it all on their plates at once. As each gentleman got through his own personal amount of tea, coffee, bread, butter, salmon, shad, liver, steak, potatoes, pickles, ham, chops, black-puddings, and sausages, he rose up and walked off. When everybody had done with everything, the fragments were cleared away: and one of the waiters appearing anew in the character of a barber, shaved such of the company as desired to be shaved; while the remainder looked on, or yawned over their newspapers. Dinner was breakfast again, without the tea and coffee; and supper and breakfast were identical.

There was a man on board this boat, with a light fresh-coloured face, and a pepper-and-salt suit of clothes, who was the most inquisitive fellow that can possibly be imagined. He never spoke otherwise than interrogatively. He was an embodied inquiry. Sitting down or standing up, still or moving, walking the deck or taking his meals, there he was, with a great note of interrogation in each eye, two in his cocked ears, two more in his turned-up nose and chin, at least half a dozen more about the corners of his mouth, and the largest one of all in his hair, which was brushed pertly off his forehead in a flaxen clump. Every button in his clothes said, "Eh? What's that? Did you speak? Say that again, will you?" He was always wide awake, like the enchanted bride who drove her husband frantic; always restless; always thirsting for answers; perpetually seeking and never finding. There never was such a curious man.

I wore a fur great-coat at that time, and before we were well clear of the wharf, he questioned me concerning it, and its price, and where I bought it, and when, and what fur it was, and what it weighed, and what it cost. Then he took notice of my watch, and asked me what *that* cost, and whether it was a French watch, and where I got it, and how I got it, and whether I bought it or had it given me, and how it went, and where the key-hole was, and when I wound it, every night or every morning, and whether I ever forgot to wind it at all, and if I did, what then? Where had I been to last, and where was I going next, and where was I going after that, and had I seen the President, and what did he say, and what did I say, and what did he say when I had said that? Eh? Lor now! do tell!

Finding that nothing would satisfy him, I evaded his questions after the first score or two, and in particular pleaded ignorance respecting the name of the fur whereof the coat was made. I am unable to say whether this was the reason, but that coat fascinated him afterwards; he usually kept close behind me as I walked, and moved as I moved, that he might look at it the better; and he frequently dived into narrow places after me at the risk of his life, that he might have the satisfaction of passing his hand up the back, and rubbing it the wrong way.

We had another odd specimen on board, of a different kind. This was a thin-faced, spare-figured man of middle age and stature, dressed in a dusty drabbish-coloured suit, such as I never saw before. He was perfectly quiet during the first part of the journey: indeed I don't remember having so much as seen him until he was brought out by circumstances, as great men often are. The conjunction of events which made him famous, happened, briefly, thus.

The canal extends to the foot of the mountain, and there, of course, it stops; the passengers being conveyed across it by land carriage, and taken on afterwards by another canal boat, the counterpart of the first, which awaits them on the other side. There are two canal lines of passage-boats; one is called The Express, and one (a cheaper one) The Pioneer. The Pioneer gets first to the mountain, and waits for the Express people to come up; both sets of passengers being conveyed across it at the same time. We were the Express company; but when we had crossed the mountain, and had come to the second boat, the proprietors took it into their heads to draft all the Pioneers into it likewise, so that we were five-and-forty at least, and the accession of passengers was not at all of that kind which improved the prospect of sleeping at night. Our people grumbled at this, as people do in such cases; but suffered the boat to be towed off with the whole freight aboard nevertheless; and away we went down the canal. At home, I should have protested lustily, but being a foreigner here, I held my peace. Not so this passenger. He cleft a path among the people on deck (we were nearly all on deck), and without addressing anybody whomsoever, soliloquised as follows:

"This may suit *you*, this may, but it don't suit *me*. This may be all very well with Down Easters, and men of Boston raising, but it won't suit my figure nohow; and no two ways about *that;* and so I tell you. Now! I'm from the brown forests of the Mississippi, *I* am, and when the sun shines on me, it does shine—a little. It don't glimmer where *I* live, the sun don't. No. I'm a brown forester, I am. I an't a Johnny Cake. There are no smooth skins where I live. We're rough men there. Rather. If Down Easters and men of Boston raising like this, I'm glad of it, but I'm none of that raising nor of that breed. No. This company wants a little fixing, *it* does. I'm the wrong sort of man for 'em, *I* am. They won't like me, *they* won't. This is piling of it up, a little too moûntaïnoŭs, this is." At the end of every one of these short sentences he turned upon his heel, and walked the other way; checking himself abruptly when he had finished another short sentence, and turning back again.

It is impossible for me to say what terrific meaning was hidden in the words of this brown forester, but I know that the other passengers looked on in a sort of admiring horror, and that presently the boat was put back to the wharf, and as many of the Pioneers as could be coaxed or bullied into going away, were got rid of.

When we started again, some of the boldest spirits on board, made bold to say to the obvious occasion of this improvement in our prospects, "Much obliged to you, sir;" whereunto the brown forester (waving his hand, and still walking up and down as before), replied, "No you an't. You're none o' my raising. You may act for yourselves, *you* may. I have pinted out the way. Down Easters and Johnny Cakes can follow if they please. I an't a Johnny Cake, *I* an't. I am from the brown forests of the Mississippi, *I* am"—and so on, as before. He was unanimously voted one of the tables for his bed at night— there is a great contest for the tables—in consideration for his public services: and he had the warmest corner by the stove throughout the rest of the journey. But I never could find out that he did anything except sit there; nor did I hear him speak again until, in the midst of the bustle and turmoil of getting the luggage ashore in the dark at Pittsburg, I stumbled over him as he sat smoking a cigar on the cabin steps, and heard him muttering to himself, with a short laugh of defiance, "I an't a Johnny Cake, *I* an't. I'm from the brown forests of the Mississippi, *I* am, damme!" I am inclined to argue from this, that he had never left off saying so; but I could not make an affidavit of that part of the story, if required to do so by my Queen and Country.

As we have not reached Pittsburg yet, however, in the order of our narrative, I may go on to remark that breakfast was perhaps the least desirable meal of the day, as in addition to the many savoury odours arising from the eatables already mentioned, there were whiffs of gin, whiskey, brandy, and rum, from the little bar hard by, and a decided seasoning of stale tobacco. Many of the gentlemen passengers were far from particular in respect of their linen, which was in some cases as yellow as the little rivulets that had trickled from the corners of their mouths in chewing, and dried there. Nor was the atmosphere quite free from zephyr whisperings of the thirty beds which had just been cleared away, and of which we were further and more pressingly reminded by the occasional appearance on the table-cloth of a kind of Game, not mentioned in the Bill of Fare.

And yet despite these oddities—and even they had, for me at least, a humour of their own—there was much in this mode of travelling which I heartily enjoyed at the time, and look back upon with great pleasure. Even the running up, bare-necked, at five o'clock in the morning, from the tainted cabin to the dirty deck; scooping up the icy water, plunging one's head into it, and drawing it out, all fresh and glowing with the cold; was a good thing. The fast, brisk walk upon the towing-path, between that time and breakfast, when every vein and artery seemed to tingle with health; the exquisite beauty of the opening day, when light came gleaming off from every-thing; the lazy motion of the boat, when one lay idly on the deck, looking through, rather than at, the deep blue sky; the gliding on at night, so noiselessly, past frowning hills, sullen with dark trees, and sometimes angry in one red, burning spot high up, where unseen men lay crouching round a fire; the shining out of the bright stars un-disturbed by noise of wheels or steam, or any other sound than the limpid rippling of the water as the boat went on: all these were pure delights.

Then there were new settlements and detached log-cabins and frame-houses, full of interest for strangers from an old country: cabins with simple ovens, outside, made of clay; and lodgings for the pigs nearly as good as many of the human quarters; broken windows, patched with worn-out hats, old clothes, old boards, fragments of blankets and paper; and home-made dressers standing in the open air without the door, whereon was ranged the household store, not hard to count, of earthen jars and pots. The eye was pained to see the stumps of great trees thickly strewn in every field of wheat, and seldom to lose the eternal swamp and dull morass, with hundreds of rotten trunks and twisted branches steeped in its unwholesome water. It was quite sad and oppressive, to come upon great tracts where settlers had been burning down the trees, and where their wounded bodies lay about, like those of murdered creatures, while here and there some charred and blackened giant reared aloft two withered arms, and seemed to call down curses on his foes. Sometimes, at night, the way wound through some lovely gorge, like a mountain pass in Scotland, shining and coldly glittering in the light of the moon, and so closed in by high steep hills all round, that there seemed to be no egress save through the narrower path by which we had come, until one rugged hill-side seemed to open, and shutting out the moonlight as we passed into its gloomy throat, wrapped our new course in shade and darkness.

We had left Harrisburg on Friday. On Sunday morning we arrived at the foot of the mountains, which is crossed by railroad. There are ten inclined planes; five ascending, and five descending; the carriages are dragged up the former, and let slowly down the latter, by means of stationary engines; the comparatively level spaces between, being traversed, sometimes by horse, and sometimes by engine power, as the case demands. Occasionally the rails are laid upon the extreme verge of a giddy precipice; and looking from the carriage window, the traveller gazes sheer down, without a stone or scrap of fence between, into the mountain depths below. The journey is very carefully made, however; only two carriages travelling together; and while proper precautions are taken, is not to be dreaded for its dangers.

It was very pretty travelling thus, at a rapid pace along the heights of the mountain in a keen wind, to look down into a valley full of light and softness; catching glimpses, through the tree-tops, of scattered cabins; children running to the doors; dogs bursting out to bark, whom we could see without hearing; terrified pigs scampering homewards; families sitting out in their rude gardens; cows gazing upward with a stupid indifference; men in their shirt-sleeves looking on at their unfinished houses, planning out to-morrow's work; and we riding onward, high above them, like a whirlwind. It was amusing too, when we had dined, and rattled down a steep pass, having no other moving power than the weight of the carriages themselves, to see the engine released, long after us, come buzzing down alone, like a great insect, its back of green and gold so shining in the sun, that if it had spread a pair of wings and soared away, no one would have had occasion, as I fancied, for the least surprise. But it stopped short of us in a very business-like manner when we reached the canal: and, before we left the wharf, went panting up this hill again, with the passengers who had waited our arrival for the means of traversing the road by which we had come.

On the Monday evening, furnace fires and clanking hammers on the banks of the canal, warned us that we approached the termination of this part of our journey. After going through another dreamy place—a long aqueduct across the Alleghany River, which was stranger than the bridge at Harrisburg, being a vast, low, wooden chamber full of water—we emerged upon that ugly confusion of backs of buildings and crazy galleries and stairs, which always abuts on water, whether it be river, sea, canal, or ditch: and were at Pittsburg.

Pittsburg is like Birmingham in England; at least its townspeople say so. Setting aside the streets, the shops, the houses, waggons, factories, public buildings, and population, perhaps it may be. It certainly has a great quantity of smoke hanging about it, and is famous for its iron-works. Besides the prison to which I have already referred, this town contains a pretty arsenal and other institutions. It is very beautifully situated on the Alleghany River, over which there are two bridges; and the villas of the wealthier citizens sprinkled about the high grounds in the neighbourhood, are pretty enough. We lodged at a most excellent hotel, and were admirably served. As usual it was full of boarders, was very large, and had a broad colonnade to every story of the house.

We tarried here three days. Our next point was Cincinnati: and as this was a steamboat journey, and western steamboats usually blow up one or two a week in the season, it was advisable to collect opinions in reference to the comparative safety of the vessel bound that way, then lying in the river. One called the Messenger was the best recommended. She had been advertised to start positively, every day for a fortnight or so, and had not gone yet, nor did her captain seem to have any very fixed intention on the subject. But this is the custom: for if the law were to bind down a free and independent citizen to keep his word with the public, what would become of the liberty of the subject? Besides, it is in the way of trade. And if passengers be decoyed in the way of trade, and people be inconvenienced in the way of trade, what man, who is a sharp tradesman himself, shall say, "We must put a stop to this?"

Impressed by the deep solemnity of the public announcement, I (being then ignorant of these usages) was for hurrying on board in a breathless state, immediately; but receiving private and confidential information that the boat would certainly not start until Friday, April the First, we made ourselves very comfortable in the mean while, and went on board at noon that day.

## CHAPTER XI

### FROM PITTSBURG TO CINCINNATI IN A WESTERN STEAMBOAT.
### CINCINNATI

THE Messenger was one among a crowd of high-pressure steamboats, clustered together by a wharf-side, which, looked down upon from the rising ground that forms the landing-place, and backed by the lofty bank on the opposite side of the river, appeared no larger than so many floating models. She had some forty passengers on board, exclusive of the poorer persons on the lower deck; and in half an hour, or less, proceeded on her way.

We had, for ourselves, a tiny state-room with two berths in it, opening out of the ladies' cabin. There was, undoubtedly, something satisfactory in this "location," inasmuch as it was in the stern, and we had been a great many times very gravely recommended to keep as far aft as possible, "because the steamboats generally blew up forward." Nor was this an unnecessary caution, as the occurrence and circumstances of more than one such fatality during our stay sufficiently testified. Apart from this source of self-congratulation, it was an unspeakable relief to have any place, no matter how confined, where one could be alone: and as the row of little chambers of which this was one, had each a second glass-door besides that in the ladies' cabin, which opened on a narrow gallery outside the vessel, where the other passengers seldom came, and where one could sit in peace and gaze upon the shifting prospect, we took possession of our new quarters with much pleasure.

If the native packets I have already described be unlike anything we are in the habit of seeing on water, these western vessels are still more foreign to all the ideas we are accustomed to entertain of boats. I hardly know what to liken them to, or how to describe them.

In the first place, they have no mast, cordage, tackle, rigging, or other such boat-like gear; nor have they anything in their shape at all calculated to remind one of a boat's head, stern, sides, or keel. Except that they are in the water, and display a couple of paddle-boxes, they might be intended, for anything that appears to the contrary, to perform some unknown service, high and dry, upon a mountain top. There is no visible deck, even: nothing but a long, black, ugly roof, covered with burnt-out feathery sparks; above which tower two iron chimneys, and a hoarse escape valve, and a glass steerage-house. Then, in order as the eye descends towards the water, are the sides, and doors, and windows of the state-rooms, jumbled as oddly together as though they formed a small street, built by the varying tastes of a dozen men: the whole is supported on beams and pillars resting on a dirty barge, but a few inches above the water's edge: and in the narrow space between this upper structure and this barge's deck, are the furnace fires and machinery, open at the sides to every wind that blows, and every storm of rain it drives along its path.

Passing one of these boats at night, and seeing the great body of fire, exposed as I have just described, that rages and roars beneath the frail pile of painted wood: the machinery, not warded off or guarded in any way, but doing its work in the midst of the crowd of idlers and emigrants and children, who throng the lower deck: under the management, too, of reckless men whose acquaintance with its mysteries may have been of six months' standing: one feels directly that the wonder is, not that there should be so many fatal accidents, but that any journey should be safely made.

Within, there is one long narrow cabin, the whole length of the boat; from which the state-rooms open, on both sides. A small portion of it at the stern is partitioned off for the ladies; and the bar is at the

opposite extreme. There is a long table down the centre, and at either
end a stove. The washing apparatus is forward, on the deck. It is a
little better than on board the canal boat, but not much. In all
modes of travelling, the American customs, with reference to the
means of personal cleanliness and wholesome ablution, are extremely
negligent and filthy; and I strongly incline to the belief that a considerable amount of illness is referable to this cause.

We are to be on board the Messenger three days: arriving at
Cincinnati (barring accidents) on Monday morning. There are three
meals a day. Breakfast at seven, dinner at half-past twelve, supper
about six. At each, there are a great many small dishes and plates
upon the table, with very little in them; so that although there is
every appearance of a mighty "spread," there is seldom really more
than a joint: except for those who fancy slices of beet-root, shreds of
dried beef, complicated entanglements of yellow pickle; maize,
Indian corn, apple-sauce, and pumpkin.

Some people fancy all these little dainties together (and sweet
preserves beside), by way of relish to their roast pig. They are
generally those dyspeptic ladies and gentlemen who eat unheard-of
quantities of hot corn bread (almost as good for the digestion as a
kneaded pin-cushion), for breakfast, and for supper. Those who do
not observe this custom, and who help themselves several times
instead, usually suck their knives and forks meditatively, until they
have decided what to take next: then pull them out of their mouths:
put them in the dish; help themselves; and fall to work again. At
dinner, there is nothing to drink upon the table, but great jugs full
of cold water. Nobody says anything, at any meal, to anybody. All
the passengers are very dismal, and seem to have tremendous secrets
weighing on their minds. There is no conversation, no laughter, no
cheerfulness, no sociality, except in spitting; and that is done in
silent fellowship round the stove, when the meal is over. Every man
sits down, dull and languid; swallows his fare as if breakfasts, dinners,
and suppers, were necessities of nature never to be coupled with
recreation or enjoyment; and having bolted his food in a gloomy
silence, bolts himself, in the same state. But for these animal observances, you might suppose the whole male portion of the company
to be the melancholy ghosts of departed book-keepers, who had
fallen dead at the desk: such is their weary air of business and
calculation. Undertakers on duty would be sprightly beside them;
and a collation of funeral-baked meats, in comparison with these
meals, would be a sparkling festivity.

The people are all alike, too. There is no diversity of character.
They travel about on the same errands, say and do the same things
in exactly the same manner, and follow in the same dull cheerless
round. All down the long table, there is scarcely a man who is in
anything different from his neighbour. It is quite a relief to have,
sitting opposite, that little girl of fifteen with the loquacious chin:
who, to do her justice, acts up to it, and fully identifies nature's

handwriting, for of all the small chatterboxes that ever invaded the repose of drowsy ladies' cabin, she is the first and foremost. The beautiful girl, who sits a little beyond her—farther down the table there—married the young man with the dark whiskers, who sits beyond *her*, only last month. They are going to settle in the very Far West, where he has lived four years, but where she has never been. They were both overturned in a stage-coach the other day (a bad omen anywhere else, where overturns are not so common), and his head, which bears the marks of a recent wound, is bound up still. She was hurt too, at the same time, and lay insensible for some days; bright as her eyes are, now.

Further down still, sits a man who is going some miles beyond their place of destination, to "improve" a newly-discovered copper mine. He carries the village—that is to be—with him: a few frame cottages, and an apparatus for smelting the copper. He carries its people too. They are partly American and partly Irish, and herd together on the lower deck; where they amused themselves last evening till the night was pretty far advanced, by alternately firing off pistols and singing hymns.

They, and the very few who have been left at table twenty minutes, rise, and go away. We do so too; and passing through our little state-room, resume our seats in the quiet gallery without.

A fine broad river always, but in some parts much wider than in others: and then there is usually a green island, covered with trees, dividing it into two streams. Occasionally, we stop for a few minutes, maybe to take in wood, maybe for passengers, at some small town or village (I ought to say city, every place is a city here); but the banks are for the most part deep solitudes, overgrown with trees, which, hereabouts, are already in leaf and very green. For miles, and miles, and miles, these solitudes are unbroken by any sign of human life or trace of human footstep; nor is anything seen to move about them but the blue jay, whose colour is so bright, and yet so delicate, that it looks like a flying flower. At lengthened intervals a log cabin, with its little space of cleared land about it, nestles under a rising ground, and sends its thread of blue smoke curling up into the sky. It stands in the corner of the poor field of wheat, which is full of great unsightly stumps, like earthly butchers'-blocks. Sometimes the ground is only just now cleared: the felled trees lying yet upon the soil: and the log-house only this morning begun. As we pass this clearing, the settler leans upon his axe or hammer, and looks wistfully at the people from the world. The children creep out of the temporary hut, which is like a gipsy tent upon the ground, and clap their hands and shout. The dog only glances round at us, and then looks up into his master's face again, as if he were rendered uneasy by any suspension of the common business, and had nothing more to do with pleasures. And still there is the same, eternal foreground. The river has washed away its banks, and stately trees have fallen down into the stream. Some have been there so long, that they are mere dry, grizzly skeletons.

Some have just toppled over, and having earth yet about their roots, are bathing their green heads in the river, and putting forth new shoots and branches. Some are almost sliding down, as you look at them. And some were drowned so long ago, that their bleached arms start out from the middle of the current, and seem to try to grasp the boat, and drag it under water.

Through such a scene as this, the unwieldy machine takes its hoarse, sullen way: venting, at every revolution of the paddles, a loud high-pressure blast; enough, one would think, to waken up the host of Indians who lie buried in a great mound yonder: so old, that mighty oaks and other forest trees have struck their roots into its earth; and so high, that it is a hill, even among the hills that Nature planted round it. The very river, as though it shared one's feelings of compassion for the extinct tribes who lived so pleasantly here, in their blessed ignorance of white existence, hundreds of years ago, steals out of its way to ripple near this mound: and there are few places where the Ohio sparkles more brightly than in the Big Grave Creek.

All this I see as I sit in the little stern-galley mentioned just now. Evening slowly steals upon the landscape and changes it before me, when we stop to set some emigrants ashore.

Five men, as many women, and a little girl. All their worldly goods are a bag, a large chest and an old chair: one, old, high-backed, rush-bottomed chair: a solitary settler in itself. They are rowed ashore in the boat, while the vessel stands a little off awaiting its return, the water being shallow. They are landed at the foot of a high bank, on the summit of which are a few log cabins, attainable only by a long winding path. It is growing dusk; but the sun is very red, and shines in the water and on some of the tree-tops, like fire.

The men get out of the boat first; help out the women; take out the bag, the chest, the chair; bid the rowers "good-bye;" and shove the boat off for them. At the first plash of the oars in the water, the oldest woman of the party sits down in the old chair, close to the water's edge, without speaking a word. None of the others sit down, though the chest is large enough for many seats. They all stand where they landed, as if stricken into stone; and look after the boat. So they remain, quite still and silent: the old woman and her old chair, in the centre; the bag and chest upon the shore, without anybody heeding them: all eyes fixed upon the boat. It comes alongside, is made fast, the men jump on board, the engine is put in motion, and we go hoarsely on again. There they stand yet, without the motion of a hand. I can see them through my glass, when, in the distance and increasing darkness, they are mere specks to the eye: lingering there still: the old woman in the old chair, and all the rest about her: not stirring in the least degree. And thus I slowly lose them.

The night is dark, and we proceed within the shadow of the wooded bank, which makes it darker. After gliding past the sombre maze of boughs for a long time, we come upon an open space where the tall trees are burning. The shape of every branch and twig is expressed

in a deep red glow, and as the light wind stirs and ruffles it, they seem
to vegetate in fire. It is such a sight as we read of in legends of
enchanted forests: saving that it is sad to see these noble works wasting away so awfully, alone; and to think how many years must come
and go before the magic that created them will rear their like upon
this ground again. But the time will come: and when, in their changed
ashes, the growth of centuries unborn has struck its roots, the restless
men of distant ages will repair to these again unpeopled solitudes; and
their fellows, in cities far away, that slumber now, perhaps, beneath
the rolling sea, will read in language strange to any ears in being now,
but very old to them, of primeval forests where the axe was never
heard, and where the jungled ground was never trodden by a human
foot.

Midnight and sleep blot out these scenes and thoughts: and when
the morning shines again, it gilds the house-tops of a lively city,
before whose broad paved wharf the boat is moored; with other boats,
and flags, and moving wheels, and hum of men around it; as though
there were not a solitary or silent rood of ground within the compass
of a thousand miles.

Cincinnati is a beautiful city; cheerful, thriving, and animated.
I have not often seen a place that commends itself so favourably and
pleasantly to a stranger at the first glance as this does: with its clean
houses of red and white, its well-paved roads, and foot-ways of bright
tile. Nor does it become less prepossessing on a closer acquaintance.
The streets are broad and airy, the shops extremely good, the private
residences remarkable for their elegance and neatness. There is something of invention and fancy in the varying styles of these latter
erections, which, after the dull company of the steamboat, is perfectly delightful, as conveying an assurance that there are such
qualities still in existence. The disposition to ornament these pretty
villas and render them attractive, leads to the culture of trees and
flowers, and the laying out of well-kept gardens, the sight of which,
to those who walk along the streets, is inexpressibly refreshing and
agreeable. I was quite charmed with the appearance of the town, and
its adjoining suburb of Mount Auburn: from which the city, lying in
an amphitheatre of hills, forms a picture of remarkable beauty, and
is seen to great advantage.

There happened to be a great Temperance Convention held here
on the day after our arrival; and as the order of march brought the
procession under the windows of the hotel in which we lodged, when
they started in the morning, I had a good opportunity of seeing it.
It comprised several thousand men; the members of various "Washington Auxiliary Temperance Societies;" and was marshalled by
officers on horseback, who cantered briskly up and down the line,
with scarves and ribbons of bright colours fluttering out behind them
gaily. There were bands of music too, and banners out of number:
and it was a fresh, holiday-looking concourse altogether.

I was particularly pleased to see the Irishmen, who formed a distinct society among themselves, and mustered very strong with their green scarves; carrying their national Harp and their Portrait of Father Mathew, high above the people's heads. They looked as jolly and good-humoured as ever; and, working (here) the hardest for their living and doing any kind of sturdy labour that came in their way, were the most independent fellows there, I thought.

The banners were very well painted, and flaunted down the street famously. There was the smiting of the rock, and the gushing forth of the waters; and there was a temperate man with "considerable of a hatchet" (as the standard-bearer would probably have said), aiming a deadly blow at a serpent which was apparently about to spring upon him from the top of a barrel of spirits. But the chief feature of this part of the show was a huge allegorical device, borne among the ship-carpenters, on one side whereof the steamboat Alcohol was represented bursting her boiler and exploding with a great crash, while upon the other, the good ship Temperance sailed away with a fair wind, to the heart's content of the captain, crew, and passengers.

After going round the town, the procession repaired to a certain appointed place, where, as the printed programme set forth, it would be received by the children of the different free schools, "singing Temperance Songs." I was prevented from getting there, in time to hear these Little Warblers, or to report upon this novel kind of vocal entertainment: novel, at least, to me: but I found in a large open space, each society gathered round its own banners, and listening in silent attention to its own orator. The speeches, judging from the little I could hear of them, were certainly adapted to the occasion, as having that degree of relationship to cold water which wet blankets may claim: but the main thing was the conduct and appearance of the audience throughout the day; and that was admirable and full of promise.

Cincinnati is honourably famous for its free schools, of which it has so many that no person's child among its population can, by possibility, want the means of education, which are extended, upon an average, to four thousand pupils, annually. I was only present in one of these establishments during the hours of instruction. In the boys' department, which was full of little urchins (varying in their ages, I should say, from six years old to ten or twelve), the master offered to institute an extempory examination of the pupils in algebra; a proposal, which, as I was by no means confident of my ability to detect mistakes in that science, I declined with some alarm. In the girls' school, reading was proposed; and as I felt tolerably equal to that art, I expressed my willingness to hear a class. Books were distributed accordingly, and some half-dozen girls relieved each other in reading paragraphs from English History. But it seemed to be a dry compilation, infinitely above their powers; and when they had blundered through three or four dreary passages concerning the Treaty of Amiens, and other thrilling topics of the same nature (obviously without comprehending ten words), I expressed myself quite satisfied. It is very possible that they only mounted to this exalted stave in the Ladder of Learning for the astonishment of a visitor; and that at other times they keep upon its lower rounds; but I should have been much better pleased and satisfied if I had heard them exercised in simpler lessons, which they understood.

As in every other place I visited, the Judges here were gentlemen of high character and attainments. I was in one of the courts for a few minutes, and found it like those to which I have already referred. A nuisance cause was trying; there were not many spectators; and the witnesses, counsel, and jury, formed a sort of family circle, sufficiently jocose and snug.

The society with which I mingled, was intelligent, courteous, and agreeable. The inhabitants of Cincinnati are proud of their city as one of the most interesting in America: and with good reason: for beautiful and thriving as it is now, and containing, as it does, a population of fifty thousand souls, but two-and-fifty years have passed away since the ground on which it stands (bought at that time for a few dollars) was a wild wood, and its citizens were but a handful of dwellers in scattered log huts upon the river's shore.

## CHAPTER XII

FROM CINCINNATI TO LOUISVILLE IN ANOTHER WESTERN STEAMBOAT; AND FROM LOUISVILLE TO ST. LOUIS IN ANOTHER. ST. LOUIS.

LEAVING Cincinnati at eleven o'clock in the forenoon, we embarked for Louisville in the Pike steamboat, which, carrying the mails, was a packet of a much better class than that in which we had come from Pittsburg. As this passage does not occupy more than twelve or thirteen hours, we arranged to go ashore that night: not coveting the distinction of sleeping in a state-room, when it was possible to sleep anywhere else.

There chanced to be on board this boat, in addition to the usual dreary crowd of passengers, one Pitchlynn, a chief of the Choctaw tribe of Indians, who *sent in his card* to me, and with whom I had the pleasure of a long conversation.

He spoke English perfectly well, though he had not begun to learn the language, he told me, until he was a young man grown. He had read many books; and Scott's poetry appeared to have left a strong impression on his mind; especially the opening of The Lady of the Lake, and the great battle scene in Marmion, in which, no doubt from the congeniality of the subjects to his own pursuits and tastes, he had great interest and delight. He appeared to understand correctly all he had read; and whatever fiction had enlisted his sympathy in its belief, had done so keenly and earnestly. I might almost say fiercely. He was dressed in our ordinary every-day costume, which hung about his fine figure loosely, and with indifferent grace. On my telling him that I regretted not to see him in his own attire, he threw up his right arm, for a moment, as though he were brandishing some heavy weapon, and answered, as he let it fall again, that his race were losing many things besides their dress, and would soon be seen upon the earth no more: but he wore it at home, he added proudly.

He told me that he had been away from his home, west of the Mississippi, seventeen months: and was now returning. He had been chiefly at Washington on some negotiations pending between his Tribe and the Government: which were not settled yet (he said in a melancholy way), and he feared never would be: for what could a few poor Indians do, against such well-skilled men of business as the whites? He had no love for Washington; tired of towns and cities very soon; and longed for the Forest and the Prairie.

I asked him what he thought of Congress? He answered, with a smile, that it wanted dignity, in an Indian's eyes.

He would very much like, he said, to see England before he died; and spoke with much interest about the great things to be seen there. When I told him of that chamber in the British Museum wherein are preserved household memorials of a race that ceased to be, thousands of years ago, he was very attentive, and it was not hard to see that he had a reference in his mind to the gradual fading away of his own people.

This led us to speak of Mr. Catlin's gallery, which he praised highly: observing that his own portrait was among the collection, and that all the likenesses were "elegant." Mr. Cooper, he said, had painted the Red Man well; and so would I, he knew, if I would go home with him and hunt buffaloes, which he was quite anxious I should do. When I told him that supposing I went, I should not be very likely to damage the buffaloes much, he took it as a great joke and laughed heartily.

He was a remarkably handsome man; some years past forty, I should judge; with long black hair, an aquiline nose, broad cheek-bones, a sunburnt complexion, and a very bright, keen, dark, and piercing eye. There were but twenty thousand of the Choctaws left, he said, and their number was decreasing every day. A few of his brother chiefs had been obliged to become civilised, and to make themselves acquainted with what the whites knew, for it was their only chance of existence. But they were not many; and the rest were as they always had been. He dwelt on this: and said several times that unless they tried to assimilate themselves to their conquerors, they must be swept away before the strides of civilised society.

When we shook hands at parting, I told him he must come to England, as he longed to see the land so much: that I should hope to see him there, one day: and that I could promise him he would be well received and kindly treated. He was evidently pleased by this assurance, though he rejoined with a good-humoured smile and an

arch shake of his head, that the English used to be very fond of the
Red Men when they wanted their help, but had not cared much for
them, since.

He took his leave; as stately and complete a gentleman of Nature's
making, as ever I beheld; and moved among the people in the boat,
another kind of being. He sent me a lithographed portrait of himself
soon afterwards; very like, though scarcely handsome enough; which
I have carefully preserved in memory of our brief acquaintance.

There was nothing very interesting in the scenery of this day's
journey, which brought us at midnight to Louisville. We slept at the
Galt House; a splendid hotel; and were as handsomely lodged as
though we had been in Paris, rather than hundreds of miles beyond
the Alleghanies.

The city presenting no objects of sufficient interest to detain us on
our way, we resolved to proceed next day by another steamboat, the
Fulton, and to join it, about noon, at a suburb called Portland, where
it would be delayed some time in passing through a canal.

The interval, after breakfast, we devoted to riding through the
town, which is regular and cheerful: the streets being laid out at
right angles, and planted with young trees. The buildings are smoky
and blackened, from the use of bituminous coal, but an Englishman
is well used to that appearance, and indisposed to quarrel with it.
There did not appear to be much business stirring; and some unfinished buildings and improvements seemed to intimate that the
city had been overbuilt in the ardour of "going-a-head," and was
suffering under the re-action consequent upon such feverish forcing
of its powers.

On our way to Portland, we passed a "Magistrate's office," which
amused me, as looking far more like a dame school than any police
establishment: for this awful Institution was nothing but a little
lazy, good-for-nothing front parlour, open to the street; wherein two
or three figures (I presume the magistrate and his myrmidons) were
basking in the sunshine, the very effigies of languor and repose. It
was a perfect picture of Justice retired from business for want of
customers; her sword and scales sold off; napping comfortably with
her legs upon the table.

Here, as elsewhere in these parts, the road was perfectly alive with
pigs of all ages; lying about in every direction, fast asleep; or grunting
along in quest of hidden dainties. I had always a sneaking kindness
for these odd animals, and found a constant source of amusement,
when all others failed, in watching their proceedings. As we were
riding along this morning, I observed a little incident between two
youthful pigs, which was so very human as to be inexpressibly
comical and grotesque at the time, though I dare say, in telling, it
is tame enough.

One young gentleman (a very delicate porker with several straws
sticking about his nose, betokening recent investigations in a dung-
hill) was walking deliberately on, profoundly thinking, when suddenly

his brother, who was lying in a miry hole unseen by him, rose up immediately before his startled eyes, ghostly with damp mud. Never was pig's whole mass of blood so turned. He turned back at least three feet, gazed for a moment, and then shot off as hard as he could go: his excessively little tail vibrating with speed and terror like a distracted pendulum. But before he had gone very far, he began to reason with himself as to the nature of this frightful appearance; and as he reasoned, he relaxed his speed by gradual degrees; until at last he stopped, and faced about. There was his brother, with the mud upon him glazing in the sun, yet staring out of the very same hole, perfectly amazed at his proceedings! He was no sooner assured of this; and he assured himself so carefully that one may almost say he shaded his eyes with his hand to see the better; than he came back at a round trot, pounced upon him, and summarily took off a piece of his tail; as a caution to him to be careful what he was about for the future, and never to play tricks with his family any more.

We found the steamboat in the canal, waiting for the slow process of getting through the lock, and went on board, where we shortly afterwards had a new kind of visitor in the person of a certain Kentucky Giant whose name is Porter, and who is of the moderate height of seven feet eight inches, in his stockings.

There never was a race of people who so completely gave the lie to history as these giants, or whom all the chroniclers have so cruelly libelled. Instead of roaring and ravaging about the world, constantly catering for their cannibal larders, and perpetually going to market in an unlawful manner, they are the meekest people in any man's acquaintance: rather inclining to milk and vegetable diet, and bearing anything for a quiet life. So decidedly are amiability and mildness their characteristics, that I confess I look upon that youth who distinguished himself by the slaughter of these inoffensive persons, as a false-hearted brigand, who, pretending to philanthropic motives, was secretly influenced only by the wealth stored up within their castles, and the hope of plunder. And I lean the more to this opinion from finding that even the historian of those exploits, with all his partiality for his hero, is fain to admit that the slaughtered monsters in question were of a very innocent and simple turn; extremely guileless and ready of belief; lending a credulous ear to the most improbable tales; suffering themselves to be easily entrapped into pits; and even (as in the case of the Welsh Giant) with an excess of the hospitable politeness of a landlord, ripping themselves open, rather than hint at the possibility of their guests being versed in the vagabond arts of sleight-of-hand and hocus-pocus.

The Kentucky Giant was but another illustration of the truth of this position. He had a weakness in the region of the knees, and a trustfulness in his long face, which appealed even to five-feet nine for encouragement and support. He was only twenty-five years old, he said, and had grown recently, for it had been found necessary to make an addition to the legs of his inexpressibles. At fifteen he was a

short boy, and in those days his English father and his Irish mother
had rather snubbed him, as being too small of stature to sustain the
credit of the family. He added that his health had not been good,
though it was better now; but short people are not wanting who
whisper that he drinks too hard.

I understand he drives a hackney-coach, though how he does it,
unless he stands on the footboard behind, and lies along the roof
upon his chest, with his chin in the box, it would be difficult to
comprehend. He brought his gun with him, as a curiosity. Christened
"The Little Rifle," and displayed outside a shop-window, it would
make the fortune of any retail business in Holborn. When he had
shown himself and talked a little while, he withdrew with his pocket-
instrument, and went bobbing down the cabin, among men of six
feet high and upwards, like a lighthouse walking among lamp-posts.

Within a few minutes afterwards, we were out of the canal, and
in the Ohio river again.

The arrangements of the boat were like those of the Messenger,
and the passengers were of the same order of people. We fed at the
same times, on the same kind of viands, in the same dull manner,
and with the same observances. The company appeared to be
oppressed by the same tremendous concealments, and had as little
capacity of enjoyment or light-heartedness. I never in my life did
see such listless, heavy dulness as brooded over these meals: the very
recollection of it weighs me down, and makes me, for the moment,
wretched. Reading and writing on my knee, in our little cabin, I
really dreaded the coming of the hour that summoned us to table;
and was as glad to escape from it again, as if it had been a penance
or a punishment. Healthy cheerfulness and good spirits forming a
part of the banquet, I could soak my crusts in the fountain with Le
Sage's strolling player, and revel in their glad enjoyment: but sitting
down with so many fellow-animals to ward off thirst and hunger as
a business; to empty, each creature, his Yahoo's trough as quickly
as he can, and then slink sullenly away; to have these social sacra-
ments stripped of everything but the mere greedy satisfaction of the
natural cravings; goes so against the grain with me, that I seriously
believe the recollection of these funeral feasts will be a waking nightmare to me all my life.

There was some relief in this boat, too, which there had not been
in the other, for the captain (a blunt, good-natured fellow) had his
handsome wife with him, who was disposed to be lively and agreeable, as were a few other lady-passengers who had their seats about
us at the same end of the table. But nothing could have made head
against the depressing influence of the general body. There was a
magnetism of dulness in them which would have beaten down the
most facetious companion that the earth ever knew. A jest would
have been a crime, and a smile would have faded into a grinning
horror. Such deadly, leaden people; such systematic plodding,
weary, insupportable heaviness; such a mass of animated indigestion

323*

in respect of all that was genial, jovial, frank, social, or hearty; never, sure, was brought together elsewhere since the world began.

Nor was the scenery, as we approached the junction of the Ohio and Mississippi rivers, at all inspiriting in its influence. The trees were stunted in their growth; the banks were low and flat; the settlements and log cabins fewer in number: their inhabitants more wan and wretched than any we had encountered yet. No songs of birds were in the air, no pleasant scents, no moving lights and shadows from swift passing clouds. Hour after hour, the changeless glare of the hot, unwinking sky, shone upon the same monotonous objects. Hour after hour, the river rolled along, as wearily and slowly as the time itself.

At length, upon the morning of the third day, we arrived at a spot so much more desolate than any we had yet beheld, that the forlornest places we had passed, were, in comparison with it, full of interest. At the junction of the two rivers, on ground so flat and low and marshy, that at certain seasons of the year it is inundated to the house-tops, lies a breeding-place of fever, ague, and death; vaunted in England as a mine of Golden Hope, and speculated in, on the faith of monstrous representations, to many people's ruin. A dismal swamp on which the half-built houses rot away: cleared here and there for the space of a few yards; and teeming, then, with rank unwholesome vegetation, in whose baleful shade the wretched wanderers who are tempted hither, droop, and die, and lay their bones; the hateful Mississippi circling and eddying before it, and turning off upon its southern course a slimy monster hideous to behold; a hotbed of disease, an ugly sepulchre, a grave uncheered by any gleam of promise: a place without one single quality, in earth or air or water, to commend it: such is this dismal Cairo.

But what words shall describe the Mississippi, great father of rivers, who (praise be to Heaven) has no young children like him! An enormous ditch, sometimes two or three miles wide, running liquid mud, six miles an hour: its strong and frothy current choked and obstructed everywhere by huge logs and whole forest trees: now twining themselves together in great rafts, from the interstices of which a sedgy, lazy foam works up, to float upon the water's top; now rolling past like monstrous bodies, their tangled roots showing like matted hair; now glancing singly by like giant leeches; and now writhing round and round in the vortex of some small whirlpool, like wounded snakes. The banks low, the trees dwarfish, the marshes swarming with frogs, the wretched cabins few and far apart, their inmates hollow-cheeked and pale, the weather very hot, mosquitoes penetrating into every crack and crevice of the boat, mud and slime on everything: nothing pleasant in its aspect, but the harmless lightning which flickers every night upon the dark horizon.

For two days we toiled up this foul stream, striking constantly against the floating timber, or stopping to avoid those more dangerous obstacles, the snags, or sawyers, which are the hidden trunks of trees that have their roots below the tide. When the nights are very dark, the look-out stationed in the head of the boat, knows by the ripple of the water if any great impediment be near at hand, and rings a bell beside him, which is the signal for the engine to be stopped: but always in the night this bell has work to do, and after every ring, there comes a blow which renders it no easy matter to remain in bed.

The decline of day here was very gorgeous; tingeing the firmament deeply with red and gold, up to the very keystone of the arch above us. As the sun went down behind the bank, the slightest blades of grass upon it seemed to become as distinctly visible as the arteries in the skeleton of a leaf; and when, as it slowly sank, the red and golden bars upon the water grew dimmer, and dimmer yet, as if they were sinking too; and all the glowing colours of departing day paled, inch by inch, before the sombre night; the scene became a thousand times more lonesome and more dreary than before, and all its influences darkened with the sky.

We drank the muddy water of this river while we were upon it. It is considered wholesome by the natives, and is something more opaque than gruel. I have seen water like it at the Filter-shops, but nowhere else.

On the fourth night after leaving Louisville, we reached St. Louis, and here I witnessed the conclusion of an incident, trifling enough in itself, but very pleasant to see, which had interested me during the whole journey.

There was a little woman on board, with a little baby; and both little woman and little child were cheerful, good-looking, bright-eyed, and fair to see. The little woman had been passing a long time with her sick mother in New York, and had left her home in St. Louis, in that condition in which ladies who truly love their lords desire to be. The baby was born in her mother's house; and she had not seen her husband (to whom she was now returning), for twelve months: having left him a month or two after their marriage.

Well, to be sure, there never was a little woman so full of hope, and tenderness, and love, and anxiety, as this little woman was: and all day long she wondered whether " He " would be at the wharf and whether "He" had got her letter; and whether, if she sent the baby ashore by somebody else, "He" would know it, meeting it in the street: which, seeing that he had never set eyes upon it in his life, was not very likely in the abstract, but was probable enough, to the young mother. She was such an artless little creature; and was in such a sunny, beaming, hopeful state; and let out all this matter clinging close about her heart, so freely; that all the other lady passengers entered into the spirit of it as much as she; and the captain (who heard all about it from his wife) was wondrous sly, I promise you: inquiring, every time we met at table, as in forgetfulness, whether she expected anybody to meet her at St. Louis, and whether she would want to go ashore the night we reached it (but he supposed she wouldn't), and cutting many other dry jokes of that nature. There was one little weazen, dried-apple-faced old woman, who took occasion to doubt the constancy of husbands in such circumstances of bereavement; and there was another lady (with a lap-dog) old enough to moralize on the lightness of human affections, and yet not so old that she could help nursing the baby, now and then, or laughing with the rest, when the little woman called it by its father's name, and asked it all manner of fantastic questions concerning him in the joy of her heart.

It was something of a blow to the little woman, that when we were within twenty miles of our destination, it became clearly necessary to put this baby to bed. But she got over it with the same good humour; tied a handkerchief round her head; and came out into the little gallery with the rest. Then, such an oracle as she became in reference to the localities! and such facetiousness as was displayed by the married ladies! and such sympathy as was shown by the single ones! and such peals of laughter as the little woman herself (who would just as soon have cried) greeted every jest with!

At last, there were the lights of St. Louis, and here was the wharf, and those were the steps: and the little woman covering her face with her hands, and laughing (or seeming to laugh) more than ever, ran into her own cabin, and shut herself up. I have no doubt that in the charming inconsistency of such excitement, she stopped her ears, lest she should hear "Him" asking for her: but I did not see her do it.

Then, a great crowd of people rushed on board, though the boat was not yet made fast, but was wandering about, among the other boats, to find a landing-place: and everybody looked for the husband: and nobody saw him: when, in the midst of us all—Heaven knows how she ever got there—there was the little woman clinging with both arms tight round the neck of a fine, good-looking, sturdy young fellow! and in a moment afterwards, there she was again, actually clapping her little hands for joy, as she dragged him through the small door of her small cabin, to look at the baby as he lay asleep!

We went to a large hotel, called the Planter's House: built like an English hospital, with long passages and bare walls, and skylights above the room-doors for the free circulation of air. There were a great many boarders in it; and as many lights sparkled and glistened from the windows down into the street below, when we drove up, as if it had been illuminated on some occasion of rejoicing. It is an excellent house, and the proprietors have most bountiful notions of providing the creature comforts. Dining alone with my wife in our own room, one day, I counted fourteen dishes on the table at once.

In the old French portion of the town, the thoroughfares are narrow and crooked, and some of the houses are very quaint and picturesque: being built of wood, with tumble-down galleries before the windows, approachable by stairs or rather ladders from the street. There are queer little barbers' shops and drinking-houses too, in this quarter; and abundance of crazy old tenements with blinking case-

ments, such as may be seen in Flanders. Some of these ancient
habitations, with high garret gable-windows perking to the roofs,
have a kind of French shrug about them ; and being lop-sided with
age, appear to hold their heads askew, besides, as if they were grimac-
ing in astonishment at the American Improvements.

It is hardly necessary to say, that these consist of wharfs and
warehouses, and new buildings in all directions; and of a great many
vast plans which are still "progressing." Already, however, some very
good houses, broad streets, and marble-fronted shops, have gone so
far a-head as to be in a state of completion; and the town bids fair in
a few years to improve considerably: though it is not likely ever to
vie, in point of elegance or beauty, with Cincinnati.

The Roman Catholic religion, introduced here by the early
French settlers, prevails extensively. Among the public institutions
are a Jesuit college; a convent for "the Ladies of the Sacred Heart;"
and a large chapel attached to the college, which was in course of
erection at the time of my visit, and was intended to be consecrated
on the second of December in the next year. The architect of
this building, is one of the reverend fathers of the school, and the
works proceed under his sole direction. The organ will be sent from
Belgium.

In addition to these establishments, there is a Roman Catholic
cathedral, dedicated to Saint Francis Xavier; and a hospital, founded
by the munificence of a deceased resident, who was a member of that
church. It also sends missionaries from hence among the Indian
tribes.

The Unitarian church is represented, in this remote place, as in
most other parts of America, by a gentleman of great worth and
excellence. The poor have good reason to remember and bless it; for
it befriends them and aids the cause of rational education, without
any sectarian or selfish views. It is liberal in all its actions; of kind
construction; and of wide benevolence.

There are three free-schools already erected, and in full operation
in this city. A fourth is building, and will soon be opened.

No man ever admits the unhealthiness of the place he dwells in
(unless he is going away from it), and I shall therefore, I have no
doubt, be at issue with the inhabitants of St. Louis, in questioning
the perfect salubrity of its climate, and in hinting that I think it must
rather dispose to fever, in the summer and autumnal seasons. Just
adding, that it is very hot, lies among great rivers, and has vast tracts
of undrained swampy land around it, I leave the reader to form his
own opinion.

As I had a great desire to see a Prairie before turning back from
the furthest point of my wanderings; and as some gentlemen of the
town had, in their hospitable consideration, an equal desire to gratify
me; a day was fixed, before my departure, for an expedition to the
Looking-Glass Prairie, which is within thirty miles of the town.
Deeming it possible that my readers may not object to know what

kind of thing such a gipsy party may be at that distance from home, and among what sort of objects it moves, I will describe the jaunt in another chapter.

## CHAPTER XIII

### A JAUNT TO THE LOOKING-GLASS PRAIRIE AND BACK

I MAY premise that the word Prairie is variously pronounced *paraaer*, *parearer*, and *paroarer*. The latter mode of pronunciation is perhaps the most in favour.

We were fourteen in all, and all young men: indeed it is a singular though very natural feature in the society of these distant settlements, that it is mainly composed of adventurous persons in the prime of life, and has very few grey heads among it. There were no ladies: the trip being a fatiguing one: and we were to start at five o'clock in the morning punctually.

I was called at four, that I might be certain of keeping nobody waiting; and having got some bread and milk for breakfast, threw up the window and looked down into the street, expecting to see the whole party busily astir, and great preparations going on below. But as everything was very quiet, and the street presented that hopeless aspect with which five o'clock in the morning is familiar elsewhere, I deemed it as well to go to bed again, and went accordingly.

I woke again at seven o'clock, and by that time the party had assembled, and were gathered round, one light carriage, with a very stout axletree; one something on wheels like an amateur carrier's cart; one double phaeton of great antiquity and unearthly construction; one gig with a great hole in its back and a broken head; and one rider on horseback who was to go on before. I got into the first coach with three companions; the rest bestowed themselves in the other vehicles; two large baskets were made fast to the lightest; two large stone jars in wicker cases, technically known as demi-johns, were consigned to the "least rowdy" of the party for safe-keeping; and the procession moved off to the ferry-boat, in which it was to cross the river bodily, men, horses, carriages, and all, as the manner in these parts is.

We got over the river in due course, and mustered again before a little wooden box on wheels, hove down all aslant in a morass, with "MERCHANT TAILOR" painted in very large letters over the door. Having settled the order of proceeding, and the road to be taken, we started off once more and began to make our way through an ill-favoured Black Hollow, called, less expressively, the American Bottom.

The previous day had been—not to say hot, for the term is weak and lukewarm in its power of conveying an idea of the temperature. The town had been on fire; in a blaze. But at night it had come on to rain in torrents, and all night long it had rained without cessation. We had a pair of very strong horses, but travelled at the rate of little more than a couple of miles an hour, through one unbroken slough of black mud and water. It had no variety but in depth. Now it was only half over the wheels, now it hid the axletree, and now the coach sank down in it almost to the windows. The air resounded in all directions with the loud chirping of the frogs, who, with the pigs (a coarse, ugly breed, as unwholesome-looking as though they were the spontaneous growth of the country), had the whole scene to themselves. Here and there we passed a log hut: but the wretched cabins were wide apart and thinly scattered, for though the soil is very rich in this place, few people can exist in such a deadly atmosphere. On either side of the track, if it deserve the name, was the thick "bush;" and everywhere was stagnant, slimy, rotten, filthy water.

As it is the custom in these parts to give a horse a gallon or so of cold water whenever he is in a foam with heat, we halted for that purpose, at a log inn in the wood, far removed from any other residence. It consisted of one room, bare-roofed and bare-walled of course, with a loft above. The ministering priest was a swarthy young savage, in a shirt of cotton print like bed-furniture, and a pair of ragged trousers. There were a couple of young boys, too, nearly naked, lying idle by the well; and they, and he, and *the* traveller at the inn, turned out to look at us.

The traveller was an old man with a grey gristly beard two inches long, a shaggy moustache of the same hue, and enormous eyebrows; which almost obscured his lazy, semi-drunken glance, as he stood regarding us with folded arms: poising himself alternately upon his toes and heels. On being addressed by one of the party, he drew nearer, and said, rubbing his chin (which scraped under his horny hand like fresh gravel beneath a nailed shoe), that he was from Delaware, and had lately bought a farm "down there," pointing into one of the marshes where the stunted trees were thickest. He was "going," he added, to St. Louis, to fetch his family, whom he had left behind; but he seemed in no great hurry to bring on these incumbrances, for when we moved away, he loitered back into the cabin, and was plainly bent on stopping there so long as his money lasted. He was a great politician of course, and explained his opinions at some length to one of our company; but I only remember that he concluded with two sentiments, one of which was, Somebody for ever; and the other, Blast everybody else! which is by no means a bad abstract of the general creed in these matters.

When the horses were swollen out to about twice their natural dimensions (there seems to be an idea here, that this kind of inflation improves their going), we went forward again, through mud and mire, and damp, and festering heat, and brake and bush, attended always by the music of the frogs and pigs, until nearly noon, when we halted at a place called Belleville.

Belleville was a small collection of wooden houses, huddled together in the very heart of the bush and swamp. Many of them had singularly bright doors of red and yellow; for the place had been lately visited by a travelling painter, "who got along," as I was told, "by eating his way." The criminal court was sitting, and was at that moment trying some criminals for horse-stealing: with whom it would most likely go hard: for live stock of all kinds being necessarily very much exposed in the woods, is held by the community in rather higher value than human life; and for this reason, juries generally make a point of finding all men indicted for cattle-stealing, guilty, whether or no.

The horses belonging to the bar, the judge, and witnesses, were tied to temporary racks set up roughly in the road; by which is to be understood, a forest path, nearly knee-deep in mud and slime.

There was an hotel in this place, which, like all hotels in America, had its large dining-room for the public table. It was an odd, shambling, low-roofed out-house, half-cowshed and half-kitchen, with a coarse brown canvas table-cloth, and tin sconces stuck against the walls, to hold candles at supper-time. The horseman had gone forward to have coffee and some eatables prepared, and they were by this time nearly ready. He had ordered "wheat-bread and chicken fixing," in preference to "corn-bread and common doings." The latter kind of refection includes only pork and bacon. The former comprehends broiled ham, sausages, veal cutlets, steaks, and such other viands of that nature as may be supposed, by a tolerably wide poetical construction, "to fix" a chicken comfortably in the digestive organs of any lady or gentleman.

On one of the door-posts at this inn, was a tin plate, whereon was inscribed in characters of gold, "Doctor Crocus;" and on a sheet of paper, pasted up by the side of this plate, was a written announcement that Dr. Crocus would that evening deliver a lecture on Phrenology for the benefit of the Belleville public; at a charge, for admission, of so much a head.

Straying up-stairs, during the preparation of the chicken fixings, I happened to pass the doctor's chamber; and as the door stood wide open, and the room was empty, I made bold to peep in.

It was a bare, unfurnished, comfortless room, with an unframed portrait hanging up at the head of the bed; a likeness, I take it, of the Doctor, for the forehead was fully displayed, and great stress was laid by the artist upon its phrenological developments. The bed itself was covered with an old patch-work counterpane. The room was destitute of carpet or of curtain. There was a damp fireplace without any stove, full of wood ashes; a chair, and a very small table; and on the last-named piece of furniture was displayed, in grand array, the doctor's library, consisting of some half-dozen greasy old books.

Now, it certainly looked about the last apartment on the whole earth out of which any man would be likely to get anything to do him good. But the door, as I have said, stood coaxingly open, and plainly said in conjunction with the chair, the portrait, the table, and the books, "Walk in, gentlemen, walk in! Don't be ill, gentlemen, when you may be well in no time. Doctor Crocus is here, gentlemen, the celebrated Dr. Crocus! Doctor Crocus has come all this way to cure you, gentlemen. If you haven't heard of Dr. Crocus, it's your fault, gentlemen, who live a little way out of the world here: not Dr. Crocus's. Walk in, gentlemen, walk in!"

In the passage below, when I went down-stairs again, was Dr. Crocus himself. A crowd had flocked in from the Court House, and a voice from among them called out to the landlord, "Colonel! introduce Doctor Crocus."

"Mr. Dickens," says the colonel, "Doctor Crocus."

Upon which Doctor Crocus, who is a tall, fine-looking Scotchman, but rather fierce and warlike in appearance for a professor of the peaceful art of healing, bursts out of the concourse with his right arm extended, and his chest thrown out as far as it will possibly come, and says:

"Your countryman, sir!"

Whereupon Doctor Crocus and I shake hands; and Doctor Crocus looks as if I didn't by any means realise his expectations, which, in a linen blouse, and a great straw hat, with a green ribbon, and no gloves, and my face and nose profusely ornamented with the stings of mosquitoes and the bites of bugs, it is very likely I did not.

"Long in these parts, sir?" says I.

"Three or four months, sir," says the Doctor.

"Do you think of soon returning to the old country?" says I.

Doctor Crocus makes no verbal answer, but gives me an imploring look, which says so plainly "Will you ask me that again, a little louder, if you please?" that I repeat the question.

"Think of soon returning to the old country, sir!" repeats the Doctor.

"To the old country, sir," I rejoin.

Doctor Crocus looks round upon the crowd to observe the effect he produces, rubs his hands, and says, in a very loud voice:

"Not yet awhile, sir, not yet. You won't catch me at that just yet, sir. I am a little too fond of freedom for *that*, sir. Ha, ha! It's not so easy for a man to tear himself from a free country such as this is, sir. Ha, ha! No, no! Ha, ha! None of that till one's obliged to do it, sir. No, no!"

As Doctor Crocus says these latter words, he shakes his head, knowingly, and laughs again. Many of the bystanders shake their heads in concert with the doctor, and laugh too, and look at each other as much as to say, "A pretty bright and first-rate sort of chap is Crocus!" and unless I am very much mistaken, a good many people went to the lecture that night, who never thought about phrenology, or about Doctor Crocus either, in all their lives before.

From Belleville, we went on, through the same desolate kind of
waste, and constantly attended, without the interval of a moment,
by the same music; until, at three o'clock in the afternoon, we
halted once more at a village called Lebanon to inflate the horses
again, and give them some corn besides: of which they stood much in
need. Pending this ceremony, I walked into the village, where I
met a full-sized dwelling-house coming down-hill at a round trot,
drawn by a score or more of oxen.

The public-house was so very clean and good a one, that the
managers of the jaunt resolved to return to it and put up there for
the night, if possible. This course decided on, and the horses being
well refreshed, we again pushed forward, and came upon the Prairie
at sunset.

It would be difficult to say why, or how—though it was possibly
from having heard and read so much about it—but the effect on me
was disappointment. Looking towards the setting sun, there lay,
stretched out before my view, a vast expanse of level ground; unbroken, save by one thin line of trees, which scarcely amounted to a
scratch upon the great blank; until it met the glowing sky, wherein
it seemed to dip: mingling with its rich colours, and mellowing in its
distant blue. There it lay, a tranquil sea or lake without water, if
such a simile be admissible, with the day going down upon it: a few
birds wheeling here and there: and solitude and silence reigning
paramount around. But the grass was not yet high; there were bare
black patches on the ground; and the few wild flowers that the eye
could see, were poor and scanty. Great as the picture was, its very
flatness and extent, which left nothing to the imagination, tamed it
down and cramped its interest. I felt little of that sense of freedom
and exhilaration which a Scottish heath inspires, or even our
English downs awaken. It was lonely and wild, but oppressive in its
barren monotony. I felt that in traversing the Prairies, I could never
abandon myself to the scene, forgetful of all else; as I should do
instinctively, were the heather underneath my feet, or an iron-
bound coast beyond; but should often glance towards the distant
and frequently-receding line of the horizon, and wish it gained and
passed. It is not a scene to be forgotten, but it is scarcely one, I
think (at all events, as I saw it), to remember with much pleasure,
or to covet the looking-on again, in after-life.

We encamped near a solitary log-house, for the sake of its water,
and dined upon the plain. The baskets contained roast fowls,
buffalo's tongue (an exquisite dainty, by the way), ham, bread,
cheese, and butter; biscuits, champagne, sherry; lemons and sugar
for punch; and abundance of rough ice. The meal was delicious, and
the entertainers were the soul of kindness and good humour. I have
often recalled that cheerful party to my pleasant recollection since,
and shall not easily forget, in junketings nearer home with friends of
older date, my boon companions on the Prairie.

Returning to Lebanon that night, we lay at the little inn at which we had halted in the afternoon. In point of cleanliness and comfort it would have suffered by no comparison with any English alehouse, of a homely kind, in England.

Rising at five o'clock next morning, I took a walk about the village: none of the houses were strolling about to-day, but it was early for them yet, perhaps: and then amused myself by lounging in a kind of farm-yard behind the tavern, of which the leading features were, a strange jumble of rough sheds for stables; a rude colonnade, built as a cool place of summer resort; a deep well; a great earthen mound for keeping vegetables in, in winter time; and a pigeon-house, whose little apertures looked, as they do in all pigeon-houses, very much too small for the admission of the plump and swelling-breasted birds who were strutting about it, though they tried to get in never so hard. That interest exhausted, I took a survey of the inn's two parlours, which were decorated with coloured prints of Washington, and President Madison, and of a white-faced young lady (much speckled by the flies), who held up her gold neck-chain for the admiration of the spectator, and informed all admiring comers that she was "Just Seventeen:" although I should have thought her older. In the best room were two oil portraits of the kit-cat size, representing the landlord and his infant son; both looking as bold as lions, and staring out of the canvas with an intensity that would have been cheap at any price. They were painted, I think, by the artist who had touched up the Belleville doors with red and gold; for I seemed to recognise his style immediately.

After breakfast, we started to return by a different way from that which we had taken yesterday, and coming up at ten o'clock with an encampment of German emigrants carrying their goods in carts, who had made a rousing fire which they were just quitting, stopped there to refresh. And very pleasant the fire was; for, hot though it had been yesterday, it was quite cold to-day, and the wind blew keenly. Looming in the distance, as we rode along, was another of the ancient Indian burial-places, called The Monks' Mound; in memory of a body of fanatics of the order of La Trappe, who founded a desolate convent there, many years ago, when there were no settlers within a thousand miles, and were all swept off by the pernicious climate: in which lamentable fatality, few rational people will suppose, perhaps, that society experienced any very severe deprivation.

The track of to-day had the same features as the track of yester-day. There was the swamp, the bush, and the perpetual chorus of frogs, the rank unseemly growth, the unwholesome steaming earth. Here and there, and frequently too, we encountered a solitary broken-down waggon, full of some new settler's goods. It was a pitiful sight to see one of these vehicles deep in the mire; the axletree broken; the wheel lying idly by its side; the man gone miles away, to look for assistance; the woman seated among their wandering household gods with a baby at her breast, a picture of forlorn, dejected patience; the team of oxen crouching down mournfully in the mud, and breathing forth such clouds of vapour from their mouths and nostrils, that all the damp mist and fog around seemed to have come direct from them.

In due time we mustered once again before the merchant tailor's, and having done so, crossed over to the city in the ferry-boat: passing, on the way, a spot called Bloody Island, the duelling-ground of St. Louis, and so designated in honour of the last fatal combat fought there, which was with pistols, breast to breast. Both combatants fell dead upon the ground; and possibly some rational people may think of them, as of the gloomy madmen on the Monks' Mound, that they were no great loss to the community.

## CHAPTER XIV

### RETURN TO CINCINNATI. A STAGE-COACH RIDE FROM THAT CITY TO COLUMBUS, AND THENCE TO SANDUSKY. SO, BY LAKE ERIE, TO THE FALLS OF NIAGARA

As I had a desire to travel through the interior of the state of Ohio, and to "strike the lakes," as the phrase is, at a small town called Sandusky, to which that route would conduct us on our way to Niagara, we had to return from St. Louis by the way we had come, and to retrace our former track as far as Cincinnati.

The day on which we were to take leave of St. Louis being very fine; and the steamboat, which was to have started I don't know how early in the morning, postponing, for the third or fourth time, her departure until the afternoon; we rode forward to an old French village on the river, called properly Carondelet, and nicknamed Vide Poche, and arranged that the packet should call for us there.

The place consisted of a few poor cottages, and two or three public-houses; the state of whose larders certainly seemed to justify the second designation of the village, for there was nothing to eat in any of them. At length, however, by going back some half a mile or so, we found a solitary house where ham and coffee were procurable; and there we tarried to await the advent of the boat, which would come in sight from the green before the door, a long way off.

It was a neat, unpretending village tavern, and we took our repast in a quaint little room with a bed in it, decorated with some old oil paintings, which in their time had probably done duty in a Catholic chapel or monastery. The fare was very good, and served with great cleanliness. The house was kept by a characteristic old couple, with whom we had a long talk, and who were perhaps a very good sample of that kind of people in the West.

The landlord was a dry, tough, hard-faced old fellow (not so very old either, for he was but just turned sixty, I should think), who had been out with the militia in the last war with England, and had seen all kinds of service,—except a battle; and he had been very near seeing that, he added: very near. He had all his life been restless and locomotive, with an irresistible desire for change; and was still the son of his old self: for if he had nothing to keep him at home, he said (slightly jerking his hat and his thumb towards the window of the room in which the old lady sat, as we stood talking in front of the house), he would clean up his musket, and be off to Texas to-morrow morning. He was one of the very many descendants of Cain proper to this continent, who seem destined from their birth to serve as pioneers in the great human army: who gladly go on from year to year extending its outposts, and leaving home after home behind them; and die at last, utterly regardless of their graves being left thousands of miles behind, by the wandering generation who succeed.

His wife was a domesticated, kind-hearted old soul, who had come with him, "from the queen city of the world," which, it seemed, was Philadelphia; but had no love for this Western country, and indeed had little reason to bear it any; having seen her children, one by one, die here of fever, in the full prime and beauty of their youth. Her heart was sore, she said, to think of them; and to talk on this theme, even to strangers, in that blighted place, so far from her old home, eased it somewhat, and became a melancholy pleasure.

The boat appearing towards evening, we bade adieu to the poor old lady and her vagrant spouse, and making for the nearest landing-place, were soon on board The Messenger again, in our old cabin, and steaming down the Mississippi.

If the coming up this river, slowly making head against the stream, be an irksome journey, the shooting down it with the turbid current is almost worse; for then the boat, proceeding at the rate of twelve or fifteen miles an hour, has to force its passage through a labyrinth of floating logs, which, in the dark, it is often impossible to see beforehand or avoid. All that night, the bell was never silent for five minutes at a time; and after every ring the vessel reeled again, sometimes beneath a single blow, sometimes beneath a dozen dealt in quick succession, the lightest of which seemed more than enough to beat in her frail keel, as though it had been pie-crust. Looking down upon the filthy river after dark, it seemed to be alive with monsters, as these black masses rolled upon the surface, or came starting up again, head first, when the boat, in ploughing her way among a shoal of such obstructions, drove a few among them for the moment under water. Sometimes the engine stopped during a long interval, and then before her and behind, and gathering close about her on all sides, were so many of these ill-favoured obstacles that she was fairly hemmed in; the centre of a floating island; and was constrained to pause until they parted, somewhere, as dark clouds will do before the wind, and opened by degrees a channel out.

In good time next morning, however, we came again in sight of the detestable morass called Cairo; and stopping there to take in wood, lay alongside a barge, whose starting timbers scarcely held together. It was moored to the bank, and on its side was painted "Coffee House;" that being, I suppose, the floating paradise to which the people fly for shelter when they lose their houses for a month or two beneath the hideous waters of the Mississippi. But looking southwards from this point, we had the satisfaction of seeing that intolerable river dragging its slimy length and ugly freight abruptly off towards New Orleans; and passing a yellow line which stretched across the current, were again upon the clear Ohio, never, I trust, to see the Mississippi more, saving in troubled dreams and nightmares. Leaving it for the company of its sparkling neighbour, was like the transition from pain to ease, or the awakening from a horrible vision to cheerful realities.

We arrived at Louisville on the fourth night, and gladly availed ourselves of its excellent hotel. Next day we went on in the Ben Franklin, a beautiful mail steamboat, and reached Cincinnati shortly after midnight. Being by this time nearly tired of sleeping upon shelves, we had remained awake to go ashore straightway; and groping a passage across the dark decks of other boats, and among labyrinths of engine-machinery and leaking casks of molasses, we reached the streets, knocked up the porter at the hotel where we had stayed before, and were, to our great joy, safely housed soon afterwards.

We rested but one day at Cincinnati, and then resumed our journey to Sandusky. As it comprised two varieties of stage-coach travelling, which, with those I have already glanced at, comprehend the main characteristics of this mode of transit in America, I will take the reader as our fellow-passenger, and pledge myself to perform the distance with all possible despatch.

Our place of destination in the first instance is Columbus. It is distant about a hundred and twenty miles from Cincinnati, but there is a macadamised road (rare blessing!) the whole way, and the rate of travelling upon it is six miles an hour.

We start at eight o'clock in the morning, in a great mail-coach, whose huge cheeks are so very ruddy and plethoric, that it appears to be troubled with a tendency of blood to the head. Dropsical it certainly is, for it will hold a dozen passengers inside. But, wonderful to add, it is very clean and bright, being nearly new; and rattles through the streets of Cincinnati gaily.

Our way lies through a beautiful country, richly cultivated, and luxuriant in its promise of an abundant harvest. Sometimes we pass a field where the strong bristling stalks of Indian corn look like a crop of walking-sticks, and sometimes an enclosure where the green wheat is springing up among a labyrinth of stumps; the primitive worm-fence is universal, and an ugly thing it is; but the farms are neatly kept, and, save for these differences, one might be travelling just now in Kent.

We often stop to water at a roadside inn, which is always dull and silent. The coachman dismounts and fills his bucket, and holds it to the horses' heads. There is scarcely ever any one to help him; there are seldom any loungers standing round; and never any stable-company with jokes to crack. Sometimes, when we have changed our team, there is a difficulty in starting again, arising out of the prevalent mode of breaking a young horse: which is to catch him, harness him against his will, and put him in a stage-coach without further notice: but we get on somehow or other, after a great many kicks and a violent struggle; and jog on as before again.

Occasionally, when we stop to change, some two or three half-drunken loafers will come loitering out with their hands in their pockets, or will be seen kicking their heels in rocking-chairs, or lounging on the window-sill, or sitting on a rail within the colonnade: they have not often anything to say though, either to us or to each other, but sit there idly staring at the coach and horses. The landlord of the inn is usually among them, and seems, of all the party, to be the least connected with the business of the house. Indeed he is with reference to the tavern, what the driver is in relation to the coach and passengers: whatever happens in his sphere of action, he is quite indifferent, and perfectly easy in his mind.

The frequent change of coachmen works no change or variety in the coachman's character. He is always dirty, sullen, and taciturn. If he be capable of smartness of any kind, moral or physical, he has a faculty of concealing it which is truly marvellous. He never speaks to you as you sit beside him on the box, and if you speak to him, he answers (if at all) in monosyllables. He points out nothing on the road, and seldom looks at anything: being, to all appearance, thoroughly weary of it and of existence generally. As to doing the honours of his coach, his business, as I have said, is with the horses. The coach follows because it is attached to them and goes on wheels: not because you are in it. Sometimes, towards the end of a long stage, he suddenly breaks out into a discordant fragment of an election song, but his face never sings along with him: it is only his voice, and not often that.

He always chews and always spits, and never encumbers himself with a pocket-handkerchief. The consequences to the box passenger, especially when the wind blows towards him, are not agreeable.

Whenever the coach stops, and you can hear the voices of the inside passengers; or whenever any bystander addresses them, or any one among them; or they address each other; you will hear one phrase repeated over and over and over again to the most extraordinary extent. It is an ordinary and unpromising phrase enough, being neither more nor less than "Yes, sir;" but it is adapted to every variety of circumstance, and fills up every pause in the conversation. Thus:—

The time is one o'clock at noon. The scene, a place where we are to stay and dine, on this journey. The coach drives up to the door of an inn. The day is warm, and there are several idlers lingering about the tavern, and waiting for the public dinner. Among them, is a stout gentleman in a brown hat, swinging himself to and fro in a rocking-chair on the pavement.

As the coach stops, a gentleman in a straw hat looks out of the window:

STRAW HAT. (To the stout gentleman in the rocking-chair.) I reckon that's Judge Jefferson, an't it?

BROWN HAT. (Still swinging; speaking very slowly; and without any emotion whatever.) Yes, sir.

STRAW HAT. Warm weather, Judge.

BROWN HAT. Yes, sir.

STRAW HAT. There was a snap of cold, last week.

BROWN HAT. Yes, sir.

STRAW HAT. Yes, sir.

A pause. They look at each other, very seriously.

STRAW HAT. I calculate you'll have got through that case of the corporation, Judge, by this time, now?

BROWN HAT. Yes, sir.

STRAW HAT. How did the verdict go, sir?

BROWN HAT. For the defendant, sir.

STRAW HAT. (Interrogatively.) Yes, sir?

BROWN HAT. (Affirmatively.) Yes, sir.

BOTH. (Musingly, as each gazes down the street.) Yes, sir.

Another pause. They look at each other again, still more seriously than before.

BROWN HAT. This coach is rather behind its time to-day, I guess.

STRAW HAT. (Doubtingly.) Yes, sir.

BROWN HAT. (Looking at his watch.) Yes, sir; nigh upon two hours.

STRAW HAT. (Raising his eyebrows in very great surprise.) Yes, sir!

BROWN HAT. (Decisively, as he puts up his watch.) Yes, sir.

ALL THE OTHER INSIDE PASSENGERS. (Among themselves.) Yes, sir.

COACHMAN. (In a very surly tone.) No it an't.

STRAW HAT. (To the coachman.) Well, I don't know, sir. We were a pretty tall time coming that last fifteen mile. That's a fact.

The coachman making no reply, and plainly declining to enter into any controversy on a subject so far removed from his sympathies and feelings, another passenger says, "Yes, sir;" and the gentleman in the straw hat in acknowledgment of his courtesy, says "Yes, sir," to him, in return. The straw hat then inquires of the brown hat, whether that coach in which he (the straw hat) then sits, is not a new one? To which the brown hat again makes answer, "Yes, sir."

STRAW HAT. I thought so. Pretty loud smell of varnish, sir?

BROWN HAT. Yes, sir.

ALL THE OTHER INSIDE PASSENGERS. Yes, sir.

BROWN HAT. (To the company in general.) Yes, sir.

The conversational powers of the company having been by this
time pretty heavily taxed, the straw hat opens the door and gets
out; and all the rest alight also. We dine soon afterwards with the
boarders in the house, and have nothing to drink but tea and coffee.
As they are both very bad and the water is worse, I ask for brandy;
but it is a Temperance Hotel, and spirits are not to be had for love
or money. This preposterous forcing of unpleasant drinks down the
reluctant throats of travellers is not at all uncommon in America,
but I never discovered that the scruples of such wincing landlords
induced them to preserve any unusually nice balance between the
quality of their fare, and their scale of charges: on the contrary, I
rather suspected them of diminishing the one and exalting the other,
by way of recompense for the loss of their profit on the sale of
spirituous liquors. After all, perhaps, the plainest course for persons
of such tender consciences, would be, a total abstinence from
tavern-keeping.

Dinner over, we get into another vehicle which is ready at the door
(for the coach has been changed in the interval), and resume our
journey; which continues through the same kind of country until
evening, when we come to the town where we are to stop for tea and
supper; and having delivered the mail bags at the Post-office, ride
through the usual wide street, lined with the usual stores and houses
(the drapers always having hung up at their door, by way of sign,
a piece of bright red cloth), to the hotel where this meal is prepared.
There being many boarders here, we sit down, a large party, and a
very melancholy one as usual. But there is a buxom hostess at the
head of the table, and opposite, a simple Welsh schoolmaster with
his wife and child; who came here, on a speculation of greater promise
than performance, to teach the classics: and they are sufficient
subjects of interest until the meal is over, and another coach is ready.
In it we go on once more, lighted by a bright moon, until midnight;
when we stop to change the coach again, and remain for half an
hour or so in a miserable room, with a blurred lithograph of Washington over the smoky fireplace, and a mighty jug of cold water on the
table: to which refreshment the moody passengers do so apply themselves that they would seem to be, one and all, keen patients of Dr.
Sangrado. Among them is a very little boy, who chews tobacco like
a very big one; and a droning gentleman, who talks arithmetically
and statistically on all subjects, from poetry downwards; and who
always speaks in the same key, with exactly the same emphasis, and
with very grave deliberation. He came outside just now, and told
me how that the uncle of a certain young lady who had been spirited
away and married by a certain captain, lived in these parts; and how
this uncle was so valiant and ferocious that he shouldn't wonder if
he were to follow the said captain to England, "and shoot him down

in the street wherever he found him;" in the feasibility of which
strong measure I, being for the moment rather prone to contradiction, from feeling half asleep and very tired, declined to acquiesce:
assuring him that if the uncle did resort to it, or gratified any other
little whim of the like nature, he would find himself one morning
prematurely throttled at the Old Bailey: and that he would do well
to make his will before he went, as he would certainly want it
before he had been in Britain very long.

On we go, all night, and by-and-by the day begins to break,
and presently the first cheerful rays of the warm sun come slanting
on us brightly. It sheds its light upon a miserable waste of sodden
grass, and dull trees, and squalid huts, whose aspect is forlorn and
grievous in the last degree. A very desert in the wood, whose growth
of green is dank and noxious like that upon the top of standing
water: where poisonous fungus grows in the rare footprint on the
oozy ground, and sprouts like witches' coral, from the crevices in
the cabin wall and floor; it is a hideous thing to lie upon the very
threshold of a city. But it was purchased years ago, and as the owner
cannot be discovered, the State has been unable to reclaim it. So
there it remains, in the midst of cultivation and improvement, like
ground accursed, and made obscene and rank by some great crime.

We reached Columbus shortly before seven o'clock, and stayed
there, to refresh, that day and night: having excellent apartments in
a very large unfinished hotel called the Neill House, which were
richly fitted with the polished wood of the black walnut, and opened
on a handsome portico and stone verandah, like rooms in some
Italian mansion. The town is clean and pretty, and of course is
"going to be" much larger. It is the seat of the State legislature of
Ohio, and lays claim, in consequence, to some consideration and
importance.

There being no stage-coach next day, upon the road we wished to
take, I hired "an extra," at a reasonable charge, to carry us to Tiffin;
a small town from whence there is a railroad to Sandusky. This
extra was an ordinary four-horse stage-coach, such as I have described, changing horses and drivers, as the stage-coach would, but
was exclusively our own for the journey. To ensure our having
horses at the proper stations, and being incommoded by no strangers,
the proprietors sent an agent on the box, who was to accompany us
the whole way through; and thus attended, and bearing with us,
besides a hamper full of savoury cold meats, and fruit, and wine,
we started off again in high spirits, at half-past six o'clock next
morning, very much delighted to be by ourselves, and disposed to
enjoy even the roughest journey.

It was well for us, that we were in this humour, for the road we
went over that day, was certainly enough to have shaken tempers
that were not resolutely at Set Fair, down to some inches below
Stormy. At one time we were all flung together in a heap at the
bottom of the coach, and at another we were crushing our heads

against the roof. Now, one side was down deep in the mire, and we were holding on to the other. Now, the coach was lying on the tails of the two wheelers; and now it was rearing up in the air, in a frantic state, with all four horses standing on the top of an insurmountable eminence, looking coolly back at it, as though they would say "Unharness us. It can't be done." The drivers on these roads, who certainly get over the ground in a manner which is quite miraculous, so twist and turn the team about in forcing a passage, corkscrew fashion, through the bogs and swamps, that it was quite a common circumstance on looking out of the window, to see the coachman with the ends of a pair of reins in his hands, apparently driving nothing, or playing at horses, and the leaders staring at one unexpectedly from the back of the coach, as if they had some idea of getting up behind. A great portion of the way was over what is called a corduroy road, which is made by throwing trunks of trees into a marsh, and leaving them to settle there. The very slightest of the jolts with which the ponderous carriage fell from log to log, was enough, it seemed, to have dislocated all the bones in the human body. It would be impossible to experience a similar set of sensations, in any other circumstances, unless perhaps in attempting to go up to the top of St. Paul's in an omnibus. Never, never once, that day, was the coach in any position, attitude, or kind of motion to which we are accustomed in coaches. Never did it make the smallest approach to one's experience of the proceedings of any sort of vehicle that goes on wheels.

Still, it was a fine day, and the temperature was delicious, and though we had left Summer behind us in the west, and were fast leaving Spring, we were moving towards Niagara and home. We alighted in a pleasant wood towards the middle of the day, dined on a fallen tree, and leaving our best fragments with a cottager, and our worst with the pigs (who swarm in this part of the country like grains of sand on the sea-shore, to the great comfort of our commissariat in Canada), we went forward again, gaily.

As night came on, the track grew narrower and narrower, until at last it so lost itself among the trees, that the driver seemed to find his way by instinct. We had the comfort of knowing, at least, that there was no danger of his falling asleep, for every now and then a wheel would strike against an unseen stump with such a jerk, that he was fain to hold on pretty tight and pretty quick, to keep himself upon the box. Nor was there any reason to dread the least danger from furious driving, inasmuch as over that broken ground the horses had enough to do to walk; as to shying, there was no room for that; and a herd of wild elephants could not have run away in such a wood, with such a coach at their heels. So we stumbled along, quite satisfied.

These stumps of trees are a curious feature in American travelling. The varying illusions they present to the unaccustomed eye as it grows dark, are quite astonishing in their number and reality. Now,

there is a Grecian urn erected in the centre of a lonely field; now there
is a woman weeping at a tomb; now a very commonplace old gentleman in a white waistcoat, with a thumb thrust into each arm-hole
of his coat; now a student poring on a book; now a crouching negro;
now, a horse, a dog, a cannon, an armed man; a hunch-back throwing off his cloak and stepping forth into the light. They were often
as entertaining to me as so many glasses in a magic lantern, and
never took their shapes at my bidding, but seemed to force themselves upon me, whether I would or no; and strange to say, I sometimes recognised in them counterparts of figures once familiar to me
in pictures attached to childish books, forgotten long ago.

It soon became too dark, however, even for this amusement, and
the trees were so close together that their dry branches rattled
against the coach on either side, and obliged us all to keep our heads
within. It lightened too, for three whole hours; each flash being very
bright, and blue, and long; and as the vivid streaks came darting in
among the crowded branches, and the thunder rolled gloomily above
the tree tops, one could scarcely help thinking that there were better
neighbourhoods at such a time than thick woods afforded.

At length, between ten and eleven o'clock at night, a few feeble
lights appeared in the distance, and Upper Sandusky, an Indian
village, where we were to stay till morning, lay before us.

They were gone to bed at the log Inn, which was the only house
of entertainment in the place, but soon answered to our knocking,
and got some tea for us in a sort of kitchen or common room,
tapestried with old newspapers, pasted against the wall. The bed-
chamber to which my wife and I were shown, was a large, low,
ghostly room; with a quantity of withered branches on the hearth,
and two doors without any fastening, opposite to each other, both
opening on the black night and wild country, and so contrived, that
one of them always blew the other open: a novelty in domestic
architecture, which I do not remember to have seen before, and
which I was somewhat disconcerted to have forced on my attention
after getting into bed, as I had a considerable sum in gold for our
travelling expenses, in my dressing-case. Some of the luggage, however, piled against the panels, soon settled this difficulty, and my
sleep would not have been very much affected that night, I believe,
though it had failed to do so.

My Boston friend climbed up to bed, somewhere in the roof,
where another guest was already snoring hugely. But being bitten
beyond his power of endurance, he turned out again, and fled for
shelter to the coach, which was airing itself in front of the house.
This was not a very politic step, as it turned out; for the pigs scenting
him, and looking upon the coach as a kind of pie with some manner
of meat inside, grunted round it so hideously, that he was afraid to
come out again, and lay there shivering, till morning. Nor was it
possible to warm him, when he did come out, by means of a glass of
brandy: for in Indian villages, the legislature, with a very good and

wise intention, forbids the sale of spirits by tavern keepers. The precaution, however, is quite inefficacious, for the Indians never fail to procure liquor of a worse kind, at a dearer price, from travelling pedlars.

It is a settlement of the Wyandot Indians who inhabit this place. Among the company at breakfast was a mild old gentleman, who had been for many years employed by the United States Government in conducting negotiations with the Indians, and who had just concluded a treaty with these people by which they bound themselves, in consideration of a certain annual sum, to remove next year to some land provided for them, west of the Mississippi, and a little way beyond St. Louis. He gave me a moving account of their strong attachment to the familiar scenes of their infancy, and in particular to the burial-places of their kindred; and of their great reluctance to leave them. He had witnessed many such removals, and always with pain, though he knew that they departed for their own good. The question whether this tribe should go or stay, had been discussed among them a day or two before, in a hut erected for the purpose, the logs of which still lay upon the ground before the inn. When the speaking was done, the ayes and noes were ranged on opposite sides, and every male adult voted in his turn. The moment the result was known, the minority (a large one) cheerfully yielded to the rest, and withdrew all kind of opposition.

We met some of these poor Indians afterwards, riding on shaggy ponies. They were so like the meaner sort of gipsies, that if I could have seen any of them in England, I should have concluded, as a matter of course, that they belonged to that wandering and restless people.

Leaving this town directly after breakfast, we pushed forward again, over a rather worse road than yesterday, if possible, and arrived about noon at Tiffin, where we parted with the extra. At two o'clock we took the railroad; the travelling on which was very slow, its construction being indifferent, and the ground wet and marshy; and arrived at Sandusky in time to dine that evening. We put up at a comfortable little hotel on the brink of Lake Erie, lay there that night, and had no choice but to wait there next day, until a steamboat bound for Buffalo appeared. The town, which was sluggish and uninteresting enough, was something like the back of an English watering-place, out of the season.

Our host, who was very attentive and anxious to make us comfortable, was a handsome middle-aged man, who had come to this town from New England, in which part of the country he was "raised." When I say that he constantly walked in and out of the room with his hat on; and stopped to converse in the same free-and-easy state; and lay down on our sofa, and pulled his newspaper out of his pocket, and read it at his ease; I merely mention these traits as characteristic of the country: not at all as being matter of complaint, or as having been disagreeable to me. I should undoubtedly be offended by such proceedings at home, because there they are not the custom, and where they are not, they would be impertinencies; but in America, the only desire of a good-natured fellow of this kind, is to treat his guests hospitably and well; and I had no more right, and I can truly say no more disposition, to measure his conduct by our English rule and standard, than I had to quarrel with him for not being of the exact stature which would qualify him for admission into the Queen's grenadier guards. As little inclination had I to find fault with a funny old lady who was an upper domestic in this establishment, and who, when she came to wait upon us at any meal, sat herself down comfortably in the most convenient chair, and producing a large pin to pick her teeth with, remained performing that ceremony, and steadfastly regarding us meanwhile with much gravity and composure (now and then pressing us to eat a little more), until it was time to clear away. It was enough for us, that whatever we wished done was done with great civility and readiness, and a desire to oblige, not only here, but everywhere else; and that all our wants were, in general, zealously anticipated.

We were taking an early dinner at this house, on the day after our arrival, which was Sunday, when a steamboat came in sight, and presently touched at the wharf. As she proved to be on her way to Buffalo, we hurried on board with all speed, and soon left Sandusky far behind us.

She was a large vessel of five hundred tons, and handsomely fitted up, though with high-pressure engines; which always conveyed that kind of feeling to me, which I should be likely to experience, I think, if I had lodgings on the first-floor of a powder-mill. She was laden with flour, some casks of which commodity were stored upon the deck. The captain coming up to have a little conversation, and to introduce a friend, seated himself astride of one of these barrels, like a Bacchus of private life; and pulling a great clasp-knife out of his pocket, began to "whittle" it as he talked, by paring thin slices off the edges. And he whittled with such industry and hearty good will, that but for his being called away very soon, it must have disappeared bodily, and left nothing in its place but grist and shavings.

After calling at one or two flat places, with low dams stretching out into the lake, whereon were stumpy lighthouses, like windmills without sails, the whole looking like a Dutch vignette, we came at midnight to Cleveland, where we lay all night, and until nine o'clock next morning.

I entertained quite a curiosity in reference to this place, from having seen at Sandusky a specimen of its literature in the shape of a newspaper, which was very strong indeed upon the subject of Lord Ashburton's recent arrival at Washington, to adjust the points in dispute between the United States Government and Great Britain: informing its readers that as America had "whipped" England in her infancy, and whipped her again in her youth, so it was clearly necessary that she must whip her once again in her maturity; and pledging its credit to all True Americans, that if Mr. Webster did his duty in the approaching negotiations, and sent the English Lord home again in double quick time, they should, within two years, sing "Yankee Doodle in Hyde Park, and Hail Columbia in the scarlet courts of Westminster!" I found it a pretty town, and had the satisfaction of beholding the outside of the office of the journal from which I have just quoted. I did not enjoy the delight of seeing the wit who indited the paragraph in question, but I have no doubt he is a prodigious man in his way, and held in high repute by a select circle.

There was a gentleman on board, to whom, as I unintentionally learned through the thin partition which divided our state-room from the cabin in which he and his wife conversed together, I was unwittingly the occasion of very great uneasiness. I don't know why or wherefore, but I appeared to run in his mind perpetually, and to dissatisfy him very much. First of all I heard him say: and the most ludicrous part of the business was, that he said it in my very ear, and could not have communicated more directly with me, if he had leaned upon my shoulder, and whispered me: "Boz is on board still, my dear." After a considerable pause, he added, complainingly, "Boz keeps himself very close;" which was true enough, for I was not very well, and was lying down, with a book. I thought he had done with me after this, but I was deceived; for a long interval having elapsed, during which I imagine him to have been turning restlessly from side to side, and trying to go to sleep; he broke out again, with "I suppose *that* Boz will be writing a book by-and-by, and putting all our names in it!" at which imaginary consequence of being on board a boat with Boz, he groaned, and became silent.

We called at the town of Erie, at eight o'clock that night, and lay there an hour. Between five and six next morning, we arrived at Buffalo, where we breakfasted; and being too near the Great Falls to wait patiently anywhere else, we set off by the train, the same morning at nine o'clock, to Niagara.

It was a miserable day; chilly and raw; a damp mist falling; and the trees in that northern region quite bare and wintry. Whenever the train halted, I listened for the roar; and was constantly straining my eyes in the direction where I knew the Falls must be, from seeing the river rolling on towards them; every moment expecting to behold the spray. Within a few minutes of our stopping, not before, I saw two great white clouds rising up slowly and majestically from the depths of the earth. That was all. At length we alighted: and then for the first time, I heard the mighty rush of water, and felt the ground tremble underneath my feet.

The bank is very steep, and was slippery with rain, and half-melted ice. I hardly know how I got down, but I was soon at the bottom, and climbing, with two English officers who were crossing and had joined me, over some broken rocks, deafened by the noise, half-blinded by the spray, and wet to the skin. We were at the foot of the American Fall. I could see an immense torrent of water tearing headlong down from some great height, but had no idea of shape, or situation, or anything but vague immensity.

When we were seated in the little ferry-boat, and were crossing the swollen river immediately before both cataracts, I began to feel what it was: but I was in a manner stunned, and unable to comprehend the vastness of the scene. It was not until I came on Table Rock, and looked—Great Heaven, on what a fall of bright-green water!—that it came upon me in its full might and majesty.

Then, when I felt how near to my Creator I was standing, the first effect, and the enduring one—instant and lasting—of the tremendous spectacle, was Peace. Peace of Mind, tranquillity, calm recollections of the Dead, great thoughts of Eternal Rest and Happiness: nothing of gloom or terror. Niagara was at once stamped upon my heart, an Image of Beauty; to remain there, changeless and indelible, until its pulses cease to beat, for ever.

Oh, how the strife and trouble of daily life receded from my view, and lessened in the distance, during the ten memorable days we passed on that Enchanted Ground! What voices spoke from out the thundering water; what faces, faded from the earth, looked out upon me from its gleaming depths; what Heavenly promise glistened in those angels' tears, the drops of many hues, that showered around, and twined themselves about the gorgeous arches which the changing rainbows made!

I never stirred in all that time from the Canadian side, whither I had gone at first. I never crossed the river again; for I knew there were people on the other shore, and in such a place it is natural to shun strange company. To wander to and fro all day, and see the cataracts from all points of view; to stand upon the edge of the great Horse-Shoe Fall, marking the hurried water gathering strength as it approached the verge, yet seeming, too, to pause before it shot into the gulf below; to gaze from the river's level up at the torrent as it came streaming down; to climb the neighbouring heights and watch it through the trees, and see the wreathing water in the rapids hurrying on to take its fearful plunge; to linger in the shadow of the solemn rocks three miles below; watching the river as, stirred by no visible cause, it heaved and eddied and awoke the echoes, being troubled yet, far down beneath the surface, by its giant leap; to have Niagara before me, lighted by the sun and by the moon, red in the day's decline, and grey as evening slowly fell upon it; to look upon it every day, and wake up in the night and hear its ceaseless voice: this was enough.

I think in every quiet season now, still do those waters roll and leap, and roar and tumble, all day long; still are the rainbows spanning them, a hundred feet below. Still, when the sun is on them, do they shine and glow like molten gold. Still, when the day is gloomy, do they fall like snow, or seem to crumble away like the front of a great chalk cliff, or roll down the rock like dense white smoke. But always does the mighty stream appear to die as it comes

down, and always from its unfathomable grave arises that tremendous ghost of spray and mist which is never laid: which has haunted
this place with the same dread solemnity since Darkness brooded on
the deep, and that first flood before the Deluge—Light—came
rushing on Creation at the word of God.

## CHAPTER XV

IN CANADA; TORONTO; KINGSTON; MONTREAL; QUEBEC; ST. JOHN'S.
IN THE UNITED STATES AGAIN; LEBANON; THE SHAKER VILLAGE;
WEST POINT

I WISH to abstain from instituting any comparison, or drawing any
parallel whatever, between the social features of the United States
and those of the British Possessions in Canada. For this reason, I
shall confine myself to a very brief account of our journeyings in the
latter territory.

But before I leave Niagara, I must advert to one disgusting circumstance which can hardly have escaped the observation of any decent
traveller who has visited the Falls.

On Table Rock, there is a cottage belonging to a Guide, where
little relics of the place are sold, and where visitors register their
names in a book kept for the purpose. On the wall of the room in
which a great many of these volumes are preserved, the following
request is posted: "Visitors will please not copy nor extract the
remarks and poetical effusions from the registers and albums kept
here."

But for this intimation, I should have let them lie upon the tables
on which they were strewn with careful negligence, like books in a
drawing-room: being quite satisfied with the stupendous silliness of
certain stanzas with an anti-climax at the end of each, which were
framed and hung up on the wall. Curious, however, after reading
this announcement, to see what kind of morsels were so carefully
preserved, I turned a few leaves, and found them scrawled all over
with the vilest and the filthiest ribaldry that ever human hogs
delighted in.

It is humiliating enough to know that there are among men, brutes
so obscene and worthless, that they can delight in laying their miserable profanations upon the very steps of Nature's greatest altar.
But that these should be hoarded up for the delight of their fellow-
swine, and kept in a public place where any eyes may see them, is a
disgrace to the English language in which they are written (though
I hope few of these entries have been made by Englishmen), and a
reproach to the English side, on which they are preserved.

The quarters of our soldiers at Niagara, are finely and airily situated. Some of them are large detached houses on the plain above the Falls, which were originally designed for hotels; and in the evening time, when the women and children were leaning over the balconies watching the men as they played at ball and other games upon the grass before the door, they often presented a little picture of cheerfulness and animation which made it quite a pleasure to pass that way.

At any garrisoned point where the line of demarcation between one country and another is so very narrow as at Niagara, desertion from the ranks can scarcely fail to be of frequent occurrence: and it may be reasonably supposed that when the soldiers entertain the wildest and maddest hopes of the fortune and independence that await them on the other side, the impulse to play traitor, which such a place suggests to dishonest minds, is not weakened. But it very rarely happens that the men who do desert, are happy or contented afterwards; and many instances have been known in which they have confessed their grievous disappointment, and their earnest desire to return to their old service if they could but be assured of pardon, or lenient treatment. Many of their comrades, notwithstanding, do the like, from time to time; and instances of loss of life in the effort to cross the river with this object, are far from being uncommon. Several men were drowned in the attempt to swim across, not long ago; and one, who had the madness to trust himself upon a table as a raft, was swept down to the whirlpool, where his mangled body eddied round and round some days.

I am inclined to think that the noise of the Falls is very much exaggerated; and this will appear the more probable when the depth of the great basin in which the water is received, is taken into account. At no time during our stay there, was the wind at all high or boisterous, but we never heard them, three miles off, even at the very quiet time of sunset, though we often tried.

Queenston, at which place the steamboats start for Toronto (or I should rather say at which place they call, for their wharf is at Lewiston, on the opposite shore), is situated in a delicious valley, through which the Niagara river, in colour a very deep green, pursues its course. It is approached by a road that takes its winding way among the heights by which the town is sheltered; and seen from this point is extremely beautiful and picturesque. On the most conspicuous of these heights stood a monument erected by the Provincial Legislature in memory of General Brock, who was slain in a battle with the American forces, after having won the victory. Some vagabond, supposed to be a fellow of the name of Lett, who is now, or who lately was, in prison as a felon, blew up this monument two years ago, and it is now a melancholy ruin, with a long fragment of iron railing hanging dejectedly from its top, and waving to and fro like a wild ivy branch or broken vine stem. It is of much higher importance than it may seem, that this statue should be repaired at the public cost, as it ought to have been long ago. Firstly, because it is beneath the dignity of England to allow a memorial raised in honour of one of her defenders, to remain in this condition, on the very spot where he died. Secondly, because the sight of it in its present state, and the recollection of the unpunished outrage which brought it to this pass, is not very likely to soothe down border feelings among English subjects here, or compose their border quarrels and dislikes.

I was standing on the wharf at this place, watching the passengers embarking in a steamboat which preceded that whose coming we awaited, and participating in the anxiety with which a sergeant's wife was collecting her few goods together—keeping one distracted eye hard upon the porters, who were hurrying them on board, and the other on a hoopless washing-tub for which, as being the most utterly worthless of all her movables, she seemed to entertain particular affection—when three or four soldiers with a recruit came up and went on board.

The recruit was a likely young fellow enough, strongly built and well made, but by no means sober: indeed he had all the air of a man who had been more or less drunk for some days. He carried a small bundle over his shoulder, slung at the end of a walking-stick, and had a short pipe in his mouth. He was as dusty and dirty as recruits usually are, and his shoes betokened that he had travelled on foot some distance, but he was in a very jocose state, and shook hands with this soldier, and clapped that one on the back, and talked and laughed continually, like a roaring idle dog as he was.

The soldiers rather laughed at this blade than with him: seeming to say, as they stood straightening their canes in their hands, and looking coolly at him over their glazed stocks, "Go on, my boy, while you may! you'll know better by-and-by:" when suddenly the novice, who had been backing towards the gangway in his noisy merriment, fell overboard before their eyes, and splashed heavily down into the river between the vessel and the dock.

I never saw such a good thing as the change that came over these soldiers in an instant. Almost before the man was down, their professional manner, their stiffness and constraint, were gone, and they were filled with the most violent energy. In less time than is required to tell it, they had him out again, feet first, with the tails of his coat flapping over his eyes, everything about him hanging the wrong way, and the water streaming off at every thread in his threadbare dress. But the moment they set him upright and found that he was none the worse, they were soldiers again, looking over their glazed stocks more composedly than ever.

The half-sobered recruit glanced round for a moment, as if his first impulse were to express some gratitude for his preservation, but seeing them with this air of total unconcern, and having his wet pipe presented to him with an oath by the soldier who had been by far the most anxious of the party, he stuck it in his mouth, thrust his hands into his moist pockets, and without even shaking the water off his clothes, walked on board whistling; not to say as if nothing had happened, but as if he had meant to do it, and it had been a perfect success.

Our steamboat came up directly this had left the wharf, and soon bore us to the mouth of the Niagara; where the stars and stripes of America flutter on one side and the Union Jack of England on the other: and so narrow is the space between them that the sentinels in either fort can often hear the watchword of the other country given. Thence we emerged on Lake Ontario, an inland sea; and by half-past six o'clock were at Toronto.

The country round this town being very flat, is bare of scenic interest; but the town itself is full of life and motion, bustle, business, and improvement. The streets are well paved, and lighted with gas; the houses are large and good; the shops excellent. Many of them have a display of goods in their windows, such as may be seen in thriving county towns in England; and there are some which would do no discredit to the metropolis itself. There is a good stone prison here; and there are, besides, a handsome church, a court-house, public offices, many commodious private residences, and a government observatory for noting and recording the magnetic variations. In the College of Upper Canada, which is one of the public establishments of the city, a sound education in every department of polite learning can be had, at a very moderate expense: the annual charge for the instruction of each pupil, not exceeding nine pounds sterling. It has pretty good endowments in the way of land, and is a valuable and useful institution.

The first stone of a new college had been laid but a few days before, by the Governor General. It will be a handsome, spacious edifice, approached by a long avenue, which is already planted and made available as a public walk. The town is well adapted for wholesome exercise at all seasons, for the footways in the thoroughfares which lie beyond the principal street, are planked like floors, and kept in very good and clean repair.

It is a matter of deep regret that political differences should have run high in this place, and led to most discreditable and disgraceful results. It is not long since guns were discharged from a window in this town at the successful candidates in an election, and the coachman of one of them was actually shot in the body, though not dangerously wounded. But one man was killed on the same occasion; and from the very window whence he received his death, the very flag which shielded his murderer (not only in the commission of his crime, but from its consequences), was displayed again on the occasion of the public ceremony performed by the Governor General, to which I have just adverted. Of all the colours in the rainbow, there is but one which could be so employed: I need not say that flag was orange.

The time of leaving Toronto for Kingston is noon. By eight o'clock next morning, the traveller is at the end of his journey, which is performed by steamboat upon Lake Ontario, calling at Port Hope and Coburg, the latter a cheerful, thriving little town. Vast quantities of flour form the chief item in the freight of these vessels. We had no fewer than one thousand and eighty barrels on board, between Coburg and Kingston.

The latter place, which is now the seat of government in Canada, is a very poor town, rendered still poorer in the appearance of its market-place by the ravages of a recent fire. Indeed, it may be said of Kingston, that one half of it appears to be burnt down, and the other half not to be built up. The Government House is neither elegant nor commodious, yet it is almost the only house of any importance in the neighbourhood.

There is an admirable jail here, well and wisely governed, and excellently regulated, in every respect. The men were employed as shoemakers, ropemakers, blacksmiths, tailors, carpenters, and stonecutters; and in building a new prison, which was pretty far advanced towards completion. The female prisoners were occupied in needlework. Among them was a beautiful girl of twenty, who had been there nearly three years. She acted as bearer of secret despatches for the self-styled Patriots on Navy Island, during the Canadian Insurrection: sometimes dressing as a girl, and carrying them in her stays; sometimes attiring herself as a boy, and secreting them in the lining of her hat. In the latter character she always rode as a boy would, which was nothing to her, for she could govern any horse that any man could ride, and could drive four-in-hand with the best whip in those parts. Setting forth on one of her patriotic missions, she appropriated to herself the first horse she could lay her hands on; and this offence had brought her where I saw her. She had quite a lovely face, though, as the reader may suppose from this sketch of her history, there was a lurking devil in her bright eye, which looked out pretty sharply from between her prison bars.

There is a bomb-proof fort here of great strength, which occupies a bold position, and is capable, doubtless, of doing good service; though the town is much too close upon the frontier to be long held, I should imagine, for its present purpose in troubled times. There is also a small navy-yard, where a couple of Government steamboats were building, and getting on vigorously.

We left Kingston for Montreal on the tenth of May, at half-past nine in the morning, and proceeded in a steamboat down the St. Lawrence river. The beauty of this noble stream at almost any point, but especially in the commencement of this journey when it winds its way among the thousand Islands, can hardly be imagined. The number and constant successions of these islands, all green and richly wooded; their fluctuating sizes, some so large that for half an hour together one among them will appear as the opposite bank of the river, and some so small that they are mere dimples on its broad bosom; their infinite variety of shapes; and the numberless combinations of beautiful forms which the trees growing on them present: all form a picture fraught with uncommon interest and pleasure.

In the afternoon we shot down some rapids where the river boiled and bubbled strangely, and where the force and headlong violence of the current were tremendous. At seven o'clock we reached Dickenson's Landing, whence travellers proceed for two or three hours by stage-coach: the navigation of the river being rendered so dangerous and difficult in the interval, by rapids, that steamboats do not make the passage. The number and length of those *portages*, over which the roads are bad, and the travelling slow, render the way between the towns of Montreal and Kingston, somewhat tedious.

Our course lay over a wide, uninclosed tract of country at a little distance from the river-side, whence the bright warning lights on the dangerous parts of the St. Lawrence shone vividly. The night was dark and raw, and the way dreary enough. It was nearly ten o'clock when we reached the wharf where the next steamboat lay; and went on board, and to bed.

She lay there all night, and started as soon as it was day. The morning was ushered in by a violent thunderstorm, and was very wet, but gradually improved and brightened up. Going on deck after breakfast, I was amazed to see floating down with the stream, a most gigantic raft, with some thirty or forty wooden houses upon it, and at least as many flagmasts, so that it looked like a nautical street. I saw many of these rafts afterwards, but never one so large. All the timber, or "lumber," as it is called in America, which is brought down the St. Lawrence, is floated down in this manner. When the raft reaches its place of destination, it is broken up; the materials are sold; and the boatmen return for more.

At eight we landed again, and travelled by a stage-coach for four hours through a pleasant and well-cultivated country, perfectly French in every respect: in the appearance of the cottages; the air, language, and dress of the peasantry; the sign-boards on the shops and taverns: and the Virgin's shrines, and crosses, by the wayside. Nearly every common labourer and boy, though he had no shoes to his feet, wore round his waist a sash of some bright colour: generally red: and the women, who were working in the fields and gardens, and doing all kinds of husbandry, wore, one and all, great flat straw hats with most capacious brims. There were Catholic Priests and Sisters of Charity in the village streets; and images of the Saviour at the corners of cross-roads, and in other public places.

At noon we went on board another steamboat, and reached the village of Lachine, nine miles from Montreal, by three o'clock. There, we left the river, and went on by land.

Montreal is pleasantly situated on the margin of the St. Lawrence, and is backed by some bold heights, about which there are charming rides and drives. The streets are generally narrow and irregular, as in most French towns of any age; but in the more modern parts of the city, they are wide and airy. They display a great variety of very good shops; and both in the town and suburbs there are many excellent private dwellings. The granite quays are remarkable for their beauty, solidity, and extent.

There is a very large Catholic cathedral here, recently erected; with two tall spires, of which one is yet unfinished. In the open space in front of this edifice, stands a solitary, grim-looking, square brick tower, which has a quaint and remarkable appearance, and which the wiseacres of the place have consequently determined to pull down immediately. The Government House is very superior to that at Kingston, and the town is full of life and bustle. In one of the suburbs is a plank road—not footpath—five or six miles long, and a famous road it is too. All the rides in the vicinity were made doubly interesting by the bursting out of spring, which is here so rapid, that it is but a day's leap from barren winter, to the blooming youth of summer.

The steamboats to Quebec perform the journey in the night; that is to say, they leave Montreal at six in the evening, and arrive at Quebec at six next morning. We made this excursion during our stay in Montreal (which exceeded a fortnight), and were charmed by its interest and beauty.

The impression made upon the visitor by this Gibraltar of America: its giddy heights; its citadel suspended, as it were, in the air; its picturesque steep streets and frowning gateways; and the splendid views which burst upon the eye at every turn: is at once unique and lasting.

It is a place not to be forgotten or mixed up in the mind with other places, or altered for a moment in the crowd of scenes a traveller can recall. Apart from the realities of this most picturesque city, there are associations clustering about it which would make a desert rich in interest. The dangerous precipice along whose rocky front, Wolfe and his brave companions climbed to glory; the Plains of Abraham, where he received his mortal wound; the fortress so chivalrously defended by Montcalm; and his soldier's grave, dug for him while yet alive, by the bursting of a shell; are not the least among them, or among the gallant incidents of history. That is a noble Monument too, and worthy of two great nations, which perpetuates the memory of both brave generals, and on which their names are jointly written.

The city is rich in public institutions and in Catholic churches and charities, but it is mainly in the prospect from the site of the Old Government House, and from the Citadel, that its surpassing beauty lies. The exquisite expanse of country, rich in field and forest, mountain-height and water, which lies stretched out before the view, with miles of Canadian villages, glancing in long white streaks, like veins along the landscape; the motley crowd of gables, roofs, and chimney tops in the old hilly town immediately at hand; the beautiful St. Lawrence sparkling and flashing in the sunlight; and the tiny ships below the rock from which you gaze, whose distant rigging looks like spiders' webs against the light, while casks and barrels on their decks dwindle into toys, and busy mariners become so many puppets; all this, framed by a sunken window in the fortress and looked at from the shadowed room within, forms one of the brightest and most enchanting pictures that the eye can rest upon.

In the spring of the year, vast numbers of emigrants who have newly arrived from England or from Ireland, pass between Quebec and Montreal on their way to the backwoods and new settlements of Canada. If it be an entertaining lounge (as I very often found it) to take a morning stroll upon the quay at Montreal, and see them grouped in hundreds on the public wharfs about their chests and boxes, it is matter of deep interest to be their fellow-passenger on one of these steamboats, and mingling with the concourse, see and hear them unobserved.

The vessel in which we returned from Quebec to Montreal was crowded with them, and at night they spread their beds between decks (those who had beds, at least), and slept so close and thick about our cabin door, that the passage to and fro was quite blocked up. They were nearly all English; from Gloucestershire the greater part; and had had a long winter-passage out; but it was wonderful to see how clean the children had been kept, and how untiring in their love and self-denial all the poor parents were.

Cant as we may, and as we shall to the end of all things, it is very much harder for the poor to be virtuous than it is for the rich; and the good that is in them, shines the brighter for it. In many a noble mansion lives a man, the best of husbands and of fathers, whose private worth in both capacities is justly lauded to the skies. But bring him here, upon this crowded deck. Strip from his fair young wife her silken dress and jewels, unbind her braided hair, stamp early wrinkles on her brow, pinch her pale cheek with care and much privation, array her faded form in coarsely patched attire, let there be nothing but his love to set her forth or deck her out, and you shall put it to the proof indeed. So change his station in the world, that he shall see in those young things who climb about his knee: not records of his wealth and name: but little wrestlers with him for his daily bread; so many poachers on his scanty meal; so many units to divide his every sum of comfort, and farther to reduce its small amount. In lieu of the endearments of childhood in its sweetest aspect, heap upon him all its pains and wants, its sicknesses and ills, its fretfulness, caprice, and querulous endurance: let its prattle be, not of engaging infant fancies, but of cold, and thirst, and hunger: and if his fatherly affection outlive all this, and he be patient, watchful, tender; careful of his children's lives, and mindful always of their joys and sorrows; then send him back to Parliament, and Pulpit, and to Quarter Sessions, and when he hears fine talk of the depravity of those who live from hand to mouth, and labour hard to do it, let him speak up, as one who knows, and tell those holders forth that they, by parallel with such a class, should be High Angels in their daily lives, and lay but humble siege to Heaven at last.

Which of us shall say what he would be, if such realities, with small relief or change all through his days, were his! Looking round upon these people: far from home, houseless, indigent, wandering, weary with travel and hard living: and seeing how patiently they nursed and tended their young children: how they consulted ever their wants first, then half supplied their own; what gentle ministers of hope and faith the women were; how the men profited by their example; and how very, very seldom even a moment's petulance or harsh complaint broke out among them: I felt a stronger love and honour of my kind come glowing on my heart, and wished to God there had been many Atheists in the better part of human nature there, to read this simple lesson in the book of Life.

We left Montreal for New York again, on the thirtieth of May; crossing to La Prairie, on the opposite shore of the St. Lawrence, in a steamboat; we then took the railroad to St. John's, which is on the brink of Lake Champlain. Our last greeting in Canada was from the English officers in the pleasant barracks at that place (a class of gentlemen who had made every hour of our visit memorable by their hospitality and friendship); and with "Rule Britannia" sounding in our ears, soon left it far behind.

But Canada has held, and always will retain, a foremost place in my remembrance. Few Englishmen are prepared to find it what it is. Advancing quietly; old differences settling down, and being fast forgotten; public feeling and private enterprise alike in a sound and wholesome state; nothing of flush or fever in its system, but health and vigour throbbing in its steady pulse: it is full of hope and promise. To me—who had been accustomed to think of it as something left behind in the strides of advancing society, as something neglected and forgotten, slumbering and wasting in its sleep—the demand for labour and the rates of wages; the busy quays of Montreal; the vessels taking in their cargoes, and discharging them; the amount of shipping in the different ports; the commerce, roads, and public works, all made *to last;* the respectability and character of the public journals; and the amount of rational comfort and happiness which honest industry may earn: were very great surprises. The steamboats on the lakes, in their conveniences, cleanliness, and safety; in the gentlemanly character and bearing of their captains; and in the politeness and perfect comfort of their social regulations; are unsurpassed even by the famous Scotch vessels, deservedly so much esteemed at home. The inns are usually bad; because the custom of boarding at hotels is not so general here as in the States, and the British officers, who form a large portion of the society of every town, live chiefly at the regimental messes: but in every other respect, the traveller in Canada will find as good provision for his comfort as in any place I know.

There is one American boat—the vessel which carried us on Lake Champlain, from St. John's to Whitehall—which I praise very highly, but no more than it deserves, when I say that it is superior even to that in which we went from Queenston to Toronto, or to that in which we travelled from the latter place to Kingston, or I have no doubt I may add to any other in the world. This steamboat, which is called the Burlington, is a perfectly exquisite achievement of neatness, elegance, and order. The decks are drawing-rooms; the cabins are boudoirs, choicely furnished and adorned with prints, pictures, and musical instruments; every nook and corner in the vessel is a perfect curiosity of graceful comfort and beautiful contrivance. Captain Sherman, her commander, to whose ingenuity and excellent taste these results are solely attributable, has bravely and worthily distinguished himself on more than one trying occasion: not least among them, in having the moral courage to carry British troops, at a time (during the Canadian rebellion) when no other conveyance was open to them. He and his vessel are held in universal respect, both by his own countrymen and ours; and no man ever enjoyed the popular esteem, who, in his sphere of action, won and wore it better than this gentleman.

By means of this floating palace we were soon in the United States again, and called that evening at Burlington; a pretty town, where we lay an hour or so. We reached Whitehall, where we were to disembark, at six next morning; and might have done so earlier, but that these steamboats lie by for some hours in the night, in consequence of the lake becoming very narrow at that part of the journey, and difficult of navigation in the dark. Its width is so contracted at one point, indeed, that they are obliged to warp round by means of a rope.

After breakfasting at Whitehall, we took the stage-coach for Albany: a large and busy town, where we arrived between five and six o'clock that afternoon; after a very hot day's journey, for we were now in the height of summer again. At seven we started for New York on board a great North River steamboat, which was so crowded with passengers that the upper deck was like the box lobby of a theatre between the pieces, and the lower one like Tottenham Court Road on a Saturday night. But we slept soundly, notwithstanding, and soon after five o'clock next morning reached New York.

Tarrying here, only that day and night, to recruit after our late fatigues, we started off once more upon our last journey in America. We had yet five days to spare before embarking for England, and I had a great desire to see "the Shaker Village," which is peopled by a religious sect from whom it takes its name.

To this end, we went up the North River again, as far as the town of Hudson, and there hired an extra to carry us to Lebanon, thirty miles distant: and of course another and a different Lebanon from that village where I slept on the night of the Prairie trip.

The country through which the road meandered, was rich and beautiful; the weather very fine; and for many miles the Kaatskill mountains, where Rip Van Winkle and the ghostly Dutchmen played at ninepins one memorable gusty afternoon, towered in the blue distance, like stately clouds. At one point, as we ascended a steep hill, athwart whose base a railroad, yet constructing, took its course, we came upon an Irish colony. With means at hand of building decent cabins, it was wonderful to see how clumsy, rough, and wretched, its hovels were. The best were poor protection from the weather; the worst let in the wind and rain through wide breaches in the roofs of sodden grass, and in the walls of mud; some had neither door nor window; some had nearly fallen down, and were imperfectly propped up by stakes and poles; all were ruinous and filthy. Hideously ugly old women and very buxom young ones, pigs, dogs, men, children, babies, pots, kettles, dunghills, vile refuse, rank straw, and standing water, all wallowing together in an inseparable heap, composed the furniture of every dark and dirty hut.

Between nine and ten o'clock at night, we arrived at Lebanon: which is renowned for its warm baths, and for a great hotel, well adapted, I have no doubt, to the gregarious taste of those seekers after health or pleasure who repair here, but inexpressibly comfortless to me. We were shown into an immense apartment, lighted by two dim candles, called the drawing-room: from which there was a descent by a flight of steps, to another vast desert, called the dining-room: our bed-chambers were among certain long rows of little white-washed cells, which opened from either side of a dreary passage; and were so like rooms in a prison that I half expected to be locked up when I went to bed, and listened involuntarily for the turning of the key on the outside. There need be baths somewhere in the neighbourhood, for the other washing arrangements were on as limited a scale as I ever saw, even in America: indeed, these bed-rooms were so very bare of even such common luxuries as chairs, that I should say they were not provided with enough of anything, but that I bethink myself of our having been most bountifully bitten all night.

The house is very pleasantly situated, however, and we had a good breakfast. That done, we went to visit our place of destination, which was some two miles off, and the way to which was soon indicated by a finger-post, whereon was painted, "To the Shaker Village."

As we rode along, we passed a party of Shakers, who were at work upon the road; who wore the broadest of all broad-brimmed hats; and were in all visible respects such very wooden men, that I felt about as much sympathy for them, and as much interest in them, as if they had been so many figure-heads of ships. Presently we came to the beginning of the village, and alighting at the door of a house where the Shaker manufactures are sold, and which is the head-quarters of the elders, requested permission to see the Shaker worship.

Pending the conveyance of this request to some person in author-ity, we walked into a grim room, where several grim hats were hanging on grim pegs, and the time was grimly told by a grim clock which uttered every tick with a kind of struggle, as if it broke the grim silence reluctantly, and under protest. Ranged against the wall were six or eight stiff, high-backed chairs, and they partook so strongly of the general grimness that one would much rather have sat on the floor than incurred the smallest obligation to any of them.

Presently, there stalked into this apartment, a grim old Shaker, with eyes as hard, and dull, and cold, as the great round metal buttons on his coat and waistcoat; a sort of calm goblin. Being informed of our desire, he produced a newspaper wherein the body of elders, whereof he was a member, had advertised but a few days before, that in consequence of certain unseemly interruptions which their worship had received from strangers, their chapel was closed to the public for the space of one year.

As nothing was to be urged in opposition to this reasonable arrangement, we requested leave to make some trifling purchase of Shaker goods; which was grimly conceded. We accordingly repaired to a store in the same house and on the opposite side of the passage, where the stock was presided over by something alive in a russet case, which the elder said was a woman; and which I suppose *was* a woman, though I should not have suspected it.

On the opposite side of the road was their place of worship: a cool, clean edifice of wood, with large windows and green blinds: like a spacious summer-house. As there was no getting into this place, and nothing was to be done but walk up and down, and look at it and the other buildings in the village (which were chiefly of wood, painted a dark red like English barns, and composed of many stories like English factories), I have nothing to communicate to the reader, beyond the scanty results I gleaned the while our purchases were making.

These people are called Shakers from their peculiar form of adoration, which consists of a dance, performed by the men and women of all ages, who arrange themselves for that purpose in opposite parties: the men first divesting themselves of their hats and coats, which they gravely hang against the wall before they begin; and tying a ribbon round their shirt-sleeves, as though they were going to be bled. They accompany themselves with a droning, humming noise, and dance until they are quite exhausted, alternately advancing and retiring in a preposterous sort of trot. The effect is said to be unspeakably absurd: and if I may judge from a print of this ceremony which I have in my possession; and which I am informed by those who have visited the chapel, is perfectly accurate; it must be infinitely grotesque.

They are governed by a woman, and her rule is understood to be absolute, though she has the assistance of a council of elders. She lives, it is said, in strict seclusion, in certain rooms above the chapel, and is never shown to profane eyes. If she at all resemble the lady who presided over the store, it is a great charity to keep her as close as possible, and I cannot too strongly express my perfect concurrence in this benevolent proceeding.

All the possessions and revenues of the settlement are thrown into a common stock, which is managed by the elders. As they have made converts among people who were well to do in the world, and are frugal and thrifty, it is understood that this fund prospers: the more especially as they have made large purchases of land. Nor is this at Lebanon the only Shaker settlement: there are, I think, at least, three others.

They are good farmers, and all their produce is eagerly purchased and highly esteemed. "Shaker seeds," "Shaker herbs," and "Shaker distilled waters," are commonly announced for sale in the shops of towns and cities. They are good breeders of cattle, and are kind and merciful to the brute creation. Consequently, Shaker beasts seldom fail to find a ready market.

They eat and drink together, after the Spartan model, at a great public table. There is no union of the sexes, and every Shaker, male and female, is devoted to a life of celibacy. Rumour has been busy upon this theme, but here again I must refer to the lady of the store, and say, that if many of the sister Shakers resemble her, I treat all such slander as bearing on its face the strongest marks of wild improbability. But that they take as proselytes, persons so young that they cannot know their own minds, and cannot possess much strength of resolution in this or any other respect, I can assert from my own observation of the extreme juvenility of certain youthful Shakers whom I saw at work among the party on the road.

They are said to be good drivers of bargains, but to be honest and just in their transactions, and even in horse-dealing to resist those thievish tendencies which would seem, for some undiscovered reason, to be almost inseparable from that branch of traffic. In all matters they hold their own course quietly, live in their gloomy, silent commonwealth, and show little desire to interfere with other people.

This is well enough, but nevertheless I cannot, I confess, incline towards the Shakers; view them with much favour, or extend towards them any very lenient construction. I so abhor, and from my soul detest that bad spirit, no matter by what class or sect it may be entertained, which would strip life of its healthful graces, rob youth of its innocent pleasures, pluck from maturity and age their pleasant ornaments, and make existence but a narrow path towards the grave: that odious spirit which, if it could have had full scope and sway upon the earth, must have blasted and made barren the imaginations of the greatest men, and left them, in their power of raising up enduring images before their fellow-creatures yet unborn, no better than the beasts: that, in these very broad-brimmed hats and very sombre coats—in stiff-necked, solemn-visaged piety, in short, no matter what its garb, whether it have cropped hair as in a Shaker village, or long nails as in a Hindoo temple—I recognise the worst among the enemies of Heaven and Earth, who turn the water at the marriage feasts of this poor world, not into wine, but gall. And if there must be people vowed to crush the harmless fancies and the love of innocent delights and gaieties, which are a part of human nature: as much a part of it as any other love or hope that is our common portion: let them, for me, stand openly revealed among the ribald and licentious; the very idiots know that *they* are not on the Immortal road, and will despise them, and avoid them readily.

Leaving the Shaker village with a hearty dislike of the old Shakers, and a hearty pity for the young ones: tempered by the strong probability of their running away as they grow older and wiser, which they not uncommonly do: we returned to Lebanon, and so to Hudson, by the way we had come upon the previous day. There, we took the steamboat down the North River towards New York, but stopped, some four hours' journey short of it, at West Point, where we remained that night, and all next day, and next night too.

In this beautiful place: the fairest among the fair and lovely Highlands of the North River: shut in by deep green heights and ruined forts, and looking down upon the distant town of Newburgh, along a glittering path of sunlit water, with here and there a skiff, whose white sail often bends on some new tack as sudden flaws of wind come down upon her from the gullies in the hills: hemmed in, besides, all round with memories of Washington, and events of the revolutionary war: is the Military School of America.

It could not stand on more appropriate ground, and any ground more beautiful can hardly be. The course of education is severe, but well devised, and manly. Through June, July, and August, the young men encamp upon the spacious plain whereon the college stands; and all the year their military exercises are performed there, daily. The term of study at this institution, which the State requires from all cadets, is four years; but, whether it be from the rigid nature of the discipline, or the national impatience of restraint, or both causes combined, not more than half the number who begin their studies here, ever remain to finish them.

The number of cadets being about equal to that of the members of Congress, one is sent here from every Congressional district: its member influencing the selection. Commissions in the service are distributed on the same principle. The dwellings of the various Professors are beautifully situated; and there is a most excellent hotel for strangers, though it has the two drawbacks of being a total abstinence house (wines and spirits being forbidden to the students), and of serving the public meals at rather uncomfortable hours: to wit, breakfast at seven, dinner at one, and supper at sunset.

The beauty and freshness of this calm retreat, in the very dawn and greenness of summer—it was then the beginning of June—were exquisite indeed. Leaving it upon the sixth, and returning to New York, to embark for England on the succeeding day, I was glad to think that among the last memorable beauties which had glided past us, and softened in the bright perspective, were those whose pictures, traced by no common hand, are fresh in most men's minds; not easily to grow old, or fade beneath the dust of Time: the Kaatskill Mountains, Sleepy Hollow, and the Tappaan Zee.

## CHAPTER XVI

### THE PASSAGE HOME

I NEVER had so much interest before, and very likely I shall never have so much interest again, in the state of the wind, as on the long looked-for morning of Tuesday the Seventh of June. Some nautical authority had told me a day or two previous, "anything with west in it, will do;" so when I darted out of bed at daylight, and throwing up the window, was saluted by a lively breeze from the north-west which had sprung up in the night, it came upon me so freshly, rustling with so many happy associations, that I conceived upon the spot a special regard for all airs blowing from that quarter of the compass, which I shall cherish, I dare say, until my own wind has breathed its last frail puff, and withdrawn itself for ever from the mortal calendar.

The pilot had not been slow to take advantage of this favourable weather, and the ship which yesterday had been in such a crowded dock that she might have retired from trade for good and all, for any chance she seemed to have of going to sea, was now full sixteen miles away. A gallant sight she was, when we, fast gaining on her in a steam-boat, saw her in the distance riding at anchor: her tall masts pointing up in graceful lines against the sky, and every rope and spar expressed in delicate and thread-like outline: gallant, too, when, we being all aboard, the anchor came up to the sturdy chorus " Cheerily men, oh cheerily !" and she followed proudly in the towing steamboat's wake: but bravest and most gallant of all, when the tow-rope being cast adrift, the canvas fluttered from her masts, and spreading her white wings she soared away upon her free and solitary course.

In the after cabin we were only fifteen passengers in all, and the greater part were from Canada, where some of us had known each other. The night was rough and squally, so were the next two days, but they flew by quickly, and we were soon as cheerful and snug a party, with an honest, manly-hearted captain at our head, as ever came to the resolution of being mutually agreeable, on land or water.

We breakfasted at eight, lunched at twelve, dined at three, and took our tea at half-past seven. We had abundance of amusements, and dinner was not the least among them : firstly, for its own sake; secondly, because of its extraordinary length: its duration, inclusive of all the long pauses between the courses, being seldom less than two hours and a half; which was a subject of never-failing entertainment. By way of beguiling the tediousness of these banquets, a select association was formed at the lower end of the table, below the mast, to whose distinguished president modesty forbids me to make any further allusion, which, being a very hilarious and jovial institution, was (prejudice apart) in high favour with the rest of the community, and particularly with a black steward, who lived for three weeks in a broad grin, at the marvellous humour of these incorporated worthies.

Then, we had chess for those who played it, whist, cribbage, books, backgammon, and shovelboard. In all weathers, fair or foul, calm or windy, we were every one on deck, walking up and down in pairs, lying in the boats, leaning over the side, or chatting in a lazy group together. We had no lack of music, for one played the accordion, another the violin, and another (who usually began at six o'clock A.M.) the keybugle: the combined effect of which instruments, when they all played different tunes in different parts of the ship, at the same time, and within hearing of each other, as they sometimes did (everybody being intensely satisfied with his own performance), was sublimely hideous.

When all of these means of entertainment failed, a sail would heave in sight: looming, perhaps, the very spirit of a ship, in the misty distance, or passing us so close that through our glasses we could see the people on her decks, and easily make out her name, and whither she was bound. For hours together we could watch the dolphins and porpoises as they rolled and leaped and dived around the vessel; or those small creatures ever on the wing, the Mother Carey's chickens, which had borne us company from New York bay, and for a whole fortnight fluttered about the vessel's stern. For some days we had a dead calm, or very light winds, during which the crew amused themselves with fishing, and hooked an unlucky dolphin, who expired, in all his rainbow colours, on the deck: an event of such importance in our barren calendar, that afterwards we dated from the dolphin, and made the day on which he died, an era.

Besides all this, when we were five or six days out, there began to be much talk of icebergs, of which wandering islands an unusual number had been seen by the vessels that had come into New York a day or two before we left that port, and of whose dangerous neighbourhood we were warned by the sudden coldness of the weather, and the sinking of the mercury in the barometer. While these tokens lasted, a double look-out was kept, and many dismal tales were whispered after dark, of ships that had struck upon the ice and gone down in the night; but the wind obliging us to hold a southward course, we saw none of them, and the weather soon grew bright and warm again.

The observation every day at noon, and the subsequent working of the vessel's course, was, as may be supposed, a feature in our lives of paramount importance; nor were there wanting (as there never are) sagacious doubters of the captain's calculations, who, so soon as his back was turned, would, in the absence of compasses, measure the chart with bits of string, and ends of pocket-handkerchiefs, and points of snuffers, and clearly prove him to be wrong by an odd thousand miles or so. It was very edifying to see these unbelievers shake their heads and frown, and hear them hold forth strongly upon navigation: not that they knew anything about it, but that they always mistrusted the captain in calm weather, or when the wind was adverse. Indeed, the mercury itself is not so variable as this class of passengers, whom you will see, when the ship is going nobly through the water, quite pale with admiration, swearing that the captain beats all captains ever known, and even hinting at subscriptions for a piece of plate; and who, next morning, when the breeze has lulled, and all the sails hang useless in the idle air, shake their despondent heads again, and say, with screwed-up lips, they hope that captain is a sailor—but they shrewdly doubt him.

It even became an occupation in the calm, to wonder when the wind *would* spring up in the favourable quarter, where, it was clearly shown by all the rules and precedents, it ought to have sprung up long ago. The first mate, who whistled for it zealously, was much respected for his perseverance, and was regarded even by the unbelievers as a first-rate sailor. Many gloomy looks would be cast upward through the cabin skylights at the flapping sails while dinner was in progress; and some, growing bold in ruefulness, predicted that we should land about the middle of July. There are always on board ship, a Sanguine One, and a Despondent One. The latter character carried it hollow at his period of the voyage, and triumphed over the Sanguine One at every meal, by inquiring where he supposed the Great Western (which left New York a week after us) was *now:* and where he supposed the 'Cunard' steam-packet was *now:* and what he thought of sailing vessels, as compared with steamships *now:* and so beset his life with pestilent attacks of that kind, that he too was obliged to affect despondency, for very peace and quietude.

These were additions to the list of entertaining incidents, but there was still another source of interest. We carried in the steerage nearly a hundred passengers: a little world of poverty: and as we came to know individuals among them by sight, from looking down upon the deck where they took the air in the daytime, and cooked their food, and very often ate it too, we became curious to know their histories, and with what expectations they had gone out to America, and on what errands they were going home, and what their circumstances were. The information we got on these heads from the carpenter, who had charge of these people, was often of the strangest kind. Some of them had been in America but three days, some but three months, and some had gone out in the last voyage of that very ship in which they were now returning home. Others had sold their clothes to raise the passage money, and had hardly rags to cover them; others had no food, and lived upon the charity of the rest: and one man, it was discovered nearly at the end of the voyage, not before—for he kept his secret close, and did not court compassion—had had no sustenance whatever but the bones and scraps of fat he took from the plates used in the after-cabin dinner, when they were put out to be washed.

The whole system of shipping and conveying these unfortunate persons, is one that stands in need of thorough revision. If any class deserve to be protected and assisted by the Government, it is that class who are banished from their native land in search of the bare means of subsistence. All that could be done for these poor people by the great compassion and humanity of the captain and officers was done, but they require much more. The law is bound, at least upon the English side, to see that too many of them are not put on board one ship: and that their accommodations are decent: not demoralising and profligate. It is bound, too, in common humanity, to declare that no man shall be taken on board without his stock of provisions being previously inspected by some proper officer, and pronounced moderately sufficient for his support upon the voyage. It is bound to provide, or to require that there be provided, a medical attendant; whereas in these ships there are none, though sickness of adults, and deaths of children, on the passage, are matters of the very commonest occurrence. Above all it is the duty of any Government, be it monarchy or republic, to interpose and put an end to that system by which a firm of traders in emigrants purchase of the owners the whole 'tween-decks of a ship, and send on board as many wretched people as they can lay hold of, on any terms they can get, without the smallest reference to the conveniences of the steerage, the number of berths, the slightest separation of the sexes, or anything but their own immediate profit. Nor is even this the worst of the vicious system: for, certain crimping agents of these houses, who have a percentage on all the passengers they inveigle, are constantly travelling about those districts where poverty and discontent are rife, and tempting the credulous into more misery, by holding out monstrous inducements to emigration which can never be realised.

The history of every family we had on board was pretty much the same. After hoarding up, and borrowing, and begging, and selling everything to pay the passage, they had gone out to New York, expecting to find its streets paved with gold; and had found them paved with very hard and very real stones. Enterprise was dull; labourers were not wanted; jobs of work were to be got, but the payment was not. They were coming back, even poorer than they went. One of them was carrying an open letter from a young English artisan, who had been in New York a fortnight, to a friend near Manchester, whom he strongly urged to follow him. One of the officers brought it to me as a curiosity. "This is the country, Jem," said the writer. "I like America. There is no despotism here; that's the great thing. Employment of all sorts is going a-begging, and wages are capital. You have only to choose a trade, Jem, and be it. I haven't made choice of one yet, but I shall soon. *At present I haven't quite made up my mind whether to be a carpenter—or a tailor.*"

There was yet another kind of passenger, and but one more, who, in the calm and the light winds, was a constant theme of conversation and observation among us. This was an English sailor, a smart, thorough-built, English man-of-war's-man from his hat to his shoes, who was serving in the American navy, and having got leave of absence was on his way home to see his friends. When he presented himself to take and pay for his passage, it had been suggested to him that being an able seaman he might as well work it and save the money, but this piece of advice he very indignantly rejected: saying, "He'd be damned but for once he'd go aboard ship, as a gentleman." Accordingly, they took his money, but he no sooner came aboard, than he stowed his kit in the forecastle, arranged to mess with the crew, and the very first time the hands were turned up, went aloft like a cat, before anybody. And all through the passage there he was, first at the braces, outermost on the yards, perpetually lending a hand everywhere, but always with a sober dignity in his manner, and a sober grin on his face, which plainly said, "I do it as a gentleman. For my own pleasure, mind you!"

At length and at last, the promised wind came up in right good earnest, and away we went before it, with very stitch of canvas set, slashing through the water nobly. There was a grandeur in the motion of the splendid ship, as overshadowed by her mass of sails, she rode at a furious pace upon the waves, which filled one with an indescribable sense of pride and exultation. As she plunged into a foaming valley, how I loved to see the green waves, bordered deep with white, come rushing on astern, to buoy her upward at their pleasure, and curl about her as she stooped again, but always own her for their haughty mistress still! On, on we flew, with changing lights upon the water, being now in the blessed region of fleecy skies; a bright sun lighting us by day, and a bright moon by night; the vane pointing directly homeward, alike the truthful index to the favouring wind and to our cheerful hearts; until at sunrise, one fair Monday morning—the twenty-seventh of June, I shall not easily forget the day—there lay before us, old Cape Clear, God bless it, showing, in the mist of early morning, like a cloud: the brightest and most welcome cloud, to us, that ever hid the face of Heaven's fallen sister—Home.

Dim speck as it was in the wide prospect, it made the sunrise a more cheerful sight, and gave to it that sort of human interest which it seems to want at sea. There, as elsewhere, the return of day is inseparable from some sense of renewed hope and gladness; but the light shining on the dreary waste of water, and showing it in all its vast extent of loneliness, presents a solemn spectacle, which even night, veiling it in darkness and uncertainty, does not surpass. The rising of the moon is more in keeping with the solitary ocean; and has an air of melancholy grandeur, which in its soft and gentle influence, seems to comfort while it saddens. I recollect when I was a very young child having a fancy that the reflection of the moon in water was a path to Heaven, trodden by the spirits of good people on their way to God; and this old feeling often came over me again, when I watched it on a tranquil night at sea.

The wind was very light on this same Monday morning, but it was still in the right quarter, and so, by slow degrees, we left Cape Clear behind, and sailed along within sight of the coast of Ireland. And how merry we all were, and how loyal to the George Washington, and how full of mutual congratulations, and how venturesome in predicting the exact hour at which we should arrive at Liverpool, may be easily imagined and readily understood. Also, how heartily we drank the captain's health that day at dinner; and how restless we became about packing up: and how two or three of the most sanguine spirits rejected the idea of going to bed at all that night as something it was not worth while to do, so near the shore, but went nevertheless, and slept soundly; and how to be so near our journey's end, was like a pleasant dream, from which we feared to wake.

The friendly breeze freshened again next day, and on we went once more before it gallantly: descrying now and then an English ship going homeward under shortened sail, while we, with every inch of canvas crowded on, dashed gaily past, and left her far behind. Towards evening, the weather turned hazy, with a drizzling rain; and soon became so thick, that we sailed, as it were, in a cloud. Still we swept onward like a phantom ship, and many an eager eye glanced up to where the Look-out on the mast kept watch for Holyhead.

At length his long-expected cry was heard, and at the same moment there shone out from the haze and mist ahead, a gleaming light, which presently was gone, and soon returned, and soon was gone again. Whenever it came back, the eyes of all on board, brightened and sparkled like itself: and there we all stood, watching this revolving light upon the rock at Holyhead, and praising it for its brightness and its friendly warning, and lauding it, in short, above all other signal lights that ever were displayed, until it once more glimmered faintly in the distance, far behind us.

Then, it was time to fire a gun, for a pilot; and almost before its smoke had cleared away, a little boat with a light at her mast-head came bearing down upon us, through the darkness, swiftly. And presently, our sails being backed, she ran alongside; and the hoarse pilot, wrapped and muffled in pea-coats and shawls to the very bridge of his weather-ploughed-up nose, stood bodily among us on the deck. And I think if that pilot had wanted to borrow fifty pounds for an indefinite period on no security, we should have engaged to lend it to him, among us, before his boat had dropped astern, or (which is the same thing) before every scrap of news in the paper he brought with him had become the common property of all on board.

We turned in pretty late that night, and turned out pretty early next morning. By six o'clock we clustered on the deck, prepared to go ashore; and looked upon the spires, and roofs, and smoke, of Liverpool. By eight we all sat down in one of its Hotels, to eat and drink together for the last time. And by nine we had shaken hands all round, and broken up our social company for ever.

The country, by the railroad, seemed, as we rattled through it, like a luxuriant garden. The beauty of the fields (so small they looked!), the hedge-rows, and the trees; the pretty cottages, the beds

of flowers, the old churchyards, the antique houses, and every well-
known object; the exquisite delights of that one journey, crowding
in the short compass of a summer's day, the joy of many years, with
the winding up with Home and all that makes it dear; no tongue can
tell, or pen of mine describe.

## CHAPTER XVII

### SLAVERY

THE upholders of slavery in America—of the atrocities of which
system, I shall not write one word for which I have not had ample
proof and warrant—may be divided into three great classes.

The first, are those more moderate and rational owners of human
cattle, who have come into the possession of them as so many coins
in their trading capital, but who admit the frightful nature of the
Institution in the abstract, and perceive the dangers to society with
which it is fraught: dangers which however distant they may be, or
howsoever tardy in their coming on, are as certain to fall upon its
guilty head, as is the Day of Judgment.

The second, consists of all those owners, breeders, users, buyers
and sellers of slaves, who will, until the bloody chapter has a bloody
end, own, breed, use, buy, and sell them at all hazards; who dogged,
deny the horrors of the system in the teeth of such a mass of evidence
as never was brought to bear on any other subject, and to which the
experience of every day contributes its immense amount; who would
at this or any other moment, gladly involve America in a war, civil
or foreign, provided that it had for its sole end and object the assertion of their right to perpetuate slavery, and to whip and work and
torture slaves, unquestioned by any human authority, and unas-
sailed by any human power; who, when they speak of Freedom, mean
the Freedom to oppress their kind, and to be savage, merciless, and
cruel; and of whom every man on his own ground, in republican
America, is a more exacting, and a sterner, and a less responsible
despot than the Caliph Haroun Alraschid in his angry robe of scarlet.

The third, and not the least numerous or influential, is composed
of all that delicate gentility which cannot bear a superior, and cannot
brook an equal; of that class whose Republicanism means, "I will not
tolerate a man above me: and of those below, none must approach
too near;" whose pride, in a land where voluntary servitude is shunned
as a disgrace, must be ministered to by slaves; and whose inalienable
rights can only have their growth in negro wrongs.

It has been sometimes urged that, in the unavailing efforts which
have been made to advance the cause of Human Freedom in the
republic of America (strange cause for history to treat of!), sufficient

regard has not been had to the existence of the first class of persons;
and it has been contended that they are hardly used, in being confounded with the second. This is, no doubt, the case; noble instances
of pecuniary and personal sacrifice have already had their growth
among them; and it is much to be regretted that the gulf between
them and the advocates of emancipation should have been widened
and deepened by any means: the rather, as there are, beyond dispute,
among these slave-owners, many kind masters who are tender in the
exercise of their unnatural power. Still, it is to be feared that this
injustice is inseparable from the state of things with which humanity
and truth are called upon to deal. Slavery is not a whit the more
endurable because some hearts are to be found which can partially
resist its hardening influences; nor can the indignant tide of honest
wrath stand still, because in its onward course it overwhelms a few
who are comparatively innocent, among a host of guilty.

The ground most commonly taken by these better men among the
advocates of slavery, is this: "It is a bad system; and for myself I
would willingly get rid of it, if I could; most willingly. But it is not
so bad, as you in England take it to be. You are deceived by the
representations of the emancipationists. The greater part of my slaves
are much attached to me. You will say that I do not allow them to
be severely treated; but I will put it to you whether you believe that
it can be a general practice to treat them inhumanly, when it would
impair their value, and would be obviously against the interests of
their masters."

Is it the interest of any man to steal, to game, to waste his health
and mental faculties by drunkenness, to lie, forswear hinself, indulge
hatred, seek desperate revenge, or do murder? No. All these are roads
to ruin. And why, then, do men tread them? Because such inclinations
are among the vicious qualities of mankind. Blot out, ye friends of
slavery, from the catalogue of human passions, brutal lust, cruelty,
and the abuse of irresponsible power (of all earthly temptations the
most difficult to be resisted), and when ye have done so, and not
before, we will inquire whether it be the interest of a master to lash
and maim the slaves, over whose lives and limbs he has an absolute
control!

But again: this class, together with that last one I have named, the
miserable aristocracy spawned of a false republic, lift up their voices
and exclaim "Public opinion is all-sufficient to prevent such cruelty
as you denounce." Public opinion! Why, public opinion in the slave
States *is* slavery, is it not? Public opinion, in the slave States, has
delivered the slaves over, to the gentle mercies of their masters.
Public opinion has made the laws, and denied the slaves legislative
protection. Public opinion has knotted the lash, heated the brand-
ing-iron, loaded the rifle, and shielded the murderer. Public opinion
threatens the abolitionist with death, if he venture to the South; and
drags him with a rope about his middle, in broad unblushing noon,
through the first city in the East. Public opinion has, within a few

years, burned a slave alive at a slow fire in the city of St. Louis; and public opinion has to this day maintained upon the bench that estimable Judge who charged the Jury, impanelled there to try his murderers, that their most horrid deed was an act of public opinion, and being so, must not be punished by the laws the public sentiment had made. Public opinion hailed this doctrine with a howl of wild applause, and set the prisoners free, to walk the city, men of mark, and influence, and station, as they had been before.

Public opinion! what class of men have an immense preponderance over the rest of the community, in their power of representing public opinion in the legislature? the slave-owners. They send from their twelve States one hundred members, while the fourteen free States, with a free population nearly double, return but a hundred and forty-two. Before whom do the presidential candidates bow down the most humbly, on whom do they fawn the most fondly, and for whose tastes do they cater the most assiduously in their servile protestations? The slave-owners always.

Public opinion! hear the public opinion of the free South, as expressed by its own members in the House of Representatives at Washington. "I have a great respect for the chair," quoth North Carolina, "I have a great respect for the chair as an officer of the house, and a great respect for him personally; nothing but that respect prevents me from rushing to the table and tearing that petition which has just been presented for the abolition of slavery in the district of Columbia, to pieces."—"I warn the abolitionists," says South Carolina, "ignorant, infuriated barbarians as they are, that if chance shall throw any of them into our hands, he may expect a felon's death."—"Let an abolitionist come within the borders of South Carolina," cries a third; mild Carolina's colleague; "and if we can catch him, we will try him, and notwithstanding the interference of all the governments on earth, including the Federal government, we will HANG him."

Public opinion has made this law.—It has declared that in Washington, in that city which takes its name from the father of American liberty, any justice of the peace may bind with fetters any negro passing down the street and thrust him into jail; no offence on the black man's part is necessary. The justice says, "I choose to think this man a runaway:" and locks him up. Public opinion impowers the man of law when this is done, to advertise the negro in the newspapers, warning his owner to come and claim him, or he will be sold to pay the jail fees. But supposing he is a free black, and has no owner, it may naturally be presumed that he is set at liberty. No: HE IS SOLD TO RECOMPENSE HIS JAILER. This has been done again, and again, and again. He has no means of proving his freedom; has no adviser, messenger, or assistance of any sort or kind; no investigation into his case is made, or inquiry instituted. He, a free man, who may have served for years, and bought his liberty, is thrown into jail on no process, for no crime, and on no pretence of crime: and is sold to

pay the jail fees. This seems incredible, even of America, but it is the
law.

Public opinion is deferred to, in such cases as the following: which
is headed in the newspapers:—

### "*Interesting Law-Case.*

"An interesting case is now on trial in the Supreme Court, arising
out of the following facts. A gentleman residing in Maryland had
allowed an aged pair of his slaves, substantial though not legal
freedom for several years. While thus living, a daughter was born to
them, who grew up in the same liberty, until she married a free negro,
and went with him to reside in Pennsylvania. They had several children, and lived unmolested until the original owner died, when his
heir attempted to regain them; but the magistrate before whom they
were brought, decided that he had no jurisdiction in the case. *The
owner seized the woman and her children in the night, and carried them
to Maryland.*"

"Cash for negroes," "cash for negroes," "cash for negroes," is the
heading of advertisements in great capitals down the long columns
of the crowded journals. Woodcuts of a runaway negro with manacled
hands, crouching beneath a bluff pursuer in top boots, who, having
caught him, grasps him by the throat, agreeably diversify the pleasant
text. The leading article protests against "that abominable and
hellish doctrine of abolition, which is repugnant alike to every law
of God and nature." The delicate mamma, who smiles her acquies-
cence in this sprightly writing as she reads the paper in her cool
piazza, quiets her youngest child who clings about her skirts, by
promising the boy "a whip to beat the little niggers with."—But the
negroes, little and big, are protected by public opinion.

Let us try this public opinion by another test, which is important
in three points of view: first, as showing how desperately timid of the
public opinion slave-owners are, in their delicate descriptions of
fugitive slaves in widely circulated newspapers; secondly, as showing
how perfectly contented the slaves are, and how very seldom they
run away; thirdly, as exhibiting their entire freedom from scar,
or blemish, or any mark of cruel infliction, as their pictures are
drawn, not by lying abolitionists, but by their own truthful
masters.

The following are a few specimens of the advertisements in the
public papers. It is only four years since the oldest among them
appeared; and others of the same nature continue to be published
every day, in shoals.

"Ran away, Negress Caroline. Had on a collar with one prong
turned down."

"Ran away, a black woman, Betsy. Had an iron bar on her right
leg."

"Ran away, the negro Manuel. Much marked with irons."

"Ran away, the negress Fanny. Had on an iron band about her neck."

"Ran away, a negro boy about twelve years old. Had round his neck a chain dog-collar with 'De Lampert' engraved on it."

"Ran away, the negro Hown. Has a ring of iron on his left foot. Also, Grise, *his wife*, having a ring and chain on the left leg."

"Ran away, a negro boy named James. Said boy was ironed when he left me."

"Committed to jail, a man who calls his name John. He has a clog of iron on his right foot which will weigh four or five pounds."

"Detained at the police jail, the negro wench, Myra. Has several marks of LASHING, and has irons on her feet."

"Ran away, a negro woman and two children. A few days before she went off, I burnt her with a hot iron, on the left side of her face. I tried to make the letter M."

"Ran away, a negro man named Henry; his left eye out, some scars from a dirk on and under his left arm, and much scarred with the whip."

"One hundred dollars reward, for a negro fellow, Pompey, 40 years old. He is branded on the left jaw."

"Committed to jail, a negro man. Has no toes on the left foot."

"Ran away, a negro woman named Rachel. Has lost all her toes except the large one."

"Ran away, Sam. He was shot a short time since through the hand, and has several shots in his left arm and side."

"Ran away, my negro man Dennis. Said negro has been shot in the left arm between the shoulder and elbow, which has paralysed the left hand."

"Ran away, my negro man named Simon. He has been shot badly, in his back and right arm."

"Ran away, a negro named Arthur. Has a considerable scar across his breast and each arm, made by a knife; loves to talk much of the goodness of God."

"Twenty-five dollars reward for my man Isaac. He has a scar on his forehead, caused by a blow; and one on his back, made by a shot from a pistol."

"Ran away, a negro girl called Mary. Has a small scar over her eye, a good many teeth missing, the letter A is branded on her cheek and forehead."

"Ran away, negro Ben. Has a scar on his right hand; his thumb and forefinger being injured by being shot last fall. A part of the bone came out. He has also one or two large scars on his back and hips."

"Detained at the jail, a Mulatto, named Tom. Has a scar on the right cheek, and appears to have been burned with powder on the face."

"Ran away, a negro man named Ned. Three of his fingers are drawn into the palm of his hand by a cut. Has a scar on the back of his neck, nearly half round, done by a knife."

"Was committed to jail, a negro man. Says his name is Josiah. His back very much scarred by the whip; and branded on the thigh and hips in three or four places, thus (JM). The rim of his right ear has been bit or cut off."

"Fifty dollars reward, for my fellow Edward. He has a scar on the corner of his mouth, two cuts on and under his arm, and the letter E on his arm."

"Ran away, negro boy Ellie. Has a scar on one of his arms from the bite of a dog."

"Ran away, from the plantation of James Surgette, the following negroes: Randal, has one ear cropped; Bob, has lost one eye; Kentucky Tom, has one jaw broken."

"Ran away, Anthony. One of his ears cut off, and his left hand cut with an axe."

"Fifty dollars reward for the negro Jim Blake. Has a piece cut out of each ear, and the middle finger of the left hand cut off to the second joint."

"Ran away, a negro woman named Maria. Has a scar on one side of her cheek, by a cut. Some scars on her back."

"Ran away, the Mulatto wench Mary. Has a cut on the left arm, a scar on the left shoulder, and two upper teeth missing."

I should say, perhaps, in explanation of this latter piece of description, that among the other blessings which public opinion secures to the negroes, is the common practice of violently punching out their teeth. To make them wear iron collars by day and night, and to worry them with dogs, are practices almost too ordinary to deserve mention.

"Ran away, my man Fountain. Has holes in his ears, a scar on the right side of his forehead, has been shot in the hind parts of his legs, and is marked on the back with the whip."

"Two hundred and fifty dollars reward for my negro man Jim. He is much marked with shot in his right thigh. The shot entered on the outside, halfway between the hip and knee joints."

"Brought to jail, John. Left ear cropt."

"Taken up, a negro man. Is very much scarred about the face and body, and has the left ear bit off."

"Ran away, a black girl, named Mary. Has a scar on her cheek, and the end of one of her toes cut off."

"Ran away, my Mulatto woman, Judy. She has had her right arm broke."

"Ran away, my negro man, Levi. His left hand has been burnt, and I think the end of his forefinger is off."

"Ran away, a negro man, NAMED WASHINGTON. Has lost a part of his middle finger, and the end of his little finger."

"Twenty-five dollars reward for my man John. The tip of his nose is bit off."

"Twenty-five dollars reward for the negro slave, Sally. Walks *as though* crippled in the back."

"Ran away, Joe Dennis. Has a small notch in one of his ears."

"Ran away, negro boy, Jack. Has a small crop out of his left ear."

"Ran away, a negro man, named Ivory. Has a small piece cut out of the top of each ear."

While upon the subject of ears, I may observe that a distinguished abolitionist in New York once received a negro's ear, which had been cut off close to the head, in a general post letter. It was forwarded by the free and independent gentleman who had caused it to be amputated, with a polite request that he would place the specimen in his "collection."

I could enlarge this catalogue with broken arms, and broken legs, and gashed flesh, and missing teeth, and lacerated backs, and bites of dogs, and brands of red-hot irons innumerable: but as my readers will be sufficiently sickened and repelled already, I will turn to another branch of the subject.

These advertisements, of which a similar collection might be made for every year, and month, and week, and day; and which are coolly read in families as things of course, and as a part of the current news and small-talk; will serve to show how very much the slaves profit by public opinion, and how tender it is in their behalf. But it may be worth while to inquire how the slave-owners, and the class of society to which great numbers of them belong, defer to public opinion in their conduct, not to their slaves but to each other; how they are accustomed to restrain their passions; what their bearing is among themselves; whether they are fierce or gentle; whether their social customs be brutal, sanguinary, and violent, or bear the impress of civilisation and refinement.

That we may have no partial evidence from abolitionists in this inquiry, either, I will once more turn to their own newspapers, and I will confine myself, this time, to a selection from paragraphs which appeared from day to day, during my visit to America, and which refer to occurrences happening while I was there. The italics in these extracts, as in the foregoing, are my own.

These cases did not ALL occur, it will be seen, in territory actually belonging to legalised Slave States, though most, and those the very worst among them, did, as their counterparts constantly do; but the position of the scenes of action in reference to places immediately at hand, where slavery is the law; and the strong resemblance between that class of outrages and the rest; lead to the just presumption that the character of the parties concerned was formed in slave districts, and brutalised by slave customs.

### *"Horrible Tragedy.*

"By a slip from *The Southport Telegraph*, Wisconsin, we learn that the Hon. Charles C. P. Arndt, Member of the Council for Brown county, was shot dead *on the floor of the Council chamber*, by James R. Vinyard, Member from Grant county. *The affair* grew out of a nomination for Sheriff of Grant county. Mr. E. S. Baker was nominated and supported by Mr. Arndt. This nomination was opposed by Vinyard, who wanted the appointment to vest in his own brother. In the course of debate, the deceased made some statements which Vinyard pronounced false, and made use of violent and insulting language, dealing largely in personalities, to which Mr. A. made no reply. After the adjournment, Mr. A. stepped up to Vinyard, and requested him to retract, which he refused to do, repeating the offensive words. Mr. Arndt then made a blow at Vinyard, who stepped back a pace, drew a pistol, and shot him dead.

"The issue appears to have been provoked on the part of Vinyard, who was determined at all hazards to defeat the appointment of Baker, and who, himself defeated, turned his ire and revenge upon the unfortunate Arndt."

### "The Wisconsin Tragedy.

"Public indignation runs high in the territory of Wisconsin, in relation to the murder of C. C. P. Arndt, in the Legislative Hall of the Territory. Meetings have been held in different counties of Wisconsin, denouncing *the practice of secretly bearing arms in the Legislative chambers of the country*. We have seen the account of the expulsion of James R. Vinyard, the perpetrator of the bloody deed, and are amazed to hear, that, after this expulsion by those who saw Vinyard kill Mr. Arndt in the presence of his aged father, who was on a visit to see his son, little dreaming that he was to witness his murder, *Judge Dunn has discharged Vinyard on bail*. The Miner's Free Press speaks *in terms of merited rebuke* at the outrage upon the feelings of the people of Wisconsin. Vinyard was within arm's length of Mr. Arndt, when he took such deadly aim at him, that he never spoke. Vinyard might at pleasure, being so near, have only wounded him, but he chose to kill him."

### "Murder.

"By a letter in a St. Louis paper of the 14th, we notice a terrible outrage at Burlington, Iowa. A Mr. Bridgman having had difficulty with a citizen of the place, Mr. Ross; a brother-in-law of the latter provided himself with one of Colt's revolving pistols, met Mr. B. in the street, *and discharged the contents of five of the barrels at him: each shot taking effect*. Mr. B., though horribly wounded, and dying, returned the fire, and killed Ross on the spot."

### "Terrible Death of Robert Potter.

"From the 'Caddo Gazette,' of the 12th inst., we learn the frightful death of Colonel Robert Potter. . . . He was beset in his house by an enemy, named Rose. He sprang from his couch, seized his gun, and, in his night-clothes, rushed from the house. For about two hundred yards his speed seemed to defy his pursuers; but, getting entangled in a thicket, he was captured. Rose told him *that he intended to act a generous part,* and give him a chance for his life. He then told Potter he might run, and he should not be interrupted till he reached a certain distance. Potter started at the word of command, and before a gun was fired he had reached the lake. His first impulse was to jump in the water and dive for it, which he did. Rose was close behind him, and formed his men on the bank ready to shoot him as he rose, In a few seconds he came up to breathe; and scarce had his head reached the surface of the water when it was completely riddled with the shot of their guns, and he sunk, to rise no more!''

### "Murder in Arkansas.

"We understand *that a severe rencontre came off* a few days since in the Seneca Nation, between Mr. Loose, the sub-agent of the mixed band of the Senecas, Quapaw, and Shawnees, and Mr. James Gillespie, of the mercantile firm of Thomas G. Allison and Co., of Maysville, Benton, County Ark, in which the latter was slain with a bowie-knife. Some difficulty had for some time existed between the parties. It is said that Major Gillespie brought on the attack with a cane. A severe conflict ensued, during which two pistols were fired by Gillespie and one by Loose. Loose then stabbed Gillespie with one of those never-failing weapons, a bowie-knife. The death of Major G. is much regretted, as he was a liberal-minded and energetic man. Since the above was in type, we have learned that Major Allison has stated to some of our citizens in town that Mr. Loose gave the first blow. We forbear to give any particulars, as *the matter will be the subject of judicial investigation.*"

### "Foul Deed.

"The steamer Thames, just from Missouri river, brought us a hand-bill, offering a reward of 500 dollars, for the person who assassinated Lilburn W. Baggs, late Governor of this State, at Independence, on the night of the 6th inst. Governor Baggs, it is stated in a written memorandum, was not dead, but mortally wounded.

"Since the above was written, we received a note from the clerk of the Thames, giving the following particulars. Gov. Baggs was shot by some villain on Friday, 6th inst., in the evening, while sitting in a room in his own house in Independence. His son, a boy, hearing a report, ran into the room, and found the Governor sitting in his chair, with his jaw fallen down, and his head leaning back; on discovering the injury done to his father, he gave the alarm. Foot tracks were found in the garden below the window, and a pistol picked up supposed to have been overloaded, and thrown from the hand of the scoundrel who fired it. Three buck shots of a heavy load, took effect;

one going through his mouth, one into the brain, and another probably in or near the brain; all going into the back part of the neck and head. The Governor was still alive on the morning of the 7th; but no hopes for his recovery by his friends, and but slight hopes from his physicians.

"A man was suspected, and the Sheriff most probably has possession of him by this time.

"The pistol was one of a pair stolen some days previous from a baker in Independence, and the legal authorities have the description of the other."

### "Rencontre.

"An unfortunate *affair* took place on Friday evening in Chatres Street, in which one of our most respectable citizens received a dangerous wound, from a poignard, in the abdomen. From the Bee (New Orleans) of yesterday, we learn the following particulars. It appears that an article was published in the French side of the paper on Monday last, containing some strictures on the Artillery Battalion for firing their guns on Sunday morning, in answer to those from the Ontario and Woodbury, and thereby much alarm was caused to the families of those persons who were out all night preserving the peace of the city. Major C. Gally, Commander of the battalion, resenting this, called at the office and demanded the author's name; that of Mr. P. Arpin was given to him, who was absent at the time. Some angry words then passed with one of the proprietors, and a challenge followed; the friends of both parties tried to arrange the affair, but failed to do so. On Friday evening, about seven o'clock, Major Gally met Mr. P. Arpin in Chatres Street, and accosted him. 'Are you Mr. Arpin?'

" 'Yes, sir,'

" 'Then I have to tell you that you are a——' (applying an appropriate epithet).

" 'I shall remind you of your words, sir.'

" 'But I have said I would break my cane on your shoulders.'

" 'I know it, but I have not yet received the blow.'

"At these words, Major Gally, having a cane in his hands, struck Mr. Arpin across the face, and the latter drew a poignard from his pocket and stabbed Major Gally in the abdomen.

"Fears are entertained that the wound will be mortal. *We understand that Mr. Arpin has given security for his appearance at the Criminal Court to answer the charge.*"

### "Affray in Mississippi.

"On the 27th ult., in an affray near Carthage, Leake county, Mississippi, between James Cottingham and John Wilburn, the latter was shot by the former, and so horribly wounded, that there was no hope of his recovery. On the 2nd instant, there was an affray at Carthage between A. C. Sharkey and George Goff, in which the latter was shot, and thought mortally wounded. Sharkey delivered himself up to the authorities, *but changed his mind and escaped!''*

### *"Personal Encounter.*

"An encounter took place in Sparta, a few days since, between the barkeeper of an hotel, and a man named Bury. It appears that Bury had become somewhat noisy, *and that the barkeeper, determined to preserve order, had threatened to shoot Bury,* whereupon Bury drew a pistol and shot the barkeeper down. He was not dead at the last accounts, but slight hopes were entertained of his recovery."

### *"Duel.*

"The clerk of the steamboat *Tribune* informs us that another duel was fought on Tuesday last, by Mr. Robbins, a bank officer in Vicksburg, and Mr. Fall, the editor of the Vicksburg Sentinel. According to the arrangement, the parties had six pistols each, which, after the word 'Fire!' *they were to discharge as fast as they pleased.* Fall fired two pistols without effect. Mr. Robbins' first shot took effect in Fall's thigh, who fell, and was unable to continue the combat."

### *"Affray in Clarke County.*

"An *unfortunate affray* occurred in Clarke County (Mo.), near Waterloo, on Tuesday the 19th ult., which originated in settling the partnership concerns of Messrs. M'Kane and M'Allister, who had been engaged in the business of distilling, and resulted in the death of the latter, who was shot down by Mr. M'Kane, because of his attempting to take possession of seven barrels of whiskey, the property of M'Kane, which had been knocked off to M'Allister at a sheriff's sale at one dollar per barrel. M'Kane immediately fled *and at the latest dates had not been taken.*

"*This unfortunate affray* caused considerable excitement in the neighbourhood, as both the parties were men with large families, depending upon them and stood well in the community."

I will quote but one more paragraph, which, by reason of its monstrous absurdity, may be a relief to these atrocious deeds.

### *"Affair of Honour.*

"We have just heard the particulars of a meeting which took place on Six Mile Island, on Tuesday, between two young bloods of our city: Samuel Thurston, *aged fifteen,* and William Hine, *aged thirteen* years. They were attended by young gentlemen of the same age.

The weapons used on the occasion, were a couple of Dickson's best rifles; the distance, thirty yards. They took one fire, without any damage being sustained by either party, except the ball of Thurston's gun passing through the crown of Hine's hat. *Through the intercession of the Board of Honour*, the challenge was withdrawn, and the difference amicably adjusted."

If the reader will picture to himself the kind of Board of Honour which amicably adjusted the difference between these two little boys, who in any other part of the world would have been amicably adjusted on two porter's backs and soundly flogged with birchen rods, he will be possessed, no doubt, with as strong a sense of its ludicrous character, as that which sets me laughing whenever its image rises up before me,

Now, I appeal to every human mind, imbued with the commonest of common sense, and the commonest of common hunanity; to all dispassionate, reasoning creatures, of any shade of opinion; and ask, with these revolting evidences of the state of society which exists in and about the slave districts of America before them, can they have a doubt of the real condition of the slave, or can they for a moment make a compromise between the institution or any of its flagrant, fearful features, and their own just consciences? Will they say of any tale of cruelty and horror, however aggravated in degree, that it is improbable, when they can turn to the public prints, and, running, read such signs as these, laid before them by the men who rule the slaves: in their own acts and under their own hands?

Do we not know that the worst deformity and ugliness of slavery are at once the cause and the effect of the reckless license taken by these freeborn outlaws? Do we not know that the man who has been born and bred among its wrongs; who has seen in his childhood husbands obliged at the word of command to flog their wives; women, indecently compelled to hold up their own garments that men might lay the heavier stripes upon their legs, driven and harried by brutal overseers in their time of travail, and becoming mothers on the field of toil, under the very lash itself; who has read in youth, and seen his virgin sisters read, descriptions of runaway men and women, and their disfigured persons, which could not be published elsewhere, of so much stock upon a farm, or at a show of beasts:—do we not know that that man, whenever his wrath is kindled up, will be a brutal savage? Do we not know that as he is a coward in his domestic life, stalking among his shrinking men and women slaves armed with his heavy whip, so he will be a coward out of doors, and carrying cowards' weapons hidden in his breast, will shoot men down and stab them when he quarrels? And if our reason did not teach us this and much beyond; if we were such idiots as to close our eyes to that fine mode of training which rears up such men; should we not know that they who among their equals stab and pistol in the legislative halls, and in the counting-house, and on the market-place, and in all the elsewhere peaceful pursuits of life, must be to their dependants, even though they were free servants, so many merciless and unrelenting tyrants?

What! shall we declaim against the ignorant peasantry of Ireland, and mince the matter when these American taskmasters are in question? Shall we cry shame on the brutality of those who hamstring cattle: and spare the lights of Freedom upon earth who notch the ears of men and women, cut pleasant posies in the shrinking flesh, learn to write with pens of red-hot iron on the human face, rack their poetic fancies for liveries of mutilation which their slaves shall wear for life and carry to the grave, breaking living limbs as did the soldiery who mocked and slew the Saviour of the world, and set defenceless creatures up for targets! Shall we whimper over legends of the tortures practised on each other by the Pagan Indians, and smile upon the cruelties of Christian men! Shall we, so long as these things last, exult above the scattered remnants of that race, and triumph in the white enjoyment of their possessions? Rather, for me, restore the forest and the Indian village; in lieu of stars and stripes, let some poor feather flutter in the breeze; replace the streets and squares by wigwams; and though the death-song of a hundred haughty warriors fill the air, it will be music to the shriek of one unhappy slave.

On one theme, which is commonly before our eyes, and in respect of which our national character is changing fast, let the plain Truth be spoken, and let us not, like dastards, beat about the bush by hinting at the Spaniard and the fierce Italian. When knives are drawn by Englishmen in conflict let it be said and known: "We owe this change to Republican Slavery. These are the weapons of Freedom. With sharp points and edges such as these, Liberty in America hews and hacks her slaves; or, failing that pursuit, her sons devote them to a better use, and turn them on each other."

# CHAPTER XVIII

## CONCLUDING REMARKS

THERE are many passages in this book, where I have been at some pains to resist the temptation of troubling my readers with my own deductions and conclusions: preferring that they should judge for themselves, from such premises as I have laid before them. My only object in the outset, was, to carry them with me faithfully wheresoever I went: and that task I have discharged.

But I may be pardoned, if on such a theme as the general character of the American people, and the general character of their social system, as presented to a stranger's eyes, I desire to express my own opinions in a few words, before I bring these volumes to a close.

They are, by nature, frank, brave, cordial, hospitable, and affectionate. Cultivation and refinement seem but to enhance their warmth of heart and ardent enthusiasm; and it is the possession of these latter qualities in a most remarkable degree, which renders an educated American one of the most endearing and most generous of friends. I never was so won upon, as by this class; never yielded up my full confidence and esteem so readily and pleasurably, as to them; never can make again, in half a year, so many friends for whom I seem to entertain the regard of half a life.

These qualities are natural, I implicitly believe, to the whole people. That they are, however, sadly sapped and blighted in their growth among the mass; and that there are influences at work which endanger them still more, and give but little present promise of their healthy restoration; is a truth that ought to be told.

It is an essential part of every national character to pique itself mightily upon its faults, and to deduce tokens of its virtue or its wisdom from their very exaggeration. One great blemish in the popular mind of America, and the prolific parent of an innumerable brood of evils, is Universal Distrust. Yet the American citizen plumes himself upon this spirit, even when he is sufficiently dispassionate to perceive the ruin it works; and will often adduce it, in spite of his own reason, as an instance of the great sagacity and acuteness of the people, and their superior shrewdness and independence.

"You carry," says the stranger, "this jealousy and distrust into every transaction of public life. By repelling worthy men from your legislative assemblies, it has bred up a class of candidates for the suffrage, who, in their very act, disgrace your Institutions and your people's choice. It has rendered you so fickle, and so given to change that your inconstancy has passed into a proverb; for you no sooner set up an idol firmly, than you are sure to pull it down, and dash it into fragments: and this, because directly you reward a benefactor, or a public servant, you distrust him, merely because he *is* rewarded; and immediately apply yourself to find out, either that you have been too bountiful in your acknowledgments, or he remiss in his deserts. Any man who attains a high place among you, from the President downwards, may date his downfall from that moment; for any printed lie that any notorious villain pens, although it militate directly against the character and conduct of a life, appeals at once to your distrust, and is believed. You will strain at a gnat in the way of trustfulness and confidence, however fairly won and well deserved; but you will swallow a whole caravan of camels, if they be laden with unworthy doubts and mean suspicions. Is this well, think you, or likely to elevate the character of the governors or the governed, among you?"

The answer is invariably the same: "There's freedom of opinion here, you know. Every man thinks for himself, and we are not to be easily overreached. That's how our people come to be suspicious."

Another prominent feature is the love of "smart" dealing: which gilds over many a swindle and gross breach of trust; many a defalcation, public and private; and enables many a knave to hold his head up with the best, who well deserves a halter; though it has not been without a retributive operation, for this smartness has done more in a few years to impair the public credit, and to cripple the public resources, than dull honesty, however rash, could have effected in a century. The merits of a broken speculation, or a bankruptcy, or of a successful scoundrel, are not gauged by its or his observance of the golden rule, "Do as you would be done by," but are considered with reference to their smartness. I recollect, on both occasions of our passing that ill-fated Cairo on the Mississippi, remarking on the bad effects such gross deceits must have when they exploded, in generating a want of confidence abroad, and discouraging foreign investment: but I was given to understand that this was a very smart scheme by which a deal of money had been made: and that its smartest feature was, that they forgot these things abroad, in a very short time, and speculated again, as freely as ever. The following dialogue I have held a hundred times: "Is it not a very disgraceful circumstance that such a man as So-and-so should be acquiring a large property by the most infamous and odious means, and notwithstanding all the crimes of which he has been guilty, should be tolerated and abetted by your Citizens? He is a public nuisance, is he not?" "Yes, sir." "A convicted liar?" "Yes, sir." "He has been kicked, and cuffed, and caned?" "Yes, sir." "And he is utterly dishonourable, debased, and profligate?" "Yes, sir." "In the name of wonder, then, what is his merit?" "Well, sir, he is a smart man."

In like manner, all kinds of deficient and impolitic usages are referred to the national love of trade; though, oddly enough, it would be a weighty charge against a foreigner that he regarded the Americans as a trading people. The love of trade is assigned as a reason for that comfortless custom, so very prevalent in country towns, of married persons living in hotels, having no fireside of their own, and seldom meeting from early morning until late at night, but at the hasty public meals. The love of trade is a reason why the literature of America is to remain for ever unprotected: "For we are a trading people, and don't care for poetry:" though we *do*, by the way, profess to be very proud of our poets: while healthful amusements, cheerful means of recreation, and wholesome fancies, must fade before the stern utilitarian joys of trade.

These three characteristics are strongly presented at every turn, full in the stranger's view. But, the foul growth of America has a more tangled root than this; and it strikes its fibres, deep in its licentious Press.

Schools may be erected, East, West, North, and South; pupils be taught, and masters reared, by scores upon scores of thousands; colleges may thrive, churches may be crammed, temperance may be diffused, and advancing knowledge in all other forms walk through the land with giant strides: but while the newspaper press of America is in, or near, its present abject state, high moral improvement in that country is hopeless. Year by year, it must and will go back; year by year, the tone of public feeling must sink lower down; year by year, the Congress and the Senate must become of less account before all decent men; and year by year, the memory of the Great Fathers of the Revolution must be outraged more and more, in the bad life of their degenerate child.

Among the herd of journals which are published in the States, there are some, the reader scarcely need be told, of character and credit. From personal intercourse with accomplished gentlemen connected with publications of this class, I have derived both pleasure and profit. But the name of these is Few, and of the others Legion; and the influence of the good, is powerless to counteract the moral poison of the bad.

Among the gentry of America; among the well-informed and moderate: in the learned professions; at the bar and on the bench: there is, as there can be, but one opinion, in reference to the vicious character of these infamous journals. It is sometimes contended— I will not say strangely, for it is natural to seek excuses for such a disgrace—that their influence is not so great as a visitor would suppose. I must be pardoned for saying that there is no warrant for this plea, and that every fact and circumstance tends directly to the opposite conclusion.

When any man, of any grade of desert in intellect or character, can climb to any public distinction, no matter what, in America, without first grovelling down upon the earth, and bending the knee before this monster of depravity; when any private excellence is safe from its attacks; when any social confidence is left unbroken by it, or any tie of social decency and honour is held in the least regard; when any man in that free country has freedom of opinion, and presumes to think for himself, and speak for himself, without humble reference to a censorship which, for its rampant ignorance and base dishonesty, he utterly loathes and despises in his heart; when those who most acutely feel its infamy and the reproach it casts upon the nation, and who most denounce it to each other, dare to set their heels upon, and crush it openly, in the sight of all men: then, I will believe that its influence is lessening, and men are returning to their manly senses. But while that Press has its evil eye in every house, and its black hand in every appointment in the state, from a president to a postman; while, with ribald slander for its only stock in trade, it is the standard literature of an enormous class, who must find their reading in a newspaper, or they will not read at all; so long must its odium be upon the country's head, and so long must the evil it works, be plainly visible in the Republic.

To those who are accustomed to the leading English journals, or to the respectable journals of the Continent of Europe; to those who are accustomed to anything else in print and paper; it would be impossible, without an amount of extract for which I have neither space nor inclination, to convey an adequate idea of this frightful engine in

America. But if any man desire confirmation of my statement on this head, let him repair to any place in this city of London, where scattered numbers of these publications are to be found; and there, let him form his own opinion.*

It would be well, there can be no doubt, for the American people as a whole, if they loved the Real less, and the Ideal somewhat more. It would be well, if there were greater encouragement to lightness of heart and gaiety, and a wider cultivation of what is beautiful, without being eminently and directly useful. But here, I think the general remonstrance, "we are new country," which is so often advanced as an excuse for defects which are quite unjustifiable, as being, of right, only the slow growth of an old one, may be very reasonably urged: and I yet hope to hear of there being some other national amusement in the United States, besides newspaper politics.

They certainly are not a humorous people, and their temperament always impressed me as being of a dull and gloomy character. In shrewdness of remark, and a certain cast-iron quaintness, the Yankees, or people of New England, unquestionably take the lead; as they do in most other evidences of intelligence. But in travelling about, out of the large cities—as I have remarked in former parts of these volumes—I was quite oppressed by the prevailing seriousness and melancholy air of business: which was so general and unvarying, that at every new town I came to, I seemed to meet the very same people whom I had left behind me, at the last. Such defects as are perceptible in the national manners, seem, to me, to be referable, in a great degree, to this cause: which has generated a dull, sullen persistence in coarse usages, and rejected the graces of life as undeserving of attention. There is no doubt that Washington, who was always most scrupulous and exact on points of ceremony, perceived the tendency towards this mistake, even in his time, and did his utmost to correct it.

I cannot hold with other writers on these subjects that the prevalence of various forms of dissent in America, is in any way attributable to the non-existence there of an established church: indeed, I think the temper of the people, if it admitted of such an Institution being founded amongst them, would lead them to desert it, as a matter of course, merely because it *was* established. But, supposing it to exist, I doubt its probable efficacy in summoning the wandering sheep to one great fold, simply because of the immense amount of dissent which prevails at home; and because I do not find in America any one form of religion with which we in Europe, or even in England, are unacquainted. Dissenters resort thither in great numbers, as other people do, simply because it is a land of resort; and great settlements

---

*NOTE TO THE ORIGINAL EDITION.—Or let him refer to an able, and perfectly truthful article, in *The Foreign Quarterly Review*, published in the present month of October; to which my attention has been attracted, since these sheets have been passing through the press. He will find some specimens there, by no means remarkable to any man who has been in America, but sufficiently striking to one who has not.

of them are founded, because ground can be purchased, and towns and villages reared, where there were none of the human creation before. But even the Shakers emigrated from England; our country is not unknown to Mr. Joseph Smith, the apostle of Mormonism, or to his benighted disciples; I have beheld religious scenes myself in some of our populous towns which can hardly be surpassed by an American camp-meeting; and I am not aware that any instance of superstitious imposture on the one hand, and superstitious credulity on the other, has had its origin in the United States, which we cannot more than parallel by the precedents of Mrs. Southcote, Mary Tofts the rabbit-breeder, or even Mr. Thom of Canterbury: which latter case arose, some time after the dark ages had passed away.

The Republican Institutions of America undoubtedly lead the people to assert their self-respect and their equality; but a traveller is bound to bear those Institutions in his mind, and not hastily to resent the near approach of a class of strangers, who, at home, would keep aloof. This characteristic, when it was tinctured with no foolish pride, and stopped short of no honest service, never offended me; and I very seldom, if ever, experienced its rude or unbecoming display. Once or twice it was comically developed, as in the following case; but this was an amusing incident, and not the rule, or near it.

I wanted a pair of boots at a certain town, for I had none to travel in, but those with the memorable cork soles, which were much too hot for the fiery decks of a steamboat. I therefore sent a message to an artist in boots, importing, with my compliments, that I should be happy to see him, if he would do me the polite favour to call. He very kindly returned for answer, that he would "look round" at six o'clock that evening.

I was lying on the sofa, with a book and a wine-glass, at about that time, when the door opened, and a gentleman in a stiff cravat, within a year or two on either side of thirty, entered, in his hat and gloves; walked up to the looking-glass; arranged his hair; took off his gloves; slowly produced a measure from the uttermost depths of his coat-pocket and requested me, in a languid tone, to "unfix" my straps. I complied, but looked with some curiosity at his hat, which was still upon his head. It might have been that, or it might have been the heat—but he took it off. Then, he sat himself down on a chair opposite to me; rested an arm on each knee; and, leaning forward very much, took from the ground, by a great effort, the specimen of metropolitan workmanship which I had just pulled off: whistling, pleasantly, as he did so. He turned it over and over; surveyed it with a contempt no language can express; and inquired if I wished him to fix me a boot like *that?* I courteously replied, that provided the boots were large enough, I would leave the rest to him; that if convenient and practicable, I should not object to their bearing some resemblance to the model then before him; but that I would be entirely guided by, and would beg to leave the whole subject to, his judgment and discretion. "You an't partickler, about this scoop in the heel, I suppose

then?" says he: "we don't foller that, here." I repeated my last
observation. He looked at himself in the glass again; went closer to
it to dash a grain or two of dust out of the corner of his eye; and
settled his cravat. All this time, my leg and foot were in the air.
"Nearly ready, sir?" I inquired. "Well, pretty nigh," he said; "keep
steady." I kept as steady as I could, both in foot and face; and having
by this time got the dust out, and found his pencil-case, he measured
me, and made the necessary notes. When he had finished, he fell into
his old attitude, and taking up the boot again, mused for some time.
"And this," he said, at last, "is an English boot, is it? This is a London
boot, eh?" "That, sir," I replied, "is a London boot." He mused over
it again, after the manner of Hamlet with Yorick's skull; nodded his
head, as who should say, "I pity the Institutions that led to the production of this boot!"; rose; put up his pencil, notes, and paper—
glancing at himself in the glass, all the time—put on his hat; drew
on his gloves very slowly; and finally walked out. When he had been
gone about a minute, the door reopened, and his hat and his head
reappeared. He looked round the room, and at the boot again, which
was still lying on the floor; appeared thoughtful for a minute; and
then said "Well, good arternoon." "Good afternoon, sir," said I: and
that was the end of the interview.

There is but one other head on which I wish to offer a remark; and
that has reference to the public health. In so vast a country, where
there are thousands of millions of acres of land yet unsettled and
uncleared, and on every rood of which, vegetable decomposition is
annually taking place; where there are so many great rivers, and such
opposite varieties of climate; there cannot fail to be a great amount
of sickness at certain seasons. But I may venture to say, after conversing with many members of the medical profession in America,
that I am not singular in the opinion that much of the disease which
does prevail, might be avoided, if a few common precautions were
observed. Greater means of personal cleanliness, are indispensable
to this end; the custom of hastily swallowing large quantities of
animal food, three times a-day, and rushing back to sedentary pursuits after each meal, must be changed; the gentler sex must go more
wisely clad, and take more healthful exercise; and in the latter clause,
the males must be included also. Above all, in public institutions, and
throughout the whole of every town and city, the system of ventila-
tion, and drainage, and removal of impurities requires to be
thoroughly revised. There is no local Legislature in America which
may not study Mr. Chadwick's excellent Report upon the Sanitary
Condition of our Labouring Classes, with immense advantage.

I HAVE now arrived at the close of this book. I have little reason to
believe, from certain warnings I have had since I returned to England,
that it will be tenderly or favourably received by the American
people; and as I have written the Truth in relation to the mass of
those who form their judgments and express their opinions, it will

be seen that I have no desire to court, by any adventitious means, the popular applause.

It is enough for me, to know that what I have set down in these pages, cannot cost me a single friend on the other side of the Atlantic, who is, in anything, deserving of the name. For the rest, I put my trust, implicitly, in the spirit in which they have been conceived and penned; and I can bide my time.

I have made no reference to my reception, nor have I suffered it to influence me in what I have written; for, in either case, I should have offered but a sorry acknowledgment, compared with that I bear within my breast, towards those partial readers of my former books, across the Water, who met me with an open hand, and not with one that closed upon an iron muzzle.

THE END

# POSTSCRIPT

At a Public Dinner given to me on Saturday the 18th of April, 1868, in the City of New York, by two hundred representatives of the Press of the United States of America, I made the following observations among others:

"So much of my voice has lately been heard in the land, that I might have been contented with troubling you no further from my present standing-point, were it not a duty with which I henceforth charge myself, not only here but on every suitable occasion, whatsoever and wheresoever, to express my high and grateful sense of my second reception in America, and to bear my honest testimony to the national generosity and magnanimity. Also, to declare how astounded I have been by the amazing changes I have seen around me on every side,—changes moral, changes physical, changes in the amount of land subdued and peopled, changes in the rise of vast new cities, changes in the growth of older cities almost out of recognition, changes in the graces and amenities of life, changes in the Press, without whose advancement no advancement can take place anywhere. Nor am I, believe me, so arrogant as to suppose that in five and twenty years there have been no changes in me, and that I had nothing to learn and no extreme impressions to correct when I was here first. And this brings me to a point on which I have, ever since I landed in the United States last November, observed a strict silence, though sometimes tempted to break it, but in reference to which I will, with your good leave, take you into my confidence now. Even the Press, being human, may be sometimes mistaken or misinformed, and I rather think that I have in one or two rare instances observed its information to be not strictly accurate with reference to myself. Indeed, I have, now and again, been more surprised by printed news that I have read of myself, than by any printed news that I have ever read in my present state of existence. Thus, the vigour and perseverance with which I have for some months past been collecting materials for, and hammering away at, a new book on America has much astonished me; seeing that all that time my declaration has been perfectly well known to my publishers on both sides of the Atlantic, that no consideration on earth, would induce me to write one. But what I have intended, what I have resolved upon (and this is the confidence I seek to place in you) is, on my return to England, in my own person, in my own Journal, to bear, for the behoof of my countrymen, such testimony to the gigantic changes in this country as I have hinted at to-night. Also, to record that wherever I have been, in the smallest places equally with the largest, I have been received with unsurpassable politeness, delicacy, sweet temper, hospitality, consideration, and with unsurpassable respect for the privacy daily enforced upon me by the nature of my avocation here and the state of my health. This testimony, so long as I live, and so long as my descendants have any legal right in my books, I shall cause to be republished, as an appendix to every copy of those two books of mine in which I have referred to America. And this I will do and cause to be done, not in mere love and thankfulness, but because I regard it as an act of plain justice and honour."

I said these words with the greatest earnestness that I could lay upon them, and I repeat them in print here with equal earnestness. So long as this book shall last, I hope that they will form a part of it, and will be fairly read as inseparable from my experiences and impressions of America.

CHARLES DICKENS.

*May*, 1868.

# MASTER HUMPHREY'S CLOCK

MASTER HUMPHREY'S CLOCK

# MASTER HUMPHREY'S CLOCK

BY
CHARLES DICKENS

ILLUSTRATED BY
H. K. BROWNE (PHIZ) &
GEORGE CATTERMOLE

LONDON:
HAZELL, WATSON & VINEY, LTD.

# MASTER
# HUMPHREY'S CLOCK

BY

CHARLES DICKENS

ILLUSTRATED BY

H. K. BROWNE ("PHIZ")

GEORGE CATTERMOLE

# MASTER HUMPHREY'S CLOCK

## I

## MASTER HUMPHREY, FROM HIS CLOCK-SIDE IN THE CHIMNEY-CORNER

THE reader must not expect to know where I live. At present, it is true, my abode may be a question of little or no import to anybody; but if I should carry my readers with me, as I hope to do, and there should spring up between them and me feelings of homely affection and regard attaching something of interest to matters ever so slightly connected with my fortunes or my speculations, even my place of residence might one day have a kind of charm for them. Bearing this possible contingency in mind, I wish them to understand, in the outset, that they must never expect to know it.

I am not a churlish old man. Friendless I can never be, for all mankind are my kindred, and I am on ill terms with no one member of my great family. But for many years I have led a lonely, solitary life;—what wound I sought to heal, what sorrow to forget, originally, matters not now; it is sufficient that retirement has become a habit with me, and that I am unwilling to break the spell which for so long a time has shed its quiet influence upon my home and heart.

I live in a venerable suburb of London, in an old house which in bygone days was a famous resort for many roysterers and peerless ladies, long since departed. It is a silent, shady place, with a paved courtyard so full of echoes, that sometimes I am tempted to believe that faint responses to the noises of old times linger there yet, and that these ghosts of sound haunt my footsteps as I pace it up and down. I am the more confirmed in this belief, because, of late years, the echoes that attend my walks have been less loud and marked than they were wont to be; and it is pleasanter to imagine in them the rustling of silk brocade, and the light step of some lovely girl, than to recognise in their altered note the failing tread of an old man.

Those who like to read of brilliant rooms and gorgeous furniture would derive but little pleasure from a minute description of my simple dwelling. It is dear to me for the same reason that they would hold it in slight regard. Its worm-eaten doors, and low ceilings crossed by clumsy beams; its walls of wainscot, dark stairs, and gaping closets; its small chambers, communicating with each other by winding passages or narrow steps; its many nooks, scarce larger than its corner-cupboards; its very dust and dulness, are all dear to me. The moth and spider are my constant tenants; for in my house the one basks in his long sleep, and the other plies his busy loom secure and undisturbed. I have a pleasure in thinking on a summer's day how many butterflies have sprung for the first time into light and sunshine from some dark corner of these old walls.

When I first came to live here, which was many years ago, the neighbours were curious to know who I was, and whence I came, and why I lived so much alone. As time went on, and they still remained unsatisfied on these points, I became the centre of a popular ferment, extending for half a mile round, and in one direction for a full mile. Various rumours were circulated to my prejudice. I was a spy, an infidel, a conjurer, a kidnapper of children, a refugee, a priest, a monster. Mothers caught up their infants and ran into their houses as I passed; men eyed me spitefully, and muttered threats and curses. I was the object of suspicion and distrust—ay, of downright hatred too.

But when in course of time they found I did no harm, but, on the contrary, inclined towards them despite their unjust usage, they began to relent. I found my footsteps no longer dogged, as they had often been before, and observed that the women and children no longer retreated, but would stand and gaze at me as I passed their doors. I took this for a good omen, and waited patiently for better times. By degrees I began to make friends among these humble folks: and though they were just shy of speaking, would give them "good day," and so pass on. In a little time, those whom I had thus accosted would make a point of coming to their doors and windows at the usual hour, and nod or courtesy to me; children, too, came timidly within my reach, and ran away quite scared when I patted their heads and bade them be good at school. These little people soon grew more familiar. From exchanging mere words of course with my older neighbours, I gradually became their friend and adviser, the depositary of their cares and sorrows, and sometimes, it may be, the reliever, in my small way, of their distresses. And now I never walk abroad but pleasant recognitions and smiling faces wait on Master Humphrey.

It was a whim of mine, perhaps as a whet to the curiosity of my neighbours, and a kind of retaliation upon them for their suspicions— it was, I say, a whim of mine, when I first took up my abode in this place, to acknowledge no other name than Humphrey. With my detractors, I was Ugly Humphrey. When I began to convert them into friends, I was Mr. Humphrey and Old Mr. Humphrey. At length I settled down into plain Master Humphrey, which was understood to be the title most pleasant to my ear; and so completely a matter of course has it become, that sometimes when I am taking my morning walk in my little courtyard, I overhear my barber—who has a profound respect for me, and would not, I am sure, abridge my honours for the world—holding forth on the other side of the wall, touching the state of "Master Humphrey's health," and communicating to some friend the substance of the conversation that he and Master Humphrey have had together in the course of the shaving which he has just concluded.

That I may not make acquaintance with my readers under false pretences, or give them cause to complain hereafter that I have withheld any matter which it was essential for them to have learnt at first, I wish them to know—and I smile sorrowfully to think that the time has been when the confession would have given me pain—that I am a mis-shapen, deformed old man.

I have never been made a misanthrope by this cause. I have never been stung by an insult, nor wounded by any jest upon my crooked figure. As a child I was melancholy and timid, but that was because the gentle consideration paid to my misfortune sunk deep into my spirit and made me sad, even in those early days. I was but a very young creature when my poor mother died, and yet I remember that often when I hung about her neck, and oftener still when I played about the room before her, she would catch me to her bosom, and bursting into tears, would soothe me with every term of fondness and affection. God knows I was a happy child at those times,—happy to nestle in her breast,—happy to weep when she did,—happy in not knowing why.

These occasions are so strongly impressed upon my memory, that they seem to have occupied whole years. I have numbered very, very few when they ceased for ever, but before then their meaning had been revealed to me.

I do not know whether all children are imbued with a quick perception of childish grace and beauty, and a strong love for it, but I was. I had no thought that I remember, either that I possessed it myself or that I lacked it, but I admired it with an intensity that I cannot describe. A little knot of playmates—they must have been beautiful, for I see them now—were clustered one day round my mother's knee in eager admiration of some picture representing a group of infant angels, which she held in her hand. Whose the picture was, whether it was familiar to me or otherwise, or how all the children came to be there, I forget; I have some dim thought it was my birthday, but the beginning of my recollection is that we were all together in a garden, and it was summer weather,—I am sure of that, for one of the little girls had roses in her sash. There were many lovely angels in this picture, and I remember the fancy coming upon me to point out which of them represented each child there, and that when I had gone through my companions, I stopped and hesitated, wondering which was most like me. I remember the children looking at each other, and my turning red and hot, and their crowding round to kiss me, saying that they loved me all the same; and then, and when the old sorrow came into my dear mother's mild and tender look, the truth broke upon me for the first time, and I knew, while watching my awkward and ungainly sports, how keenly she had felt for her poor crippled boy.

I used frequently to dream of it afterwards, and now my heart aches for that child as if I had never been he, when I think how often he awoke from some fairy change to his own old form, and sobbed himself to sleep again.

Well, well,—all these sorrows are past. My glancing at them may not be without its use, for it may help in some measure to explain why I have all my life been attached to the inanimate objects that people my chamber, and how I have come to look upon them rather in the light of old and constant friends, than as mere chairs and tables which a little money could replace at will.

Chief and first among all these is my Clock,—my old, cheerful, companionable Clock. How can I ever convey to others an idea of the comfort and consolation that this old Clock has been for years to me!

It is associated with my earliest recollections. It stood upon the staircase at home (I call it home still mechanically), nigh sixty years ago. I like it for that; but it is not on that account, nor because it is a quaint old thing in a huge oaken case curiously and richly carved, that I prize it as I do. I incline to it as if it were alive, and could underſtand and give me back the love I bear it.

And what other thing that has not life could cheer me as it does? what other thing that has not life (I will not say how few things that have) could have proved the same patient, true, untiring friend? How often have I sat in the long winter evenings feeling such society in its cricket-voice, that raising my eyes from my book and looking gratefully towards it, the face reddened by the glow of the shining fire has seemed to relax from its staid expression and to regard me kindly! how often in the summer twilight, when my thoughts have wandered back to a melancholy past, have its regular whisperings recalled them to the calm and peaceful present! how often in the dead tranquillity of night has its bell broken the oppressive silence, and seemed to give me assurance that the old clock was still a faithful watcher at my chamber-door! My easy-chair, my desk, my ancient furniture, my very books, I can scarcely bring myself to love even these last like my old clock.

It stands in a snug corner, midway between the fireside and a low arched door leading to my bedroom. Its fame is diffused so extensively throughout the neighbourhood, that I have often the satisfaction of hearing the publican, or the baker, and sometimes even the parish-clerk, petitioning my housekeeper (of whom I shall have much to say by and by) to inform him the exact time by Master Humphrey's clock. My barber, to whom I have referred, would sooner believe it than the sun. Nor are these its only distinctions. It has acquired, I am happy to say, another, inseparably connecting it not only with my enjoyments and reflections, but with those of other men; as I shall now relate.

I lived alone here for a long time without any friend or acquaintance. In the course of my wanderings by night and day, at all hours and seasons, in city streets and quiet country parts, I came to be

familiar with certain faces, and to take it to heart as quite a heavy
disappointment if they failed to present themselves each at its
accustomed spot. But these were the only friends I knew, and beyond
them I had none.

It happened, however, when I had gone on thus for a long time,
that I formed an acquaintance with a deaf gentleman, which ripened
into intimacy and close companionship. To this hour, I am ignorant
of his name. It is his humour to conceal it, or he has a reason and
purpose for so doing. In either case, I feel that he has a right to require
a return of the trust he has reposed; and as he has never sought to
discover my secret, I have never sought to penetrate his. There may
have been something in this tacit confidence in each other flattering
and pleasant to us both, and it may have imparted in the beginning
an additional zest, perhaps, to our friendship. Be this as it may, we
have grown to be like brothers, and still I only know him as the deaf
gentleman.

I have said that retirement has become a habit with me. When I
add, that the deaf gentleman and I have two friends, I communicate
nothing which is inconsistent with that declaration. I spend many
hours of every day in solitude and study, have no friends or change
of friends but these, only see them at stated periods, and am supposed
to be of a retired spirit by the very nature and object of our association.

We are men of secluded habits, with something of a cloud upon our
early fortunes, whose enthusiasm, nevertheless, has not cooled with
age, whose spirit of romance is not yet quenched, who are content to
ramble through the world in a pleasant dream, rather than ever
waken again to its harsh realities. We are alchemists who would
extract the essence of perpetual youth from dust and ashes, tempt
coy Truth in many light and airy forms from the bottom of her well,
and discover one crumb of comfort or one grain of good in the commonest and least-regarded matter that passes through our crucible.
Spirits of past times, creatures of imagination, and people of to-day
are alike the objects of our seeking, and, unlike the objects of search
with most philosophers, we can insure their coming at our command.

The deaf gentleman and I first began to beguile our days with
these fancies, and our nights in communicating them to each other.
We are now four. But in my room there are six old chairs, and we
have decided that the two empty seats shall always be placed at our
table when we meet, to remind us that we may yet increase our
company by that number, if we should find two men to our mind.
When one among us dies, his chair will always be set in its usual
place, but never occupied again; and I have caused my will to be so
drawn out, that when we are all dead the house shall be shut up, and
the vacant chairs still left in their accustomed places. It is pleasant
to think that even then our shades may, perhaps, assemble together
as of yore we did, and join in ghostly converse.

One night in every week, as the clock strikes ten, we meet. At the
second stroke of two, I am alone.

And now shall I tell how that my old servant, besides giving us note of time, and ticking cheerful encouragement of our proceedings, lends its name to our society, which for its punctuality and my love is christened "Master Humphrey's Clock"? Now shall I tell how that in the bottom of the old dark closet, where the steady pendulum throbs and beats with healthy action, though the pulse of him who made it stood still long ago, and never moved again, there are piles of dusty papers constantly placed there by our hands, that we may link our enjoyment with my old friend, and draw means to beguile time from the heart of time itself? Shall I, or can I, tell with what a secret pride I open this repository when we meet at night, and still find new store of pleasure in my dear old Clock?

Friend and companion of my solitude! mine is not a selfish love; I would not keep your merits to myself, but disperse something of pleasant association with your image through the whole wide world; I would have men couple with your name cheerful and healthy thoughts; I would have them believe that you keep true and honest time; and how it would gladden me to know that they recognised some hearty English work in Master Humphrey's clock!

## THE CLOCK-CASE

It is my intention constantly to address my readers from the chimney-corner, and I would fain hope that such accounts as I shall give them of our histories and proceedings, our quiet speculations or more busy adventures, will never be unwelcome. Lest, however, I should grow prolix in the outset by lingering too long upon our little association, confounding the enthusiasm with which I regard this chief happiness of my life with that minor degree of interest which those to whom I address myself may be supposed to feel for it, I have deemed it expedient to break off as they have seen.

But, still clinging to my old friend, and naturally desirous that all its merits should be known, I am tempted to open (somewhat irregularly and against our laws, I must admit) the clock-case. The first roll of paper on which I lay my hand is in the writing of the deaf gentleman. I shall have to speak of him in my next paper; and how can I better approach that welcome task then by prefacing it with a production of his own pen, consigned to the safe keeping of my honest Clock by his own hand?

The manuscript runs thus:

### INTRODUCTION TO THE GIANT CHRONICLES

Once upon a time, that is to say, in this our time,—the exact year, month, and day are of no matter,—there dwelt in the city of London a substantial citizen, who united in his single person the dignities of wholesale fruiterer, alderman, common-councilman, and member of

Master Humphrey's Clock 215

the worshipful Company of Patten-makers; who had superadded to
these extraordinary distinctions the important post and title of
Sheriff, and who at length, and to crown all, stood next in rotation
for the high and honourable office of Lord Mayor.

He was a very substantial citizen indeed. His face was like the full
moon in a fog, with two little holes punched out for his eyes, a very
ripe pear stuck on for his nose, and a wide gash to serve for a mouth.
The girth of his waistcoat was hung up and lettered in his tailor's
shop as an extraordinary curiosity. He breathed like a heavy snorer,
and his voice in speaking came thickly forth, as if it were oppressed
and stifled by feather-beds. He trod the ground like an elephant, and
eat and drank like—like nothing but an alderman, as he was.

This worthy citizen had risen to his great eminence from small
beginnings. He had once been a very lean, weazen little boy, never
dreaming of carrying such a weight of flesh upon his bones or of
money in his pockets, and glad enough to take his dinner at a baker's
door, and his tea at a pump. But he had long ago forgotten all this,
as it was proper that a wholesale fruiterer, alderman, common-
councilman, member of the worshipful Company of Patten-makers,
past sheriff, and, above all, a Lord Mayor that was to be, should; and
he never forgot it more completely in all his life than on the eighth
of November in the year of his election to the great golden civic chair,
which was the day before his grand dinner at Guildhall.

It happened that as he sat that evening all alone in his counting-
house, looking over the bill of fare for next day, and checking off the
fat capons in fifties, and the turtle-soup by the hundred quarts, for
his private amusement,—it happened that as he sat alone occupied
in these pleasant calculations, a strange man came in and asked him
how he did, adding, "If I am half as much changed as you, sir, you
have no recollection of me, I am sure."

The strange man was not over and above well dressed, and was
very far from being fat or rich-looking in any sense of the word, yet
he spoke with a kind of modest confidence, and assumed an easy,
gentlemanly sort of an air, to which nobody but a rich man can law-
fully presume. Besides this, he interrupted the good citizen just as
he had reckoned three hundred and seventy-two fat capons, and was
carrying them over to the next column; and as if that were not aggravation enough, the learned recorder for the city of London had only
ten minutes previously gone out at that very same door, and had
turned round and said, "Good night, my lord." Yes, he had said,
"my lord";—he, a man of birth and education, of the Honourable
Society of the Middle Temple, Barrister-at-Law,—he who had an
uncle in the House of Commons, and an aunt almost but not quite
in the House of Lords (for she had married a feeble peer, and made
him vote as she liked),—he, this man, this learned recorder, had said,
"my lord." "I'll not wait till to-morrow to give you your title, my
Lord Mayor," says he, with a bow and a smile; "you are Lord Mayor
de facto, if not de jure. Good night, my lord."

The Lord Mayor elect thought of this, and turning to the stranger, and sternly bidding him "go out of his private counting-house," brought forward the three hundred and seventy-two fat capons, and went on with his account.

"Do you remember," said the other, stepping forward,—"*do* you remember little Joe Toddyhigh?"

The port wine fled for a moment from the fruiterer's nose as he muttered, "Joe Toddyhigh! What about Joe Toddyhigh?"

"*I* am Joe Toddyhigh," cried the visitor. "Look at me, look hard at me,—harder, harder. You know me now? You know little Joe again? What a happiness to us both, to meet the very night before your grandeur! O! give me your hand, Jack,—both hands,—both, for the sake of old times."

"You pinch me, sir. You're a-hurting of me," said the Lord Mayor elect pettishly. "Don't,—suppose anybody should come,—Mr. Toddyhigh, sir."

"Mr. Toddyhigh!" repeated the other ruefully.

"O, don't bother," said the Lord Mayor elect, scratching his head. "Dear me! Why, I thought you was dead. What a fellow you are!"

Indeed, it was a pretty state of things, and worthy the tone of vexation and disappointment in which the Lord Mayor spoke. Joe Toddyhigh had been a poor boy with him at Hull, and had oftentimes divided his last penny and parted his last crust to relieve his wants; for though Joe was a destitute child in those times, he was as faithful and affectionate in his friendship as ever man of might could be. They parted one day to seek their fortunes in different directions. Joe went to sea, and the now wealthy citizen begged his way to London. They separated with many tears, like foolish fellows as they were, and agreed to remain fast friends, and if they lived, soon to communicate again.

When he was an errand-boy, and even in the early days of his apprenticeship, the citizen had many a time trudged to the Post-office to ask if there were any letter from poor little Joe, and had gone home again with tears in his eyes, when he found no news of his only friend. The world is a wide place, and it was a long time before the letter came; when it did, the writer was forgotten. It turned from white to yellow from lying in the Post-office with nobody to claim it, and in course of time was torn up with five hundred others, and sold for waste-paper. And now at last, and when it might least have been expected, here was this Joe Toddyhigh turning up and claiming acquaintance with a great public character, who on the morrow would be cracking jokes with the Prime Minister of England, and who had only, at any time during the next twelve months, to say the word, and he could shut up Temple Bar, and make it no thoroughfare for the king himself!

"I am sure I don't know what to say, Mr. Toddyhigh," said the Lord Mayor elect; "I really don't. It's very inconvenient. I'd sooner have given twenty pound,—it's very inconvenient, really."

A thought had come into his mind, that perhaps his old friend might say something passionate which would give him an excuse for being angry himself. No such thing. Joe looked at him steadily, but very mildly, and did not open his lips.

"Of course I shall pay you what I owe you," said the Lord Mayor elect, fidgeting in his chair. "You lent me—I think it was a shilling or some small coin—when we parted company, and that of course I shall pay with good interest. I can pay my way with any man, and always have done. If you look into the Mansion House the day after to-morrow,—some time after dusk,—and ask for my private clerk you'll find he has a draft for you. I haven't got time to say anything more just now, unless,"—he hesitated, for, coupled with a strong desire to glitter for once in all his glory in the eyes of his former companion, was a distrust of his appearance, which might be more shabby than he could tell by that feeble light,—"unless you'd like to come to the dinner to-morrow. I don't mind your having this ticket, if you like to take it. A great many people would give their ears for it, I can tell you."

His old friend took the card without speaking a word, and instantly departed. His sunburnt face and grey hair were present to the citizen's mind for a moment; but by the time he reached three hundred and eighty-one fat capons, he had quite forgotten him.

Joe Toddyhigh had never been in the capital of Europe before, and he wandered up and down the streets that night amazed at the number of churches and other public buildings, the splendour of the shops, the riches that were heaped up on every side, the glare of light in which they were displayed, and the concourse of people who hurried to and fro, indifferent, apparently, to all the wonders that surrounded them. But in all the long streets and broad squares, there were none but strangers; it was quite a relief to turn down a by-way and hear his own footsteps on the pavement. He went home to his inn, thought that London was a dreary, desolate place, and felt disposed to doubt the existence of one true-hearted man in the whole worshipful Company of Patten-makers. Finally, he went to bed, and dreamed that he and the Lord Mayor elect were boys again.

He went next day to the dinner; and when in a burst of light and music, and in the midst of splendid decorations and surrounded by brilliant company, his former friend appeared at the head of the Hall, and was hailed with shouts and cheering, he cheered and shouted with the best, and for the moment could have cried. The next moment he cursed his weakness in behalf of a man so changed and selfish, and quite hated a jolly-looking old gentleman opposite for declaring himself in the pride of his heart a Patten-maker.

As the banquet proceeded, he took more and more to heart the rich citizen's unkindness; and that, not from any envy, but because he felt that a man of his state and fortune could all the better afford to recognise an old friend, even if he were poor and obscure. The more he thought of this, the more lonely and sad he felt. When the company dispersed and adjourned to the ball-room, he paced the hall and passages alone, ruminating in a very melancholy condition upon the disappointment he had experienced.

It chanced, while he was lounging about in this moody state, that he stumbled upon a flight of stairs, dark, steep, and narrow, which he ascended without any thought about the matter, and so came into a little music-gallery, empty and deserted. From this elevated post, which commanded the whole hall, he amused himself in looking down upon the attendants who were clearing away the fragments of the feast very lazily, and drinking out of all the bottles and glasses with most commendable perseverance.

His attention gradually relaxed, and he fell fast asleep.

When he awoke, he thought there must be something the matter with his eyes; but, rubbing them a little, he soon found that the moonlight was really streaming through the east window, that the lamps were all extinguished, and that he was alone. He listened, but no distant murmur in the echoing passages, not even the shutting of a door, broke the deep silence; he groped his way down the stairs, and found that the door at the bottom was locked on the other side. He began now to comprehend that he must have slept a long time, that he had been overlooked, and was shut up there for the night.

His first sensation, perhaps, was not altogether a comfortable one, for it was a dark, chilly, earthy-smelling place, and something too large, for a man so situated, to feel at home in. However, when the momentary consternation of his surprise was over, he made light of the accident, and resolved to feel his way up the stairs again, and make himself as comfortable as he could in the gallery until morning. As he turned to execute this purpose, he heard the clocks strike three.

Any such invasion of a dead stillness as the striking of distant clocks, causes it to appear the more intense and insupportable when the sound has ceased. He listened with strained attention in the hope that some clock, lagging behind its fellows, had yet to strike,—looking all the time into the profound darkness before him, until it seemed to weave itself into a black tissue, patterned with a hundred reflections of his own eyes. But the bells had all pealed out their warning for that once, and the gust of wind that moaned through the place seemed cold and heavy with their iron breath.

The time and circumstances were favourable to reflection. He tried to keep his thoughts to the current, unpleasant though it was, in which they had moved all day, and to think with what a romantic feeling he had looked forward to shaking his old friend by the hand before he died, and what a wide and cruel difference there was between the meeting they had had, and that which he had so often and so long anticipated. Still, he was disordered by waking to such sudden loneliness, and could not prevent his mind from running upon odd tales of people of undoubted courage, who, being shut up by night in vaults or churches, or other dismal places, had scaled great heights

*Gog and Magog.*

to get out, and fled from silence as they had never done from danger.
This brought to his mind the moonlight through the window, and
bethinking himself of it, he groped his way back up the crooked stairs
—but very stealthily, as though he were fearful of being overheard.

He was very much astonished when he approached the gallery
again, to see a light in the building: still more so, on advancing hastily
and looking round, to observe no visible source from which it could
proceed. But how much greater yet was his astonishment at the
spectacle which this light revealed.

The statues of the two giants, Gog and Magog, each above fourteen
feet in height, those which succeeded to still older and more barbarous figures, after the Great Fire of London, and which stand in
the Guildhall to this day, were endowed with life and motion. These
guardian genii of the City had quitted their pedestals, and reclined
in easy attitudes in the great stained-glass window. Between them
was an ancient cask, which seemed to be full of wine; for the younger
Giant, clapping his huge hand upon it, and throwing up his mighty
leg, burst into an exulting laugh, which reverberated through the
hall like thunder.

Joe Toddyhigh instinctively stooped down, and, more dead than
alive, felt his hair stand on end, his knees knock together, and a cold
damp break out upon his forehead. But even at that minute curiosity
prevailed over every other feeling, and somewhat reassured by the
good-humour of the Giants and their apparent unconsciousness of
his presence, he crouched in a corner of the gallery, in as small a space
as he could, and, peeping between the rails, observed them closely.

It was then that the elder Giant, who had a flowing grey beard,
raised his thoughtful eyes to his companion's face, and in a grave and
solemn voice addressed him thus:

## FIRST NIGHT OF THE GIANT CHRONICLES

"Magog, does boisterous mirth beseem the Giant Warder of this
ancient city? Is this becoming demeanour for a watchful spirit over
whose bodiless head so many years have rolled, so many changes
swept like empty air—in whose impalpable nostrils the scent of blood
and crime, pestilence, cruelty, and horror, has been familiar as breath
to mortals—in whose sight Time has gathered in the harvest of centuries, and garnered so many crops of human pride, affections, hopes,
and sorrows? Bethink you of our compact. The night wanes; feasting,
revelry, and music have encroached upon our usual hours of solitude
and morning will be here apace. Ere we are stricken mute again, bethink you of our compact."

Pronouncing these latter words with more of impatience than
quite accorded with his apparent age and gravity, the Giant raised
a long pole (which he still bears in his hand) and tapped his brother
Giant rather smartly on the head; indeed, the blow was so smartly
administered, that the latter quickly withdrew his lips from the cask,

to which they had been applied, and, catching up his shield and halberd, assumed an attitude of defence. His irritation was but momentary, for he laid these weapons aside as hastily as he had assumed them, and said as he did so:

"You know, Gog, old friend, that when we animate these shapes which the Londoners of old assigned (and not unworthily) to the guardian genii of their city, we are susceptible of some of the sensations which belong to human kind. Thus when I taste wine, I feel blows; when I relish the one, I disrelish the other. Therefore, Gog, the more especially as your arm is none of the lightest, keep your good staff by your side, else we may chance to differ. Peace be between us!"

"Amen!" said the other, leaning his staff in the window-corner. "Why did you laugh just now?"

"To think," replied the Giant Magog, laying his hand upon the cask, "of him who owned this wine, and kept it in a cellar hoarded from the light of day, for thirty years,—'till it should be fit to drink,' quoth he. He was twoscore and ten years old when he buried it beneath his house, and yet never thought that he might be scarcely 'fit to drink' when the wine became so. I wonder it never occurred to him to make himself unfit to be eaten. There is very little of him left by this time."

"The night is waning," said Gog mournfully.

"I know it," replied his companion, "and I see you are impatient. But look. Through the eastern window—placed opposite to us, that the first beams of the rising sun may every morning gild our giant faces—the moon-rays fall upon the pavement in a stream of light that to my fancy sinks through the cold stone and gushes into the old crypt below. The night is scarcely past its noon, and our great charge is sleeping heavily."

They ceased to speak, and looked upward at the moon. The sight of their large, black, rolling eyes filled Joe Toddyhigh with such horror that he could scarcely draw his breath. Still they took no note of him, and appeared to believe themselves quite alone.

" Our compact," said Magog after a pause, "is, if I understand it, that, instead of watching here in silence through the dreary nights, we entertain each other with stories of our past experience; with tales of the past, the present, and the future; with legends of London and her sturdy citizens from the old simple times. That every night at midnight, when St. Paul's bell tolls out one, and we may move and speak, we thus discourse, nor leave such themes till the first gray gleam of day shall strike us dumb. Is that our bargain, brother?"

"Yes," said the Giant Gog, "that is the league between us who guard this city, by day in spirit, and by night in body also; and never on ancient holidays have its conduits run wine more merrily than we will pour forth our legendary lore. We are old chroniclers from this time hence. The crumbled wall encircle us once more, the postern-gates are closed, the drawbridge is up, and pent in its narrow den beneath, the water foams and struggles with the sunken starlings.

Jerkins and quarter-staves are in the streets again, the nightly watch is set, the rebel, sad and lonely in his Tower dungeon, tries to sleep and weeps for home and children. Aloft upon the gates and walls are noble heads flaring fiercely down upon the dreaming city, and vexing the hungry dogs that scent them in the air, and tear the ground beneath with dismal howlings. The axe, the block, the rack, in their dark chambers give signs of recent use. The Thames, floating past long lines of cheerful windows whence come a burst of music and a stream of light, bears suddenly to the Palace wall the last red stain brought on the tide from Traitor's Gate. But your pardon, brother. The night wears, and I am talking idly."

The other Giant appeared to be entirely of this opinion, for during the foregoing rhapsody of his fellow-sentinel he had been scratching his head with an air of comical uneasiness, or rather with an air that would have been very comical if he had been a dwarf or an ordinary sized man. He winked too, and though it could not be doubted for a moment that he winked to himself, still he certainly cocked his enormous eye towards the gallery where the listener was concealed. Nor was this all, for he gaped; and when he gaped, Joe was horribly reminded of the popular prejudice on the subject of giants, and of their fabled power of smelling out Englishmen, however closely concealed.

His alarm was such that he nearly swooned, and it was some little time before his power of sight or hearing was restored. When he recovered he found that the elder Giant was pressing the younger to commence the Chronicles, and that the latter was endeavouring to excuse himself, on the ground that the night was far spent, and it would be better to wait until the next. Well assured by this that he was certainly about to begin directly, the listener collected his faculties by a great effort, and distinctly heard Magog express himself to the following effect:

In the sixteenth century and in the reign of Queen Elizabeth of glorious memory (albeit her golden days are sadly rusted with blood), there lived in the city of London a bold young 'prentice who loved his master's daughter. There were no doubt within the walls a great many 'prentices in this condition, but I speak of only one, and his name was Hugh Graham.

This Hugh was apprenticed to an honest Bowyer who dwelt in the ward of Cheype, and was rumoured to possess great wealth. Rumour was quite as infallible in those days as at the present time, but it happened then as now to be sometimes right by accident. It stumbled upon the truth when it gave the old Bowyer a mint of money. His trade had been a profitable one in the time of King Henry the Eighth, who encouraged English archery to the utmost and he had been prudent and discreet. Thus it came to pass that Mistress Alice, his only daughter, was the richest heiress in all his wealthy ward. Young Hugh had often maintained with staff and cudgel that she was the handsomest. To do him justice, I believe she was.

If he could have gained the heart of pretty Mistress Alice by knocking this conviction into stubborn people's heads, Hugh would have had no cause to fear. But though the Bowyer's daughter smiled in secret to hear of his doughty deeds for her sake, and though her little waiting-woman reported all her smiles (and many more) to Hugh, and though he was at a vast expense in kisses and small coin to recompense her fidelity, he made no progress in his love. He durst not whisper it to Mistress Alice save on sure encouragement, and that she never gave him. A glance of her dark eye as she sat at the door on a summer's evening after prayer-time, while he and the neighbouring 'prentices exercised themselves in the street with blunted sword and buckler, would fire Hugh's blood so that none could stand before him; but then she glanced at others quite as kindly as on him, and where was the use of cracking crowns if Mistress Alice smiled upon the cracked as well as on the cracker?

Still Hugh went on, and loved her more and more. He thought of her all day, and dreamed of her all night long. He treasured up her every word and gesture, and had a palpitation of the heart whenever he heard her footstep on the stairs or her voice in an adjoining room. To him, the old Bowyer's house was haunted by an angel; there was enchantment in the air and space in which she moved. It would have been no miracle to Hugh if flowers had sprung from the rush-strewn floors beneath the tread of lovely Mistress Alice.

Never did 'prentice long to distinguish himself in the eyes of his lady-love so ardently as Hugh. Sometimes he pictured to himself the house taking fire by night, and he, when all drew back in fear, rushing through flame and smoke, and bearing her from the ruins in his arms. At other times he thought of a rising of fierce rebels, an attack upon the city, a strong assault upon the Bowyer's house in particular, and he falling on the threshold pierced with numberless wounds in defence of Mistress Alice. If he could only enact some prodigy of valour, do some wonderful deed, and let her know that she had inspired it, he thought he could die contented.

Sometimes the Bowyer and his daughter would go out to supper with a worthy citizen at the fashionable hour of six o'clock, and on such occasions Hugh, wearing his blue 'prentice cloak as gallantly as 'prentice might, would attend with a lantern and his trusty club to escort them home. These were the brightest moments of his life. To hold the light while Mistress Alice picked her steps, to touch her hand as he helped her over broken ways, to have her leaning on his arm,—it sometimes even came to that,—this was happiness indeed!

When the nights were fair, Hugh followed in the rear, his eyes riveted on the graceful figure of the Bowyer's daughter as she and the old man moved on before him. So they threaded the narrow winding streets of the city, now passing beneath the overhanging gables of old wooden houses whence creaking signs projected into the street, and now emerging from some dark and frowning gateway into the clear moonlight. At such times, or when the shouts of straggling brawlers

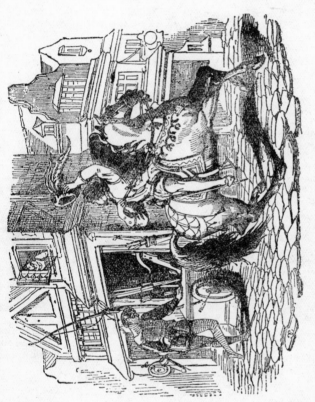

*A Gallant Cavalier.*

met her ear, the Bowyer's daughter would look timidly back at Hugh, beseeching him to draw nearer; and then how he grasped his club and longed to do battle with a dozen rufflers, for the love of Mistress Alice!

The old Bowyer was in the habit of lending money on interest to the gallants of the Court, and thus it happened that many a richly-dressed gentleman dismounted at his door. More waving plumes and gallant steeds, indeed, were seen at the Bowyer's house, and more embroidered silks and velvets sparkled in his dark shop and darker private closet, than at any merchant's in the city. In those times no less than in the present it would seem that the richest-looking cavaliers often wanted money the most.

Of these glittering clients there was one who always came alone. He was nobly mounted, and, having no attendant, gave his horse in charge to Hugh while he and the Bowyer were closeted within. Once as he sprung into the saddle Mistress Alice was seated at an upper window, and before she could withdraw he had doffed his jewelled cap and kissed his hand. Hugh watched him caracoling down the street, and burnt with indignation. But how much deeper was the glow that reddened in his cheeks when, raising his eyes to the case-ment, he saw that Alice watched the stranger too!

He came again and often, each time arrayed more gaily than before, and still the little casement showed him Mistress Alice. At length one heavy day, she fled from home. It had cost her a hard struggle, for all her old father's gifts were strewn about her chamber as if she had parted from them one by one, and knew that the time must come when these tokens of his love would wring her heart,—yet she was gone.

She left a letter commending her poor father to the care of Hugh, and wishing he might be happier than ever he could have been with her, for he deserved the love of a better and a purer heart than she had to bestow. The old man's forgiveness (she said) she had no power to ask, but she prayed God to bless him,—and so ended with a blot upon the paper where her tears had fallen.

At first the old man's wrath was kindled, and he carried his wrong to the Queen's throne itself; but there was no redress he learnt at Court, for his daughter had been conveyed abroad. This afterwards appeared to be the truth, as there came from France, after an inter-val of several years, a letter in her hand. It was written in trembling characters, and almost illegible. Little could be made out save that she often thought of home and her old dear pleasant room,—and that she had dreamt her father was dead and had not blessed her,—and that her heart was breaking.

The poor old Bowyer lingered on, never suffering Hugh to quit his sight, for he knew now that he had loved his daughter, and that was the only link that bound him to earth. It broke at length and he died, bequeathing his old 'prentice his trade and all his wealth, and solemnly charging him with his last breath to revenge his child if ever he who had worked her misery crossed his path in life again.

From the time of Alice's flight, the tilting-ground, the fields, the fencing-school, the summer-evening sports, knew Hugh no more. His spirit was dead within him. He rose to great eminence and repute among the citizens, but was seldom seen to smile, and never mingled in their reveries or rejoicings. Brave, humane, and generous, he was beloved by all. He was pitied too by those who knew his story, and these were so many that when he walked along the streets alone at dusk, even the rude common people doffed their caps and mingled a rough air of sympathy with their respect.

One night in May—it was her birthnight, and twenty years since she had left her home—Hugh Graham sat in the room she had hallowed in his boyish days. He was now a grey-haired man, though still in the prime of life. Old thoughts had borne him company for many hours, and the chamber had gradually grown quite dark, when he was roused by a low knocking at the outer door.

He hastened down, and opening it saw by the light of a lamp which he had seized upon the way, a female figure crouching in the portal. It hurried swiftly past him and glided up the stairs. He looked for pursuers. There were none in sight. No, not one.

He was inclined to think it a vision of his own brain, when suddenly a vague suspicion of the truth flashed upon his mind. He barred the door, and hastened wildly back. Yes, there she was,—there, in the chamber he had quitted,—there in her old innocent happy home, so changed that none but he could trace one gleam of what she had been,—there upon her knees,—with her hands clasped in agony and shame before her burning face.

"My God, my God!" she cried, "now strike me dead! Though I have brought death and shame and sorrow on this roof, O, let me die at home in mercy!"

There was no tear upon her face then, but she trembled and glanced round the chamber. Everything was in its old place. Her bed looked as if she had risen from it but that morning. The sight of these familiar objects, marking the dear remembrance in which she had been held, and the blight she had brought upon herself, was more than the woman's better nature that had carried her there could bear. She wept and fell upon the ground.

A rumour was spread about, in a few days' time, that the Bowyer's cruel daughter had come home, and that Master Graham had given her lodging in his house. It was rumoured too that he had resigned her fortune, in order that she might bestow it in acts of charity, and that he had vowed to guard her in her solitude, but that they were never to see each other more. These rumours greatly incensed all virtuous wives and daughters in the ward, especially when they appeared to receive corroboration from the circumstance of Master Graham taking up his abode in another tenement hard by. The estimation in which he was held, however, forbade any questioning on the subject; and as the Bowyer's house was close shut up, and nobody came forth when public shows and festivities were in progress, or to flaunt in the public walks, or to buy new fashions at the mercer's booths, all the well-conducted females agreed among themselves that there could be no woman there.

These reports had scarcely died away when the wonder of every good citizen, male and female, was utterly absorbed and swallowed up by a Royal Proclamation, in which her Majesty, strongly censuring the practice of wearing long Spanish rapiers of preposterous length (as being a bullying and swaggering custom, tending to bloodshed and public disorder), commanded that on a particular day therein named, certain grave citizens should repair to the city gates, and there, in public, break all rapiers worn or carried by persons claiming admission, that exceeded, though it were only by a quarter of an inch, three standard feet in length.

Royal Proclamations usually take their course, let the public wonder never so much. On the appointed day two citizens of high repute took up their stations at each of the gates, attended by a party of the city guard, the main body to enforce the Queen's will, and take custody of all such rebels (if any) as might have the temerity to dispute it: and a few to bear the standard measures and instruments for reducing all unlawful sword-blades to the prescribed dimensions. In pursuance of these arrangements, Master Graham and another were posted at Lud Gate, on the hill before St. Paul's.

A pretty numerous company were gathered together at this spot; for, besides the officers in attendance to enforce the proclamation, there was a motley crowd of lookers-on of various degrees, who raised from time to time such shouts and cries as the circumstances called forth. A spruce young courtier was the first who approached: he unsheathed a weapon of burnished steel that shone and glistened in the sun, and handed it with the newest air to the officer, who, finding it exactly three feet long, returned it with a bow. Thereupon the gallant raised his hat and crying "God save the Queen!" passed on amidst the plaudits of the mob. Then came another—a better courtier still—who wore a blade but two feet long, whereat the people laughed, much to the disparagement of his honour's dignity. Then came a third, a sturdy old officer of the army, girded with a rapier at least a foot and a half beyond her Majesty's pleasure; at him they raised a great shout, and most of the spectators (but especially those who were armourers or cutlers) laughed very heartily at the breakage which would ensue. But they were disappointed; for the old campaigner, coolly unbuckling his sword and bidding his servant carry it home again, passed through unarmed, to the great indignation of all the beholders. They relieved themselves in some degree by hooting a tall blustering fellow with a prodigious weapon, who stopped short on coming in sight of the preparations, and after a little consideration turned back again. But all this time no rapier had been broken, although it was high noon, and all cavaliers of any quality or appearance were taking their way towards Saint Paul's churchyard.

During these proceedings, Master Graham had stood apart, strictly confining himself to the duty imposed upon him, and taking little heed of anything beyond. He stepped forward now as a richly-dressed gentleman on foot, followed by a single attendant, was seen advancing up the hill.

As this person drew nearer, the crowd stopped their clamour, and bent forward with eager looks. Master Graham standing alone in the gateway, and the stranger coming slowly towards him, they seemed, as it were, set face to face. The nobleman (for he looked one) had a haughty and disdainful air, which bespoke the slight estimation in which he held the citizen. The citizen, on the other hand, preserved the resolute bearing of one who was not to be frowned down or daunted, and who cared very little for any nobility but that of worth and manhood. It was perhaps some consciousness on the part of each, of these feelings in the other, that infused a more stern expression into their regards as they came closer together.

"Your rapier, worthy sir!"

At the instant that he pronounced these words Graham started, and falling back some paces, laid his hand upon the dagger in his belt.

"You are the man whose horse I used to hold before the Bowyer's door? You are that man? Speak!"

"Out, you 'prentice hound!" said the other.

"You are he! I know you well now!" cried Graham. "Let no man step between us two, or I shall be his murderer." With that he drew his dagger, and rushed in upon him.

The stranger had drawn his weapon from the scabbard ready for the scrutiny, before a word was spoken. He made a thrust at his assailant, but the dagger which Graham clutched in his left hand being the dirk in use at that time for parrying such blows, promptly turned the point aside. They closed. The dagger fell rattling on the ground, and Graham, wrestling his adversary's sword from his grasp, plunged it through his heart. As he drew it out it snapped in two, leaving a fragment in the dead man's body.

All this passed so swiftly that the bystanders looked on without an effort to interfere; but the man was no sooner down than an uproar broke forth which rent the air. The attendant rushing through the gate proclaimed that his master, a nobleman, had been set upon and slain by a citizen; the word spread quickly from mouth to mouth; Saint Paul's Cathedral, and every book-shop, ordinary, and smoking-house in the churchyard poured out its stream of cavaliers and their followers, who mingling together in a dense tumultuous body, struggled, sword in hand, towards the spot.

With equal impetuosity, and stimulating each other by loud cries and shouts, the citizens and common people took up the quarrel on their side, and encircling Master Graham a hundred deep, forced him from the gate. In vain he waved the broken sword above his head, crying that he would die on London's threshold for their sacred homes. They bore him on, and ever keeping him in the midst, so that no man could attack him, fought their way into the city.

The clash of swords and roar of voices, the dust and heat and pressure, the trampling under foot of men, the distracted looks and shrieks of women at the windows above as they recognised their relatives or lovers in the crowd, the rapid tolling of alarm-bells, the furious rage and passion of the scene, were fearful. Those who, being on the outskirts of each crowd, could use their weapons with effect, fought desperately, while those behind, maddened with baffled rage, struck at each other over the heads of those before them, and crushed their own fellows. Wherever the broken sword was seen above the people's heads, towards that spot the cavaliers made a new rush. Every one of these charges was marked by sudden gaps in the throng where men were trodden down, but as fast as they were made, the tide swept over them, and still the multitude pressed on again, a confused mass of swords, clubs, staves, broken plumes, fragments of rich cloaks and doublets, and angry bleeding faces, all mixed up together in inextricable disorder.

The design of the people was to force Master Graham to take refuge in his dwelling, and to defend it until the authorities could interfere, or they could gain time for parley. But either from ignorance or in the confusion of the moment they stopped at his old house, which was closely shut. Some time was lost in beating the doors open and passing him to the front. About a score of the boldest of the other party threw themselves into the torrent while this was being done, and reaching the door at the same moment with himself cut him off from his defenders.

"I will never turn in such a righteous cause, so help me Heaven!" cried Graham, in a voice that at last made itself heard, and confronting them as he spoke. "Least of all will I turn upon this threshold which owes its desolation to such men as ye. I give no quarter, and I will have none! Strike!"

For a moment they stood at bay. At that moment a shot from an unseen hand, apparently fired by some person who had gained access to one of the opposite houses, struck Graham in the brain, and he fell dead. A low wail was heard in the air,—many people in the concourse cried that they had seen a spirit glide across the little casement window of the Bowyer's house——

A dead silence succeeded. After a short time some of the flushed and heated throng laid down their arms and softly carried the body within doors. Others fell off or slunk away in knots of two or three, others whispered together in groups, and before a numerous guard which then rode up could muster in the street, it was nearly empty.

Those who carried Master Graham to the bed up-stairs were shocked to see a woman lying beneath the window with her hands clasped together. After trying to recover her in vain, they laid her near the citizen, who still retained, tightly grasped in his right hand, the first and last sword that was broken that day at Lud Gate.

The Giant uttered these concluding words with sudden precipitation; and on the instant the strange light which had filled the hall faded away. Joe Toddyhigh glanced involuntarily at the eastern window, and saw the first pale gleam of morning. He turned his head again towards the other window in which the Giants had been seated. It was empty. The cask of wine was gone, and he could dimly make out that the two great figures stood mute and motionless upon their pedestals.

After rubbing his eyes and wondering for full half an hour, during which time he observed morning come creeping on apace, he yielded to the drowsiness which overpowered him and fell into a refreshing slumber. When he awoke it was broad day; the building was open, and workmen were busily engaged in removing the vestiges of last night's feast.

Stealing gently down the little stairs, and assuming the air of some early lounger who had dropped in from the street, he walked up to the foot of each pedestal in turn, and attentively examined the figure it supported. There could be no doubt about the features of either; he recollected the exact expression they had worn at different passages of their conversation, and recognised in every line and lineament the Giants of the night. Assured that it was no vision, but that he had heard and seen with his own proper senses, he walked forth, determining at all hazards to conceal himself in the Guildhall again that evening. He further resolved to sleep all day, so that he might be very wakeful and vigilant, and above all that he might take notice of the figures at the precise moment of their becoming animated and subsiding into their old state, which he greatly reproached himself for not having done already.

---

## CORRESPONDENCE

### TO MASTER HUMPHREY

SIR,—Before you proceed any further in your account of your friends and what you say and do when you meet together, excuse me if I proffer my claim to be elected to one of the vacant chairs in that old room of yours. Don't reject me without full consideration; for if you do, you will be sorry for it afterwards—you will, upon my life.

I enclose my card, sir, in this letter. I never was ashamed of my name, and I never shall be. I am considered a devilish gentlemanly fellow, and I act up to the character. If you want a reference, ask any of the men of our club. Ask any fellow who goes there to write his letters, what sort of conversation mine is. Ask him if he thinks I have the sort of voice that will suit your deaf friend and make him hear, if he can hear anything at all. Ask the servants what they think of me. There's not a rascal among 'em, sir, but will tremble to

*A Charming Fellow.*

hear my name. That reminds me—don't you say too much about that housekeeper of yours; it's a low subject, damned low.

I tell you what, sir. If you vote me into one of those empty chairs, you'll have among you a man with a fund of gentlemanly information that'll rather astonish you. I can let you into a few anecdotes about some fine women of title, that are quite high life, sir—the tiptop sort of thing. I know the name of every man who has been out on an affair of honour within the last five-and-twenty years; I know the private particulars of every cross and squabble that has taken place upon the turf, at the gaming-table, or elsewhere, during the whole of that time. I have been called the gentlemanly chronicle. You may consider yourself a lucky dog; upon my soul, you may congratulate yourself, though I say so.

It's an uncommon good notion that of yours, not letting anybody know where you live. I have tried it, but there has always been an anxiety respecting me, which has found me out. Your deaf friend is a cunning fellow to keep his name so close. I have tried that too, but have always failed. I shall be proud to make his acquaintance—tell him so, with my compliments.

You must have been a queer fellow when you were a child, confounded queer. It's odd, all that about the picture in your first paper—prosy, but told in a devilish gentlemanly sort of way. In places like that I could come in with great effect with a touch of life—don't you feel that?

I am anxiously waiting for your next paper to know whether your friends live upon the premises, and at your expense, which I take it for granted is the case. If I am right in this impression, I know a charming fellow (an excellent companion and most delightful company) who will be proud to join you. Some years ago he seconded a great many prize-fighters, and once fought an amateur match himself; since then he has driven several mails, broken at different periods all the lamps on the right-hand side of Oxford-street, and six times carried away every bell-handle in Bloomsbury-square, besides turning off the gas in various thoroughfares. In point of gentlemanliness he is unrivalled, and I should say that next to myself he is of all men the best suited to your purpose.

> Expecting your reply,
> I am,
> Etc, etc.

Master Humphrey informs this gentleman that this application, both as it concerns himself and his friend, is rejected.

## II

## MASTER HUMPHREY, FROM HIS CLOCK-SIDE IN THE CHIMNEY-CORNER

My old companion tells me it is midnight. The fire glows brightly, crackling with a sharp and cheerful sound, as if it loved to burn. The merry cricket on the hearth (my constant visitor), this ruddy blaze, my clock, and I, seem to share the world among us, and to be the only things awake. The wind, high and boisterous but now, has died away and hoarsely mutters in its sleep. I love all times and seasons each in its turn, and am apt, perhaps, to think the present one the best; but past or coming I always love this peaceful time of night, when long-buried thoughts, favoured by the gloom and silence, steal from their graves, and haunt the scenes of faded happiness and hope.

The popular faith in ghosts has a remarkable affinity with the whole current of our thoughts at such an hour as this, and seems to be their necessary and natural consequence. For who can wonder that man should feel a vague belief in tales of disembodied spirits wandering through those places which they once dearly affected, when he himself, scarcely less separated from his old world than they, is for ever lingering upon past emotions and bygone times, and hovering, the ghost of his former self, about the places and people that warmed his heart of old? It is thus that at this quiet hour I haunt the house where I was born, the rooms I used to tread, the scenes of my infancy, my boyhood, and my youth; it is thus that I prowl around my buried treasure (though not of gold or silver), and mourn my loss; it is thus that I revisit the ashes of extinguished fires, and take my silent stand at old bedsides. If my spirit should ever glide back to this chamber when my body is mingled with the dust, it will but follow the course it often took in the old man's lifetime, and add but one more change to the subjects of its contemplation.

In all my idle speculations I am greatly assisted by various legends connected with my venerable house, which are current in the neighbourhood, and are so numerous that there is scarce a cupboard or corner that has not some dismal story of its own. When I first entertained thoughts of becoming its tenant, I was assured that it was haunted from roof to cellar, and I believe that the bad opinion in which my neighbours once held me, had its rise in my not being torn to pieces, or at least distracted with terror, on the night I took possession; in either of which cases I should doubtless have arrived by a short cut at the very summit of popularity.

But traditions and rumours all taken into account, who so abets me in every fancy and chimes with my every thought, as my dear deaf friend? and how often have I cause to bless the day that brought us two together! Of all days in the year I rejoice to think that it should have been Christmas Day, with which from childhood we associate something friendly, hearty, and sincere.

I had walked out to cheer myself with the happiness of others, and, in the little tokens of festivity and rejoicing, of which the streets and houses present so many upon that day, had lost some hours. Now I stopped to look at a merry party hurrying through the snow on foot to their place of meeting, and now turned back to see a whole coachful of children safely deposited at the welcome house. At one time, I admired how carefully the working man carried the baby in its gaudy hat and feathers, and how his wife, trudging patiently on behind, forgot even her care of her gay clothes, in exchanging greetings with the child as it crowed and laughed over the father's shoulder; at another, I pleased myself with some passing scene of gallantry or courtship, and was glad to believe that for a season half the world of poverty was gay.

As the day closed in, I still rambled through the streets, feeling a companionship in the bright fires that cast their warm reflection on the windows as I passed, and losing all sense of my own loneliness in imagining the sociality and kind-fellowship that everywhere prevailed. At length I happened to stop before a Tavern, and, encountering a Bill of Fare in the window, it all at once brought it into my head to wonder what kind of people dined alone in Taverns upon Christmas Day.

Solitary men are accustomed, I suppose, unconsciously to look upon solitude as their own peculiar property. I had sat alone in my room on many, many anniversaries of this great holiday, and had never regarded it but as one of universal assemblage and rejoicing. I had excepted, and with an aching heart, a crowd of prisoners and beggars; but *these* were not the men for whom the Tavern doors were open. Had they any customers, or was it a mere form?—a form, no doubt.

Trying to feel quite sure of this, I walked away; but before I had gone many paces, I stopped and looked back. There was a provoking air of business in the lamp above the door which I could not overcome. I began to be afraid there might be many customers —young men, perhaps, struggling with the world, utter strangers in this great place, whose friends lived at a long distance off, and whose means were too slender to enable them to make the journey. The supposition gave rise to so many distressing little pictures, that, in preference to carrying them home with me, I determined to encounter the realities. So I turned and walked in.

I was at once glad and sorry to find that there was only one person in the dining-room; glad to know that there were not more, and sorry that he should be there by himself. He did not look so old as I, but like me he was advanced in life, and his hair was nearly white. Though I made more noise in entering and seating myself than was quite necessary, with the view of attracting his attention and saluting him in the good old form of that time of year, he did not raise his head, but sat with it resting on his hand, musing over his half-finished meal.

I called for something which would give me an excuse for remaining in the room (I had dined early, as my housekeeper was engaged at night to partake of some friend's good cheer), and sat where I could observe without intruding on him. After a time he looked up. He was aware that somebody had entered, but could see very little of me, as I sat in the shade and he in the light. He was sad and thoughtful, and I forbore to trouble him by speaking.

Let me believe it was something better than curiosity which riveted my attention and impelled me strongly towards this gentleman. I never saw so patient and kind a face. He should have been surrounded by friends, and yet here he sat dejected and alone when all men had their friends about them. As often as he roused himself from his reverie he would fall into it again, and it was plain that, whatever were the subject of his thoughts, they were of a melancholy kind, and would not be controlled.

He was not used to solitude. I was sure of that; for I know by myself that if he had been, his manner would have been different, and he would have taken some slight interest in the arrival of another. I could not fail to mark that he had no appetite; that he tried to eat in vain; that time after time the plate was pushed away, and he relapsed into his former posture.

His mind was wandering among old Christmas days, I thought. Many of them sprung up together, not with a long gap between each, but in unbroken succession like days of the week. It was a great change to find himself for the first time (I quite settled that it *was* the first) in an empty silent room with no soul to care for. I could not help following him in imagination through crowds of pleasant faces, and then coming back to that dull place with its bough of mistletoe sickening in the gas, and sprigs of holly parched up already by a Simoom of roast and boiled. The very waiter had gone home; and his representative, a poor, lean, hungry man, was keeping Christmas in his jacket.

I grew still more interested in my friend. His dinner done, a decanter of wine was placed before him. It remained untouched for a long time, but at length with a quivering hand he filled a glass and raised it to his lips. Some tender wish to which he had been accustomed to give utterance on that day, or some beloved name that he had been used to pledge, trembled upon them at the moment. He put it down very hastily—took it up once more—again put it down—pressed his hand upon his face—yes—and tears stole down his cheeks, I am certain.

Without pausing to consider whether I did right or wrong, I stepped across the room, and sitting down beside him laid my hand gently on his arm.

"My friend," I said, "forgive me if I beseech you to take comfort and consolation from the lips of an old man. I will not preach to you what I have not practised, indeed. Whatever be your grief, be of a good heart—be of a good heart, pray!"

"I see that you speak earnestly," he replied, "and kindly I am very sure, but——"

I nodded my head to show that I understood what he would say; for I had already gathered, from a certain fixed expression in his face, and from the attention with which he watched me while I spoke, that his sense of hearing was destroyed. "There should be a freemasonry between us," said I, pointing from himself to me to explain my meaning; "if not in our gray hairs, at least in our misfortunes. You see that I am but a poor cripple."

I never felt so happy under my affliction since the trying moment of my first becoming conscious of it, as when he took my hand in his with a smile that has lighted my path in life from that day, and we sat down side by side.

This was the beginning of my friendship with the deaf gentleman; and when was ever the slight and easy service of a kind word in season repaid by such attachment and devotion as he has shown to me!

He produced a little set of tablets and a pencil to facilitate our conversation, on that our first acquaintance; and I well remember how awkward and constrained I was in writing down my share of the dialogue, and how easily he guessed my meaning before I had written half of what I had to say. He told me in a faltering voice that he had not been accustomed to be alone on that day —that it had always been a little festival with him; and seeing that I glanced at his dress in the expectation that he wore mourning, he added hastily that it was not that; if it had been he thought he could have borne it better. From that time to the present we have never touched upon this theme. Upon every return of the same day we have been together; and although we make it our annual custom to drink to each other hand in hand after dinner, and to recall with affectionate garrulity every circumstance of our first meeting, we always avoid this one as if by mutual consent.

Meantime we have gone on strengthening in our friendship and regard, and forming an attachment which, I trust and believe, will only be interrupted by death, to be renewed in another existence. I scarcely know how we communicate as we do; but he has long since ceased to be deaf to me. He is frequently my companion in my walks, and even in crowded streets replies to my slightest look or gesture, as though he could read my thoughts. From the vast number of objects which pass in rapid succession before our eyes, we frequently select the same for some particular notice or remark; and when one of these little coincidences occurs, I cannot describe the pleasure which animates my friend, or the beaming countenance he will preserve for half-an-hour afterwards at least.

He is a great thinker from living so much within himself, and, having a lively imagination, has a facility of conceiving and enlarging upon odd ideas, which renders him invaluable to our little body, and greatly astonishes our two friends. His powers in this respect are much assisted by a large pipe, which he assures us once belonged to a German Student. Be this as it may, it has undoubtedly a very ancient and mysterious appearance, and is of such capacity that it takes three hours and a half to smoke it out. I have reason to believe that my barber, who is the chief authority of a knot of gossips, who congregate every evening at a small tobacconist's hard by, has related anecdotes of this pipe and the grim figures that are carved upon its bowl, at which all the smokers in the neighbourhood have stood aghast; and I know that my housekeeper, while she holds it in high veneration, has a superstitious feeling connected with it which would render her exceedingly unwilling to be left alone in its company after dark.

Whatever sorrow my dear friend has known, and whatever grief may linger in some secret corner of his heart, he is now a cheerful, placid, happy creature. Misfortune can never have fallen upon such a man but for some good purpose; and when I see its traces in his gentle nature and his earnest feeling, I am the less disposed to murmur at such trials as I may have undergone myself. With regard to the pipe, I have a theory of my own; I cannot help thinking that it is in some manner connected with the event that brought us together; for I remember that it was a long time before he even talked about it; that when he did, he grew reserved and melancholy; and that it was a long time yet before he brought it forth. I have no curiosity, however, upon this subject; for I know that it promotes his tranquillity and comfort, and I need no other inducement to regard it with my utmost favour.

Such is the deaf gentleman. I can call up his figure now, clad in sober gray, and seated in the chimney-corner. As he puffs out the smoke from his favourite pipe, he casts a look on me brimful of cordiality and friendship, and says all manner of kind and genial things in a cheerful smile; then he raises his eyes to my clock, which is just about to strike, and, glancing from it to me and back again, seems to divide his heart between us. For myself, it is not too much to say that I would gladly part with one of my poor limbs, could he but hear the old clock's voice.

Of our two friends, the first has been all his life one of that easy, wayward, truant class whom the world is accustomed to designate as nobody's enemies but their own. Bred to a profession for which he never qualified himself, and reared in the expectation of a fortune he has never inherited, he has undergone every vicissitude of which such an existence is capable. He and his younger brother, both orphans from their childhood, were educated by a wealthy relative, who taught them to expect an equal division of his property; but too indolent to court, and too honest to flatter, the elder gradually lost ground in the affections of a capricious old man, and the younger,

*The Two Friends.*

The Two Friends

who did not fail to improve his opportunity, now triumphs in the possession of enormous wealth. His triumph is to hoard it in solitary wretchedness, and probably to feel with the expenditure of every shilling a greater pang than the loss of his whole inheritance ever cost his brother.

Jack Redburn—he was Jack Redburn at the first little school he went to, where every other child was mastered and surnamed, and he has been Jack Redburn all his life, or he would perhaps have been a richer man by this time—has been an inmate of my house these eight years past. He is my librarian, secretary, steward, and first minister; director of all my affairs, and inspector-general of my household. He is something of a musician, something of an author, something of an actor, something of a painter, very much of a carpenter, and an extraordinary gardener, having had all his life a wonderful aptitude for learning everything that was of no use to him. He is remarkably fond of children, and is the best and kindest nurse in sickness that ever drew the breath of life. He has mixed with every grade of society, and known the utmost distress; but there never was a less selfish, a more tender-hearted, a more enthusiastic, or a more guileless man; and I dare say, if few have done less good, fewer still have done less harm in the world than he. By what chance Nature forms such whimsical jumbles I don't know; but I do know that she sends them among us very often, and that the king of the whole race is Jack Redburn.

I should be puzzled to say how old he is. His health is none of the best, and he wears a quantity of iron-gray hair, which shades his face and gives it rather a worn appearance; but we consider him quite a young fellow notwithstanding; and if a youthful spirit, surviving the roughest contact with the world, confers upon its possessor any title to be considered young, then he is a mere child. The only interruptions to his careless cheerfulness are on a wet Sunday, when he is apt to be unusually religious and solemn, and sometimes of an evening, when he has been blowing a very slow tune on the flute. On these last-named occasions he is apt to incline towards the mysterious or the terrible. As a specimen of his powers in this mood, I refer my readers to the extract from the clock-case which follows this paper: he brought it to me not long ago at midnight, and informed me that the main incident had been suggested by a dream of the night before.

His apartments are two cheerful rooms looking towards the garden, and one of his great delights is to arrange and rearrange the furniture in these chambers, and put it in every possible variety of position. During the whole time he has been here, I do not think he has slept for two nights running with the head of his bed in the same place; and every time he moves it, is to be the last. My housekeeper was at first well-nigh distracted by these frequent changes; but she has become quite reconciled to them by degrees, and has so fallen in with his humour, that they often consult together with great gravity upon the next final alteration. Whatever his arrangements are, however, they are always a pattern of neatness; and every one of the manifold articles connected with his manifold occupations is to be found in its own particular place. Until within the last two or three years he was subject to an occasional fit (which usually came upon him in very fine weather), under the influence of which he would dress himself with peculiar care, and, going out under pretence of taking a walk, disappeared for several days together. At length, after the interval between each outbreak of this disorder had gradually grown longer and longer, it wholly disappeared; and now he seldom stirs abroad, except to stroll out a little way on a summer's evening. Whether he yet mistrusts his own constancy in this respect, and is therefore afraid to wear a coat, I know not; but we seldom see him in any other upper garment than an old spectral-looking dressing-gown, with very disproportionate pockets, full of a miscellaneous collection of odd matters, which he picks up wherever he can lay his hands upon them.

Everything that is a favourite with our friend is a favourite with us; and thus it happens that the fourth among us is Mr. Owen Miles, a most worthy gentleman, who had treated Jack with great kindness before my deaf friend and I encountered him by an accident, to which I may refer on some future occasion. Mr. Miles was once a very rich merchant; but receiving a severe shock in the death of his wife, he retired from business, and devoted himself to a quiet, unostentatious life. He is an excellent man, of thoroughly sterling character: not of quick apprehension, and not without some amusing prejudices, which I shall leave to their own development. He holds us all in profound veneration; but Jack Redburn he esteems as a kind of pleasant wonder, that he may venture to approach familiarly. He believes, not only that no man ever lived who could do so many things as Jack, but that no man ever lived who could do anything so well; and he never calls my attention to any of his ingenious proceedings, but he whispers in my ear, nudging me at the same time with his elbow: "If he had only made it his trade, sir—if he had only made it his trade!"

They are inseparable companions; one would almost suppose that, although Mr. Miles never by any chance does anything in the way of assistance, Jack could do nothing without him. Whether he is reading, writing, painting, carpentering, gardening, flute-playing, or what not, there is Mr. Miles beside him, buttoned up to the chin in his blue coat, and looking on with a face of incredulous delight, as though he could not credit the testimony of his own senses, and had a misgiving that no man could be so clever but in a dream.

These are my friends; I have now introduced myself and them.

## THE CLOCK-CASE

A CONFESSION FOUND IN A PRISON IN THE TIME OF CHARLES THE
SECOND

I HELD a lieutenant's commission in his Majesty's army, and served
abroad in the campaigns of 1677 and 1678. The treaty of Nimeguen
being concluded, I returned home, and retiring from the service,
withdrew to a small estate lying a few miles east of London, which
I had recently acquired in right of my wife.

This is the last night I have to live, and I will set down the naked
truth without disguise. I was never a brave man, and had always
been from my childhood of a secret, sullen, distrustful nature. I
speak of myself as if I had passed from the world; for while I write
this, my grave is digging, and my name is written in the black-book
of death.

Soon after my return to England, my only brother was seized
with mortal illness. This circumstance gave me slight or no pain; for
since we had been men, we had associated but very little together.
He was open-hearted and generous, handsomer than I, more accomplished, and generally beloved. Those who sought my acquaintance abroad or at home, because they were friends of his, seldom
attached themselves to me long, and would usually say, in our first
conversation, that they were surprised to find two brothers so
unlike in their manners and appearance. It was my habit to lead
them on to this avowal; for I knew what comparisons they must
draw between us; and having a rankling envy in my heart, I sought
to justify it to myself.

We had married two sisters. This additional tie between us, as it
may appear to some, only estranged us the more. His wife knew me
well. I never struggled with any secret jealousy or gall when she was
present but that woman knew it as well as I did. I never raised my
eyes at such times but I found hers fixed upon me; I never bent them
on the ground or looked another way but I felt that she overlooked
me always. It was an inexpressible relief to me when we quarrelled,
and a greater relief still when I heard abroad that she was dead. It
seems to me now as if some strange and terrible foreshadowing of
what has happened since must have hung over us then. I was afraid
of her; she haunted me; her fixed and steady look comes back upon
me now, like the memory of a dark dream, and makes my blood
run cold.

She died shortly after giving birth to a child—a boy. When my
brother knew that all hope of his own recovery was past, he called
my wife to his bedside, and confided this orphan, a child of four
years old, to her protection. He bequeathed to him all the property

he had, and willed that, in case of his child's death, it should pass to my wife, as the only acknowledgment he could make her for her care and love. He exchanged a few brotherly words with me, deploring our long separation; and being exhausted, fell into a slumber from which he never awoke.

We had no children; and as there had been a strong affection between the sisters, and my wife had almost supplied the place of a mother to this boy, she loved him as if he had been her own. The child was ardently attached to her; but he was his mother's image in face and spirit, and always mistrusted me.

I can scarcely fix the date when the feeling first came upon me; but I soon began to be uneasy when this child was by. I never roused myself from some moody train of thought but I marked him looking at me; not with mere childish wonder, but with something of the purpose and meaning that I had so often noted in his mother. It was no effort of my fancy, founded on close resemblance of feature and expression. I never could look the boy down. He feared me, but seemed by some instinct to despise me while he did so; and even when he drew back beneath my gaze—as he would when we were alone, to get nearer to the door—he would keep his bright eyes upon me still.

Perhaps I hide the truth from myself, but I do not think that, when this began, I meditated to do him any wrong. I may have thought how serviceable his inheritance would be to us, and may have wished him dead; but I believe I had no thought of compassing his death. Neither did the idea come upon me at once, but by very slow degrees, presenting itself at first in dim shapes at a very great distance, as men may think of an earthquake or the last day; then drawing nearer and nearer, and losing something of its horror and improbability; then coming to be part and parcel—nay nearly the whole sum and substance—of my daily thoughts, and resolving itself into a question of means and safety; not of doing or abstaining from the deed.

While this was going on within me, I never could bear that the child should see me looking at him, and yet I was under a fascination which made it a kind of business with me to contemplate his slight and fragile figure and think how easily it might be done. Sometimes I would steal up-stairs and watch him as he slept; but usually I hovered in the garden near the window of the room in which he learnt his little tasks; and there, as he sat upon a low seat beside my wife, I would peer at him for hours together from behind a tree; starting, like the guilty wretch I was, at every rustling of a leaf, and still gliding back to look and start again.

Hard by our cottage, but quite out of sight, and (if there were any wind astir) of hearing too, was a deep sheet of water. I spent days in shaping with my pocket-knife a rough model of a boat, which I finished at last and dropped in the child's way. Then I withdrew to a secret place, which he must pass if he stole away alone to swim this bauble, and lurked there for his coming. He came neither that day nor the next, though I waited from noon till nightfall. I was sure that I had him in my net, for I had heard him prattling of the toy, and knew that in his infant pleasure he kept it by his side in bed. I felt no weariness or fatigue, but waited patiently, and on the third day he passed me, running joyously along, with his silken hair streaming in the wind, and he singing—God have mercy upon me! —singing a merry ballad,—who could hardly lisp the words.

I stole down after him, creeping under certain shrubs which grow in that place, and none but devils know with what terror I, a strong, full-grown man, tracked the footsteps of that baby as he approached the water's brink. I was close upon him, had sunk upon my knee and raised my hand to thrust him in, when he saw my shadow in the stream and turned him round.

His mother's ghost was looking from his eyes. The sun burst forth from behind a cloud; it shone in the bright sky, the glistening earth, the clear water, the sparkling drops of rain upon the leaves. There were eyes in everything. The whole great universe of light was there to see the murder done. I know not what he said; he came of bold and manly blood, and, child as he was, he did not crouch or fawn upon me. I heard him cry that he would try to love me,—not that he did,—and then I saw him running back towards the house. The next I saw was my own sword naked in my hand, and he lying at my feet stark dead,—dabbled here and there with blood, but otherwise no different from what I had seen him in his sleep—in the same attitude too, with his cheek resting upon his little hand.

I took him in my arms and laid him—very gently now that he was dead—in a thicket. My wife was from home that day, and would not return until the next. Our bedroom window, the only sleeping-room on that side of the house, was but a few feet from the ground, and I resolved to descend from it at night and bury him in the garden. I had no thought that I had failed in my design, no thought that the water would be dragged and nothing found, that the money must now lie waste, since I must encourage the idea that the child was lost or stolen. All my thoughts were bound up and knotted together in the one absorbing necessity of hiding what I had done.

How I felt when they came to tell me that the child was missing, when I ordered scouts in all directions, when I gasped and trembled at every one's approach, no tongue can tell or mind of man conceive. I buried him that night. When I parted the boughs and looked into the dark thicket, there was a glow-worm shining like the visible spirit of God upon the murdered child. I glanced down into his grave when I had placed him there, and still it gleamed upon his breast; an eye of fire looking up to Heaven in supplication to the stars that watched me at my work.

I had to meet my wife, and break the news, and give her hope that the child would soon be found. All this I did,—with some appearance, I suppose, of being sincere, for I was the object of no suspicion. This done, I sat at the bedroom window all day long, and watched the spot where the dreadful secret lay.

It was in a piece of ground which had been dug up to be newly turfed, and which I had chosen on that account, as the traces of my spade were less likely to attract attention. The men who laid down the grass must have thought me mad. I called to them continually to expedite their work, ran out and worked beside them, trod down the earth with my feet, and hurried them with frantic eagerness. They had finished their task before night, and then I thought myself comparatively safe.

I slept,—not as men do who awake refreshed and cheerful, but I did sleep, passing from vague and shadowy dreams of being hunted down, to visions of the plot of grass, through which now a hand, and now a foot, and now the head itself was starting out. At this point I always woke and stole to the window, to make sure that it was not really so. That done, I crept to bed again; and thus I spent the night in fits and starts, getting up and lying down full twenty times, and dreaming the same dream over and over again,—which was far worse than lying awake, for every dream had a whole night's suffering of its own. Once I thought the child was alive, and that I had never tried to kill him. To wake from that dream was the most dreadful agony of all.

The next day I sat at the window again, never once taking my eyes from the place, which, although it was covered by the grass, was as plain to me—its shape, its size, its depth, its jagged sides, and all—as if it had been open to the light of day. When a servant walked across it, I felt as if he must sink in; when he had passed, I looked to see that his feet had not worn the edges. If a bird lighted there, I was in terror lest by some tremendous interposition it should be instrumental in the discovery; if a breath of air sighed across it, to me it whispered murder. There was not a sight or a sound—how ordinary, mean, or unimportant soever—but was fraught with fear. And in this state of ceaseless watching I spent three days.

On the fourth there came to the gate one who had served with me abroad, accompanied by a brother officer of his whom I had never seen. I felt that I could not bear to be out of sight of the place. It was a summer evening, and I bade my people take a table and a flask of wine into the garden. Then I sat down *with my chair upon the grave*, and being assured that nobody could disturb it now without my knowledge, tried to drink and talk.

They hoped that my wife was well,—that she was not obliged to keep her chamber,—that they had not frightened her away. What could I do but tell them with a faltering tongue about the child? The officer whom I did not know was a down-looking man, and kept his eyes upon the ground while I was speaking. Even that terrified me. I could not divest myself of the idea that he saw something there which caused him to suspect the truth. I asked him hurriedly if he supposed that—and stopped. "That the child has been murdered?"

said he, looking mildly at me: "O no! what could a man gain by murdering a poor child?" *I* could have told him what a man gained by such a deed, no one better: but I held my peace and shivered as with an ague.

Mistaking my emotion, they were endeavouring to cheer me with the hope that the boy would certainly be found,—great cheer that was for me!—when we heard a low deep howl, and presently there sprung over the wall two great dogs, who, bounding into the garden, repeated the baying sound we had heard before.

"Bloodhounds!" cried my visitors.

What need to tell me that! I had never seen one of that kind in all my life, but I knew what they were and for what purpose they had come. I grasped the elbows of my chair, and neither spoke nor moved.

"They are of the genuine breed," said the man whom I had known abroad, "and being out for exercise have no doubt escaped from their keeper."

Both he and his friend turned to look at the dogs, who with their noses to the ground moved restlessly about, running to and fro, and up and down, and across, and round in circles, careering about like wild things, and all this time taking no notice of us, but ever and again repeating the yell we had heard already, then dropping their noses to the ground again and tracking earnestly here and there. They now began to snuff the earth more eagerly than they had done yet, and although they were still very restless, no longer beat about in such wide circuits, but kept near to one spot, and constantly diminished the distance between themselves and me.

At last they came up close to the great chair on which I sat, and raising their frightful howl once more, tried to tear away the wooden rails that kept them from the ground beneath. I saw how I looked, in the faces of the two who were with me.

"They scent some prey," said they, both together.

"They scent no prey!" cried I.

"In Heaven's name, move!" said the one I knew, very earnestly, "or you will be torn to pieces."

"Let them tear me from limb to limb, I'll never leave this place!" cried I. "Are dogs to hurry men to shameful deaths! Hew them down, cut them in pieces."

"There is some foul mystery here!" said the officer whom I did not know, drawing his sword. "In King Charles's name, assist me to secure this man."

They both set upon me and forced me away, though I fought and bit and caught at them like a madman. After a struggle, they got me quietly between them; and then, my God! I saw the angry dogs tearing at the earth and throwing it up into the air like water.

What more have I to tell? That I fell upon my knees, and with chattering teeth confessed the truth, and prayed to be forgiven. That I had since denied, and now confess to it again. That I have been tried for the crime, found guilty, and sentenced. That I have not the courage to anticipate my doom, or to bear up manfully against it. That I have no compassion, no consolation, no hope, no friend. That my wife has happily lost for the time those faculties which would enable her to know my misery or hers. That I am alone in this stone dungeon with my evil spirit, and that I die to-morrow.

[*Old Curiosity Shop* begins here.]

## CORRESPONDENCE

Master Humphrey has been favoured with the following letter written on strongly-scented paper, and sealed in light-blue wax with the representation of two very plump doves interchanging beaks. It does not commence with any of the usual forms of address, but begins as is here set forth.

Bath, Wednesday night.

Heavens! into what an indiscretion do I suffer myself to be betrayed! To address these faltering lines to a total stranger, and that stranger one of a conflicting sex!—and yet I am precipitated into the abyss, and have no power of self-snatchation (forgive me if I coin that phrase) from the yawning gulf before me.

Yes, I am writing to a man; but let me not think of that, for madness is in the thought. You will understand my feelings? O yes, I am sure you will; and you will respect them too, and not despise them,—will you?

Let me be calm. That portrait,—smiling as once he smiled on me; that cane,—dangling as I have seen it dangle from his hand I know not how oft; those legs that have glided through my nightly dreams and never stopped to speak; the perfectly gentlemanly, though false original,—can I be mistaken? O no, no.

Let me be calmer yet; I would be calm as coffins. You have published a letter from one whose likeness is engraved, but whose name (and wherefore?) is suppressed. Shall *I* breathe that name! Is it—but why ask when my heart tells me too truly that it is!

I would not upbraid him with his treachery; I would not remind him of those times when he plighted the most eloquent of vows, and procured from me a small pecuniary accommodation; and yet I would see him—see him did I say—*him*—alas! such is woman's nature. For as the poet beautifully says—but you will already have anticipated the sentiment. Is it not sweet? O yes!

It was in this city (hallowed by the recollection) that I met him first; and assuredly if mortal happiness be recorded anywhere, then those rubbers with their three-and-sixpenny points are scored on tablets of celestial brass. He always held an honour—generally two. On that eventful night we stood at eight. He raised his eyes (luminous in their seductive sweetness) to my agitated face. "*Can* you?" said

he, with peculiar meaning. I felt the gentle pressure of his foot on
mine; our corns throbbed in unison. *"Can* you?" he said again; and
every lineament of his expressive countenance added the words
"resist me?" I murmured "No," and fainted.

They said, when I recovered, it was the weather. *I* said it was
the nutmeg in the negus. How little did they suspect the truth! How
little did they guess the deep mysterious meaning of that inquiry!
He called next morning on his knees; I do not mean to say that he
actually came in that position to the house-door, but that he went
down upon those joints directly the servant had retired. He brought
some verses in his hat, which he said were original, but which I have
since found were Milton's; likewise a little bottle labelled laudanum;
also a pistol and a sword-stick. He drew the latter, uncorked the
former, and clicked the trigger of the pocket fire-arm. He had come,
he said, to conquer or to die. He did not die. He wrested from me
an avowal of my love, and let off the pistol out of a back window
previous to partaking of a slight repast.

Faithless, inconstant man! How many ages seem to have elapsed
since his unaccountable and perfidious disappearance! Could I still
forgive him both that and the borrowed lucre that he promised to
pay next week! Could I spurn him from my feet if he approached
in penitence, and with a matrimonial object! Would the blandishing
enchanter still weave his spells around me, or should I burst them
all and turn away in coldness! I dare not trust my weakness with
the thought.

My brain is in a whirl again. You know his address, his occupations,
his mode of life,—are acquainted, perhaps, with his inmost thoughts.
You are a humane and philanthropic character; reveal all you know
—all; but especially the street and number of his lodgings. The post
is departing, the bellman rings,—pray Heaven it be not the knell
of love and hope to

BELINDA.

P.S. Pardon the wanderings of a bad pen and a distracted mind.
Address to the Post-office. The bellman, rendered impatient by
delay, is ringing dreadfully in the passage.

P.P.S. I open this to say that the bellman is gone, and that you
must not expect it till the next post; so don't be surprised when
you don't get it.

Master Humphrey does not feel himself at liberty to furnish his
fair correspondent with the address of the gentleman in question, but
he publishes her letter as a public appeal to his faith and gallantry.

## III

### MASTER HUMPHREY'S VISITOR

WHEN I am in a thoughtful mood, I often succeed in diverting the current of some mournful reflections, by conjuring up a number of fanciful associations with the objects that surround me, and dwelling upon the scenes and characters they suggest.

I have been led by this habit to assign to every room in my house and every old staring portrait on its walls a separate interest of its own. Thus, I am persuaded that a stately dame, terrible to behold in her rigid modesty, who hangs above the chimney-piece of my bedroom, is the former lady of the mansion. In the courtyard below is a stone face of surpassing ugliness, which I have somehow —in a kind of jealousy, I am afraid—associated with her husband. Above my study is a little room with ivy peeping through the lattice, from which I bring their daughter, a lovely girl of eighteen or nineteen years of age, and dutiful in all respects save one, that one being her devoted attachment to a young gentleman on the stairs, whose grandmother (degraded to a disused laundry in the garden) piques herself upon an old family quarrel, and is the implacable enemy of their love. With such materials as these I work out many a little drama, whose chief merit is, that I can bring it to a happy end at will. I have so many of them on hand, that if on my return home one of these evenings I were to find some bluff old wight of two centuries ago comfortably seated in my easy chair, and a lovelorn damsel vainly appealing to his heart, and leaning her white arm upon my clock itself, I verily believe I should only express my surprise that they had kept me waiting so long, and never honoured me with a call before.

I was in such a mood as this, sitting in my garden yesterday morning under the shade of a favourite tree, revelling in all the bloom and brightness about me, and feeling every sense of hope and enjoyment quickened by this most beautiful season of Spring, when my meditations were interrupted by the unexpected appearance of my barber at the end of the walk, who I immediately saw was coming towards me with a hasty step that betokened something remarkable.

My barber is at all times a very brisk, bustling, active little man,— for he is, as it were, chubby all over, without being stout or unwieldy, —but yesterday his alacrity was so very uncommon that it quite took me by surprise. For could I fail to observe when he came up to me that his gray eyes were twinkling in a most extraordinary manner, that his little red nose was in an unusual glow, that every line in his round bright face was twisted and curved into an expres-

*Mr Pickwick introduces Himself to Master Humphrey.*

sion of pleased surprise, and that his whole countenance was radiant with glee? I was still more surprised to see my housekeeper, who usually preserves a very staid air, and stands somewhat upon her dignity, peeping round the hedge at the bottom of the walk, and exchanging nods and smiles with the barber, who twice or thrice looked over his shoulder for that purpose. I could conceive no announcement to which these appearances could be the prelude, unless it were that they had married each other that morning.

I was, consequently, a little disappointed when it only came out that there was a gentleman in the house who wished to speak with me.

"And who is it?" said I.

The barber, with his face screwed up still tighter than before, replied that the gentleman would not send his name, but wished to see me. I pondered for a moment, wondering who this visitor might be, and I remarked that he embraced the opportunity of exchanging another nod with the housekeeper, who still lingered in the distance.

"Well!" said I, "bid the gentleman come here."

This seemed to be the consummation of the barber's hopes, for he turned sharp round, and actually ran away.

Now, my sight is not very good at a distance, and therefore, when the gentleman first appeared in the walk, I was not quite clear whether he was a stranger to me or otherwise. He was an elderly gentleman, but came tripping along in the pleasantest manner conceivable, avoiding the garden-roller and the borders of the beds with inimitable dexterity, picking his way among the flower-pots, and smiling with unspeakable good humour. Before he was half-way up the walk he began to salute me; then I thought I knew him; but when he came towards me with his hat in his hand, the sun shining on his bald head, his bland face, his bright spectacles, his fawn-coloured tights, and his black gaiters,—then my heart warmed towards him, and I felt quite certain that it was Mr. Pickwick.

"My dear sir," said that gentleman as I rose to receive him, "pray be seated. Pray sit down. Now, do not stand on my account. I must insist upon it, really." With these words Mr. Pickwick gently pressed me down into my seat, and taking my hand in his, shook it again and again with a warmth of manner perfectly irresistible. I endeavoured to express in my welcome something of that heartiness and pleasure which the sight of him awakened, and made him sit down beside me. All this time he kept alternately releasing my hand and grasping it again, and surveying me through his spectacles with such a beaming countenance as I never till then beheld.

"You knew me directly!" said Mr. Pickwick. "What a pleasure it is to think that you knew me directly!"

I remarked that I had read his adventures very often, and his features were quite familiar to me from the published portraits. As I thought it a good opportunity of adverting to the circumstance, I condoled with him upon the various libels on his character which had found their way into print. Mr. Pickwick shook his head, and for a moment looked very indignant, but smiling again directly, added that no doubt I was acquainted with Cervantes's introduction to the second part of Don Quixote, and that it fully expressed his sentiments on the subject.

"But now," said Mr. Pickwick, "don't you wonder how I found you out?"

"I shall never wonder, and, with your good leave, never know," said I, smiling in my turn. "It is enough for me that you give me this gratification. I have not the least desire that you should tell me by what means I have obtained it."

"You are very kind," returned Mr. Pickwick, shaking me by the hand again; "you are so exactly what I expected! But for what particular purpose do you think I have sought you, my dear sir? Now what *do* you think I have come for?"

Mr. Pickwick put this question as though he were persuaded that it was morally impossible that I could by any means divine the deep purpose of his visit, and that it must be hidden from all human ken. Therefore, although I was rejoiced to think that I had anticipated his drift, I feigned to be quite ignorant of it, and after a brief consideration shook my head despairingly.

"What should you say," said Mr. Pickwick, laying the forefinger of his left hand upon my coat-sleeve, and looking at me with his head thrown back, and a little on one side,—"what should you say if I confessed that after reading your account of yourself and your little society, I had come here, a humble candidate for one of those empty chairs?"

"I should say," I returned, "that I know of only one circumstance which could still further endear that little society to me, and that would be the associating with it my old friend,—for you must let me call you so,—my old friend, Mr. Pickwick."

As I made him this answer every feature of Mr. Pickwick's face fused itself into one all-pervading expression of delight. After shaking me heartily by both hands at once, he patted me gently on the back, and then—I well understood why—coloured up to the eyes, and hoped with great earnestness of manner that he had not hurt me.

If he had, I would have been content that he should have repeated the offence a hundred times rather than suppose so; but as he had not, I had no difficulty in changing the subject by making an inquiry which had been upon my lips twenty times already.

"You have not told me," said I, "anything about Sam Weller."

"O! Sam," replied Mr. Pickwick, "is the same as ever. The same true, faithful fellow that he ever was. What should I tell you about Sam, my dear sir, except that he is more indispensable to my happiness and comfort every day of my life?"

"And Mr. Weller senior?" said I.

"Old Mr. Weller," returned Mr. Pickwick, "is in no respect more altered than Sam, unless it be that he is a little more opinionated than he was formerly, and perhaps at times more talkative. He spends a good deal of his time now in our neighbourhood, and has so constituted himself a part of my bodyguard, that when I ask permission for Sam to have a seat in your kitchen on clock nights (supposing your three friends think me worthy to fill one of the chairs), I am afraid I must often include Mr. Weller too."

I very readily pledged myself to give both Sam and his father a free admission to my house at all hours and seasons, and this point settled, we fell into a lengthy conversation which was carried on with as little reserve on both sides as if we had been intimate friends from our youth, and which conveyed to me the comfortable assurance that Mr. Pickwick's buoyancy of spirit, and indeed all his old cheerful characteristics, were wholly unimpaired. As he had spoken of the consent of my friends as being yet in abeyance, I repeatedly assured him that his proposal was certain to receive their most joyful sanction, and several times entreated that he would give me leave to introduce him to Jack Redburn and Mr. Miles (who were near at hand) without further ceremony.

To this proposal, however, Mr. Pickwick's delicacy would by no means allow him to accede, for he urged that his eligibility must be formally discussed, and that, until this had been done, he could not think of obtruding himself further. The utmost I could obtain from him was a promise that he would attend upon our next night of meeting, that I might have the pleasure of presenting him immediately on his election.

Mr. Pickwick, having with many blushes placed in my hands a small roll of paper, which he termed his "qualification," put a great many questions to me touching my friends, and particularly Jack Redburn, whom he repeatedly termed "a fine fellow," and in whose favour I could see he was strongly predisposed. When I had satisfied him on these points, I took him up into my room, that he might make acquaintance with the old chamber which is our place of meeting.

"And this," said Mr. Pickwick, stopping short, "is the clock! Dear me! And this is really the old clock!"

I thought he would never have come away from it. After advancing towards it softly, and laying his hand upon it with as much respect and as many smiling looks as if it were alive, he set himself to consider it in every possible direction, now mounting on a chair to look at the top, now going down upon his knees to examine the bottom, now surveying the sides with his spectacles almost touching the case, and now trying to peep between it and the wall to get a slight view of the back. Then he would retire a pace or two and look up at the dial to see it go, and then draw near again and stand with his head on one side to hear it tick: never failing to glance towards me at intervals of a few seconds each, and nod his head with such complacent gratification as I am quite unable to describe. His admiration was not confined to the clock either, but extended itself to every article in the room; and really, when he had gone through them every one, and at last sat himself down in all the six chairs, one after another, to try how they felt, I never saw such a picture of good-humour and happiness as he presented, from the top of his shining head down to the very last button of his gaiters.

I should have been well pleased, and should have had the utmost enjoyment of his company, if he had remained with me all day, but my favourite, striking the hour, reminded him that he must take his leave. I could not forbear telling him once more how glad he had made me, and we shook hands all the way down-stairs.

We had no sooner arrived in the Hall than my housekeeper, gliding out of her little room (she had changed her gown and cap, I observed), greeted Mr. Pickwick with her best smile and courtesy; and the barber, feigning to be accidentally passing on his way out, made him a vast number of bows. When the housekeeper courtesied, Mr. Pickwick bowed with the utmost politeness, and when he bowed, the housekeeper courtesied again; between the housekeeper and the barber, I should say that Mr. Pickwick faced about and bowed with undiminished affability fifty times at least.

I saw him to the door; an omnibus was at the moment passing the corner of the lane, which Mr. Pickwick hailed and ran after with extraordinary nimbleness. When he had got about half-way, he turned his head, and seeing that I was still looking after him, and that I waved my hand, stopped, evidently irresolute whether to come back and shake hands again, or to go on. The man behind the omnibus shouted, and Mr. Pickwick ran a little way towards him: then he looked round at me, and ran a little way back again. Then there was another shout, and he turned round once more and ran the other way. After several of these vibrations, the man settled the question by taking Mr. Pickwick by the arm and putting him into the carriage; but his last action was to let down the window and wave his hat to me as it drove off.

I lost no time in opening the parcel he had left with me. The following were its contents :—

### MR. PICKWICK'S TALE

A good many years have passed away since old John Podgers lived in the town of Windsor, where he was born, and where, in course of time, he came to be comfortably and snugly buried. You may be sure that in the time of King James the First, Windsor was a very quaint queer old town, and you may take it upon my authority that John Podgers was a very quaint queer old fellow; consequently he and Windsor fitted each other to a nicety, and seldom parted company even for half a day.

John Podgers was broad, sturdy, Dutch-built, short, and a very hard eater, as men of his figure often are. Being a hard sleeper like-wise, he divided his time pretty equally between these two recrea-tions, always falling asleep when he had done eating, and always taking another turn at the trencher when he had done sleeping, by which means he grew more corpulent and more drowsy every day of his life. Indeed it used to be currently reported that when he sauntered up and down the sunny side of the street before dinner (as he never failed to do in fair weather), he enjoyed his soundest nap; but many people held this to be a fiction, as he had several times been seen to look after fat oxen on market-days, and had even been heard, by persons of good credit and reputation, to chuckle at the sight, and say to himself with great glee, "Live beef, live beef!" It was upon this evidence that the wisest people in Windsor (beginning with the local authorities, of course) held that John Podgers was a man of strong, sound sense, not what is called smart, perhaps, and it might be of a rather lazy and apoplectic turn, but still a man of solid parts, and one who meant much more than he cared to show. This impression was confirmed by a very dignified way he had of shaking his head and imparting, at the same time, a pendulous motion to his double chin; in short, he passed for one of those people who, being plunged into the Thames, would make no vain efforts to set it afire, but would straightway flop down to the bottom with a deal of gravity, and be highly respected in consequence by all good men.

Being well to do in the world, and a peaceful widower,—having a great appetite, which, as he could afford to gratify it, was a luxury and no inconvenience, and a power of going to sleep, which, as he had no occasion to keep awake, was a most enviable faculty,—you will readily suppose that John Podgers was a happy man. But appearances are often deceptive when they least seem so, and the truth is that, notwithstanding his extreme sleekness, he was rendered uneasy in his mind and exceedingly uncomfortable by a constant apprehension that beset him night and day.

You know very well that in those times there flourished divers evil old women who, under the name of Witches, spread great disorder through the land, and inflicted various dismal tortures upon Christian men; sticking pins and needles into them when they least expected it, and causing them to walk in the air with their feet upwards, to the great terror of their wives and families, who were naturally very much disconcerted when the master of the house unexpectedly came home, knocking at the door with his heels and combing his hair on the scraper. These were their commonest pranks, but they every day played a hundred others, of which none were less objectionable, and many were much more so, being improper besides; the result was that vengeance was denounced against all old women, with whom even the king himself had no sympathy (as he certainly ought to have had), for with his own most Gracious hand he penned a most Gracious consignment of them to everlasting wrath, and devised most Gracious means for their confusion and slaughter, in virtue whereof scarcely a day passed but one witch at the least was most graciously hanged, drowned, or roasted in some part of his dominions.

Still the press teemed with strange and terrible news from the North or the South, or the East or the West, relative to witches and their unhappy victims in some corner of the country, and the Public's hair stood on end to that degree that it lifted its hat off its head, and made its face pale with terror.

You may believe that the little town of Windsor did not escape the general contagion. The inhabitants boiled a witch on the king's birthday and sent a bottle of the broth to court, with a dutiful address expressive of their loyalty. The king, being rather frightened by the present, piously bestowed it upon the Archbishop of Canterbury, and returned an answer to the address, wherein he gave them golden rules for discovering witches, and laid great stress upon certain protecting charms, and especially horseshoes. Immediately the towns-people went to work nailing up horseshoes over every door, and so many anxious parents apprenticed their children to farriers to keep them out of harm's way, that it became quite a genteel trade, and flourished exceedingly.

In the midst of all this bustle John Podgers ate and slept as usual, but shook his head a great deal oftener than was his custom, and was observed to look at the oxen less, and at the old women more. He had a little shelf put up in his sitting-room, whereon was displayed, in a row which grew longer every week, all the witchcraft literature of the time; he grew learned in charms and exorcisms, hinted at certain questionable females on broomsticks whom he had seen from his chamber window, riding in the air at night, and was in constant terror of being bewitched. At length, from perpetually dwelling upon this one idea, which, being alone in his head, had all its own way, the fear of witches became the single passion of his life. He, who up to that time had never known what it was to dream, began to have visions of witches whenever he fell asleep; waking, they were incessantly present to his imagination likewise; and, sleeping or waking, he had not a moment's peace. He began to set witch-traps in the highway, and was often seen lying in wait round the corner for hours together, to watch their effect. These engines were of simple construction, usually consisting of two straws disposed in the form of a cross, or a piece of a Bible cover with a pinch of salt upon it; but they were infallible, and if an old woman chanced to stumble over them (as not unfrequently happened, the chosen spot being a broken and stony place), John started from a doze, pounced out upon her, and hung round her neck till assistance arrived, when she was immediately carried away and drowned. By dint of constantly inveigling old ladies and disposing of them in this summary manner, he acquired the reputation of a great public character; and as he received no harm in these pursuits beyond a scratched face or so, he came, in the course of time, to be considered witch-proof.

There was but one person who entertained the least doubt of John Podgers's gifts, and that person was his own nephew, a wild, roving young fellow of twenty who had been brought up in his uncle's house and lived there still,—that is to say, when he was at home, which was not as often as it might have been. As he was an apt scholar, it was he who read aloud every fresh piece of strange and terrible intelligence that John Podgers bought; and this he always did of an evening in the little porch in front of the house, round which the neighbours would flock in crowds to hear the direful news,—for people like to be frightened, and when they can be frightened for nothing and at another man's expense, they like it all the better.

One fine midsummer evening, a group of persons were gathered in this place, listening intently to Will Marks (that was the nephew's name), as with his cap very much on one side, his arm coiled slyly round the waist of a pretty girl who sat beside him, and his face screwed into a comical expression intended to represent extreme gravity, he read—with Heaven knows how many embellishments of his own—a dismal account of a gentleman down in Northampton-shire under the influence of witchcraft and taken forcible possession of by the Devil, who was playing his very self with him. John Podgers, in a high sugar-loaf hat and short cloak, filled the opposite seat, and surveyed the auditory with a look of mingled pride and horror very edifying to see; while the hearers, with their heads thrust forward and their mouths open, listened and trembled, and hoped there was a great deal more to come. Sometimes Will stopped for an instant to look round upon his eager audience, and then, with a more comical expression of face than before and a settling of himself comfortably, which included a squeeze of the young lady before mentioned, he launched into some new wonder surpassing all the others.

The setting sun shed his last golden rays upon this little party, who, absorbed in their present occupation, took no heed of the approach of night, or the glory in which the day went down, when the sound of a horse, approaching at a good round trot, invading the silence of the hour, caused the reader to make a sudden stop, and the listeners to raise their heads in wonder. Nor was their wonder diminished when a horseman dashed up to the porch, and abruptly checking his steed, inquired where one John Podgers dwelt.

"Here!" cried a dozen voices, while a dozen hands pointed out sturdy John, still basking in the terrors of the pamphlet.

The rider, giving his bridle to one of those who surrounded him, dismounted, and approached John, hat in hand, but with great haste.

"Whence come ye?" said John.

"From Kingston, master."

"And wherefore?"

"On most pressing business."

"Of what nature?"

"Witchcraft."

Witchcraft! Everybody looked aghast at the breathless messenger, and the breathless messenger looked equally aghast at everybody—

except Will Marks, who, finding himself unobserved, not only squeezed the young lady again, but kissed her twice. Surely he must have been bewitched himself, or he never could have done it—and the young lady too, or she never would have let him.

"Witchcraft!" cried Will, drowning the sound of his last kiss, which was rather a loud one.

The messenger turned towards him, and with a frown repeated the word more solemnly than before; then told his errand, which was, in brief, that the people of Kingston had been greatly terrified for some nights past by hideous revels, held by witches beneath the gibbet within a mile of the town, and related and deposed to by chance wayfarers who had passed within ear-shot of the spot; that the sound of their voices in their wild orgies had been plainly heard by many persons; that three old women laboured under strong suspicion, and that precedents had been consulted and solemn council had, and it was found that to identify the hags some single person must watch upon the spot alone; that no single person had the courage to perform the task; and that he had been despatched express to solicit John Podgers to undertake it that very night, as being a man of great renown, who bore a charmed life, and was proof against unholy spells.

John received this communication with much composure, and said in a few words, that it would have afforded him inexpressible pleasure to do the Kingston people so slight a service, if it were not for his unfortunate propensity to fall asleep, which no man regretted more than himself upon the present occasion, but which quite settled the question. Nevertheless, he said, there *was* a gentleman present (and here he looked very hard at a tall farrier), who, having been engaged all his life in the manufacture of horseshoes, must be quite invulnerable to the power of witches, and who, he had no doubt, from his own reputation for bravery and good-nature, would readily accept the commission. The farrier politely thanked him for his good opinion, which it would always be his study to deserve, but added that, with regard to the present little matter, he couldn't think of it on any account, as his departing on such an errand would certainly occasion the instant death of his wife, to whom, as they all knew, he was tenderly attached. Now, so far from this circumstance being notorious, everybody had suspected the reverse, as the farrier was in the habit of beating his lady rather more than tender husbands usually do; all the married men present, however, applauded his resolution with great vehemence, and one and all declared that they would stop at home and die if needful (which happily it was not) in defence of their lawful partners.

This burst of enthusiasm over, they began to look, as by one consent, toward Will Marks, who, with his cap more on one side than ever, sat watching the proceedings with extraordinary unconcern. He had never been heard openly to express his disbelief in witches, but had often cut such jokes at their expense as left it to be inferred;

publicly stating on several occasions that he considered a broomstick an inconvenient charger, and one especially unsuited to the dignity of the female character, and indulging in other free remarks of the same tendency, to the great amusement of his wild companions.

As they looked at Will they began to whisper and murmur among themselves, and at length one man cried, "Why don't you ask Will Marks?"

As this was what everybody had been thinking of, they all took up the word, and cried in concert, "Ah! why don't you ask Will?"

"*He* don't care," said the farrier.

"Not he," added another voice in the crowd.

"He don't believe in it, you know," sneered a little man with a yellow face and a taunting nose and chin, which he thrust out from under the arm of a long man before him.

"Besides," said a red-faced gentleman with a gruff voice, "he's a single man."

"That's the point!" said the farrier; and all the married men murmured, ah! that was it, and they only wished they were single themselves; they would show him what spirit was, very soon.

The messenger looked towards Will Marks beseechingly.

"It will be a wet night, friend, and my grey nag is tired after yesterday's work——"

Here there was a general titter.

"But," resumed Will, looking about him with a smile, "if nobody else puts in a better claim to go, for the credit of the town I am your man, and I would be, if I had to go afoot. In five minutes I shall be in the saddle, unless I am depriving any worthy gentleman here of the honour of the adventure, which I wouldn't do for the world."

But here arose a double difficulty, for not only did John Podgers combat the resolution with all the words he had, which were not many, but the young lady combated it too with all the tears she had, which were very many indeed. Will, however, being inflexible, parried his uncle's objections with a joke, and coaxed the young lady into a smile in three short whispers. As it was plain that he set his mind upon it, and would go, John Podgers offered him a few first-rate charms out of his own pocket, which he dutifully declined to accept; and the young lady gave him a kiss, which he also returned.

"You see what a rare thing it is to be married," said Will, "and how careful and considerate all these husbands are. There's not a man among them but his heart is leaping to forestall me in this adventure, and yet a strong sense of duty keeps him back. The husbands in this one little town are a pattern to the world, and so must the wives be too, for that matter, or they could never boast half the influence they have!"

Waiting for no reply to this sarcasm, he snapped his fingers and withdrew into the house, and thence into the stable, while some busied themselves in refreshing the messenger, and others in baiting his steed. In less than the specified time he returned by another way, with a good cloak hanging over his arm, a good sword girded by his side, and leading his good horse caparisoned for the journey.

"Now," said Will, leaping into the saddle at a bound, "up and away. Upon your mettle, friend, and push on. Good night!"

He kissed his hand to the girl, nodded to his drowsy uncle, waved his cap to the rest—and off they flew pell-mell, as if all the witches in England were in their horses' legs. They were out of sight in a minute.

The men who were left behind shook their heads doubtfully, stroked their chins, and shook their heads again. The farrier said that certainly Will Marks was a good horseman, nobody should ever say he denied that: but he was rash, very rash, and there was no telling what the end of it might be; what did he go for, that was what he wanted to know? He wished the young fellow no harm, but why did he go? Everybody echoed these words, and shook their heads again, having done which they wished John Podgers good night, and straggled home to bed.

The Kingston people were in their first sleep when Will Marks and his conductor rode through the town and up to the door of a house where sundry grave functionaries were assembled, anxiously expecting the arrival of the renowned Podgers. They were a little disappointed to find a gay young man in his place; but they put the best face upon the matter, and gave him full instructions how he was to conceal himself behind the gibbet, and watch and listen to the witches, and how at a certain time he was to burst forth and cut and slash among them vigorously, so that the suspected parties might be found bleeding in their beds next day, and thoroughly confounded. They gave him a great quantity of wholesome advice besides, and—which was more to the purpose with Will—a good supper. All these things being done, and midnight nearly come, they sallied forth to show him the spot where he was to keep his dreary vigil.

The night was by this time dark and threatening. There was a rumbling of distant thunder, and a low sighing of wind among the trees, which was very dismal. The potentates of the town kept so uncommonly close to Will that they trod upon his toes, or stumbled against his ankles, or nearly tripped up his heels at every step he took, and, besides these annoyances, their teeth chattered so with fear, that he seemed to be accompanied by a dirge of castanets.

At last they made a halt at the opening of a lonely, desolate space, and, pointing to a black object at some distance, asked Will if he saw that, yonder.

"Yes," he replied. "What then?"

Informing him abruptly that it was the gibbet where he was to watch, they wished him good night in an extremely friendly manner, and ran back as fast as their feet would carry them.

Will walked boldly to the gibbet, and, glancing upwards when he came under it, saw—certainly with satisfaction—that it was empty, and that nothing dangled from the top but some iron chains, which swung mournfully to and fro as they were moved by the breeze. After a careful survey of every quarter he determined to take his station with his face towards the town; both because that would place him with his back to the wind, and because, if any trick or surprise were attempted, it would probably come from that direction in the first instance. Having taken these precautions, he wrapped his cloak about him so that it left the handle of his sword free, and ready to his hand, and leaning against the gallows-tree with his cap not quite so much on one side as it had been before, took up his position for the night.

### SECOND CHAPTER OF MR. PICKWICK'S TALE

We left Will Marks leaning under the gibbet with his face towards the town, scanning the distance with a keen eye, which sought to pierce the darkness and catch the earliest glimpse of any person or persons that might approach towards him. But all was quiet, and, save the howling of the wind as it swept across the heath in gusts, and the creaking of the chains that dangled above his head, there was no sound to break the sullen stillness of the night. After half an hour or so this monotony became more disconcerting to Will than the most furious uproar would have been, and he heartily wished for some one antagonist with whom he might have a fair stand-up fight, if it were only to warm himself.

Truth to tell, it was a bitter wind, and seemed to blow to the very heart of a man whose blood, heated but now with rapid riding, was the more sensitive to the chilling blast. Will was a daring fellow, and cared not a jot for hard knocks or sharp blades; but he could not persuade himself to move or walk about, having just that vague expectation of a sudden assault which made it a comfortable thing to have something at his back, even though that something were a gallows-tree. He had no great faith in the superstitions of the age, still such of them as occurred to him did not serve to lighten the time, or to render his situation the more endurable. He remembered how witches were said to repair at that ghostly hour to churchyards and gibbets, and such-like dismal spots, to pluck the bleeding mandrake or scrape the flesh from dead men's bones, as choice ingredients for their spells; how, stealing by night to lonely places, they dug graves with their finger-nails, or anointed themselves before riding in the air, with a delicate pomatum made of the fat of infants newly boiled. These, and many other fabled practices of a no less agreeable nature, and all having some reference to the circumstances in which he was placed, passed and repassed in quick succession through the mind of Will Marks, and adding a shadowy dread to that distrust and watchfulness which his situation inspired, rendered it, upon the whole, sufficiently uncomfortable. As he had foreseen, too, the rain began to descend heavily, and driving before the wind in a thick mist, obscured even those few objects which the darkness of the night had before imperfectly revealed.

"Look!" shrieked a voice. "Great Heaven, it has fallen down, and stands erect as if it lived!"

The speaker was close behind him; the voice was almost at his ear. Will threw off his cloak, drew his sword, and darting swiftly round, seized a woman by the wrist, who, recoiling from him with a dreadful shriek, fell struggling upon her knees. Another woman, clad, like her whom he had grasped, in mourning garments, stood rooted to the spot on which they were, gazing upon his face with wild and glaring eyes that quite appalled him.

"Say," cried Will, when they had confronted each other thus for some time, "what are ye?"

"Say what are *you*," returned the woman, "who trouble even this obscene resting-place of the dead, and strip the gibbet of its honoured burden? Where is the body?"

He looked in wonder and affright from the woman who questioned him to the other whose arm he clutched.

"Where is the body?" repeated his questioner more firmly than before. "You wear no livery which marks you for the hireling of the government. You are no friend to us, or I should recognise you, for the friends of such as we are few in number. What are you then, and wherefore are you here?"

"I am no foe to the distressed and helpless," said Will. "Are ye among that number? ye should be by your looks."

"We are!" was the answer.

"Is it ye who have been wailing and weeping here under cover of the night?" said Will.

"It is," replied the woman sternly; and pointing, as she spoke, towards her companion, "she mourns a husband, and I a brother. Even the bloody law that wreaks its vengeance on the dead does not make that a crime, and if it did 'twould be alike to us who are past its fear or favour."

Will glanced at the two females, and could barely discern that the one whom he addressed was much the elder, and that the other was young and of a slight figure. Both were deadly pale, their garments wet and worn, their hair dishevelled and streaming in the wind, themselves bowed down with grief and misery; their whole appearance most dejected, wretched, and forlorn. A sight so different from any he had expected to encounter touched him to the quick, and all idea of anything but their pitiable condition vanished before it.

"I am a rough, blunt yeoman," said Will. "Why I came here is told in a word; you have been overheard at a distance in the silence of the night, and I have undertaken a watch for hags or spirits. I came here expecting an adventure, and prepared to go through with any. If there be aught that I can do to help or aid you, name it, and on the faith of a man who can be secret and trusty, I will stand by you to the death."

"How comes this gibbet to be empty?" asked the elder female.

"I swear to you," replied Will, "that I know as little as yourself. But this I know, that when I came here an hour ago or so, it was as it is now; and if, as I gather from your question, it was not so last night, sure I am that it has been secretly disturbed without the knowledge of the folks in yonder town. Bethink you, therefore, whether you have no friends in league with you or with him on whom the law has done its worst, by whom these sad remains have been removed for burial."

The women spoke together, and Will retired a pace or two while they conversed apart. He could hear them sob and moan, and saw that they wrung their hands in fruitless agony. He could make out little that they said, but between whiles he gathered enough to assure him that his suggestion was not very wide of the mark, and that they not only suspected by whom the body had been removed, but also whither it had been conveyed. When they had been in conversation a long time, they turned towards him once more. This time the younger female spoke.

"You have offered us your help?"

"I have."

"And given a pledge that you are still willing to redeem?"

"Yes. So far as I may, keeping all plots and conspiracies at arm's length."

"Follow us, friend."

Will, whose self-possession was now quite restored, needed no second bidding, but with his drawn sword in his hand, and his cloak so muffled over his left arm as to serve for a kind of shield without offering any impediment to its free action, suffered them to lead the way. Through mud and mire, and wind and rain, they walked in silence a full mile. At length they turned into a dark lane, where, suddenly starting out from beneath some trees where he had taken shelter, a man appeared, having in his charge three saddled horses. One of these (his own apparently), in obedience to a whisper from the women, he consigned to Will, who, seeing that they mounted, mounted also. Then, without a word spoken, they rode on together, leaving the attendant behind.

They made no halt nor slackened their pace until they arrived near Putney. At a large wooden house which stood apart from any other they alighted, and giving their horses to one who was already waiting, passed in by a side door, and so up some narrow creaking stairs into a small panelled chamber, where Will was left alone. He had not been here very long, when the door was softly opened, and there entered to him a cavalier whose face was concealed beneath a black mask.

Will stood upon his guard, and scrutinised this figure from head to foot. The form was that of a man pretty far advanced in life, but of a firm and stately carriage. His dress was of a rich and costly kind, but so soiled and disordered that it was scarcely to be recognised for one of those gorgeous suits which the expensive taste and fashion of the time prescribed for men of any rank or station. He was booted and spurred, and bore about him even as many tokens of the state of the roads as Will himself. All this he noted, while the eyes behind the mask regarded him with equal attention. This survey over, the cavalier broke silence.

"Thou'rt young and bold, and wouldst be richer than thou art?"

"The two first I am," returned Will. "The last I have scarcely thought of. But be it so. Say that I would be richer than I am; what then?"

"The way lies before thee now," replied the Mask.

"Show it me."

"First let me inform thee, that thou wert brought here to-night lest thou shouldst too soon have told thy tale to those who placed thee on the watch."

"I thought as much when I followed," said Will. "But I am no blab, not I."

"Good," returned the Mask. "Now listen. He who was to have executed the enterprise of burying that body, which, as thou hast suspected, was taken down to-night, has left us in our need."

Will nodded, and thought within himself that if the Mask were to attempt to play any tricks, the first eyelet-hole on the left-hand side of his doublet, counting from the buttons up the front, would be a very good place in which to pink him neatly.

"Thou art here, and the emergency is desperate. I propose his task to thee. Convey the body (now coffined in this house), by means that I shall show, to the Church of St. Dunstan in London to-morrow night, and thy service shall be richly paid. Thou'rt about to ask whose corpse it is. Seek not to know. I warn thee, seek not to know. Felons hang in chains on every moor and heath. Believe, as others do, that this was one, and ask no further. The murders of state policy, its victims or avengers, had best remain unknown to such as thee!"

"The mystery of this service," said Will, "bespeaks its danger. What is the reward?"

"One hundred golden unities," replied the cavalier. "The danger to one who cannot be recognised as the friend of a fallen cause is not great, but there is some hazard to be run. Decide between that and the reward."

"What if I refuse?" said Will.

"Depart in peace, in God's name," returned the Mask in a melancholy tone, "and keep our secret, remembering that those who brought thee here were crushed and stricken women, and that those who bade thee go free could have had thy life with one word, and no man the wiser."

Men were readier to undertake desperate adventures in those times than they are now. In this case the temptation was great, and the punishment, even in case of detection, was not likely to be very severe, as Will came of a loyal stock, and his uncle was in good repute, and a passable tale to account for his possession of the body and his ignorance of the identity might be easily devised.

The cavalier explained that a covered cart had been prepared for the purpose; that the time of departure could be arranged so that he should reach London Bridge at dusk, and proceed through the City after the day had closed in; that people would be ready at his journey's end to place the coffin in a vault without a minute's delay; that officious inquirers in the streets would be easily repelled by the tale that he was carrying for interment the corpse of one who had died of the plague; and in short showed him every reason why he should succeed, and none why he should fail. After a time they were joined by another gentleman, masked like the first, who added new arguments to those which had been already urged; the wretched wife, too, added her tears and prayers to their calmer representations; and in the end, Will, moved by compassion and good-nature, by a love of the marvellous, by a mischievous anticipation of the terrors of the Kingston people when he should be missing next day, and finally, by the prospect of gain, took upon himself the task, and devoted all his energies to its successful execution.

The following night, when it was quite dark, the hollow echoes of old London Bridge responded to the rumbling of the cart which contained the ghastly load, the object of Will Marks' care. Sufficiently disguised to attract no attention by his garb, Will walked at the horse's head, as unconcerned as a man could be who was sensible that he had now arrived at the most dangerous part of his undertaking, but full of boldness and confidence.

It was now eight o'clock. After nine, none could walk the streets without danger of their lives, and even at this hour, robberies and murder were of no uncommon occurrence. The shops upon the bridge were all closed; the low wooden arches thrown across the way were like so many black pits, in every one of which ill-favoured fellows lurked in knots of three or four; some standing upright against the wall, lying in wait; others skulking in gateways, and thrusting out their uncombed heads and scowling eyes: others crossing and re-crossing, and constantly jostling both horse and man to provoke a quarrel; others stealing away and summoning their companions in a low whistle. Once, even in that short passage, there was the noise of scuffling and the clash of swords behind him, but Will, who knew the City and its ways, kept straight on and scarcely turned his head.

The streets being unpaved, the rain of the night before had converted them into a perfect quagmire, which the splashing waterspouts from the gables, and the filth and offal cast from the different houses, swelled in no small degree. These odious matters being left to putrefy in the close and heavy air, emitted an insupportable stench, to which every court and passage poured forth a contribution of its own. Many parts, even of the main streets, with their projecting stories tottering overhead and nearly shutting out the sky, were more like huge chimneys than open ways. At the corners of some of these, great bonfires were burning to prevent infection from the plague, of which it was rumoured that some citizens had lately died; and few, who availing themselves of the light thus afforded paused for a moment to look around them, would have been disposed to doubt the existence of the disease, or wonder at its dreadful visitations.

But it was not in such scenes as these, or even in the deep and miry road, that Will Marks found the chief obstacles to his progress. There were kites and ravens feeding in the streets (the only scavengers the City kept), who, scenting what he carried, followed the cart or fluttered on its top, and croaked their knowledge of its burden and their ravenous appetite for prey. There were distant fires, where the poor wood and plaster tenements wasted fiercely, and whither crowds made their way, clamouring eagerly for plunder, beating down all who came within their reach, and yelling like devils let loose. There were single-handed men flying from bands of ruffians, who pursued them with naked weapons, and hunted them savagely; there were drunken, desperate robbers issuing from their dens and staggering through the open streets where no man dared molest them; there were vagabond servitors returning from the Bear Garden, where had been good sport that day, dragging after them their torn and bleeding dogs, or leaving them to die and rot upon the road. Nothing was abroad but cruelty, violence, and disorder.

Many were the interruptions which Will Marks encountered from these stragglers, and many the narrow escapes he made. Now some stout bully would take his seat upon the cart, insisting to be driven to his own home, and now two or three men would come down upon him together, and demand that on peril of his life he showed them what he had inside. Then a party of the city watch, upon their rounds, would draw across the road, and not satisfied with his tale, question him closely, and revenge themselves by a little cuffing and hustling for maltreatment sustained at other hands that night. All these assailants had to be rebutted, some by fair words, some by foul, and some by blows. But Will Marks was not the man to be stopped or turned back now he had penetrated so far, and though he got on slowly, still he made his way down Fleet-street and reached the church at last.

As he had been forewarned, all was in readiness. Directly he stopped, the coffin was removed by four men, who appeared so suddenly that they seemed to have started from the earth. A fifth mounted the cart, and scarcely allowing Will time to snatch from it a little bundle containing such of his own clothes as he had thrown off on assuming his disguise, drove briskly away. Will never saw cart or man again.

He followed the body into the church, and it was well he lost no time in doing so, for the door was immediately closed. There was no light in the building save that which came from a couple of torches borne by two men in cloaks, who stood upon the brink of a vault. Each supported a female figure, and all observed a profound silence.

By this dim and solemn glare, which made Will feel as though light itself were dead, and its tomb the dreary arches that frowned above, they placed the coffin in the vault, with uncovered heads, and closed it up. One of the torch-bearers then turned to Will, and stretched forth his hand, in which was a purse of gold. Something told him directly that those were the same eyes which he had seen beneath the mask.

"Take it," said the cavalier in a low voice, "and be happy. Though these have been hasty obsequies, and no priest has blessed the work, there will not be the less peace with thee thereafter, for having laid his bones beside those of his little children. Keep thy own counsel, for thy sake no less than ours, and God be with thee!"

"The blessing of a widowed mother on thy head, good friend!" cried the younger lady through her tears; "the blessing of one who has now no hope or rest but in this grave!"

Will stood with the purse in his hand, and involuntarily made a gesture as though he would return it, for though a thoughtless fellow, he was of a frank and generous nature. But the two gentlemen, extinguishing their torches, cautioned him to be gone, as their common safety would be endangered by a longer delay; and at the same time their retreating footsteps sounded through the church. He turned, therefore, towards the point at which he had entered, and seeing by a faint gleam in the distance that the door was again partially open, groped his way towards it and so passed into the street.

Meantime the local authorities of Kingston had kept watch and ward all the previous night, fancying every now and then that dismal shrieks were borne towards them on the wind, and frequently winking to each other, and drawing closer to the fire as they drank the health of the lonely sentinel, upon whom a clerical gentleman present was especially severe by reason of his levity and youthful folly. Two or three of the gravest in company, who were of a theological turn, propounded to him the question, whether such a character was not but poorly armed for single combat with the Devil, and whether he himself would not have been a stronger opponent; but the clerical gentleman, sharply reproving them for their presumption in discussing such questions, clearly showed that a fitter champion than Will could scarcely have been selected, not only for that being a child of Satan, he was the less likely to be alarmed by the appearance of his own father, but because Satan himself would be at his ease in such company, and would not scruple to kick up his heels to an extent which it was quite certain he would never venture before clerical eyes, under whose influence (as was notorious) he became quite a tame and milk-and-water character.

But when next morning arrived, and with it no Will Marks, and when a strong party repairing to the spot, as a strong party ventured to do in broad day, found Will gone and the gibbet empty, matters grew serious indeed. The day passing away and no news arriving, and the night going on also without any intelligence, the thing grew more tremendous still; in short, the neighbourhood worked itself up to such a comfortable pitch of mystery and horror, that it is a great question whether the general feeling was not one of excessive disappointment, when, on the second morning, Will Marks returned.

However this may be, back Will came in a very cool and collected state, and appearing not to trouble himself much about anybody except old John Podgers, who, having been sent for, was sitting in the Town Hall crying slowly, and dozing between whiles. Having embraced his uncle and assured him of his safety, Will mounted on a table and told his story to the crowd.

And surely they would have been the most unreasonable crowd that ever assembled together, if they had been in the least respect disappointed with the tale he told them; for besides describing the Witches' Dance to the minutest motion of their legs, and performing it in character on the table, with the assistance of a broomstick, he related how they had carried off the body in a copper caldron, and so bewitched him, that he lost his senses until he found himself lying under a hedge at least ten miles off, whence he had straightway returned as they then beheld. The story gained such universal applause that it soon afterwards brought down express from London the great witch-finder of the age, the Heaven-born Hopkins, who having examined Will closely on several points, pronounced it the most extraordinary and the best accredited witch-story ever known, under which title it was published at the Three Bibles on London Bridge, in small quarto, with a view of the caldron from an original drawing, and a portrait of the clerical gentleman as he sat by the fire.

On one point Will was particularly careful: and that was to describe for the witches he had seen, three impossible old females, whose likenesses never were or will be. Thus he saved the lives of the suspected parties, and of all other old women who were dragged before him to be identified.

This circumstance occasioned John Podgers much grief and sorrow, until happening one day to cast his eyes upon his housekeeper, and observing her to be plainly afflicted with rheumatism, he procured her to be burnt as an undoubted witch. For this service to the state he was immediately knighted, and became from that time Sir John Podgers.

Will Marks never gained any clue to the mystery in which he had been an actor, nor did any inscription in the church, which he often visited afterwards, nor any of the limited inquiries that he dared to make, yield him the least assistance. As he kept his own secret, he was compelled to spend the gold discreetly and sparingly. In the course of time he married the young lady of whom I have already told you, whose maiden name is not recorded, with whom he led a prosperous and happy life. Years and years after this adventure, it was his wont to tell her upon a stormy night that it was a great comfort to him to think those bones, to whomsoever they might have once belonged, were not bleaching in the troubled air, but were mouldering away with the dust of their own kith and kindred in a quiet grave.

Being very full of Mr. Pickwick's application, and highly pleased with the compliment he had paid me, it will be readily supposed that long before our next night of meeting I communicated it to my three friends, who unanimously voted his admission into our body. We all looked forward with some impatience to the occasion which would enroll him among us, but I am greatly mistaken if Jack Redburn and myself were not by many degrees the most impatient of the party.

At length the night came, and a few minutes after ten Mr. Pickwick's knock was heard at the street-door. He was shown into a lower room, and I directly took my crooked stick and went to accompany him up-stairs, in order that he might be presented with all honour and formality.

"Mr. Pickwick," said I, on entering the room, "I am rejoiced to see you,—rejoiced to believe that this is but the opening of a long series of visits to this house, and but the beginning of a close and lasting friendship."

That gentleman made a suitable reply with a cordiality and frankness peculiarly his own, and glanced with a smile towards two persons behind the door, whom I had not at first observed, and whom I immediately recognised as Mr. Samuel Weller and his father.

It was a warm evening, but the elder Mr. Weller was attired, notwithstanding, in a most capacious greatcoat, and his chin enveloped in a large speckled shawl, such as is usually worn by stage coachmen on active service. He looked very rosy and very stout, especially about the legs, which appeared to have been compressed into his top-boots with some difficulty. His broad-brimmed hat he held under his left arm, and with the forefinger of his right hand he touched his forehead a great many times in acknowledgment of my presence.

"I am very glad to see you in such good health, Mr. Weller," said I.

"Why, thankee, sir," returned Mr. Weller, "the axle an't broke yet. We keeps up a steady pace,—not too sewere, but vith a moderate degree o' friction,—and the consekens is that ve're still a runnin' and comes in to the time reg'lar.—My son Samivel, sir, as you may have read on in history," added Mr. Weller, introducing his firstborn.

I received Sam very graciously, but before he could say a word his father struck in again.

"Samivel Veller, sir," said the old gentleman, "has conferred upon me the ancient title o' grandfather vich had long laid dormouse, and wos s'posed to be nearly hex-tinct in our family. Sammy, relate a anecdote o' vun o' them boys,—that 'ere little anecdote about young Tony sayin' as he *vould* smoke a pipe unbeknown to his mother."

"Be quiet, can't you?" said Sam; "I never see such a old magpie —never!"

"That 'ere Tony is the blessedest boy," said Mr. Weller, heedless of this rebuff, "the blessedest boy as ever *I* see in *my* days! of all the charmin'est infants as ever I heerd tell on, includin' them as was kivered over by the robin-redbreasts arter they'd committed sooicide with blackberries, there never wos any like that 'ere little Tony. He's alvays a playin' vith a quart pot, that boy is! To see him a settin' down on the doorstep pretending to drink out of it, and fetching a long breath artervards, and smoking a bit of firevood, and sayin', 'Now I'm grandfather,'—to see him a doin' that at two year old is better than any play as wos ever wrote. 'Now I'm grandfather!' He vouldn't take a pint pot if you wos to make him a present on it, but he gets his quart, and then he says, 'Now I'm grandfather!'"

Mr. Weller was so overpowered by this picture that he straightway fell into a most alarming fit of coughing, which must certainly have been attended with some fatal result but for the dexterity and promptitude of Sam, who, taking a firm grasp of the shawl just under his father's chin, shook him to and fro with great violence, at the same time administering some smart blows between his shoulders. By this curious mode of treatment Mr. Weller was finally recovered, but with a very crimson face, and in a state of great exhaustion.

"He'll do now, Sam," said Mr. Pickwick, who had been in some alarm himself.

"He'll do, sir!" cried Sam, looking reproachfully at his parent. "Yes, he *will* do one o' these days,—he'll do for his-self and then he'll wish he hadn't. Did anybody ever see sich a inconsiderate old file,—laughing into conwulsions afore company, and stampin' on the floor as if he'd brought his own carpet vith him and wos under a wager to punch the pattern out in a given time? He'll begin again in a minute. There—he's a goin' off—I said he would!"

In fact, Mr. Weller, whose mind was still running upon his precocious grandson, was seen to shake his head from side to side, while a laugh, working like an earthquake, below the surface, produced various extraordinary appearances in his face, chest, and shoulders, —the more alarming because unaccompanied by any noise whatever. These emotions, however, gradually subsided, and after three or four short relapses he wiped his eyes with the cuff of his coat, and looked about him with tolerable composure.

"Afore the governor vith-draws," said Mr. Weller, "there is a pint, respecting vich Sammy has a qvestion to ask. Vile that qvestion is a perwadin' this here conwersation, p'raps the gen'lmen vill permit me to re-tire."

"Wot are you goin' away for?" demanded Sam, seizing his father by the coat-tail.

"I never see such a undootiful boy as you, Samivel," returned Mr. Weller. "Didn't you make a solemn promise, amountin' almost

*Tony Weller and his Grandson.*

to a speeches o' wow, that you'd put that 'ere qvestion on my account?''

"Well, I'm agreeable to do it," said Sam, "but not if you go cuttin' away like that, as the bull turned round and mildly observed to the drover ven they wos a goadin' him into the butcher's door. The fact is, sir," said Sam, addressing me, "that he wants to know somethin' respectin' that 'ere lady as is housekeeper here."

"Ay. What is that?"

"Vy, sir," said Sam, grinning still more, "he wishes to know vether she——"

"In short," interposed old Mr. Weller decisively, a perspiration breaking out upon his forehead, "vether that 'ere old creetur is or is not a widder."

Mr. Pickwick laughed heartily, and so did I, as I replied decisively, that "my housekeeper was a spinster."

"There!" cried Sam, "now you're satisfied. You hear she's a spinster."

"A wot?" said his father, with deep scorn.

"A spinster," replied Sam.

Mr. Weller looked very hard at his son for a minute or two, and then said,

"Never mind vether she makes jokes or not, that's no matter. Wot I say is, is that 'ere female a widder, or is she not?"

"Wot do you mean by her making jokes?" demanded Sam, quite aghast at the obscurity of his parent's speech.

"Never you mind, Samivel," returned Mr. Weller gravely; "puns may be wery good things or they may be wery bad 'uns, and a female may be none the better or she may be none the vurse for making of 'em; that's got nothin' to do vith widders."

"Vy now," said Sam, looking round, "would anybody believe as a man at his time o' life could be running his head agin spinsters and punsters being the same thing?"

"There an't a straw's difference between 'em," said Mr. Weller. "Your father didn't drive a coach for so many years, not to be ekal to his own langvidge as far as *that* goes, Sammy."

Avoiding the question of etymology, upon which the old gentleman's mind was quite made up, he was several times assured that the housekeeper had never been married. He expressed great satisfaction on hearing this, and apologised for the question, remarking that he had been greatly terrified by a widow not long before, and that his natural timidity was increased in consequence.

"It wos on the rail," said Mr. Weller, with strong emphasis; "I wos a goin' down to Birmingham by the rail, and I wos locked up in a close carriage vith a living widder. Alone ve wos; the widder and me wos alone; and I believe it wos only because ve *wos* alone and there wos no clergyman in the conwayance, that that 'ere widder didn't marry me afore ve reached the half-way station. Ven I think how she began a screaming as ve wos a goin' under them tunnels in the dark,—how she kept on a faintin' and ketchin' hold o' me,—and how I tried to bust open the door as was tight-locked and perwented all escape— Ah! It was a awful thing, most awful!''

Mr. Weller was so very much overcome by this retrospect that he was unable, until he had wiped his brow several times, to return any reply to the question whether he approved of railway communication, notwithstanding that it would appear from the answer which he ultimately gave, that he entertained strong opinions on the subject.

"I con-sider," said Mr. Weller, "that the rail is unconstitootional and an inwaser o' priwileges, and I should wery much like to know what that 'ere old Carter as once stood up for our liberties and wun 'em too,—I should like to know wot he vould say, if he wos alive now, to Englishmen being locked up vith widders, or vith anybody again their wills. Wot a old Carter vould have said, a old Coachman may say, and I as-sert that in that pint o' view alone, the rail is an inwaser. As to the comfort, vere's the comfort o' sittin' in a harm-cheer lookin' at brick walls or heaps o' mud, never comin' to a public-house, never seein' a glass o' ale, never goin' through a pike, never meetin' a change o' no kind (horses or othervise), but alvays comin' to a place, ven you come to one at all, the wery pictur o' the last, vith the same p'leesemen standin' about, the same blessed old bell a ringin', the same unfort'nate people standin' behind the bars, a waitin' to be let in; and everythin' the same except the name, vich is wrote up in the same sized letters as the last name, and vith the same colours. As to the *h*onour and dignity o' travellin', vere can that be vithout a coachman; and wot's the rail to sich coachmen and guards as is some-times forced to go by it, but a outrage and a insult? As to the pace, wot sort o' pace do you think I, Tony Veller, could have kept a coach goin' at, for five hundred thousand pound a mile, paid in adwance afore the coach was on the road? And as to the ingein,—a nasty, weezin', creakin', gaspin', puffin', bustin' monster, alvays out o' breath, vith a shiny green-and-gold back, like a unpleasant beetle in that 'ere gas magnifier,—as to the ingein as is alvays a pourin' out red-hot coals at night, and black smoke in the day, the sensiblest thing it does, in my opinion, is, ven there's somethin' in the vay, and it sets up that 'ere frightful scream vich seems to say, 'Now here's two hundred and forty passengers in the wery greatest extremity o' danger, and here's their two hundred and forty screams in vun!' ''

By this time I began to fear that my friends would be rendered impatient by my protracted absence. I therefore begged Mr. Pick-wick to accompany me up-stairs, and left the two Mr. Wellers in the care of the housekeeper, laying strict injunctions upon her to treat them with all possible hospitality.

## IV

## THE CLOCK

As we were going up-stairs, Mr. Pickwick put on his spectacles, which he had held in his hand hitherto; arranged his neckerchief, smoothed down his waistcoat, and made many other little preparations of that kind which men are accustomed to be mindful of, when they are going among strangers for the first time, and are anxious to impress them pleasantly. Seeing that I smiled, he smiled too, and said that if it had occurred to him before he left home, he would certainly have presented himself in pumps and silk stockings.

"I would, indeed, my dear sir," he said very seriously; "I would have shown my respect for the society, by laying aside my gaiters."

"You may rest assured," said I, "that they would have regretted your doing so very much, for they are quite attached to them."

"No, really!" cried Mr. Pickwick, with manifest pleasure. "Do you think they care about my gaiters? Do you seriously think that they identify me at all with my gaiters?"

"I am sure they do," I replied.

"Well, now," said Mr. Pickwick, "that is one of the most charming and agreeable circumstances that could possibly have occurred to me!"

I should not have written down this short conversation, but that it developed a slight point in Mr. Pickwick's character, with which I was not previously acquainted. He has a secret pride in his legs. The manner in which he spoke, and the accompanying glance he bestowed upon his tights, convince me that Mr. Pickwick regards his legs with much innocent vanity.

"But here are our friends," said I, opening the door and taking his arm in mine; "let them speak for themselves.—Gentlemen, I present to you Mr. Pickwick."

Mr. Pickwick and I must have been a good contrast just then. I, leaning quietly on my crutch-stick, with something of a care-worn, patient air; he, having hold of my arm, and bowing in every direction with the most elastic politeness, and an expression of face whose sprightly cheerfulness and good-humour knew no bounds. The difference between us must have been more striking yet, as we advanced towards the table, and the amiable gentleman, adapting his jocund step to my poor tread, had his attention divided between treating my infirmities with the utmost consideration, and affecting to be wholly unconscious that I required any.

I made him personally known to each of my friends in turn. First, to the deaf gentleman, whom he regarded with much interest, and accosted with great frankness and cordiality. He had evidently some vague idea, at the moment, that my friend being deaf must be dumb also; for when the latter opened his lips to express the pleasure it afforded him to know a gentleman of whom he had heard so much, Mr. Pickwick was so extremely disconcerted, that I was obliged to step in to his relief.

His meeting with Jack Redburn was quite a treat to see. Mr. Pickwick smiled, and shook hands, and looked at him through his spectacles, and under them, and over them, and nodded his head approvingly, and then nodded to me, as much as to say, "This is just the man; you were quite right"; and then turned to Jack and said a few hearty words and then did and said everything over again with unimpaired vivacity. As to Jack himself, he was quite as much delighted with Mr. Pickwick as Mr. Pickwick could possibly be with him. Two people never can have met together since the world began, who exchanged a warmer or more enthusiastic greeting.

It was amusing to observe the difference between this encounter and that which succeeded, between Mr. Pickwick and Mr. Miles. It was clear that the latter gentleman viewed our new member as a kind of rival in the affections of Jack Redburn, and besides this, he had more than once hinted to me, in secret, that although he had no doubt Mr. Pickwick was a very worthy man, still he did consider that some of his exploits were unbecoming a gentleman of his years and gravity. Over and above these grounds of distrust, it is one of his fixed opinions, that the law never can by possibility do anything wrong; he therefore looks upon Mr. Pickwick as one who has justly suffered in purse and peace for a breach of his plighted faith to an unprotected female and holds that he is called upon to regard him with some suspicion on that account. These causes led to a rather cold and formal reception; which Mr. Pickwick acknowledged with the same stateliness and intense politeness as was displayed on the other side. Indeed, he assumed an air of such majestic defiance, that I was fearful he might break out into some solemn protest or declaration, and therefore inducted him into his chair without a moment's delay.

This piece of generalship was perfectly successful. The instant he took his seat, Mr. Pickwick surveyed us all with a most benevolent aspect, and was taken with a fit of smiling full five minutes long. His interest in our ceremonies was immense. They are not very numerous or complicated, and a description of them may be comprised in very few words. As our transactions have already been, and must necessarily continue to be, more or less anticipated by being presented in these pages at different times, and under various forms, they do not require a detailed account.

Our first proceeding when we are assembled is to shake hands all round, and greet each other with cheerful and pleasant looks. Remembering that we assemble not only for the promotion of our happiness, but with the view of adding something to the common stock, an air of languor or indifference in any member of our body would be regarded by the others as a kind of treason. We have never

had an offender in this respect; but if we had, there is no doubt that
he would be taken to task pretty severely.

Our salutation over, the venerable piece of antiquity from which
we take our name is wound up in silence. The ceremony is always
performed by Master Humphrey himself (in treating of the club, I
may be permitted to assume the historical style, and speak of myself
in the third person), who mounts upon a chair for the purpose, armed
with a large key. While it is in progress, Jack Redburn is required
to keep at the farther end of the room under the guardianship of Mr.
Miles, for he is known to entertain certain aspiring and unhallowed
thoughts connected with the clock, and has even gone so far as to
state that if he might take the works out for a day or two, he thinks
he could improve them. We pardon him his presumption in consideration of his good intentions, and his keeping this respectful
distance, which last penalty is insisted on, lest by secretly wounding
the object of our regard in some tender part, in the ardour of his zeal
for its improvement, he should fill us with dismay and consternation.

This regulation afforded Mr. Pickwick the highest delight, and
seemed, if possible, to exalt Jack in his good opinion.

The next ceremony is the opening of the clock-case (of which
Master Humphrey has likewise the key), the taking from it as many
papers as will furnish forth our evening's entertainment, and arranging in the recess such new contributions as have been provided since
our last meeting. This is always done with peculiar solemnity. The
deaf gentleman then fills and lights his pipe, and we once more take
our seats round the table before mentioned, Master Humphrey acting
as president,—if we can be said to have any president, where all are
on the same social footing,—and our friend Jack as secretary. Our
preliminaries being now concluded, we fall into any train of conversation that happens to suggest itself, or proceed immediately to
one of our readings. In the latter case, the paper selected is consigned
to Master Humphrey, who flattens it carefully on the table and makes
dog's ears in the corner of every page, ready for turning over easily;
Jack Redburn trims the lamp with a small machine of his own
invention which usually puts it out; Mr. Miles looks on with great
approval notwithstanding; the deaf gentleman draws in his chair, so
that he can follow the words on the paper or on Master Humphrey's
lips as he pleases; and Master Humphrey himself, looking round with
mighty gratification, and glancing up at his old clock, begins to read
aloud.

Mr. Pickwick's face, while his tale was being read, would have
attracted the attention of the dullest man alive. The complacent
motion of his head and forefinger as he gently beat time, and corrected the air with imaginary punctuation, the smile that mantled
on his features at every jocose passage, and the sly look he stole
around to observe its effect, the calm manner in which he shut his
eyes and listened when there was some little piece of description, the
changing expression with which he acted the dialogue to himself, his

agony that the deaf gentleman should know what it was all about, and his extraordinary anxiety to correct the reader when he hesitated at a word in the manuscript, or substituted a wrong one, were alike worthy of remark. And when at last, endeavouring to communicate with the deaf gentleman by means of the finger alphabet, with which he constructed such words as are unknown in any civilised or savage language, he took up a slate and wrote in large text, one word in a line, the question, "How—do—you—like—it?"—when he did this, and handing it over the table awaited the reply, with a countenance only brightened and improved by his great excitement, even Mr. Miles relaxed, and could not forbear looking at him for the moment with interest and favour.

"It has occurred to me," said the deaf gentleman, who had watched Mr. Pickwick and everybody else with silent satisfaction— "it has occurred to me," said the deaf gentleman, taking his pipe from his lips, "that now is our time for filling our only empty chair."

As our conversation had naturally turned upon the vacant seat, we lent a willing ear to this remark, and looked at our friend inquiringly.

"I feel sure," said he, "that Mr. Pickwick must be acquainted with somebody who would be an acquisition to us; that he must know the man we want. Pray let us not lose any time, but set this question at rest. Is it so, Mr. Pickwick?"

The gentleman addressed was about to return a verbal reply, but remembering our friend's infirmity, he substituted for this kind of answer some fifty nods. Then taking up the slate and printing on it a gigantic "Yes," he handed it across the table, and rubbing his hands as he looked round upon our faces, protested that he and the deaf gentleman quite understood each other, already.

"The person I have in my mind," said Mr. Pickwick, "and whom I should not have presumed to mention to you until some time hence, but for the opportunity you have given me, is a very strange old man. His name is Bamber."

"Bamber!" said Jack. "I have certainly heard the name before."

"I have no doubt, then," returned Mr. Pickwick, "that you remember him in those adventures of mine (the Posthumous Papers of our old club, I mean), although he is only incidentally mentioned; and, if I remember right, appears but once."

"That's it," said Jack. "Let me see. He is the person who has a grave interest in old mouldy chambers and the Inns of Court, and who relates some anecdotes having reference to his favourite theme, —and an odd ghost story,—is that the man?"

"The very same. Now," said Mr. Pickwick, lowering his voice to a mysterious and confidential tone, "he is a very extraordinary and remarkable person; living, and talking, and looking, like some strange spirit, whose delight is to haunt old buildings; and absorbed in that one subject which you have just mentioned, to an extent which is quite wonderful. When I retired into private life, I sought him out, and I do assure you that the more I see of him, the more strongly I am impressed with the strange and dreamy character of his mind."

"Where does he live?" I inquired.

"He lives," said Mr. Pickwick, " in one of those dull, lonely old places with which his thoughts and stories are all connected; quite alone, and often shut up close for several weeks together. In this dusty solitude he broods upon the fancies he has so long indulged, and when he goes into the world, or anybody from the world without goes to see him, they are still present to his mind and still his favourite topic. I may say, I believe, that he has brought himself to entertain a regard for me, and an interest in my visits; feelings which I am certain he would extend to Master Humphrey's Clock if he were once tempted to join us. All I wish you to understand is, that he is a strange secluded visionary, in the world but not of it; and as unlike anybody here as he is unlike anybody elsewhere that I have ever met or known."

Mr. Miles received this account of our proposed companion with rather a wry face, and after murmuring that perhaps he was a little mad, inquired if he were rich.

"I never asked him," said Mr. Pickwick.

"You might know, sir, for all that," retorted Mr. Miles, sharply.

"Perhaps so, sir," said Mr. Pickwick, no less sharply than the other, "but I do not. Indeed," he added, relapsing into his usual mildness, "I have no means of judging. He lives poorly, but that would seem to be in keeping with his character. I never heard him allude to his circumstances, and never fell into the society of any man who had the slightest acquaintance with them. I have really told you all I know about him, and it rests with you to say whether you wish to know more, or know quite enough already."

We were unanimously of opinion that we would seek to know more; and as a sort of compromise with Mr. Miles (who, although he said "Yes—O certainly—he should like to know more about the gentleman—he had no right to put himself in opposition to the general wish," and so forth, shook his head doubtfully and hemmed several times with peculiar gravity), it was arranged that Mr. Pickwick should carry me with him on an evening visit to the subject of our discussion, for which purpose an early appointment between that gentleman and myself was immediately agreed upon; it being understood that I was to act upon my own responsibility, and to invite him to join us or not, as I might think proper. This solemn question determined, we returned to the clock-case (where we have been forestalled by the reader), and between its contents, and the conversation they occasioned, the remainder of our time passed very quickly.

When we broke up, Mr. Pickwick took me aside to tell me that he had spend a most charming and delightful evening. Having made this communication with an air of the strictest secrecy, he took Jack Redburn into another corner to tell him the same, and then retired into another corner with the deaf gentleman and the slate, to repeat the assurance. It was amusing to observe the contest in his mind whether he should extend his confidence to Mr. Miles, or treat him with dignified reserve. Half a dozen times he stepped up behind him with a friendly air, and as often stepped back again without saying a word; at last, when he was close at that gentleman's ear and upon the very point of whispering something conciliating and agreeable, Mr. Miles happened suddenly to turn his head, upon which Mr. Pickwick skipped away, and said with some fierceness, "Good night, sir—I was about to say good night, sir,—nothing more"; and so made a bow and left him.

"Now, Sam," said Mr. Pickwick, when he had got downstairs.

"All right, sir," replied Mr. Weller. " Hold hard, sir. Right arm fust—now the left—now one strong conwulsion, and the great-coat's on, sir."

Mr. Pickwick acted up these directions, and being further assisted by Sam, who pulled at one side of the collar, and Mr. Weller, who pulled hard at the other, was speedily enrobed. Mr. Weller, senior, then produced a full-sized stable lantern, which he had carefully deposited in a remote corner, on his arrival, and inquired whether Mr. Pickwick would have "the lamps alight."

"I think not to-night," said Mr. Pickwick.

"Then if this here lady vill per-mit," rejoined Mr. Weller, "we'll leave it here, ready for next journey. This here lantern, mum," said Mr. Weller, handing it to the housekeeper, " vunce belonged to the celebrated Bill Blinder as is now at grass, as all on us vill be in our turns. Bill, mum, wos the hostler as had charge o' them two vell-known piebald leaders that run in the Bristol fast coach, and vould never go to no other tune but a sutherly vind and a cloudy sky, which wos consekvently played incessant, by the guard, wenever they wos on duty. He wos took wery bad one arternoon, arter having been off his feed, and wery shaky on his legs for some veeks; and he says to his mate, 'Matey,' he says, 'I think I'm a-goin' the wrong side o' the post, and that my foot's wery near the bucket. Don't say I an't,' he says, 'for I know I am, and don't let me be interrupted,' he says, 'for I've saved a little money, and I'm a-goin' into the stable to make my last vill and testymint.' 'I'll take care as nobody interrupts,' says his mate, 'but you on'y hold up your head, and shake your ears a bit, and you're good for twenty years to come.' Bill Blinder makes him no answer, but he goes avay into the stable, and there he soon artervards lays himself down a'tween the two piebalds, and dies,—previously a writin' outside the corn-chest, 'This is the last vill and testymint of Villiam Blinder.' They wos nat'rally wery much amazed at this, and arter looking among the litter, and up in the loft, and vere not, they opens the corn-chest, and finds that he'd been and chalked his vill inside the lid; so the lid was obligated to be took off the hinges, and sent up to Doctor Commons to be proved, and under that 'ere wery instrument this here lantern was passed to Tony Veller; vich circumstarnce, mum, gives it a wally in my eyes, and makes me rekvest, if you vill be so kind, as to take partickler care on it."

The housekeeper graciously promised to keep the object of Mr. Weller's regard in the safest possible custody, and Mr. Pickwick, with a laughing face, took his leave. The bodyguard followed, side by side; old Mr. Weller buttoned and wrapped up from his boots to his chin; and Sam with his hands in his pockets and his hat half off his head, remonstrating with his father, as he went, on his extreme loquacity.

I was not a little surprised, on turning to go up-stairs, to encounter the barber in the passage at that late hour; for his attendance is usually confined to some half-hour in the morning. But Jack Redburn, who finds out (by instinct, I think) everything that happens in the house, informed me with great glee, that a society in imitation of our own had been that night formed in the kitchen, under the title of "Mr. Weller's Watch," of which the barber was a member; and that he could pledge himself to find means of making me acquainted with the whole of its future proceedings, which I begged him, both on my own account and that of my readers, by no means to neglect doing.

[*Old Curiosity Shop* is continued here, completing No. IV.]

## V

## MR. WELLER'S WATCH

IT seems that the housekeeper and the two Mr. Wellers were no sooner left together on the occasion of their first becoming acquainted than the housekeeper called to her assistance Mr. Slithers the barber, who had been lurking in the kitchen in expectation of her summons; and with many smiles and much sweetness introduced him as one who would assist her in the responsible office of entertaining her distinguished visitors.

"Indeed," said she, "without Mr. Slithers I should have been placed in quite an awkward situation."

"There is no call for any hock'erdness, mum," said Mr. Weller with the utmost politeness; "no call wotsumever. A lady," added the old gentleman, looking about him with the air of one who establishes an incontrovertible position,—"a lady can't be hock'erd. Natur' has otherwise purwided."

The housekeeper inclined her head and smiled yet more sweetly. The barber, who had been fluttering about Mr. Weller and Sam in a state of great anxiety to improve their acquaintance, rubbed his hands and cried, "Hear, hear! Very true, sir"; whereupon Sam turned about and steadily regarded him for some seconds in silence.

"I never knew," said Sam, fixing his eyes in a ruminative manner upon the blushing barber,—"I never knew but vun o' your trade, but *he* wos worth a dozen, and wos indeed dewoted to his callin'!"

"Was he in the easy shaving way, sir," inquired Mr. Slithers, "or in the cutting and curling line?"

"Both," replied Sam; "easy shavin' was his natur', and cuttin' and curlin' was his pride and glory. His whole delight wos in his trade. He spent all his money in bears, and run in debt for 'em besides, and there they wos a growling avay down in the front cellar all day long, and ineffectooally gnashing their teeth, vile the grease o' their relations and friends wos being re-tailed in gallipots in the shop above, and the first-floor winder wos ornamented vith their heads; not to speak o' the dreadful aggrawation it must have been to 'em to see a man alvays a walkin' up and down the pavement outside, vith the portrait of a bear in his last agonies, and underneath in large letters, 'Another fine animal wos slaughtered yesterday at Jinkinson's!' Hows'ever, there they wos, and there Jinkinson wos, till he wos took wery ill with some inn'ard disorder, lost the use of his legs, and wos confined to his bed, vere he laid a wery long time, but sich wos his pride in his profession, even then, that wenever he wos worse than usual the doctor used to go down-stairs and say, 'Jinkinson's wery low this mornin'; we must give the bears a stir'; and as sure as ever they stirred 'em up a bit and made 'em roar, Jinkinson opens his eyes if he wos ever so bad, calls out, 'There's the bears!' and rewives agin."

"Astonishing!" cried the barber.

"Not a bit," said Sam, "human natur' neat as imported. Vun day the doctor happenin' to say, 'I shall look in as usual to-morrow mornin',' Jinkinson catches hold of his hand and says, 'Doctor,' he says, will you grant me one favour?' 'I will, Jinkinson,' says the doctor. 'Then, doctor,' says Jinkinson, 'vill you come unshaved, and let me shave you?' 'I will,' says the doctor. 'God bless you,' says Jinkinson. Next day the doctor came, and arter he'd been shaved all skilful and reg'lar, he says, 'Jinkinson,' he says, 'it's wery plain this does you good. Now,' he says, 'I've got a coachman as has got a beard that 'ud warm your heart to work on, and though the footman,' he says, 'hasn't got much of a beard, still he's a trying it on vith a pair o' viskers to that extent that razors is Christian charity. If they take it in turns to mind the carriage when it's a waitin' below,' he says, 'wot's to hinder you from operatin' on both of 'em ev'ry day as well as upon me? you've got six children,' he says, 'wot's to hinder you from shavin' all their heads and keepin' 'em shaved? you've got two assistants in the shop down-stairs, wot's to hinder you from cuttin' and curlin' them as often as you like? Do this," he says, 'and you're a man agin.' Jinkinson squeedged the doctor's hand and begun that wery day; he kept his tools upon the bed, and wenever he felt his-self gettin' worse, he turned to at vun o' the children who wos a runnin' about the house vith heads like clean Dutch cheeses, and shaved him agin. Vun day the lawyer come to make his vill; all the time he wos a takin' it down, Jinkinson was secretly a clippin' avay at his hair vith a large pair of scissors. 'Wot's that 'ere snippin' noise?' says the lawyer every now and then; 'it's like a man havin' his hair cut.' 'It *is* wery like a man havin' his hair cut,' says poor Jinkinson, hidin' the scissors, and lookin' quite innocent. By the time the lawyer found it out, he was wery nearly bald. Jinkinson wos kept alive in this vay for a long time, but at last vun day he has in all the children vun arter another, shaves each on 'em wery clean, and gives him vun kiss on the crown o' his head; then he has in the two assistants, and arter cuttin' and curlin' of 'em in the first style of elegance, says he should like to hear the woice o' the greasiest bear, vich rekvest is immediately complied with; then he says that he feels wery happy in his mind and vishes to be left alone; and then he dies, previously cuttin' his own hair and makin' one flat curl in the wery middle of his forehead."

This anecdote produced an extraordinary effect, not only upon Mr. Slithers, but upon the housekeeper also, who evinced so much anxiety to please and be pleased, that Mr. Weller, with a manner betokening some alarm, conveyed a whispered inquiry to his son whether he had gone "too fur."

"Wot do you mean by too fur?" demanded Sam.

"In that 'ere little compliment respectin' the want of hock'erdness in ladies, Sammy," replied his father.

"You don't think she's fallen in love with you in consekens o' that, do you?" said Sam.

"More unlikelier things have come to pass, my boy," replied Mr. Weller in a hoarse whisper; "I'm always afeerd of inadwertent capti-wation, Sammy. If I know'd how to make myself ugly or unpleasant, I'd do it, Samivel, rayther than live in this here state of perpetival terror!"

Mr. Weller had, at that time, no further opportunity of dwelling upon the apprehensions which beset his mind, for the immediate occasion of his fears proceeded to lead the way down-stairs, apologis-ing as they went for conducting him into the kitchen, which apart-ment, however, she was induced to proffer for his accommodation in preference to her own little room, the rather as it afforded greater facilities for smoking, and was immediately adjoining the ale-cellar. The preparations which were already made sufficiently proved that these were not mere words of course, for on the deal table were a sturdy ale-jug and glasses, flanked with clean pipes and a plentiful supply of tobacco for the old gentleman and his son, while on a dresser hard by was goodly store of cold meat and other eatables. At sight of these arrangements Mr. Weller was at first distracted between his love of joviality and his doubts whether they were not to be con-sidered as so many evidences of captivation having already taken place; but he soon yielded to his natural impulse, and took his seat at the table with a very jolly countenance.

"As to imbibin' any o' this here flagrant veed, mum, in the presence of a lady," said Mr. Weller, taking up a pipe and laying it down again, "it couldn't be. Samivel, total abstinence, if *you* please."

"But I like it of all things," said the housekeeper.

"No," rejoined Mr. Weller, shaking his head,—"no."

"Upon my word I do," said the housekeeper. "Mr. Slithers knows I do."

Mr. Weller coughed, and notwithstanding the barber's confirmation of the statement, said "No" again, but more feebly than before. The housekeeper lighted a piece of paper, and insisted on applying it to the bowl of the pipe with her own fair hands; Mr. Weller resisted; the housekeeper cried that her fingers would be burnt; Mr. Weller gave way. The pipe was ignited, Mr. Weller drew a long puff of smoke, and detecting himself in the very act of smiling on the housekeeper, put a sudden constraint upon his countenance and looked sternly at the candles, with a determination not to captivate, himself, or encourage thoughts of captivation in others. From this iron frame of mind he was roused by the voice of his son.

"I don't think," said Sam, who was smoking with great composure and enjoyment, "that if the lady wos agreeable it 'ud be wery far out o' the vay for us four to make up a club of our own like the governors does up-stairs, and let him," Sam pointed with the stem of his pipe towards his parent, "be the president."

The housekeeper affably declared that it was the very thing she had been thinking of. The barber said the same. Mr. Weller said nothing, but he laid down his pipe as if in a fit of inspiration, and performed the following manœuvres.

Unbuttoning the three lower buttons of his waistcoat and pausing for a moment to enjoy the easy flow of breath consequent upon this process, he laid violent hands upon his watch-chain, and slowly and with extreme difficulty drew from his fob an immense double-cased silver watch, which brought the lining of the pocket with it, and was not to be disentangled but by great exertions and an amazing redness of face. Having fairly got it out at last, he detached the outer case and wound it up with a key of corresponding magnitude; then put the case on again, and having applied the watch to his ear to ascertain that it was still going, gave it some half-dozen hard knocks on the table to improve its performance.

"That," said Mr. Weller, laying it on the table with its face upwards, "is the title and emblem o' this here society. Sammy, reach them two stools this vay for the wacant cheers. Ladies and gen'lmen, Mr. Weller's Watch is vound up and now a-goin'. Order!"

By way of enforcing this proclamation, Mr. Weller, using the watch after the manner of a president's hammer, and remarking with great pride that nothing hurt it, and that falls and concussions of all kinds materially enhanced the excellence of the works and assisted the regulator, knocked the table a great many times, and declared the association formally constituted.

"And don't let's have no grinnin' at the cheer, Samivel," said Mr.

Weller to his son, "or I shall be committin' you to the cellar, and then p'r'aps we may get into what the 'Merrikins call a fix, and the English a qvestion o' privileges."

Having uttered this friendly caution, the President settled himself in his chair with great dignity, and requested that Mr. Samuel would relate an anecdote.

"I've told one," said Sam.

"Wery good, sir; tell another," returned the chair.

"We wos a talking jist now, sir," said Sam, turning to Slithers, "about barbers. Pursuing that 'ere fruitful theme, sir, I'll tell you in a wery few words a romantic little story about another barber as p'r'aps you may never have heerd."

"Samivel!" said Mr. Weller, again bringing his watch and the table into smart collision, "address your obserwations to the cheer, sir, and not to priwate indiwiduals!"

"And if I might rise to order," said the barber in a soft voice, and looking round him with a conciliatory smile as he leant over the table, with the knuckles of his left hand resting upon it,—"if I *might* rise to order, I would suggest that 'barbers' is not exactly the kind of language which is agreeable and soothing to our feelings. You, sir, will correct me if I'm wrong, but I believe there *is* such a word in the dictionary as hairdressers."

"Well, but suppose he wasn't a hairdresser," suggested Sam.

"Wy then, sir, be parliamentary and call him vun all the more," returned his father. "In the same vay as ev'ry gen'lman in another place is a *h*onourable, ev'ry barber in this place is a hairdresser. Ven you read the speeches in the papers, and see as vun gen'lman says of another, 'the *h*onourable member, if he vill allow me to call him so,' you will understand, sir, that that means, 'if he vill allow me to keep up that 'ere pleasant and uniwersal fiction.'"

It is a common remark, confirmed by history and experience, that great men rise with the circumstances in which they are placed. Mr. Weller came out so strong in his capacity of chairman, that Sam was for some time prevented from speaking by a grin of surprise, which held his faculties enchained, and at last subsided in a long whistle of a single note. Nay, the old gentleman appeared even to have astonished himself, and that to no small extent, as was demonstrated by the vast amount of chuckling in which he indulged, after the utterance of these lucid remarks.

"Here's the story," said Sam. "Vunce upon a time there wos a young hairdresser as opened a wery smart little shop vith four wax dummies in the winder, two gen'lmen and two ladies—the gen'lmen vith blue dots for their beards, wery large viskers, oudacious heads of hair, uncommon clear eyes, and nostrils of amazin' pinkness; the ladies vith their heads o' one side, their right forefingers on their lips, and their forms deweloped beautiful, in vich last respect they had the adwantage over the gen'lmen, as wasn't allowed but wery little shoulder, and terminated rayther abrupt in fancy drapery. He had also a many hair-brushes and tooth-brushes bottled up in the winder, neat glass-cases on the counter, a floor-clothed cuttin'-room up-stairs, and a weighin'-macheen in the shop, right opposite the door. But the great attraction and ornament wos the dummies, which this here young hairdresser wos constantly a runnin' out in the road to look at, and constantly a runnin' in again to touch up and polish; in short, he wos so proud on 'em, that ven Sunday come, he wos always wretched and mis'rable to think they wos behind the shutters, and looked anxiously for Monday on that account. Vun o' these dummies wos a fav'rite vith him beyond the others; and ven any of his acquain-tance asked him wy he didn't get married—as the young ladies he know'd, in partickler, often did—he used to say, 'Never! I never vill enter into the bonds of vedlock,' he says, 'until I meet vith a young 'ooman as realises my idea o' that 'ere fairest dummy vith the light hair. Then, and not till then,' he says, 'I vill approach the altar.' All the young ladies he know'd as had got dark hair told him this wos wery sinful, and that he wos wurshippin' a idle; but them as wos at all near the same shade as the dummy coloured up wery much, and wos observed to think him a very nice young man.''

"Samivel," said Mr. Weller, gravely, "a member o' this associashun bein' one o' that 'ere tender sex which is now immedetly referred to, I have to rekvest that you vill make no reflections."

"I ain't a makin' any, am I?" inquired Sam.

"Order, sir!" rejoined Mr. Weller, with severe dignity. Then, sink-ing the chairman in the father, he added, in his usual tone of voice: "Samivel, drive on!"

Sam interchanged a smile with the housekeeper, and proceeded:

"The young hairdresser hadn't been in the habit o' makin' this avowal above six months, ven he en-countered a young lady as wos the wery picter o' the fairest dummy. 'Now,' he says, 'it's all up. I am a slave!' The young lady wos not only the picter o' the fairest dummy, but she was wery romantic, as the young hairdresser was, too, and he says, 'O!' he says, 'here's a community o' feelin', here's a flow o' soul!' he says, 'here's a interchange o' sentiment!' The young lady didn't say much, o' course, but she expressed herself agreeable, and shortly artevards vent to see him vith a mutual friend. The hair-dresser rushes out to meet her, but d'rectly she sees the dummies she changes colour and falls a tremblin' wiolently. 'Look up, my love,' says the hairdresser, 'behold your imige in my winder, but not cor-recter than in my art!' 'My imige!' she says. 'Yourn!' replies the hair-dresser. 'But whose imige is *that?*' she says, a pinting at vun o' the gen'lmen. 'No vun's, my love,' he says, 'it is but a idea.' 'A idea!' she cries: 'it is a portrait, I feel it is a portrait, and that 'ere noble face must be in the millingtary!' 'Wot do I hear!' says he, a crumplin' his curls. 'Villiam Gibbs,' she says, quite firm, 'never renoo the subject. I respect you as a friend,' she says, 'but my affections is set upon that manly brow.' 'This,' says the hairdresser, 'is a reg'lar blight, and in it I perceive the hand of Fate. Farevell!' Vith these vords he rushes into the shop, breaks the dummy's nose vith a blow of his curlin'-irons, melts him down at the parlour fire, and never smiles artervards."

"The young lady, Mr. Weller?" said the housekeeper.

"Why, ma'am," said Sam, "findin' that Fate had a spite agin her, and everybody she come into contact vith, she never smiled neither, but read a deal o' poetry and pined avay,—by rayther slow degrees, for she ain't dead yet. It took a deal o' poetry to kill the hairdresser, and some people say arter all that it wos more the gin and water as caused him to be run over; p'r'aps it was a little o' both, and came o' mixing the two."

The barber declared that Mr. Weller had related one of the most interesting stories that had ever come within his knowledge, in which opinion the housekeeper entirely concurred.

"Are you a married man, sir?" inquired Sam.

The barber replied that he had not that honour.

"I s'pose you mean to be?" said Sam.

"Well," replied the barber, rubbing his hands smirkingly, "I don't know, I don't think it's very likely."

"That's a bad sign," said Sam; "if you'd said you meant to be vun o' these days, I should ha' looked upon you as bein' safe. You're in a wery precarious state."

"I am not conscious of any danger, at all events," returned the barber.

"No more wos I, sir," said the elder Mr. Weller, interposing; "those vere my symptoms, exactly. I've been took that vay twice. Keep your vether eye open, my friend, or you're gone."

There was something so very solemn about this admonition, both in its matter and manner, and also in the way in which Mr. Weller still kept his eye fixed upon the unsuspecting victim, that nobody cared to speak for some little time, and might not have cared to do so for some time longer, if the housekeeper had not happened to sigh, which called off the old gentleman's attention and gave rise to a gallant inquiry whether "there wos anythin' wery piercin' in that 'ere little heart?"

"Dear me, Mr. Weller!" said the housekeeper, laughing.

"No, but is there anything' as agitates it?" pursued the old gentleman. "Has it always been obderrate, always opposed to the happiness o' human creeturs? Eh? Has it?"

At this critical juncture for her blushes and confusion, the housekeeper discovered that more ale was wanted, and hastily withdrew into the cellar to draw the same, followed by the barber, who insisted on carrying the candle. Having looked after her with a very complacent expression of face, and after him with some disdain, Mr. Weller caused his glance to travel slowly round the kitchen, until at length it rested on his son.

"Sammy," said Mr. Weller, "I mistrust that barber."

"Wot for?" returned Sam; "wot's he got to do with you? You're a

nice man, you are, arter pretendin' all kinds o' terror, to go a payin'
compliments and talkin' about hearts and piercers."

The imputation of gallantry appeared to afford Mr. Weller the
utmost delight, for he replied in a voice choked by suppressed
laughter, and with the tears in his eyes,

"Wos I a talkin' about hearts and piercers,—wos I though,
Sammy, eh?"

"Wos you? of course you wos."

"She don't know no better, Sammy, there ain't no harm in it,—no
danger, Sammy; she's only a punster. She seemed pleased, though,
didn't she? O' course, she wos pleased, it's nat'ral she should be, wery
nat'ral."

"He's wain of it!" exclaimed Sam, joining in his father's mirth.
"He's actually wain!"

"Hush!" replied Mr. Weller, composing his features, "they're
comin' back,—the little heart's a coming' back. But mark these
wurds o' mine once more, and remember 'em ven your father says he
said 'em. Samivel, I mistrust that 'ere deceitful barber."

[*Old Curiosity Shop* is continued to the end of the number.]

## VI

### MASTER HUMPHREY, FROM HIS CLOCK-SIDE IN THE CHIMNEY-CORNER

Two or three evenings after the institution of Mr. Weller's Watch, I
thought I heard, as I walked in the garden, the voice of Mr. Weller
himself at no great distance; and stopping once or twice to listen
more attentively, I found that the sounds proceeded from my
housekeeper's little sitting-room, which is at the back of the house. I
took no further notice of the circumstance at that time, but it
formed the subject of a conversation between me and my friend Jack
Redburn next morning, when I found that I had not been deceived
in my impression. Jack furnished me with the following particulars;
and as he appeared to take extraordinary pleasure in relating them,
I have begged him in future to jot down any such domestic scenes or
occurrences that may please his humour, in order that they may be
told in his own way. I must confess that, as Mr. Pickwick and he are
constantly together, I have been influenced, in making this request
by a secret desire to know something of their proceedings.

On the evening in question, the housekeeper's room was arranged
with particular care, and the housekeeper herself was very smartly
dressed. The preparations, however, were not confined to mere
showy demonstrations, as tea was prepared for three persons, with a
small display of preserves and jams and sweet cakes, which heralded

some uncommon occasion. Miss Benton (my housekeeper bears that name) was in a state of great expectation, too, frequently going to the front door and looking anxiously down the lane, and more than once observing to the servant-girl that she expected company, and hoped no accident had happened to delay them.

A modest ring at the bell at length allayed her fears, and Miss Benton, hurrying into her own room and shutting herself up, in order that she might preserve that appearance of being taken by surprise which is so essential to the polite reception of visitors, awaited their coming with a smiling countenance.

"Good ev'nin', mum," said the older Mr. Weller, looking in at the door after a prefatory tap. "I'm afeered we've come in rayther arter the time, mum, but the young colt being full o' wice, has been a boltin' and shyin' and gettin' his leg over the traces to sich a extent that if he an't wery soon broke in, he'll wex me into a broken heart, and then he'll never be brought out no more except to learn his letters from the writin' on his grandfather's tombstone."

With these pathetic words, which were addressed to something outside the door about two feet six from the ground, Mr. Weller introduced a very small boy firmly set upon a couple of very sturdy legs, who looked as if nothing could ever knock him down. Besides having a very round face strongly resembling Mr. Weller's, and a stout little body of exactly his build, this young gentleman, standing with his little legs very wide apart, as if the top-boots were familiar to them, actually winked upon the housekeeper with his infant eye, in imitation of his grandfather.

"There's a naughty boy, mum," said Mr. Weller, bursting with delight, "there's a immoral Tony. Wos there ever a little chap o' four year and eight months old as vinked his eye at a strange lady afore?"

As little affected by this observation as by the former appeal to his feelings, Master Weller elevated in the air a small model of a coach whip which he carried in his hand, and addressing the housekeeper with a shrill "ya—hip!" inquired if she was "going down the road"; at which happy adaptation of a lesson he had been taught from infancy, Mr. Weller could restrain his feelings no longer, but gave him twopence on the spot.

"It's in wain to deny it, mum," said Mr. Weller, "this here is a boy arter his grandfather's own heart, and beats out all the boys as ever wos or will be. Though at the same time, mum," added Mr. Weller, trying to look gravely down upon his favourite, "it was wery wrong on him to want to—over all the posts as we come along, and wery cruel on him to force poor grandfather to lift him cross-legged over every vun of 'em. He vouldn't pass vun single blessed vost, mum, and at the top o' the lane there's seven-and-forty on 'em all in a row, and wery close together."

Here Mr. Weller, whose feelings were in a perpetual conflict between pride in his grandson's achievements and a sense of his own responsibility, and the importance of impressing him with moral truths, burst into a fit of laughter, and suddenly checking himself, remarked in a severe tone that little boys as made their grandfathers put 'em over posts never went to heaven at any price.

By this time the housekeeper had made tea, and little Tony, placed on a chair beside her, with his eyes nearly on a level with the top of the table, was provided with various delicacies which yielded him extreme contentment. The housekeeper (who seemed rather afraid of the child, notwithstanding her caresses) then patted him on the head, and declared that he was the finest boy she had ever seen.

"Wy, mum," said Mr. Weller, "I don't think you'll see a many sich, and that's the truth. But if my son Samivel vould give me my vay, mum, and only dis-pense vith his—*might* I wenter to say the vurd?"

"What word, Mr. Weller?" said the housekeeper, blushing slightly.

"Petticuts, mum," returned that gentleman, laying his hand upon the garments of his grandson. "If my son Samivel, mum, vould only dis-pense vith these here, you'd see sich a alteration in his appearance, as the imagination can't depicter."

"But what would you have the child wear instead, Mr. Weller?" said the housekeeper.

"I've offered my son Samivel, mum, agen and agen," returned the old gentleman, "to purwide him at my own cost vith a suit o' clothes as 'ud be the makin' on him, and form his mind in infancy for those pursuits as I hope the family o' the Vellers vill alvays dewote themselves to. Tony, my boy, tell the lady wot them clothes are, as grandfather says, father ought to let you vear."

"A little white hat and a little sprig weskut and little knee cords and little top-boots and a little green coat with little bright buttons and a little welwet collar," replied Tony, with great readiness and no stops.

"That's the cos-toom, mum," said Mr. Weller, looking proudly at the housekeeper. "Once make sich a model on him as that, and you'd say he *wos* a angel!"

Perhaps the housekeeper thought that in such a guise young Tony would look more like the angel at Islington than anything else of that name, or perhaps she was disconcerted to find her previously-conceived ideas disturbed, as angels are not commonly represented in top-boots and sprig waistcoats. She coughed doubtfully, but said nothing.

"How many brothers and sisters have you, my dear?" she asked, after a short silence.

"One brother and no sister at all," replied Tony. "Sam his name is, and so's my father's. Do you know my father?"

"O yes, I know him," said the housekeeper, graciously.

"Is my father fond of you?" pursued Tony.

"I hope so," rejoined the smiling housekeeper.

Tony considered a moment, and then said, "Is my grandfather fond of you?"

This would seem a very easy question to answer, but instead of replying to it, the housekeeper smiled in great confusion, and said that really children did ask such extraordinary questions that it was the most difficult thing in the world to talk to them. Mr. Weller took upon himself to reply that he was very fond of the lady; but the housekeeper entreating that he would not put such things into the child's head, Mr. Weller shook his own while she looked another way, and seemed to be troubled with a misgiving that captivation was in progress. It was, perhaps, on this account that he changed the subject precipitately.

"It's wery wrong in little boys to make game o' their grandfathers, an't it, mum?" said Mr. Weller, shaking his head waggishly, until Tony looked at him, when he counterfeited the deepest dejection and sorrow.

"O, very sad!" assented the housekeeper. "But I hope no little boys do that?"

"There is vun young Turk, mum," said Mr. Weller, "as havin' seen his grandfather a little overcome with drink on the occasion of a friend's birthday, goes a reelin' and staggerin' about the house, and makin' believe that he's the old gen'lm'n."

"O, quite shocking!" cried the housekeeper.

"Yes, mum," said Mr. Weller; "and previously to so doin', this 'ere young traitor that I'm a speakin' of, pinches his little nose to make it red, and then he gives a hiccup and says, 'I'm all right,' he says; 'give us another song!' Ha, ha! 'Give us another song,' he says. Ha, ha!"

In his excessive delight, Mr. Weller was quite unmindful of his moral responsibility, until little Tony kicked up his legs, and laughing immoderately, cried, "That was me, that was"; whereupon the grandfather, by a great effort, became extremely solemn.

"No, Tony, not you," said Mr. Weller. "I hope it warn't you, Tony. It must ha' been that 'ere naughty little chap as comes sometimes out o' the empty watch-box round the corner,—that same little chap as wos found standin' on the table afore the lookin'-glass, pretending to shave himself vith a oyster-knife."

"He didn't hurt himself, I hope?" observed the housekeeper.

"Not he, mum," said Mr. Weller proudly; "bless your heart, you might trust that 'ere boy vith a steam-engine a'most, he's sich a knowin' young"—but suddenly recollecting himself and observing that Tony perfectly understood and appreciated the compliment, the old gentleman groaned and observed that "it wos all wery shockin'—wery."

"O, he's a bad 'an," said Mr. Weller, "is that 'ere watch-box boy, makin' sich a noise and litter in the back yard; he does, waterin' wooden horses and feedin' of 'em vith grass, and perpetivally spillin' his little brother out of a veelbarrow and frightenin' his mother out of her vits, at the wery moment wen she's expectin' to increase her stock of happiness vith another play-fellow,—O, he's a bad u'n! He's

even gone so far as to put on a pair of paper spectacles as he got his
father to make for him, and walk up and down the garden vith his
hands behind him in imitation of Mr. Pickwick,—but Tony don't do
sich things, O no!"

"O no!" echoed Tony.

"He knows better, he does," said Mr. Weller. "He knows that if he
wos to come sich games as these nobody vouldn't love him, and that
his grandfather in partickler couldn't abear the sight on him; for
vich reasons Tony's alvays good."

"Always good," echoed Tony; and his grandfather immediately
took him on his knee and kissed him, at the same time, with many
nods and winks, slyly pointing at the child's head with his thumb, in
order that the housekeeper, otherwise deceived by the admirable
manner in which he (Mr. Weller) had sustained his character, might
not suppose that any other young gentleman was referred to, and
might clearly understand that the boy of the watch-box was but an
imaginary creation, and a fetch of Tony himself, invented for his
improvement and reformation.

Not confining himself to a mere verbal description of his grandson's abilities, Mr. Weller, when tea was finished, invited him by
various gifts of pence and halfpence to smoke imaginary pipes, drink
visionary beer from real pots, imitate his grandfather without
reserve, and in particular to go through the drunken scene, which
threw the old gentleman into ectasies and filled the housekeeper with
wonder. Nor was Mr. Weller's pride satisfied with even this display,
for when he took his leave he carried the child, like some rare and
astonishing curiosity, first to the barber's house and afterwards to
the tobacconist's, at each of which places he repeated his performances with the utmost effect to applauding and delighted audiences.
It was half-past nine o'clock when Mr. Weller was last seen carrying
him home upon his shoulder, and it has been whispered abroad that
at that time the infant Tony was rather intoxicated.

[*Old Curiosity Shop* is continued from here to the end without further break.]

----

[*Master Humphrey* is revived thus at the close of the *Old Curiosity Shop*, merely
to introduce *Barnaby Rudge*.]

I was musing the other evening upon the characters and incidents
with which I had been so long engaged; wondering how I could ever
have looked forward with pleasure to the completion of my tale, and
reproaching myself for having done so, as if it were a kind of cruelty
to those companions of my solitude whom I had now dismissed, and
could never again recall; when my clock struck ten. Punctual to the
hour my friends appeared.

On our last night of meeting, we had finished the story which the
reader has just concluded. Our conversation took the same current as
the meditations which the entrance of my friends had interrupted, and
The Old Curiosity Shop was the staple of our discourse.

I may confide to the reader now, that in connection with this little history I had something upon my mind; something to communicate which I had all along with difficulty repressed; something I had deemed it, during the progress of the story, necessary to its interest to disguise, and which, now that it was over, I wished, and was yet reluctant, to disclose.

To conceal anything from those to whom I am attached, is not in my nature. I can never close my lips where I have opened my heart. This temper, and the consciousness of having done some violence to it in my narrative, laid me under a restraint which I should have had great difficulty in overcoming, but for a timely remark from Mr. Miles, who, as I hinted in a former paper, is a gentleman of business habits, and of great exactness and propriety in all his transactions.

"I could have wished," my friend objected, "that we had been made acquainted with the single gentleman's name. I don't like his withholding his name. It made me look upon him at first with suspicion, and caused me to doubt his moral character, I assure you I am fully satisfied by this time of his being a worthy creature; but in this respect he certainly would not appear to have acted at all like a man of business.

"My friends," said I, drawing to the table, at which they were by this time seated in their usual chairs, "do you remember that this story bore another title besides that one we have so often heard of late?"

Mr. Miles had his pocket-book out in an instant, and referring to an entry therein, rejoined, "Certainly. Personal Adventures of Master Humphrey. Here it is. I made a note of it at the time."

I was about to resume what I had to tell them, when the same Mr. Miles again interrupted me, observing that the narrative originated in a personal adventure of my own, and that was no doubt the reason for its being thus designated.

This led me to the point at once.

"You will one and all forgive me," I returned, "if for the greater convenience of the story, and for its better introduction, that adventure was fictitious. I had my share, indeed,—no light or trivial one,—in the pages we have read, but it was not the share I feigned to have at first. The younger brother, the single gentleman, the nameless actor in this little drama, stands before you now."

It was easy to see they had not expected this disclosure.

"Yes," I pursued. "I can look back upon my part in it with a calm, half-smiling pity for myself as for some other man. But I am he, indeed; and now the chief sorrows of my life are yours."

I need not say what true gratification I derived from the sympathy and kindness with which this acknowledgement was received; nor how often it had risen to my lips before; nor how difficult I had found it—how impossible, when I came to those passages which touched me most, and most nearly concerned me—to sustain the character I had assumed. It is enough to say that I replaced in the clock-case the

328*

record of so many trials,—sorrowfully, it is true, but with a softened sorrow which was almost pleasure; and felt that in living through the past again; and communicating to others the lesson it had helped to teach me, I had been a happier man.

We lingered so long over the leaves from which I had read, that as I consigned them to their former resting-place, the hand of my trusty clock pointed to twelve, and there came towards us upon the wind the deep voice and distant bell of St. Paul's as it struck the hour of midnight.

"This," said I, returning with a manuscript I had taken at the moment from the same repository, "to be opened to such music, should be a tale where London's face by night is darkly seen, and where some deed of such a time as this is dimly shadowed out. Which of us here has seen the working of that great machine whose voice has just now ceased?"

Mr. Pickwick had, of course, and so had Mr. Miles. Jack and my deaf friend were in the minority.

I had seen it but a few days before, and could not help telling them of the fancy I had about it.

I paid my fee of twopence upon entering, to one of the money-changers who sit within the Temple; and falling, after a few turns up and down, into the quiet train of thought which such a place awakens, paced the echoing stones like some old monk whose present world lay all within its walls. As I looked afar up into the lofty dome, I could not help wondering what were his reflections whose genius reared that mighty pile, when, the last small wedge of timber fixed, the last nail driven into its home for many centuries, the clang of hammers, and the hum of busy voices gone, and the Great Silence whole years of noise had helped to make, reigning undisturbed around, he mused, as I did now, upon his work, and lost himself amid its vast extent. I could not quite determine whether the contemplation of it would impress him with a sense of greatness or of insignificance; but when I remembered how long a time it had taken to erect, in how short a space it might be traversed even to its remotest parts, for how brief a term he, or any of those who cared to bear his name, would live to see it, or know of its existence, I imagined him far more melancholy than proud, and looking with regret upon his labour done. With these thoughts in my mind, I began to ascend, almost unconsciously, the flight of steps leading to the several wonders of the building, and found myself before a barrier where another money-taker sat, who demanded which among them I would choose to see. There were the stone gallery, he said, and the whispering gallery, the geometrical staircase, the room of models, the clock—the clock being quite in my way, I stopped him there, and chose that sight from all the rest.

I groped my way into the Turret which it occupies, and saw before me, in a kind of loft, what seemed to be a great, old oaken press with folding doors. These being thrown back by the attendant) who was sleeping when I came upon him, and looked a drowsy fellow, as though his close companionship with Time had made him quite indifferent to it), disclosed a complicated crowd of wheels and chains in iron and brass,—great, sturdy, rattling engines,—suggestive of breaking a finger put in here or there, and grinding the bone to powder,—and these were the Clock! Its very pulse, if I may use the word, was like no other clock. It did not mark the flight of every moment with a gentle second stroke, as though it would check old Time, and have him stay his pace in pity, but measured it with one sledge-hammer beat, as if its business were to crush the seconds as they came trooping on, and remorselessly to clear a path before the Day of Judgment.

I sat down opposite to it, and hearing its regular and never-changing voice, that one deep constant note, uppermost amongst all the noise and clatter in the streets below,—marking that, let that tumult rise or fall, go on or stop,—let it be night or noon, to-morrow or to-day, this year or next,—it still performed its functions with the same dull constancy, and regulated the progress of the life around, the fancy came upon me that this was London's Heart, and that when it should cease to beat, the City would be no more.

It is night. Calm and unmoved amidst the scenes that darkness favours, the great heart of London throbs in its Giant breast. Wealth and beggary, vice and virtue, guilt and innocence, repletion and the direst hunger, all treading on each other and crowding together, are gathered round it. Draw but a little circle above the clustering house-tops, and you shall have within its space everything, with its opposite extreme and contradiction, close beside. Where yonder feeble light is shining, a man is but this moment dead. The taper at a few yards' distance is seen by eyes that have this instant opened on the world. There are two houses separated by an inch or two of wall. In one, there are quiet minds at rest; in the other, a waking conscience that one might think would trouble the very air. In that close corner where the roofs shrink down and cower together as if to hide their secrets from the handsome street hard by, there are such dark crimes, such miseries and horrors, as could be hardly told in whispers. In the handsome street, there are folks asleep who have dwelt there all their lives, and have no more knowledge of these things than if they had never been, or were transacted at the remotest limits of the world,—who, if they were hinted at, would shake their heads, look wise, and frown, and say they were impossible, and out of Nature,—as if all great towns were not. Does not this Heart of London, that nothing moves, nor stops, nor quickens,—that goes on the same let what will be done, —does it not express the City's character well?

The day begins to break, and soon there is the hum and noise of life. Those who have spent the night on doorsteps and cold stones crawl off to beg; they who have slept in beds come forth to their occupation, too, and business is astir. The fog of sleep rolls slowly off and London shines awake. The streets are filled with carriages, and people gaily clad. The jails are full, too, to the throat, nor have the workhouses or hospitals much room to spare. The courts of law are crowded.

Taverns have their regular frequenters by this time, and every mart of traffic has its throng. Each of these places is a world, and has its own inhabitants; each is distinct from, and almost unconscious of the existence of any other. There are some few people well to do, who remember to have heard it said, that numbers of men and women—thousands, they think it was—get up in London every day, unknowing where to lay their heads at night; and that there are quarters of the town where misery and famine always are. They don't believe it quite,—there may be some truth in it, but it is exaggerated, of course. So, each of these thousand worlds goes on, intent upon itself, until night comes again,—first with its lights and pleasures, and its cheerful streets; then with its guilt and darkness.

Heart of London, there is a moral in thy every stroke! as I look on at thy indomitable working, which neither death, nor press of life, nor grief, nor gladness out of doors will influence one jot, I seem to hear a voice within thee which sinks into my heart, bidding me, as I elbow my way among the crowd, have some thought for the meanest wretch that passes, and, being a man, to turn away with scorn and pride from none that bear the human shape.

I am by no means sure that I might not have been tempted to enlarge upon the subject, had not the papers that lay before me on the table been a silent reproach for even this digression. I took them up again when I had got thus far, and seriously prepared to read.

The handwriting was strange to me, for the manuscript had been fairly copied. As it is against our rules, in such a case, to inquire into the authorship until the reading is concluded, I could only glance at the different faces round me, in search of some expression which should betray the writer, Whoever he might be, he was prepared for this, and gave no sign for my enlightenment.

I had the papers in my hand, when my deaf friend interposed with a suggestion.

"It has occurred to me," he said, "bearing in mind your sequel to the tale we have finished, that if such of us as have anything to relate of our own lives could interweave it with our contribution to the Clock, it would be well to do so. This need be no restraint upon us, either as to time, or place, or incident, since any real passage of this kind may be surrounded by fictitious circumstances, and represented by fictitious characters. What if we make this an article of agreement among ourselves?"

The proposition was cordially received, but the difficulty appeared to be that here was a long story written before we had thought of it.

"Unless," said I, "it should have happened that the writer of this tale—which is not impossible, for men are apt to do so when they write—has actually mingled with it something of his own endurance and experience."

Nobody spoke, but I thought I detected in one quarter that this was really the case.

"If I have no assurance to the contrary," I added, therefore, "I shall take it for granted that he has done so, and that even these papers come within our new agreement. Everybody being mute, we hold that understanding, if you please."

And here I was about to begin again, when Jack informed us softly, that during the progress of our last narrative, Mr. Weller's Watch had adjourned its sitting from the kitchen, and regularly met outside our door, where he had no doubt that august body would be found at the present moment. As this was for the convenience of listening to our stories, he submitted that they might be suffered to come in, and hear them more pleasantly.

To this we one and all yielded a ready assent, and the party being discovered, as Jack had supposed, and invited to walk in, entered (though not without great confusion at having been detected), and were accommodated with chairs at a little distance.

Then, the lamp being trimmed, the fire well stirred and burning brightly, the hearth clean swept, the curtains closely drawn, the clock wound up, we entered on our new story.

[This was *Barnaby Rudge*, continued in vol. xi of this Edition.]

---

[This is, as indicated, the final appearance of *Master Humphrey's Clock*. It forms the conclusion of *Barnaby Rudge*.]

It is again midnight. My fire burns cheerfully; the room is filled with my old friend's sober voice; and I am left to muse upon the story we have just now finished.

It makes me smile, at such a time as this, to think if there were any one to see me sitting in my easy-chair, my gray head hanging down, my eyes bent thoughtfully upon the glowing embers, and my crutch—emblem of my helplessness—lying upon the hearth at my feet, how solitary I should seem. Yet though I am the sole tenant of this chimney-corner, though I am childless and old, I have so sense of loneliness at this hour; but am the centre of a silent group whose company I love.

Thus, even age and weakness have their consolations. If I were a younger man, if I were more active, more strongly bound and tied to life, these visionary friends would shun me, or I should desire to fly from them. Being what I am, I can court their society, and delight in it; and pass whole hours in picturing to myself the shadows that perchance flock every night into this chamber, and in imagining with pleasure what kind of interest they have in the frail, feeble mortal who is its sole inhabitant.

All the friends I have ever lost I find again among these visitors. I love to fancy their spirits hovering about me, feeling still some earthly kindness for their old companion, and watching his decay. "He is weaker, he declines apace, he draws nearer and nearer to us, and will soon be conscious of our existence." What is there to alarm me in this? It is encouragement and hope.

These thoughts have never crowded on me half so fast as they have done to-night. Faces I had long forgotten have become familiar to me once again; traits I had endeavoured to recall for years have come before me in an instant; nothing is changed but me; and even I can be my former self at will.

Raising my eyes but now to the face of my old clock, I remember quite involuntarily, the veneration, not unmixed with a sort of childish awe, with which I used to sit and watch it as it ticked, unheeded in a dark staircase corner. I recollect looking more grave and steady when I met its dusty face, as if, having that strange kind of life within it, and being free from all excesses of vulgar appetite, and warning all the house by night and day, it were a sage. How often I have listened to it as it told the beads of time, and wondered at its constancy! How often watched it slowly pointing round the dial, and, while I panted for the eagerly expected hour to come, admired, despite myself, its steadiness of purpose and lofty freedom from all human strife, impatience, and desire.

I thought it cruel once. It was very hard of heart, to my mind, I remember. It was an old servant even then; and I felt as though it ought to show some sorrow; as though it wanted sympathy with us in our distress, and were a dull, heartless, mercenary creature. Ah! how soon I learnt to know that in its ceaseless going on, and in its being checked or stayed by nothing, lay its greatest kindness, and the only balm for grief and wounded peace of mind.

To-night, to-night, when this tranquillity and calm are on my spirits, and memory presents so many shifting scenes before me, I take my quiet stand at will by many a fire that has been long extinguished, and mingle with the cheerful group that cluster round it. If I could be sorrowful in such a mood, I should grow sad to think what a poor blot I was upon their youth and beauty once, and now how few remain to put me to the blush; I should grow sad to think that such among them as I sometimes meet with in my daily walks are scarcely less infirm than I; that time brought us to a level; and that all distinctions fade and vanish as we take our trembling steps towards the grave.

But memory was given us for better purposes than this, and mine is not a torment, but a source of pleasure. To muse upon the gaiety and youth I have known suggests to me glad scenes of harmless mirth that may be passing now. From contemplating them apart, I soon become an actor in these little dramas, and humouring my fancy, lose myself among the beings it invokes.

When my fire is bright and high, and a warm blush mantles in the walls and ceiling of this ancient room; when my clock makes cheerful music, like one of those chirping insects who delight in the warm hearth, and are sometimes, by a good superstition, looked upon as the harbingers of fortune and plenty to that household in whose mercies they put their humble trust; when everything is in a ruddy genial glow, and there are voices in the crackling flame, and smiles in its flashing light, other smiles and other voices congregate around me, invading, with their pleasant harmony, the silence of the time.

For then a knot of youthful creatures gather round my fireside, and the room re-echoes to their merry voices. My solitary chair no longer holds its ample place before the fire, but is wheeled into a smaller corner, to leave more room for the broad circle formed about the cheerful hearth. I have sons, and daughters, and grandchildren, and we are assembled on some occasion of rejoicing common to us all. It is a birthday, perhaps, or perhaps it may be Christmas time; but be it what it may, there is rare holiday among us; we are full of glee.

In the chimney-corner, opposite myself, sits one who has grown old beside me. She is changed, of course; much changed; and yet I recognise the girl even in that gray hair and wrinkled brow. Glancing from the laughing child who half hides in her ample skirts, and half peeps out,—and from her to the little matron of twelve years old, who sits so womanly and so demure at no great distance from me,—and from her again, to a fair girl in the full bloom of early womanhood, the centre of the group, who has glanced more than once towards the opening door, and by whom the children, whispering and tittering among themselves, *will* leave a vacant chair, although she bids them not,—I see her image thrice repeated, and feel how long it is before one form and set of features wholly pass away, if ever, from among the living. While I am dwelling upon this, and tracing out the gradual change from infancy to youth, from youth to perfect growth, from that to age, and thinking, with an old man's pride, that she is comely yet, I feel a slight thin hand upon my arm, and, looking down, see seated at my feet a crippled boy,—a gentle, patient child,—whose aspect I know well. He rests upon a little crutch,—I know it too,—and leaning on it as he climbs my footstool, whispers, in my ear "I am hardly one of these, dear grandfather, although I love them dearly. They are very kind to me, but you will be kinder still, I know."

I have my hand upon his neck, and stoop to kiss him, when my clock strikes, my chair is in its old spot, and I am alone.

What if I be? What if this fireside be tenantless, save for the presence of one weak old man? From my house-top I can look upon a hundred homes, in every one of which these social companions are matters of reality. In my daily walks I pass a thousand men whose cares are all forgotten, whose labours are made light, whose dull routine work from day to day is cheered and brightened by their glimpses of domestic joy at home. Amid the struggles of this struggling town what cheerful sacrifices are made; what toil endured with readiness; what patience shown and fortitude displayed for the mere sake of home and its affections! Let me thank Heaven that I can people my fireside with shadows such as these; with shadows of bright objects that exist in crowds about me; and let me say, "I am alone no more."

I never was less so—I write it with a grateful heart—than I am to-night. Recollections of the past and visions of the present come to bear me company; the meanest man to whom I have ever given alms appears, to add his mite of peace and comfort to my stock; and whenever the fire within me shall grow cold, to light my path upon this earth no more, I pray that it may be at such an hour as this, and when I love the world as well as I do now.

### THE DEAF GENTLEMAN FROM HIS OWN APARTMENT

Our dear friend laid down his pen at the end of the foregoing paragraph, to take it up no more. I little thought ever to employ mine upon so sorrowful a task as that which he has left me, and to which I now devote it.

As he did not appear among us at his usual hour next morning, we knocked gently upon his door. No answer being given, it was softly opened; and then, to our surprise, we saw him seated before the ashes of his fire, with a little table I was accustomed to set at his elbow when I left him for the night at a short distance from him, as though he had pushed it away with the idea of rising and retiring to his bed. His crutch and footstool lay at his feet as usual, and he was dressed in his chamber-gown, which he had put on before I left him. He was reclining in his chair, in his accustomed posture, with his face towards the fire, and seemed absorbed in meditation,—indeed, at first, we almost hoped he was.

Going up to him, we found him dead. I have often, very often, seen him sleeping, and always peacefully, but I never saw him look so calm and tranquil. His face wore a serene, benign expression, which had impressed me very strongly when we last shook hands; not that he had ever had any other look, God knows; but there was something in this so very spiritual, so strangely and indefinably allied to youth, although his head was gray and venerable, that it was new even to him. It came upon me all at once when on some slight pretence he called me back upon the previous night to take me by the hand again, and once more say, "God bless you."

A bell-rope hung within his reach, but he had not moved towards it; nor had he stirred, we all agreed, except, as I have said, to push away his table, which he could have done, and no doubt did, with a very slight motion of his hand. He had relapsed for a moment into his late train of meditation, and, with a thoughtful smile upon his face, had died.

I had long known it to be his wish that whenever this event should come to pass we might be all assembled in the house. I therefore lost no time in sending for Mr. Pickwick and for Mr. Miles, both of whom arrived before the messenger's return.

It is not my purpose to dilate upon the sorrow and affectionate emotions of which I was at once the witness and the sharer. But I may say, of the humbler mourners, that his faithful housekeeper was fairly heart-broken; that the poor barber would not be comforted:

and that I shall respect the homely truth and warmth of heart of Mr. Weller and his son to the last moment of my life.

"And the sweet old creetur, sir," said the elder Mr. Weller to me in the afternoon, "has bolted. Him as had no wice, and was so free from temper that a infant might ha' drove him, has been took at last with that 'ere unawoidable fit o' staggers as we all must come to, and gone off his feed for ever! I see him," said the old gentleman, with a moisture in his eye, which could not be mistaken,—"I see him gettin', every journey, more and more groggy; I says to Samivel, 'My boy! the Grey's a-goin' at the knees; and now my predilictions is fatally werified, and him as I could never do enough to serve or show my likin' for, is up the great uniwersal spout o' natur'.'"

I was not the less sensible of the old man's attachment because he expressed it in his peculiar manner. Indeed, I can truly assert of both him and his son, that notwithstanding the extraordinary dialogues they held together, and the strange commentaries and corrections with which each of them illustrated the other's speech, I do not think it possible to exceed the sincerity of their regret; and that I am sure their thoughtfulness and anxiety in anticipating the discharge of many little offices of sympathy would have done honour to the most delicate-minded persons.

Our friend had frequently told us that his will would be found in a box in the Clock-case, the key of which was in his writing-desk. As he had told us also that he desired it to be opened immediately after his death, whenever that should happen, we met together that night for the fulfilment of his request.

We found it where he had told us, wrapped in a sealed paper, and with it a codicil of recent date, in which he named Mr. Miles and Mr. Pickwick his executors,—as having no need of any greater benefit from his estate than a generous token (which he bequeathed to them) of his friendship and remembrance.

After pointing out the spot in which he wished his ashes to repose, he gave to "his dear old friends," Jack Redburn and myself, his house, his books, his furniture,—in short, all that his house contained; and with this legacy more ample means of maintaining it in its present state than we, with our habits and at our terms of life, can ever exhaust. Besides these gifts, he left to us, in trust, an annual sum of no insignificant amount, to be distributed in charity among his accustomed pensioners—they are a long list—and such other claimants on his bounty as might, from time to time, present themselves. And as true charity not only covers a multitude of sins, but includes a multitude of virtues, such as forgiveness, liberal construction, gentleness and mercy to the faults of others, and the remembrance of our own imperfections and advantages, he bade us not inquire too closely into the venial errors of the poor, but finding that they *were* poor, first to relieve and then endeavour—at an advantage—to reclaim them.

To the housekeeper he left an annuity, sufficient for her comfortable maintenance and support through life. For the barber, who had attended him many years, he made a similar provision. And I may make two remarks in this particular place: first, that I think this pair are very likely to club their means together and make a match of it; and secondly, that I think my friend had this result in his mind, for I have heard him say, more than once, that he could not concur with the generality of mankind in censuring equal marriages made in later life, since there were many cases in which such unions could not fail to be a wise and rational source of happiness to both parties.

The elder Mr. Weller is so far from viewing this prospect with any feelings of jealousy, that he appears to be very much relieved by its contemplation; and his son, if I am not mistaken, participates in this feeling. We are all of opinion, however, that the old gentleman's danger, even at its crisis, was very slight, and that he merely laboured under one of those transitory weaknesses to which persons of his temperament are now and then liable, and which becomes less and less alarming at every return, until they wholly subside. I have no doubt he will remain a jolly old widower for the rest of his life, as he has already inquired of me, with much gravity, whether a writ of habeas corpus would enable him to settle his property upon Tony beyond the possibility of recall; and has, in my presence, conjured his son, with tears in his eyes, that in the event of his ever becoming amorous again, he will put him in a strait-waistcoat until the fit is past, and distinctly inform the lady that his property is "made over."

Although I have very little doubt that Sam would dutifully comply with these injunctions in a case of extreme necessity, and that he would do so with perfect composure and coolness, I do not apprehend things will ever come to that pass, as the old gentleman seems perfectly happy in the society of his son, his pretty daughter-in-law, and his grandchildren, and has solemnly announced his determination to "take arter the old 'un in all respects"; from which I infer that it is his intention to regulate his conduct by the model of Mr. Pickwick, who will certainly set him the example of a single life.

I have diverged for a moment from the subject with which I set out, for I know that my friend was interested in these little matters, and I have a natural tendency to linger upon any topic that occupied his thoughts or gave him pleasure and amusement. His remaining wishes are very briefly told. He desired that we would make him the frequent subject of our conversation; at the same time, that we would never speak of him with an air of gloom or restraint, but frankly, and as one whom we still loved and hoped to meet again. He trusted that the old house would wear no aspect of mourning, but that it would be lively and cheerful; and that we would not remove or cover up his picture, which hangs in our dining-room, but make it our companion as he had been. His own room, our place of meeting, remains at his desire, in its accustomed state; our seats are placed about the table as of old; his easy-chair, his desk, his crutch, his footstool, hold their accustomed places, and the clock stands in its familiar corner. We go into the chamber at stated times to see that all is as it should be, and to take care that the light and air are not shut out, for on that point he expressed a strong solicitude. But it was his fancy that the apartment should not be inhabited; that it should be religiously preserved in this condition, and that the voice of his old companion should be heard no more.

My own history may be summed up in a very few words; and even those I should have spared the reader but for my friend's allusion to me some time since. I have no deeper sorrow than the loss of a child,—an only daughter, who is living, and who fled from her father's house but a few weeks before our friend and I first met. I had never spoken of this even to him, because I have always loved her, and I could not bear to tell him of her error until I could tell him also of her sorrow and regret. Happily I was enabled to do so some time ago. And it will not be long, with Heaven's leave, before she is restored to me; before I find in her and her husband the support of my declining years.

For my pipe, it is an old relic of home, a thing of no great worth, a poor trifle, but sacred to me for her sake.

Thus, since the death of our venerable friend, Jack Redburn and I have been the sole tenants of the old house; and, day by day, have lounged together in his favourite walks. Mindful of his injunctions, we have long been able to speak of him with ease and cheerfulness, and to remember him as he would be remembered. From certain allusions which Jack has dropped, to his having been deserted and cast off in early life, I am inclined to believe that some passages of his youth may possibly be shadowed out in the history of Mr. Chester and his son, but seeing that he avoids the subject, I have not pursued it.

My task is done. The chamber in which we have whiled away so many hours, not, I hope, without some pleasure and some profit, is deserted; our happy hour of meeting strikes no more; the chimney-corner has grown cold; and MASTER HUMPHREY'S CLOCK has stopped for ever.

# THE LIFE

OF

# CHARLES DICKENS

## Editor's Note

"*He's sich a* harbitrary *gent!*" *Thus, according to tradition, was John Forster summed up by a cabman he patronised and with whom he had some words about his fare. The phrase would have delighted Dickens. It is a thumbnail portrait of the man who wrote the famous* Life *of our author, and who, as mentioned in the Editorial Note to* Our Mutual Friend, *had the sweep of the arm and the domineering way of Mr. Podsnap. John Forster was a heavyweight man of literature, who combined keen business ability with—on the whole— good literary judgment. Dickens, needing such a man, appreciated his qualities, and made him his confidant; and their friendship found a lasting memorial in the* Life *of Dickens. As Lockhart was to Sir Walter Scott, so, in many ways, was Forster to Dickens; although Forster's work has hardly the dramatic qualities and wide interest of Lockhart's. Only these two biographers could command the unique material used in the* Lives *they wrote; and both men succeed in bringing their great subjects into the presence of the reader—without intruding their own personalities, as many modern biographers do. Lockhart and Forster also have the same faults: both were guilty of tampering with correspondence in a way then general but nowadays barred. Also, both men were extremely reticent about certain aspects in the domestic lives of their subjects: a franker attitude would have avoided much misunderstanding and suspicion-breeding mystery, but it must be said in their excuse that they were hampered by consideration for people then still living. Notwithstanding these faults, Lockhart's* Life *of Scott and Forster's* Life *of Dickens are with Boswell's* Johnson *in the front rank of English biography. This abridgment of Forster's work aims to preserve its intimate study and the most essential of its illustrative materials in anecdote, letters, etc.*

CHARLES DICKENS

*(Drawing from the Portrait by Harry Furniss)*

# THE LIFE
## OF
# CHARLES DICKENS

BY

JOHN FORSTER

LONDON:
HAZELL, WATSON & VINEY, LTD.

# THE LIFE
OF
## CHARLES DICKENS

BY

JOHN FORSTER

LONDON
CHAPMAN & HALL, LTD.

# BOOK FIRST

## CHILDHOOD AND YOUTH

### 1812–36. ÆT. 1–24

# THE LIFE OF
# CHARLES DICKENS

## I

EARLIEST YEARS

1812–22

CHARLES DICKENS, the most popular novelist of the century, and one of the greatest humorists that England has produced, was born at Landport, in Portsea, on Friday, the seventh of February, 1812.

His father, John Dickens, a clerk in the navy pay-office, was at this time stationed in the Portsmouth Dockyard. He had made acquaintance with the lady, Elizabeth Barrow, who became afterwards his wife, through her elder brother, Thomas Barrow, also engaged on the establishment at Somerset House; and she bore him in all a family of eight children, of whom two died in infancy. The eldest, Fanny (born 1810), was followed by Charles (entered in the baptismal register of Portsea as Charles John Huffham, though on the very rare occasions when he subscribed that name he wrote Huffam); by another son, named Alfred, who died in childhood; by Letitia (born 1816); by another daughter, Harriet, who died also in childhood; by Frederick (born 1820); by Alfred Lamert (born 1822); and by Augustus (born 1827).

Walter Scott tell us, in his fragment of autobiography, speaking of the strange remedies applied to his lameness, that he remembered lying on the floor in the parlour of his grandfather's farmhouse, swathed up in a sheepskin warm from the body of the sheep, being then not three years old. David Copperfield's memory goes beyond this. He represents himself seeing so far back into the blank of his infancy as to discern therein his mother and her servant, dwarfed to his sight by stooping down or kneeling on the floor, and himself going unsteadily from the one to the other. He admits this may be fancy, though he believes the power of observation in numbers of very young children to be quite wonderful for its closeness and accuracy, and thinks that the recollection of most of us can go farther back into such times than many of us suppose. But what he adds is certainly not fancy. "If it should appear from anything I may set down in this narrative that I was a child of close observation, or that as a

317

man I have a strong memory of my childhood, I undoubtedly lay claim to both of these characteristics." Applicable as it might be to David Copperfield, this was unaffectedly true of Charles Dickens.

He has often told me that he remembered the small front garden to the house at Portsea, from which he was taken away when he was two years old, and where, watched by a nurse through a low kitchen window almost level with the gravel walk, he trotted about with something to eat, and his little elder sister with him. He was carried from the garden one day to see the soldiers exercise; and I perfectly recollect that, on our being at Portsmouth together while he was writing *Nickleby*, he recognised the exact shape of the military parade seen by him as a very infant, on the same spot, a quarter of a century before.

When his father was again brought up by his duties to London from Portsmouth, they went into lodgings in Norfolk Street, Middlesex Hospital; and it lived also in the child's memory that they had come away from Portsea in the snow. Their home, shortly after, was again changed, the elder Dickens being placed upon duty in Chatham Dockyard; and the house where he lived in Chatham, which had a plain-looking whitewashed plaster front and a small garden before and behind, was in St. Mary's Place, otherwise called the Brook, and next door to a Baptist meeting-house called Providence Chapel, of which a Mr. Giles he presently mentioned was minister. Charles at this time was between four and five years old; and here he stayed till he was nine. Here the most durable of his early impressions were received; and the associations that were around him when he died were those which at the outset of his life had affected him most strongly.

The house called Gadshill Place stands on the strip of highest ground in the main road between Rochester and Gravesend. Very often had we travelled past it together, many years before it became his home; and never without some allusion to what he told me when first I saw it in his company, that amid the recollections connected with his childhood it held always a prominent place, for, upon first seeing it as he came from Chatham with his father, and looking up at it with much admiration, he had been promised that he might himself live in it or in some such house when he came to be a man, if he would only work hard enough. Which for a long time was his ambition. . . .

He was a very little and a very sickly boy. He was subject to attacks of violent spasms which disabled him for any active exertion. He was never a good little cricket-player; he was never a first-rate hand at marbles, or peg-top, or prisoner's base; but he had great pleasure in watching the other boys, officers' sons for the most part, at these games, reading while they played; and he had always the belief that this early sickness had brought to himself one inestimable advantage, in the circumstances of his weak health having strongly inclined him to reading. It will not appear, as my narrative moves on, that he owed much to his parents, or was other than in his first letter to Washington Irving he described himself to have been, a "very small and not-over-particularly-taken-care-of boy"; but he has frequently been heard to say that his first desire for knowledge, and his earliest passion for reading, were awakened by his mother, from whom he learnt the rudiments, not only of English, but also, a little later, of Latin. She taught him regularly every day for a long time, and taught him, he was convinced, thoroughly well. I once put to him a question in connection with this to which he replied in almost exactly the words he placed five years later in the mouth of David Copperfield; "I faintly remember her teaching me the alphabet; and when I look upon the fat black letters in the primer, the puzzling novelty of their shapes, the easy good nature of O and S always seem to present themselves before me as they used to do." . . .

One of the many passages in *Copperfield* which are literally true, has its proper place here. "My father had left a small collection of books in a little room upstairs to which I had access (for it adjoined my own), and which nobody else in our house ever troubled. From that blessed little room, *Roderick Random, Peregrine Pickle, Humphrey Clinker, Tom Jones, The Vicar of Wakefield, Don Quixote, Gil Blas* and *Robinson Crusoe* came out, a glorious host, to keep me company. They kept alive my fancy, and my hope of something beyond that place and time—they, and the *Arabian Nights*, and the *Tales of the Genii*—and did me no harm; for, whatever harm was in some of them, was not there for me; *I* knew nothing of it. It is astonishing to me now, how I found time, in the midst of my porings and blunderings over heavier themes, to read those books as I did. It is curious to me how I could ever have consoled myself under my small troubles (which were great troubles to me), by impersonating my favourite characters in them. . . . I have been Tom Jones (a child's Tom Jones, a harmless creature) for a week together. I have sustained my own idea of Roderick Random for a month at a stretch, I verily believe. I had a greedy relish for a few volumes of voyages and travels—I forget what, now—that were on those shelves; and for days and days I can remember to have gone about my region of our house, armed with the centre-piece out of an old set of boot-trees the perfect realisation of Captain Somebody, of the Royal British Navy, in danger of being beset by savages, and resolved to sell his life at a great price. . . . When I think of it, the picture always rises in my mind, of a summer evening, the boys at play in the churchyard, and I sitting on my bed reading as if for life. Every barn in the neighbourhood, every stone in the church, and every foot of the churchyard, had some association of its own, in my mind, connected with these books, and stood for some locality made famous in them. I have seen Tom Pipes go climbing up the church steeple; I have watched Strap, with the knapsack on his back, stopping to rest himself upon the wicket-gate; and I *know* that Commodore Trunnion held that club with Mr. Pickle in the parlour of our little village alehouse." Every word of this personal recollection had been written down as fact, some years before it found its way into *David Copperfield*; the only change in the fiction being his omission of the name of a cheap series of novelists then in course of publication, by means of which his father had become happily the owner of so large a lump of literary treasure in his small collection of books.

The usual result followed. The child took to writing himself; and became famous in his childish circle, for having written a tragedy called *Misnar, the Sultan of India*, founded (and very literally founded, no doubt) on one of the *Tales of the Genii*. Nor was this his only distinction. He told a story offhand so well, and sang small comic songs so especially well, that he used to be elevated on chairs and tables, both at home and abroad, for more effective display of these talents; and when he first told me of this, at one of the Twelfth-night parties on his eldest son's birthday, he said he never recalled it that his own shrill little voice of childhood did not again tingle in his ears, and he blushed to think what a horrible little nuisance he must have been to many unoffending grown-up people who were called upon to admire him.

His chief ally and encourager in such displays was a youth of some ability, much older than himself, named James Lamert, stepson to his mother's sister, and therefore a sort of cousin, who was his great patron and friend in his childish days. Mary, the eldest daughter of Charles Barrow, himself a lieutenant in the navy, had for her first husband a commander in the navy called Allen, on whose death by drowning at Rio Janeiro she had joined her sister, the navy pay-clerk's wife, at Chatham; in which place she subsequently took for her second husband Doctor Lamert, an army surgeon, whose son James, even after he had been sent to Sandhurst for his education, continued still to visit Chatham from time to time. He had a turn for private theatricals; and as his father's quarters were in the ordnance hospital there, a great rambling place otherwise at that time almost uninhabited, he had plenty of room in which to get up his entertainments. The staff-doctor himself played his part, and his portrait will be found in *Pickwick*.

By Lamert, I have often heard him say, he was first taken to the theatre at the very tenderest age. He could hardly, however, have been younger than Charles Lamb, whose first experience was of having seen *Artaxerxes* when six years old; and certainly not younger than Walter Scott, who was only four when he saw *As You Like It* on the Bath stage, and remembered having screamed out, *"Ain't they brothers?"* when scandalised by Orlando and Oliver beginning to fight. But he was at any rate old enough to recollect how his young heart leapt with terror as the wicked King Richard, struggling for life against the virtuous Richmond, backed up and bumped against the box in which he was; and subsequent visits to the same sanctuary, as he tells us, revealed to him many wondrous secrets, "of which not the least terrific were, that the witches in *Macbeth* bore an awful resemblance to the thanes and other proper inhabitants of Scotland;

and that the good King Duncan couldn't rest in his grave, but was constantly coming out of it, and calling himself somebody else."

During the last two years of Charles's residence at Chatham, he was sent to a school kept in Clover Lane by the young Baptist minister already named, Mr. William Giles. I have the picture of him here very strongly in my mind as a sensitive, thoughtful, feeble-bodied little boy, with an amount of experience as well as fancy unusual in such a child, and with a dangerous kind of wandering intelligence that a teacher might turn to good or evil, happiness or misery, as he directed it. Nor does the influence of Mr. Giles, such as it was, seem to have been other than favourable. Charles had himself a not ungrateful sense in after years that this first of his masters, in his little-cared-for childhood, had pronounced him to be a boy of capacity; and when, about half-way through the publication of *Pickwick*, his old teacher sent a silver snuff-box with admiring inscription to "the inimitable Boz," it reminded him of praise far more precious obtained by him at his first year's examination in the Clover Lane academy, when his recitation of a piece out of the *Humorist's Miscellany* about Doctor Bolus had received, unless his youthful vanity bewildered him, a double encore. A habit, the only bad one taught him by Mr. Giles, of taking for a time, in very moderate quantities, the snuff called Irish Blackguard, was the result of this gift from his old master ; but he abandoned it after some few years, and it was never resumed.

It was in the boys' playing-ground near Clover Lane in which the school stood that, according to one of his youthful memories, he had been, in the hay-making time, delivered from the dungeons of Seringapatam, an immense pile ("of haycock"), by his countrymen the victorious British ("boy next door and his two cousins"), and had been recognised with ecstasy by his affianced one ("Miss Green"), who had come all the way from England ("second house in the terrace"), to ransom and marry him. It was in this playing-field, too, as he has himself recorded, he first heard in confidence from one whose father was greatly connected, "being under Government," of the existence of a terrible banditti called *the radicals*, whose principles were that the prince regent wore stays; that nobody had a right to any salary; and that the army and navy ought to be put down; horrors at which he trembled in his bed, after supplicating that the radicals might be speedily taken and hanged. Nor was it the least of the disappointments in his visit of after life to the scenes of his boyhood to have found this play-field swallowed up by a railway station. It was gone, with its two beautiful trees of hawthorn; and where the hedge, the turf and all the buttercups and daisies had been, there was nothing but the stoniest of jolting roads.

He was not much over nine years old when his father was recalled from Chatham to Somerset House, and he had to leave this good master, and the old place endeared to him by recollections that clung to him afterwards all his life long. It was here he had made the acquaintance not only of the famous books that David Copperfield specially names, . . . but also of the *Tatler*, *The Spectator*, *The Idler*, the *Citizen of the World*, and Mrs. Inchbald's *Collection of Farces*. These latter had been, as well, in the little library to which access was open to him; and of all of them his earliest remembrance was the having read them over and over at Chatham, not for the first, the second, or the third time. They were a host of friends when he had no single friend; and, in leaving the place, he has been often heard to say he seemed to be leaving them too, and everything that had given his ailing little life its picturesqueness or sunshine. It was the birthplace of his fancy; and he hardly knew what store he had set by its busy varieties of change and scene, until he saw the falling cloud that was to hide its pictures from him for ever. The gay, bright regiments always going and coming, the continual paradings and firings, the successions of sham-sieges and sham-defences, the plays got up by his cousin in the hospital, the navy pay-yacht in which he had sailed to Sheerness with his father, and the ships floating out in the Medway, with their far visions of sea—he was to lose them all. He was never to watch the boys at their games any more, or see them sham over again the sham-sieges and defences. He was to be taken away to London inside the stage-coach *Commodore;* and Kentish woods and fields, Cobham park and hall, Rochester cathedral and castle, and all the wonderful romance together, including a red-cheeked baby he had been wildly in love with, were to vanish like a dream. "On the night before we came away," he told me, "my good master came flitting in among the packing-cases to give me Goldsmith's *Bee* as a keepsake. Which I kept for his sake, and its own, a long time afterwards." A longer time afterwards he recollected the stage-coach journey, and in one of his published papers said that never had he forgotten, through all the intervening years, the smell of the damp straw in which he was packed and forwarded, like game, carriage paid. "There was no other inside passenger, and I consumed my sandwiches in solitude and dreariness, and it rained hard all the way, and I thought life sloppier than I expected to find it."

The earliest impressions received and retained by him in London were of his father's money involvements; and how first he heard mentioned "the deed," representing in fact that crisis of his father's affairs which is ascribed in fiction to Mr. Micawber's. He knew it in later days to have been a composition with creditors; though at this earlier date he was conscious of having confounded it with parchments of a much more demoniacal description. One result from the awful document soon showed itself in enforced retrenchment. The family had to take up its abode in a house in Bayham Street, Camden Town.

Bayham Street was about the poorest part of the London suburbs then, and the house was a mean small tenement, with a wretched little back-garden abutting on a squalid court. Here was no place for new acquaintances to him: not a boy was near with whom he might hope to become in any way familiar. A washerwoman lived next door, and a Bow Street officer lived over the way. Many, many times has he spoken to me of this, and how he seemed at once to fall into a solitary condition apart from all other boys of his own age, and to sink into a neglected state at home which had always been quite unaccountable to him. "As I thought," he said on one occasion very bitterly, "in the little back garret in Bayham Street, of all I had lost in losing Chatham, what would I have given, if I had had anything to give, to have been sent back to any other school, to have been taught something anywhere!" He was at another school already, not knowing it. The self-education forced upon him was teaching, all unconsciously as yet, what, for the future that awaited him, it most behoved him to know.

That he took, from the very beginning of this Bayham Street life, his first impression of that struggling poverty which is nowhere more vividly shown than in the commoner streets of the ordinary London suburb, and which enriched his earliest writings with a freshness of original humour and quite unstudied pathos that gave them much of their sudden popularity, there cannot be a doubt. "I certainly understood it," he has often said to me, "quite as well then as I do now." But he was not conscious yet that he did so understand it, or of the influence it was exerting on his life even then. It seems almost too much to assert of a child, say at nine or ten years old, that his observation of everything was as close and good, or that he had as much intuitive understanding of the character and weaknesses of the grown-up people around him, as when the same keen and wonderful faculty had made him famous among men. But my experience of him led me to put implicit faith in the assertion he unvaryingly himself made, that he had never seen any cause to correct or change what in his boyhood was his own secret impression of anybody, whom he had, as a grown man, the opportunity of testing in later years.

How it came that, being what he was, he should now have fallen into the misery and neglect of the time about to be described, was a subject on which thoughts were frequently interchanged between us; and on one occasion he gave me a sketch of the character of his father which, as I can here repeat it in the exact words employed by him, will be the best preface I can make to what I feel that I have no alternative but to tell. "I know my father to be as kindhearted and generous a man as ever lived in the world. Everything that I can remember of his conduct to his wife, or children, or friends, in sickness or affliction, is beyond all praise. By me, as a sick child, he has watched night and day, unweariedly and patiently, many nights and days. He never undertook any business, charge or trust that he did not zealously, conscientiously, punctually, honourably discharge. His industry has always been untiring. He was proud of me, in his way, and had a great admiration of the comic singing. But, in the ease of his temper, and the straitness of his means, he appeared to have utterly lost at this time the idea of educating me at all, and to have utterly put from him the notion that I had any claim upon him, in that regard, whatever. So I degenerated into cleaning his boots of a morning, and my own; and making myself useful in the work of the little house; and looking after my younger brothers and sisters (we were now six in all); and going on such poor errands as arose out of our poor way of living."

The cousin by marriage of whom I have spoken, James Lamert, who had lately completed his education at Sandhurst, and was waiting in hopes of a commission, lived now with the family in Bayham Street, and had not lost his taste for the stage, or his ingenuities in connection with it. Taking pity on the solitary lad, he made and painted a little theatre for him. It was the only fanciful reality of his present life; but it could not supply what he missed most sorely, the companionship of boys of his own age, with whom he might share in the advantages of school, and contend for its prizes. His sister Fanny was at about this time elected as a pupil to the Royal Academy of Music; and he has told me what a stab to his heart it was, thinking of his own disregarded condition, to see her go away to begin her education, amid the tearful good wishes of everybody in the house.

Nevertheless, as time went on, his own education still unconsciously went on as well, under the sternest and most potent of teachers; and, neglected and miserable as he was, he managed gradually to transfer to London all the dreaminess and all the romance with which he had invested Chatham. There were then at the top of Bayham Street some almshouses, and were still when he revisited it with me nearly twenty-seven years ago; and to go to this spot, he told me, and look from it over the dust-heaps and dock-leaves and fields (no longer there when we saw it together) at the cupola of St. Paul's looming through the smoke, was a treat that served him for hours of vague reflection afterwards. To be taken out for a walk into the real town, especially if it were anywhere about Covent Garden or the Strand, perfectly entranced him with pleasure. But most of all, he had a profound attraction of repulsion to St. Giles's. If he could only induce whomsoever took him out to take him through Seven Dials, he was supremely happy. "Good Heaven!" he would exclaim, "what wild visions of prodigies of wickedness, want, and beggary, arose in my mind out of that place!" He was all this time, the reader will remember, still subject to continual attacks of illness, and, by reason of them, a very small boy even for his age.

That part of his boyhood is now very near of which, when the days of fame and prosperity came to him, he felt the weight upon his memory as a painful burthen until he could lighten it by sharing it with a friend; and an accident I will presently mention led him first to reveal it. There is, however, an interval of some months still to be described, of which, from conversations or letters that passed between us, after or because of this confidence, and that already have yielded fruit to these pages, I can supply some vague and desultory notices. The use thus made of them, it is due to myself to remark, was contemplated then; for though, long before his death, I had ceased to believe it likely that I should survive to write about him, he had never withdrawn the wish at this early time strongly expressed, or the confidences, not only then, but to the very eve of his death reposed in me, that were to enable me to fulfil it. The fulfilment indeed he had himself rendered more easy by partially uplifting the veil in *David Copperfield*.

The visits made from Bayham Street were chiefly to two connections of the family, his mother's elder brother and his godfather. The latter, who was a rigger, and mast, oar and block maker, lived at Limehouse in a substantial handsome sort of way, and was kind to his godchild. It was always a great treat to him to go to Mr. Huffham's; and the London night-sights as he returned were a perpetual joy and marvel. Here, too, the comic-singing accomplishment was brought into play so greatly to the admiration of one of the godfather's guests, an honest boat-builder, that he pronounced the little lad to be a "progidy." The visits to the uncle, who was at this time fellow-clerk with his father in Somerset House, were nearer home. Mr. Thomas Barrow, the eldest of his mother's family, had broken his leg in a fall; and, while laid up with this illness, his lodging was in Gerrard Street, Soho, in the upper part of the house of a worthy gentleman then recently deceased, a bookseller named Manson, father to the partner in the celebrated firm of Christie and Mason, whose widow at the time carried on the business. Attracted by the look of the lad as he went upstairs, these good people lent him books to amuse him; among them Miss Porter's *Scottish Chiefs*, Holbein's *Dance of Death*, and George Colman's *Broad Grins*. The latter seized his fancy very much; and he was so impressed by its description of Covent Garden, in the piece called the "Elder Brother," that he stole down to the market by himself to compare it with the book. He remembered, as he said in telling me this, snuffing up the flavour of the faded cabbage-leaves as if it were the very breath of comic fiction. Nor was he far wrong, as comic fiction then, and for some time after, was. It was reserved for himself to give sweeter and fresher breath to it. Many years were to pass first, but he was beginning already to make the trial.

His uncle was shaved by a very odd old barber out of Dean Street, Soho, who was never tired of reviewing the events of the last war, and especially of detecting Napoleon's mistakes, and rearranging his whole life for him on a plan of his own. The boy wrote a description of this old barber, but never had courage to show it. At about the same time, taking for his model the description of the canon's housekeeper in *Gil Blas*, he sketched a deaf old woman who waited on them in Bayham Street, and who made delicate hashes with walnut ketchup. As little did he dare to show this, either; though he thought it, himself, extremely clever.

In Bayham Street, meanwhile, affairs were going on badly; the poor boy's visits to his uncle, while the latter was still kept a prisoner by his accident, were interrupted by another attack of fever; and on his recovery the mysterious "deed" had again come uppermost. His father's resources were so low, and all his expedients so thoroughly exhausted, that trial was to be made whether his mother might not come to the rescue. The time was arrived for her to exert herself, she said; and she "must do something." The godfather down at Limehouse was reported to have an Indian connection. People in the East Indies always sent their children home to be educated. She would set up a school. They would all grow rich by it. And then, thought the sick boy, "perhaps even I might go to school myself."

A house was soon found at number four, Gower Street North; a large brass plate on the door announced MRS. DICKENS'S ESTABLISH-MENT; and the result I can give in the exact words of the then small actor in the comedy, whose hopes it had raised so high. "I left, at a great many other doors, a great many circulars calling attention to the merits of the establishment. Yet nobody ever came to school, nor do I recollect that anybody ever proposed to come, or that the least preparation was made to receive anybody. But I know that we got on very badly with the butcher and baker; that very often we had not too much for dinner; and that at last my father was arrested." The interval between the sponging-house and the prison was passed by the sorrowful lad in running errands and carrying messages for the prisoner, delivered with swollen eyes and through shining tears; and the last words said to him by his father before he was finally carried to the Marshalsea, were to the effect that the sun was set upon him for ever. "I really believed at the time," said Dickens to me, "that they had broken my heart." He took after-wards ample revenge for this false alarm by making all the world laugh at them in *David Copperfield*.

The readers of Mr. Micawber's history who remember David's first visit to the Marshalsea prison, and how upon seeing the turnkey he recalled the turnkey in the blanket in *Roderick Random*, will read with curious interest what follows, written as a personal experience of fact two or three years before the fiction had even entered into his thoughts.

"My father was waiting for me in the lodge, and we went up to his room (on the top story but one), and cried very much. And he told me, I remember, to take warning by the Marshalsea, and to observe that if a man had twenty pounds a year, and spent nineteen pounds nineteen shillings and sixpence, he would be happy; but that a shilling spent the other way would make him wretched. I see the fire we sat before now; with two bricks inside the rusted grate, one on each side, to prevent its burning too many coals. Some other debtor shared the room with him, who came in by and by; and as the dinner was a joint-stock repast, I was sent up to 'Captain Porter' in the room overhead, with Mr. Dickens's compliments, and I was his son, and could he, Captain P., lend me a knife and fork?

"Captain Porter lent the knife and fork, with his compliments in return. There was a very dirty lady in his little room; and two wan girls, his daughters, with shock heads of hair. I thought I should not have liked to borrow Captain Porter's comb. The Captain himself was in the last extremity of shabbiness; and if I could draw at all, I would draw an accurate portrait of the old, old brown great-coat he wore, with no other coat below it. His whiskers were large. I saw his bed rolled up in a corner; and what plates and dishes and pots he had, on a shelf; and I knew (God knows how) that the two girls with the shock heads were Captain Porter's natural children, and that the dirty lady was not married to Captain P. My timid, wondering station on his threshold was not occupied more than a couple of minutes, I dare say; but I came down again to the room below with all this as surely in my knowledge, as the knife and fork were in my hand."

How there was something agreeable and gipsy-like in the dinner after all, and how he took back the Captain's knife and fork early in the afternoon, and how he went home to comfort his mother with an account of his visit, David Copperfield has also accurately told. Then, at home, came many miserable daily struggles that seemed to last an immense time, yet did not perhaps cover many weeks. Almost everything by degrees was sold or pawned, little Charles being the principal agent in those sorrowful transactions. Such of the books as had been brought from Chatham, *Peregrine Pickle, Roderick Random, Tom Jones, Humphrey Clinker,* and all the rest, went first. They were carried off from the little chiffonier, which his father called the library, to a bookseller in the Hampstead Road, the same that David Copperfield describes as in the City Road; and the account of the sales, as they actually occurred and were told to me long before David was born, was reproduced word for word in his imaginary narrative. "The keeper of this bookstall, who lived in a little house behind it, used to get tipsy every night, and to be violently scolded by his wife every morning. More than once, when I went there early, I had audience of him in a turn-up bedstead, with a cut in his forehead or a black eye, bearing witness to his excesses over night (I am afraid he was quarrelsome in his drink); and he, with a shaking hand, endeavouring to find the needful shillings in one or other of the pockets of his clothes, which lay upon the floor, while his wife, with a baby in her arms and her shoes down at heel, never left off rating him. Sometimes he had lost his money, and then he would ask me to call again; but his wife had always got some (had taken his, I dare say, while he was drunk), and secretly completed the bargain on the stairs, as we went down together."

The same pawnbroker's shop, too, which was so well known to David, became not less familiar to Charles; and a good deal of notice was here taken of him by the pawnbroker, or by his principal clerk who officiated behind the counter, and who, while making out the duplicate, liked of all things to hear the lad conjugate a Latin verb, and translate or decline his *musa* and *dominus*. Everything to this accompaniment went gradually; until at last, even of the furniture of Gower Street number four, there was nothing left except a few chairs, a kitchen table and some beds. Then they encamped, as it were, in the two parlours of the emptied house, and lived there night and day.

All which is but the prelude to what remains to be described.

## II

### HARD EXPERIENCES IN BOYHOOD

#### 1822-4

THE incidents to be told now would probably never have been known to me, or indeed any of the occurrences of his childhood and youth, but for the accident of a question which I put to him one day in the March or April of 1847.

I asked if he remembered ever having seen in his boyhood our friend the elder Mr. Dilke, his father's acquaintance and contemporary, who had been a clerk in the same office in Somerset House to which Mr. John Dickens belonged. Yes, he said, he recollected seeing him at a house in Gerrard Street, where his uncle Barrow lodged during an illness, and Mr. Dilke had visited him. Never at any other time. Upon which I told him that someone else had been intended in the mention made to me, for that the reference implied not merely his being met accidentally, but his having had some juvenile employment in a warehouse near the Strand; at which place Mr. Dilke, being with the elder Dickens one day, had noticed him, and received, in return for the gift of a half-crown, a very low bow. He was silent for several minutes; I felt that I had unintentionally touched a painful place in his memory; and to Mr. Dilke I never spoke of the subject again. It was not, however, then, but some weeks later, that Dickens made further allusion to my thus having struck unconsciously upon a time of which he never could lose the remembrance while he remembered anything, and the recollection of which, at intervals, haunted him and made him miserable, even to that hour.

Very shortly afterwards, I learnt in all their detail the incidents that had been so painful to him, and what then was said to me or written respecting them revealed the story of his boyhood. The idea of *David Copperfield*, which was to take all the world into his confidence, had not at this time occurred to him; but what it had so startled me to know, his readers were afterwards told with only such change or addition as for the time might sufficiently disguise himself under cover of his hero. For, the poor little lad, with good ability and a most sensitive nature, turned at the age of ten into a "labouring hind" in the service of "Murdstone and Grinby," and conscious already of what made it seem very strange to him that he could so easily have been thrown away at such an age, was indeed himself. His was the secret agony of soul at finding himself "companion to Mick Walker and Mealy Potatoes," and his the tears that mingled with the water in which he and they rinsed and washed out bottles. It had all been written, as fact, before he thought of any other use for it; and it was not until several months later, when the fancy of *David Copperfield*, itself suggested by what he had so written of his early troubles, began to take shape in his mind, that he abandoned his first intention of writing his own life. Those warehouse experiences fell then so aptly into the subject he had chosen, that he could not resist the temptation of immediately using them; and the manuscript recording them, which was but the first portion of what he had designed to write, was embodied in the substance of the eleventh and earlier chapters of his novel. What already had been sent to me, however, and proof-sheets of the novel interlined at the time, enable me now to separate the fact from the fiction; and to supply to the story of the author's childhood those passages, omitted from the book, which, apart from their illustration of the growth of his character, present to us a picture of tragical suffering, and of tender as well as humorous fancy, unsurpassed in even the wonders of his published writings.

The person indirectly responsible for the scenes to be described was the young relative James Lamert, the cousin by his aunt's marriage of whom I have made frequent mention, who got up the plays at Chatham, and after passing at Sandhurst had been living with the family in Bayham Street in the hope of obtaining a commission in the army. This did not come until long afterwards, when, in consideration of his father's services, he received it, and relinquished it then in favour of a younger brother; but he had meanwhile, before the family removed from Camden Town, ceased to live with them. The husband of a sister of his (of the same name as himself, being indeed his cousin, George Lamert), a man of some property, had recently embarked in an odd sort of commercial speculation; and had taken him into his office, and his house, to assist in it. I give now the fragment of the autobiography of Dickens.

"This speculation was a rivalry of ' Warren's Blacking, 30, Strand,' —at that time very famous. One Jonathan Warren (the famous one was Robert), living at 30, Hungerford Stairs, or Market, Strand (for I forget which it was called then), claimed to have been the original inventor or proprietor of the blacking recipe, and to have been deposed and ill-used by his renowned relation. At last he put himself in the way of selling his recipe, and his name, and his 30, Hungerford Stairs, Strand (30, Strand, very large, and the intermediate direction very small), for an annuity; and he set forth by his agents that a little capital would make a great business of it. The man of some property was found in George Lamert, the cousin and brother-in-law of James. He bought this right and title, and went into the blacking business and the blacking premises.

"—In an evil hour for me, as I often bitterly thought. Its chief manager, James Lamert, the relative who had lived with us in Bayham Street, seeing how I was employed from day to day, and knowing what our domestic circumstances then were, proposed that I should go into the blacking warehouse, to be as useful as I could, at a salary, I think, of six shillings a week. I am not clear whether it was six or seven. I am inclined to believe, from my uncertainty on this head, that it was six at first, and seven afterwards. At any rate, the offer was accepted very willingly by my father and mother, and on a Monday morning I went down to the blacking warehouse to begin my business life.

"It is wonderful to me how I could have been so easily cast away at such an age. It is wonderful to me that, even after my descent into the poor little drudge I had been since we came to London, no one had compassion enough on me—a child of singular abilities: quick, eager, delicate, and soon hurt, bodily or mentally—to suggest that something might have been spared, as certainly it might have been, to place me at any common school. Our friends, I take it, were tired out. No one made any sign. My father and mother were quite satisfied. They could hardly have been more so, if I had been twenty years of age, distinguished at a grammar-school, and going to Cambridge.

"The blacking warehouse was the last house on the left-hand side of the way, at old Hungerford Stairs. It was a crazy, tumble-down old house, abutting of course on the river, and literally overrun with rats. Its wainscotted rooms and its rotten floors and staircase, and the old grey rats swarming down in the cellars, and the sound of their squeaking and scuffling coming up the stairs at all times, and the dirt and decay of the place, rise up visibly before me, as if I were there again. The counting-house was on the first floor, looking over the coal-barges and the river. There was a recess in it, in which I was to sit and work. My work was to cover the pots of paste-blacking: first with a piece of oil-paper, and then with a piece of blue paper; to tie them round with a string; and then to clip the paper close and neat all round, until it looked as smart as a pot of ointment from an apothecary's shop. When a certain number of grosses of pots had attained this pitch of perfection, I was to paste on each a printed label; and then go on again with more pots. Two or three other boys were kept at similar duty downstairs on similar wages. One of them came up, in a ragged apron and a paper cap, on the first Monday morning, to show me the trick of using the string and tying the knot. His name was Bob Fagin; and I took the liberty of using his name, long afterwards, in *Oliver Twist*.

"Our relative had kindly arranged to teach me something in the dinner-hour; from twelve to one, I think it was; every day. But an arrangement so incompatible with counting-house business soon died away, from no fault of his or mine; and for the same reason, my small work-table, and my grosses of pots, my papers, string, scissors, paste-pot and labels, by little and little, vanished out of the recess in the counting-house, and kept company with the other small work-tables, grosses of pots, papers, string, scissors and paste-pots downstairs. It was not long before Bob Fagin and I, and another boy whose name was Paul Green, but who was currently believed to have been christened Poll (a belief which I transferred, long afterwards, again, to Mr. Sweedlepipe, in *Martin Chuzzlewit*), worked generally, side by side. Bob Fagin was an orphan, and lived with his brother-in-law, a waterman. Poll Green's father had the additional distinction of being a fireman, and was employed at Drury Lane theatre; where another relation of Poll's, I think his little sister, did imps in the pantomimes.

"No words can express the secret agony of my soul as I sunk into this companionship; compared these everyday associates with those of my happier childhood; and felt my early hopes of growing up to be a learned and distinguished man crushed in my breast. The deep remembrance of the sense I had of being utterly neglected and hope-less; of the shame I felt in my position; of the misery it was to my young heart to believe that, day by day, what I had learned, and thought, and delighted in, and raised my fancy and my emulation up by, was passing away from me, never to be brought back any more; cannot be written. My whole nature was so penetrated with the grief and humiliation of such considerations, that even now, famous and caressed and happy, I often forget in my dreams that I have a dear wife and children; even that I am a man; and wander desolately back to that time of my life.

"My mother and my brothers and sisters (excepting Fanny in the Royal Academy of Music) were still encamped, with a young servant-girl from Chatham Workhouse, in the two parlours in the emptied house in Gower Street North. It was a long way to go and return with-in the dinner-hour, and, usually, I either carried my dinner with me, or went and bought it at some neighbouring shop. In the latter case, it was commonly a saveloy and a penny loaf; sometimes, a four-penny plate of beef from a cook's shop; sometimes, a plate of bread and cheese, and a glass of beer, from a miserable old public-house over the way; the Swan, if I remember right, or the Swan and some-thing else that I have forgotten. Once, I remember tucking my own bread (which I had brought from home in the morning) under my arm, wrapped up in a piece of paper like a book, and going into the best dining-room in Johnson's alamode beef-house in Clare Court, Drury Lane, and magnificently ordering a small plate of alamode beef to eat with it. What the waiter thought of such a strange little apparition, coming in all alone, I don't know; but I can see him now, staring at me as I ate my dinner, and bringing up the other waiter to look. I gave him a halfpenny, and I wish, now, that he hadn't taken it."

I lose here for a little while the fragment of direct narrative, but I perfectly recollect that he used to describe Saturday night as his great treat. It was a grand thing to walk home with six shillings in his pocket, and to look in at the shop windows, and think what it would buy. Hunt's roasted corn, as a British and patriotic substitute for coffee, was in great vogue just then; and the little fellow used to buy it, and to roast it on the Sunday. There was a cheap periodical of selected pieces called the *Portfolio* which he had also a great fancy for taking home with him. The new proposed "deed," meanwhile, had failed to propitiate his father's creditors; all hope of arrangement passed away; and the end was that his mother and her encampment in Gower Street North broke up and went to live in the Marshalsea. I am able at this point to resume his own account.

"The key of the house was sent back to the landlord, who was very glad to get it; and I (small Cain that I was, except that I had never done harm to anyone) was handed over as a lodger to a reduced old lady, long known to our family, in Little College Street, Camden Town, who took children in to board, and had once done so at Brighton; and who, with a few alterations and embellishments, unconsciously began to sit for Mrs. Pipchin in *Dombey*, when she took in me.

"She had a little brother and sister under her care then; somebody's natural children, who were very irregularly paid for; and a widow's little son. The two boys and I slept in the same room. My own exclusive breakfast, of a penny cottage loaf and a pennyworth of milk, I provided for myself. I kept another small loaf, and a quarter of a pound of cheese, on a particular shelf of a particular cupboard: to make my supper on when I came back at night. They made a hole in the six or seven shillings, I know well; and I was out at the blacking warehouse all day, and had to support myself upon that money all the week. I suppose my lodging was paid for, by my father. I certainly did not pay it myself; and I certainly had no other assistance whatever (the making of my clothes, I think, excepted), from Monday morning until Saturday night. No advice, no counsel, no encouragement, no consolation, no support, from anyone that I can call to mind, so help me God.

"Sundays Fanny and I passed in the prison. I was at the academy in Tenterden Street, Hanover Square, at nine o'clock in the morning, to fetch her; and we walked back there together at night.

"I was so young and childish, and so little qualified—how could I be otherwise?—to undertake the whole charge of my own existence that, in going to Hungerford Stairs of a morning, I could not resist the stale pastry put out at half-price on trays at the confectioners' doors in Tottenham Court Road; and I often spent in that the money I should have kept for my dinner. Then I went without my dinner, or bought a roll, or a slice of pudding. There were two pudding shops between which I was divided, according to my finances. One was in a court close to St. Martin's Church (at the back of the church), which is now removed altogether. The pudding at that shop was made with currants, and was rather a special pudding, but was dear: two penn'orth not being larger than a penn'orth of more ordinary pudding. A good shop for the latter was in the Strand, somewhere near where the Lowther Arcade is now. It was a stout, hale pudding, heavy and flabby; with great raisins in it, stuck in whole, at great distances apart. It came up hot, at about noon every day; and many and many a day did I dine off it.

"We had half an hour, I think, for tea. When I had money enough, I used to go to a coffee-shop, and have half a pint of coffee, and a slice of bread and butter. When I had no money, I took a turn in Covent Garden Market, and stared at the pineapples. The coffee-shops to which I most resorted were, one in Maiden Lane; one in a court (non-existent now) close to Hungerford Market; and one in St. Martin's Lane, of which I only recollect that it stood near the church, and that in the door there was an oval glass plate, with COFFEE-ROOM painted on it, addressed towards the street. If I ever find myself in a very different kind of coffee-room now, but where there is such an inscription on glass, and read it backward on the wrong side MOOR-EEFFOC (as I often used to do then, in a dismal reverie), a shock goes through my blood.

"I know I do not exaggerate, unconsciously and unintentionally, the scantiness of my resources and the difficulties of my life. I know that if a shilling or so were given me by anyone, I spent it in a dinner or a tea. I know that I worked, from morning to night, with common men and boys, a shabby child. I know that I tried, but ineffectually, not to anticipate my money, and to make it last the week through by putting it away in a drawer I had in the counting-house, wrapped into six little parcels, each parcel containing the same amount, and labelled with a different day. I know that I have lounged about the streets, insufficiently and unsatisfactorily fed. I know that, but for the mercy of God, I might easily have been, for any care that was taken of me, a little robber or a little vagabond.

"But I held some station at the blacking warehouse too. Besides that my relative at the counting-house did what a man so occupied, and dealing with a thing so anomalous, could, to treat me as one upon a different footing from the rest, I never said, to man or boy, how it was that I came to be there, or gave the least indication of being sorry that I was there. That I suffered in secret, and that I suffered exquisitely, no one ever knew but I. How much I suffered, it is, as I have said already, utterly beyond my power to tell. No man's imagination can overstep the reality. But I kept my own counsel, and I did my work. I knew from the first that, if I could not do my work as well as any of the rest, I could not hold myself above a slight and contempt. I soon became at least as expeditious and as skilful with my hands as either of the other boys. Though perfectly familiar with them, my conduct and manners were different enough from theirs to place a space between us. They, and the men, always spoke of me as 'the young gentleman.' A certain man (a soldier once) named Thomas, who was the foreman, and another named Harry, who was the carman and wore a red jacket, used to call me 'Charles' sometimes, in speaking to me; but I think it was mostly when we were very confidential, and when I had made some efforts to entertain them over our work with the results of some of the old readings, which were fast perishing out of my mind. Poll Green uprose once, and rebelled against the 'young-gentleman' usage; but Bob Fagin settled him speedily.

"My rescue from this kind of existence I considered quite hopeless, and abandoned as such, altogether; though I am solemnly convinced that I never, for one hour, was reconciled to it, or was otherwise than miserably unhappy. I felt keenly, however, the being so cut off from my parents, my brothers, and sisters; and, when my day's work was done, going home to such a miserable blank; and *that*, I thought, might be corrected. One Sunday night I remonstrated with my father on this head, so pathetically and with so many tears, that his kind nature gave way. He began to think that it was not quite right. I do believe he had never thought so before, or thought about it. It was the first remonstrance I had ever made about my lot, and perhaps it opened up a little more than I intended. A back-attic was found for me at the house of an insolvent court agent, who lived in Lant Street in the Borough, where Bob Sawyer lodged many years afterwards. A bed and bedding were sent over for me, and made up on the floor. The little window had a pleasant prospect of a timber-yard; and when I took possession of my new abode, I thought it was a Paradise."

There is here another blank, which it is, however, not difficult to supply from letters and recollections of my own. What was to him of course the great pleasure of his paradise of a lodging was its bringing him again, though after a fashion sorry enough, within the circle of home. From this time he used to breakfast "at home," in other words in the Marshalsea; going to it as early as the gates were open, and for the most part much earlier. They had no want of bodily comforts there. His father's income, still going on, was amply sufficient for that; and in every respect indeed but elbow-room, I have heard him say the family lived more comfortably in prison than they had done for a long time out of it. They were waited on still by the maid-of-all-work from Bayham Street, the orphan girl of the Chatham Workhouse, from whose sharp little worldly and also kindly ways he took his first impression of the marchioness in the *Old Curiosity Shop*. She too had a lodging in the neighbourhood that she might be early on the scene of her duties; and when Charles met her, as he would do occasionally, in his lounging-place by London Bridge, he would occupy the time before the gates opened by telling her quite astonishing fictions about the wharves and the tower. "But I hope I believed them myself," he would say. Besides breakfast, he had supper also in the prison; and got to his lodging generally at nine o'clock. The gates closed always at ten.

I must not omit what he told me of the landlord of this little lodging. He was a fat, good-natured, kind old gentleman. He was lame, and had a quiet old wife; and he had a very innocent grown-up son, who was lame, too. They were all very kind to the boy. He was taken with one of his old attacks of spasm one night, and the whole three of them were about his bed until morning. They were all dead when he told me this, but in another form they live still very pleasantly as the Garland family in the *Old Curiosity Shop*.

He had a similar illness one day in the warehouse, which I can describe in his own words. "Bob Fagin was very good to me on the occasion of a bad attack of my old disorder. I suffered such excruciating pain that time, that they made a temporary bed of straw in my old recess in the counting-house, and I rolled about on the floor, and Bob filled empty blacking-bottles with hot water, and applied relays of them to my side, half the day. I got better, and quite easy towards evening; but Bob (who was much bigger and older than I) did not like the idea of my going home alone, and took me under his protection. I was too proud to let him know about the prison; and after making several efforts to get rid of him, to all of which Bob Fagin n his goodness was deaf, shook hands with him on the steps of a house near Southwark Bridge on the Surrey side, making believe that I lived there. As a finishing piece of reality in case of his looking back, I knocked at the door, I recollect, and asked, when the woman opened it, if that was Mr. Robert Fagin's house."

The Saturday nights continued, as before, to be precious to him. "My usual way home was over Blackfriars Bridge, and down that turning in the Blackfriars Road which has Rowland Hill's chapel on one side, and the likeness of a golden dog licking a golden pot over a shop door on the other. There are a good many little low-browed old shops in that street, of a wretched kind; and some are unchanged now. I looked into one a few weeks ago, where I used to buy boot-laces on Saturday nights, and saw the corner where I once sat down on a stool to have a pair of ready-made half-boots fitted on. I have been seduced more than once, in that street on a Saturday night, by a show-van at a corner; and have gone in, with a very motley assemblage, to see the Fat Pig, the Wild Indian, and the Little Lady. There were two or three hat-manufactories there, then (I think they are there still); and among the things which, encountered anywhere, or under any circumstances, will instantly recall that time, is the smell of hat-making."

His father's attempts to avoid going through the court having failed, all needful ceremonies had to be undertaken to obtain the benefit of the Insolvent Debtors' Act; and in one of these little Charles had his part to play. One condition of the statute was that the wearing apparel and personal matters retained were not to exceed twenty pounds sterling in value. "It was necessary, as a matter of form, that the clothes I wore should be seen by the official appraiser.

I had a half-holiday to enable me to call upon him, at his own time, at a house somewhere beyond the Obelisk. I recollect his coming out to look at me with his mouth full, and a strong smell of beer upon him, and saying good-naturedly that 'that would do,' and 'it was all right.' Certainly the hardest creditor would not have been disposed (even if he had been legally entitled) to avail himself of my poor white hat, little jacket, or corduroy trowsers. But I had a fat old silver watch in my pocket, which had been given me by my grandmother before the blacking days, and I had entertained my doubts as I went along whether that valuable possession might not bring me over the twenty pounds. So I was greatly relieved, and made him a bow of acknowledgment as I went out.''

Still the want felt most by him was the companionship of boys of his own age. He had no such acquaintance. Sometimes, he remembered to have played on the coal-barges at dinner-time with Poll Green and Bob Fagin; but those were rare occasions. He generally strolled alone, about the back streets of the Adelphi; or explored the Adelphi Arches. One of his favourite localities was a little public-house by the water-side called the "Fox-under-the-Hill," approached by an underground passage which we once missed in looking for it together; and he had a vision which he has mentioned in *Copperfield* of sitting eating something on a bench outside, one fine evening, and looking at some coal-heavers dancing before the house. "I wonder what they thought of me," says David. He had himself already said the same in his fragment of autobiography.

Another characteristic little incident he made afterwards one of David's experiences, but I am able to give it here without the disguises that adapt it to the fiction. "I was such a little fellow, with my poor white hat, little jacket, and corduroy trowsers, that frequently, when I went into the bar of a strange public-house for a glass of ale or porter to wash down the saveloy and the loaf I had eaten in the street, they didn't like to give it me. I remember, one evening (I had been somewhere for my father, and was going back to the Borough over Westminster Bridge), that I went into a public-house in Parliament Street, which is still there though altered, at the corner of the short street leading into Cannon Row, and said to the landlord behind the bar, 'What is your very best—the VERY *best*—ale, a glass?' For, the occasion was a festive one, for some reason: I forget why. It may have been my birthday, or somebody else's. 'Twopence,' says he. 'Then,' says I, 'just draw me a glass of that, if you please, with a good head to it.' The landlord looked at me, in return, over the bar, from head to foot, with a strange smile on his face; and instead of drawing the beer, looked round the screen and said something to his wife, who came out from behind it, with her work in her hand, and joined him in surveying me. Here we stand, all three, before me now, in my study in Devonshire Terrace. The landlord, in his shirt-sleeves, leaning against the bar window-frame; his wife, looking over the little half-door; and I, in some confusion, looking up at them from outside the partition. They asked me a good many questions, as what my name was, how old I was, where I lived, how I was employed, etc. To all of which, that I might commit nobody, I invented appropriate answers. They served me with the ale, though I suspect it was not the strongest on the premises; and the landlord's wife, opening the little half-door and bending down, gave me a kiss that was half-admiring and half-compassionate, but all womanly and good, I am sure."

A later, and not less characteristic, occurrence of the true story of this time found also a place, three or four years after it was written, in his now famous fiction. It preceded but by a short term the discharge, from the Marshalsea, of the elder Dickens; to whom a rather considerable legacy from a relative had accrued not long before ("some hundreds," I understood), and had been paid into court during his imprisonment. The scene to be described arose on the occasion of a petition drawn up by him before he left, praying, not for the abolition of imprisonment for debt, as David Copperfield relates, but for the less dignified but more accessible boon of a bounty to the prisoners to drink His Majesty's health on His Majesty's forthcoming birthday.

"I mention the circumstance because it illustrates, to me, my early interest in observing people. When I went to the Marshalsea of a night, I was always delighted to hear from my mother what she knew about the histories of the different debtors in the prison; and when I heard of this approaching ceremony, I was so anxious to see them all come in, one after another (though I knew the greater part of them already, to speak to, and they me), that I got leave of absence on purpose, and established myself in a corner, near the petition. It was stretched out, I recollect, on a great ironing-board, under the window, which in another part of the room made a bedstead at night. The internal regulations of the place, for cleanliness and order, and for the government of a common room in the ale-house, where hot water and some means of cooking, and a good fire, were provided for all who paid a very small subscription, were excellently administered by a governing committee of debtors, of which my father was chairman for the time being. As many of the principal officers of this body as could be got into the small room without filling it up supported him, in front of the petition; and my old friend Captain Porter (who had washed himself, to do honour to so solemn an occasion) stationed himself close to it, to read it to all who were unacquainted with its contents. The door was then thrown open, and they began to come in, in a long file; several waiting on the landing outside, while one entered, affixed his signature, and went out. To everybody in succession Captain Porter said, 'Would you like to hear it read?' If he weakly showed the least disposition to hear it, Captain Porter, in a loud, sonorous voice, gave him every word of it. I remember a certain luscious roll he gave to such words as 'Majesty—gracious Majesty—your gracious Majesty's unfortunate subjects—your Majesty's well-

known munificence'—as if the words were something real in his
mouth, and delicious to taste: my poor father meanwhile listening
with a little of an author's vanity, and contemplating (not severely)
the spikes on the opposite wall. Whatever was comical in this scene,
and whatever was pathetic, I sincerely believe I perceived in my
corner, whether I demonstrated or not, quite as well as I should
perceive it now. I made out my own little character and story for
every man who put his name to the sheet of paper. I might be able
to do that now, more truly: not more earnestly, or with a closer
interest. Their different peculiarities of dress, of face, of gait, of
manner, were written indelibly upon my memory. I would rather
have seen it than the best play ever played; and I thought about it
afterwards, over the pots of paste-blacking, often and often. When
I looked, with my mind's eye, into the Fleet Prison during Mr.
Pickwick's incarceration, I wonder whether half a dozen men were
wanting from the Marshalsea crowd that came filing in again, to the
sound of Captain Porter's voice!"

When the family left the Marshalsea they all went to lodge with
the lady in Little College Street, a Mrs. Roylance, who has obtained
unexpected immortality as Mrs. Pipchin; and they afterwards
occupied a small house in Somers Town. But, before this time, Charles
was present with some of them in Tenterden Street to see his sister
Fanny receive one of the prizes given to the pupils of the Royal
Academy of Music. "I could not bear to think of myself—beyond the
reach of all such honourable emulation and success. The tears ran
down my face. I felt as if my heart were rent. I prayed, when I went
to bed that night, to be lifted out of the humiliation and neglect in
which I was. I never had suffered so much before. There was no envy
in this." There was little need that he should say so. Extreme enjoyment in witnessing the exercise of her talents, the utmost pride in
every success obtained by them, he manifested always to a degree
otherwise quite unusual with him; and on the day of her funeral,
which we passed together, I had most affecting proof of his tender
and grateful memory of her in these childish days. A few more
sentences, certainly not less touching than any that have gone before,
will bring the story of them to its close. They stand here exactly as
written by him.

"I am not sure that it was before this time, or after it, that the
blacking warehouse was removed to Chandos Street, Covent Garden.
It is no matter. Next to the shop at the corner of Bedford Street,
in Chandos Street, are two rather old-fashioned houses and shops
adjoining one another. They were one then, or thrown into one, for
the blacking business; and had been a butter shop. Opposite to them
was, and is, a public-house, where I got my ale, under these new
circumstances. The stones in the street may be smoothed by my small
feet going across to it at dinner-time, and back again. The establishment was larger now, and we had one or two new boys. Bob Fagin
and I had attained to great dexterity in tying up the pots. I forget

how many we could do in five minutes. We worked, for the light's sake, near the second window as you come from Bedford Street; and we were so brisk at it, that the people used to stop and look in. Sometimes there would be quite a little crowd there. I saw my father coming in at the door one day when we were very busy, and I wondered how he could bear it.

"Now, I generally had my dinner in the warehouse. Sometimes I brought it from home, so I was better off. I see myself coming across Russell Square from Somers Town, one morning, with some cold hotch-potch in a small basin tied up in a handkerchief. I had the same wanderings about the streets as I used to have, and was just as solitary and self-dependent as before; but I had not the same difficulty in merely living. I never, however, heard a word of being taken away, or of being otherwise than quite provided for.

"At last, one day, my father and the relative so often mentioned quarrelled; quarrelled by letter, for I took the letter from my father to him which caused the explosion, but quarrelled very fiercely. It was about me. It may have had some backward reference, in part, for anything I know, to my employment at the window. All I am certain of is that, soon after I had given him the letter, my cousin (he was a sort of cousin, by marriage) told me he was very much insulted about me; and that it was impossible to keep me, after that. I cried very much, partly because it was so sudden, and partly because in his anger he was violent about my father, though gentle to me. Thomas, the old soldier, comforted me, and said he was sure it was for the best. With a relief so strange that it was like oppression, I went home.

"My mother set herself to accommodate the quarrel, and did so next day. She brought home a request for me to return next morning, and a high character of me, which I am very sure I deserved. My father said I should go back no more, and should go to school. I do not write resentfully or angrily: for I know how all these things have worked together to make me what I am: but I never afterwards forgot, I never shall forget, I never can forget, that my mother was warm for my being sent back.

"From that hour until this at which I write, no word of that part of my childhood which I have now gladly brought to a close, has passed my lips to any human being. I have no idea how long it lasted; whether for a year, or much more, or less. From that hour, until this, my father and my mother have been stricken dumb upon it. I have never heard the least allusion to it, however far off and remote, from either of them. I have never, until I now impart it to this paper, in any burst of confidence with anyone, my own wife not excepted, raised the curtain I then dropped, thank God.

"Until old Hungerford Market was pulled down, until old Hungerford Stairs were destroyed, and the very nature of the ground changed, I never had the courage to go back to the place where my servitude began. I never saw it. I could not endure to go near it. For many

years, when I came near to Robert Warrens' in the Strand, I crossed
over to the opposite side of the way, to avoid a certain smell of the
cement they put upon the blacking-corks, which reminded me of what
I was once. It was a very long time before I liked to go up Chandos
Street. My old way home by the Borough made me cry, after my
eldest child could speak.

"In my walks at night I have walked there often, since then, and
by degrees I have come to write this. It does not seem a tithe of
what I might have written, or of what I meant to write."

The substance of some after-talk explanatory of points in the
narrative, of which a note was made at the time, may be briefly
added. He could hardly have been more than twelve years old when
he left the place, and was still unusually small for his age; much
smaller, though two years older, than his own eldest son was at the
time of these confidences. His mother had been in the blacking
warehouse many times; his father not more than once or twice.
The rivalry of Robert Warren by Jonathan's representatives, the
cousins George and James, was carried to wonderful extremes in the
way of advertisement; and they were all very proud, he told me, of
the cat scratching the boot, which was *their* house's device. The poets
in the house's regular employ he remembered, too, and made his
first study from one of them for the poet of Mrs Jarley's waxwork.
The whole enterprise, however, had the usual end of such things.
The younger cousin tired of the concern; and a Mr. Wood, the proprietor who took James's share and became George's partner, sold
it ultimately to Robert Warren. It continued to be his at the time
Dickens and myself last spoke of it together, and he had made an
excellent bargain of it.

## III

### SCHOOL-DAYS AND START IN LIFE

#### 1824-30

IN what way those strange experiences of his boyhood affected him
afterwards, the narrative of his life must show: but there were
influences that made themselves felt even on his way to manhood.

What at once he brought out of the humiliation that had impressed
him so deeply, though scarcely as yet quite consciously, was a natural
dread of the hardships that might still be in store for him, sharpened
by what he had gone through; and this, though in its effect for the
present imperfectly understood, became by degrees a passionate
resolve, even while he was yielding to circumstances, *not to be* what
circumstances were conspiring to make him. All that was involved in

what he had suffered and sunk into could not have been known to him at the time; but it was plain enough later, as we see; and in conversation with me after the revelation was made, he used to find, at extreme points in his life, the explanation of himself in those early trials. He had derived great good from them, but not without alloy. The fixed and eager determination, the restless and resistless energy, which opened to him opportunities of escape from many mean environments, not by turning off from any path of duty, but by resolutely rising to such excellence or distinction as might be attainable in it, brought with it some disadvantage among many noble advantages. Of this he was himself aware, but not to the full extent. What it was that in society made him often uneasy, shrinking, and over-sensitive, he knew; but all the danger he ran in bearing down and over-mastering the feeling, he did not know. A too great confidence in himself, a sense that everything was possible to the will that would make it so, laid occasionally upon him self-imposed burdens greater than might be borne by anyone with safety. In that direction there was in him, at such times, something even hard and aggressive; in his determinations a something that had almost the tone of fierceness; something in his nature that made his resolves insuperable, however hasty the opinions on which they had been formed. So rare were these manifestations, however, and so little did they prejudice a character as entirely open and generous as it was at all times ardent and impetuous, that only very infrequently, towards the close of the middle term of a friendship which lasted without the interruption of a day for more than three and thirty years, were they ever unfavourably presented to me. But there they were; and when I have seen strangely present, at such chance intervals, a stern and even cold isolation of self-reliance side by side with a susceptivity almost feminine and the most eager craving for sympathy, it has seemed to me as though his habitual impulses for everything kind and gentle had sunk, for the time, under a sudden hard and inexorable sense of what Fate had dealt to him in those early years. On more than one occasion indeed I had confirmation of this. "I must entreat you," he wrote to me in June 1862, "to pause for an instant, and go back to what you know of my childish days, and to ask yourself whether it is natural that something of the character formed in me then, and lost under happier circumstances, should have reappeared in the last five years. The never-to-be-forgotten misery of that old time bred a certain shrinking sensitiveness in a certain ill-clad, ill-fed child, that I have found come back in the never-to-be-forgotten misery of this later time."

One good there was, however, altogether without drawback, and which claims simply to be mentioned before my narrative is resumed. The story of his childish misery has itself sufficiently shown that he never throughout it lost his precious gift of animal spirits, or his native capacity for humorous enjoyment; and there were positive gains to him from what he underwent which were also rich and lasting. To what in the outset of his difficulties and trials gave the decisive bent to his genius, I have already made special reference; and we are to observe, of what followed, that with the very poor and unprosperous, out of whose sufferings and strugglings, and the virtues as well as vices born of them, his not least splendid successes were wrought, his childish experiences had made him actually one. They were not his clients whose cause he pleaded with such pathos and humour, and on whose side he got the laughter and tears of all the world, but in some sort his very self. Nor was it a small part of this manifest advantage that he should have obtained his experience as a child and not as a man; that only the good part, the flower and fruit of it, was plucked by him; and that nothing of the evil part, none of the earth in which the seed was planted, remained to soil him.

His next move in life can also be given in his own language. "There was a school in the Hampstead Road kept by Mr. Jones, a Welshman, to which my father dispatched me to ask for a card of terms. The boys were at dinner, and Mr. Jones was carving for them, with a pair of holland sleeves on, when I acquitted myself of this commission. He came out, and gave me what I wanted; and hoped I should become a pupil. I did. At seven o'clock one morning, very soon afterwards, I went as day scholar to Mr. Jones's establishment, which was in Mornington Place, and had its school-room sliced away by the Birmingham Railway, when that change came about. The school-room however was not threatened by directors or civil engineers then, and there was a board over the door graced with the words WELLINGTON HOUSE ACADEMY."

At Wellington House Academy he remained nearly two years, being a little over fourteen years of age when he quitted it. In his minor writings, as well as in *Copperfield*, will be found general allusions to it, and there is a paper among his pieces reprinted from *Household Words* which purports specifically to describe it. To the account therein given of himself when he went to the school, as advanced enough, so safely had his memory retained its poor fragments of early schooling, to be put into Virgil, as getting sundry prizes, and as attaining to the eminent position of its first boy, one of his two schoolfellows with whom I have had communication, makes objection; but both admit that the general features of the place are reproduced with wonderful accuracy, and more especially in those points for which the school appears to have been much more notable than for anything connected with the scholarship of its pupils.

In the reprinted piece Dickens describes it as remarkable for white mice. He says that red-polls, linnets, and even canaries, were kept by the boys in desks, drawers, hat-boxes, and other strange refuges for birds; but that white mice were the favourite stock, and that the boys trained the mice much better than the master trained the boys. He recalled in particular one white mouse who lived in the cover of a Latin dictionary, ran up ladders, drew Roman chariots, shouldered muskets, turned wheels, and even made a very creditable appearance on the stage as the Dog of Montargis, who might have achieved greater things but for having had the misfortune to mistake his way in a triumphal procession to the Capitol, when he fell into a deep inkstand, and was dyed black and drowned.

Nevertheless, he mentions the school as one also of some celebrity in its neighbourhood, though nobody could have said why; and adds that among the boys the master was supposed to know nothing, and one of the ushers was supposed to know everything. "We are still inclined to think the first named supposition perfectly correct. We went to look at the place only this last midsummer, and found that the railway had cut it up, root and branch. A great trunk line had swallowed the playground, sliced away the school-room, and pared off the corner of the house. Which, thus curtailed of its proportions, presented itself in a green stage of stucco, profile-wise towards the road, like a forlorn flat-iron without a handle, standing on end."

One who knew him in those early days, Mr. Owen P. Thomas, thus writes to me (February 1871): "I had the honour of being Mr. Dickens's schoolfellow for about two years (1824–6), both being day-scholars at Mr. Jones's 'Classical and Commercial Academy,' as then inscribed in front of the house. . . . My recollection of Dickens whilst at school is that of a healthy-looking boy, small but well-built, with a more than usual flow of spirits, inducing to harmless fun, seldom or ever I think to mischief, to which so many lads at that age are prone. I cannot recall anything that then indicated he would hereafter become a literary celebrity; but perhaps he was too young then. He usually held his head more erect than lads ordinarily do, and there was a general smartness about him. His week-day dress of jacket and trousers, I can clearly remember, was what is called pepper-and-salt; and instead of the frill that most boys of his age wore then, he had a turn-down collar, so that he looked less youthful in consequence. He invented what we termed a ' lingo,' produced by the addition of a few letters of the same sound to every word; and it was our ambition, walking and talking thus along the street, to be considered foreigners. As an alternate amusement, the present writer well remembers extemporising tales of some sort, and reciting them offhand, with Dickens and Danson or Tobin walking on either side of him. . . ."

To Mr. Thomas's letter the reader will thank me for adding one not less interesting, with which Dr. Henry Danson has favoured me. We have here, with the same fun and animal spirits, a little of the proneness to mischief which his other schoolfellow says he was free from; but the mischief is all of the harmless kind, and might perhaps have been better described as but part of an irrepressible vivacity.

"My impression is that I was a schoolfellow of Dickens for nearly two years: he left before me, I think at about fifteen years of age. Mr. Jones's school, called the Wellington Academy, was in the Hampstead Road, at the north-east corner of Granby Street. The school-house was afterwards removed for the London and North-Western Railway. It was considered at the time a very superior sort of school, one of the best, indeed, in that part of London; but it was most shamefully mismanaged, and the boys made but very little progress. The proprietor, Mr. Jones, was a Welshman; a most ignorant fellow, and a mere tyrant; whose chief employment was to scourge the boys. Dickens has given a very lively account of this place in his paper entitled 'Our School,' but it is very mythical in many respects, and more especially in the compliment he pays in it to himself. I do not remember that Dickens distinguished himself in any way, or carried off any prizes. My belief is that he did not learn Greek or Latin there, and you will remember there is no allusion to the classics in any of his writings. He was a handsome, curly-headed lad, full of animation and animal spirits, and probably was connected with every mischievous prank in the school. I do not think he came in for any of Mr. Jones's scourging propensity; in fact, together with myself, he was only a day-pupil, and with these there was a whole-some fear of tales being carried home to the parents. His personal appearance at that time is vividly brought home to me in the portrait of him taken a few years later by Mr. Lawrence. He resided with his friends in a very small house in a street leading out of Seymour Street, north of Mr. Judkin's chapel.

"Depend on it he was quite a self-made man, and his wonderful knowledge and command of the English language must have been acquired by long and patient study after leaving his last school.

"I have no recollection of the boy you name. His chief associates were, I think, Tobin, Mr. Thomas Bray, and myself. The first-named was his chief ally, and his acquaintance with him appears to have continued many years afterwards. At about that time penny and Saturday magazines were published weekly, and were greedily read by us. We kept bees, white mice, and other living things clandestinely in our desks; and the mechanical arts were a good deal cultivated, in the shape of coach-building, and making pumps and boats, the motive power of which was the white mice.

"I think at that time Dickens took to writing small tales, and we had a sort of club for lending and circulating them. Dickens was also very strong in using a sort of lingo, which made us quite unintelligible to bystanders. We were very strong, too, in theatricals. We mounted small theatres, and got up very gorgeous scenery to illustrate the *Miller and his Men* and *Cherry and Fair Star.* I remember the present Mr. Beverley, the scene-painter, assisted us in this. Dickens was always a leader at these plays, which were occasionally presented with much solemnity before an audience of boys, and in the presence of the ushers. My brother, assisted by Dickens, got up the *Miller and his Men*, in a very gorgeous form. Master Beverley constructed the mill for us in such a way that it could tumble to pieces with the assistance of crackers. At one representation the fireworks in the last scene, ending with the destruction of the mill, were so very real that the police interfered, and knocked violently at the doors. Dickens's after-taste for theatricals might have had its origin in these small affairs.

"I quite remember Dickens on one occasion heading us in Drummond Street in pretending to be poor boys, and asking the passers-by for charity—especially old ladies; one of whom told us she 'had no money for beggar boys.' On these adventures, when the old ladies were quite staggered by the impudence of the demand, Dickens would explode with laughter and take to his heels.

"I met him one Sunday morning shortly after he left the school, and we very piously attended the morning service at Seymour Street chapel. I am sorry to say Master Dickens did not attend in the slightest degree to the service, but incited me to laughter by declaring his dinner was ready and the potatoes would be spoiled, and in fact behaved in such a manner that it was lucky for us we were not ejected from the chapel.

"I heard of him some time after from Tobin, whom I met carrying a foaming pot of London particular in Lincoln's Inn Fields, and I then understood that Dickens was in the same or some neighbouring office. . . ."

Dickens had not quitted school many months before his father had made sufficient interest with an attorney of Gray's Inn, Mr. Edward Blackmore, to obtain him regular employment in his office. In this capacity of clerk, our only trustworthy glimpse of him we owe to the last-named gentleman, who has described briefly, and I do not doubt authentically, the services so rendered by him to the law. It cannot be said that they were noteworthy, though it might be difficult to find a more distinguished person who has borne the title, unless we make exception for the very father of literature himself, whom Chaucer, with amusing illustration of the way in which words change their meanings, calls "that conceited clerke Homère."

"I was well acquainted," writes Mr. Edward Blackmore of Alresford, "with his parents, and, being then in practice in Gray's Inn, they asked me if I could find employment for him. He was a bright, clever-looking youth, and I took him as a clerk. He came to me in May 1827, and left in November 1828; and I have now an account-book which he used to keep of petty disbursements in the office, in which he charged himself with the modest salary first of thirteen shillings and sixpence, and afterwards of fifteen shillings a week. Several incidents took place in the office of which he must have been a keen observer, as I recognised some of them in his *Pickwick* and *Nickleby*; and I am much mistaken if some of his characters had not their originals in persons I well remember. His taste for theatricals was much promoted by a fellow-clerk named Potter, since dead, with whom he chiefly associated. They took every opportunity, then unknown to me, of going together to a minor theatre, where (I afterwards heard) they not unfrequently engaged in parts. After he left me I saw him at times in the lord chancellor's court, taking notes of cases as a reporter. I then lost sight of him until his *Pickwick* made its appearance." This letter indicates the position he held at Mr. Blackmore's; and we have but to turn to the passage in *Pickwick* which describes the several grades of attorney's clerk, to understand it more clearly. He was very far below the articled clerk, who has paid a premium and is attorney in perspective. He was not so high as the salaried clerk, with nearly the whole of his weekly thirty shillings spent on his personal pleasures. He was not even on a level with the middle-aged copying clerk, always needy and uniformly shabby. He was simply among, however his own nature may have lifted him above, the "office-lads in their first surtouts, who feel a befitting contempt for boys at day-schools, club as they go home at night for savelovs and porter, and think there's nothing like life." Thus far, not more or less, had he now reached. He was one of the office-lads, and probably in his first surtout.

But, even thus, the process of education went on, defying what seemed to interrupt it; and in the amount of his present equipment for his needs of life, what he brought from the Wellington House Academy can have borne but the smallest proportion to his acquirement at Mr. Blackmore's. Yet to seek to identify, without help from himself, any passages in his books with those boyish law-experiences, would be idle and hopeless enough. In the earliest of his writings, and down to the very latest, he worked exhaustively the field which is opened by an attorney's office to a student of life and manners; but we have not now to deal with his numerous varieties of the *genus* clerk drawn thus for the amusement of others, but with the acquisitions which at present he was storing up for himself from the opportunities such offices opened to him. Nor would it be possible to have better illustrative comment on all these years than is furnished by his father's reply to a friend it was now hoped to interest on his behalf, which more than once I have heard him whimsically but good-humouredly imitate. "Pray, Mr. Dickens, where was your son educated?" "Why, indeed, Sir—ha! ha!—he may be said to have educated himself!" Of the two kinds of education which Gibbon says that all men who rise above the common level receive: the first that of his teachers, and the second, more personal and more important, *his own*; he had the advantage only of the last. It nevertheless sufficed for him.

Very nearly another eighteen months were now to be spent mainly in practical preparation for what he was, at this time, led finally to choose as an employment from which a fair income was certain with such talents as he possessed; his father already having taken to it, in these latter years, in aid of the family resources. In his father's house, which was at Hampstead through the first portion of the Mornington Street school-time, then in the house out of Seymour

Street mentioned by Mr. Danson, and afterwards, upon the elder Dickens going into the gallery as a reporter for the *Morning Herald*, in Bentinck Street, Manchester Square, Charles had continued to live: and, influenced doubtless by the example before him, he took sudden determination to qualify himself thoroughly for what his father was lately become, a newspaper parliamentary reporter. He set resolutely therefore to the study of shorthand; and, for the additional help of such general information about books as a fairly educated youth might be expected to have, as well as to satisfy some higher personal cravings, he became an assiduous attendant in the British Museum reading-room. He would frequently refer to these days as decidedly the usefullest to himself he had ever passed; and judging from the results they must have been so. No man who knew him in later years, and talked to him familiarly of books and things, would have suspected his education in boyhood, almost entirely self-acquired as it was, to have been so rambling or haphazard as I have here described it. The secret consisted in this, that, whatever for the time he had to do, he lifted himself, there and then, to the level of, and at no time disregarded the rules that guided the hero of his novel: "Whatever I have tried to do in life, I have tried with all my heart to do well. What I have devoted myself to, I have devoted myself to completely. Never to put one hand to anything on which I could throw my whole self, and never to affect depreciation of my work, whatever it was, I find now to have been my golden rules."

Of the difficulties that beset his shorthand studies, as well as of what first turned his mind to them, he has told also something in *Copperfield*. He had heard that many men distinguished in various pursuits had begun life by reporting the debates in parliament, and he was not deterred by a friend's warning that the mere mechanical accomplishment for excellence in it might take a few years to master thoroughly: "a perfect and entire command of the mystery of shorthand writing and reading being about equal in difficulty to the mastery of six languages." Undaunted, he plunged into it, self-teaching in this as in graver things; and, having bought Mr. Gurney's half-guinea book, worked steadily his way through its distractions. "The changes that were rung upon dots, which in such a position meant such a thing, and in such another position something else entirely different; the wonderful vagaries that were played by circles; the unaccountable consequences that resulted from marks like flies' legs; the tremendous effects of a curve in a wrong place, not only troubled my waking hours, but reappeared before me in my sleep. When I had groped my way, blindly, through these difficulties, and had mastered the alphabet, there then appeared a procession of new horrors, called arbitrary characters; the most despotic characters I have ever known; who insisted, for instance, that a thing like the beginning of a cobweb meant 'expectation,' and that a pen-and-ink sky-rocket stood for 'disadvantageous.' When I had fixed these wretches in my mind, I found that they had driven everything else out of it; then, beginning again, I forgot them; while I was picking them up, I dropped the other fragments of the system; in short, it was almost heart-breaking.''

What it was that made it not quite heart-breaking to the hero of the fiction, its readers know; and something of the same kind was now to enter into the actual experience of its writer. First let me say, however, that after subduing to his wants in marvellously quick time this unruly and unaccommodating servant of stenography, what he most desired was still not open to him. "There never *was* such a shorthand-writer," has been often said to me by Mr. Beard, the friend he first made in that line when he entered the gallery, and with whom to the close of his life he maintained the friendliest intercourse. But there was no opening for him in the gallery yet. He had to pass nearly two years as a reporter for one of the offices in Doctors' Commons, having made attempt even in the direction of the stage to escape such drudgery, before he became a sharer in parliamentary toils and triumphs; and what sustained his young hero through something of the same sort of trial was also his own support. He too had his Dora, at apparently the same hopeless elevation; striven for as the one only thing to be attained, and even more unattainable, for neither did he succeed nor happily did she die; but the one idol, like the other, supplying a motive to exertion for the time, and otherwise opening out to the idolater, both in fact and fiction, a highly unsubstantial, happy, foolish time. I used to laugh and tell him I had no belief in any but the book Dora, until the incident of a sudden reappearance of the real one in his life, nearly six years after *Copperfield* was written, convinced me there had been a more actual foundation for those chapters of his book than I was ready to suppose. Still I would hardly admit it; and, that the matter could possibly affect him then, persisted in a stout refusal to believe. His reply (1855) throws a little light on this juvenile part of his career, and I therefore venture to preserve it.

"I don't quite apprehend what you mean by my over-rating the strength of the feeling of five-and-twenty years ago. If you mean of my own feeling, and will only think what the desperate intensity of my nature is, and that this began when I was Charley's age; that it excluded every other idea from my mind for four years, at a time of life when four years are equal to four times four; and that I went at it with a determination to overcome all the difficulties, which fairly lifted me up into that newspaper life, and floated me away over a hundred men's heads: then you are wrong, because nothing can exaggerate that. I have positively stood amazed at myself ever since!—And so I suffered, and so worked, and so beat and hammered away at the maddest romances that ever got into any boy's head and stayed there, that to see the mere cause of it all, now, loosens my hold upon myself. Without for a moment sincerely believing that it would have been better if we had never got separated, I cannot see the occasion of so much emotion as I should see anyone else. No one can imagine in the most distant degree what pain the recollection gave me in *Copperfield*. And, just as I can never open that book as I open any other book, I cannot see the face (even at four-and-forty), or hear the voice, without going wandering away over the ashes of all that youth and hope in the wildest manner." More and more plainly seen, however, in the light of four-and-forty, the romance glided visibly away, its work being fairly done; and, at the close of the month following that in which this letter was written, during which he had very quietly made a formal call with his wife at his youthful Dora's house, and contemplated with a calm equanimity, in the hall, her stuffed favourite Jip, he began the fiction in which there was a Flora to set against its predecessor's Dora, both derived from the same original. The fancy had a comic humour in it he found it impossible to resist, but it was kindly and pleasant to the last; and if the later picture showed him plenty to laugh at in this retrospect of his youth, there was nothing he thought of more tenderly than the earlier, as long as he was conscious of anything.

## IV

### NEWSPAPER REPORTING AND WRITING

#### 1831-5

DICKENS was nineteen years old when at last he entered the gallery. His father, with whom he still lived in Bentinck Street, had already, as we have seen, joined the gallery as a reporter for one of the morning papers, and was now in the more comfortable circumstances derived from the addition to his official pension which this praise-worthy labour ensured; but his own engagement on the *Chronicle* dates somewhat later. His first parliamentary service was given to the *True Sun*, a journal which had on its editorial staff some dear friends of mine, through whom I became myself a contributor to it, and afterwards, in common with all concerned, whether in its writing, reporting, printing or publishing, a sharer in its difficulties. The most formidable of these arrived one day in a general strike of the reporters; and I well remember noticing at this dread time, on the staircase of the magnificent mansion we were lodged in, a young man of my own age whose keen animation of look would have arrested attention anywhere, and whose name, upon inquiry, I then for the first time heard. It was coupled with the fact which gave it interest even then, that "young Dickens" had been spokesman for the recalcitrant reporters, and conducted their case triumphantly.

He was afterwards during two sessions engaged for the *Mirror of Parliament*, which one of his uncles by the mother's side originated and conducted; and finally, in his twenty-third year, he became a reporter for the *Morning Chronicle*.

His attempt to get upon the stage dates immediately before these newspaper engagements. His Doctors' Commons reportership was a living so wearily uncertain, that a possibility of the other calling had occurred to him in quite a businesslike way. He went to theatres almost every night for a long time; studied and practised himself in parts; was so much attracted by the "At Homes" of the elder Mathews, that he resolved to make his first plunge in a similar direction; and finally wrote to make offer of himself to Covent Garden. "I wrote to Bartley, who was stage-manager, and told him how young I was, and exactly what I thought I could do; and that I believed I had a strong perception of character and oddity, and a natural power of reproducing in my own person what I observed in others. This was at the time when I was at Doctors' Commons as a shorthand writer for the proctors. And I recollect I wrote the letter from a little office I had there, where the answer came also. There must have been something in my letter that struck the authorities, for Bartley wrote to me almost immediately to say that they were busy getting up the *Hunchback* (so they were), but that they would communicate with me again, in a fortnight. Punctual to the time another letter came, with an appointment to do anything of Mathews's I pleased before him and Charles Kemble, on a certain day at the theatre. My sister Fanny was in the secret, and was to go with me to play the songs. I was laid up when the day came, with a terrible bad cold and an inflammation of the face; the beginning, by the by, of that annoyance in one ear to which I am subject to this day. I wrote to say so, and added that I would resume my application next season. I made a great splash in the gallery soon afterwards; the *Chronicle* opened to me; I had a distinction in the little world of the newspaper, which made one like it; began to write; didn't want money; had never thought of the stage but as a means of getting it; gradually left off turning my thoughts that way, and never resumed the idea. I never told you this, did I? See how near I may have been to another sort of life." The letter in which he gave me this interesting detail belongs to another place; but the anticipation of so much of it here is required to complete his boyish history.

The beginning to write was a thing far more momentous to him (though then he did not know it) than his "great splash" in the gallery. In the December number for 1833 of what then was called the *Old Monthly Magazine*, his first published piece of writing had seen the light. He has described himself dropping this paper ("Mr. Minns and his cousin," as he afterwards entitled it, but which appeared in the magazine as "A Dinner at Poplar Walk") stealthily one evening at twilight, with fear and trembling, into a dark letter-box in a dark office up a dark court in Fleet Street; and he has told his agitation when it appeared in all the glory of print. "On which occasion I walked down to Westminster Hall, and turned into it for half an hour, because my eyes were so dimmed with joy and pride that they could not bear the street, and were not fit to be seen there." He had purchased the magazine at a shop in the Strand; and exactly two years afterwards, in the younger member of a publishing firm who had called at his chambers in Furnival's Inn, to which he had moved soon after entering the gallery, with the proposal that originated *Pickwick*, he recognised the person he had bought that magazine from, and whom before or since he had never seen.

This interval of two years more than comprised what remained of his career in the gallery and the engagements connected with it; but that this occupation was of the utmost importance in its influence on his life, in the discipline of his powers as well as of his character, there can be no doubt whatever. "To the wholesome training of severe newspaper-work, when I was a very young man, I constantly refer my first successes," he said to the New York editors when he last took leave of them. It opened to him a wide and varied range of experience, which his wonderful observation, exact as it was humorous, made entirely his own. He saw the last of the old coaching days, and of the old inns that were a part of them; but it will be long before the readers of his living page see the last of the life of either. "There never was," he once wrote to me (in 1845), "anybody connected with newspapers who, in the same space of time, had so much express and post-chaise experience as I. And what gentlemen they were to serve, in such things, at the old *Morning Chronicle*! Great or small, it did not matter. I have had to charge for half a dozen break-downs in half a dozen times as many miles. I have had to charge for the damage of a great-coat from the drippings of a blazing wax-candle, in writing through the smallest hours of the night in a swift-flying carriage and pair. I have had to charge for all sorts of breakages fifty times in a journey without question, such being the ordinary results of the pace which we went at. I have charged for broken hats, broken luggage, broken chaises, broken harness—everything but a broken head, which is the only thing they would have grumbled to pay for."

Something to the same effect he said publicly twenty years later, on the occasion of his presiding, in May 1865, at the second annual dinner of the Newspaper Press Fund, when he condensed within the compass of his speech a summary of the whole of his reporting life. "I am not here," he said, "advocating the case of a mere ordinary client of whom I have little or no knowledge. I hold a brief to-night for my brothers. I went into the gallery of the House of Commons as a parliamentary reporter when I was a boy, and I left it—I can hardly believe the inexorable truth—nigh thirty years ago. I have pursued the calling of a reporter under circumstances of which many of my brethren here can form no adequate conception. I have often transcribed for the printer, from my shorthand notes, important public speeches in which the strictest accuracy was required, and a mistake in which would have been to a young man severely compromising, writing on the palm of my hand, by the light of a dark lantern, in a post-chaise and four, galloping through a wild country, and through the dead of the night, at the then surprising rate of fifteen miles an hour. The very last time I was at Exeter, I strolled into the castle-yard there to identify, for the amusement of a friend, the spot on which I once 'took,' as we used to call it, an election speech of Lord John Russell at the Devon contest, in the midst of a lively fight maintained by all the vagabonds in that division of the county, and under such a pelting rain, that I remember two good-natured colleagues who chanced to be at leisure held a pocket-handkerchief over my note-book, after the manner of a state canopy in an ecclesiastical procession. I have worn my knees by writing on them on the old back-row of the old gallery of the old House of Commons; and I have worn my feet by standing to write in a preposterous pen in the old House of Lords, where we used to be huddled together like so many sheep—kept in waiting, say, until the Woolsack might want re-stuffing. Returning home from exciting political meetings in the country to the waiting press in London, I do verily believe I have been upset in almost every description of vehicle known in this country. I have been, in my time, belated on miry by-roads, towards the small hours, forty or fifty miles from London, in a wheelless carriage, with exhausted horses and drunken post-boys, and have got back in time for publication, to be received with never-forgotten compliments by the late Mr. Black, coming in the broadest of Scotch from the broadest of hearts I ever knew. These trivial things I mention as an assurance to you that I never have forgotten the fascination of that old pursuit. The pleasure that I used to feel in the rapidity and dexterity of its exercise has never faded out of my breast. Whatever little cunning of hand or head I took to it, or acquired in it, I have so retained that I fully believe I could resume it to-morrow, very little the worse from long disuse. To this present year of my life, when I sit in this hall, or where not, hearing a dull speech (the phenomenon does occur), I sometimes beguile the tedium of the moment by mentally following the speaker in the old, old way; and sometimes, if you can believe me, I even find my hand going on the tablecloth, taking an imaginary note of it all." The latter I have known him do frequently. It was indeed a quite ordinary habit with him.

Mr. James Grant, a writer who was himself in the gallery with Dickens, and who states that among its eighty or ninety reporters he occupied the very highest rank, not merely for accuracy in reporting, but for marvellous quickness in transcribing, has lately also told us that while there he was exceedingly reserved in his manners, and that, though showing the usual courtesies to all he was concerned with in his duties, the only personal intimacy he formed was with Mr. Thomas Beard, then too reporting for the *Morning Chronicle*. I have already mentioned the friendly and familiar relations maintained with this gentleman to the close of his life; and, in confirmation of Mr. Grant's statement, I can further say that the only other associate of these early reporting days to whom I ever heard him refer with special regard was the late Mr. Vincent Dowling, many years editor of *Bell's Life*, with whom he did not continue much personal intercourse, but of whose character as well as talents he had formed a very high opinion. Nor is there anything to add to the notice of this time which the reader's fancy may not easily supply. A letter has been kept as written by him while engaged on one of his "expresses"; but it is less for its saying anything new, than for its confirming with a pleasant vividness what has been said already, that its contents will justify mention here.

He writes, on a "Tuesday morning" in May 1835, from the Bush Inn, Bristol; the occasion that has taken him to the west, connected with a reporting party, being Lord John Russell's Devonshire contest above-named, and his associate-chief being Mr. Beard, entrusted with command for the *Chronicle* in this particular express. He expects to forward "the conclusion of Russell's dinner" by Cooper's company's coach leaving the Bush at half-past six next morning; and by the first Ball's coach on Thursday morning he will forward the report of the Bath dinner, endorsing the parcel for immediate delivery, with extra rewards for the porter. Beard is to go over to Bath next morning. He is himself to come back by the mail from Marlborough; he has no doubt, if Lord John makes a speech of any ordinary dimensions, it can be done by the time Marlborough is reached; "and taking into consideration the immense importance of having the addition of saddle-horses from thence, it is, beyond all doubt, worth an effort. . . . I need not say," he continues, "that it will be sharp work and will require two of us; for we shall both be up the whole of the previous night, and shall have to sit up all night again to get it off in time." He adds that as soon as they have had a little sleep they will return to town as quickly as they can; but they have, if the express succeeds, to stop at sundry places along the road to pay money and notify satisfaction. And so, for himself and Beard, he is his editor's very sincerely. . . .

The mention of his career in the gallery may close with the comment that his observation while there had not led him to form any high opinion of the House of Commons or its heroes; and that, of the Pickwickian sense which so often takes the place of common sense in our legislature, he omitted no opportunity of declaring his contempt at every part of his life.

The other occupation had meanwhile not been lost sight of, and for this we are to go back a little. Since the first sketch appeared in the *Monthly Magazine*, nine others have enlivened the pages of later numbers of the same magazine, the last in February 1835, and that which appeared in the preceding August having first had the signature of Boz. . . . The magazine was owned as well as conducted at

this time by a Mr. Holland, who had come back from Bolivar's South
American campaigns with the rank of captain, and had hoped to
make it a popular mouthpiece for his ardent liberalism. But this
hope, as well as his own health, quite failed; and he had sorrowfully
to decline receiving any more of the sketches when they had to cease
as voluntary offerings. I do not think that either he or the magazine
lived many weeks after an evening I passed with him in Doughty
Street, in 1837, when he spoke in a very touching way of the failure of
this and other enterprises of his life, and of the help that Dickens had
been to him.

Nothing being forthcoming from the *Monthly*, it was of course but
natural that the sketches too should cease to be forthcoming; and,
even before the above-named February number appeared, a new
opening had been found for them. An evening off-shoot to the
*Morning Chronicle* had been lately in hand; and to a countryman of
Black's engaged in the preparations for it, Mr. George Hogarth,
Dickens was communicating from his rooms in Furnival's Inn, on the
evening of Tuesday the 20th of January, 1835, certain hopes and
fancies he had formed. This was at the beginning of his knowledge of
an accomplished and kindly man, with whose family his relations
were soon to become so intimate as to have an influence on all his
future career. Mr. Hogarth had asked him, as a favour to himself, to
write an original sketch for the first number of the enterprise, and in
writing back to say with what readiness he should comply, and how
anxiously he should desire to do his best for the person who had
made the request, he mentioned what had arisen in his mind. It had
occurred to him that he might not be unreasonably or improperly
trespassing farther on Mr. Hogarth if, trusting to his kindness to
refer the application to the proper quarter, he begged to ask whether
it was probable, if he commenced a regular series of articles under
some attractive title for the *Evening Chronicle*, its conductors would
think he had any claim to *some* additional remuneration (of course, of
no great amount) for doing so. In short, he wished to put it to the
proprietors—first, whether a continuation of some chapters of light
papers in the style of his street-sketches would be considered of use
to the new journal; and secondly, if so, whether they would not think
it fair and reasonable that, taking his share of the ordinary reporting
business of the *Chronicle* besides, he should receive something for the
papers beyond his ordinary salary as a reporter? The request was
thought fair, he began the sketches, and his salary was raised from
five to seven guineas a week.

They went on, with undiminished spirit and freshness, throughout
the year; and much as they were talked of outside as well as in the
world of newspapers, nothing in connection with them delighted the
writer half so much as the hearty praise of his own editor. Mr. Black
is one of the men who have passed without recognition out of a world
their labours largely benefited, but with those who knew him no man
was so popular, as well for his broad, kindly humour, as for his honest

great-hearted enjoyment of whatever was excellent in others.
Dickens to the last remembered, that it was most of all the cordial
help of this good old mirth-loving man, which had started him joyfully on his career of letters. It was John Black that flung the
slipper after me, he would often say, "Dear old Black! my first
hearty out-and-out appreciator," is an expression in one of his
letters written to me in the year he died.

## V

### FIRST BOOK, AND ORIGIN OF "PICKWICK"

### 1836

THE opening of 1836 found him collecting into two volumes the first
series of *Sketches by Boz*, of which he had sold the copyright for a
conditional payment of (I think) a hundred and fifty pounds to a
young publisher named Macrone, whose acquaintance he had made
through Mr. Ainsworth a few weeks before. At this time also, we are
told in a letter before quoted, the editorship of the *Monthly Magazine*
having come into Mr. James Grant's hands, this gentleman, applying
to him through its previous editor to know if he would again contribute to it, learnt two things the first that he was going to be
married, and the second that, having entered into an arrangement to
write a monthly serial, his duties in future would leave him small
spare time. Both pieces of news were soon confirmed. *The Times* of
26 March, 1836, gave notice that on the 31st would be published the
first shilling number of the *Posthumous Papers of the Pickwick Club,
edited by Boz;* and the same journal of a few days later announced
that on 2 April Mr. Charles Dickens had married Catherine, the
eldest daughter of Mr. George Hogarth, whom already we have met
as his fellow-worker on the *Chronicle.* The honeymoon was passed in
the neighbourhood to which at all times of interest in his life he
turned with a strange recurring fondness; and while the young couple
are at the quiet little village of Chalk, on the road between Gravesend
and Rochester, I will relate exactly the origin of the ever-memorable
Mr. Pickwick.

A new publishing house had started recently, among other enterprises ingenious rather than important, a Library of Fiction; among
the authors they wished to enlist in it was the writer of the sketches
in the *Monthly;* and, to the extent of one paper during the past year,
they had effected this through their editor, Mr. Charles Whitehead,
a very ingenious and a very unfortunate man. "I was not aware,"
wrote the elder member of the firm to Dickens, thirteen years later,

in a letter to which reference was made[1] in the preface to *Pickwick* in one of his later editions, "that you were writing in the *Chronicle*, or what your name was; but Whitehead, who was an old *Monthly* man, recollected it, and got you to write 'The Tuggs's at Ramsgate.'"

And now comes another person on the scene. "In November 1835," continues Mr. Chapman, "we published a little book called the *Squib Annual*, with plates by Seymour; and it was during my visit to him, to see after them, that he said he should like to do a series of cockney sporting-plates of a superior sort to those he had already published. I said I thought they might do, if accompanied by letter-press and published in monthly parts; and this being agreed to, we wrote to the author of *Three Courses and a Dessert* and proposed it; but receiving no answer, the scheme dropped for some months, till Seymour said he wished us to decide, as another job had offered which would fully occupy his time; and it was on this we decided to ask you to do it. Having opened already a connection with you for our Library of Fiction, we naturally applied to you to do the *Pickwick;* but I do not think we even mentioned our intention to Mr. Seymour, and I am quite sure that from the beginning to the end nobody but yourself had anything whatever to do with it. Our prospectus was out at the end of February, and it had all been arranged before that date."

The member of the firm who carried the application to him in Furnival's Inn was not the writer of this letter, but Mr. Hall, who had sold him two years before, not knowing that he was the purchaser, the magazine in which his first effusion was printed; and he has himself described what passed at the interview. "The idea propounded to me was that the monthly something should be a vehicle for certain plates to be executed by Mr. Seymour; and there was a notion, either on the part of that admirable humorous artist, or of my visitor, that a NIMROD CLUB, the members of which were to go out shooting, fishing, and so forth, and getting themselves into difficulties through their want of dexterity, would be the best means of introducing these. I objected, on consideration, that although born and partly bred in the country I was no great sportsman, except in regard to all kinds of locomotion; that the idea was not novel, and had already been much used; that it would be infinitely better for the plates to arise naturally out of the text; and that I would like to take my own way, with a freer range of English scenes and people, and was afraid I should ultimately do so in any case, whatever course I might prescribe to myself at starting. My views being

[1] Not quoted in detail, on that or any other occasion; though referred to. It was, however, placed in my hands, for use if occasion should arise, when Dickens went to America in 1867. The letter bears date 7 July, 1849, and was Mr. Chapman's answer to the question Dickens had asked him, whether the account of the origin of *Pickwick* which he had given in the preface to the cheap edition in 1847 was not strictly correct. "It is *so* correctly described," was Mr. Chapman's opening remark, "that I can throw but little additional light on it." The name of his hero, I may add, Dickens took from that of a celebrated coach-proprietor of Bath.

deferred to, I thought of Mr. Pickwick, and wrote the first number; from the proof-sheets of which Mr. Seymour made his drawing of the club and his happy portrait of its founder. I connected Mr. Pickwick with a club, because of the original suggestion; and I put in Mr. Windle expressly for the use of Mr. Seymour."

Mr. Hall was dead when this statement was first made, in the preface to the cheap edition in 1847; but Mr. Chapman clearly recollected his partner's account of the interview, and confirmed every part of it, in his letter of 1849, with one exception. In giving Mr. Seymour credit for the figure by which all the habitable globe knows Mr. Pickwick, and which certainly at the outset helped to make him a reality, it had given the artist too much. The reader will hardly be so startled as I was on coming to the closing line of Mr. Chapman's confirmatory letter. "As this letter is to be historical, I may as well claim what little belongs to me in the matter, and that is the figure of Pickwick. Seymour's first sketch was of a long, thin man. The present immortal one he made from my description of a friend of mine at Richmond, a fat old beau who would wear, in spite of the ladies' protests, drab tights and black gaiters. His name was John Foster." . . .

The first number had not yet appeared when his *Sketches by Boz, Illustrative of Every-day Life and Every-day People*, came forth in two duodecimos with some capital cuts by Cruikshank, and with a preface in which he spoke of the nervousness he should have had in venturing alone before the public, and of his delight in getting the help of Cruikshank, who had frequently contributed to the success, though his well-earned reputation rendered it impossible for him ever to have shared the hazard, of similar undertakings. It very soon became apparent that there was no hazard here. The *Sketches* were much more talked about than the first two or three numbers of *Pickwick*, and I remember still with what hearty praise the book was first named to me by my dear friend Albany Fonblanque, as keen and clear a judge as ever lived either of books or men. Richly did it merit all the praise it had, and more, I will add, than he was ever disposed to give to it himself. He decidedly underrated it. He gave, in subsequent writings, so much more perfect form and fullness to everything it contained, that he did not care to credit himself with the marvel of having yet so early anticipated so much. But the first sprightly runnings of his genius are undoubtedly here. Mr. Bumble is in the parish sketches, and Mr. Dawkins the dodger in the Old Bailey scenes. There is laughter and fun to excess, never misapplied; there are the minute points and shades of character, with all the discrimination and nicety of detail afterwards so famous; there is everywhere the most perfect ease and skill of handling. The observation shown throughout is nothing short of wonderful. Things are painted literally as they are; and, whatever the picture, whether of every-day vulgar, shabby genteel, or downright low, with neither the condescending air which is affectation, nor the too familiar one which is slang. The book altogether is a perfectly unaffected, unpretentious, honest performance. Under its manly, sensible straightforward vein of talk there is running at the same time a natural flow of sentiment never sentimental, of humour always easy and unforced, and of pathos for the most part dramatic or picturesque, under which lay the germ of what his mature genius took afterwards most delight in. Of course there are inequalities in it, and some things that would have been better away: but it is a book that might have stood its ground, even if it had stood alone, as containing usually truthful observation of a sort of life between the middle class and the low, which, having few attractions for bookish observers, was quite unhackneyed ground. It had otherwise also the very special merit of being in no respect bookish or commonplace in its descriptions of the old city with which its writer was so familiar. It was a picture of everyday London at its best and worst, in its humours and enjoyments as well as its sufferings and sins, pervaded everywhere not only with the absolute reality of the things depicted, but also with that subtle sense and mastery of feeling which gives to the reader's sympathies invariably right direction, and awakens consideration, tenderness and kindness precisely for those who most need such help.

Between the first and the second numbers of *Pickwick*, the artist, Mr. Seymour, died by his own hand; and the number came out with three instead of four illustrations. Dickens had seen the unhappy man only once, forty-eight hours before his death; when he went to Furnival's Inn with an etching for the "stroller's-tale" in that number, which, altered at Dickens's suggestion, he brought away again for the few further touches that occupied him to a late hour of the night before he destroyed himself. A notice attached to the number informed the public of this latter fact. There was at first a little difficulty in replacing him, and for a single number Mr. Buss was interposed. But before the fourth number a choice had been made, which as time went on was so thoroughly justified that, through the greater part of the wonderful career which was then beginning, the connection was kept up, and Mr. Hablot Browne's name is not unworthily associated with the masterpieces of Dickens's genius. An incident which I heard related by Mr. Thackeray at one of the Royal Academy dinners belongs to this time. "I can remember when Mr. Dickens was a very young man, and had commenced delighting the world with some charming humorous works in covers which were coloured light green and came out once a month, that this young man wanted an artist to illustrate his writings; and I recollect walking up to his chambers in Furnival's Inn, with two or three drawings in my hand which, strange to say, he did not find suitable." Dickens has himself described another change now made in the publication. "We started with a number of twenty-four pages and four illustrations. Mr. Seymour's sudden and lamented death before the second number was published brought about a quick decision upon a point already in agitation; the number became one of thirty-two pages wth only two illustrations, and remained so to the end."

The Session of 1836 terminated his connection with the gallery, and some fruits of his increased leisure showed themselves before the close of the year. His eldest sister's musical attainments and connections had introduced him to many cultivators and professors of that art; he was led to take much interest in Mr. Braham's enterprise at the St. James's Theatre; and in aid of it he wrote a farce for Mr. Harley, founded upon one of his sketches, and the story and songs for an opera composed by his friend Mr. Hullah. Both the *Strange Gentleman*, acted in September, and the *Village Coquettes*, produced in December 1836, had a good success; and the last is memorable to me for having brought me first into personal communication with Dickens.

# BOOK SECOND

## FIRST FIVE YEARS OF FAME

### 1836–41. ÆT. 24–9

# I

WRITING THE "PICKWICK PAPERS"

## 1837

THE first letter I had from him was at the close of 1836 from Furnival's Inn, when he sent me the book of his opera of the *Village Coquettes*, which had been published by Mr. Bentley; and this was followed, two months later, by his collected *Sketches*, both first and second series; which he desired me to receive "as a very small testimony of the donor's regard and obligations, as well as of his desire to cultivate and avail himself of a friendship which has been so pleasantly thrown in his way. . . . In short, if you will receive them for my sake and not for their own, you will greatly oblige me." I had met him in the interval at the house of our common friend Mr. Ainsworth, and I remember vividly the impression then made upon me.

Very different was his face in those days from that which photography has made familiar to the present generation. A look of youthfulness first attracted you, and then a candour and openness of expression which made you sure of the qualities within. The features were very good. He had a capital forehead, a firm nose with full wide nostrils, eyes wonderfully beaming with intellect and running over with humour and cheerfulness, and a rather prominent mouth strongly marked with sensibility. The head was altogether well formed and symmetrical, and the air and carriage of it were extremely spirited. The hair so scant and grizzled in later days was then of a rich brown and most luxuriant abundance, and the bearded face of his last two decades had hardly a vestige of hair or whiskers; but there was that in the face as I first recollect it which no time could change, and which remained implanted on it unalterably to the last. This was the quickness, keenness, and practical power, the eager, restless, energetic outlook on each several feature, that seemed to tell so little of a student or writer of books, and so much of a man of action and business in the world. Light and motion flashed from every part of it. "It was as if made of steel," was said of it, four or five years after the time to which I am referring, by a most original and delicate observer, the late Mrs. Carlyle. "What a face is his to meet in a drawing-room!" wrote Leigh Hunt to me, the morning after I made them known to each other. "It has the life and soul in it of fifty human beings." In such sayings are expressed not alone the restless and resistless vivacity and force of which I have spoken, but that also which lay beneath them of steadiness and hard endurance. . . .

It was not until the fourth or fifth number of *Pickwick* (in the latter Sam Weller made his first appearance) that its importance began to be understood by "the trade," and on the eve of the issue of its sixth number, 22 August, 1836, he had signed an agreement with Mr. Bentley to undertake the editorship of a monthly magazine to be started the following January, to which he was to supply a serial story; and soon afterwards he had agreed with the same publisher to write two other tales, the first at a specified early date; the expressed remuneration in each case being certainly inadequate to the claims of a writer of any marked popularity. Under these Bentley agreements he was now writing, month by month, the first half of *Oliver Twist*, and, under his Chapman and Hall agreement, the last half of *Pickwick*, not even by a week in advance of the printer with either, when a circumstance became known to him of which he thus wrote to me.

"I heard half an hour ago, on authority which leaves me in no doubt about the matter (from the binder of *Pickwick* in fact), that Macrone intends publishing a new issue of my *Sketches* in monthly parts of nearly the same size and in just the same form as the *Pickwick Papers*. I need not tell you that this is calculated to injure me most seriously, or that I have a very natural and most decided objection to being supposed to presume upon the success of the *Pickwick*, and thus foist this old work upon the public in its new dress for the mere purpose of putting money in my own pocket. Neither need I say that the fact of my name being before the town, attached to three publications at the same time, must prove seriously prejudicial to my reputation. As you are acquainted with the circumstances under which these copyrights were disposed of, and as I know I may rely on your kind help, may I beg you to see Macrone, and to state in the strongest and most emphatic manner my feeling on this point. I wish him to be reminded of the sums he paid for those books; of the sale he has had for them; of the extent to which he has already pushed them; and of the very great profits he must necessarily have acquired from them. I wish him also to be reminded that no intention of publishing them in this form was in the remotest manner hinted to me, by him or on his behalf, when he obtained possession of the copyright. I then wish you to put it to his feelings of common honesty and fair-dealing whether after this communication he will persevere in his intention." What else the letter contained need not be quoted, but it strongly moved me to do my best.

I found Mr. Macrone inaccessible to all arguments of persuasion, however. That he had bought the book for a small sum at a time when the smallest was not unimportant to the writer, shortly before his marriage, and that he had since made very considerable profits by it, in no way disturbed his position that he had a right to make as much as he could of what was his, without regard to how it had become so. There was nothing for it but to change front, and, admitting it might be a less evil to the unlucky author to repurchase than to let the monthly issue proceed, to ask what further gain was looked for: but so wide a mouth was opened at this that I would have no part in the costly process of filling it. I told Dickens so, and strongly counselled him to keep quiet for a time.

But the worry and vexation were too great with all the work he had in hand, and I was hardly surprised next day to receive the letter sent me; which yet should be prefaced with the remark that suspense of any kind was at all times intolerable to the writer. The interval between the accomplishment of anything, and "its first motion," Dickens never could endure, and he was too ready to make any sacrifice to abridge or end it. This did not belong to the strong side of his character, and advantage was frequently taken of the fact. "I sent down just now to know whether you were at home (two o'clock), as Chapman and Hall were with me, and, the case being urgent, I wished to have the further benefit of your kind advice and assistance. Macrone and his friend (arcades ambo) waited on them this morning, and after a long discussion peremptorily refused to take one farthing less than two thousand pounds. The friend repeated the statement of figures which he made to you yesterday, and put it to Hall whether he could say from his knowledge of such matters that the estimate of probable profit was exorbitant. Hall, whose judgment may be relied on in such matters, could not dispute the justice of the calculation. And so the matter stood. In this dilemma it occurred to them (my *Pickwick* men), whether, if the *Sketches* MUST appear in monthly numbers, it would not be better for them to appear for their benefit and mine conjointly, than for Macrone's sole use and behoof; whether they, having all the *Pickwick* machinery in full operation, could not obtain for them a much larger sale than Macrone could ever get; and whether, even at this large price of two thousand pounds, we might not, besides retaining the copyright, reasonably hope for a good profit on the outlay. These suggestions having presented themselves, they came straight to me (having obtained a few hours' respite), and proposed that we should purchase the copyrights between us for the two thousand pounds, and publish them in monthly parts. I need not say that no other form of publication would repay the expenditure; and they wish me to explain by an address that *they*, who may be fairly put forward as the parties, have been driven into that mode of publication, or the copyright would have been lost. I considered the matter in every possible way. I sent for you, but you were out. I thought of" (what, need not be repeated, now that all is past and gone) "and consented. Was I right? I think you will say yes." I could not say no, though I was glad to have been no party to a price so exorbitant; which yet profited extremely little the person who received it. He died in hardly more than two years; and if Dickens had enjoyed the most liberal treatment at his hands, he could not have exerted himself more generously for the widow and children.

His new story was now beginning largely to share attention with his *Pickwick Papers*, and it was delightful to see how real all its people became to him. What I had most indeed to notice in him at the very outset of his career, was his indifference to any praise of his performances on the merely literary side, compared with the higher recognition of them as bits of actual life, with the meaning and purpose on their part, and the responsibility on his, of realities rather than creatures of fancy. The exception that might be drawn from *Pickwick* is rather in seeming than substance. A first book has its immunities, and the distinction of this from the rest of the writings appears in what has been said of its origin. The plan of it was simply to amuse. It was to string together whimsical sketches of the pencil by entertaining sketches of the pen; and, at its beginning, where or how it was to end as little known to himself as to any of its readers. But genius is a master as well as a servant, and when the laughter and fun were at their highest something graver made its appearance. He had to defend himself for this; and he said that, though the mere oddity of a new acquaintance was apt to impress one at first, the more serious qualities were discovered when we became friends with the man. In other words, he might have said that the change was become necessary for his own satisfaction. The book itself, in teaching him what his power was, had made him more conscious of what would be expected from its use; and this never afterwards quitted him. In what he was to do hereafter, as in all he was doing now, with *Pickwick* still to finish and *Oliver* only beginning, it constantly attended him. Nor could it well be otherwise, with all those fanciful creations so real, to a nature in itself so practical and earnest; and in this spirit I had well understood the letter accompanying what had been published of *Oliver* since its commencement the preceding February, which reached me the day after I visited him. Something to the effect of what has just been said, I had remarked publicly of the portion of the story sent to me; and his instant warm-hearted acknowledgment, of which I permit myself to quote a line or two, showed me in what perfect agreement we were. "How can I thank you? Can I do better than by saying that the sense of poor Oliver's reality, which I know you have had from the first, has been the highest of all praise to me. None that has been lavished upon me have I felt half so much as that appreciation of my intent and meaning. You know I have ever done so, for it was your feeling for me and mine for you that first brought us together, and I hope will keep us so, till death do us part. Your notices make me grateful but very proud; so have a care of them."

There was nothing written by him after this date which I did not see before the world did, either in manuscript or proofs; and in connection with the latter I shortly began to give him the help which he publicly mentioned twenty years later in dedicating his collected writings to me. One of his letters reminds me when these corrections began, and they were continued very nearly to the last. They lightened for him a labour of which he had more than enough imposed upon him at this time by others, and they were never anything but an enjoyment to me. "I have," he wrote, "so many sheets of the *Miscellany* to correct before I can begin *Oliver*, that I fear I shall not be able to leave home this morning. I therefore send your revise of the *Pickwick* by Fred, who is on his way with it to the printers. You will see that my alterations are very slight, but I think for the better." This was the fourteenth number of the *Pickwick Papers*. Fred was his next younger brother, who lived with him at the time.

The number following this was the famous one in which the hero finds himself in the Fleet, and another of his letters will show what enjoyment the writing of it had given to himself. I had sent to ask him where we were to meet for a proposed ride that day. "HERE," was his reply. "I am slippered and jacketted, and, like that same starling who is so very seldom quoted, can't get out. I am getting on, thank Heaven, 'like a house o' fire,' and think the next *Pickwick* will bang all the others. I shall expect you at one, and we will walk to the stable together. If you know anybody at Saint Paul's, I wish you'd send round and ask them not to ring the bell so. I can hardly hear my own ideas as they come into my head, and say what they mean."

The exulting tone of confidence in what he had thus been writing was indeed well justified. He had as yet done nothing so remarkable, in blending humour with tragedy, as his picture of what the poor side of a debtor's prison was in the days of which we have seen that he had himself had bitter experience; and we have but to recall, as it rises sharply to the memory, what is contained in this portion of a work that was not only among his earliest but his least considered as to plan, to understand what it was that not alone had given him his fame so early, but which in itself held the germ of the future that awaited him. Every point was a telling one, and the truthfulness of the whole unerring. The dreadful restlessness of the place, undefined yet unceasing, unsatisfying and terrible, was pictured throughout with Defoe's minute reality; while points of character were handled in that greater style which connects with the richest oddities of humour an insight into principles of character universal as nature itself. When he resolved that Sam Weller should be occupant of the prison with Mr. Pickwick, he was perhaps thinking of his favourite Smollett, and how, when Peregrine Pickle was inmate of the Fleet, Hatchway and Pipes refused to leave him; but Fielding himself might have envied his way of setting about it. . . .

Of what the reception of the book had been up to this time, and of the popularity Dickens had won as its author, this also will be the proper place to speak. For its kind, its extent, and the absence of everything unreal or factitious in the causes that contributed to it, it is unexampled in literature. Here was a series of sketches, without the pretence to such interest as attends a well-constructed story; put forth in a form apparently ephemeral as its purpose; having none that seemed higher than to exhibit some studies of cockney manners with help from a comic artist; and after four or five parts had appeared without newspaper notice or puffing, and itself not subserving in the public anything false or unworthy, it sprang into a popularity that

each part carried higher and higher, until people at this time talked
of nothing else, tradesmen recommended their goods by using its
name, and its sale, outstripping at a bound that of all the most famous
books of the century, had reached to an almost fabulous number. Of
part one, the binder prepared four hundred; and of part fifteen, his
order was for more than forty thousand. Every class, the high equally
with the low, were attracted to it. The charm of its gaiety and good
humour, its inexhaustible fun, its riotous overflow of animal spirits,
its brightness and keenness of observation, and, above all, the incomparable ease of its many varieties of enjoyment, fascinated everybody.
Judges on the bench and boys in the street, gravity and folly, the
young and the old, those who were entering life and those who were
quitting it, alike found it to be irresistible. "An archdeacon," wrote
Mr. Carlyle afterwards to me, "with his own venerable lips, repeated
to me, the other night, a strange profane story: of a solemn clergyman
who had been administering ghostly consolation to a sick person;
having finished, satisfactorily as he thought, and got out of the room,
he heard the sick person ejaculate: 'Well, thank God, *Pickwick* will be
out in ten days anyway!'—This is dreadful." . . .

I do not, for reasons to be hereafter stated, think the *Pickwick
Papers* comparable to the later books; but, apart from the new vein
of humour it opened, its wonderful freshness and its unflagging
animal spirits, it has two characters that will probably continue to
attract to it an unfading popularity. Its pre-eminent achievement is
of course Sam Weller; one of those people that take their place among
the supreme successes of fiction, as one that nobody ever saw but
everybody recognises, at once perfectly natural and intensely original.
Who is there that has ever thought him tedious? Who is so familiar
with him as not still to be finding something new in him? Who is so
amazed by his inexhaustible resources, or so amused by his inextin-
guishable laughter, as to doubt of his being as ordinary and perfect a
reality, nevertheless, as anything in the London streets? When indeed
the relish has been dulled that makes such humour natural and appre-
ciable, and not his native fun only, his ready and rich illustration, his
imperturbable self-possession, but his devotion to his master, his
chivalry and his gallantry, are no longer discovered, or believed no
longer to exist, in the ranks of life to which he belongs, it will be
worse for all of us than for the fame of his creator. Nor, when faith is
lost in that possible combination of eccentricities and benevolences,
shrewdness and simplicity, good sense and folly, all that suggests the
ludicrous and nothing that suggests contempt for it, which form the
delightful oddity of Pickwick, will the mistake committed be one
merely of critical misjudgment. But of this there is small fear.
Sam Weller and Mr. Pickwick are the Sancho and the Quixote of
Londoners, and as little likely to pass away as the old city itself.

Dickens was very fond of riding in these early years, and there was
no recreation he so much indulged, or with such profit to himself,
in the intervals of his hardest work. I was his companion oftener than

I could well afford the time for, the distances being great and nothing else to be done for the day; but when a note would unexpectedly arrive while I knew him to be hunted hard by one of his printers, telling me he had been sticking to work so closely that he must have rest, and, by way of getting it, proposing we should start together that morning at eleven o'clock for "a fifteen mile ride out, ditto in, and a lunch on the road," with a wind up of six o'clock dinner in Doughty Street, I could not resist the good fellowship. His notion of finding rest from mental exertion in as much bodily exertion of equal severity continued with him to the last; taking in the later years what I always thought the too great strain of as many miles in walking as he now took in the saddle, and too often indulging it at night: for, though he was always passionately fond of walking, he observed as yet a moderation in it, even accepting as sufficient my seven or eight miles' companionship. "What a brilliant morning for a country walk!" he would write, with not another word in his dispatch. Or, "Is it possible that you can't, oughtn't, shouldn't, mustn't, *won't* be tempted, this gorgeous day!" Or, "I start precisely—precisely mind—at half-past one. Come, come, *come*, and walk in the green lane. You will work the better for it all the week. COME! I shall expect you." Or, "You don't feel disposed, do you, to muffle yourself up, and start off with me for a good brisk walk, over Hampstead Heath? I know a good 'ouse there where we can have a red-hot chop for dinner, and a glass of good wine": which led to our first experience of Jack Straw's Castle, memorable for many happy meetings in coming years. But the rides were most popular and frequent. "I think," he would write, "Richmond and Twickenham, thro' the park, out at Knightsbridge, and over Barnes Common—would make a beautiful ride." Or, "Do you know, I shouldn't object to an early chop at some village inn?" Or, "Not knowing whether my head was off or on, it became so addled with work, I have gone riding the old road, and should be truly delighted to meet or be overtaken by you." Or, "Where shall it be—*oh where*—Hampstead, Greenwich, Windsor? WHERE? ? ? ? ? ? while the day is bright, not when it has dwindled away to nothing! For who can be of any use whatsomdever such a day as this, excepting out of doors?" Or it might be interrogatory summons to "A hard trot of three hours?" or intimation as laconic "To be heard of at Eel Pie House, Twickenham!" When first I knew him, I may add, his carriage for his wife's use was a small chaise with a smaller pair of ponies, which having a habit of making sudden rushes up by-streets in the day and peremptory standstills in ditches by night, were changed in the following year for a more suitable equipage.

To this mention of his habits while at work when our friendship began, I have to add what will complete the relation already given, in connection with his *Sketches*, of the uneasy sense accompanying his labour that it was yielding insufficient for himself while it enriched others, which is a needful part of his story at this time. At Midsummer 1837, replying to some inquiries, and sending his agreement with

Mr. Bentley for the *Miscellany* under which he was writing *Oliver*, he went on "It is a very extraordinary fact (I forgot it on Sunday) that I have NEVER HAD from him a copy of the agreement respecting the novel, which I never saw before or since I signed it at his house one morning long ago. Shall I ask him for a copy, or no? I have looked at some memoranda I made at the time, and I *fear* he has my second novel on the same terms, under the same agreement. This is a bad look-out, but we must try and mend it. You will tell me you are very surprised at my doing business in this way. So am I, for in most matters of labour and application I am punctuality itself. The truth is (though you do not need I should explain the matter to you, my dear fellow) that, if I had allowed myself to be worried by these things, I could never have done as much as I have. But I much fear, in my desire to avoid present vexations, I have laid up a bitter store for the future." The second novel, which he had promised in a complete form for a very early date, and had already selected subject and title for, was published four years later as *Barnaby Rudge*; but of the third he at present knew nothing but that he was expected to begin it, if not in the magazine, somewhere or other independently within a specified time.

The first appeal made, in taking action upon his letter, had reference to the immediate pressure of the *Barnaby* novel; but it also opened up the question of the great change of circumstances since these various agreements had been precipitately signed by him, the very different situation brought about by the extraordinary increase in the popularity of his writings, and the advantage it would be, to both Mr. Bentley and himself, to make more equitable adjustment of their relations. Some misunderstandings followed, but were closed by a compromise in September 1837; by which the third novel was abandoned [1] on certain conditions, and *Barnaby* was undertaken to be finished by November 1838. This involved a completion of the new story during the progress of *Oliver*, whatever might be required to follow on the close of *Pickwick*; and I doubted its wisdom. But it was accepted for the time.

He had meanwhile taken his wife abroad for a ten days' summer holiday, accompanied by the shrewd observant young artist Mr. Hablot Browne, whose admirable illustrations to *Pickwick* had more than supplied Mr. Seymour's loss; and I had a letter from him on their landing at Calais on 2 July.

"We have arranged for a post-coach to take us to Ghent, Brussels, Antwerp, and a hundred other places, that I cannot recollect now and couldn't spell if I did. We went this afternoon in a barouche to some gardens where the people dance, and where they were footing it most heartily—especially the women, who in their short petticoats and

---

[1] I have a memorandum in Dickens's writing that £500 was to have been given for it, and an additional £250 on its sale reaching 3000 copies: but he had no ground of objection to the terms that accompanied its surrender, which were favourable.

light caps look uncommonly agreeable. A gentleman in a blue surtout and silken berlins accompanied us from the hotel, and acted as
curator. He even waltzed with a very smart lady (just to show us,
condescendingly, how it ought to be done), and waltzed elegantly,
too. We rang for slippers after we came back, and it turned out that
this gentleman was the Boots."

His later seaside holiday was passed at Broadstairs, as were those
of many subsequent years, and the little watering-place has been
made memorable by his pleasant sketch of it. From his letters to myself a few lines may be given of his first doings and impressions there.

Writing on 3 September, he reports himself just risen from an
attack of illness. "I am much better, and hope to begin *Pickwick* No.
18 to-morrow. You will imagine how queer I must have been when I
tell you that I have been compelled for four-and-twenty mortal hours
to abstain from porter or other malt liquor! ! ! I done it though—
really. . . . I have discovered that the landlord of the Albion has
delicious hollands (but what is that to *you*, for you cannot sympathise with my feelings), and that a cobbler who lives opposite to my
bedroom window is a Roman Catholic, and gives an hour and a half
to his devotions every morning behind his counter. I have walked
upon the sands at low-water from this place to Ramsgate, and sat
upon the same at high-ditto till I have been flayed with the cold. I
have seen ladies and gentlemen walking upon the earth in slippers of
buff, and pickling themselves in the sea in complete suits of the same.
I have seen stout gentlemen looking at nothing through powerful
telescopes for hours, and, when at last they saw a cloud of smoke,
fancying a steamer behind it, and going home comfortable and happy.
I have found out that our next neighbour has a wife and something
else under the same roof with the rest of his furniture—the wife deaf
and blind, and the something else given to drinking. And if you ever
get to the end of this letter *you* will find out that I subscribe myself on
paper as on everything else (some atonement perhaps for its length
and absurdity)," etc.

In his next letter (from 12 High Street, Broadstairs, on the 7th)
there is allusion to one of the many piracies of *Pickwick*, which had
distinguished itself beyond the rest by a preface abusive of the
writer plundered. "I recollect this 'member of the dramatic-authors'-
society' bringing an action once against Chapman, who rented the
City Theatre, in which it was proved that he had undertaken to
write under special agreement seven melodramas for five pounds, to
enable him to do which a room had been hired in a gin-shop close by.
The defendant's plea was that the plaintiff was always drunk, and had
not fulfilled his contract. Well; if the *Pickwick* has been the means of
putting a few shillings in the vermin-eaten pockets of so miserable a
creature, and has saved him from a workhouse or a jail, let him
empty out his little pot of filth and welcome. I am quite content
to have been the means of relieving him. Besides, he seems to have
suffered by agreements!" . . .

## II

ONE result of his more satisfactory relations with Mr. Bentley led to a promise to edit for him a Life of the celebrated clown, Grimaldi. The manuscript had been prepared from autobiographical notes by a Mr. Egerton Wilks, and contained one or two stories told so badly, and so well worth better telling, that the hope of enlivening their dullness at the cost of very little labour constituted a sort of attraction for him. Except the preface, he did not write a line of this biography, such modifications or additions as he made having been dictated by him to his father; whom I found often in exalted enjoyment of the office of amanuensis. He had also a most indifferent opinion of the mass of material which Mr. Wilks had raked together, describing it as "twaddle"; and his own modest estimate of the book, on its completion, may be guessed from the number of notes of admiration (no less than thirty) which accompanied his written mention to me of the sale with which it started in the first week of its publication. "Seventeen hundred *Grimaldis* have already been sold, and the demand increases daily!!!!!!!!!!!!!!!!!!!!!!!!!!!!!!!!!"

It was not to have all its own way, however. A great many critical faults were found; and one point in particular was urged against his handling such a subject, that he could never himself even have seen Grimaldi. To this last objection he was moved to reply, and had prepared a letter for the *Miscellany*, "from editor to sub-editor," which it was thought best to suppress, but of which the opening remark may now be not unamusing. "I understand that a gentleman unknown is going about this town privately informing all ladies and gentlemen of discontented natures that, on a comparison of dates and putting together of many little circumstances which occur to his great sagacity, he has made the profound discovery that I can never have seen Grimaldi, whose Life I have edited, and that the book must therefore of necessity be bad. Now, sir, although I was brought up from remote country parts in the dark ages of 1819 and 1820 to behold the splendour of Christmas pantomimes and the humour of Joe, in whose honour I am informed I clapped my hands with great precocity, and although I even saw him act in the remote times of 1823; yet, as I had not then aspired to the dignity of a tail-coat, though forced by a relentless parent into my first pair of boots, I am willing, with the view of saving this honest gentleman further time and trouble, to concede that I had not arrived at man's estate when Grimaldi left the stage, and that my recollections of his acting are, to my loss, but shadowy and imperfect. Which confession I now make publicly, and without mental qualification or reserve, to all whom it may concern. But the deduction of this pleasant gentleman that therefore the Grimaldi book must be bad, I must take leave to doubt. I don't think that to edit a man's biography from his own notes it is essential you should have known him, and I don't believe that Lord Braybrooke had more than the very slightest acquaintance with Mr. Pepys, whose memoirs he edited two centuries after he died."

Enormous meanwhile, and without objection audible on any side, had been the success of the completed *Pickwick*, which we celebrated by a dinner, with himself in the chair and Talfourd in the vice-chair, everybody in hearty good humour with every other body; and a copy of which I received from him on 11 December in the most luxurious of Hayday's bindings, with a note worth preserving for its closing allusion. The passage referred to in it was a comment, in delicately chosen words, that Leigh Hunt had made on the inscription at the grave in Kensal Green. "Chapman and Hall have just sent me, with a copy of our deed, three 'extra-super' bound copies of *Pickwick*, as per specimen enclosed. The first I forward to you, the second I have presented to our good friend Ainsworth, and the third Kate has retained for herself." . . .

The "deed" mentioned was one executed in the previous month to restore to him a third ownership in the book which had thus far enriched all concerned but himself. The original understanding respecting it Mr. Edwin Chapman thus describes for me. "There was no agreement about *Pickwick* except a verbal one. Each number was to consist of a sheet and a half, for which we were to pay fifteen guineas; and we paid him for the first two numbers at once, as he required the money to go and get married with. We were also to pay more according to the sale, and I think *Pickwick* altogether cost us three thousand pounds." Adjustment to the sale would have cost four times as much, and of the actual payments I have myself no note; but, as far as my memory serves, they are overstated by Mr. Chapman. My impression is that, above and beyond the first sum due for each of the twenty numbers (making no allowance for their extension after the first to thirty-two pages), successive cheques were given, as the work went steadily on to the enormous sale it reached, which brought up the entire sum received to two thousand five hundred pounds. I had, however, always pressed so strongly the importance to him of some share in the copyright, that this at last was conceded in the deed above-mentioned, though five years were to elapse before the right should accrue; and it was only yielded as part consideration for a further agreement entered into at the same date (19 November, 1837) whereby Dickens engaged to "write a new work the title whereof shall be determined by him, of a similar character and of the same extent as the *Posthumous Papers of the Pickwick Club*," the first number of which was to be delivered on the fifteenth of the following March, and each of the numbers on the same day of each of the successive nineteen months; which was also to be the date of the payment to him, by Messrs. Chapman and Hall, of twenty several sums of one hundred and fifty pounds each for five years' use of the copyright, the entire ownership in which was then to revert to Dickens. The name of this new book, as all the world knows, was *The Life and Adventures of Nicholas Nickleby*; and between April 1838 and October 1839 it was begun and finished accordingly.

All through the interval of these arrangements *Oliver Twist* had been steadily continued. Month by month, for many months, it had run its opening course with the close of *Pickwick*, as we shall see it close with the opening of *Nickleby*; and the expectations of those who had built most confidently on the young novelist were more than confirmed. Here was the interest of a story simply but well constructed; and characters with the same impress of reality upon them, but more carefully and skilfully drawn. Nothing could be meaner than the subject, the progress of a parish or workhouse boy, nothing less so than its treatment. As each number appeared, his readers generally became more and more conscious of what already, as we have seen, had revealed itself and even the riotous fun of *Pickwick*, that the purpose was not solely to amuse; and, far more decisively than its predecessor, the new story further showed what were the not least potent elements in the still-increasing popularity that was gathering around the writer. His qualities could be appreciated as well as felt in an almost equal degree by all classes of his various readers. Thousands were attracted to him, because he placed them in the midst of scenes and characters with which they were already themselves acquainted; and thousands were reading him with no less avidity because he introduced them to passages of nature and life of which they before knew nothing, but of the truth of which their own habits and senses sufficed to assure them.

With such work as this in hand, it will hardly seem surprising that, as the time for beginning *Nickleby* came on, and as he thought of his promise for November, he should have the sense of "something hanging over him like a hideous nightmare." He felt that he could not complete the *Barnaby Rudge* novel by the November of that year as promised, and that the engagement he would have to break was unfitting him for engagements he might otherwise fulfil. He had undertaken what in truth was impossible. The labour of at once editing the *Miscellany*, and supplying it with monthly portions of *Oliver*, more than occupied all the time left him by other labours absolutely necessary. "I no sooner get myself up," he wrote, "high and dry, to attack *Oliver* manfully, than up come the waves of each month's work, and drive me back again into a sea of manuscript." There was nothing for it but that he should make further appeal to Mr. Bentley. "I have recently," he wrote to him on 11 February, 1838, "been thinking a great deal about *Barnaby Rudge. Grimaldi* has occupied so much of the short interval I had between the completion of the *Pickwick* and the commencement of the new work, that I see it will be wholly impossible for me to produce it by the time I had hoped with justice

to myself or profit to you. What I wish you to consider is this: would
it not be far more to your interest, as well as within the scope of my
ability, if *Barnaby Rudge* began in the *Miscellany* immediately on the
conclusion of *Oliver Twist*, and were continued there for the same time,
and then published in three volumes? Take these simple facts into
consideration. If the *Miscellany* is to keep its ground, it must have
some continuous tale from me when *Oliver* stops. If I sat down to
*Barnaby Rudge*, writing a little of it when I could (and with all my
other engagements it would necessarily be a very long time before I
could hope to finish it that way), it would be clearly impossible for
me to begin a new series of papers in the *Miscellany*. The conduct of
three different stories at the same time, and the production of a large
portion of each, every month, would have been beyond Scott himself.
Whereas, having *Barnaby* for the *Miscellany*, we could at once supply
the gap which the cessation of *Oliver* must create, and you would have
all the advantage of that prestige in favour of the work which is
certain to enhance the value of *Oliver Twist* considerably. Just think
of this at your leisure. I am really anxious to do the best I can for you
as well as for myself, and in this case the pecuniary advantage must
be all on your side." This letter nevertheless, which had also requested an overdue account of the sales of the *Miscellany*, led to
differences which were only adjusted after six months' wrangling;
and I was party to the understanding then arrived at by which, among
other things, *Barnaby* was placed upon the footing desired, and was
to begin when *Oliver* closed. . . .

On the 13th, after describing himself "sitting patiently at home
waiting for *Oliver Twist*, who has not yet arrived," which was his
agreeable form of saying that his fancy had fallen into sluggishness
that morning, he made remark in as pleasant phrase on some piece of
painful news I had sent him, now forgotten. "I have not yet seen the
paper, and you throw me into a fever. The comfort is, that all the
strange and terrible things come uppermost, and that the good and
pleasant things are mixed up with every moment of our existence so
plentifully that we scarcely heed them." At the close of the month Mrs.
Dickens was well enough to accompany him to Richmond, for now
the time was come to start *Nickleby*; and having been away from town
when *Pickwick's* first number came out, he made it a superstition to
be absent at many future similar times. The magazine day of that
April month, I remember, fell upon a Saturday, and the previous
evening had brought me a peremptory summons: "Meet me at the
Shakespeare on Saturday night at eight; order your horse at midnight,
and ride back with me": which was duly complied with. The smallest
hour was sounding into the night from St. Paul's before we started,
and the night was none of the pleasantest; but we carried news that
lightened every part of the road, for the sale of *Nickleby* had reached
that day the astonishing number of nearly fifty thousand! I left him
working with unusual cheerfulness at *Oliver Twist* when I quitted the
"Star and Garter" on the next day but one, after celebrating with

both friends on the previous evening an anniversary which concerned us all (their second and my twenty-sixth); and which we kept
always in future at the same place, except when they were living out
of England, for twenty successive years. It was a part of his love
of regularity and order, as well as of his kindliness of nature, to
place such friendly meetings as these under rules of habits and continuance.

## III

### "OLIVER TWIST"

#### 1838

THE whole of his time not occupied with *Nickleby* was now given to
*Oliver*, and as the story shaped itself to its close it took extraordinary
hold of him. I never knew him work so frequently after dinner, or to
such late hours (a practice he afterwards abhorred), as during the
final months of this task; which it was now his hope to complete
before October, though its close in the magazine would not be due
until the following March. "I worked pretty well last night," he
writes, referring to it in May, "very well indeed; but although I did
eleven close slips before half-past twelve I have four to write to close
the chapter; and, as I foolishly left them till this morning, have the
steam to get up afresh." A month later he writes: "I got to the sixteenth slip last night, and shall try hard to get to the thirtieth before
I go to bed." Then, on a "Tuesday night" at the opening of August,
he wrote: "Hard at work still. Nancy is no more. I showed what I have
done to Kate last night, who was in an unspeakable '*state*'; from which
and my own impression I auger well. When I have sent Sikes to the
devil, I must have yours." "No, no." he wrote, in the following
month: "don't, don't let us ride till to-morrow, not having yet disposed
of the Jew, who is such an out and outer that I don't know what to
make of him." No small difficulty to an inventor, where the creatures
of his invention are found to be as real as himself; but this also was
mastered; and then there remained but the closing quiet chapter to
tell the fortunes of those who had figured in the tale. To this he summoned me in the first week of September, replying to a request of
mine that he'd give me a call that day. "Come and give *me* a call, and
let us have 'a bit o' talk' before we have a bit o' som'at else. My
missis is going out to dinner, and I ought to go, but I have got a bad
cold. So do you come, and sit here, and read, or work, or do something,
while I write the LAST chapter of *Oliver*, which will be arter a lamb
chop." How well I remember that evening! and our talk of what
should be the fate of Charley Bates, on behalf of whom (as indeed for

the Dodger, too) Talfourd had pleaded as earnestly in mitigation of judgment as ever at the bar for any client'he most respected.

The publication had been announced for October, but the third volume illustrations intercepted it a little. . . . The completed *Oliver Twist* found a circle of admirers, not so wide in its range as those of others of his books, but of a character and mark that made their honest liking for it, and steady advocacy of it, important to his fame; and the story has held its ground in the first class of his writings. It deserves that place. . . . At the time of which I am speaking, the debtors' prisons described in *Pickwick*, the parochial management denounced in *Oliver*, and the Yorkshire schools exposed in *Nickleby*, were all actual existences; which now have no vivider existence than in the forms he thus gave to them. With wiser purposes, he superseded the old petrifying process of the magician in the Arabian tale, and struck the prisons and parish practices of his country, and its schools of neglect and crime, into palpable life for ever. A portion of the truth of the past, of the character and very history of the moral abuses of his time, will thus remain always in his writings; and it will be remembered that with only the light arms of humour and laughter, and the gentle ones of pathos and sadness, he carried cleansing and reform into those Augean stables. . . .

And now, while *Oliver* was running a great career of popularity and success, the shadow of the tale of *Barnaby Rudge*, which he was to write on similar terms and to begin in the *Miscellany* when the other should have ended, began to darken everything around him. We had much discussion respecting it, and I had no small difficulty in restraining him from throwing up the agreement altogether; but the real hardship of his position, and the considerate construction to be placed on every effort made by him to escape from obligations incurred in ignorance of the sacrifices implied by them, will be best understood from his own frank statement. On 21 January, 1839, enclosing me the copy of a letter which he proposed to send to Mr. Bentley the following morning, he thus wrote: "From what I have already said to you, you will have been led to expect that I entertained some such intention. I know you will not endeavour to dissuade me from sending it. Go it MUST. It is no fiction to say that at present I *cannot* write this tale. The immense profits which *Oliver* has realised to its publisher, and is still realising, the paltry, wretched, miserable sum it brought to me (not equal to what is every day paid for a novel that sells fifteen hundred copies at most); the recollection of this, and the consciousness that I have still the slavery and drudgery of another work on the same journeyman-terms; the consciousness that my books are enriching everybody connected with them but myself, and that I, with such a popularity as I have acquired, am struggling in old toils, and wasting my energies in the very height and freshness of my fame, and the best part of my life, to fill the pockets of others, while for those who are nearest and dearest to me I can realise little more than a genteel subsistence: all this puts me out of heart and spirits: and I cannot—cannot and will not—under such circumstances that keep me down with an iron hand, distress myself by beginning this tale until I have had time to breathe; and until the intervention, shall have restored me to a more genial and composed state of feeling. There—for six months *Barnaby Rudge* stands over. And but for you, it should stand over altogether. For I do most solemnly declare that morally, before God and man, I hold myself released from such hard bargains as these, after I have done so much for those who drove them. This net that has been wound about me so chafes me, so exasperates and irritates my mind, that to break it at whatever cost—*that* I should care nothing for—is my constant impulse. But I have not yielded to it. I merely declare that I must have a postponement very common in all literary agreements; and for the time I have mentioned—six months from the conclusion of *Oliver* in the *Miscellany*—I wash my hands of any fresh accumulation of labour, and resolve to proceed as cheerfully as I can with that which already presses upon me.''

To describe what followed upon this is not necessary. It will suffice to state the results. Upon the appearance in the *Miscellany*, in the early months of 1839, of the last portion of *Oliver Twist*, its author, having been relieved altogether from his engagement to the magazine, handed over, in a familiar epistle from a parent to his child, the editorship to Mr. Ainsworth; and the still subsisting agreement to write *Barnaby Rudge* was, upon the overture of Mr. Bentley himself, in June of the following year, 1840, also put an end to, on payment by Dickens, for the copyright of *Oliver Twist* and such printed stock as remained of the edition then on hand, of two thousand two hundred and fifty pounds. What was further incident to this transaction will be told hereafter; and a few words may meanwhile be taken, not without significance in regard to it, from the parent's familiar epistle. It describes the child as aged two years and two months (so long had he watched over it); gives sundry pieces of advice concerning its circulation, and the importance thereto of light and pleasant articles of food; and concludes, after some general moralising on the shiftings and changes of this world having taken so wonderful a turn that mail-coach guards were become no longer judges of horse-flesh: ''I reap no gain or profit by parting from you, nor will any conveyance of your property be required, for in this respect you have always been literally Bentley's *Miscellany* and never mine.''

## IV

### "NICHOLAS NICKLEBY"

#### 1838 *and* 1839

I well recollect the doubt there was, mixed with the eager expectation which the announcement of his second serial story had awakened, whether the event would justify all that interest; and if indeed it were possible that the young writer could continue to walk steadily under the burthen of the popularity laid upon him. The first number dispersed this cloud of a question in a burst of sunshine; and as much of the gaiety of nations as had been eclipsed by old Mr. Pickwick's voluntary exile to Dulwich was restored by the cheerful confidence with which young Mr. Nicholas Nickleby stepped into his shoes. Everything that had given charm to the first book was here, with more attention to the important requisite of a story, and more wealth as well as truth of character. . . .

Who that recollects the numbers of *Nickleby* as they appeared can have forgotten how each number added to the general enjoyment? All that had given *Pickwick* its vast popularity, the overflowing mirth, hearty exuberance of humour, and genial kindliness of satire, had here the advantage of a better-laid design, more connected incidents, and greater precision of character. Everybody seemed immediately to know the Nickleby family as well as his own. Dotheboys, with all that rendered it, like a piece by Hogarth, both ludicrous and terrible, became a household word. Successive groups of Mantalinis, Kenwigses, Crummleses, introduced each to its little world of reality, lighted up everywhere with truth and life, with capital observation, the quaintest drollery, and quite boundless mirth and fun. The brothers Cheeryble brought with them all the charities. With Smike came the first of those pathetic pictures that filled the world with pity for what cruelty, ignorance or neglect may inflict upon the young. And Newman Noggs ushered in that class of the creatures of his fancy in which he took himself perhaps the most delight, and which the oftener he dealt with the more he seemed to know how to vary and render attractive; gentlemen by nature, however shocking bad their hats or ungenteel their dialects; philosophers of modest endurance, and needy but most respectable coats; a sort of humble angels of sympathy and self-denial, though without a particle of splendour or even good looks about them, except what an eye as fine as their own feelings might discern. "My friends," wrote Sydney Smith, describing to Dickens the anxiety of some ladies of his acquaintance to meet him at dinner, "have not the smallest objection to be put into a number, but on the contrary

would be proud of the distinction; and Lady Charlotte, in particular,
you may marry to Newman Noggs." Lady Charlotte was not a more
real person to Sydney than Newman Noggs; and all the world whom
Dickens attracted to his books could draw from them the same
advantage as the man of wit and genius. It has been lately objected
that humanity is not seen in them in its highest or noblest types, and
the assertion may hereafter be worth considering; but what is very
certain, is that they have inculcated humanity in familiar and
engaging forms to thousands and tens of thousands of their readers,
who can hardly have failed each to make his little world around
him somewhat the better for their teaching. From first to last they
were never for a moment alien to either the sympathies or the understandings of any class; and there were crowds of people at this time
that could have not told you what imagination meant, who were
adding month by month to their limited stores the boundless gains of
imagination. . . .

Of such notices as his letters give of his progress with *Nickleby*,
which occupied him from February 1838 to October 1839, something
may now be said. Soon after the agreement for it was signed, before
the Christmas of 1837 was over, he went down into Yorkshire with
Mr. Hablot Browne to look up the Cheap Schools in that county to
which public attention had been painfully drawn by a law case in the
previous year; which had before been notorious for cruelties committed in them, whereof he had heard as early as in his childish
days; and which he was bent upon destroying if he could. I soon
heard the result of his journey; and the substance of that letter,
returned to him for the purpose, is in his preface to the story written
for the collected edition. He came back confirmed in his design, and
in February set to work upon his first chapter. On his birthday he
wrote to me. "I *have* begun! I wrote four slips last night, so you see
the beginning is made. And what is more, I can go on: so I hope the
book is in training at last." "The first chapter of *Nicholas* is done,"
he wrote two days later. "It took time, but I think answers the
purpose as well as it could." Then, after a dozen days more: "I wrote
twenty slips of *Nicholas* yesterday, left only four to do this morning
(up at 8 o'clock, too!), and have ordered my horse at one." I joined
him as he expected, and we read together at dinner that day the
first number of *Nicholas Nickleby*.

In the following number there was a difficulty which it was
marvellous should not have occurred to him in this form of publication. "I could not write a line till three o'clock," he says, describing
the close of that number, "and have yet five slips to finish, and don't
know what to put in them, for I have reached the point I meant to
leave off with." He found easy remedy for such a miscalculation at
his outset, and it was nearly his last as well as first misadventure of
the kind: his constant difficulty in *Pickwick*, as he said repeatedly,
having been not the running short but the running over: not the
whip but the drag that was wanted. *Sufflaminandus erat*, as Ben

Jonson said of Shakespeare. And in future works, with such marvellous nicety could he do always what he had planned, strictly within the space available, that I can only remember two other similar instances. The third number introduced the school; and "I remain dissatisfied until you have seen and read number three," was his way of announcing to me his own satisfaction with that first handling of Dotheboys Hall. Nor had it the least part in my admiration of his powers at this time, that he never wrote without the printer at his heels; that, always in his latest works two or three numbers in advance, he was never a single number in advance with this story; that the more urgent the call upon him the more readily he rose to it; and that his astonishing animal spirits never failed him. As late as the 20th in the November month of 1838, he thus wrote to me: "I have just begun my second chapter; cannot go out to-night; must get on; think there *will* be a *Nickleby* at the end of this month now (I doubted it before); and want to make a start towards it if I possibly can." That was on Tuesday; and on Friday morning in the same week, explaining the sudden failure of something that had been promised the previous day, he says: "I was writing incessantly until it was time to dress; and have not yet got the subject of my last chapter, which *must be* finished to-night."

But this was not all. Between that Tuesday and Friday an indecent assault had been committed on his book by a theatrical adapter named Stirling, who seized upon it without leave while yet only a third of it was written; hacked, cut and garbled its dialogue to the shape of one or two favourite actors; invented for it a plot and an ending of his own, and produced it at the Adelphi; where the outraged author, hard pressed as he was with an unfinished number, had seen it in the interval between the two letters I have quoted. He would not have run such a risk in later years, but he threw off lightly at present even such offences to his art; and though I was with him at a representation of his *Oliver Twist* the following month at the Surrey Theatre, when in the middle of the first scene he laid himself down upon the floor in a corner of the box and never rose from it until the drop-scene fell, he had been able to sit through *Nickleby*, and to see a merit in parts of the representation. Mr. Yates had a sufficiently humorous meaning in his wildest extravagance, and Mr. O. Smith could put into his queer angular oddities enough of a hard dry pathos to conjure up shadows at least of Mantalini and Newman Noggs; of Ralph Nickleby there was only a wig, a spencer and a pair of boots, but a quaint actor named Wilkinson proved equal to the drollery, though not to the fierce brutality of Squeers; and even Dickens, in the letter that amazed me by telling me of his visit to the theatre, was able to praise "the skilful management and dressing of the boys, the capital manner and speech of Fanny Squeers, the dramatic representation of her card-party in Squeers's parlour, the careful making-up of all the people, and the exceedingly good tableaux formed from Browne's sketches. . . . Mrs. Keeley's first appearance beside the fire (see wollum), and all the rest of Smike, was excellent; bating sundry choice sentiments and rubbish regarding the little robins in the fields which have been put in the boy's mouth by Mr. Stirling the adapter." His toleration could hardly be extended to the robins, and their author he properly punished by introducing and denouncing him at Mr. Crummles's farewell supper. . . .

The close of the story was written at Broadstairs, from which (he had taken a house "two doors from the Albion Hotel, where we had that merry night two years ago") he wrote to me on 9 September, 1839. "I am hard at it, but these windings-up wind slowly, and I shall think I have done great things if I have entirely finished by the 20th. Chapman and Hall came down yesterday with Browne's sketches, and dined here. They imparted their intentions as to a Nicklebeian fête which will make you laugh heartily—so I reserve them till you come. It has been blowing great guns for the last three days, and last night (I wish you could have seen it!) there was such a sea! I staggered down to the pier and, creeping under the lee of a large boat which was high and dry, watched it breaking for nearly an hour. Of course I came back wet through." On the afternoon of Wednesday the 18th he wrote again. "I shall not finish entirely before Friday, sending Hicks the last twenty pages of manuscript by the night coach. I have had pretty stiff work as you may suppose, and I have taken great pains. The discovery is made, Ralph is dead, the loves have come all right, Tim Linkinwater has proposed, and I have now only to break up Dotheboys and the book together. I am very anxious that you should see this conclusion before it leaves my hands, and I plainly see therefore that I must come to town myself on Saturday if I would not endanger the appearance of the number. So I have written to Hicks to send proofs to your chambers as soon as he can that evening; and if you don't object I will dine with you any time after five, and we will devote the night to a careful reading. I have not written to Macready, for they have not yet sent me the title-page of dedication, which is merely 'To W. C. Macready Esq. the following pages are inscribed, as a slight token of admiration and regard, by his friend the Author.' Meanwhile will you let him know that I have fixed the Nickleby dinner for Saturday, the 5th of October. Place, the Albion in Aldersgate Street. Time, six for half-past exactly. . . . I shall be more glad than I can tell you to see you again, and I look forward to Saturday, and the evenings that are to follow it, with the most joyful anticipation. I have had a good notion for *Barnaby*, of which more anon."

The shadow from the old quarter, we see, the unwritten *Barnaby* tale, intrudes itself still; though hardly, as of old, making other pleasanter anticipations less joyful. Such indeed at this time was his buoyancy of spirit that it cost him little, compared with the suffering it gave him at subsequent similar times, to separate from the people who for twenty months had been a part of himself. . . .

## V

### DURING AND AFTER "NICKLEBY"

#### 1838 *and* 1839

THE name of his old gallery companion may carry me back from the days to which the close of *Nickleby* had led me, to those when it was only beginning. "This snow will take away the cold weather," he had written, in that birthday-letter of 1838 already quoted, "and then for Twickenham." Here a cottage was taken, nearly all the summer was passed, and a familiar face there was Mr. Beard's. There too, with Talfourd and with Thackeray and Jerrold, we had many friendly days; and the social charm of Maclise was seldom wanting. Nor was there anything that exercised a greater fascination over Dickens than the grand enjoyment of idleness, the ready self-abandonment to the luxury of laziness, which we both so laughed at in Maclise, under whose easy swing of indifference, always the most amusing at the most aggravating events and times, we knew that there was artist-work as eager, energy as unwearying, and observation almost as penetrating as Dickens's own. A greater enjoyment than the fellowship of Maclise at this period it would indeed be difficult to imagine. Dickens hardly saw more than he did, while yet he seemed to be seeing nothing; and the small esteem in which this rare faculty was held by himself, a quaint oddity that in him gave to shrewdness itself an air of Irish simplicity, his unquestionable turn for literature, and a varied knowledge of books not always connected with such intense love and such unwearied practice of one special and absorbing art, combined to render him attractive far beyond the common. His fine genius and his handsome person, of neither of which at any time he seemed himself to be in the slightest degree conscious, completed the charm. Edwin Landseer, all the world's favourite, and the excellent Stanfield, came a few months later, in the Devonshire Terrace days; but another painter-friend was George Cattermole, who had then enough and to spare of fun as well as fancy to supply ordinary artists and humorists by the dozen, and wanted only a little more ballast and steadiness to possess all that could give attraction to good-fellowship. A friend now especially welcome, also, was the novelist, Mr. Ainsworth, who shared with us incessantly for the three following years in the companionship which began at his house; with whom we visited, during two of those years, friends of art and letters in his native Manchester, from among whom Dickens brought away his Brothers Cheeryble, and to whose sympathy in tastes and pursuits, accomplishments in literature, open-hearted generous ways, and cordial hospitality, many of the pleasures of later years were due. Frederick Dickens, to whom soon after this a treasury-clerkship was handsomely given, on Dickens's application, by Mr. Stanley of Alderley, known in and before those Manchester days, was for the present again living with his father, but passed much time in his brother's home; and another familiar face was that of Mr. Thomas Mitton, who had known him when himself a law-clerk in Lincoln's Inn, through whom there was introduction of the relatives of a friend and partner, Mr. Smithson, the gentleman connected with Yorkshire, mentioned in his preface to *Nickleby*, who became very intimate in his house. These, his father and mother and their two younger sons, with members of his wife's family, and his married sisters and their husbands, Mr. and Mrs. Burnett and Mr. and Mrs. Austin, are figures that all associate themselves prominently with the days of Doughty Street and the cottages of Twickenham and Petersham as remembered by me in the summers of 1838 and 1839.

In the former of these years the sports were necessarily quieter than at Petersham, where extensive garden-grounds admitted of much athletic competition, from the more difficult forms of which I in general modestly retired, but where Dickens for the most part held his own against even such accomplished athletics as Maclise and Mr. Beard. Bar-leaping, bowling and quoits were among the games carried on with the greatest ardour; and in sustained energy, or what is called keeping it up, Dickens certainly distanced every competitor. Even the lighter recreations of battledore and bagatelle were pursued with relentless activity; and at such amusements as the Petersham races, in those days rather celebrated, and which he visited daily while they lasted, he worked much harder himself than the running horses did.

What else his letters of these years enable me to recall that could possess any interest now may be told in a dozen sentences. He wrote a farce by way of helping the Covent Garden manager which the actors could not agree about, and which he turned afterwards into a story called *The Lamplighter*. He read the piece at the theatre, before the same stage-manager to whom he had written to request a very different audience in the same green-room a few years before; and Dickens could not but fancy that into Mr. Bartley's face, as he listened to the humorous reading, there crept some strange bewildered half-consciousness that in the famous writer he saw again the youthful would-be actor. He entered his name among the students at the inn of the Middle Temple, though he did not eat dinners there until many years later. We made together a circuit of nearly all the London prisons; and, in coming to the prisoners under remand while going over Newgate, accompanied by Macready and Mr. Hablot Browne, were startled by a sudden tragic cry of "My God! there's Waine-wright!" In the shabby-genteel creature, with sandy distorted hair and dirty moustache, who had turned quickly round with a defiant stare at our entrance, looking at once mean and fierce, and quite

capable of the cowardly murders he had committed, Macready had
been horrified to recognise a man familiarly known to him in former
years, and at whose table he had dined. . . . The closing months
of this year of 1839 had special interest for him. At the end of
October another daughter was born to him, who bears the name of
that dear friend of his and mine, Macready, whom he asked to be her
godfather; and before the close of the year he had moved out of
Doughty Street into Devonshire Terrace, a handsome house with a
garden of considerable size, shut out from the New Road by a high
brick-wall facing the York gate into Regent's Park. These various
matters, and his attempts at the *Barnaby* novel on the conclusion of
*Nickleby*, are the subjects of his letters between October and December.

"Thank God, all goes famously. I have worked at *Barnaby* all day,
and moreover seen a beautiful (and reasonable) house in Kent
Terrace, where Macready once lived, but larger than his." Again
(this having gone off): *"Barnaby* has suffered so much from the
house-hunting, that I mustn't chop to-day." Then (for the matter of
the Middle Temple) "I return the form. It's the right Temple, I take
for granted. *Barnaby* moves, not at race-horse speed, but yet as fast
(I think) as under these unsettled circumstances could possibly be
expected." Or again: "All well. *Barnaby* has reached his tenth page.
I have just turned lazy, and have passed into *Christabel*, and thence
to *Wallenstern*." At last the choice was made. "A house of great
promise (and great premium), 'undeniable' situation and excessive
splendour, is in view. Mitton is in treaty, and I am in ecstatic restlessness. Kate wants to know whether you have any books to send
her, so please to shoot here any literary rubbish on hand." To these I
will only add a couple of extracts from his letters while in Exeter
arranging his father's and mother's new home. They are pleasantly
written; and the vividness with which everything, once seen, was
photographed in his mind and memory, is humorously shown in
them.

"I took a little house for them this morning "(5 March, 1839: from
the New London Inn), "and if they are not pleased with it I shall be
grievously disappointed. Exactly a mile beyond the city on the
Plymouth road there are two white cottages: one is theirs and the
other belongs to their landlady. I almost forget the number of rooms;
but there is an excellent parlour with two other rooms on the ground
floor, there is really a beautiful little room over the parlour which I
am furnishing as a drawing-room, and there is a splendid garden. The
paint and paper throughout are new and fresh and cheerful-looking,
the place is clean beyond all description, and the neighbourhood
I suppose the most beautiful in this most beautiful of English
counties. Of the landlady, a Devonshire widow with whom I had the
honour of taking lunch to-day, I must make most especial mention.
She is a fat, infirm, splendidly fresh-faced country dame, rising
sixty and recovering from an attack 'on the nerves'—I thought they

never went off the stones, but I find they try country air with the best of us. In the event of my mother's being ill at any time, I really think the vicinity of this good dame, the very picture of respectability and good humour, will be the greatest possible comfort. *Her* furniture and domestic arrangements are a capital picture, but that I reserve till I see you, when I anticipate a hearty laugh. She bears the highest character with the bankers and the clergyman (who formerly lived in *my* cottage himself), and is a kind-hearted worthy capital specimen of the sort of life, or I have no eye for the real and no idea of finding it out.

"This good lady's brother and his wife live in the next nearest cottage, and the brother transacts the good lady's business, the nerves not admitting of her transacting it herself, although they leave her in her debilitated state something sharper than the finest lancet. Now the brother, having coughed all night till he coughed himself into such a perspiration that you might have 'wringed his hair,' according to the asseveration of eye-witnesses, his wife was sent for to negotiate with me; and if you could have seen me sitting in the kitchen with the two old women, endeavouring to make them comprehend that I had no evil intentions or covert designs, and that I had come down all that way to take some cottage and had *happened* to walk down that road and see that particular one, you would never have forgotten it. Then, to see the servant-girl run backwards and forwards to the sick man, and when the sick man had signed one agreement which I drew up and the old woman instantly put away in a disused tea-caddy, to see the trouble and the number of messages it took before the sick man could be brought to sign another (a duplicate) that we might have one apiece, was one of the richest scraps of genuine drollery I ever saw in all my days. How, when the business was over, we became conversational; how I was facetious, and at the same time virtuous and domestic; how I drank toasts in the beer, and stated on interrogatory that I was a married man and the father of two blessed infants; how the ladies marvelled thereat; how one of the ladies, having been in London, inquired where I lived, and, being told, remembered that Doughty Street and the Foundling Hospital were in the Old Kent Road, which I didn't contradict—all this and a great deal more must make us laugh when I return, as it makes me laugh now to think of. Of my subsequent visit to the upholsterer recommended by the landlady; of the absence of the upholsterer's wife, and the timidity of the upholsterer fearful of acting in her absence; of my sitting behind a high desk in a little dark shop, calling over the articles in requisition and checking off the prices as the upholsterer exhibited the goods and called them out; of my coming over the upholsterer's daughter, with many virtuous endearments, to propitiate the establishment and reduce the bill; of these matters I say nothing, either, for the same reason as that just mentioned. The discovery of the cottage I seriously regard as a blessing (not to speak it profanely) upon our efforts in this cause. I had heard nothing from the bank, and walked straight there,

by some strange impulse, directly after breakfast. I am sure they
may be happy there; for if I were older, and my course of activity were
run, I am sure *I* could, with God's blessing, for many and many a
year. . . ."

"The theatre is open here, and Charles Kean is to-night playing for
his last night. If it had been the 'rig'lar' drama I should have gone, but
I was afraid Sir Giles Overreach might upset me, so I stayed away.
My quarters are excellent and the head waiter is *such* a waiter!
Knowles (not Sheridan Knowles, but Knowles of the Cheetham
Hill Road) is an ass to him. This sounds bold, but truth is stranger
than fiction. By the by, not the least comical thing that has occurred
was the visit of the upholsterer (with some further calculations)
since I began this letter. I think they took me here at the New-
London for the Wonderful Being I am; they were amazingly sedulous;
and no doubt they looked for my being visited by the nobility and
gentry of the neighbourhood. My first and only visitor came to-night:
A ruddy-faced man in faded black, with extracts from a feather-bed
all over him; an extraordinary and quite miraculously dirty face; a
thick stick; and the personal appearance altogether of an amiable
bailiff in a green old age. I have not seen the proper waiter since, and
more than suspect I shall not recover this blow. He was announced
(by *the* waiter) as a 'person.' I expect my bill every minute. . . .

"The waiter is laughing outside the door with another waiter—
this is the latest intelligence of my condition."

## VI

### NEW LITERARY PROJECT

#### 1839

THE time was now come for him seriously to busy himself with a
successor to *Pickwick* and *Nickleby*, which he had not, however,
waited thus long before turning over thoroughly in his mind.
*Nickleby's* success had so far outgone even the expectation raised by
*Pickwick's* that, without some handsome practical admission of this
fact at the close, its publishers could hardly hope to retain him. This
had been frequently discussed by us, and was well understood. But,
apart from the question of his resuming with them at all, he had
persuaded himself it might be unsafe to resume in the old way,
believing the public likely to tire of the same twenty numbers over
again. There was also another and more sufficient reason for change,
which naturally had great weight with him; and this was the hope
that, by invention of a new mode as well as kind of serial publication,
he might be able for a time to discontinue the writing of a long story

with all its strain on his fancy, or in any case to shorten and vary the length of the stories written by himself, and perhaps ultimately to retain all the profits of a continuous publication, without necessarily himself contributing every line that was to be written for it. These considerations had been discussed still more anxiously; and for several months some such project had been taking form in his thoughts.

While he was at Petersham (July 1839) he thus wrote to me: "I have been thinking that subject over. Indeed I have been doing so to the great stoppage of *Nickleby* and the great worrying and fidgetting of myself. I have been thinking that if Chapman and Hall were to admit you into their confidence with respect to what they mean to do at the conclusion of *Nickleby*, without admitting me, it would help us very much. You know that I am well-disposed towards them, and that if they do something handsome, even handsomer perhaps than they dreamt of doing, they will find it their interest, and will find me tractable. You know also that I have had straightforward offers from responsible men to publish anything for me at a percentage on the profits, and take all the risk, but that I am unwilling to leave them, and have declared to you that if they behave with liberality to me I will not on any consideration, although to a certain extent I certainly and surely must gain by it. Knowing all this, I feel sure that if you were to put before them the glories of our new project, and, reminding them that when *Barnaby* is published I am clear of all engagements, were to tell them that, if they wish to secure me and perpetuate our connection, now is the time for them to step gallantly forward and make such proposals as will produce that result—I feel quite sure that if this should be done by you, as you only can do it, the result will be of the most vital importance to me and mine, and that a great deal may be effected, thus, to recompense your friend for very small profits and very large work as yet. I shall see you, please God, on Tuesday night; and if they wait upon you on Wednesday, I shall remain in town until that evening."

They came; and the tenor of the interview was so favourable that I wished him to put in writing what from time to time had been discussed in connection with the new project. This led to the very interesting letter I shall now quote, written also in the same month from Petersham. I did not remember, until I lately read it, that the notion of a possible visit to America had been in his thoughts so early.

"I should be willing to commence on the thirty-first of March, 1840, a new publication consisting entirely of original matter, of which one number price threepence should be published every week, and of which a certain amount of numbers should form a volume, to be published at regular intervals. The best general idea of the plan of the work might be given perhaps by reference to *The Tatler*, *The Spectator*, and Goldsmith's *Bee*, but it would be far more popular both in the subjects of which it treats and its mode of treating them.

"I should propose to start, as *The Spectator* does, with some pleasant fiction relative to the origin of the publication; to introduce a little

club or knot of characters and to carry their personal histories and
proceedings through the work; to introduce fresh characters constantly; to reintroduce Mr. Pickwick and Sam Weller, the latter of
whom might furnish an occasional communication with great effect;
to write amusing essays on the various foibles of the day as they arise;
to take advantage of all passing events; and to vary the form of the
papers by throwing them into sketches, essays, tales, adventures,
letters from imaginary correspondents and so forth, so as to diversify
the contents as much as possible.

"In addition to this general design, I may add that under particular
heads I should strive to establish certain features in the work, which
should be so many veins of interest and amusement running through
the whole. . . .

"The heads of the terms upon which I should be prepared to go
into the undertaking would be—That I be made a proprietor in the
work and a sharer in the profits. That when I bind myself to write
a certain portion of every number, I am ensured, *for* that writing, in
every number a certain sum of money. That those who assist me, and
contribute the remainder of every number, shall be paid by the publishers immediately after its appearance, according to a scale to be
calculated and agreed upon, on presenting my order for the amount to
which they may be respectively entitled. Or, if the publishers prefer
it, that they agree to pay me a certain sum for the *whole* of every number, and leave me to make such arrangements for that part which I
may not write, as I think best. Of course I should require that for
these payments, or any other outlay connected with the work, I am not
held accountable in any way; and that no portion of them is to be
considered as received by me on account of the profits. I need not add
that some arrangement would have to be made, if I undertake my
Travels, relative to the expenses of travelling.

"Now I want our publishing friends to take these things into consideration, and to give me the views and proposals they would be disposed to entertain when they have maturely considered the matter."

The result of their consideration was on the whole satisfactory.
An additional fifteen hundred pounds was to be paid at the close of
*Nickleby*, the new adventure was to be undertaken, and Cattermole
was to be joined with Browne as its illustrator. Nor was its plan much
modified before starting, though it was felt by us all that, for the opening numbers at least, Dickens would have to be sole contributor;
and that, whatever otherwise might be its attraction, or the success
of the detached papers proposed by him, some reinforcement of them
from time to time, by means of a story with his name continued
at reasonable if not regular intervals, would be found absolutely
necessary. . . .

Six weeks before signature of the agreement, while a title was still
undetermined, I had this letter from him. "I will dine with you. I
intended to spend the evening in strict meditation (as I did last night)
but perhaps I had better go out, lest all work and no play should make

me a dull boy. *I* have a list of titles too, but the final title I have determined on—or something very near it. I have a notion of this old file in the queer house, opening the book by an account of himself, and, among other peculiarities, of his affection for an old quaint queer-cased clock; showing how that when they have sat alone together in the long evenings, he has got accustomed to its voice, and come to consider it as the voice of a friend; how its striking, in the night, has seemed like an assurance to him that it was still a cheerful watcher at his chamber-door; and how its very face has seemed to have something of welcome in its dusty features, and to relax from its grimness when he has looked at it from his chimney-corner. Then I mean to tell how that he has kept odd manuscripts in the old, deep, dark, silent closet where the weights are; and taken them from thence to read (mixing up his enjoyments with some notion of his clock); and how, when the club came to be formed, they, by reason of their punctuality and his regard for his dumb servant, took their name from it. And thus I shall call the book either *Old Humphrey's Clock*; or *Master Humphrey's Clock*; beginning with a woodcut of old Humphrey and his clock, and explaining the why and wherefore. All Humphrey's own papers will then be dated From my clockside, and I have divers thoughts about the best means of introducing the others. I thought about this all day yesterday and all last night till I went to bed. I am sure I can make a good thing of this opening, which I have thoroughly warmed up to in consequence."

A few days later: "I incline more to *Master Humphrey's Clock* than *Old Humphrey's*—if so be that there is no danger of the Pensive confounding master with a boy." After two days more: "I was thinking all yesterday, and have begun at *Master Humphrey* to-day." Then a week later: "I have finished the first number, but have not been able to do more in the space than lead up to the Giants, who are just on the scene."

## VII

### "OLD CURIOSITY SHOP"

### 1840 *and* 1841

A DAY or two after the date of the last letter quoted, Dickens and his wife, with Maclise and myself, visited Landor in Bath, and it was during three happy days passed together there that the fancy which was shortly to take the form of little Nell first occurred to its author. But as yet with the intention only of making out of it a tale of a few chapters. On 1 March we returned from Bath; and on the 4th I had this letter: "If you can manage to give me a call in the course of th day or evening, I wish you would. I am laboriously turning over in my mind how I can best effect the improvement we spoke of last night, which I will certainly make by hook or by crook, and which I would like you to see *before* it goes finally to the printer's. I have determined not to put that witch-story into number 3, for I am by no means satisfied of the effect of its contrast with Humphrey. I think of lengthening Humphrey, finishing the description of the society, and closing with the little child-story, which is SURE to be effective, especially after the old man's quiet way." Then there came hard upon this: "What do you think of the following double title for the beginning of that little tale? 'PERSONAL ADVENTURES OF MASTER HUMPHREY: *The Old Curiosity Shop*.' I have thought of *Master Humphrey's Tale, Master Humphrey's Narrative, A Passage in Master Humphrey's Life*—but I don't think any does as well as this. I have also thought of *The Old Curiosity Dealer and the Child* instead of *The Old Curiosity Shop*. Perpend. Topping waits."—And thus was taking gradual form, with less direct consciousness of design on his own part than I can remember in any other instance throughout his career, a story which was to add largely to his popularity, more than any other of his works to make the bond between himself and his readers one of personal attachment, and very widely to increase the sense of personal attachment, and very widely to increase the sense entertained of his powers as a pathetic as well as humorous writer.

He had not written more than two or three chapters, when the capability of the subject for more extended treatment than he had at first proposed to give to it pressed itself upon him, and he resolved to throw everything else aside, devoting himself to the one story only. There were other strong reasons for this. Of the first number of the *Clock* nearly seventy thousand were sold; but with the discovery that there was no continuous tale the orders at once diminished, and a change must have been made even if the material and means for it had not been ready. There had been an interval of three numbers between the first and second chapters, which the society of Mr. Pickwick and the two Wellers made pleasant enough; but after the introduction of Dick Swiveller there were three consecutive chapters; and in the continued progress of the tale to its close there were only two more breaks, one between the fourth and fifth chapters and one between the eight and ninth, pardonable and enjoyable now for the sake of Sam and his father. The re-introduction of those old favourites, it will have been seen, formed part of his original plan; of his abandonment of which his own description may be added, from his preface to the collected edition. "The first chapter of this tale appeared in the fourth number of *Master Humphrey's Clock*, when I had already been made uneasy by the desultory character of that work, and when, I believe, my readers had thoroughly participated in the feeling. The commencement of a story was a great satisfaction to me, and I had reason to believe that my readers participated in this feeling too. Hence, being pledged to some interruptions and some pursuit of the original design, I set cheerfully about disentangling myself from those impediments as fast as I could; and, this done, from that time until its completion *The Old Curiosity Shop* was written and published from week to week, in weekly parts."

He had very early himself become greatly taken with it. "I am very glad indeed," he wrote to me after the first half-dozen chapters, "that you think so well of the *Curiosity Shop*, and especially that what may be got out of Dick strikes you. I *mean* to make much of him. I feel the story extremely myself, which I take to be a good sign; and am already warmly interested in it. I shall run it on now for four whole numbers together, to give it a fair chance." Every step lightened the road, as it became more and more real with each character that appeared in it; and I still recall the glee with which he told me what he intended to do not only with Dick Swiveller, but with Septimus Brass, changed afterwards to Sampson. Undoubtedly, however, Dick was his favourite. "Dick's behaviour in the matter of Miss Wackles will, I hope, give you satisfaction," is the remark of another of his letters. "I cannot yet discover that his aunt has any belief in him, or is in the least degree likely to send him a remittance, so that he will probably continue to be the sport of destiny." His difficulties were the quickly recurring times of publication, the confined space in each number that yet had to contribute its individual effect, and (from the suddenness with which he had begun) the impossibility of getting in advance. "I was obliged to cramp most dreadfully what I thought a pretty idea in the last chapter. I hadn't room to turn": to this or a similar effect his complaints are frequent, and of the vexations named it was by far the worst. But he steadily bore up against all, and made a triumph of the little story.

To help his work he went twice to Broadstairs, in June and in September; and at his first visit (17 June) thus wrote: "It's now four o'clock and I have been at work since half-past eight. I have really dried myself up into a condition which would almost justify me in pitching off the cliff, head first—but I must get richer before I indulge in a crowning luxury. . . . "At the opening of September he was again at the little watering place. The residence he most desired there, Fort House, stood prominently at the top of a breezy hill on the road to Kingsgate, with a cornfield between it and the sea, and this in many subsequent years he always occupied; but he was fain to be content, as yet, with Law House, a smaller villa between the hill and the cornfield, from which he now wrote of his attentions to Mr. Sampson Brass's sister. "I have been at work of course" (2 September) "and have just finished a number. I have effected a reform by virtue of which we breakfast at a quarter before eight, so that I get to work as half-past, and am commonly free by one o'clock or so, which is a great happiness. Dick is now Sampson's clerk, and I have touched Miss Brass in Number 25, lightly, but effectively I hope." . . .

At the opening of November, there seems to have been a wish on Maclise's part to try his hand at an illustration for the story; but I do not remember that it bore other fruit than a very pleasant day at Jack Straw's Castle, where Dickens read one of the later numbers to us. "Maclise and myself (alone in the carriage)," he wrote, "will be with you at two exactly. We propose driving out to Hampstead and walking there, if it don't rain in buckets'-full. I shan't send Bradburys' the MS. of next number till to-morrow, for it contains the shadow of the number after that, and I want to read it to Mac, as, if he likes the subject, it will furnish him with one, I think. You can't imagine (gravely I write and speak) how exhausted I am to-day with yesterday's labours. I went to bed last night utterly dispirited and done up." . . .

Fast shortening as the life of little Nell was now, the dying year might have seen it pass away; but I never knew him wind up any tale with such a sorrowful reluctance as this. He caught at any excuse to hold his hand from it, and stretched to the utmost limit the time left to complete it in. . . . He read to me the two chapters of Nell's death, the seventy-first and seventy-second, with the result described in a letter of the following Monday, 17 January, 1841.

"I can't help letting you know how much your yesterday's letter pleased me. I felt sure you liked the chapters when we read them on Thursday night, but it was a great delight to have my impression so strongly and heartily confirmed. You know how little value I should set on what I had done, if all the world cried out that it was good, and those whose good opinion and approbation I value most were silent. The assurance that this little closing of the scene touches and is felt by you so strongly, is better to me than a thousand most sweet voices out of doors. When I first began, *on your valued suggestion*, to keep my thoughts upon this ending of the tale, I resolved to try and do something which might be read by people about whom Death had been, with a softened feeling, and with consolation. . . . After you left last night, I took my desk upstairs; and writing until four o'clock this morning, finished the old story. It makes me very melancholy to think that all these people are lost to me for ever, and I feel as if I never could become attached to any new set of characters." The words printed in italics, as underlined by himself, give me my share in the story which had gone so closely to his heart. I was responsible for its tragic ending. He had not thought of killing her, when, about half-way through, I asked him to consider whether it did not necessarily belong even to his own conception, after taking so mere a child through such a tragedy of sorrow, to lift her also out of the commonplace of ordinary happy endings, so that the gentle pure little figure and form should never change to the fancy. All that I meant he seized at once, and never turned aside from it again.

The published book was an extraordinary success, and, in America more especially, very greatly increased the writer's fame. The pathetic vein it had opened was perhaps mainly the cause of this, but opinion at home continued still to turn on the old characteristics; the freshness of humour of which the pathos was but another form or product,

331*

the grasp of reality with which character had again been seized, the discernment of good under its least attractive forms and of evil in its most captivating disguises, the cordial wisdom and sound heart, the enjoyment and fun, luxuriant yet under proper control. No falling-off was found in these, and I doubt if any of his people have been more widely liked than Dick Swiveller and the Marchioness. . . .

# VIII

## DEVONSHIRE TERRACE AND BROADSTAIRS

### 1840

IT was an excellent saying of the first Lord Shaftesbury, that, seeing every man of any capacity holds within himself two men, the wise and the foolish, each of them ought freely to be allowed his turn; and it was one of the secrets of Dickens's social charm that he could, in strict accordance with this saying, allow each part of him its turn; could afford thoroughly to give rest and relief to what was serious in him, and, when the time came to play his gambols, could surrender himself wholly to the enjoyment of the time, and become the very genius and embodiment of one of his own most whimsical fancies.

Turning back from the narrative of his last piece of writing to recall a few occurrences of the year during which it had occupied him, I find him at its opening in one of these humorous moods, and another friend, with myself, enslaved by its influence. "What on earth does it all mean!" wrote poor puzzled Mr. Landor to me, enclosing a letter from him of the date 11 February, the day after the royal nuptials of that year. In this he had related to our old friend a wonderful hallucination arising out of that event, which had then taken entire possession of him. "Society is unhinged here," thus ran the letter, "by her majesty's marriage, and I am sorry to add that I have fallen hopelessly in love with the Queen, and wander up and down with vague and dismal thoughts of running away to some uninhabited island with a maid of honour, to be entrapped by conspiracy for that purpose. Can you suggest any particular young person, serving in such a capacity, who would suit me? It is too much perhaps to ask you to join the band of noble youths (Forster is in it, and Maclise) who are to assist me in this great enterprise, but a man of your energy would be invaluable. I have my eye upon Lady . . ., principally because she is very beautiful, and has no strong brothers. Upon this, and other points of the scheme, however, we will confer more at large when we meet; and meanwhile burn this document, that no suspicion may arise or rumour get abroad."

The maid of honour and the uninhabited island were flights of fancy, but the other daring delusion was for a time encouraged to such whimsical lengths, not alone by him but (under his influence) by the two friends named, that it took the wildest forms of humorous extravagance; and of the private confidences much interchanged, as well as of his own style of open speech in which the joke of a despairing unfitness for any further use or enjoyment of life was unflaggingly kept up, to the amazement of bystanders knowing nothing of what it meant and believing he had half lost his senses, I permit myself to give from his letters one further illustration. "I am utterly lost in misery," he writes on 12 February, "and can do nothing. I have been reading *Oliver*, *Pickwick*, and *Nickleby* to get my thoughts together for the new effort, but all in vain

> My heart is at Windsor,
> My heart isn't here;
> My heart is at Windsor,
> A following my dear.

I saw the Responsibilities this morning, and burst into tears. The presence of my wife aggravates me. I loathe my parents. I detest my house. I begin to have thoughts of the Serpentine, of the Regent's Canal, of the razors upstairs, of the chemist's down the street, of poisoning myself at Mrs. ——'s table, of hanging myself upon the pear-tree in the garden, of abstaining from food and starving myself to death, of being bled for my cold and tearing off the bandage, of falling under the feet of cab-horses in the New Road, of murdering Chapman and Hall and becoming great in story (SHE must hear something of me then—perhaps sign the warrant: or is that a fable?), of turning Chartist, of heading some bloody assault upon the palace and saving Her by my single hand——of being anything but what I have been, and doing anything but what I have done. Your distracted friend, C. D." The wild derangement of asterisks in every shape and form, with which this incoherence closed. cannot be given.

Some ailments which dated from an earlier period in his life made themselves felt in the spring of the year, as I remember, and increased horse exercise was strongly recommended to him. "I find it will be positively necessary to go, for five days in the week at least," he wrote in March, "on a perfect regimen of diet and exercise, and am anxious not to delay treating for a horse." We were now, therefore, when he was not at the seaside, much on horseback in suburban lanes and roads; and the spacious garden of his new house was also turned to healthful use at even his busiest working times. I mark this, too, as the time when the first of his ravens took up residence; and as the beginning of disputes with two of his neighbours about the smoking of the stable chimney, which his groom Topping, a highly absurd little man with flaming red hair, so complicated by secret devices of his own, meant to conciliate each complainant alternately and having the effect of aggravating both, that law proceedings were only barely avoided. "I shall give you," he writes, "my latest report of the chimney in the form of an address from Topping, made to me on our way from little Hall's at Norwood the other night, where he and Chapman and I had been walking all day, while Topping drove Kate, Mrs. Hall, and her sisters, to Dulwich. Topping had been regaled upon the premises, and was just drunk enough to be confidential. 'Beggin' your pardon, sir, but the genelman next door sir, seems to be gettin' quite comfortable and pleasant about the chimley.'—'I don't think he is, Topping.'—'Yes he is sir I think. He comes out in the yard this morning and says *Coachman* he says' (observe the vision of a great large fat man called up by the word) '*is that your raven* he says *Coachman? or is it Mr. Dickens's raven?* he says. My master's sir, I says. *Well*, he says, *it's a fine bird. I think the chimley 'ill do now Coachman,—now the jint's taken off the pipe* he says. I hope it will, sir, I says; my master's a genelman as wouldn't annoy no genelman if he could help it, I'm sure; and my own missis is so afraid of havin' a bit o' fire that o' Sundays our little bit o' weal or what not, goes to the baker's a purpose.—*Damn the chimley Coachman*, he says, *it's a smokin' now.*—It an't a smokin' your way sir, I says; *Well*, he says, *no more it is, Coachman, and as long as it smokes anybody else's way, it's all right and I'm agreeable.*' Of course I shall now have the man from the other side upon me, and very likely with an action of nuisance for smoking into his conservatory."

A graver incident, which occurred to him also among his earliest experiences as tenant of Devonshire Terrace, illustrates too well the practical turn of his kindness and humanity not to deserve relation. He has himself described it, in one of his minor writings, in setting down what he remembered as the only good that ever came of a beadle. "Of that great parish functionary," he remarks, "having newly taken the lease of a house in a certain distinguished metropolitan parish, a house which then appeared to me to be a frightfully first-class family mansion involving awful responsibilities, I became the prey." In other words he was summoned, and obliged to sit, as juryman at an inquest on the body of a little child alleged to have been murdered by its mother; of which the result was, by his persevering exertion, seconded by the humane help of the coroner, Mr. Wakley, the verdict of himself and his fellow-jurymen charged her only with the concealment of birth. "The poor desolate creature dropped upon her knees before us with protestations that we were right (protestations among the most affecting that I have ever heard in my life), and was carried away insensible. I caused some extra care to be taken of her in the prison, and counsel to be retained for her defence when she was tried at the Old Bailey; and her sentence was lenient, and her history and conduct proved that it was right." How much he felt the little incident, at the actual time of its occurrence, may be judged from the few lines written next morning: "Whether it was the poor baby, or its poor mother, or the coffin, or my fellow-jurymen, or what not, I can't say, but last night I had a most violent attack of sickness and indigestion, which not only prevented me from sleeping, but even from lying down. Accordingly Kate and I sat up through the dreary watches."

The day of the first publication of *Master Humphrey* (Saturday, 4 April) had by this time come, and, according to the rule observed in his two other great ventures, he left town with Mrs. Dickens on Friday the 3rd. With Maclise we had been together at Richmond the previous night; and I joined him at Birmingham the day following, with news of the sale of the whole sixty thousand copies to which the first working had been limited, and of orders already in hand for ten thousand more! The excitement of the success somewhat lengthened our holiday; and, after visiting Shakespeare's house at Stratford, and Johnson's at Lichfield, we found our resources so straitened in returning, that, employing as our messenger of need his younger brother Alfred, who had joined us from Tamworth where he was a student-engineer, we had to pawn our gold watches at Birmingham.

At the end of the following month he went to Broadstairs, and not many days before (on 20 May) a note from Mr. Jerdan on behalf of Mr. Bentley opened the negotiations formerly referred to, which transferred to Messrs. Chapman and Hall the agreement for *Barnaby Rudge*. I was myself absent when he left, and in a letter announcing his departure he had written: "I don't know of a word of news in all London, but there will be plenty next week, for I am going away, and I hope you'll send me an account of it. I am doubtful whether it will be a murder, a fire, a vast robbery, or the escape of Gould, but it will be something remarkable no doubt. I almost blame myself for the death of that poor girl who leaped off the monument upon my leaving town last year. She would not have done it if I had remained, neither would the two men have found the skeleton in the sewers." His prediction was quite accurate, for I had to tell him, after not many days, of the pitboy who shot at the queen. "It's a great pity they couldn't suffocate that boy, Master Oxford," he replied very sensibly, "and say no more about it. To have put him quietly between two feather-beds would have stopped his heroic speeches, and dulled the sound of his glory very much. As it is, she will have to run the gauntlet of many a fool and madman, some of whom may perchance be better shots and use other than Brummagem firearms." How much of this actually came to pass, the reader knows.

From the letters of his present Broadstairs visit, there is little more to add to the account of his progress with his story; but a sentence may be given for its characteristic expression of his invariable habit upon entering any new abode, whether to stay in it for days or for years. On a Monday night he arrived, and on the Tuesday (2 June) wrote: "Before I tasted bit or drop yesterday, I set out my writing-table with extreme taste and neatness, and improved the disposition of the furniture generally." He stayed till the end of June; when Maclise and myself joined him for the pleasure of posting back home by way of his favourite Chatham, Rochester, and Cobham, where we passed two agreeable days in revisiting well-remembered scenes.

Meanwhile there had been brought to a close the treaty for repurchase of *Oliver* and surrender of *Barnaby*, upon terms which are succinctly stated in a letter written by him to Messrs. Chapman and Hall on 2 July, the day after our return.

"The terms upon which you advance the money to-day for the purchase of the copyright and stock of *Oliver* on my behalf, are understood between us to be these. That this £2250 is to be deducted from the purchase-money of a work by me entitled *Barnaby Rudge*, of which two chapters are now in your hands, and of which the whole is to be written within some convenient time to be agreed upon between us. But if it should not be written (which God forbid!) within five years, you are to have a lien to this amount on the property belonging to me that is now in your hands, namely, my shares in the stock and copyright of *Sketches by Boz*, *The Pickwick Papers*, *Nicholas Nickleby*, *Oliver Twist*, and *Master Humphrey's Clock*; in which we do not include any share of the current profits of the last-named work, which I shall remain at liberty to draw at the times stated in our agreement. Your purchase of *Barnaby Rudge* is made upon the following terms. It is to consist of matter sufficient for ten monthly numbers of the size of *Pickwick* and *Nickleby*, which you are however at liberty to divide and publish in fifteen smaller numbers if you think fit. The terms for the purchase of this edition in numbers, and for the copyright of the whole book for six months after the publication of the last number, are £3000. At the expiration of the six months the whole copyright reverts to me." The sequel was, as all the world knows, that Barnaby became successor to little Nell, the money being repaid by the profits of the *Clock*; but I ought also to mention the generous sequel that was given to the small service thus rendered to him, by the gift, after not many days, of an antique silver-mounted jug of great beauty of form and workmanship, and with a wealth far beyond artist's design or jeweller's chasing in written words that accompanied it.[1] They were accepted to commemorate, not the help they would have far overpaid, but the gladness of his own escape from the last of the agreements that had hampered the opening of his career, and the better future which was now before him.

At the opening of August he was with Mrs. Dickens for some days

[1] "Accept from me" (8 July, 1840), "as a slight memorial of your attached companion, the poor keepsake which accompanies this. My heart is not an eloquent one on matters which touch it most, but suppose this claret jug the urn in which it lies, and believe that its warmest and truest blood is yours. This was the object of my fruitless search, and your curiosity, on Friday. At first I scarcely knew what trifle (you will deem it valuable, I know, for the giver's sake) to send you; but I thought it would be pleasant to connect it with our jovial moments, and to let it add, to the wine we shall drink from it together, a flavour which the choicest vintage could never impart. Take it from my hand—filled to the brim and running over with truth and earnestness. I have just taken one parting look at it, and it seems the most elegant thing in the world to me, for I lose sight of the vase in the crowd of welcome associations that are clustering and wreathing themselves about it."

# The Life of Charles Dickens

in Devonshire, on a visit to his father, but he had to take his work
with him; and they had only one real holiday, when Dawlish, Teign-
mouth, Babbicombe, and Torquay were explored, returning to Exeter
at night. In the beginning of September he was again at Broadstairs.

"I was just going to work," he wrote on the 9th, "when I got this
letter, and the story of the man who went to Chapman and Hall's
knocked me down flat. I wrote until now (a quarter to one) against
the grain, and have at last given it up for one day. Upon my word it
is intolerable. I have been grinding my teeth all the morning. I think
I could say in two lines something about the general report with
propriety. I'll add them to the proof" (the preface to the first volume
of the *Clock* was at this time in preparation), "giving you full power
to cut them out if you should think differently from me, and from
C and H, who in such a matter must be admitted judges." He refers
here to a report, rather extensively circulated at the time, and which
through various channels had reached his publishers, that he was
suffering from loss of reason and was under treatment in an asylum.[1]
I would have withheld it from him, as an absurdity that must quickly
be forgotten—but he had been told of it, and there was a difficulty in
keeping within judicious bounds his not unnatural wrath.

A few days later (the 15th) he wrote: "I have been rather surprised
of late to have applications from Roman Catholic clergymen, demand-
ing (rather pastorally and with a kind of grave authority) assistance,
literary employment, and so forth. At length it struck me, that,
through some channel or other, I must have been represented as
belonging to that religion. Would you believe, that in a letter from
Lamert at Cork, to my mother, which I saw last night, he says, 'What
do the papers mean by saying that Charles is demented, and further,
*that he has turned Roman Catholic?*'!" Of the begging-letter writers,
hinted at here, I ought earlier to have said something. In one of his
detached essays he has described, without a particle of exaggeration,
the extent to which he was made a victim by this class of swindler,
and the extravagance of the devices practised on him; but he had not
confessed, as he might, that for much of what he suffered he was
himself responsible, by giving so largely, as at first he did, to almost
everyone who applied to him. What at last brought him to his senses
in this respect, I think, was the request made by the adventurer who
had exhausted every other expedient, and who desired finally, after
describing himself reduced to the condition of a travelling Cheap
Jack in the smallest way of crockery, that a donkey might be left

[1] Already he had been the subject of similar reports on the occasion of the
family sorrow which compelled him to suspend the publication of *Pickwick* for two
months when, upon issuing a brief address in resuming his work (30 June, 1837),
he said: "By one set of intimate acquaintances, especially well-informed, he has
been killed outright; by another, driven mad; by a third, imprisoned for debt;
by a fourth, sent per steamer to the United States; by a fifth, rendered incapable
of mental exertion for evermore; by all, in short, represented as doing anything
but seeking in a few weeks' retirement the restoration of that cheerfulness and
peace of which a sad bereavement had temporarily deprived him."

out for him next day, which he would duly call for. This I perfectly remember, and I much fear that the applicant was the Daniel Tobin before mentioned.

Many and delightful were other letters written from Broadstairs at this date, filled with whimsical talk and humorous description, relating chiefly to an eccentric friend who stayed with him most of the time, and is sketched in one of his published papers as Mr. Kindheart; but all too private for reproduction now. He returned in the middle of October, when we resumed our almost daily ridings, foregatherings with Maclise at Hampstead and elsewhere, and social entertainments with Macready, Talfourd, Procter, Stanfield, Fonblanque, Elliotson, Tennent, d'Orsay, Quin, Harness, Wilkie, Edwin Landseer, Rogers, Sydney Smith, and Bulwer. Of the genius of the author of *Pelham* and *Eugene Aram* he had, early and late, the highest admiration, and he took occasion to express it during the present year in a new preface which he published to *Oliver Twist*. Other friends became familiar in later years; but, disinclined as he was to the dinner invitations that reached him from every quarter, all such meetings with those whom I have named, and in an especial manner the marked attentions shown him by Miss Coutts, which began with the very beginning of his career, were invariably welcome.

To speak here of the pleasure his society afforded, would anticipate the fitter mention to be made hereafter. But what in this respect distinguishes nearly all original men, he possessed eminently. His place was not to be filled up by any other. To the most trivial talk he gave the attraction of his own character. It might be a small matter; something he had read or observed during the day, some quaint odd fancy from a book, a vivid little outdoor picture, the laughing exposure of some imposture, or a burst of sheer mirthful enjoyment; but of its kind it would be something unique, because genuinely part of himself. This, and his unwearying animal spirits, made him the most delightful of companions; no claim on good-fellowship ever found him wanting; and no one so constantly recalled to his friends the description Johnson gave of Garrick, as "the cheerfullest man of his age."

Of what occupied him in the way of literary labour in the autumn and winter months of the year, some description has been given; and, apart from what has already thus been said of his work at the closing chapters of *The Old Curiosity Shop*, nothing now calls for more special allusion, except that in his town-walks in November, impelled thereto by specimens recently discovered in his country walks between Broadstairs and Ramsgate, he thoroughly explored the ballad literature of Seven Dials, and would occasionally sing, with an effect that justified his reputation for comic singing in his childhood, not a few of those wonderful productions. . . .

## IX

### "BARNABY RUDGE"

### 1841

THE letters of 1841 yield similar fruit as to his doings and sayings, and may in like manner first be consulted for the literary work he had in hand.

He had the advantage of beginning *Barnaby Rudge* with a fair amount of story in advance, which he had only to make suitable, by occasional readjustment of chapters, to publication in weekly portions; and on this he was engaged before the end of January. "I am at present " (22 January, 1841) "in what Leigh Hunt would call a kind of impossible state—thinking what on earth Master Humphrey can think of through four mortal pages. I added here and there to the last chapter of the *Curiosity Shop* yesterday, and it leaves me only four pages to write." (They were filled by a paper from Humphrey introductory of the new tale, in which will be found a striking picture of London, from midnight to the break of day.) "I also made up, and wrote the needful insertions for, the second number of *Barnaby*—so that I came back to the mill a little." Hardly yet: for after four days he writes, having meanwhile done nothing: "I have been looking (three o'clock) with an appearance of extraordinary interest and study at *one leaf* of the *Curiosities of Literature* ever since half-past ten this morning—I haven't the heart to turn over." Then, on Friday the 29th, better news came. "I didn't stir out yesterday, but sat and *thought* all day; not writing a line; not so much as the cross of a *t* or dot of an *i*. I imaged forth a good deal of *Barnaby* by keeping my mind steadily upon him; and am happy to say I have gone to work this morning in good twig, strong hope, and cheerful spirits. Last night I was unutterably and impossible-to-form-an-idea-of-ably miserable. . . . By the by don't engage yourself otherwise than to me for Sunday week, because it's my birthday. I have no doubt we shall have got over our troubles here by that time, and I purpose having a snug dinner in the study." We had the dinner, though the troubles were not over; but the next day another son was born to him. "Thank God," he wrote on the 9th, "quite well. I am thinking hard, and have just written to Browne inquiring when he will come and confer about the raven." He had by this time resolved to make that bird, whose accomplishments had been daily ripening and enlarging for the last twelve months to the increasing mirth and delight of us all, a prominent figure in *Barnaby*; and the invitation to the artist was for a conference how best to introduce him graphically.

The next letter mentioning *Barnaby* was from Brighton (25 February), whither he had flown for a week's quiet labour. "I have (it's four o'clock) done a very fair morning's work, at which I have sat very close, and been blessed besides with a clear view of the end of the volume. As the contents of one number usually require a day's thought at the very least, and often more, this puts me in great spirits. I think—that is, I hope—the story takes a great stride at this point, and takes it WELL. *Nous verrons.* Grip will be strong, and I build greatly on the Varden household."

Upon his return he had to lament a domestic calamity, which, for its connection with a famous personage in *Barnaby*, must be mentioned here. The raven had for some days been ailing, and Topping had reported of him, as Hamlet declared of himself, that he had lost his mirth and foregone all custom of exercises: but Dickens paid no great heed, remembering his recovery from an illness of the previous summer when he swallowed some white paint; so that the graver report which led him to send for the doctor came upon him unexpectedly, and nothing but his own language can worthily describe the result. Unable from the state of his feelings to write two letters, he sent the narrative to Maclise under an enormous black seal, for transmission to me.

"You will be greatly shocked" (the letter is dated Friday evening, 12 March, 1841) "and grieved to hear that the Raven is no more. He expired to-day at a few minutes after twelve o'clock at noon. He had been ailing for a few days, but we anticipated no serious result, conjecturing that a portion of the white paint he swallowed last summer might be lingering about his vitals without having any serious effect upon his constitution. Yesterday afternoon he was taken so much worse that I sent an express for the medical gentleman (Mr. Herring), who promptly attended, and administered a powerful dose of castor oil. Under the influence of this medicine, he recovered so far as to be able at eight o'clock p.m. to bite Topping. His night was peaceful. This morning at daybreak he appeared better; received (agreeably to the doctor's directions) another dose of castor oil; and partook plentifully of some warm gruel, the flavour of which he appeared to relish. Towards eleven o'clock he was so much worse that it was found necessary to muffle the stable-knocker. At half-past, or thereabouts, he was heard talking to himself about the horse and Topping's family, and to add some incoherent expressions which are supposed to have been either a foreboding of his approaching dissolution, or some wishes relative to the disposal of his little property: consisting chiefly of half-pence which he had buried in different parts of the garden. On the clock striking twelve he appeared slightly agitated, but he soon recovered, walked twice or thrice along the coach-house, stopped to bark, staggered, exclaimed *Halloa old girl!* (his favourite expression), and died.

"He behaved throughout with a decent fortitude, equanimity, and self-possession, which cannot be too much admired. I deeply regret that being in ignorance of his danger I did not attend to receive his last instructions. Something remarkable about his eyes occasioned Topping to run for the doctor at twelve. When they returned together our friend was gone. It was the medical gentleman who informed me of his decease. He did it with great caution and delicacy, preparing me by the remark that 'a jolly queer start had taken place'; but the shock was very great notwithstanding. I am not wholly free from suspicions of poison. A malicious butcher has been heard to say that he would 'do' for him: his plea was that he would not be molested in taking orders down the mews, by any bird that wore a tail. Other persons have also been heard to threaten: among others, Charles Knight, who has just started a weekly publication price fourpence: *Barnaby* being, as you know, threepence. I have directed a post-mortem examination, and the body has been removed to Mr. Herring's school of anatomy for that purpose.

"I could wish, if you can take the trouble, that you could enclose this to Forster immediately after you have read it. I cannot discharge the painful task of communication more than once. Were they ravens who took manna to somebody in the wilderness? At times I hope they were, and at others I fear they were not, or they would certainly have stolen it by the way. In profound sorrow, I am ever your bereaved friend C.D. Kate is as well as can be expected, but terribly low as you may suppose. The children seem rather glad of it. He bit their ankles. But that was play."

In what way the loss was replaced, so that *Barnaby* should have the fruit of continued study of the habits of the family of birds which Grip had so nobly represented, Dickens has told in the preface to the story; and another, older, and larger Grip, obtained through Mr. Smithson, was installed in the stable, almost before the stuffed remains of his honoured predecessor had been sent home in a glass case, by way of ornament to his bereaved master's study.

I resume our correspondence on what he was writing. "I see there is yet room for a few lines" (25 March), "and you are quite right in wishing what I cut out to be restored. I did not want Joe to be so short about Dolly, and really wrote his references to that young lady carefully—as natural things with a meaning in them. Chigwell, my dear fellow, is the greatest place in the world. Name your day for going. Such a delicious old inn opposite the churchyard—such a lovely ride—such beautiful forest scenery—such an out of the way, rural place—such a sexton! I say again, name your day." The day was named at once; and the whitest of stones marks it now in sorrowful memory. His promise was exceeded by our enjoyment; and his delight in the double recognition, of himself and of *Barnaby*, by the landlord of the nice old inn, far exceeded any pride he would have taken in what the world thinks the highest sort of honour.

"I have shut myself up" (26 March) "by myself to-day, and mean to try and 'go it' at the *Clock*; Kate being out, and the house peacefully dismal. I don't remember altering the exact part you object to, but if there be anything here you object to, knock it out ruthlessly." "Don't fail" (5 April) "to erase anything that seems to you too strong. It is difficult for me to judge what tells too much, and what does not. I am trying a very quiet number to set against this necessary one. I hope it will be good, but I am in very sad condition for work. Glad you think this powerful. What I have put in is more relief, from the raven." Two days later: "I have done that number, and am now going to work on another. I am bent (please Heaven) on finishing the first chapter by Friday night. I hope to look in upon you to-night, when we'll dispose of the toasts for Saturday. Still bilious—but a good number, I hope, notwithstanding. Jeffrey has come to town, and was here yesterday." The toasts to be disposed of were those to be given at the dinner on the 10th to celebrate the second volume of *Master Humphrey*; when Talfourd presided, and there was much jollity. According to the memorandum drawn up that Saturday night now lying before me, we all in the greatest good humour glorified each other: Talfourd proposing the *Clock*, Macready Mrs. Dickens, Dickens the publishers, and myself the artists; Macready giving Talfourd, Talfourd Macready, Dickens myself, and myself the comedian Mr. Harley, whose humorous songs had been no inconsiderable element in the mirth of the evening.

Five days later he writes: "I finished the number yesterday, and, although I dined with Jeffrey, and was obliged to go to Lord Denman's afterwards (which made me late), have done eight slips of the *Lamplighter* for Mrs. Macrone, this morning. When I have got that off my mind I shall try to go on steadily, fetching up the *Clock* lee-way." The *Lamplighter* was his old farce, which he now turned into a comic tale; and this, with other contributions given him by friends and edited by him as *Pic Nic Papers*, enabled him to help the widow of his old publisher in her straitened means by a gift of £300. He had finished his work of charity before he next wrote of *Barnaby Rudge*, but he was fetching up his lee-way lazily. "I am getting on" (29 April) "very slowly. I want to stick to the story; and the fear of committing myself, because of the impossibiity of trying back or altering a syllable, makes it much harder than it looks. It was too bad of me to give you the trouble of cutting the number, but I knew so well you would do it in the right places. For what Harley would call the 'onward work' I really think I have some famous thoughts." There is an interval of a month before the next allusion. "Solomon's expression" (3 June) "I meant to be one of those strong ones to which strong circumstances give birth in the commonest minds. Deal with it as you like. . . . Say what you please of Gordon " (I had objected to some points in his view of this madman, stated much too favourably as I thought), "he must have been at heart a kind man, and a lover of the despised and rejected, after his own fashion. He lived upon a small income, and always within it; was known to relieve the necessities of many people; exposed in his place the corrupt attempt of a minister to buy him out of Parliament; and did great charities in

Newgate. He always spoke on the people's side, and tried against his muddled brains to expose the profligacy of both parties. He never got anything by his madness, and never sought it. The wildest and most raging attacks of the time, allow him these merits; and not to let him have 'em in their full extent, remembering in what a (politically) wicked time he lived, would lie upon my conscience heavily. The libel he was imprisoned for when he died, was on the queen of France; and the French government interested themselves warmly to procure his release—which I think they might have done, but for Lord Grenville." . . .

This tale was Dickens's first attempt out of the sphere of the life of the day and its actual manners. Begun during the progress of *Oliver Twist*, it had been for some time laid aside; the form it ultimately took had been comprised only partially within its first design; and the story in its finished shape presented strongly a special purpose, the characteristic of all but his very earliest writings. Its scene is laid at the time when the incessant execution of men and women, comparatively innocent, disgraced every part of the country; demoralising thousands, whom it also prepared for the scaffold. In those days the theft of a few rags from a bleaching-ground, or the abstraction of a roll of ribbons from a counter, was visited with the penalty of blood; and such laws brutalised both their ministers and victims. It was the time, too, when a false religious outcry brought with it appalling guilt and misery. Such vices leave more behind them than the first forms assumed, and involve a lesson sufficiently required to justify a writer in dealing with them. There were also others grafted on them. In Barnaby himself it was desired to show what sources of comfort there might be, for the patient and cheerful heart, in even the worst of all human afflictions; and in the hunted life of the outcast father, whose crime had entailed not that affliction only, but other more fearful wretchedness, we have as powerful a picture as any in his writings of the inevitable and unfathomable consequences of sin. . . .

# X

## IN EDINBURGH

## 1841

His first letter from Edinburgh, where he and Mrs. Dickens had taken up quarters at the Royal Hotel on their arrival the previous night, is dated 23 June. "I have been this morning to the Parliament House, and am now introduced (I hope) to everybody in Edinburgh. The hotel is perfectly besieged, and I have been forced to take refuge in a sequestered apartment at the end of a long passage, wherein I write this letter. They talk of 300 at the dinner. We are very well off in point of rooms, having a handsome sitting-room, another next to it for *Clock* purposes, a spacious bedroom, and large dressing-room adjoining. The castle is in front of the windows, and the view noble. There was a supper ready last night which would have been a dinner anywhere." This was his first practical experience of the honours his fame had won for him, and it found him as eager to receive as all were eager to give. Very interesting still, too, are those who took leading part in the celebration; and, in his pleasant sketches of them, there are some once famous and familiar figures not so well known to the present generation. Here, among the first, are Wilson and Robertson.

"The renowned Peter Robertson is a large, portly, full-faced man with a merry eye, and a queer way of looking under his spectacles which is characteristic and pleasant. He seems a very warm-hearted earnest man too, and I felt quite at home with him forthwith. Walking up and down the hall of the courts of law (which was full of advocates, writers to the signet, clerks, and idlers) was a tall, burly, handsome man of eight and fifty, with a gait like O'Connell's, the bluest eye you can imagine, and long hair—longer than mine—falling down in a wild way under the broad brim of his hat. He had on a surtout coat, a blue checked shirt; the collar standing up, and kept in its place with a wisp of black neckerchief; no waistcoat; and a large pocket-handkerchief thrust into his breast, which was all broad and open. At his heels followed a wiry, sharp-eyed, shaggy devil of a terrier, dogging his steps as he went slashing up and down, now with one man beside him, now with another, and now quite alone, but always at a fast, rolling pace, with his head in the air, and his eyes as wide open as he could get them. I guessed it was Wilson, and it was. A bright, clear-complexioned, mountain-looking fellow, he looks as though he had just come down from the Highlands, and had never in his life taken pen in hand. But he has had an attack of paralysis in his right arm, within this month. He winced when I shook hands with him; and once or twice when we were walking up and down, slipped as if he had stumbled on a piece of orange-peel. He is a great fellow to look at, and to talk to; and, if you could divest your mind of the actual Scott, is just the figure you would put in his place." . . .

His next letter was written the morning after the dinner, on Saturday, 26 June. "The great event is over; and being gone, I am a man again. It was the most brilliant affair you can conceive; the completest success possible, from first to last. The room was crammed, and more than seventy applicants for tickets were of necessity refused yesterday. Wilson was ill, but plucked up like a lion, and spoke famously. I send you a paper herewith, but the report is dismal in the extreme. They say there will be a better one—I don't know where or when. Should there be, I will send it to you. I *think* (ahem!) that I spoke rather well. It was an excellent room, and both the subjects (Wilson and Scottish Literature, and the Memory of Wilkie) were good to go upon. There were nearly two hundred ladies present. The place is so contrived that the cross table is raised enormously; much above the heads of people sitting below: and the effect on first coming in (on me, I mean) was rather tremendous. I was quite self-possessed, however, and, notwithstanding the, enthoosemoosy, which was very startling, as cool as a cucumber. I wish to God you had been there, as it is impossible for the 'distinguished guest' to describe the scene. It beat all natur'. . . ."

Here was the close of his letter. "I have been expecting every day to hear from you, and not hearing mean to make this the briefest epistle possible. We start next Sunday (that's to-morrow week). We are going out to Jeffrey's to-day (he is very unwell), and return here to-morrow evening. If I don't find a letter from you when I come back, expect no Lights and Shadows of Scottish Life from your indignant correspondent. Murray the manager made very excellent, tasteful, and gentlemanly mention of Macready, about whom Wilson had been asking me divers questions during dinner." "A hundred thanks for your letter," he writes four days later. "I read it this morning with the greatest pleasure and delight, and answer it with ditto, ditto. Where shall I begin—about my darlings? I am delighted with Charley's precocity. He takes arter his father, he does. God bless them, you can't imagine (*you!* how can you?) how much I long to see them. It makes me quite sorrowful to think of them. . . . Yesterday, sir, the Lord Provost, council, and magistrates voted me by acclamation the freedom of the city, in testimony (I quote the letter just received from ' James Forrest, Lord Provost') 'of the sense entertained by them of your distinguished abilities as an author.' I acknowledged this morning in appropriate terms the honour they had done me, and through me the pursuit to which I was devoted. It *is* handsome, is it not?"

The parchment scroll of the city-freedom, recording the grounds on which it was voted, hung framed in his study to the last, and was one of his valued possessions. Answering some question of mine, he told me further as to the speakers, and gave some amusing glimpses of the party-spirit which still at that time ran high in the capital of the north.

"The men who spoke at the dinner were all the most rising men here, and chiefly at the Bar. They were all, alternately, Whigs and Tories; with some few Radicals, such as Gordon, who gave the memory of Burns. He is Wilson's son-in-law and the Lord Advocate's nephew—a very masterly speaker indeed, who ought to become a distinguished man. Neaves, who gave the other poets, a *little* too lawyer-like for my taste, is a great gun in the courts. Mr. Primrose is Lord Rosebery's son. Adam Black, the publisher as you know. Dr. Alison, a very popular friend of the poor. Robertson you know. Allan you know. Colquhoun is an advocate. All these men were selected for the toasts as being crack speakers, known men, and opposed to each other very strongly in politics. For this reason, the professors and so forth who sat upon the platform about me made no speeches and had none assigned them. I felt it was very remarkable to see such a number of grey-headed men gathered about my brown flowing locks; and it struck most of those who were present very forcibly. The judges, Solicitor-General, Lord Advocate, and so forth, were all here to call, the day after our arrival. The judges never go to public dinners in Scotland. Lord Meadowbank alone broke through the custom, and none of his successors have imitated him. It will give you a good notion of *party* to hear that the Solicitor-General and Lord-Advocate refused to go, though they had previously engaged, unless the croupier or the chairman were a Whig. Both (Wilson and Robertson) were Tories, simply because, Jeffrey excepted, no Whig could be found who was adapted to the office. The solicitor laid strict injunctions on Napier not to go if a Whig were not in office. No Whig was, and he stayed away. I think this is good—bearing in mind that all the old Whigs of Edinburgh were cracking their throats in the room. They give out that they were ill, and the Lord Advocate did actually lie in bed all the afternoon; but this is the real truth, and one of the judges told it to me with great glee. It seems they couldn't quite trust Wilson or Robertson, as they thought; and feared some Tory demonstration. Nothing of the kind took place; and ever since, these men have been the loudest in their praises of the whole affair."

The close of his letter tells us all his engagements, and completes his grateful picture of the hearty Scottish welcome. . . . The narrative of the trip to the Highlands must have a chapter to itself, and its incidents of adventure and comedy. The latter chiefly were due to the guide who accompanied them, a quasi-highlander himself, named a few pages back as Mr. Kindheart, whose real name was Mr. Angus Fletcher, and to whom it hardly needs that I should give other mention than will be supplied by future notices of him as his friend's letters may contain. He had much talent, but too fitful and wayward to concentrate on a settled pursuit; and though at the time we knew him first he had taken up the profession of a sculptor, he abandoned it soon afterwards. His mother, a woman distinguished by many remarkable qualities, lived now in the English lake-country; and it was no fault of hers that her son preferred a wandering life to that of home. His unfitness for an ordinary career was, perhaps, the secret of such liking for him as Dickens had. Fletcher's eccentricity and absurdities, divided often by the thinnest partition from a foolish extravagance, but occasionally clever, and always the genuine though whimsical outgrowth of the life he led, had a curious charm for Dickens. He enjoyed the oddity and humour; tolerated all the rest; and to none more freely than to Kindheart during the next few years, both in Italy and in England, opened his house and hospitality.

## XI

•

### IN THE HIGHLANDS

### 1841

FROM Loch Earn Head Dickens wrote on Monday, 5 July, having reached it, "wet through," at four that afternoon. "Having had a great deal to do in a crowded house on Saturday night at the theatre, we left Edinburgh yesterday morning at half-past seven, and travelled, with Fletcher for our guide, to a place called Stewart's Hotel nine miles further than Callender. We had neglected to order rooms, and were obliged to make a sitting-room of our own bed-chamber; in which my genius for stowing furniture away was of the very greatest service. Fletcher slept in a kennel with three panes of glass in it, which formed part and parcel of a window; the other three panes whereof belonged to a man who slept on the other side of the partition. He told me this morning that he had had a nightmare all night, and had screamed horribly, he knew. The stranger, as you may suppose, hired a gig and went off at full gallop with the first glimpse of daylight. Being very tired (for we had not had more than three hours' sleep on the previous night) we lay till ten this morning; and at half-past eleven went through the Trossachs to Loch Katrine, where I walked from the hotel after tea last night. It is impossible to say what a glorious scene it was. It rained as it never does rain anywhere but here. We conveyed Kate up a rocky pass to go and see the island of the Lady of the Lake, but she gave in after the first five minutes, and we left her, very picturesque and uncomfortable, with Tom" (the servant they had brought with them from Devonshire Terrace) "holding an umbrella over her head, while we climbed on. When we came back, she had gone into the carriage. We were wet through to the skin, and came on in that state four and twenty miles. Fletcher is very good-natured, and of extraordinary use in these outlandish parts. His habit of going into kitchens and bars, disconcerting at Broadstairs, is here of great service. Not expecting us till six, they hadn't lighted our fires when we arrived here; and if you had seen him (with whom the responsibility of the omission rested) running in and out of the sitting-room and the two bedrooms with a great pair of bellows, with which he distractedly blew each of the fires out in turn, you would have died of laughing. He had on his head a great highland cap, on his back a white coat, and cut such a figure as even the Inimitable can't depicter. . . .

"The inns, inside and out, are the queerest places imaginable. From the road, this one," at Loch Earn Head, "looks like a white wall, with windows in it by mistake. We have a good sitting-room though, on the first floor: as large (but not so lofty) as my study. The bedrooms are of that size which renders it impossible for you to move, after you have taken your boots off, without chipping pieces out of your legs. There isn't a basin in the Highlands which will hold my face; not a drawer which will open after you have put your clothes in it; not a water-bottle capacious enough to wet your tooth-brush. The huts are wretched and miserable beyond all description. The food (for those who can pay for it) 'not bad,' as M. would say: oatcake, mutton, hotchpotch, trout from the loch, small beer bottled, marmalade, and whisky. Of the last-named article I have taken about a pint to-day. The weather is what they call 'soft'— which means that the sky is a vast waterspout that never leaves off emptying itself; and the liquor has no more effect than water. . . . (I am going to work to-morrow, and hope before leaving here to write you again. The elections have been sad work indeed. That they should return Sibthorp and reject Bulwer, is, by Heaven, a national disgrace. . . . I don't wonder the devil flew over Lincoln. The people were far too addle-headed, even for him.) . . . I don't bore you with accounts of Ben this and that, and Lochs of all sorts of names, but this is a wonderful region. The way the mists were stalking about to-day, and the clouds lying down upon the hills; the deep glens, the high rocks, the rushing waterfalls, and the roaring rivers down in deep gulfs below; were all stupendous. This house is wedged round by great heights that are lost in the clouds; and the lock, twelve miles long, stretches out this dreary length before the windows. In my next I shall soar to the sublime, perhaps; in this here present writing I confine myself to the ridiculous. But I am always," etc., etc.

His next letter bore the date of "Ballechelish, Friday evening, ninth July, 1841, half-past nine, P.M." and described what we had often longed to see together, the Pass of Glencoe. ". . . I can't go to bed without writing to you from here, though the post will not leave this place until we have left it, and arrived at another. . . . The cold all day has been *intense*, and the rain sometimes most violent. It has been impossible to keep warm, by any means; even whisky failed; the wind was too piercing even for that. One stage of ten miles, over a place called the Black Mount, took us two hours and a half to do; and when we came back to a lone public called the 'King's House,' at the entrance to Glencoe—this was about three o'clock—we were wellnigh frozen. We got a fire directly, and in twenty minutes they served us up some famous kippered salmon, broiled; a broiled fowl; hot mutton, ham and poached eggs; pancakes; oatcakes, wheaten bread; butter; bottled porter; hot water, lump sugar, and whisky; of which we made a very hearty meal. All the way, the road had been among moors and mountains with huge masses of rock, which fell down God knows where, sprinkling the ground in every direction, and giving it the aspect of the burial-place of a race of giants. Now and then we passed a hut or two, with neither window nor chimney, and the smoke of the peat fire rolling out at the door. But there were not six of these dwellings in a dozen miles; and anything so bleak and wild, and mighty in its loneliness, as the whole country, it is impossible to conceive. Glencoe itself is perfectly *terrible*. The pass in an awful place. It is shut in on each side by enormous rocks from which great torrents come rushing down in all directions. In amongst these rocks on one side of the pass (the left as we came) there are scores of glens, high up, which form such haunts as you might imagine yourself wandering in, in the very height of madness of a fever. They will live in my dreams for years— I was going to say as long as I live, and I seriously think so. The very recollection of them makes me shudder. . . . Well, I will not bore you with my impressions of these tremendous wilds, but they really are fearful in their grandeur and amazing solitude. Wales is a mere toy compared with them. . . ."

The impression made upon him by the Pass of Glencoe was not overstated in this letter. It continued with him; and, even where he expected to find nature in her most desolate grandeur, on the dreary waste of an American prairie, his imagination went back with a higher satisfaction to Glencoe. But his experience of it is not yet completely told. The sequel was in a letter of two days later date from "Dalmally, Sunday, July the eleventh, 1841."

"As there was no place of this name in our route, you will be surprised to see it at the head of this present writing. But our being here is a part of such moving accidents by flood and field as will astonish you. If you should happen to have your hat on, take it off, that your hair may stand on end without any interruption. To get from Ballyhoolish (as I am obliged to spell it when Fletcher is not in the way; and he is out at this moment) to Oban, it is necessary to cross two ferries, one of which is an arm of the sea, eight or ten miles broad. Into this ferry-boat, passengers, carriages, horses, and all, get bodily, and are got across by hook or by crook if the weather be reasonably fine. Yesterday morning, however, it blew such a strong gale that the landlord of the inn, where we had paid for horses all the way to Oban (thirty miles), honestly came upstairs just as we were starting, with the money in his hand, and told us it would be impossible to cross. There was nothing to be done but to come back five and thirty miles, through Glencoe and Inverouran, to a place called Tyndrum, whence a road twelve miles long crosses to Dalmally, which is sixteen miles from Inverary. Accordingly we turned back, and in a great storm of wind and rain began to retrace the dreary road we had come the day before. . . . I was not at all ill-pleased to have to come again through that awful Glencoe. If it had been tremendous on the previous day, yesterday it was perfectly horrific. It had rained all night, and was raining then, as it only does in these parts. Through the whole glen, which is ten miles long, torrents were boiling and foaming, and sending up in every direction spray like the smoke of great fires. They were rushing down every hill and mountain side, and tearing like devils across the path, and down into the depths of the rocks. Some of the hills looked as if they were full of silver, and had cracked in a hundred places. Others as if they were frightened, and had broken out into a deadly sweat. In others there was no compromise or division of streams, but one great torrent came roaring down with a deafening noise, and a rushing of water that was quite appalling. Such a *spaet*, in short (that's the country word) has not been known for many years, and the sights and sounds were beyond description. The post-boy was not at all at his ease, and the horses were very much frightened (as well they might be) by the perpetual raging and roaring; one of them started as we came down a steep place, and we were within that much (——) of tumbling over a precipice; just then, too, the drag broke, and we were obliged to go on as we best could without it: getting out every now and then, and hanging on at the back of the carriage to prevent its rolling down too fast, and going Heaven knows where. Well, in this pleasant state of things we came to 'King's House' again, having been four hours doing the sixteen miles. The rumble where Tom sat was by this time so full of water, that he was obliged to borrow a gimlet, and bore holes in the bottom to let it run out. The horses that were to take us on, were out upon the hills, somewhere within ten miles round; and three or four bare-legged fellows went out to look for 'em, while we sat by the fire and tried to dry ourselves. At last we got off again (without the drag and with a broken spring, no smith living within ten miles), and went limping on to Inverouran. In the first three miles we were in a ditch and out again, and lost a horse's shoe. All this time it never once left off raining; and was very windy, very cold, very misty, and most intensely dismal. So we crossed the Black Mount, and came to a place we had passed the day before, where a rapid river runs over a bed of broken rock. Now this river, sir, had a bridge last winter, but the bridge broke down when the thaw came, and has never since been mended; so travellers cross upon a little platform, made of rough deal planks stretching from rock to rock; and carriages and horses ford the water at a certain point. As the platform is the reverse of steady (we had proved this the day before), is very slippery, and affords anything but a pleasant footing, having only a trembling little rail on one side, and on the other nothing between it and the foaming stream, Kate decided to remain in the carriage, and trust herself to the wheels rather than to her feet. Fletcher and I got out, and it was going away, when I advised her, as I had done several times before, to come with us; for I saw that the water was very high, the current being greatly swollen by the rain, and that the postboy had been eyeing it in a very disconcerted manner for the last half-hour. This decided her to come out; and Fletcher, she, Tom, and I, began to cross, while the carriage went about a quarter of a mile down the bank, in search of a shallow place. The platform shook so much that we could only come across two at a time, and then it felt as if it were hung on springs. As to the wind and rain! . . . well, put into one gust all the wind and rain you ever saw and heard, and you'll have some faint notion of it! When we got safely to the opposite bank, there came riding up a wild highlander in a great plaid, whom we recognised as the landlord of the inn, and who, without taking the least notice of us, went dashing on, with the plaid he was wrapped in streaming in the wind, screeching in Gaelic to the postboy on the opposite bank, and making the most frantic gestures you ever saw, in which he was joined by some other wild men on foot, who had come across by a short cut, knee deep in mire and water. As we began to see what this meant, we (that is, Fletcher and I) scrambled on after them, while the boy, horses, and carriage were plunging in the water, which left only the horses' heads and the boy's body visible. By the time we got up to them, the man on horseback and the men on foot were perfectly mad with pantomine; for as to any of their shouts being heard by the boy, the water made such a great noise that they might as well have been dumb. It made me quite sick to think how I should have felt if Kate had been inside. The carriage went round and round like a great stone, the boy was as pale as death, the horses were struggling and plashing and snorting like sea-animals, and we were all roaring to the driver to throw himself off, and let them and the coach go to the devil, when suddenly it came all right (having got into shallow water), and, all tumbling, and dripping and jogging from side to side, climbed up to the dry land. I assure you we looked rather queer, as we wiped our faces and stared at each other in a little cluster round about it. It seemed that the man on horseback had been looking at us through a telescope as we came to the track, and knowing that the place was very dangerous, and seeing that we meant to bring the carriage, had come on at a great gallop to show the driver the only place where he could cross. By the time he came up, the man had taken the water at a wrong place, and in a word was as nearly drowned (with carriage, horses, luggage, and all) as ever man was. Was *this* a good adventure?

"We all went on to the inn—the wild man galloping on first, to get a fire lighted—and there we dined on eggs and bacon, oatcake, and whisky; and changed and dried ourselves. The place was a mere knot of little outhouses, and in one of these there were fifty highlanders *all drunk*. . . . Some were drovers, some pipers, and some workmen engaged to build a hunting-lodge for Lord Breadalbane hard by, who had been driven in by stress of weather. One was a paperhanger. He had come out three days before to paper the inn's best room, a chamber almost large enough to keep a Newfoundland dog in; and, from the first half-hour after his arrival to that moment, had been hopelessly and irreclaimably drunk. They were lying about in all directions: on forms, on the ground, about a loft overhead, round the turf-fire wrapped in plaids, on the tables, and under them. We paid our bill, thanked our host very heartily, gave some money to his children, and after an hour's rest came on again. At ten o'clock at night, we reached this place, and were overjoyed to find quite an English inn, with good beds (those we have slept on, yet, have always been of straw), and every possible comfort. We breakfasted this morning at half-past ten, and at three go on to Inverary to dinner. I believe the very rough part of the journey is over, and I am really glad of it. Kate sends all kinds of regards. I shall hope to find a letter from you at Inverary when the post reaches there, to-morrow. I wrote to Oban yesterday, desiring the post-office keeper to send any he might have for us, over to that place. Love to Mac." . . .

## XII

### AGAIN AT BROADSTAIRS

### 1841

SOON after his return [from Scotland], in August, he sent me some rhymed squibs as his anonymous contribution to the fight the Liberals were then making, against what was believed to be intended by the return to office of the Tories; ignorant as we were how much wiser than his party the statesman then at the head of it was, or how greatly what we all most desired would be advanced by the very success that had been most disheartening. There will be no harm now in giving extracts from one or two of these pieces, which will sufficiently show the tone of all of them, and with what relish they were written. A celebrated address had been delivered at Tamworth, in which the orator, though in those days big with nothing much larger or graver than a sliding-scale, had made a mystery of it as an infallible specific for public affairs, which he refused to prescribe till regularly called in; and this was good-humouredly laughed at in a quack-doctor's proclamation, to the tune of "A Cobbler there was."

> He's a famous corn-doctor, of wonderful skill—
> No cutting, no rooting up, purging, or pill—
> You're merely to take, 'stead of walking or riding,
> The light schoolboy exercise, innocent sliding.
> Tol de rol, etc.

> There's no advice gratis. If high ladies send
> His legitimate fee, he's their soft-spoken friend.
> At the great public counter, with one hand behind him
> And one in his waistcoat, they're certain to find him.
> Tol de rol, etc.

He has only to add he's the true Doctor Flam,
All others being purely fictitious and sham;
The house is a large one, tall, slated, and white,
With a lobby, and lights in the passage at night.
                              Tol de rol, diddle doll, etc.


\*           \*           \*


The last of these rhymes I will give entire. This had no touch of
personal satire in it, and he would himself, for that reason, have least
objected to its revival. Thus ran his new version of "The Fine Old
English Gentleman, to be said or sung at all Conservative dinners":

I'll sing you a new ballad, and I'll warrant it first-rate,
Of the days of that old gentleman who had that old estate;
When they spent the public money at a bountiful old rate
On ev'ry mistress, pimp, and scamp, at ev'ry noble gate,
            In the fine old English Tory times;
            Soon may they come again!


The good old laws were garnished well with gibbets, whips, and chains
With fine old English penalties, and fine old English pains,
With rebel heads and seas of blood once hot in rebel veins:
For all these things were requisite to guard the rich old gains
            Of the fine old English Tory times;
            Soon may they come again!


This brave old code, like Argus, had a hundred watchful eyes,
And ev'ry English peasant had his good old English spies,
To tempt his starving discontent with fine old English lies,
Then call the good old Yeomanry to stop his peevish cries,
            In the fine old English Tory times;
            Soon may they come again.


The good old times for cutting throats that cried out in their need,
The good old times for hunting men who held their fathers' creed,
The good old times when William Pitt, as all good men agreed,
Came down direct from Paradise at more than railroad speed. . . .
            Oh the fine old English Tory times;
            When will they come again!


In those rare days, the press was seldom known to snarl or bark,
But sweetly sang of men in pow'r, like any tuneful lark;
Grave judges, too, to all their evil deeds were in the dark;
And not a man in twenty score knew how to make his mark.
            Oh the fine old English Tory times;
            Soon may they come again! . . .


But Tolerance, though slow in flight, is strong-wing'd in the main;
That night must come on these fine days, in course of time was plain;
The pure old spirit struggled, but its struggles were in vain;
A nation's grip was on it, and it died in choking pain,
            With the fine old English Tory days,
            All of the olden time.

The bright old day now dawns again; the cry runs through the land,
In England there shall be—dear bread! In Ireland—sword and brand!
And poverty, and ignorance, shall swell the rich and grand,
So, rally round the rulers with the gentle iron hand,
      Of the fine old English Tory days;
      Hail to the coming time!

    *             *            *

Small causes of displeasure had been growing out of the *Clock*, and were almost unavoidably incident to the position in which he found himself respecting it. Its discontinuance had become necessary, the strain upon himself being too great without the help from others which experience had shown to be impracticable; but I thought he had not met the difficulty wisely by undertaking, which already he had done, to begin a new story so early as the following March. On his arrival therefore we decided on another plan, with which we went armed that Saturday afternoon to his publishers; and of which the result will be best told by himself. He had returned to Broadstairs the following morning, and next day (Monday, 23 August) he wrote to me in very enthusiastic terms of the share I had taken in what he calls "the development on Saturday afternoon; when I thought Chapman very manly and sensible, Hall morally and physically feeble though perfectly well-intentioned, and both the statement and reception of the project quite triumphant. Didn't you think so too?" A fortnight later, Tuesday, 7 September, the agreement was signed in my chambers, and its terms were to the effect following. The *Clock* was to cease with the close of *Barnaby Rudge*, the respective ownerships continuing as provided; and the new work in twenty numbers, similar to those of *Pickwick* and *Nickleby*, was not to begin until after an interval of twelve months, in November 1842. During its publication he was to receive £200 monthly, to be accounted as part of the expenses; for all which, and all risks incident, the publishers made themselves responsible, under conditions the same as in the *Clock* agreement; except that, out of the profits of each number, they were to have only a fourth, three-fourths going to him, and this arrangement was to hold good until the termination of six months from the completed book, when, upon payment to him of a fourth of the value of all existing stock, they were to have half the future interest. During the twelve months' interval before the book began, he was to be paid £150 each month; but this was to be drawn from his three-fourths of the profits, and in no way to interfere with the monthly payments of £200 while the publication was going on. Such was the "project," excepting only a provision to be mentioned hereafter against the improbable event of the profits being inadequate to the repayment: and some fear as to the use he was likely to make of the leisure it afforded him seemed to me its only drawback.

That this fear was not ill-founded appears at the close of his next letter. "There's no news" (13 September) "since my last. We are going to dine with Rogers to-day, and with Lady Essex, who is also here. Rogers is much pleased with Lord Ashley, who was offered by Peel a post in the government, but resolutely refused to take office unless Peel pledged himself to factory improvement. Peel 'hadn't made up his mind'; and Lord Ashley was deaf to all other inducements, though they must have been very tempting. Much do I honour him for it. I am in an exquisitely lazy state, bathing, walking, reading, lying in the sun, doing everything but working. This frame of mind is super-induced by the prospect of rest, and the promising arrangements which I owe to you. I am still haunted by visions of America, night and day. To miss this opportunity would be a sad thing. Kate cries dismally if I mention the subject. But, God willing, I think it *must* be managed somehow !"

# BOOK THIRD

## AMERICA

1841—2. ÆT. 29–30

419

## EVE OF THE VISIT

### 1841

THE notion of America was in his mind, as we have seen, when he first projected the *Clock*, and a very hearty letter from Washington Irving about little Nell and the *Curiosity Shop*, expressing the delight with his writings and the yearnings for himself which had indeed been pouring in upon him for some time from every part of the States, had very strongly revived it. . . . Upon his return from Scotland it began to take shape as a thing that somehow or other, at no very distant date, *must be*; and at last, near the end of a letter filled with many unimportant things, the announcement, doubly underlined, came to me.

The decision once taken, he was in his usual fever until its difficulties were disposed of. The objections to separation from the children led at first to the notion of taking them, but this was as quickly abandoned; and what remained to be overcome yielded readily to the kind offices of Macready, the offer of whose home to the little ones during the time of absence, though not accepted to the full extent, gave yet the assurance needed to quiet natural apprehensions. All this, including an arrangement for publication of such notes as might occur to him on the journey, took but a few days; and I was reading in my chambers a letter he had written the previous day from Broadstairs, when a note from him reached me, written that mornng in London, to tell me he was on his way to take share of my breakfast. He had come overland by Canterbury after posting his first letter; had seen Macready the previous night; and had completed some part of the arrangements. This mode of rapid procedure was characteristic of him at all similar times, and will appear in the few following extracts from his letters.

"Now" (19 September) "to astonish you. After balancing, considering, and weighing the matter in every point of view, I HAVE MADE UP MY MIND (WITH GOD'S LEAVE) TO GO TO AMERICA—AND TO START AS SOON AFTER CHRISTMAS AS IT WILL BE SAFE TO GO." Further information was promised immediately; and a request followed, characteristic as any he could have added to his design of travelling so far away, that we should visit once more together the scenes of his boyhood. "On the ninth of October we leave here. It's a Saturday.

If it should be fine dry weather, or anything like it, will you meet us at Rochester, and stop there two or three days to see all the lions in the surrounding country? Think of this. . . .

## II

His first "American" letter was written as soon as he got sight of earth again, from the banks of Newfoundland, on Monday, 17 January, the fourteenth day from their departure: even then so far from Halifax that they could not expect to make it before Wednesday night, or to reach Boston until Saturday or Sunday. They had not been fortunate in the passage. During the whole voyage, the weather had been unprecedentedly bad, the wind for the most part dead against them, the wet intolerable, the sea horribly disturbed, the days dark, and the nights fearful. On the previous Monday night it had blown a hurricane, beginning at five in the afternoon and raging all night. His description of the storm is published, and the peculiarities of a steamer's behaviour in such circumstances are hit off as if he had been all his life a sailor. . . .

He stood out against sickness only for the day following that on which they sailed. For the three following days he kept his bed; miserable enough; and had not, until the eighth day of the voyage, six days before the date of his letter, been able to get to work at the dinner-table. What he then observed of his fellow-travellers, and had to tell of their life on board, has been set forth in his *Notes* with delightful humour; but in its first freshness I received it in this letter, and some whimsical passages, then suppressed, there will be no harm in printing now.

"We have 86 passengers; and such a strange collection of beasts never was got together upon the sea, since the days of the Ark. "I have established myself, from the first in the ladies' cabin—you remember it? I'll describe its other occupants, and our way of passing the time, to you.

"First, for the occupants. Kate and I, and Anne—when she is out of bed, which is not often. A queer little Scotch body, a Mrs. P——,* whose husband is a silversmith in New York. He married her at Glasgow three years ago, and bolted the day after the wedding; being

---

* The initials used here are in no case those of the real names, being employed in every case for the express purpose of disguising the names. Generally the remark is applicable to all initials used in the letters printed in the course of this work. The exceptions are unimportant.

(which he had not told her) heavily in debt. Since then she has been living with her mother; and she is now going out under the protection of a male cousin, to give him a year's trial. If she is not comfortable at the expiration of that time, she means to go back to Scotland again. A Mrs. B——, about twenty years old, whose husband is on board with her. He is a young Englishman domiciled in New York, and by trade (as well as I can make out) a woollen-draper. They have been married a fortnight. A Mr. and Mrs. C——, marvellously fond of each other, complete the catalogue. Mrs. C——, I have settled, is a publican's daughter, and Mr. C—— is running away with her, the till, the time-piece off the bar mantel-shelf, the mother's gold watch from the pocket at the head of the bed, and other miscellaneous property. The women are all pretty; unusually pretty. I never saw such good faces together, anywhere." . . .

The news that excited them from day to day, too, of which little more than a hint appears in the *Notes*, is worth giving as originally written.

"As for news, we have more of that than you would think for. One man lost fourteen pounds at *vingt-un* in the saloon yesterday, or another got drunk before dinner was over, or another was blinded with lobster sauce spilt over him by the steward, or another had a fall on deck and fainted. The ship's cook was drunk yesterday morning (having got at some salt-water-damaged whisky), and the captain ordered the boatswain to play upon him the hose of the fire-engine until he roared for mercy—which he didn't get; for he was sentenced to look out, for four hours at a stretch for four nights running, without a greatcoat, and to have his grog stopped. Four dozen plates were broken at dinner. One steward fell down the cabin stairs with a round of beef, and injured his foot severely. Another steward fell down after him, and cut his eye open. The baker's taken ill: so is the pastry-cook. A new man, sick to death, has been required to fill the place of the latter officer, and has been dragged out of bed and propped up in a little house upon deck, between two casks, and ordered (the captain standing over him) to make and roll out pie-crust; which he protests, with tears in his eyes, it is death to him in his bilious state to look at. Twelve dozen of bottled porter has got loose upon deck, and the bottles are rolling about distractedly, overhead. Lord Mulgrave (a handsome fellow, by the by, to look at, and nothing but a good 'un to go) laid a wager with twenty-five other men last night, whose berths, like his, are in the fore-cabin which can only be got at by crossing the deck, that he would reach his cabin first. Watches were set by the captain's, and they sallied forth, wrapped up in coats and storm caps. The sea broke over the ship so violently, that they were *five and twenty minutes* holding on by the hand-rail at the starboard paddle-box, drenched to the skin by every wave, and not daring to go on or come back, lest they should be washed overboard." News! A dozen murders in town wouldn't interest us half as much." . . .

The next day's landing at Halifax, and delivery of the mails, are sketched in the *Notes;* but not his personal part in what followed. "Then, sir, comes a breathless man who has been already into the ship and out again, shouting my name as he tears along. I stop, arm in arm with the little doctor whom I have taken ashore for oysters. The breathless man introduces himself as The Speaker of the House of Assembly; *will* drag me away to his house; and *will* have a carriage and his wife sent down for Kate, who is laid up with a hideously swollen face. Then he drags me up to the Governor's house (Lord Falkland is the Governor), and then Heaven knows where; concluding with both Houses of Parliament, which happen to meet for the session that very day, and are opened by a mock speech from the throne delivered by the Governor, with one of Lord Grey's sons for his aide-de-camp, and a great host of officers about him. I wish you could have seen the crowds cheering the Inimitable in the streets. I wish you could have seen judges, law-officers, bishops, and law-makers welcoming the Inimitable. I wish you could have seen the Inimitable shown to a great elbow-chair by the Speaker's throne, and sitting alone in the middle of the floor of the House of Commons, the observed of all observers, listening with exemplary gravity to the queerest speaking possible, and breaking in spite of himself into a smile as he thought of this commencement to the Thousand and One stories in reserve for home and Lincoln's Inn Fields and Jack Straw's Castle.—Ah, Forster! when I *do* come back again!——" . . .

What further he had to say of that week's experience, finds its first public utterance here. "How can I tell you," he continues, "what has happened since that first day? How can I give you the faintest notion of my reception here; of the crowds that pour in and out of the whole day; of the people that line the streets when I go out; of the cheering when I went to the theatre; of the copies of verses, letters of congratulation, welcomes of all kinds, balls, dinners, assemblies without end ? There is to be a public dinner to me here in Boston, next Tuesday, and great dissatisfaction has been given to the many by the high price (three pounds sterling each) of the tickets. There is to be a ball next Monday week at New York, and 150 names appear on the list of the committee. There is to be a dinner in the same place, in the same week, to which I have had an invitation with every known name in America appended to it. But what can I tell you about any of these things which will give you the slightest notion of the enthusiastic greeting they give me, or the cry that runs through the whole country ! I have had deputations from the Far West, who have come from more than two thousand miles distance: from the lakes, the rivers, the backwoods, the log-houses, the cities, factories, villages, and towns. Authorities from nearly all the States have written to me. I have heard from the universities, congress, senate, and bodies, public and private, of every sort and kind. 'It is no nonsense, and no common feeling,' wrote Dr. Channing to me yesterday. It is all heart. There never was, and never will be, such a triumph.' And it is a good thing, is it not, . . . to find those fancies it has given me and you the greatest satisfaction to think of, at the core of it all? It makes my heart quieter, and me a more retiring, sober, tranquil man to watch the effect of those thoughts in all this noise and hurry, even than if I sat, pen in hand, to put them down for the first time. I feel, in the best aspects of this welcome, something of the presence and influence of that spirit which directs my life, and through a heavy sorrow has pointed upward with unchanging finger for more than four years past. And if I know my heart, not twenty times this praise would move me to an act of folly. . . ."

The last addition made to this letter, from which many most vivid pages of the *Notes* (among them the bright quaint picture of Boston streets) were taken with small alteration, bore date 29 January. "I hardly know what to add to all this long and unconnected history. Dana, the author of that *Two Years before the Mast*" (a book which I had praised much to him, thinking it like De Foe), "is a very nice fellow indeed; and in appearance not at all the man you would expect. He is short, mild-looking, and has a care-worn face. His father is exactly like George Cruikshank after a night's jollity—only shorter. The professors at the Cambridge University, Longfellow, Felton, Jared Sparks, are noble fellows. . . ."

Unmistakably to be seen, in this earliest of his letters, is the quite fresh and unalloyed impression first received by him at this memorable visit; and it is due, as well to himself as to the country which welcomed him, that this should be considered independently of any modification or change it afterwards underwent. Of the fervency and universality of the welcome there could be no doubt, and as little that it sprang from feelings honourable both to giver and receiver. The sources of Dickens's popularity in England were in truth multiplied many-fold in America. The hearty, cordial, and humane side of his genius had fascinated them quite as much; but there was also something beyond this. The cheerful temper that had given new beauty to the commonest forms of life, the abounding humour which had added largely to all innocent enjoyment, the honourable and in those days rare distinction of America which left no home in the Union inaccessible to such advantages, had made Dickens the object everywhere of grateful admiration, for the most part of personal affection. But even this was not all. I do not say it either to lessen or increase the value of the tribute, but to express simply what it was; and there cannot be a question that the young English author, whom by his language the Americans claimed equally for their own, was almost universally regarded by them as a kind of embodied protest against what was believed to be worst in the institutions of England, depressing and overshadowing in a social sense, and adverse to purely intellectual influences. In all their newspapers of every grade at the time, the feeling of triumph over the Mother Country in this particular is predominant. You worship titles, they said, and military heroes, and millionaires, and we of the New World want to show you, by extending the kind of homage that the Old World reserves for kings and conquerors to a young man with nothing to distinguish him but his heart and his genius, what it is we think in these parts worthier of honour than birth or wealth, a title or a sword. Well, there was something in this, too, apart from a mere crowing over the Mother Country. The Americans had honestly more than a common share in the triumphs of a genius, which in more than one sense had made the deserts and wildernesses of life to blossom like the rose. They were entitled to select for a welcome, as emphatic as they might please to render it, the writer who pre-eminently in his genera-tion had busied himself to "detect and save," in human creatures, such sparks of virtue as misery or vice had not availed to extinguish; to discover what is beautiful and comely, under what commonly passes for the ungainly and deformed; to draw happiness and hope-fulness from despair itself; and, above all, so to have made known to his own countrymen the wants and sufferings of the poor, the ignorant, and the neglected, that they could be left in absolute neglect no more. . . .

## III

### SECOND IMPRESSIONS

#### 1842

His second letter, radiant with the same kindly warmth that gave always charm to his genius, was dated from the Carlton Hotel, New York, on 14 February, but its only allusion of any public interest was to the beginning of his agitation of the question of international copyright. He went to America with no express intention of starting this question in any way; and certainly with no belief that such remark upon it as a person in his position could alone be expected to make, would be resented strongly by any sections of the American people. But he was not long left in doubt on this head. He had spoken upon it twice publicly, "to the great indignation of some of the editors here, who are attacking me for so doing, right and left." On the other hand all the best men had assured him, that, if only at once followed up in England, the blow struck might bring about a change in the law; and, yielding to the agreeable delusion that the best men could be a match for the worst in such a matter, he urged me to enlist on his side what force was obtainable, and in particular, as he had made Scott's claim his war-cry, to bring Lockhart into the field. I could not do much, but what I could was done. . . .

"Carlton House, New York: Thursday, February Seventeenth, 1842. . . . As there is a sailing-packet from here to England to-morrow which is warranted (by the owners) to be a marvellous fast sailer, and as it appears most probable that she will reach home (I write the word with a pang) before the Cunard steamer of next month, I indite this letter. And lest this letter should reach you before another letter which I despatched from here last Monday, let me say in the first place that I *did* despatch a brief epistle to you on that day, together with a newspaper, and a pamphlet touching the Boz ball; and that I put in the post-office at Boston another newspaper for you containing an account of the dinner, which was just about to come off, you remember, when I wrote to you from that city.

"It was a most superb affair; and the speaking *admirable*. Indeed, the general talent for public speaking here, is one of the most striking of the things that force themselves upon an Englishman's notice. As every man looks on to being a member of Congress, every man prepares himself for it; and the result is quite surprising. You will observe one odd custom—the drinking of sentiments. It is quite extinct with us, but here everybody is expected to be prepared with an epigram as a matter of course. . . .

Washington Irving was chairman of this dinner, and having from the first a dread that he should break down in his speech, the catastrophe came accordingly. Near him sat the Cambridge professor who had come with Dickens by boat from Newhaven, with whom already a warm friendship had been formed that lasted for life, and who has pleasantly sketched what happened. Mr. Felton saw Irving constantly in the interval of preparation, and could not but despond at his daily iterated foreboding of "I shall certainly break down": though, besides the real dread, there was a sly humour which heightened its whimsical horror with an irresistible drollery. But the professor plucked up hope a little when the night came, and he saw that Irving had laid under his plate the manuscript of his speech. During dinner, nevertheless, his old foreboding cry was still heard, and "at last the moment arrived; Mr. Irving rose; and the deafening and long-continued applause by no means lessened his apprehension. He began in his pleasant voice; got through two or three sentences pretty easily, but in the next hesitated; and, after one or two attempts to go on, gave it up, with a graceful allusion to the tournament and the troop of knights all armed and eager for the fray; and ended with the toast CHARLES DICKENS, THE GUEST OF THE NATION. 'There!' said he, as he resumed his seat amid applause as great as had greeted his rising, 'There! I told you I should break down, and I've done it!' " He was in London a few months later, on his way to Spain; and I heard Thomas Moore describe at Rogers's table the difficulty there had been to overcome his reluctance, because of this breakdown, to go to the dinner of the Literary Fund on the occasion of Prince Albert's presiding. "However," said Moore, "I told him only to attempt a few words, and I suggested what they should be, and he said he'd never thought of anything so easy, and he went and did famously." I knew very well, as I listened, that this had *not* been the result; but as the distinguished American had found himself, on this second occasion, not among orators as in New York, but among men as unable as himself to speak in public, and equally able to do better things, he was doubtless more reconciled to his own failure. I have been led to this digression by Dickens's silence on his friend's breakdown. He had so great a love for Irving that it was painful to speak of him as at any disadvantage, and of the New York dinner he wrote only in its connection with his own copyright speeches. . . .

"We mean to return home in a packet-ship—not a steamer. Her name is the *George Washington*, and she will sail from here, for Liverpool, on the seventh of June. At that season of the year, they are seldom more than three weeks making the voyage; and I never will trust myself upon the wide ocean, if it please Heaven, in a steamer again. When I tell you all that I observed on board that *Britannia*, I shall astonish you. Meanwhile, consider two of their dangers. First, that if the funnel were blown overboard, the vessel must instantly be on fire, from stem to stern: to comprehend which consequence, you have only to understand that the funnel is more than 40 feet high, and that at night you see the solid fire two or three feet above its top. Imagine this swept down by a strong wind, and picture to yourself the amount of flame on deck; and that a strong wind is likely to sweep it down you soon learn, from the precautions taken to keep it up in a storm, when it is the first thing thought of. Secondly, each of these boats consumes between London and Halifax 700 tons of coals; and it is pretty clear, from this enormous difference of weight in a ship of only 1200 tons burden in all, that she must be either too heavy when she comes out of port, or too light when she goes in. The daily difference in her rolling, as she burns the coals out, is something absolutely fearful. Add to all this, that by day and night she is full of fire and people, that she has no boats, and that the struggling of that enormous machinery in a heavy sea seems as though it would rend her into fragments—and you may have a pretty considerable damned good sort of a feeble notion that it don't fit nohow; and that it an't calculated to make you smart, overmuch; and that you don't feel special bright; and by no means first-rate; and not at all tonguey (or disposed for conversation); and that however rowdy you may be by natur', it does use you up com-plete, and that's a fact; and makes you quake considerable, and disposed toe damn the ĕngīne!—All of which phrases, I beg to add, are pure Americanisms of the first water.

"When we reach Baltimore, we are in the regions of slavery. It exists there, in its least shocking and most mitigated form; but there it is. They whisper, here (they dare only whisper, you know, and that below their breaths), that on that place, and all through the South, there is a dull gloomy cloud on which the very word seems written. I shall be able to say, one of these days, that I accepted no public mark of respect in any place where slavery was;—and that's something.

"The ladies of America are decidedly and unquestionably beautiful. Their complexions are not so good as those of Englishwomen; their beauty does not last so long; and their figures are very inferior. But they are most beautiful. I still reserve my opinion of the national character—just whispering that I tremble for a Radical coming here, unless he is a Radical on principle, by reason and reflection, and from the sense of right. I fear that if he were anything else, he would return home a Tory. . . ."

A brief letter, sent me next day by the minister's bag, was in effect a postscript; and expressed still more strongly the apprehensions his voyage out had impressed him with, and which, though he afterwards saw reason greatly to modify them, were not so strange at the time as they appear to us now.

"Carlton House, New York, February twenty-eighth, 1842. . . . The *Caledonia*, I grieve and regret to say, has not arrived. If she left England to her time, she has been four and twenty days at sea. There is no news of her; and on the nights of the fourteenth and eighteenth it blew a terrible gale, which almost justifies the worst suspicions. For myself, I have hardly any hope of her; having seen enough, in our passage out to convince me that steaming across the ocean in heavy weather is as yet an experiment of the utmost hazard.

"As it was supposed that there would be no steamer whatever for England this month (since in ordinary course the *Caledonia* would have returned with the mails on the 2nd of March) I hastily got the letters ready yesterday and sent them by the *Garrick;* which may perhaps be three weeks out, but is not very likely to be longer. But belonging to the Cunard Company is a boat called the *Unicorn*, which in the summer time plies up the St. Lawrence, and brings passengers from Canada to join the British and North American steamers at Halifax. In the winter she lies at the last-mentioned place; from which news has come this morning that they have sent her on to Boston for the mails; and, rather than interrupt the communication, mean to dispatch her to England in lieu of the poor *Caledonia*. This in itself, by the way, is a daring deed; for she was originally built to run between Liverpool and Glasgow, and is no more designed for the Atlantic than a Calais packet-boat; though she once crossed it, in the summer season.

"You may judge, therefore, what the owners, think of the probability of the *Caledonia's* arrival. How slight an alteration in our plans would have made us passengers on board of her!

"It would be difficult to tell you, my dear fellow, what an impression this has made upon our minds, or with what intense anxiety and suspense we have been waiting for your letters from home. We were to have gone South to-day, but linger here until to-morrow afternoon (having sent the secretary and luggage forward) for one more chance of news. Love to dear Macready, and to dear Mac, and every one we care for. It's useless to speak of the dear children. It seems now as though we should never hear of them. . . .

"P.S. Washington Irving is a *great* fellow. We have laughed most heartily together. He is just the man he ought to be. So is Doctor Channing, with whom I have had an interesting correspondence since I saw him last at Boston. Halleck is a merry little man. Bryant a sad one, and very reserved. Washington Allston the painter (who wrote *Monaldi*) is a fine specimen of a glorious old genius. Longfellow, whose volume of poems I have got for you, is a frank accomplished man as well as a fine writer, and will be in town 'next fall.' Tell Macready that I suspect prices here must have rather altered since his time. I paid our fortnight's bill here, last night. We have dined out every day (except when I was laid up with a sore throat), and only had in all four bottles of wine. The bill was £70 English!!!

"You will see, by my other letter, how we have been fêted and feasted; and how there is war to the knife about the international copyright; and how I *will* speak about it, and decline to be put down. . . .

"Oh for news from home! I think of your letters so full of heart and friendship, with perhaps a little scrawl of Charley's or Mamey's, lying at the bottom of the deep sea; and am as full of sorrow as if they had once been living creatures.—Well! they *may* come, yet. . . ."

IV

PHILADELPHIA AND THE SOUTH

1842

DICKENS's next letter was begun in the "United States Hotel, Philadelphia," and bore date "Sunday, sixth March, 1842." It treated of much dealt with afterwards at greater length in the *Notes*, but the freshness and vivacity of the first impressions in it have surprised me. I do not, however, print any passage here which has not its own interest independently of anything contained in that book. The rule will be continued, as in the portions of letters already given, if not transcribing anything before printed, or anything having even but a near resemblance to descriptions that appear in the *Notes*.

". . . I have often asked Americans in London which were the better railroads—ours or theirs? They have taken time for reflection, and generally replied, on mature consideration, that they rather thought we excelled; in respect of the punctuality with which we arrived at our stations, and the smoothness of our travelling. I wish you could see what an American railroad is, in some parts where I now have seen them. I won't say I wish you could feel what it is, because that would be an unchristian and savage aspiration. It is never enclosed, or warded off. You walk down the main street of a large town: and, slap-dash, headlong, pell-mell, down the middle of the street; with pigs burrowing, and boys flying kites and playing marbles, and men smoking, and women talking, and children crawling, close to the very rails; there comes tearing along a mad locomotive with its train of cars, scattering a red-hot shower of sparks (from its *wood* fire) in all directions; screeching, hissing, yelling, and panting; and nobody one atom more concerned than if it were a hundred miles away. You cross a turnpike-road; and there is no gate, no policeman, no signal—nothing to keep the wayfarer or quiet traveller out of the way, but a wooden arch on which is written in great letters "Look out for the locomotive." And if any man, woman, or child, don't look out, why it's his or her fault, and there's an end of it.

"The cars are like very shabby omnibuses—only larger; holding sixty or seventy people. The seats, instead of being placed long-ways, are put crosswise, back to front. Each holds two. There is a long row of these on each side of the caravan, and a narrow passage up the centre. The windows are usually all closed, and there is very often, in addition, a hot, close, most intolerable charcoal stove in a red-hot glow. The heat and closeness are quite insupportable. But this is the characteristic of all American houses, of all the public institutions, chapels, theatres, and prisons. From the constant use of the hard anthracite coal in these beastly furnaces, a perfectly new class of diseases is springing up in the country. Their effect upon an Englishman is briefly told. He is always very sick and very faint; and has an intolerable headache, morning, noon, and night.

"In the ladies' car, there is no smoking of tobacco allowed. All gentlemen who have ladies with them, sit in this car; and it is usually very full. Before it, is the gentlemen's car; which is something narrower. As I had a window close to me yesterday which commanded this gentleman's car, I looked at it pretty often, perforce. The flashes of saliva flew so perpetually and incessantly out of the windows all the way, that it looked as though they were ripping open feather-beds inside, and letting the wind dispose of the feathers. But this spitting is universal. In the courts of law, the judge has his spittoon on the bench, the counsel have theirs, the witness has his, the prisoner his, and the crier his. The jury are accommodated at the rate of three men to a spittoon (or spit-box as they call it here); and the spectators in the gallery are provided for, as so many men who in the course of nature expectorate without cessation. There are spit-boxes in every steamboat, bar-room, public dining-room, house or office, and place of general resort, no matter what it be. In the hospitals, the students are requested, by placards, to use the boxes provided for them, and not to spit upon the stairs. I have twice seen gentlemen, at evening parties in New York, turn aside when they were not engaged in conversation, and spit upon the drawing-room carpet. And in every bar-room and hotel passage the stone floor looks as if it were paved with open oysters—from the quantity of this kind of deposit which tessellates it all over. . . ."

"WASHINGTON, *Sunday, March the Thirteenth*, 1842.

"I must tell you a slight experience I had in Philadelphia. My rooms had been ordered for a week, but, in consequence of Kate's illness, only Mr. Q—— and the luggage had gone on. Mr. Q—— always lives at the table d'hôte, so that while we were in New York our rooms were empty. The landlord not only charged me half the full rent for the time during which the rooms were reserved for us (which was quite right), but charged me also *for board for myself and Kate and Anne, at the rate of nine dollars per day* for the same period, when we were actually living, at the same expense, in New York!!! I *did* remonstrate upon this head; but was coolly told it was the custom (which I have since been assured is a lie), and had nothing for it but to pay the amount. What else could I do? I was going away by the steamboat at five o'clock in the morning; and the landlord knew perfectly well that my disputing an item of his bill would draw down upon me the sacred wrath of the newspapers, which would one and all demand in capitals if THIS was the gratitude of the man whom America had received as she had never received any other man but La Fayette?

"I went last Tuesday to the Eastern Penitentiary near Philadelphia, which is the only prison in the States, or I believe, in the world, on the principle of hopeless, strict, and unrelaxed solitary confinement, during the whole term of the sentence. It is wonderfully kept, but a most dreadful, fearful place. The inspectors, immediately on my arrival in Philadelphia, invited me to pass the day in the jail, and to dine with them when I had finished my inspection, that they might hear my opinion of the system. Accordingly I passed the whole day in going from cell to cell, and conversing with the prisoners. Every facility was given me, and no constraint whatever imposed upon any man's free speech. If I were to write you a letter of twenty sheets, I could not tell you this one day's work; so I will reserve it until that happy time when we shall sit round the table at Jack Straw's—you, and I, and Mac—and go over my diary. I never shall be able to dismiss from my mind the impressions of that day. Making notes of them, as I have done, is an absurdity, for they are written, beyond all power of erasure, in my brain. I saw men who had been there five years, six years, eleven years, two years, two months, two days; some whose term was nearly over, and some whose term had only just begun. Women too, under the same variety of circumstances. Every prisoner who comes into the jail, comes at night; is put into a bath, and dressed in the prison garb; and then a black hood is drawn over his face and head, and he is led to the cell from which he never stirs again until his whole period of confinement has expired. I looked at some of them with the same awe as I should have looked at men who had been buried alive, and dug up again.

"We dined in the jail: and I told them after dinner how much the sight had affected me, and what an awful punishment it was. I dwelt upon this; for, although the inspectors are extremely kind and benevolent men, I question whether they are sufficiently acquainted with the human mind to know what it is they are doing. Indeed, I am sure they do not know. I bore testimony, as every one who sees it must, to the admirable government of the institution (Stanfield is the keeper: grown a little younger, that's all); and added that nothing could justify such a punishment, but its working a reformation in the prisoners. That for short terms—say two years for the maximum —I conceived, especially after what they had told me of its good effects in certain cases, it might perhaps be highly beneficial; but that, carried to so great an extent, I thought it cruel and unjustifiable; and further, that their sentences for small offences were very rigorous, not to say savage. All this they took like men who were really anxious to have one's free opinion, and to do right. And we were very much pleased with each other, and parted in the friendliest way . . .

"I said I wouldn't write anything more concerning the American people, for two months. Second thoughts are best. I shall not change, and may as well speak out—to *you*. They are friendly, earnest, hospitable, kind, frank, very often accomplished, far less prejudiced than you would suppose, warm-hearted, fervent, and enthusiastic. They are chivalrous in their universal politeness to women, courteous, obliging, disinterested; and, when they conceive a perfect affection for a man (as I may venture to say of myself), entirely devoted to him. I have received thousands of people of all ranks and grades, and have never once been asked an offensive or unpolite question—except by Englishmen, who, when they have been 'located' here for some years, are worse than the devil in his blackest painting. The State is a parent to its people: has a parental care and watch over all poor children, women labouring of child, sick persons, and captives. The common men render you assistance in the streets, and would revolt from the offer of a piece of money. The desire to oblige is universal; and I have never once travelled in a public conveyance, without making some generous acquaintance whom I have been sorry to part from, and who has in many cases come on miles, to see us again. But I don't like the country. I would not live here on any consideration. It goes against the grain with me. It would with you. I think it impossible, utterly impossible, for any Englishman to live here and be happy. I have a confidence that I must be right, because I have everything, God knows, to lead me to the opposite conclusion: and yet I cannot resist coming to this one. As to the causes, they are too many to enter upon here. . . ."

The reader of the *American Notes* will remember the humorous description of the night steamer on the Potomac, and of the black driver over the Virginia Road. Both were in this letter; which, after three days, he resumed "At Washington again, Monday, March the twenty-first.

"We had intended to go to Baltimore from Richmond, by a place called Norfolk: but one of the boats being under repair, I found we should probably be detained at this Norfolk two days. Therefore we came back here yesterday, by the road we had travelled before; lay here last night; and go on to Baltimore this afternoon, at four o'clock. It is a journey of only two hours and a half. Richmond is a prettily situated town; but, like other towns in slave districts (as the planters themselves admit), has an aspect of decay and gloom which to an unaccustomed eye is *most* distressing. In the black car (for they don't let them sit with the whites) on the railroad as we went there, were a mother and family whom the steamer was conveying away, to sell; retaining the man (the husband and father I mean) on his plantation. The children cried the whole way. Yesterday, on board the boat, a slave owner and two constables were our fellow-passengers. They were coming here in search of two negroes who had run away on the previous day. On the bridge at Richmond there is a notice against fast driving over it, as it is rotten and crazy: penalty—for whites, five dollars; for slaves, fifteen stripes. My heart is lightened as if a great load had been taken from it, when I think that we are turning our backs on this accursed and detested system. I really don't think I could have borne it any longer. It is all very well to say 'be silent on the subject.' They won't let you be silent. They *will* ask you what you think of it; and *will* expatiate on slavery as if it were one of the greatest blessings of mankind. 'It's not,' said a hard, bad-looking fellow to me the other day, 'it's not the interest of a man to use his slaves ill. It's damned nonsense that you hear in England.'—I told him quietly that it was not a man's interest to get drunk, or to steal, or to game, or to indulge in any other vice, but he *did* indulge in it for all that. That cruelty, and the abuse of irresponsible power, were two of the bad passions of human nature, with the gratification of which, considerations of interest or of ruin had nothing whatever to do; and that, while every candid man must admit that even a slave might be happy enough with a good master, all human beings knew that bad masters, cruel masters, and masters who disgraced the form they bore, were matters of experience and history, whose existence was as undisputed as that of slaves themselves. He was a little taken aback by this, and asked me if I believed in the Bible. Yes, I said, but if any man could prove to me that it sanctioned slavery, I would place no further credence in it. 'Well, then,' he said, 'by God, sir, the niggers must be kept down, and the whites have put down the coloured people wherever they have found them.' 'That's the whole question,' said I. 'Yes, and by God,' says he, 'the British had better not stand out on that point when Lord Ashburton comes over, for I never felt so warlike as I do now,—and that's a fact.' I was obliged to accept a public supper in this Richmond, and I saw plainly enough, there, that the hatred which these Southern States bear to us as a nation has been fanned up and revived again by this Creole business, and can scarcely be exaggerated. . . . We were desperately tired at Richmond, as we went to a great many places, and received a very great number of visitors. We appoint usually two hours in every day for this latter purpose, and have our room so full at that period that it is difficult to move or breathe. Before we left Richmond, a gentleman told me, when I really was so exhausted that I could hardly stand, that 'three people of great fashion' were much offended by having been told, when they called last evening, that I was tired and not visible, then, but would be 'at home' from twelve to two next day! Another gentleman (no doubt of great fashion also) sent a letter to me two hours after I had gone to bed preparatory to rising at four next morning, with instructions to the slave who brought it to knock me up and wait for an answer! . . ."

# V

## CANAL AND STEAM BOAT JOURNEYS

### 1842

It would not be possible that a more vivid or exact impression, than that which is derivable from these letters, could be given of either the genius or the character of the writer. The whole man is here in the supreme hour of his life, and in all the enjoyment of its highest sensations. Inexpressibly sad to me has been the task of going over them. . . .

His next letter was begun from "On board the canal boat. Going to Pittsburgh. Monday, March twenty-eighth, 1842"; and the difficulties of rejection, to which reference has just been made, have been nowhere felt by me so much. Several of the descriptive masterpieces of the book are in it, with such touches of original freshness as might fairly have justified a reproduction of them in their first form. Among these are the Harrisburgh coach on its way through the Susquehanah Valley; the railroad across the mountain; the brown-forester of the Mississippi, the interrogative man in pepper-and-salt, and the affecting scene of the emigrants put ashore as the steamer passes up the Ohio. But all that I may here give, bearing any resemblance to what is given in the *Notes*, are, the opening sketch of the small creature on the top of the queer stage coach, to which the printed version fails to do adequate justice; and an experience to which the interest belongs of having suggested the settlement of Eden in *Martin Chuzzlewit*. ". . . We left Baltimore last Thursday the twenty-fourth at half-past eight in the morning, by railroad; and got to a place called York, about twelve. There we

dined, and took a stage-coach for Harrisburgh; twenty-five miles
further. This stage-coach was like nothing so much as the body of
one of the swings you see at a fair set upon four wheels and roofed
and covered at the sides with painted canvas. There were twelve
*inside*! I, thank my stars, was on the box. The luggage was on the
roof; among it, a good-sized dining-table, and a big rocking-chair.
We also took up an intoxicated gentleman, who sat for ten miles
between me and the coachman; and another intoxicated gentleman
who got up behind, but in the course of a mile or two fell off without
hurting himself, and was seen in the distant perspective reeling back
to the grog-shop where we had found him. There were four horses to
this land-ark, of course; but we did not perform the journey until
half-past six o'clock that night. . . . The first half of the journey
was tame enough, but the second lay through the valley of the
Susquehanah (I think I spell it right, but I haven't that *American
Geography* at hand) which is very beautiful. . . .

"You know my small respect for our House of Commons. These
local legislatures are too insufferably apish of mighty legislation, to
be seen without bile: for which reason, and because a great crowd of
senators and ladies had assembled in both houses to behold the
Inimitable, and had already begun to pour in upon him even in the
secretary's private room, I went back to the hotel, with all speed.
The members of both branches of the legislature followed me there,
however, so we had to hold the usual levee before our half-past one
o'clock dinner. We received a great number of them. Pretty nearly
every man spat upon the carpet, as usual; and one blew his nose—
with his fingers—also on the carpet, which was a very neat one, the
room given up to us being the private parlour of the landlord's wife.
This has become so common since, however, that it scarcely seems
worth mentioning. Please to observe that the gentleman in question
was a member of the Senate, which answers (as they very often tell
me) to our House of Lords.

"The innkeeper was the most attentive, civil, and obliging person
I ever saw in my life. On being asked for his bill, he said there was
no bill: the honour and pleasure, etc., being more than sufficient.
I did not permit this, of course; and begged Mr. Q—— to explain
to him, that, travelling four strong, I could not hear of it on any
account.

"And now I come to the Canal Boat. Bless your heart and soul,
my dear fellow,—if you could only see us on board the canal boat!
Let me think, for a moment, at what time of the day or night I
should best like you to see us. In the morning? Between five and six
in the morning, shall I say? Well! you *would* like to see me, standing
on the deck, fishing the dirty water out of the canal with a tin ladle
chained to the boat by a long chain; pouring the same into a tin
basin (also chained up in like manner); and scrubbing my face with
the jack-towel. At night, shall I say? I don't know that you *would*
like to look into the cabin at night, only to see me lying on a tem-

porary shelf exactly the width of this sheet of paper when it's open (*I measured it this morning*), with one man above me, and another below; and, in all, eight and twenty in a low cabin, which you can't stand upright in with your hat on. I don't think you would like to look in at breakfast time either, for then these shelves have only just been taken down and put away, and the atmosphere of the place is, as you may suppose, by no means fresh; though there *are* upon the table tea and coffee, and bread and butter, and salmon, and shad, and liver, and steak, and potatoes, and pickles, and ham, and pudding, and sausages; and three and thirty people sitting round it, eating and drinking; and savoury bottles of gin, and whisky, and brandy, and rum, in the bar hard by; and seven and twenty out of the eight and twenty men, in foul linen, with yellow streams from half-chewed tobacco trickling down their chins. Perhaps the best time for you to take a peep would be the present: eleven o'clock in the forenoon: when the barber is at his shaving, and the gentlemen are lounging about the stove waiting for their turns, and not more than seventeen are spitting in concert, and two or three are walking overhead (lying down on the luggage every time the man at the helm calls 'Bridge!'), and I am writing this in the ladies' cabin, which is a part of the gentlemen's, and only screened off by a red curtain. Indeed it exactly resembles the dwarf's private apartment in a caravan at a fair; and the gentlemen, generally, represent the spectators at a penny-a-head. The place is just as clean and just as large as that caravan you and I were in at Greenwich Fair last past. Outside, it is exactly like any canal boat you have seen near the Regent's Park, or elsewhere.

"You never can conceive what the hawking and spitting is, the whole night through. Last night was the worst. *Upon my honour and word* I was obliged, this morning, to lay my fur-coat on the deck, and wipe the half-dried flakes of spittle from it with my handkerchief: and the only surprise seemed to be, that I should consider it necessary to do so. When I turned in last night, I put it on a stool beside me, and there it lay, under a cross fire from five men—three opposite; one above; and one below. I make no complaints, and show no disgust. I am looked upon as highly facetious at night, for I crack jokes with everybody near me until we fall asleep. I am considered very hardy in the morning, for I run up, bare-necked, and plunge my head into the half-frozen water, by half-past five o'clock. I am respected for my activity, inasmuch as I jump from the boat to the towing-path, and walk five or six miles before breakfast; keeping up with the horses all the time. In a word, they are quite astonished to find a sedentary Englishman roughing it so well, and taking so much exercise; and question me very much on that head. The greater part of the men will sit and shiver round the stove all day, rather than put one foot before the other. As to having a window open, that's not to be thought of. . . .

"I told you of the many uses of the word 'fix.' I ask Mr. Q——

on board a steam-boat if breakfast be nearly ready, and he tells me yes he should think so, for when he was last below the steward was 'fixing the tables'—in other words, laying the cloth. When we have been writing, and I beg him (do you remember anything of my love of order, at this distance of time?) to collect our papers, he answers that he'll 'fix 'em presently.' So when a man's dressing he's 'fixing' himself, and when you put yourself under a doctor he 'fixes' you in no time. T'other night, before we came on board here, when I had ordered a bottle of mulled claret and waited some time for it, it was put on table with an apology from the landlord (a lieutenant-colonel) that 'he fear'd it wasn't fixed properly.' And here, on Saturday morning, a Western man, handing the potatoes to Mr. Q—— at breakfast, inquired if he wouldn't take some of 'these fixings' with his meat. I remained as grave as a judge. I catch them looking at me sometimes, and feel that they think I don't take any notice. Politics are very high here; dreadfully strong; handbills, denunciations, invectives, threats, and quarrels. The question is, who shall be the next president. The election comes off in *three years and a-half* from this time." . . .

"STILL IN THE SAME BOAT. *April the Second*, 1842.

"Many, many, happy returns of the day. It's only eight o'clock in the morning now, but we mean to drink your health after dinner, in a bumper; and scores of Richmond dinners to us! We have some wine (a present sent on board by our Pittsburgh landlord) in our own cabin; and we shall tap it to good purpose, I assure you; wishing you all manner and kinds of happiness, and a long life to ourselves that we may be partakers of it. . . .

"Let me tell you that the other night at Pittsburgh, there being present only Mr. Q—— and the portrait-painter, Kate sat down, laughing, for me to try my hand upon her. I had been holding forth upon the subject rather luminously, and asserting that I thought I could exercise the influence, but had never tried. In six minutes, I magnetised her into hysterics, and then into the magnetic sleep. I tried again next night, and she fell into the slumber in little more than two minutes. . . . I can wake her with perfect ease; but I confess (not being prepared for anything so sudden and complete) I was on the first occasion rather alarmed. . . . The Western parts being sometimes hazardous, I have fitted out the whole of my little company with LIFE PRESERVERS, which I inflate with great solemnity when we get aboard any boat, and keep, as Mrs. Cluppins did her umbrella in the court of common pleas, ready for use upon a moment's notice. . . ."

He resumed his letter, on "Sunday, April the third." . . .

"At Pittsburgh I saw another solitary confinement prison: Pittsburgh being also in Pennsylvania. A horrible thought occurred to me when I was recalling all I had seen, that night. *What if ghosts be one of the terrors of the jails?* I have pondered on it often, since then. The utter solitude by day and night; the many hours of darkness; the silence of death; the mind for ever brooding on melancholy themes, and having no relief; sometimes an evil conscience very busy: imagine a prisoner covering up his head in the bedclothes and looking out from time to time, with a ghastly dread of some inexplicable silent figure that always sits upon his bed, or stands (if a thing can be said to stand, that never walks as men do) in the same corner of his cell. The more I think of it, the more certain I feel that not a few of these men (during a portion of their imprisonment at least) are nightly visited by spectres. I did ask one man in this last jail, if he dreamed much. He gave me a most extraordinary look, and said—under his breath—in a whisper—'No.' . . .

# VI

## FAR WEST: TO NIAGARA FALLS

### 1842

THE next letter described his experiences in the Far West, his stay in St. Louis, his visit to a Prairie, the return to Cincinnati, and, after a stage-coach ride from that city to Columbus, the travel thence to Sandusky, and so, by Lake Erie, to the Falls of Niagara. All these subjects appear in the *Notes*, but nothing printed there is repeated in the extracts now to be given :

". . . They won't let me alone about slavery. A certain Judge in St. Louis went so far yesterday, that I fell upon him (to the indescribable horror of the man who brought him) and told him a piece of my mind. I said that I was very averse to speaking on the subject here, and always forbore, if possible: but when he pitied our national ignorance of the truths of slavery, I must remind him that we went upon indisputable records, obtained after many years of careful investigation, and at all sorts of self-sacrifice; and that I believed we were much more competent to judge of its atrocity and horror, than he who had been brought up in the midst of it. I told him that I could sympathise with men who admitted it to be a dreadful evil, but frankly confessed their inability to devise a means of getting rid of it: but that men who spoke of it as a blessing, as a matter of course, as a state of things to be desired, were out of the pale of reason; and that for them to speak of ignorance or prejudice was an absurdity too ridiculous to be combated. . . .

"It is not six years ago, since a slave in this very same St. Louis being arrested (I forget for what), and knowing he had no chance of a fair trial be his offence what it might, drew his bowie knife and

ripped the constable across the body. A scuffle ensuing, the desperate
negro stabbed two others with the same weapon. The mob who
gathered round (among whom were men of mark, wealth, and influence in the place) overpowered him by numbers; carried him away
to a piece of open ground beyond the city; *and burned him alive.*
This, I say, was done within six years in broad day; in a city with its
courts, lawyers, tipstaffs, judges, jails, and hangman; and not a hair
on the head of one of those men has been hurt to this day. And it is,
believe me, it is the miserable, wretched independence in small
things; the paltry republicanism which recoils from honest service
to an honest man, but does not shrink from every trick, artifice. and
knavery in business; that makes these slaves necessary, and will
render them so, until the indignation of other countries sets them
free. . . .

"Same Boat, *Saturday, Sixteenth April,* 1842.

"Let me tell you, my dear Forster, before I forget it, a pretty
little scene we had on board the boat between Louisville and St.
Louis, as we were going to the latter place. It is not much to tell,
but it was very pleasant and interesting to witness."

What follows has been printed in the *Notes,* and ought not, by
the rule I have laid down, to be given here. But, beautiful as the
printed description is, it has not profited by the alteration of some
touches, and the omission of others in the first fresh version of it,
which, for that reason, I here preserve—one of the most charming
soul-felt pictures of character and emotion that ever warmed the
heart in fact or fiction. It was, I think, Jeffrey's favourite passage in
all the writings of Dickens: and certainly, if anyone would learn the
secret of their popularity, it is to be read in the observation and
description of this little incident.

"There was a little woman on board, with a little baby; and both
little woman and little child were cheerful, good-looking, bright-
eyed, and fair to see. The little woman had been passing a long time
with a sick mother in New York, and had left her home in St. Louis
in that condition in which ladies who truly love their lords desire to
be. The baby had been born in her mother's house, and she had not
seen her husband (to whom she was now returning) for twelve
months: having left him a month or two after their marriage. Well,
to be sure, there never was a little woman so full of hope, and
tenderness, and love, and anxiety, as this little woman was: and
there she was, all the livelong day, wondering whether 'he' would be
at the wharf; and whether 'he' had got her letter; and whether, if she
sent the baby on shore by somebody else, *'he' would know it, meeting
it in the street*: which, seeing that he had never set eyes upon it in
his life, was not very likely in the abstract, but was probable enough
to the young mother. She was such an artless little creature; and was
in such a sunny, beaming, hopeful state; and let out all this matter,

clinging close about her heart, so freely; that all the other lady passengers entered into the spirit of it as much as she: and the captain (who heard all about it from his wife) was wondrous sly, I promise you: inquiring, every time we met at table, whether she expected anybody to meet her at St. Louis, and supposing she wouldn't want to go ashore the night we reached it, and cutting many other dry jokes which convulsed all his hearers, but especially the ladies. There was one little, weazen, dried-apple old woman among them, who took occasion to doubt the constancy of husbands under such circumstances of bereavement; and there was another lady (with a lap dog), old enough to moralise on the lightness of human affections, and yet not so old that she could help nursing the baby now and then, or laughing with the rest when the little woman called it by its father's name, and asked it all manner of fantastic questions concerning him, in the joy of her heart. It was something of a blow to the little woman, that when we were within twenty miles of our destination, it became clearly necessary to put the baby to bed; but she got over that with the same good humour, tied a little handkerchief over her little head, and came out into the gallery with the rest. Then, such an oracle as she became in reference to the localities! and such facetiousness as was displayed by the married ladies! and such sympathy as was shown by the single ones! and such peals of laughter as the little woman herself (who would just as soon have cried) greeted every jest with! At last, there were the lights of St. Louis—and here was the wharf—and those were the steps—and the little woman, covering her face with her hands, and laughing, or seeming to laugh, more than ever, ran into her own cabin, and shut herself up tight. I have no doubt that, in the charming inconsistency of such excitement, she stopped her ears lest she should hear 'him' asking for her; but I didn't see her do it. Then a great crowd of people rushed on board, though the boat was not yet made fast, and was staggering about among the other boats to find a landing-place; and everybody looked for the husband, and nobody saw him; when all of a sudden, right in the midst of them—God knows how she ever got there—there was the little woman hugging with both arms round the neck of a fine, good-looking, sturdy fellow! And in a moment afterwards, there she was again, dragging him through the small door of her small cabin, to look at the baby as he lay asleep!—What a good thing it is to know that so many of us would have been quite downhearted and sorry if that husband had failed to come." . . .

"SANDUSKY.

*"Sunday, Twenty-fourth April,* 1842.

". . . We remained at Cincinnati all Tuesday the nineteenth, and all that night. At eight o'clock on Wednesday morning the twentieth, we left in the mail stage for Columbus: Anne, Kate, and Mr. Q——inside; I on the box. The distance is a hundred and twenty miles;

the road macadamised; and for an American road, very good. We were three and twenty hours performing the journey. We travelled all night; reached Columbus at seven in the morning; breakfasted; and went to bed until dinner time. At night we held a levee for half an hour, and the people poured in as they always do: each gentleman with a lady on each arm, exactly like the Chorus to *God Save the Queen*. I wish you could see them, that you might know what a splendid comparison this is. They wear their clothes precisely as the chorus people do; and stand—supposing Kate and me to be in the centre of the stage, with our backs to the footlights—just as the company would, on the first night of the season. They shake hands exactly after the manner of the guests at a ball at the Adelphi or the Haymarket; receive any facetiousness on my part, as if there were a stage direction 'all laugh'; and have rather more difficulty in 'getting off' than the last gentlemen, in white pantaloons, polished boots, and berlins, usually display, under the most trying circumstances. . . .

"An inn at which we halted was a rough log-house. The people were all abed, and we had to knock them up. We had the queerest sleeping-room, with two doors, one opposite the other; both opening directly on the wild black country, and neither having any lock or bolt. The effect of these opposite doors was, that one was always blowing the other open: an ingenuity in the art of building, which I don't remember to have met with before. You should have seen me, in my shirt, blockading them with portmanteaux, and desperately endeavouring to make the room tidy! But the blockading was really needful, for in my dressing-case I have about £250 in gold; and for the amount of the middle figure in that scarce metal, there are not a few men in the West who would murder their fathers. Apropos of this golden store, consider at your leisure the strange state of things in this country. It has no money; really *no money*. The bank paper won't pass; the newspapers are full of advertisements from tradesmen who sell by barter; and American gold is not to be had, or purchased. I bought sovereigns, English sovereigns, at first: but as I could get none of them at Cincinnati to this day, I have had to purchase French gold; 20-franc pieces; with which I am travelling as if I were in Paris!

"But let's go back to Lower Sandusky. Mr. Q—— went to bed up in the roof of the log-house somewhere, but was so beset by bugs that he got up after an hour and *lay in the coach* . . . where he was obliged to wait till breakfast time. We breakfasted, driver and all, in the one common room. It was papered with newspapers, and was as rough a place as need be. At half-past seven we started again, and we reached Sandusky at six o'clock yesterday afternoon. It is on Lake Erie, twenty-four hours' journey by steam-boat from Buffalo. We found no boat here, nor has there been one, since. We are waiting, with everything packed up, ready to start on the shortest notice; and are anxiously looking out for smoke in the distance. . . .

*"Tuesday, April Twenty-sixth,* 1842.
"NIAGARA FALLS!!! (UPON THE ENGLISH SIDE).

"I don't know at what length I might have written you from Sandusky, my beloved friend, if a steamer had not come in sight just as I finished the last unintelligible sheet (oh! the ink in these parts!): whereupon I was obliged to pack up bag and baggage, to swallow a hasty apology for a dinner, and to hurry my train on board with all the speed I might. She was a fine steamship, four hundred tons burden, name the *Constitution*, had very few passengers on board, and had bountiful and handsome accommodation. It's all very fine talking about Lake Erie, but it won't do for persons who are liable to sea-sickness. We were all sick. It's almost as bad in that respect as the Atlantic. The waves are very short, and horribly constant. We reached Buffalo at six this morning; went ashore to breakfast; sent to the post-office forthwith; and received—oh! who or what can say with how much pleasure and what unspeakable delight!—our English letters!

"We lay all Sunday night at a town (and a beautiful town too) called Cleveland; on Lake Erie. The people poured on board, in crowds, by six on Monday morning, to see me; and a party of 'gentlemen' actually planted themselves before our little cabin, and stared in at the door and windows *while I was washing, and Kate lay in bed.* I was so incensed at this, and at a certain newspaper published in that town which I had accidentally seen in Sandusky (advocating war with England to the death, saying that Britain must be 'whipped again,' and promising all true Americans that within two years they should sing *Yankee Doodle* in Hyde Park and *Hail Columbia* in the courts of Westminster), that when the mayor came on board to present himself to me, according to custom, I refused to see him, and bade Mr. Q—— tell him why and wherefore. His honour took it very coolly, and retired to the top of the wharf, with a big stick and a whittling knife, with which he worked so lustily (staring at the closed door of our cabin all the time) that long before the boat left the big stick was no bigger than a cribbage peg!

"I never in my life was in such a state of excitement as coming from Buffalo here, this morning. You come by railroad; and are nigh two hours upon the way. I looked out for the spray, and listened for the roar, as far beyond the bounds of possibility, as though, landing in Liverpool, I were to listen for the music of your pleasant voice in Lincoln's Inn Fields. At last, when the train stopped, I saw two great white clouds rising up from the depths of the earth—nothing more. They rose up slowly, gently, majestically, into the air. I dragged Kate down a deep and slippery path leading to the ferry boat; bullied Anne for not coming fast enough; perspired at every pore; and felt, it is impossible to say how, as the sound grew louder and louder in my ears, and yet nothing could be seen for the mist.

"There were two English officers with us (ah! what *gentlemen,* what noblemen of nature they seemed), and they hurried off with me; leaving Kate and Anne on a crag of ice; and clambered after me over the rocks at the foot of the small Fall, while the ferryman was getting the boat ready. I was not disappointed—but I could make out nothing. In an instant, I was blinded by the spray, and wet to the skin. I saw the water tearing madly down from some immense height, but could get no idea of shape, or situation, or anything but vague immensity. But when we were seated in the boat, and crossing at the very foot of the cataract—then I began to feel what it was. Directly I had changed my clothes at the inn I went out again, taking Kate with me; and hurried to the Horseshoe Fall. I went down alone, into the very basin. It would be hard for a man to stand nearer God than he does there. There was a bright rainbow at my feet; and from that I looked up to—great Heaven! to *what* a fall of bright green water! The broad, deep, mighty stream seems to die in the act of falling; and, from its unfathomable grave, arises that tremendous ghost of spray and mist which is never laid, and has been haunting this place with the same dread solemnity—perhaps from the creation of the world.

"We purpose remaining here a week. In my next, I will try to give you some idea of my impressions, and to tell you how they change with every day. At present it is impossible. I can only say that the first effect of this tremendous spectacle on me, was peace of mind—tranquillity—great thoughts of eternal rest and happiness—nothing of terror. I can shudder at the recollection of Glencoe (dear friend, with Heaven's leave we must see Glencoe together), but whenever I think of Niagara, I shall think of its beauty."

# VII

## "AMERICAN NOTES"

### 1842

REALITY did not fall short of his anticipation of home. His return was the occasion of unbounded enjoyment; and what he had planned before sailing as the way we should meet, received literal fulfilment. By the sound of his cheery voice I first knew that he was come; and from my house we went together to Maclise, also "without a moment's warning." A Greenwich dinner in which several friends (Talfourd, Milnes, Procter, Maclise, Stanfield, Marryat, Barham, Hood, and Cruikshank among them) took part, and other immediate greetings, followed; but the most special celebration was reserved for autumn, when, by way of challenge to what he had seen while abroad, a home-journey was arranged with Stanfield, Maclise, and myself for his companions, into such of the most striking scenes of a picturesque

English county as the majority of us might not before have visited:
Cornwall being ultimately chosen.

Before our departure he was occupied by his preparation of the
*American Notes*; and to the same interval belongs the arrival in
London of Mr. Longfellow, who became his guest, and (for both of
us I am privileged to add) our attached friend. Longfellow's name
was not then the familiar word it has since been in England; but he
had already written several of his most felicitous pieces, and he
possessed all the qualities of delightful companionship, the culture
and the charm, which have no higher type than the accomplished
and genial American. He reminded me, when lately again in England,
of two experiences out of many we had enjoyed together this quarter
of a century before. One of them was a day at Rochester, when, met
by one of those prohibitions which are the wonder of visitors and
the shame of Englishmen, we overleapt gates and barriers, and,
setting at defiance repeated threats of all the terrors of law coarsely
expressed to us by the custodian of the place, explored minutely the
castle ruins. The other was a night among those portions of the
population which outrage law and defy its terrors all the days of their
lives, the tramps and thieves of London; when, under guidance and
protection of the most trusted officers of the two great metropolitan
prisons afforded to us by Mr. Chesterton and Lieut. Tracy, we went
over the worst haunts of the most dangerous classes. Nor will it be
unworthy of remark, in proof that attention is not drawn vainly to
such scenes, that, upon Dickens going over them a dozen years later
when he wrote a paper about them for his *Household Words*, he found
important changes effected whereby these human dens, if not less
dangerous, were become certainly more decent. On the night of our
earlier visit, Maclise, who accompanied us, was struck with such
sickness on entering the first of the Mint lodging-houses in the
Borough, that he had to remain, for the time we were in them, under
guardianship of the police outside. Longfellow returned home by the
*Great Western* from Bristol on 21 October, enjoying as he passed
through Bath the hospitality of Landor; and at the end of the
following week we started on our Cornish travel. . . .

With the opening of September I had renewed report of his book,
and of other matters. "The Philadelphia chapter I think very good,
but I am sorry to say it has not made as much in print as I hoped. . . .
In America they have forged a letter with my signature, which they
coolly declare appeared in the *Chronicle* with the copyright circular;
and in which I express myself in such terms as you may imagine, in
reference to the dinners and so forth. It has been widely distributed
all over the States; and the felon who invented it is a 'smart man' of
course. You are to understand that it is not done as a joke, and is
scurrilously reviewed. Mr. Park Benjamin begins a lucubration upon
it with these capitals, DICKENS IS A FOOL, AND A LIAR. . . . I have
a new protégé, in the person of a wretched deaf and dumb boy whom
I found upon the sands the other day, half dead, and have got (for

the present) into the union infirmary at Minster. A most deplorable case.''

The printers were now hard at work, and in the last week of September he wrote: "I send you proofs as far as Niagara. . . . I am rather holiday-making this week . . . taking principal part in a regatta here yesterday, very pretty and gay indeed. We think of coming up in time for Macready's opening, when perhaps you will give us a chop; and of course you and Mac will dine with *us* the next day? I shall leave nothing of the book to do after coming home, please God, but the two chapters on slavery and the people which I could manage easily in a week, if need were. . . . The policeman who supposed the Duke of Brunswick to be one of the swell mob, ought instantly to be made an inspector. The suspicion reflects the highest credit (I seriously think) on his penetration and judgment.'' Three days later: "For the last two days we have had gales blowing from the north-east, and seas rolling on us that drown the pier. To-day it is tremendous. Such a sea was never known here at this season, and it is running in at this moment in waves of twelve feet high. You would hardly know the place. But we shall be punctual to your dinner hour on Saturday. If the wind should hold in the same quarter, we may be obliged to come up by land; and in that case I should start the caravan at six in the morning. . . . What do you think of this for my title—*American Notes for General Circulation?*''

On 10 October I heard from him that the chapter intended to be introductory to the *Notes* was written, and waiting our conference whether or not it should be printed. We decided against it; on his part so reluctantly, that I had to undertake for its publication when a more fitting time should come. This in my judgment has arrived, and the chapter first sees the light on this page. There is no danger at present, as there would have been when it was written, that its proper self-assertion should be mistaken for an apprehension of hostile judgments which he was anxious to deprecate or avoid. He is out of reach of all that now; and reveals to us here, as one whom fear or censure can touch no more, his honest purpose in the use of satire even where his humorous temptations were strongest. What he says will on other grounds also be read with unusual interest, for it will be found to connect itself impressively not with his first experiences only, but with his second visit to America at the close of his life. He held always the same high opinion of what was best in that country, and always the same contempt for what was worst in it.

## "INTRODUCTORY, AND NECESSARY TO BE READ

"I have placed the foregoing title at the head of this page, because I challenge and deny the right of any person to pass judgment on this book, or to arrive at any reasonable conclusion in reference to it, without first being at the trouble of becoming acquainted with its design and purpose.

"It is not statistical. Figures of arithmetic have already been heaped upon America's devoted head, almost as lavishly as figures of speech have been piled above Shakespeare's grave.

"It comprehends no small talk concerning individuals, and no violation of the social confidences of private life. The very prevalent practice of kidnapping live ladies and gentlemen, forcing them into cabinets, and labelling and ticketing them whether they will or no, for the gratification of the idle and the curious, is not to my taste. Therefore I have avoided it.

"It has not a grain of any political ingredient in its whole composition.

"Neither does it contain, nor have I intended that it should contain, any lengthened and minute account of my personal reception in the United States; not because I am, or ever was, insensible to that spontaneous effusion of affection and generosity of heart, in a most affectionate and generous-hearted people; but because I conceive that it would ill become me to flourish matter necessarily involving so much of my own praises, in the eyes of my unhappy readers.

"This book is simply what it claims to be—a record of the impressions I received from day to day, during my hasty travels in America, and sometimes (but not always) of the conclusions to which they, and after-reflection on them, have led me; a description of the country I passed through; of the institutions I visited; of the kind of people among whom I journeyed; and of the manners and customs that came within my observation. Very many works having just the same scope and range, have been already published, but I think that these two volumes stand in need of no apology on that account. The interest of such productions, if they have any, lies in the varying impressions made by the same novel things on different minds; and not in new discoveries or extraordinary adventures.

"I can scarcely be supposed to be ignorant of the hazard I run in writing of America at all. I know perfectly well that there is, in that country, a numerous class of well-intentioned persons prone to be dissatisfied with all accounts of the Republic whose citizens they are, which are not couched in terms of exalted and extravagant praise. I know perfectly well that there is in America, as in most other places laid down in maps of the great world, a numerous class of persons so tenderly and delicately constituted, that they cannot bear the truth in any form. And I do not need the gift of prophecy to discern afar off, that they who will be aptest to detect malice, ill-will, and all uncharitableness in these pages, and to show, beyond any doubt, that they are perfectly inconsistent with that grateful and enduring recollection which I profess to entertain of the welcome I found awaiting me beyond the Atlantic—will be certain native journalists, veracious and gentlemanly, who were at great pains to prove to me.

on all occasions during my stay there, that the aforesaid welcome was utterly worthless.

"But, venturing to dissent even from these high authorities, I formed my own opinion of its value in the outset, and retain it to this hour; and in asserting (as I invariably did on all public occasions) my liberty and freedom of speech while I was among the Americans, and in maintaining it at home, I believe that I best show my sense of the high worth of that welcome, and of the honourable singleness of purpose with which it was extended to me. From first to last I saw, in the friends who crowded round me in America, old readers, over-grateful and over-partial perhaps, to whom I had happily been the means of furnishing pleasure and entertainment; not a vulgar herd who would flatter and cajole a stranger into turning with closed eyes from all the blemishes of the nation, and into chaunting its praises with the discrimination of a street ballad-singer. From first to last I saw, in those hospitable hands, a home-made wreath of laurel; and not an iron muzzle disguised beneath a flower or two.

"Therefore I take—and hold myself not only justified in taking, but bound to take—the plain course of saying what I think, and noting what I saw; and as it is not my custom to exalt what in my judgment are foibles and abuses at home, so I have no intention of softening down, or glozing over, those that I have observed abroad.

"If this book should fall into the hands of any sensitive American who cannot bear to be told that the working of the institutions of his country is far from perfect; that in spite of the advantage she has over all other nations in the elastic freshness and vigour of her youth, she is far from being a model for the earth to copy; and that even in those pictures of the national manners with which he quarrels most, there is still (after the lapse of several years, each of which may be fairly supposed to have had its stride in improvement) much that is just and true at this hour; let him lay it down, now, for I shall not please him. Of the intelligent, reflecting, and educated among his countrymen, I have no fear; for I have ample reason to believe, after many delightful conversations not easily to be forgotten, that there are very few topics (if any) on which their sentiments differ materially from mine.

"I may be asked—'If you have been in any respect disappointed in America, and are assured beforehand that the expression of your disappointment will give offence to any class, why do you write at all?' My answer is, that I went there expecting greater things than I found, and resolved as far as in me lay to do justice to the country, at the expense of any (in my view) mistaken or prejudiced statements that might have been made to its disparagement. Coming home with a corrected and sobered judgment, I consider myself no less bound to do justice to what, according to my best means of judgment, I found to be the truth."

Of the book for whose opening page this matter introductory was written it will be enough merely to add that it appeared on 18 October; that before the close of the year four large editions had been sold; and that in my opinion it thoroughly deserved the estimate formed of it by one connected with America by the strongest social affections, and otherwise in all respects an honourable, high-minded, upright judge. "You have been very tender," wrote Lord Jeffrey, "to our sensitive friends beyond sea, and my whole heart goes along with every word you have written. I think that you have perfectly accomplished all that you profess or undertake to do, and that the world has never yet seen a more faithful, graphic, amusing, kind-hearted narrative."

# BOOK FOURTH

## LONDON AND GENOA

1843-5. ÆT. 31-3

## FIRST YEAR OF "MARTIN CHUZZLEWIT"

### 1843

THE Cornish trip had come off, meanwhile, with such unexpected and continued attraction for us that we were well into the third week of absence before we turned our faces homeward. Railways helped us then not much; but where the roads were inaccessible to post-horses, we walked. Tintagel was visited, and no part of mountain or sea consecrated by the legends of Arthur was left unexplored.

"Behold finally, the title of the new book," was the first note I had from Dickens (12 November) after our return; "don't lose it, for I have no copy." Title and even story had been undetermined while we travelled, from the lingering wish he still had to begin it among those Cornish scenes; but this intention had now been finally abandoned, and the reader lost nothing by his substitution, for the lighthouse or mine in Cornwall, of the Wiltshire village forge on the windy autumn evening which opens the tale of *Martin Chuzzlewit*. Into that name he finally settled, but only after much deliberation, as a mention of his changes will show. Martin was the prefix to all, but the surname varied from its first form of Sweezleden, Sweezleback, and Sweezlewag, to those of Chuzzletoe, Chuzzleboy, Chubblewig, and Chuzzlewig; nor was Chuzzlewit chosen at last until after more hesitation and discussion. What he had sent me in his letter as finally adopted, ran thus: "The Life and Adventures of Martin Chuzzlewig, his family, friends, and enemies. Comprising all his wills and his ways. With an historical record of what he did and what he didn't. The whole forming a complete key to the house of Chuzzlewig." All which latter portion of the title was of course dropped as the work became modified, in its progress, by changes at first not contemplated; but as early as the third number he drew up the plan of "old Martin's plot to degrade and punish Pecksniff," and the difficulties he encountered in departing from other portions of his scheme were such as to render him, in his subsequent stories, more bent upon constructive care at the outset, and on adherence as far as might be to any design he had formed.

The first number, which appeared in January 1843, had not been quite finished when he wrote to me on 8 December: "The *Chuzzlewit* copy makes so much more than I supposed, that the number is nearly done. Thank God!" Beginning so hurriedly as at last he did, altering his course at the opening and seeing little as yet of the main track of his design, perhaps no story was ever begun by him with stronger heart or confidence. Illness kept me to my rooms for some days, and he was so eager to try the effect of Pecksniff and Pinch that he came down with the ink hardly dry on the last slip to read the manuscript to me. Well did Sydney Smith, on writing to say how very much the number had pleased him, foresee the promise there was in those characters. "Pecksniff and his daughters, and Pinch, are admirable —quite first-rate painting, such as no one but yourself can execute!" And let me here at once remark that the notion of taking Pecksniff for a type of character was really the origin of the book; the design being to show, more or less by every person introduced, the number and variety of humours and vices that have their root in selfishness. . . .

Eighteen hundred and forty-three opened with the most vigorous prosecution of his *Chuzzlewit* labour. "I hope the number will be very good," he wrote to me of number two (8 January). "I have been hammering away, and at home all day. Ditto yesterday; except for two hours in the afternoon, when I ploughed through snow half a foot deep, round about the wilds of Willesden." For the present, however, I shall glance only briefly from time to time at his progress with the earlier portions of the story on which he was thus engaged until the midsummer of 1844. Disappointments arose in connection with it, unexpected and strange, which had important influence upon him: but I reserve the mention of these for awhile, that I may speak of the leading incidents of 1843.

"I am in a difficulty," he wrote (12 February), "and am coming down to you sometime to-day or to-night. I couldn't write a line yesterday; not a word, though I really tried hard. In a kind of despair I started off at half-past two with my pair of petticoats to Richmond; and dined there!! Oh what a lovely day it was in those parts." His pair of petticoats were Mrs. Dickens and her sister Georgina: the latter, since his return from America, having become part of his household, of which she remained a member until his death; and he had just reason to be proud of the steadiness, depth, and devotion of her friendship. In a note-book begun by him in January 1855, where for the first time in his life he jotted down hints and fancies proposed to be made available in future writings, I find a character sketched of which the most part was applicable to his sister-in-law, if the whole was not suggested by her. "She—sacrificed to children, and sufficiently rewarded. From a child herself, always 'the children' (of somebody else) to engross her. And so it comes to pass that she is never married; never herself has a child; is always devoted 'to the children' (of somebody else); and they love her; and she has always youth dependent on her till her death—and dies quite happily." . . .

I soon after joined him at a cottage he rented in Finchley; and here, walking and talking in the green lanes as the midsummer months were coming on, his introduction of Mrs. Gamp, and the uses to which he should apply that remarkable personage, first

occurred to him. In his preface to the book he speaks of her as a fair
representation, at the time it was published, of the hired attendant
on the poor in sickness: but he might have added that the rich were
no better off, for Mrs. Gamp's original was in reality a person hired
by a most distinguished friend of his own, a lady, to take charge of an
invalid very dear to her; and the common habit of this nurse in the
sick-room, among other Gampish peculiarites, was to rub her nose
along the top of the tall fender. Whether or not, on that first mention
of her, I had any doubts whether such a character could be made a
central figure in his story, I do not now remember; but if there were
any at the time, they did not outlive the contents of the packet which
introduced her to me in the flesh a few weeks after our return. "Tell
me," he wrote from Yorkshire, where he had been meanwhile passing
pleasant holiday with a friend, "what you think of Mrs. Gamp?
You'll not find it easy to get through the hundreds of misprints in her
conversation, but I want your opinion at once. I think you know
already something of mine. I mean to make a mark with her."

\*     \*     \*     \*

From October 4 to 6, he was at Manchester, presiding at the opening of its great Athenæum, when Mr. Cobden and Mr. Disraeli also
"assisted." Here he spoke mainly on a matter always nearest his
heart, the education of the very poor. He protested against the danger
of calling a little learning dangerous; declared his preference for the
very least of the little over none at all; proposed to substitute for
the old a new doggerel,

> Though house and lands be never got,
> Learning can give what they can *not;*

told his listeners of the real and paramount danger we had lately
taken Longfellow to see in the nightly refuges of London, "thousands
of immortal creatures condemned without alternative or choice to
tread, not what our great poet calls the primrose path to the everlasting bonfire, but one of jagged flints and stones laid down by brutal
ignorance"; and contrasted this with the unspeakable consolation
and blessings that a little knowledge had shed on men of the lowest
estate and most hopeless means, "watching the stars with Ferguson
the shepherd's boy, walking the streets with Crabbe, a poor barber
here in Lancashire with Arkwright, a tallow-chandler's son with
Franklin, shoe-making with Bloomfield in his garret, following the
plough with Burns, and high above the noise of loom and hammer,
whispering courage in the ears of workers I could this day name in
Sheffield and in Manchester."

The same spirit impelled him to give eager welcome to the remarkable institution of Ragged Schools, which, begun by a shoemaker of
Portsmouth and a chimney-sweep of Windsor and carried on by a
peer of the realm, has had results of incalculable importance to
society. The year of which I am writing was its first, as this in which
I write is its last; and in the interval, out of three hundred thousand
children to whom it has given some sort of education, it is computed

also to have given to a third of that number the means of honest employment. "I sent Miss Coutts," he had written (24 September), "a sledge-hammer account of the Ragged Schools; and as I saw her name for two hundred pounds in the clergy education subscription list, took pains to show her that religious mysteries and difficult creeds wouldn't do for such pupils. I told her, too, that it was of immense importance they should be *washed*. She writes back to know what the rent of some large airy premises would be, and what the expense of erecting a regular bathing or purifying place; touching which points I am in correspondence with the authorities. I have no doubt she will do whatever I ask her in the matter. She is a most excellent creature, I protest to God, and I have a most perfect affection and respect for her." . . .

Active as he had been in the now ending year, and great as were its varieties of employment; his genius in its highest mood, his energy unwearied in good work, and his capacity for enjoyment without limit; he was able to signalise its closing months by an achievement supremely fortunate, which but for disappointments the year had also brought might never have been thought of. He had not begun until a week after his return from Manchester, where the fancy first occurred to him, and before the end of November he had finished, his memorable *Christmas Carol*. It was the work of such odd moments of leisure as were left him out of the time taken up by two numbers of his *Chuzzlewit*; and though begun with but the special design of adding something to the *Chuzzlewit* balance, I can testify to the accuracy of his own account of what befell him in its composition, with what a strange mastery it seized him for itself, how he wept over it, and laughed, and wept again, and excited himself to an extraordinary degree, and how he walked thinking of it fifteen and twenty miles about the black streets of London, many and many a night after all sober folks had gone to bed. And when it was done, as he told our American friend Mr. Felton, he let himself loose like a madman. "Forster is out again," he added, by way of illustrating our practical comments on his book-celebration of the jovial old season, "and if he don't go in again after the manner in which we have been keeping Christmas, he must be very strong indeed. Such dinings, such dancings, such conjurings, such blind-man's buffings, such theatre-goings, such kissings-out of old years and kissings-in of new ones, never took place in these parts before."

Yet had it been to him, this closing year, a time also of much anxiety and strange disappointments of which I am now to speak ; and before, with that view, we go back for a while to its earlier months, one step into the new year may be taken for what marked it with interest and importance to him. Eighteen hundred and forty-four was but fifteen days old when a third son (his fifth child, which received the name of its godfather Francis Jeffrey) was born; and here is an answer sent by him, two days later, to an invitation from Maclise, Stanfield, and myself to dine with us at Richmond: "Devon-

SHIRE LODGE, *Seventeenth of January*, 1844, FELLOW COUNTRYMEN! The appeal with which you have honoured me, awakens within my breast emotions that are more easily to be imagined than described. Heaven bless you. I shall indeed be proud, my friends, to respond to such a requisition. I had withdrawn from Public Life—I fondly thought for ever—to pass the evening of my days in hydropathical pursuits, and the contemplation of virtue. For which latter purpose, I had bought a looking-glass.—But, my friends, private feeling must ever yield to a stern sense of public duty. The Man is lost in the Invited Guest, and I comply. Nurses, wet and dry; apothecaries; mothers-in-law; babies; with all the sweet (and chaste) delights of private life; these, my countrymen, are hard to leave. But you have called me forth, and I will come. Fellow countrymen, your friend and faithful servant, CHARLES DICKENS."

## II

"CHUZZLEWIT" DISAPPOINTMENTS AND "CHRISTMAS CAROL"

### 1843-4

"CHUZZLEWIT" had fallen short of all the expectations formed of it in regard to sale. By much the most masterly of his writings hitherto, the public had rallied to it in far less numbers than to any of its predecessors. The primary cause of this, there is little doubt, had been the change to weekly issues in the form of publication of his last two stories; for into everything in this world mere habit enters more largely than we are apt to suppose. Nor had the temporary withdrawal to America been favourable to an immediate resumption by his readers of their old and intimate relations. This also is to be added, that the excitement by which a popular reputation is kept up to the highest selling mark will always be subject to lulls too capricious for explanation. But whatever the causes, here was the undeniable fact of a grave depreciation of sale in his writings, unaccompanied by any falling off either in themselves or in the writer's reputation. It was very temporary; but it was present, and to be dealt with accordingly. The forty and fifty thousand purchasers of *Pickwick* and *Nickleby*, the sixty and seventy thousand of the early numbers of the enterprise in which the *Old Curiosity Shop* and *Barnaby Rudge* appeared, had fallen to little over twenty thousand. They rose somewhat on Martin's ominous announcement, at the end of the fourth number, that he'd *go to America*; but though it was believed that this resolve, which Dickens adopted as suddenly as his hero, might increase the number of his readers, that reason influenced him less than the challenge to make good his *Notes* which every mail had been bringing him from unsparing assailants beyond the Atlantic. The substantial effect of the American episode upon the sale was yet by no means great. A couple of thousand additional purchasers were added, but the highest number at any time reached before the story closed was twenty-three thousand. Its sale, since, has ranked next after *Pickwick* and *Copperfield*.

We were now, however, to have a truth brought home to us which few that have had real or varied experience in such matters can have failed to be impressed by—that publishers are bitter bad judges of an author, and are seldom safe persons to consult in regard to the fate or fortunes that may probably await him. Describing the agreement for this book in September 1841, I spoke of a provision against the improbable event of its profits proving inadequate to certain necessary repayments. In this unlikely case, which was to be ascertained by the proceeds of the first five numbers, the publishers were to have power to appropriate fifty pounds a month out of the two hundred pounds payable for authorship in the expenses of each number; but though this had been introduced with my knowledge, I knew also too much of the antecedent relations of the parties to regard it as other than a mere form to satisfy the attorneys in the case. The fifth number, which landed Martin and Mark in America, and the sixth, which described their first experiences, were published; and on the eve of the seventh, in which Mrs. Gamp was to make her first appearance, I heard with infinite pain that from Mr. Hall, the younger partner of the firm which had enriched itself by *Pickwick* and *Nickleby*, and a very kind well-disposed man, there had dropped an inconsiderate hint to the writer of those books that it might be desirable to put the clause in force. It had escaped him without his thinking of all that it involved; certainly the senior partner, whatever amount of as thoughtless sanction he had at the moment given to it, always much regretted it, and made endeavours to exhibit his regret; but the mischief was done, and for the time was irreparable.

"I am so irritated," Dickens wrote to me on 28 June, "so rubbed in the tenderest part of my eyelids with bay-salt, by what I told you yesterday, that a wrong kind of fire is burning in my head, and I don't think I *can* write. Nevertheless, I am trying. In case I should succeed, and should not come down to you this morning, shall you be at the club or elsewhere after dinner? I am bent on paying the money. And before going into the matter with anybody I should like you to propound from me the one preliminary question to Bradbury and Evans. It is more than a year and a half since Clowes wrote to urge me to give him a hearing, in case I should ever think of altering my plans. A printer is better than a bookseller, and it is quite as much the interest of one (if not more) to join me. But whoever it is, or whatever, I am bent upon paying Chapman and Hall *down*. And when I have done that, Mr. Hall shall have a piece of my mind."

What he meant by the proposed repayment will be understood by what formerly was said of his arrangements with those gentlemen on the repurchase of his early copyrights. Feeling no surprise at this announcement, I yet prevailed with him to suspend proceedings until his return from Broadstairs in October; and what then I had to say led to memorable resolves. The communication he had desired me to make to his printers had taken them too much by surprise to enable them to form a clear judgment respecting it; and they replied by suggestions which were in effect a confession of that want of confidence in themselves. They enlarged upon the great results that would follow a re-issue of his writings in a cheap form; they strongly urged such an undertaking; and they offered to invest to any desired amount in the establishment of a magazine or other periodical to be edited by him. The possible dangers, in short, incident to their assuming the position of publishers as well as printers of new works from his pen, seemed at first to be so much greater than on closer examination they were found to be, that at the outset they shrank from encountering them. And hence the remarkable letter I shall now quote (1 November, 1843).

"Don't be startled by the novelty and extent of my project. Both startled *me* at first; but I am well assured of its wisdom and necessity. I am afraid of a magazine—just now. I don't think the time a good one, or the chances favourable. I am afraid of putting myself before the town as writing tooth and nail for bread, headlong, after the close of a book taking so much out of one as *Chuzzlewit*. I am afraid I could not do it, with justice to myself. I know that whatever we may say at first, a new magazine, or a new anything, would require so much propping, that I should be *forced* (as in the *Clock*) to put myself into it, in my old shape. I am afraid of Bradbury and Evans's desire to force on the cheap issue of my books, or any of them, prematurely. I am sure if it took place yet awhile, it would damage me and damage the property, *enormously*. It is very natural in them to want it; but, since they do want it, I have no faith in their regarding me in any other respect than they would regard any other man in a speculation. I see that this is really your opinion as well; and I don't see what I gain, in such a case, by leaving Chapman and Hall. If I had made money, I should unquestionably fade away from the public eye for a year, and enlarge my stock of description and observation by seeing countries new to me; which it is most necessary to me that I should see, and which with an increasing family I can scarcely hope to see at all, unless I see them now. Already for some time I have had this hope and intention before me; and, though not having yet made money, I find or fancy that I can put myself in the position to accomplish it. And this is the course I have before me. At the close of *Chuzzlewit* (by which time the debt will have been materially reduced) I purpose drawing from Chapman and Hall my share of the subscription—bills, or money, will do equally well. I design to tell them that it is not likely I shall do anything for a year; that, in the meantime, I make no arrangement whatever with anyone; and our business matters rest *in statu quo*. The same to Bradbury and Evans. I shall let the house if

I can; if not, leave it to be let. I shall take all the family, and two servants—three at most—to some place which I know beforehand to be CHEAP and in a delightful climate, in Normandy or Brittany, to which I shall go over, first, and where I shall rent some house for six or eight months. During that time, I shall walk through Switzerland, cross the Alps, travel through France and Italy; take Kate perhaps to Rome and Venice, but not elsewhere; and in short see everything that is to be seen. I shall write my descriptions to you from time to time, exactly as I did in America; and you will be able to judge whether or not a new and attractive book may not be made on such ground. At the same time I shall be able to turn over the story I have in my mind, and which I have a strong notion might be published with great advantage, *first in Paris*—but that's another matter to be talked over. And of course I have not yet settled, either, whether any book about the travel, or this, should be the first. 'All very well,' you say, 'if you had money enough.' Well, but if I can see my way to what would be necessary without binding myself in any form to anything; without paying interest, or giving any security but one of my Eagle five thousand pounds; you would give up that objection. And I stand committed to no bookseller, printer, moneylender, banker, or patron whatever; and decidedly strengthen my position with my readers, instead of weakening it, drop by drop, as I otherwise must. Is it not so? and is not the way before me, plainly this? I infer that in reality you do yourself think that what I first thought of is *not* the way? I have told you my scheme very badly, as I said I would. I see its great points, against many prepossessions the other way—as, leaving England, home, friends, everything I am fond of—but it seems to me, at a critical time, *the* step to set me right. A blessing on Mr. Mariotti my Italian master, and his pupil! . . . If you have any breath left, tell Topping how you are."

I had certainly not much after reading this letter, written amid all the distractions of his work, with both the *Carol* and *Chuzzlewit* in hand; but such insufficient breath as was left to me I spent against the project, and in favour of far more consideration than he had given to it before anything should be settled. "I expected you," he wrote next day (2 November), "to be startled. If I was startled myself, when I first got this project of foreign travel into my head, MONTHS AGO, how much more must you be, on whom it comes fresh: numbering only hours! Still, I am very resolute upon it—very. I am convinced that my expenses abroad would not be more than half of my expenses here; the influence of change and nature upon me, enormous. You know, as well as I, that I think *Chuzzlewit* in a hundred points immeasurably the best of my stories. That I feel my power now, more than I ever did. That I have a greater confidence in myself than I ever had. That I *know*, if I have health, I could sustain my place in the minds of thinking men, though fifty writers started up to-morrow. But how many readers do *not* think! How many take it upon trust from knaves and idiots, that one writes too fast, or runs a thing to death! How coldly did this very book go on for months, until it forced itself up in people's opinion, without forcing itself up in sale! If I wrote for forty thousand Forsters, or for forty thousand people who know I write because I can't help it, I should have no need to leave the scene. But this very book warns me that if I *can* leave it for a time, I had better do so, and must do so. Apart from that again, I feel that longer rest after this story would do me good. You say two or three months, because you have been used to see me for eight years never leaving off. But it is not rest enough. It is impossible to go on working the brain to that extent for ever. The very spirit of the thing, in doing it, leaves a horrible despondency behind, when it is done; which must be prejudicial to the mind, so soon renewed and so seldom let alone. What would poor Scott have given to have gone abroad, of his own free will, a young man, instead of creeping there, a driveller, in his miserable decay! I said myself in my note to you—anticipating what you put to me—that it was a question *what* I should come out with, first. The travel-book, if to be done at all, would cost me very little trouble; and surely would go very far to pay charges, whenever published. We have spoken of the baby, and of leaving it here with Catherine's mother. Moving the children into France could not, in any ordinary course of things, do them anything but good. And the question is, what it would do to that by which they live: not what it would do to them. . . . I had forgotten that point in the B. and E. negotiation; but they certainly suggested instant publication of the reprints, or at all events of some of them; by which of course I know, and as you point out, I could provide of myself what is wanted. I take this as putting the thing distinctly as a matter of trade, and feeling it so. And, as a matter of trade with them or anybody else, as a matter of trade between me and the public, should I not be better off a year hence, with the reputation of having seen so much in the meantime? The reason which induces you to look upon this scheme with dislike—separation for so long a time—surely has equal weight with me. I see very little pleasure in it, beyond the natural desire to have been in those great scenes; I anticipate no enjoyment at the time. I have come to look upon it as a matter of policy and duty. I have a thousand other reasons, but shall very soon myself be with you."

There were difficulties, still to be strongly urged, against taking any present step to a final resolve; and he gave way a little. But the pressure was soon renewed. "I have been," he wrote (10 November), "all day in *Chuzzlewit* agonies—conceiving only. I hope to bring forth to-morrow. Will you come here at six? I want to say a word or two about the cover of the *Carol* and the advertising, and to consult you on a nice point in the tale. It will come wonderfully I think. Mac will call here soon after, and we can then all three go to Bulwer's together. And do, my dear fellow, do for God's sake turn over about Chapman and Hall, and look upon my project as a *a settled thing*. If you object to see them, I must write to them." My reluctance to any present change in his publishing arrangements was connected with the little story, which, amid all his troubles and "*Chuzzlewit* agonies," he was steadily carrying to its close; and which remains a splendid proof of the consciousness of power felt by him, and of his confidence that it had never been greater than when his readers were thus falling off from him. He had entrusted the *Carol* for publication on his own account, under the usual terms of commission, to the firm he had been so long associated with; and at such a moment to tell them, short of absolute necessity, his intention to quit them altogether, I thought a needless putting in peril of the little book's chances. He yielded to this argument; but the issue, as will be found, was less fortunate than I hoped.

Let disappointments, or annoyances, however, beset him as they might, once heartily in his work and all was forgotten. His temperament of course coloured everything, cheerful or sad, and his present outlook was disturbed by imaginary fears: but it was very certain that his labours and successes thus far had enriched others more than himself, and while he knew that his mode of living had been scrupulously governed by what he believed to be his means, the first suspicion that these might be inadequate made a change necessary to so upright a nature. It was the turning-point of his career; and the issue, though not immediately, ultimately justified him. Much of his present restlessness I was too ready myself to ascribe to that love of change which was always arising from his passionate desire to vary and extend his observation; but even as to this the result showed him right in believing that he should obtain intellectual advantage from the effects of such further travel. Here indeed he spoke from experience, for already he had returned from America with wider views than when he started, and with more maturity of mind. The money difficulties on which he dwelt were also, it is now to be admitted, unquestionable. Beyond his own domestic expenses necessarily increasing, there were many, never-satisfied, constantly-recurring claims from family quarters, not the more easily avoidable because unreasonable and unjust; and it was after describing to me one such with great bitterness, a few days following the letter last quoted, that he thus replied on the following day (19 November) to the comment I had made upon it: "I was most horribly put out for a little while; for I had got up early to go to work, and was full of interest in what I had to do. But having eased my mind by that note to you, and taken a turn or two up and down the room, I went at it again, and soon got so interested that I blazed away till 9 last night; only stopping ten minutes for dinner! I suppose I wrote eight printed pages of *Chuzzlewit* yesterday. The consequence is that I *could* finish to-day, but am taking it easy, and making myself laugh very much." The very next day, unhappily, there came to himself a repetition of precisely similar trouble in exaggerated form, and to me a fresh reminder of what was gradually settling into a fixed resolve. "I am quite serious and sober when I say, that I have very grave thoughts of keeping my whole

# The Life of Charles Dickens

menagerie in Italy three years." . . .

In construction and conduct of story *Martin Chuzzlewit* is defective, character and description constituting the chief part of its strength. But what it lost as a story by the American episode it gained in the other direction; young Martin, by happy use of a bitter experience, casting off his slough of selfishness in the poisonous swamp of Eden. Dickens often confessed, however, the difficulty it had been to him to have to deal with this gap in the main course of his narrative. . . .

Thackeray used to say that there was nothing finer in rascaldom than this ruin of Pecksniff by his son-in-law at the very moment when the oily hypocrite believes himself to be achieving his masterpiece of dissembling over the more vulgar avowed ruffian. " 'Jonas!' cried Mr. Pecksniff much affected, 'I am not a diplomatical character; my heart is in my hand. By far the greater part of the inconsiderable savings I have accumulated in the course of—I hope—a not dishonourable or useless career, is already given, devised, or bequeathed (correct me, my dear Jonas, if I am technically wrong), with expressions of confidence which I will not repeat; and in securities which it is unnecessary to mention; to a person whom I cannot, whom I will not, whom I need not name.' Here he gave the hand of his son-in-law a fervent squeeze, as if he would have added, 'God bless you: be very careful of it when you get it!' "

Certainly Dickens thus far had done nothing of which, as in this novel, the details were filled in with such incomparable skill; where the wealth of comic circumstance was lavished in such overflowing abundance on single types of character; or where generally, as throughout the story, the intensity of his observation of individual humours and vices had taken so many varieties of imaginative form. Everything in *Chuzzlewit* indeed had grown under treatment, as will be commonly the case in the handling of a man of genius, who never knows where any given conception may lead him, out of the wealth of resource in development and incident which it has itself created. "As to the way," he wrote to me of its two most prominent figures, as soon as all their capabilities were revealed to him, "as to the way in in which these characters have opened out, this is to me one of the most surprising processes of the mind in this sort of invention. Given what one knows, what one does not know springs up; and I am as absolutely certain of its being true, as I am of the law of gravitation— if such a thing be possible, more so." The remark displays exactly what in all his important characters was the very process of creation with him. . . .

But this is a chapter of disappointments, and I have now to state, that as *Martin Chuzzlewit's* success was to seem to him at first only distant and problematical, so even the prodigious immediate success of the *Christmas Carol* itself was not to be an unmitigated pleasure. Never had little book an outset so full of brilliancy of promise.

Published but a few days before Christmas, it was hailed on every side with enthusiastic greeting. The first edition of six thousand copies was sold the first day, and on 3 January, 1844, he wrote to me that "two thousand of the three printed for second and third editions are already taken by the trade." But a very few weeks were to pass before the darker side of the picture came. "Such a night as I have passed!" he wrote to me on Saturday morning, 10 February. "I really believed I should never get up again, until I had passed through all the horrors of a fever. I found the *Carol* accounts awaiting me, and they were the cause of it. The first six thousand copies show a profit of £230! And the last four will yield as much more. I had set my heart and soul upon a Thousand, clear. What a wonderful thing it is, that such a great success should occasion me such intolerable anxiety and disappointment! My year's bills, unpaid, are so terrific, that all the energy and determination I can possibly exert will be required to clear me before I go abroad; which, if next June come and find me alive, I shall do. Good Heaven, if I had only taken heart a year ago! Do come soon, as I am very anxious to talk with you. We can send round to Mac after you arrive, and tell him to join us at Hampstead or elsewhere. I was so utterly knocked down last night, that I came up to the contemplation of all these things quite bold this morning. If I can let the house for this season, I will be off to some seaside place as soon as a tenant offers. I am not afraid, if I reduce my expenses; but if I do not, I shall be ruined past all mortal hope of redemption."

The ultimate result was that his publishers were changed, and the immediate result that his departure for Italy became a settled thing; but a word may be said on these *Carol* accounts before mention is made of his new publishing arrangements. Want of judgment had been shown in not adjusting the expenses of production with a more equable regard to the selling price, but even as it was, before the close of the year, he had received £726 from a sale of fifteen thousand copies; and the difference between this and the amount realised by the same proportion of the sale of the successor to the *Carol*, undoubtedly justified him in the discontent now expressed. Of that second sale, as well as of the third and fourth, more than double the numbers of the *Carol* were at once sold, and of course there was no complaint of any want of success; but the truth really was, as to all the Christmas stories issued in this form, that the price charged, while too large for the public addressed by them, was too little to remunerate their outlay; and when in later years he put forth similar fancies for Christmas, charging for them fewer pence than the shillings required for these, he counted his purchasers with fairly corresponding gains to himself, not by tens but by hundreds of thousands. The sale of one of those pieces, five years before his death, went up in its first week to 250,000.

It was necessary now that negotiations should be resumed with his printers, but before any step was taken Messrs. Chapman and Hall were informed of his intention not to open fresh publishing relations with them after *Chuzzlewit* should have closed. Then followed deliberations and discussions, many and grave, which settled themselves at last into the form of an agreement with Messrs. Bradbury and Evans executed on 1 June 1844; by which upon advance made to him of £2,800 he assigned to them a fourth share in whatever he might write during the next ensuing eight years, to which the agreement was to be strictly limited. There were the usual protecting clauses, but no interest was to be paid, and no obligations were imposed as to what works should be written, if any, or the form of them; the only farther stipulation having reference to the event of a periodical being undertaken whereof Dickens might be only partially editor or author, in which case his proprietorship of copyright and profits was to be two-thirds instead of three-fourths. There was an understanding, at the time this agreement was signed, that a successor to the *Carol* would be ready for the Christmas of 1844; but no other promise was asked or made in regard to any other book, nor had he himself decided what form to give to his experiences of Italy, if he should even finally determine to publish them at all.

Between this agreement and his journey six weeks elapsed, and there were one or two characteristic incidents before his departure: but mention must first be interposed of the success quite without alloy that also attended the little book, and carried off in excitement and delight every trace of doubt or misgiving. "Blessing on your kind heart," wrote Jeffrey to the author of the *Carol*. "You should be happy yourself, for you may be sure you have done more good by this little publication, fostered more kindly feelings, and prompted more positive acts of beneficence, than can be traced to all the pulpits and confessionals in Christendom since Christmas 1842." "Who can listen," exclaimed Thackeray, "to objections regarding such a book as this? It seems to me a national benefit, and to every man or woman who reads it a personal kindness." Such praise expressed what men of genius felt and said: but the small volume had other tributes, less usual and not less genuine. There poured upon its author daily, all through that Christmas time, letters from complete strangers to him which I remember reading with a wonder of pleasure; not literary at all, but of the simplest domestic kind: of which the general burden was to tell him, amid many confidences, about their homes, how the *Carol* had come to be read aloud there, and was to be kept upon a little shelf by itself, and was to do them no end of good. Anything more to be said of it will not add much to this. . . .

## III

1844

. . . In the previous February, on the 26th and 28th respectively, he had taken the chair at two great meetings, in Liverpool of the Mechanics' Institution, and in Birmingham of the Polytechnic Institution, to which reference is made by him in a letter of the 21st. I quote the allusion because it shows thus early the sensitive regard to his position as a man of letters, and his scrupulous consideration for the feelings as well as interest of the class, which he manifested in many various and often greatly self-sacrificing ways all through his life. "Advise me on the following point. And as I must write to-night, having already lost a post, advise me by bearer. This Liverpool Institution, which is wealthy and has a high grammar school the masters of which receive in salaries upwards of £2000 a year (indeed its extent horrifies me; I am struggling through its papers this morning), writes me yesterday by its secretary a business letter about the order of the proceedings on Monday; and it begins thus. "I beg to send you prefixed, with the best respects of our committee, a bank order for twenty pounds in payment of the expenses contingent on your visit to Liverpool.'—And there, sure enough, it is. Now my impulse was, *and is* decidedly to return it. Twenty pounds is not of moment to me; and any sacrifice of independence is worth it twenty times twenty times told. But haggling in my mind is doubt whether that would be proper, and not boastful (in an inexplicable way); and whether as an author, I have a right to put myself on a basis which the professors of literature in other forms *connected with the Institution* cannot afford to occupy. Don't you see? But of course you do. The case stands thus. The Manchester Institution, being in debt, appeals to me as it were *in formâ pauperis*, and makes no such provision as I have named. The Birmingham Institution, just struggling into life with great difficulty, applies to me on the same grounds. But the Leeds people (thriving) write to me, making the expenses a distinct matter of business; and the Liverpool, as a point of delicacy, say nothing about it to the last minute, and then send the money. Now, what in the name of goodness ought I to do?—I am as much puzzled with the cheque as Colonel Jack was with his gold. If it would have settled the matter to put it on the fire yesterday, I should certainly have done it. Your opinion is requested. I think I shall have grounds for a very good speech at Brummagem; but I am not sure about Liverpool; having misgivings of over-gentility." My opinion was clearly for sending the money back, which accordingly was done.

Both speeches, duly delivered to enthusiastic listeners at the places named, were good, and both, with suitable variations, had the same theme: telling his popular audience in Birmingham that the principle of their institute, education comprehensive and unsectarian, was the only safe one, for that without danger no society could go on punishing men for preferring vice to virtue without giving them the means of knowing what virtue was; and reminding his genteeler audience in Liverpool, that if happily they had been themselves well taught, so much the more should they seek to extend the benefit to all, since, whatever the precedence due to rank, wealth, or intellect, there was yet a nobility beyond them, expressed unaffectedly by the poet's verse and in the power of education to confer.

> Howe'er it be, it seems to me,
>   'Tis only noble to be good:
> True hearts are more than coronets,
>   And simple faith than Norman blood.

He underwent some suffering, which he might have spared himself, at his return. "I saw the *Carol* last night," he wrote to me of a dramatic performance of the little story at the Adelphi. "Better than usual, and Wright seems to enjoy Bob Cratchit, but *heart-breaking* to me. Oh Heaven! if any forecast of *this* was ever in my mind! Yet O. Smith was drearily better than I expected. It is a great comfort to have that kind of meat underdone; and his face is quite perfect." Of what he suffered from these adaptations of his books, multiplied remorselessly at every theatre, I have forborne to speak, but it was the subject of complaint with him incessantly; and more or less satisfied as he was with individual performances, such as Mr. Yates's Quilp or Mantalini and Mrs. Keeley's Smike or Dot, there was only one, that of Barnaby Rudge by the Miss Fortescue who became afterwards Lady Gardner, on which I ever heard him dwell with a thorough liking. It is true that to the dramatisations of his next and other following Christmas stories he gave help himself; but, even then, all such efforts to assist special representations were mere attempts to render more tolerable what he had no power to prevent, and, with a few rare exceptions, they were never very successful. Another and graver wrong was the piracy of his writings, every one of which had been reproduced with merely such colourable changes of title, incidents, and name of characters, as were believed to be sufficient to evade the law and adapt them to "penny" purchasers. So shamelessly had this been going on every since the days of *Pickwick*, in so many outrageous ways and with all but impunity, that a course repeatedly urged by Talfourd and myself was at last taken in the present year with the *Christmas Carol* and the *Chuzzlewit* pirates. Upon a case of such peculiar flagrancy, however, that the vice-chancellor would not even hear Dickens's counsel; and what it cost our dear friend Talfourd to suppress his speech exceeded by very much the labour and pains with which he had prepared it. "The pirates," wrote Dickens to      after leaving the court on 18 January, "are beaten flat. They are bruised, bloody, battered, smashed, squelched, and utterly undone. Knight Bruce would not hear Talfourd, but instantly gave judgement. He had interrupted Anderton constantly by asking him to produce a passage which was not an expanded or contracted idea from my book. And at every successive passage he cried out, 'That is Mr. Dickens's case. Find another!' He said that there was not a shadow of doubt upon the matter. That there was no authority which would bear a construction in their favour; the piracy going beyond all previous instances. They might mention it again in a week, he said, if they liked, and might have an issue if they pleased; but they would probably consider it unnecessary after that strong expression of his opinion. Of course I will stand by what we have agreed as to the only terms of compromise with the printers. I am determined that I will have an apology for their affidavits. The other men may pay their costs and get out of it, but I will stick to my friend the author." Two days later he wrote: "The further affidavits put in by way of extenuation by the printing rascals *are* rather strong, and give one a pretty correct idea of what the men must be who hold on by the heels of literature. Oh! the agony of Talfourd at Knight Bruce's not hearing him! He had sat up till three in the morning, he says, preparing his speech; and would have done all kinds of things with the affidavits. It certainly was a splendid subject. We have heard nothing from the vagabonds yet. I once thought of printing the affidavits without a word of comment, and sewing them up with *Chuzzlewit*. Talfourd is strongly disinclined to compromise with the printers on any terms. In which case it would be referred to the master to ascertain what profits had been made by the piracy, and to order the same to be paid to me. But wear and tear of law is my consideration." The undertaking to which he had at last to submit was, that upon ample public apology and payment of all costs, the offenders should be let go: but the real result was that, after infinite vexation and trouble, he had himself to pay all the costs incurred on his own behalf; and, a couple of years later, upon repetition of the wrong he had suffered in so gross a form that proceedings were again advised by Talfourd and others, he wrote to me from Switzerland the condition of mind to which his experience had brought him. "My feeling about the —— is the feeling common, I suppose, to three-fourths of the reflecting part of the community in our happiest of all possible countries; and that is, that it is better to suffer a great wrong than to have recourse to the much greater wrong of the law. I shall not easily forget the expense, and anxiety, and horrible injustice of the *Carol* case, wherein, in asserting the plainest right on earth, I was really treated as if I were the robber instead of the robbed. Upon the whole, I certainly would much rather NOT proceed. What do you think of sending in a grave protest against what has been done in this case, on account of the immense amount of piracy to which I am daily exposed, and because I have been already met in the Court of Chancery with the legal doctrine that silence under such wrongs barred my remedy: to which Talfourd's written opinion might be appended as proof that we stopped under no discouragement. It is useless to affect that I don't know I have a morbid susceptibility of exasperation, to which the meanness and badness of the law in such a matter would be stinging in the last degree. And I know of nothing that *could* come, even of a successful action, which would be worth the mental trouble and disturbance it would cost." . . .

The reader may be amused if I add what he said of the pirates in those earlier days when grave matters touched him less gravely. On the eve of the first number of *Nickleby* he had issued a proclamation. "Whereas we are the only true and lawful Boz. And whereas it hath been reported to us, who are commencing a new work, that some dishonest dullards resident in the by-streets and cellars of this town impose upon the unwary and credulous, by producing cheap and wretched imitations of our delectable works. And whereas we derive but small comfort under this injury from the knowledge that the dishonest dullards aforesaid cannot, by reason of their mental smallness, follow near our heels, but are constrained to creep along by dirty and little-frequented ways, at a most respectful and humble distance behind. And whereas, in like manner, as some other vermin are not worth the killing for the sake of their carcases, so these kennel pirates are not worth the powder and shot of the law, inasmuch as whatever damages they may commit they are in no condition to pay any. This is to give notice, that we have at length devised a mode of execution for them, so summary and terrible, that if any gang or gangs thereof presume to hoist but one shred of the colours of the good ship *Nickleby*, we will hang them on gibbets so lofty and enduring that their remains shall be a monument of our just vengeance to all succeeding ages; and it shall not lie in the power of any lord high admiral, on earth, to cause them to be taken down again." The last paragraph of the proclamation informed the potentates of Paternoster Row, that from the then ensuing day of the thirtieth of March, until further notice, "we shall hold our Levees, as heretofore, on the last evening but one of every month, between the hours of seven and nine, at our Board of Trade, number one hundred and eighty-six in the Strand, London; where we again request the attendance (in vast crowds) of their accredited agents and ambassadors. Gentlemen to wear knots upon their shoulders; and patent cabs to draw up with their doors towards the grand entrance, for the convenience of loading."

The preparation for departure [for Italy] was now actively going forward, and especially his inquiries for two important adjuncts thereto, a courier and a carriage. As to the latter it occurred to him that he might perhaps get for little money "some good old shabby devil of a coach—one of those vast phantoms that hide themselves in a corner of the Pantechnicon" and exactly such a one he found there; sitting himself inside it, a perfect Sentimental Traveller, while the managing man told him its history. "As for comfort—let me see—it is about the size of your library; with night-lamps and day-lamps and pockets and imperials and leathern cellars, and the most extraordinary contrivances. Joking apart, it is a wonderful machine. And when you see it (if you do see it) you will roar at first, and will then proclaim it to be 'perfectly brilliant, my dear fellow.' " It was marked sixty pounds; he got it for five-and-forty; and my own emotions respecting it he had described by anticipation quite correctly. In finding a courier he was even more fortunate; and these successes were followed by a third apparently very promising but in the result less satisfactory. His house was let to not very careful people.

The tenant having offered herself for Devonshire Terrace unexpectedly, during the last week or two of his stay in England he went into temporary quarters in Osnaburgh Terrace: and here a domestic difficulty befell of which the mention may be amusing, when I have disposed of an incident that preceded it too characteristic for omission. The Mendicity Society's officers had caught a notorious begging-letter writer, had identified him as an old offender against Dickens of which proofs were found on his person, and had put matters in train for his proper punishment; when the wretched creature's wife made such appeal before the case was heard at the police-court, that Dickens broke down in his character of prosecutor, and at the last moment, finding what was said of the man's distress at the time to be true, relented. "When the Mendicity officers themselves told me the man was in distress, I desired them to suppress what they knew about him, and slipped out of the bundle (in the police-office) his first letter, which was the greatest lie of all. For he looked wretched, and his wife had been waiting about the street to see me, all the morning. It was an exceedingly bad case, however, and the imposition, all through, very great indeed. Insomuch that I could not *say* anything in his favour, even when I saw him. Yet I was not sorry that the creature found the loophole for escape. The officers had taken him illegally without any warrant; and really they messed it all through, quite facetiously."

He will himself also best relate the small domestic difficulty into which he fell in his temporary dwelling upon his unexpectedly discovering it to be unequal to the strain of a dinner party for which invitations had gone out just before the sudden "let" of Devonshire Terrace. The letter is characteristic in other ways, or I should hardly have gone so far into domesticities here; and it enables me to add that with the last on its list of guests, Mr. Thomas Chapman, the chairman of Lloyd's, he held frequent kindly intercourse, and that few things more absurd or unfounded have been invented, even of Dickens, than that he found any part of the original of Mr. Dombey in the nature, the appearance, or the manners of this excellent and much-valued friend. "Advise, advise," he wrote (9 Osnaburgh Terrace, 28 May, 1844), "advise with a distracted man. Investigation below stairs renders it, as my father would say, 'manifest to any person of ordinary intelligence, if the term may be considered allowable,' that the Saturday's dinner cannot come off here with safety. It would be a

# The Life of Charles Dickens 471

toss-up, and might come down heads, but it would put us into an
agony with that kind of people. . . . Now, I feel a difficulty in
dropping it altogether, and really fear that this might have an indefinably suspicious and odd appearance. Then said I at breakfast this
morning, I'll send down to the Clarendon. Then says Kate, have it at
Richmond. Then say I that might be inconvenient to the people.
Then she says, how could it be if we dine late enough? Then I am very
much offended without exactly knowing why; and come up here, in a
state of hopeless mystification. . . . What do you think? Ellis would
be quite as dear as anybody else; and unless the weather changes,
the place is objectionable. I must make up my mind to do one thing
or other, for we shall meet Lord Denham at dinner to-day. Could it
be dropped decently? That, I think very doubtful. Could it be done for
a couple of guineas apiece at the Clarendon? . . . In a matter of
more importance I could make up my mind. But in a matter of this
kind I bother and bewilder myself, and come to no conclusion
whatever. Advise! Advise! . . . List of the invited. There's Lord
Normanby. And there's Lord Denham. There's Easthope, wife, and
sister. There's Sydney Smith. There's you and Mac. There's Babbage.
There's a Lady Osborne and her daughter. There's Southwood Smith.
And there's Quin. And there are Thomas Chapman and his wife. So
many of these people have never dined with us, that the fix is particularly tight. Advise! Advise!" My advice was for throwing over the
party altogether, but additional help was obtained and the dinner
went off very pleasantly. . . .

The last incident before Dickens's departure was a farewell dinner
to him at Greenwich, which took also the form of a celebration for
the completion of *Chuzzlewit*, or, as the Ballantynes used to call it in
Scott's case, a christening dinner; when Lord Normanby took the
chair, and I remember sitting next the great painter Turner, who
had come with Stanfield, and had enveloped his throat, that sultry
summer day, in a huge red belcher-handkerchief, which nothing
would induce him to remove. He was not otherwise demonstrative,
but enjoyed himself in a quiet silent way, less perhaps at the speeches
than at the changing lights on the river. Carlyle did not come; telling
me in his reply to the invitation that he truly loved Dickens, having
discerned in the inner man of him a real music of the genuine kind,
but that he'd rather testify to this in some other form than that of
dining out in the dog-days.

## IV

### IDLENESS AT ALBARO: VILLA BAGNERELLO

#### 1844

THE travelling party arrived at Marseilles on the evening of Sunday, 14 July. Not being able to get *vetturino* horses in Paris, they had come on post; paying for nine horses but bringing only four, and thereby saving a shilling a mile out of what the four would have cost in England. So great thus far, however, had been the cost of travel, that "what with distance, caravan, sight-seeing, and everything," two hundred pounds would be nearly swallowed up before they were at their destination. The success otherwise had been complete. The children had not cried in their worst troubles, the carriage had gone lightly over abominable roads, and the courier had proved himself a perfect gem. "Surrounded by strange and perfectly novel circumstances," Dickens wrote to me from Marseilles, "I feel as if I had a new head on side by side with my old one."

To what shrewd and kindly observation the old one had helped him at every stage of his journey, his published book of travel tells, and of all that there will be nothing here; but a couple of experiences at his outset, of which he told me afterwards, have enough character in them to be worth mention.

Shortly before there had been some public interest about the captain of a Boulogne steamer apprehended on a suspicion of having stolen specie, but reinstated by his owners after a public apology to him on their behalf; and Dickens had hardly set foot on the boat that was to carry them across, when he was attracted by the look of its captain, and discovered him after a minute's talk to be that very man. "Such an honest, simple, good fellow, I never saw," said, Dickens, as he imitated for me the homely speech in which his confidences were related. The Boulogne people, he said, had given him a piece of plate, "but Lord bless us! it took a deal more than that to get him round again in his own mind; and for weeks and weeks he was uncommon low to be sure. Newgate, you see! What a place for a seafaring man as had held up his head afore the best on 'em, and had more friends, I mean to say, and I do tell you the daylight truth, than any man on this station—ah! or any other, I don't care where!"

His first experience in a foreign tongue he made immediately on landing, when he had gone to the bank for money, and after delivering with most laborious distinctness a rather long address in French to the clerk behind the counter, was disconcerted by that functionary's cool inquiry in the native-born Lombard Street manner, "How would you like to take it, sir?" He took it, as everybody must, in five-franc pieces, and a most inconvenient coinage he found it; for he required so much that he had to carry it in a couple of small sacks, and was always "turning hot about suddenly" taking it into his head that he had lost them.

The evening of Tuesday, 16 July, saw him in a villa at Albaro, the suburb of Genoa in which, upon the advice of our Gore House friends, he had resolved to pass the summer months before taking up his quarters in the city. His wish was to have had Lord Byron's house there, but it had fallen into neglect and become the refuge of a third-rate wineshop. The matter had then been left to Angus Fletcher who just now lived near Genoa, and he had taken at a rent absurdly above its value an unpicturesque and uninteresting dwelling, which at once impressed its new tenant with its likeness to a pink jail. "It is," he said to me, "the most perfectly lonely, rusty, stagnant old staggerer of a domain that you can possibly imagine. What would I give if you could only look round the courtyard! *I* look down into it, whenever I am near that side of the house, for the stable is so full of 'vermin and swarmers' (pardon the quotation from my inimitable friend) that I always expect to see the carriage going out bodily, with legions of industrious fleas harnessed to and drawing it off, on their own account. We have a couple of Italian work-people in our establishment; and to hear one or other of them talking away to our servants with the utmost violence and volubility in Genoese, and our servants answering with great fluency in English (very loud: as if the others were only deaf, not Italian), is one of the most ridiculous things possible. The effect is greatly enhanced by the Genoese manner, which is exceedingly animated and pantomimic; so that two friends of the lower class conversing pleasantly in the street, always seem on the eve of stabbing each other forthwith. And a stranger is immensely astonished at their not doing it." . . .

A letter sketched for me the story of his travel through France, and I may at once say that I thus received, from week to week, the "first sprightly runnings" of every description in his *Pictures from Italy*. But my rule as to the American letters must be here observed yet more strictly; and nothing resembling his printed book, however distantly, can be admitted into these pages. Even so my difficulty of rejection will not be less; for as he had not actually decided, until the very last, to publish his present experiences at all, a larger number of the letters were left unrifled by him. He had no settled plan from the first, as in the other case. . . .

[In one of his early letters he wrote:] ". . . Good Heavens! How I wish you'd come for a week or two, and taste the white wine at a penny farthing the pint. It is excellent. . . ." Then, after seven days: "I have got my paper and inkstand and figures now (the box from Osnaburgh Terrace only came last Thursday), and can think— I have begun to do so every morning—with a business-like air, of the Christmas book. My paper is arranged, and my pens are spread out in the usual form. I think you know the form—don't you? My books have not passed the custom-house yet, and I tremble for some volumes of Voltaire. . . . I write in the best bedroom. The sun is off the corner window at the side of the house by a very little after twelve; and I can then throw the blinds open, and look up from my paper, at the sea, the mountains, the washed-out villas, the vineyards, at the blistering white-hot fort with a sentry on the drawbridge standing in a bit of shadow no broader than his own musket, and at the sky, as often as I like. It is a very peaceful view, and yet a very cheerful one. Quiet as quiet can be."

Not yet, however, had the time for writing come. A sharp attack of illness befell his youngest little daughter, Kate, and troubled him much. Then, after beginning the Italian grammar himself, he had to call in the help of a master; and his learning of the language took up time. But he had an aptitude for it, and after a month's application told me (24 August) that he could ask in Italian for whatever he wanted in any shop or coffee-house, and could read it pretty well. "I wish you could see me" (16 September), "without my knowing it, walking about alone here. I am now as bold as a lion in the streets. The audacity with which one begins to speak when there is no help for it, is quite astonishing." . . .

In the middle of August he dined with the French consul-general, and there will now be no impropriety in printing his agreeable sketch of the dinner. "There was present, among other Genoese, the Marquis di Negri: a very fat and much older Jerdan, with the same thickness of speech and size of tongue. He was Byron's friend, keeps open house here, writes poetry, improvises, and is a very good old Blunderbore; just the sort of instrument to make an artesian well with, anywhere. Well, sir, after dinner, the consul proposed my health, with a little French conceit to the effect that I had come to Italy to have personal experience of its lovely climate, and that there was this similarity between the Italian sun and its visitor, that the sun shone into the darkest places and made them bright and happy with its benignant influence, and that my books had done the like with the breasts of men, and so forth. Upon which Blunderbore gives his bright-but-toned blue coat a great rap on the breast, turns up his fishy eyes, stretches out his arm like the living statue defying the lightning at Astley's, and delivers four impromptu verses in my honour, at which everybody is enchanted, and I more than anybody—perhaps with the best reason, for I didn't understand a word of them. The consul then takes from his breast a roll of paper, and says, 'I shall read them!' Blunderbore then says, 'Don't!' But the consul does, and Blunderbore beats time to the music of the verse with his knuckles on the table; and perpetually ducks forward to look round the cap of a lady sitting between himself and me to see what I think of them. I exhibit lively emotion. The verses are in French—short line—on the taking of Tangiers by the Prince de Joinville; and are received with great applause; especially by a nobleman present who is reported to be unable to read and write. They end in my mind (rapidly translating them into prose) thus:

| | |
|---|---|
| The cannon of France | Rendering thanks |
| Shake the foundation | To Heaven. |
| Of the wondering sea, | The King |
| The artillery on the shore | And all the Royal Family |
| Is put to silence. | Are bathed |
| Honour to Joinville | In tears. |
| And the Brave! | They call upon the name |
| The Great Intelligence | Of Joinville! |
| Is borne | France also |
| Upon the wings of Fame | Weeps, and echoes it. |
| To Paris. | Joinville is crowned |
| Her national citizens | With Immortality; |
| Exchange caresses | And Peace and Joinville, |
| In the streets! | And the Glory of France, |
| The temples are crowded | Diffuse themselves |
| With religious patriots | Conjointly. |

If you can figure to yourself the choice absurdity of receiving anything into one's mind in this way, you can imagine the labour I underwent in my attempts to keep the lower part of my face square, and to lift up one eye gently, as with admiring attention. But I am bound to add that this is really pretty literal; for I read them afterwards." At his French friend's house he afterwards made the acquaintance of Lamartine. . . .

The marquis had a splendid house, but Dickens found the grounds so carved into grottoes and fanciful walks as to remind him of nothing so much as our old White Conduit House, except that he would have been well pleased, on the present occasion, to have discovered a waiter crying, "Give your orders, gents!" it being not easy to him at any time to keep up, the whole night through, on ices and variegated lamps merely. But the scene for awhile was amusing enough, and not rendered less so by the delight of the marquis himself, "who was constantly diving out into dark corners and then among the lattice-work and flower pots, rubbing his hands and going round and round with explosive chuckles in his huge satisfaction with the entertainment." With horror it occurred to Dickens, however, that four more hours of this kind of entertainment would be too much; that the Genoa gates closed at twelve; and that as the carriage had not been ordered till the dancing was expected to be over and the gates to reopen, he must make a sudden bolt if he would himself get back to Albaro. "I had barely time," he told me, "to reach the gate before midnight; and was running as hard as I could go, downhill, over uneven ground, along a new street, called the Strada Sevra, when I came to a pole fastened straight across the street, nearly breast-high, without any light or watchman—quite in the Italian style. I went over it, headlong, with such force that I rolled myself completely white in the dust; but although I tore my clothes to shreds, I hardly scratched myself except in one place on the knee. I had no time to think of it then, for I was up directly and off again to save the gate: but when I got outside the wall and saw the state I was in, I wondered I had not broken my neck. I 'took it easy' after this, and walked home, by lonely ways enough, without meeting a single soul. But there is nothing to be feared, I believe, from midnight walks in this part of Italy. In other places you incur the danger of being stabbed by mistake; whereas the people here are quiet and good-tempered, and very rarely commit any outrage."

Such adventures, nevertheless, are seldom without consequences, and there followed in this case a short but sharp attack of illness. It came on with the old " unspeakable and agonising pain in the side," for which Bob Fagin had prepared and applied the hot bottles in the old warehouse time; and it yielded quickly to powerful remedies. But for a few days he had to content himself with the minor sights of Albaro. . . .

In the second week of September he went to meet his brother Frederick at Marseilles, and bring him back over the Cornice road to pass a fortnight's holiday at Genoa: and his description of the first inn upon the Alps they slept in is too good to be lost. "We lay last night," he wrote (9 September), "at the first halting-place on this journey, in an inn which is not entitled, as it ought to be, The house of call for fleas and vermin in general, but is entitled The grand hotel of the Post! I hardly know what to compare it to. It seemed something like a house in Somers Town originally built for a wine-vaults and never finished, but grown very old. There was nothing to eat in it and nothing to drink. They had lost the teapot; and when they found it, they couldn't make out what had become of the lid, which, turning up at last and being fixed on to the teapot, couldn't be got off again for the pouring-in of more water. Fleas of elephantine dimensions were gambolling boldly in the dirty beds; and the mosquitoes! —But here let me draw a curtain (as I would have done if there had been any). We had scarcely any sleep, and rose up with hands and arms hardly human." . . .

V

WORK IN GENOA: PALAZZO PESCHIERE

1844

. . . THE subject for his new Christmas story he had chosen, but he had not found a title for it, or the machnery to work it with; when, at the moment of what seemed to be his greatest trouble, both reliefs came. Sitting down one mornng resolute for work, though against the grain, his hand being out and everything inviting to idleness, such a peal of chimes arose from the city as he found to be "maddening." All Genoa lay beneath him, and up from it, with some sudden set of the wind, came in one fell sound the clang and clash of all its steeples, pouring into his ears, again and again, in a tuneless, grating, discordant, jerking, hideous vibration that made his ideas "spin round and round till they lost themselves in a whirl of vexation and giddiness, and dropped down dead." He had never before so suffered, nor did he again; but this was his description to me next day, and his excuse for having failed in a promise to send me his title. Only two days later, however, came a letter in which not a syllable was written but "We have heard THE CHIMES at midnight, Master Shallow!" and I knew he had discovered what he wanted.

Other difficulties were still to be got over. He craved for the London streets. He so missed his long night-walks before beginning anything that he seemed, as he said, dumbfounded without them. "I can't help thinking of the boy in the school-class whose button was cut off by Walter Scott and his friends. Put me down on Waterloo Bridge at eight o'clock in the evening, with leave to roam about as long as I like, and I would come home, as you know, panting to go on. I am sadly strange as it is, and can't settle. You will have lots of hasty notes from me while I am at work: but you know your man; and whatever strikes me, I shall let off upon you as if I were in Devonshire Terrace. It's a great thing to have my title, and see my way how to work the bells. Let them clash upon me now from all the churches and convents in Genoa, I see nothing but the old London belfry I have set them in. In my mind's eye, Horatio, I like more and more my notion of making, in this little book, a great blow for the poor. Something powerful, I think I can do, but I want to be tender too, and cheerful; as like the *Carol* in that respect as may be, and as unlike it as such a thing can be. The duration of the action will resemble it a little, but I trust to the novelty of the machinery to carry that off; and if my design be anything at all, it has a grip upon the very throat of the time." (8 October.)

Thus bent upon his work, for which he never had been in more earnest mood, he was disturbed by hearing that he must attend the levee of the governor, who had unexpectedly arrived in the city, and who would take it as an affront, his eccentric friend Fletcher told him, if that courtesy were not immediately paid. "It was the morning on which I was going to begin, so I wrote round to our consul,"— praying, of course, that excuse should be made for him. Don't bother yourself, replied that sensible functionary, for all the consuls and governors alive; but shut yourself up by all means. "So," continues Dickens telling me the tale, "he went next morning in great state, and full costume, to present two English gentlemen. 'Where's the great poet?' said the Governor. 'I want to see the great poet.' 'The great poet, your excellency,' said the consul, 'is at work, writing a book, and begged me to make his excuses.' 'Excuses!' said the Governor, 'I wouldn't interfere with such an occupation for all the world. Pray tell him that my house is open to the honour of his presence when it is perfectly convenient for him; but not otherwise. And let no gentleman,' said the Governor, a surweyin' of his suite with majestic eye, 'call upon Signor Dickens till he is understood to be disengaged.' And he sent somebody with his own cards next day. Now I *do* seriously call this, real politeness and pleasant consideration —not positively American, but still gentlemanly and polished. The same spirit pervades the inferior departments; and I have not been required to observe the usual police regulations, or to put myself to the slightest trouble about anything." (18 October.) . . .

He kept his promise that I should hear from him while writing, and I had frequent letters when he was fairly in his work. "With my steam very much up, I find it a great trial to be so far off from you, and consequently to have no one (always excepting Kate and Georgy) to whom to expatiate on my day's work. And I want a crowded street to plunge into at night. And I want to be 'on the spot' as it were. But apart from such things, the life I lead is favourable to work." In his next letter: "I am in regular, ferocious excitement with the *Chimes*; get up at seven; have a cold bath before breakfast; and blaze away, wrathful and red-hot, until three o'clock or so: when I usually knock off (unless it rains) for the day. . . . I am fierce to finish in a spirit bearing some affinity to those of truth and mercy, and to shame the cruel and the canting. I have not forgotten my catechism. 'Yes, verily, and with God's help, so I will!'"

Within a week he had completed his first part, or quarter. "I send you to-day" (18 October), "by mail, the first and longest of the four divisions. This is great for the first week, which is usually uphill. I have kept a copy in shorthand in case of accidents. I hope to send you a parcel every Monday until the whole is done. I do not wish to influence you, but it has a great hold upon me, and has affected me, in the doing, in divers strong ways, deeply, forcibly. . . ."

A visit from him to London was to be expected almost immediately! That all remonstrance would be idle, under the restless excitement his work had awakened, I well knew. It was not merely the wish he had, natural enough, to see the last proofs and the wood-cuts before the day of publication, which he could not otherwise do; but it was the stronger and more eager wish, before that final launch, to have a vivider sense than letters could give him of the effect of what he had been doing. "If I come, I shall put up at Cuttris's" (then the Piazza Hotel in Covent Garden), "that I may be close to you. Don't say to anybody, except our immediate friends, that I am coming. Then I shall not be bothered. If I should preserve my present fierce writing humour, in any pass I may run to Venice, Bologna, and Florence, before I turn my face towards Lincoln's Inn Fields; and come to England by Milan and Turin. But this of course depends in a great measure on your reply." My reply, dwelling on the fatigue and cost, had the reception I foresaw. "Notwithstanding what you say, I am still in the same mind about coming to London.

# The Life of Charles Dickens 479

Not because the proofs concern me at all (I should be an ass as well
as a thankless vagabond if they did), but because of that unspeakable
restless something which would render it almost as impossible for me
to remain here and not see the thing complete, as it would be for a
full balloon, left to itself, not to go up. I do not intend coming from
*here*, but by way of Milan and Turin (previously going to Venice),
and so, across the wildest pass of the Alps that may be open, to
Strasburg. . . . As you dislike the Young England gentleman I
shall knock him out, and replace him by a man (I can dash him in at
your rooms in an hour) who recognises no virtue in anything but the
good old times, and talks of them, parrot-like, whatever the matter
is. A real good old city Tory, in a blue coat and bright buttons and a
white cravat, and with a tendency of blood to the head. File away
at Filer, as you please; but bear in mind that the *Westminster
Review* considered Scrooge's presentation of the turkey to Bob
Cratchit as grossly incompatible with political economy. I don't
care at all for the skittle-playing." These were among things I had
objected to.

But the close of his letter revealed more than its opening of the
reason, not at once so frankly confessed, for the long winter-journey
he was about to make; and if it be thought that, in printing the
passage, I take a liberty with my friend, it will be found that equal
liberty is taken with myself, whom it good-naturedly caricatures; so
that the reader can enjoy his laugh at either or both. "Shall I confess
to you, I particularly want Carlyle above all to see it before the rest of
the world, when it is done; and I should like to inflict the little story
on him and on dear old gallant Macready with my own lips, and to
have Stanny and the other Mac sitting by. Now, if you was a real
gent, you'd get up a little circle for me, one wet evening, when I
come to town: and would say, 'My boy (SIR, will you have the goodness to leave those books alone and go downstairs—WHAT the devil
are you doing! And mind, sir, I can see nobody—Do you hear?
Nobody. I am particularly engaged with a gentleman from Asia)—
My boy, would you give us that little Christmas book (a little
Christmas book of Dickens's, Macready, which I'm anxious you
should hear); and don't slur it, now, or be too fast, Dickens, please!'—
I say, if you was a real gent, something to this effect might happen. I
shall be under sailing orders the moment I have finished. And I
shall produce myself (please God) in London on the very day you
name. For one week: to the hour."

The wish was complied with, of course; and that night in Lincoln's
Inn Fields led to rather memorable issues. His next letter told me
the little tale was done. "Third of November, 1844. Half-past two,
afternoon. Thank God! I have finished the *Chimes*. This moment. I
take up my pen again to-day, to say only that much; and to add that
I have had what women call 'a real good cry.'" Very genuine all
this, it is hardly necessary to say. The little book thus completed was
not one of his greater successes, and it raised him up some objectors;

but there was that in it which more than repaid the suffering its writing cost him, and the enmity its opinions provoked; and in his own heart it had a cherished corner to the last. . . .

### VI

#### ITALIAN TRAVEL

#### 1844

So it all fell out accordingly. He parted from his disconsolate wife, as he told me in his first letter from Ferrara, on Wednesday, 6 November: left her shut up in her palace like a baron's lady in the time of the Crusades; and had his first real experience of the wonders of Italy. He saw Parma, Modena, Bologna, Ferrara, Venice, Verona, and Mantua. As to all which the impressions conveyed to me in his letters have been more or less given in his published *Pictures*. . . .

On Sunday the 17th, he was at Lodi, from which he wrote to me that he had been, like Leigh Hunt's pig, up "all manner of streets" since he left his palazzo; that with one exception he had not on any night given up more than five hours to rest; that all the days except two had been bad ("the last two foggy as Blackfriars Bridge on Lord Mayor's Day"); and that the cold had been dismal. But what cheerful, keen, observant eyes he carried everywhere; and, in the midst of new and unaccustomed scenes, and of objects and remains of art for which no previous study had prepared him, with what a delicate play of imagination and fancy the accuracy of his ordinary vision was exalted and refined, I think strikingly shown by the few unstudied passages I am preserving from these friendly letters. . . .

"I am already brim-full of cant about pictures, and shall be happy to enlighten you on the subject of the different schools, at any length you please. It seems to me that the preposterous exaggeration in which our countrymen delight in reference to this Italy, hardly extends to the really good things. Perhaps it is in its nature, that there it should fall short. I have never yet seen any praise of Titian's great picture of the 'Assumption of the Virgin' at Venice, which soared half as high as the beautiful and amazing reality. It is perfection. Tintoretto's picture too, of the 'Assembly of the Blest,' at Venice also, with all the lines in it (it is of immense size and the figures are countless) tending majestically and dutifully to Almighty God in the centre, is grand and noble in the extreme. There are some wonderful portraits there, besides; and some confused, and hurried, and slaughterous battle pieces, in which the surprising art that presents the generals to your eye, so that it is almost impossible you can miss them in a crowd though they are in the thick of it, is very pleasant to dwell upon. I have seen some delightful pictures; and some (at Verona and Mantua) really too absurd and ridiculous even to laugh at. Hampton Court is a fool to 'em—and oh there are some rum 'uns there, my friend. Some werry rum 'uns. . . . Two things are clear to me already. One is, that the rules of art are much too slavishly followed; making it a pain to you, when you go into galleries day after day, to be so very precisely sure where this figure will be turning round, and that figure will be lying down, and that other will have a great lot of drapery twined about him, and so forth. This becomes a perfect nightmare. The second is, that these great men, who were of necessity very much in the hands of the monks and priests, painted monks and priests a vast deal too often. I constantly see, in pictures of tremendous power, heads quite below the story and the painter; and I invariably observe that those heads are of the convent stamp, and have their counterparts, exactly, in the convent inmates of this hour. I see the portraits of monks I know at Genoa, in all the lame parts of strong paintings: so I have settled with myself that in such cases the lameness was not with the painter, but with the vanity and ignorance of his employers, who *would* be apostles on canvas at all events."

In the same letter he described the Inns. "It is a great thing—quite a matter of course—with English travellers, to decry the Italian inns. Of course you have no comforts that you are used to in England; and travelling alone, you dine in your bedroom always; which is opposed to our habits. But they are immeasurably better than you would suppose. The attendants are very quick; very punctual; and so obliging, if you speak to them politely, that you would be a beast not to look cheerful, and take everything pleasantly. . . . The windows won't open, and the doors won't shut; and these latter (a cat could get in, between them and the floor) have a windy command of a colonnade which is open to the night, so that my slippers positively blow off my feet, and make little circuits in the room—like leaves. There is a very ashy wood-fire, burning on an immense hearth which has no fender (there is no such thing in Italy); and it only knows two extremes—an agony of heat when wood is put on, and an agony of cold when it has been on two minutes. There is also an uncomfortable stain in the wall, where the fifth door (not being strictly indispensable) was walled up a year or two ago, and never painted over. But the bed is clean; and I have had an excellent dinner; and without being obsequious or servile, which is not at all the characteristic of the people in the north of Italy, the waiters are so amiably disposed to invent little attentions which they suppose to be English, and are so lighthearted and good-natured, that it is a pleasure to have to do with them. . . .

Of the help his courier continued to be to him I had whimsical instances in almost every letter, but he appears too often in the published book to require such celebration here. He is, however, an essential figure to two little scenes sketched for me at Lodi, and I may preface them by saying that Louis Roche, a native of Avignon, justified to the close his master's high opinion. He was again engaged for nearly a year in Switzerland, and soon after, poor fellow, though with a jovial robustness of look and breadth of chest that promised unusual length of days, was killed by heart-disease. "The brave C. continues to be a prodigy. He puts out my clothes at every inn as if I were going to stay there twelve months; calls me to the instant every morning; lights the fire before I get up; gets hold of roast fowls and produces them in coaches at a distance from all other help, in hungry moments; and is invaluable to me. He is such a good fellow, too, that little rewards don't spoil him. I always give him, after I have dined, a tumbler of Sauterne or Hermitage or whatever I may have; sometimes (as yesterday) when we have come to a public-house at about eleven o'clock, very cold, having started before daybreak and had nothing, I make him take his breakfast with me; and this renders him only more anxious than ever, by redoubling attentions, to show me that he thinks he has got a good master. . . . I didn't tell you that the day before I left Genoa, we had a dinner-party—our English consul and his wife; the banker; Sir George Crawford and his wife; the De la Rues; Mr. Curry; and some others, fourteen in all. At about nine in the morning, two men in immense paper caps inquired at the door for the brave C., who presently introduced them in triumph as the governor's cooks, his private friends, who had come to dress the dinner! Jane wouldn't stand this, however; so we were obliged to decline. Then there came, at half-hourly intervals, six gentlemen having the appearance of English clergymen, being other private friends who had come to wait. . . . We accepted *their* services; and you never saw anything so nicely and quietly done. He had asked, as a special distinction, to be allowed the supreme control of the dessert; and he had ices made like fruit, had pieces of crockery turned upside-down so as to look like other pieces of crockery non-existent in this part of Europe, and carried a case of toothpicks in his pocket. Then his delight was, to get behind Kate at one end of the table, to look at me at the other, and to say to Georgy in a low voice whenever he handed her anything, "What does master think of datter 'rangement? Is he cōntĕnt?' . . . If you could see what these fellows of couriers are when their families are not upon the move, you would feel what a prize he is. I can't make out whether he was ever a smuggler, but nothing will induce him to give the custom-house officers anything: in consequence of which that portmanteau of mine has been unnecessarily opened twenty times. Two of them will come to the coach-door, at the gate of a town. 'Is there anything contraband in this carriage, signore?' 'No, no. There's nothing here. I am an Englishman, and this is my servant.' 'A buono mano signore?' 'Roche' (in English), 'give him something, and get rid of him.' He sits unmoved. 'A buono mano signore?' 'Go along with you!' says the brave C. 'Signore, I am a custom-house officer!' 'Well, then, more shame for you!'—he always makes the same answer. And then he turns to me and says in English:

while the custom-house officer's face is a portrait of anguish framed in the coach window, from his intense desire to know what is being told to his disparagement: 'Datter chip,' shaking his fist at him, 'is greatest tief—and you know it you rascal—as never did en-razh me so, that I cannot bear myself!' I suppose chip to mean chap, but it may include the custom-house officer's father and have some reference to the old block, for anything I distinctly know."

He closed his Lodi letter next day at Milan, whither his wife and her sister had made an eighty miles' journey from Genoa, to pass a couple of days with him in Prospero's old dukedom before he left for London. "We shall go our several ways on Thursday morning, and I am still bent on appearing at Cuttris's on Sunday the first, as if I had walked thither from Devonshire Terrace. In the meantime I shall not write to you again . . . to enhance the pleasure (if anything *can* enhance the pleasure) of our meeting. . . . I am opening my arms so wide!" . . .

There was certainly no want of animation when we met. I have but to write the words to bring back the eager face and figure, as they flashed upon me so suddenly this wintry Saturday night that almost before I could be conscious of his presence I felt the grasp of his hand. It is almost all I find it possible to remember of the brief, bright meeting. Hardly did he seem to have come when he was gone. But all that the visit proposed he accomplished. He saw his little book in its final form for publication; and, to a select few brought together on Monday, 2 December, at my house, had the opportunity of reading it aloud. . . .

He wrote from Paris, at which he had stopped on his way back to see Macready, whom an engagement to act there with Mr. Mitchell's English company had prevented from joining us in Lincoln's Inn Fields. There had been no such frost and snow since 1829, and he gave dismal report of the city. With Macready he had gone two nights before to the Odéon to see Alexander Dumas' *Christine* played by Madam St. George, "once Napoleon's mistress; now of an immense size, from dropsy I suppose; and with little weak legs which she can't stand upon. Her age, withal, somewhere about 80 or 90. I never in my life beheld such a sight. Every stage conventionality she ever picked up (and she had them all) has got the dropsy too, and is swollen and bloated hideously. . . .

He left Paris on the night of the 13th with the *malle poste*, which did not reach Marseilles till fifteen hours behind its time, after three days and three nights travelling over horrible roads. Then, in a confusion between the two rival packets for Genoa, he unwillingly detained one of them more than an hour from sailing; and only managed at last to get to her just as she was moving out of harbour. As he went up the side, he saw a strange sensation among the angry travellers whom he had detained so long; heard a voice exclaim "I am blarmed of it ain'tDICKENS!" and stood in the centre of a group of *Five Americans*! But the pleasantest part of the story is that they were, one and all, glad to see him; that their chief man, or leader, who had met him in New York, at once introduced them all round with the remark, "Personally our countrymen, and you, can fix it friendly, sir, I do expectuate;" and that, through the stormy passage to Genoa which followed, they were excellent friends. For the greater part of the time, it is true, Dickens had to keep to his cabin; but he contrived to get enjoyment out of them nevertheless. . . .

## VII

### LAST MONTHS IN ITALY

### 1845

ON 22 December he had resumed his ordinary Genoa life. . . . A journey southward began on 20 January, and five days later I had a letter written from La Scala, at a little inn, "supported on low brick arches like a British haystack," the bed in their room "like a mangle," the ceiling without lath or plaster, nothing to speak of available for comfort or decency, and nothing particular to eat or drink. "But for all this I have become attached to the country and I don't care who knows it."

Before Radicofani was reached, there were disturbing rumours of bandits and even uncomfortable whispers as to their night's lodging-place : "Can you imagine" (he named a first-rate bore, for whose name I shall substitute) "M. F. G. in a very frowsy brown cloak concealing his whole figure, and with very white hair and a very white beard, darting out of this place with a long staff in his hand, and begging? There he was, whether you can or not; out of breath with the rapidity of his dive, and staying with his staff all the Radicofani boys, that he might fight it out with me alone. It was very wet, and so was I: for I had kept, according to custom, my box-seat. It was blowing so hard that I could scarcely stand; and there was a custom-house on the spot, besides. Over and above all this, I had no small money; and the brave C. never has, when I want it for a beggar. When I had excused myself several times, he suddenly drew himself up and said, with a wizard look (fancy the aggravation of M. F. G. as a wizard!), 'Do you know what you are doing, my lord? Do you mean to go on to-day?' 'Yes,' I said, 'I do.' 'My lord,' he said, 'do you know that your *vetturino* is unacquainted with this part of the country; that there is a wind raging on the mountain, which will sweep you away; that the courier, the coach, and all the passengers, were blown from the road last year; and that the danger is great and almost certain?' 'No,' I said, 'I don't.' 'My lord, you don't understand me, I think?' 'Yes, I do, d—— you!' nettled by this (you feel

it? I confess it). 'Speak to my servant. It's his business. Not mine'—
for he really was too like M. F. G. to be borne. If you could have seen
him!—'Santa Maria, these English lords! It's not their business if
they're killed! They leave it to their servants!' He drew off the boys;
whispered them to keep away from the heretic; and ran up the hill
again, almost as fast as he had come down. He stopped at a little
distance as we moved on; and pointing to Roche with his long staff
cried loudly after me, 'It's *his* business if you're killed, is it, my
lord? Ha! ha! ha! whose business is it when the English lords are
born! Ha! ha! ha!' The boys taking it up in a shrill yell, I left the joke
and them at this point. But I must confess that I thought he had the
best of it. And he had so far reason for what he urged, that when we
got on the mountain pass the wind became terrific, so that we were
obliged to take Kate out of the carriage lest she should be blown over,
carriage and all, and had ourselves to hang on to it, on the windy
side, to prevent its going Heaven knows where!"

The first impression of Rome was disappointing. It was the evening
of 30 January, and the cloudy sky, dull cold rain and muddy foot-
ways, he was prepared for; but he was not prepared for the long streets
of commonplace shops and houses like Paris or any other capital, the
busy people, the equipages, the ordinary walkers up and down. "It
was no more my Rome, degraded and fallen and lying asleep in the
sun among a heap of ruins, than Lincoln's Inn Fields is. So I really
went to bed in a very indifferent humour." That all this yielded to
later and worthier impressions I need hardly say; and he had never
in his life, he told me afterwards, been so moved or overcome by any
sight as by that of the Coliseum, "except perhaps by the first contemplation of the Falls of Niagara." . . .

Two more months were to finish his Italian holiday, and I do not
think he enjoyed any part of it so much as its close. He had formed a
real friendship for Genoa, was greatly attached to the social circle
he had drawn round him there, and liked rest after his travel all the
more for the little excitement of living its activities over again, week
by week, in these letters to me. Of incidents during these remaining
weeks there were few, but such as he mentioned had in them points of
humour or character still worth remembering. Two men were hanged
in the city; and two ladies of quality, he told me, agreed to keep up
for a time a prayer for the souls of these two miserable creatures so
incessant that Heaven should never for a moment be left alone: to
which end "they relieved each other" after such wise, that, for the
whole of the stated time, one of them was always on her knees in the
cathedral church of San Lorenzo. From which he inferred that "a
morbid sympathy for criminals is not wholly peculiar to England,
though it affects more people in that country perhaps than in any
other." . . .

Another little incident is also characteristic. An English ship of
war, the *Fantôme*, appeared in the harbour; and from her commander,
Sir Frederick Nicolson, Dickens received, among attentions very

pleasant to him, an invitation to lunch on board and bring his wife, for whom, at a time appointed, a boat was to be sent to the Ponte Reale (the royal bridge). But no boat being there at the time, Dickens sent off his servant in another boat to the ship to say he feared some mistake. "While we were walking up and down a neighbouring piazza in his absence, a brilliant fellow in a dark blue shirt with a white hem to it all round the collar, regular corkscrew curls, and a face as brown as a berry, comes up to me and says, 'Beg your pardon sir, Mr. Dickens?' 'Yes.' 'Beg your pardon sir, but I'm one of the ship's company of the *Phantom* sir, cox'en of the cap'en's gig sir, she's a-lying off the pint sir—been there half an hour.' 'Well but my good fellow,' I said, 'you're at the wrong place!' 'Beg your pardon sir, I was afeerd it was the wrong place sir, but I've asked them Genoese here, sir, twenty times if it was Port Real; and they knows no more than a dead jackass!'—Isn't it a good thing to have made a regular Portsmouth name of it?" . . .

His last letter from Genoa was written on 7 June, not from the Peschiere, but from a neighbouring palace, "Brignole Rosso," into which he had fled from the miseries of moving. "They are all at sixes and sevens up at the Peschiere, as you may suppose; and Roche is in a condition of tremendous excitement, engaged in settling the inventory with the house-agent, who has just told me he is the devil himself. I had been appealed to, and had contented myself with this expression of opinion, 'Signor Noli, you are an old impostor!' '*Illustrissimo*,' said Signor Noli in reply, 'your servant is the devil himself: sent on earth to torture me.' I look occasionally towards the Peschiere (it is visible from this room), expecting to see one of them flying out of a window. . . .

# BOOK FIFTH

## LONDON, LAUSANNE AND PARIS

### 1845-7. ÆT. 33-5

# I

## 1845–6

HIS first letter after again taking possession of Devonshire Terrace revived a subject on which opinions had been from time to time interchanged during his absence, and to which there was allusion in the agreement executed before his departure. The desire was still as strong with him as when he started *Master Humphrey's Clock* to establish a periodical, that, while relieving his own pen by enabling him to receive frequent help from other writers, might retain always the popularity of his name. "I really think I have an idea, and not a bad one, for the periodical. I have turned it over, the last two days, very much in my mind: and think it positively good. I incline still to weekly; price three-halfpence, if possible; partly original, partly select; notices of books, notices of theatres, notices of all good things, notices of all bad ones; *Carol* philosophy, cheerful views, sharp anatomisation of humbug, jolly good temper; papers always in season, pat to the time of year; and a vein of glowing, hearty, generous, mirthful, beaming reference in everything to Home and Fireside. And I would call it, sir:

---

## THE CRICKET

A cheerful creature that chirrups on the Hearth.

*Natural History.*

---

"Now, don't decide hastily till you've heard what I would do. I would come out, sir, with a prospectus on the subject of the Cricket that should put everybody in a good temper, and make such a dash at people's fenders and arm-chairs as hasn't been made for many a long day. I could approach them in a different mode under this name, and in a more winning and immediate way, than under any other. I would at once sit down upon their very hobs; and take a personal and confidential position with them which should separate me, instantly, from all other periodicals periodically published, and supply a distinct and sufficient reason for my coming into existence. And I would chirp, chirp, chirp away in every number until I chirped it up to ——well, you shall say how many hundred thousand! . . . "

My objection, incident more or less to every such scheme, was the risk of losing its general advantage by making it too specially dependent on individual characteristics; but there was much in favour of the present notion, and its plan had been modified so far, in the discussions that followed, as to involve less absolute personal identification with Dickens,—when discussion, project, everything was swept away by a larger scheme, in its extent and its danger more suitable to the wild and hazardous enterprises of that prodigious year (1845) of excitement and disaster. In this more tremendous adventure, already hinted at on a previous page, we all became involved; and the chirp of the Cricket, delayed in consequence until Christmas, was heard then in circumstances quite other than those first intended. The change he thus announced to me about half-way through the summer, in the same letter which told me the success of d'Orsay's kind exertion to procure a fresh engagement for his courier Roche. "What do you think of a notion that has occurred to me in connection with our abandoned little weekly? It would be a delicate and beautiful fancy for a Christmas book, making the Cricket a little household god—silent in the wrong and sorrow of the tale, and loud again when all went well and happy." The reader will not need to be told that thus originated the story of the *Cricket on the Hearth*, a Fairy Tale of Home, which had a great popularity in the Christmas days of 1845. Its sale at the outset doubled that of both its predecessors.

But as yet the larger adventure had not made itself known, and the interval was occupied with the private play of which the notion had been started between us at his visit in December, and which led to his disclosure of a passage in his early career belonging to that interval between his school-days and start in life when he had to pass nearly two weary years as a reporter for one of the offices in Doctors' Commons, from which he sought relief by an attempt to get upon the stage. I had asked him, after his return to Genoa, whether he continued to think that we should have the play; and his reply began thus: "ARE we to have that play? ? ? Have I spoken of it, ever since I came home from London, as a settled thing! I do not know if I have ever told you seriously, but I have often thought, that I should certainly have been as successful on the boards as I have been between them. I assure you, when I was on the stage at Montreal (not having played for years) I was as much astonished at the reality and ease, to myself, of what I did as if I had been another man. See how oddly things come about!" . . .

Graver things now claim a notice which need not be proportioned to their gravity, because, though they had an immediate effect on Dickens's fortunes, they do not otherwise form part of his story. But first let me say, he was at Broadstairs for three weeks in the autumn; we had the private play on his return; and a month later, on 28 October, a sixth child and fourth son, named Alfred Tennyson after his godfathers d'Orsay and Tennyson, was born in Devonshire

Terrace. A death in the family followed, the older and more gifted of his ravens having indulged the same illicit taste for putty and paint which had been fatal to his predecessor. Voracity killed him, as it killed Scott's. He died unexpectedly before the kitchen-fire. "He kept his eye to the last upon the meat as it roasted, and suddenly turned over on his back with a sepulchral cry of *Cuckoo!*" The letter which told me this (31 October) announced to me also that he was at a deadlock in his Christmas story: "Sick, bothered and depressed. Visions of Brighton come upon me; and I have a great mind to go there to finish my second part, or to Hampstead. I have a desperate thought of 'Jack Straw's.' I never was in such bad writing cue as I am this week, in all my life." The reason was not far to seek. In the preparation for the proposed new Daily Paper he was now actively assisting, and had all but consented to the publication of his name.

I entertained at this time, for more than one powerful reason, the greatest misgiving of his intended share in the adventure. It was not fully revealed until later on what difficult terms, physical as well as mental, Dickens held the tenure of his imaginative life; but already I knew enough to doubt the wisdom of what he was at present undertaking. In all intellectual labour, his will prevailed so strongly when he fixed it on any object of desire, that what else its attainment might exact was never duly measured; and this led to frequent strain and unconscious waste of what no man could less afford to spare. To the world gladdened by his work, its production might always have seemed quite as easy as its enjoyment; but it may be doubted if ever any man's mental effort cost him more. His habits were robust, but not his health; that secret had been disclosed to me before he went to America; and to the last he decidedly refused to admit the enormous price he had paid for his triumphs and successes. The morning after his last note I heard again. "I have been so very unwell this morning, with giddiness and headache, and botheration of one sort or other, that I didn't get up till noon: and, shunning Fleet Street" (the office of the proposed new paper), "am now going for a country walk, in the course of which you will find me, if you feel disposed to come away in the carriage that goes to you with this. It is to call for a pull of the first part of the *Cricket*, and will bring you, if you like, by way of Hampstead to me, and subsequently to dinner. There is much I should like to discuss, if you can manage it. It's the loss of my walks, I suppose; but I am as giddy as if I were drunk, and can hardly see." I gave far from sufficient importance at the time to the frequency of complaints of this kind, or to the recurrence, at almost regular periods after the year following the present of those spasms in the side of which he has recorded an instance in the recollections of his childhood, and of which he had an attack in Genoa; but though not conscious of it to its full extent, this consideration was among those that influenced me in a determination to endeavour to turn him from what could not but be regarded as full of peril. His health, however, had no real prominence in my letter; and it is strange now to observe that it appears as an argument in his reply. I had simply put before him, in the strongest form, all the considerations drawn from his genius and fame that should deter him from the labour and responsibility of a daily paper, not less than from the party and political involvements incident to it; and here was the material part of the answer made: "Many thanks for your affectionate letter, which is full of generous truth. These considerations weigh with me, *heavily*: but I think I descry in these times, greater stimulants to such an effort; greater chance of some fair recognition of it, greater means of preserving in it, or retiring from it unscratched by any weapon one should care for; than at any other period. And most of all I have, sometimes, that possibility of failing health or fading popularity before me, which beckons me to such a venture when it comes within my reach. At the worst, I have written to little purpose, if I cannot *write myself right* in people's minds, in such a case as this."

And so it went on: but it does not fall within my plan to describe more than the issue, which was to be accounted so far at least fortunate that it established a journal which has advocated steadily improvements in the condition of all classes, rich as well as poor, and has been able, during late momentous occurrences, to give wider scope to its influence by its enterprise and liberalty. To that result, the great writer whose name gave its earliest attraction to the *Daily News* was not enabled to contribute much; but from him it certainly received the first impress of the opinions it has since consistently maintained. Its prospectus is before me in his handwriting, but it bears upon itself sufficiently the character of his hand and mind. The paper would be kept free, it said, from personal influence or party bias; and would be devoted to the advocacy of all rational and honest means by which wrong might be redressed, just rights maintained, and the happiness and welfare of society promoted.

The day for the appearance of its first number was that which was to follow Peel's speech for the repeal of the Corn Laws; but, brief as my allusions to the subject are, the remark should be made that even before this day came there were interruptions to the work of preparation, at one time very grave, which threw such "changes of vexation" on Dickens's personal relations to the venture as went far to destroy both his faith and his pleasure in it. No opinion need be offered as to where most of the blame lay, and it would be useless now to apportion the share that might possibly have belonged to himself; but, owing to this cause, his editorial work began with such diminished ardour that its brief continuance could not but be looked for. A little note written "before going home" at six o'clock in the morning of Wednesday, 21 January, 1846, to tell me they had "been at press three-quarters of an hour, and were out before *The Times*," marks the beginning; and a note written in the night of Monday, 9 February, "tired to death and quite worn out," to say that he had just resigned his editorial functions, describes the end. I had not been unprepared. A week before (Friday, 30 January) he had written: "I want a long talk with you. I was obliged to come down here in a hurry to give out a travelling letter I meant to have given out last night, and could not call upon you. Will you dine with us to-morrow at six sharp? I have been revolving plans in my mind this morning for quitting the paper and going abroad again to write a new book in shilling numbers. Shall we go to Rochester to-morrow week (my birthday) if the weather be, as it surely must be, better?" To Rochester accordingly we had gone, he and Mrs. Dickens and her sister, with Maclise and Jerrold and myself; going over the old Castle, Watts's Charity, and Chatham fortifications on the Saturday, passing Sunday in Cobham church and Cobham Park; having our quarters both days at the "Bull" Inn made famous in *Pickwick*; and thus, by indulgence of the desire which was always strangely urgent in him, associating his new resolve in life with those earliest scenes of his youthful time. On one point our feeling had been in thorough agreement. If long continuance with the paper was not likely, the earliest possible departure from it was desirable. But as the letters descriptive of his Italian travel (turned afterwards into *Pictures from Italy*) had begun with its first number, his name could not at once be withdrawn; and, for the time during which they were still to appear he consented to contribute other occasional letters on important social questions. Public executions and Ragged Schools were among the subjects chosen by him, and all were handled with conspicuous ability, But the interval they covered was a short one.

To the supreme control which he had quitted, I succeeded, retaining it very reluctantly for the greater part of that weary, anxious, laborious year; but in little more than four months from the day the paper started, the whole of Dickens's connection with the *Daily News*, even that of contributing letters with his signature, had ceased. As he said in the preface to the republished *Pictures*, it was a mistake, in so departing from his old pursuits, to have disturbed the old relations between himself and his readers. It had, however, been "a brief mistake"; the departure had been only "for a moment"; and now those pursuits were "joyfully" to be resumed in Switzerland. . . .

## II

### RETREAT TO SWITZERLAND

### 1846

. . . Very pleasant were the earliest impressions of Switzerland with which his first letter closed. "The country is delightful in the extreme—as leafy, green, and shady, as England; full of deep glens,

and branchy places (rather a Leigh Huntish expression), and bright
with all sorts of flowers in profusion. It abounds in singing birds besides—very pleasant after Italy; and the moonlight on the lake is
noble. Prodigious mountains rise up from its opposite shore (it is eight
or nine miles across, at this point), and the Simplon, the St. Gothard,
Mont Blanc and all the Alpine wonders are piled there, in tremendous
grandeur. The cultivation is uncommonly rich and profuse. There are
all manner of walks, vineyard, green lanes, cornfields, and pastures
full of hay. The general neatness is as remarkable as in England.
There are no priests or monks in the streets, and the people appear to
be industrious and thriving. French (and very intelligible and pleasant French) seems to be the universal language. I never saw so many
booksellers' shops crammed within the same space, as in the steep
up-and-down streets of Lausanne." . . .

In the heart of these things he was now to live and work for at least
six months; and, as the love of nature was as much a passion with
him in his intervals of leisure, as the craving for crowds and streets
when he was busy with the creatures of his fancy, no man was better
qualified to enjoy what was thus open to him from his little farm. . . .

Regular evening walks of nine or ten miles were named in the
next letter (22 June) as having been begun; and thoughts of his
books were already stirring in him. "An odd shadowy undefined idea
is at work within me, that I could connect a great battlefield somehow with my little Christmas story. Shapeless visions of the repose
and peace pervading it in after-time; with the corn and grass growing
over the slain, and people singing at the plough; are so perpetually
floating before me, that I cannot but think there may turn out to be
something good in them when I see them more plainly. . . . I want
to get Four Numbers of the monthly book done here, and the Christmas book. If all goes well, and nothing changes, and I can accomplish
this by the end of November, I shall run over to you in England for a
few days with a light heart, and leave Roche to move the caravan to
Paris in the meanwhile. It will be just the very point in the story
when the life and crowd of that extraordinary place will come vividly
to my assistance in writing." Such was his design and, though
difficulties not now seen started up which he had a hard fight to get
through, he managed to accomplish it. . . .

Only a couple of weeks, themselves not idle ones, had passed over
him when he made a dash at the beginning of his work; from which
indeed he had only been detained so long by the non-arrival of a box
despatched from London before his own departure, containing not
his proper writing materials only, but certain quaint little bronze
figures that thus early stood upon his desk, and were as much needed
for the easy flow of his writing as blue ink or quill pens. "I have not
been idle (28th of June) since I have been here, though at first I was
'kept out' of the big box as you know. I had a good deal to write for
Lord John about the Ragged Schools. I set to work and did that. A
good deal for Miss Coutts, in reference to her charitable projects. I

set to work and did *that*. Half of the children's New Testament to write, or pretty nearly. I set to work and did *that*. Next I cleared off the greater part of such correspondence as I had rashly pledged myself to; and then . . .

I performed this feat yesterday—only wrote the first slip—but there it is, and it is a plunge straight over head and ears into the story. . . . Besides all this, I have really gone with great vigour at the French, where I find myself greatly assisted by the Italian; and am subject to two descriptions of mental fits in reference to the Christmas book: one, of the suddenest and wildest enthusiasm; one, of solitary and anxious consideration. . . . By the way, as I was unpacking the big box I took hold of a book, and said to 'Them,'— 'Now, whatever passage my thumb rests on, I shall take as having reference to my work.' It was TRISTRAM SHANDY, and opened at these words, 'What a work it is likely to turn out! Let us begin it!' "

The same letter told me that he still inclined strongly to "the field of battle notion" for his Christmas volume, but was not as yet advanced in it; being curious first to see whether its capacity seemed to strike me at all. My only objection was to his adventure of opening two stories at once, of which he did not yet see the full danger; but for the moment the Christmas fancy was laid aside, and not resumed, except in passing allusions, until after the close of August, when the first two numbers of *Dombey* were done. The interval supplied fresh illustration of his life in his new home, not without much interest; and as I have shown what a pleasant social circle, "wonderfully friendly and hospitable to the last, already had grouped itself round him in Lausanne, and how full of matter to be heard and learned he found such institutions as its prison and blind school, the picture will receive attractive touches if I borrow from his letters written during this outset of *Dombey* some further notices as well as of general progress of his work, as of what was specially interesting and amusing to him at the time and of how the country and the people impressed him. In all of these his character will be found strongly marked.

## III

### SWISS PEOPLE AND SCENERY

#### 1846

. . . Of the ordinary Swiss people he formed from the first a high opinion which everything during his stay among them confirmed. He thought it the greatest injustice to call them "the Americans of the Continent." In his first letters he said of the peasantry all about Lausanne that they were as pleasant a people as need be. He never passed, on any of the roads, man, woman, or child, without a salutation; and anything churlish or disagreeable he never noticed in them. "They have not," he continued, "the sweetness and grace of the Italians, or the agreeable manners of the better specimens of French peasantry, but they are admirably educated (the schools of this canton are extraordinarily good in every little village), and always prepared to give a civil and pleasant answer. There is no greater mistake. . . .

A letter of a little later date, describing a marriage on the farm, gave some further comical illustration of the rifle-firing propensities of the Swiss, and had otherwise also whimsical touches of character. "One of the farmer's people—a sister, I think—was married from here the other day. It is wonderful to see how naturally the smallest girls are interested in marriages. Katey and Mamey were as excited as if they were eighteen. The fondness of the Swiss for gunpowder on interesting occasions, is one of the drollest things. For three days before, the farmer himself, in the midst of his various agricultural duties, plunged out of a little door near my windows, about once in every hour, and fired off a rifle. I thought he was shooting rats who were spoiling the vines; but he was merely relieving his mind, it seemed, on the subject of the approaching nuptials. All night afterwards, he and a small circle of friends kept perpetually letting off guns under the casement of the bridal chamber. A Bride is always drest here in black silk; but this bride wore merino of that colour, observing to her mother when she bought it (the old lady is 82, and works on the farm), 'You know, mother, I am sure to want mourning for you, soon; and the same gown will do.' "

Meanwhile, day by day, he was steadily moving on with his first number; feeling sometimes the want of streets in an "extraordinary nervousness it would be hardly possible to describe," that would come upon him after he had been writing all day; but all other times finding the repose of the place very favourable to industry. "I am writing slowly at first, of course" (5 July), "but I hope I shall have finished the first number in the course of a fortnight at furthest. I have done the first chapter, and begun another. . . .

. . . But when the fourth chapter yet was incomplete, he could repress no longer the desire to write to me of what he was doing (18 July). "I think the general idea of *Dombey* is interesting and new, and has great material in it. But I don't like to discuss it with you till you have read number one, for fear I should spoil its effect. When done—about Wednesday or Thursday, please God—I will send it in two days' posts, seven letters each day. If you have it set at once (I am afraid you couldn't read it, otherwise than in print) I know you will impress on B. & E. the necessity of the closest secrecy. The very name getting out, would be ruinous. The points for illustration, and the enormous care required, make me excessively anxious. The man for Dombey, if Browne could see him, the class man to a T, is Sir A— E——, of D——'s. Great pains will be necessary with Miss Tox. The Toodle Family should not be too much caricatured, because of Polly. I should like Browne to think of Susan Nipper, who will not be wanted in the first number. After the second number, they will all be nine or ten years older; but this will not involve much change in the characters, except in the children and Miss Nipper. What a brilliant thing to be telling you all these names so familiarly, when you know nothing about 'em! I quite enjoy it. By the by, I hope you may like the introduction of Solomon Gills. I think he lives in a good sort of house. . . ."

His letter (2 August) described his own first real experience of mountain travel. "I begin my letter to-night, but only begin, for we returned from Chamonix in time for dinner just now, and are pretty considerably done up. We went by a mountian pass not often crossed by ladies, called the Col de Balme, where your imagination may picture Kate and Georgy on mules *for ten hours at a stretch* riding up and down the most frightful precipices. . . . You may suppose that the mule-travelling is pretty primitive. Each person takes a carpet-bag strapped on the mule behind himself or herself: and that is all the baggage that can be carried. A guide, a thorough-bred mountaineer, walks all the way, leading the lady's mule; I say lady's *par excellence*, in compliment to Kate; and all the rest struggle on as they please. The cavalcade stops at a lone hut for an hour and a half in the middle of the day, and lunches brilliantly on whatever it can get. Going by that Col de Balme pass, you climb up and up and up for five hours and more, and look—from a mere unguarded ledge of path on the side of the precipice—into such awful valleys, that at last you are firm in the belief that you have got everything in the world, and that there can be nothing earthly overhead. . . . I was very anxious to make the expedition to what is called 'The Garden': a green spot covered with wild flowers, lying across the Mer de Glace, and among the most awful mountains: but I could find no Englishman at the hotels who was similarly disposed, and the Brave [*i.e.* Roche, his servant] *wouldn't* go. No, sir! He gave in point blank (having been horribly blown in a climbing excursion the day before), and couldn't stand it. He is too heavy for such work, unquestionably. In all other respects, I think he has exceeded himself on this journey: and if you could have seen him riding a very small mule up a road exactly like the broken stairs of Rochester Castle, with a brandy bottle slung over his shoulder, a small pie in his hat, a roast fowl looking out of his pocket, and a mountain staff of six feet long carried crosswise on the saddle before him, you'd have said so. He was (next to me) the admiration of Chamonix, but he utterly quenched me on the road."

On the road as they returned there had been a small adventure, the day before this letter was written. Dickens was jingling slowly up the Tête Noire pass (his mule having thirty-seven bells on its head), riding at the moment quite alone, when—"an Englishman came bolting out of a little chaletain, a most inaccessible and extraordinary place, and said with great glee, "There has been an accident here sir!' I had been thinking of anything else you please! and, having no reason to suppose him an Englishman except his language, which went for nothing in the confusion, stammered out a reply in French and stared at him, in a very damp shirt and trousers, as he stared at me in a similar costume. On his repeating the announcement, I began to have a glimmering of common sense; and so arrived at a know-ledge of the fact that a German lady had been thrown from her mule and had broken her leg, at a short distance off, and had found her way in great pain to that cottage, where the Englishman, a Prussian, and a Frenchman, had presently come up; and the Frenchman, by extraordinary good fortune, was a surgeon! They were all from Chamonix, and the three latter were walking in company. It was quite charming to see how attentive they were. The lady was from Lausanne; where she had come from Frankfort to make excursions with her two boys, who are at the college here, during the vacation. She had no other attendants, and the boys were crying and very frightened. The Englishman was in the full glee of having just cut up one white dress, two chemises, and three pocket-handkerchiefs, for bandages; the Frenchman had just set the leg skilfully; the Prussian had scoured a neighbouring wood for some men to carry her forward; and they were all at it, behind the hut, making a sort of hand-barrow on which to bear her. When it was constructed, she was strapped upon it; had her poor head covered over with a handker-chief, and was carried away; and we all went on in company: Kate and Georgy consoling and tending the sufferer, who was very cheerful, but had lost her husband only a year." With the same delightful observation, and missing no touch of kindly character that might give each actor his place in the little scene, the sequel is described; but it does not need to add more. It was hoped that by means of relays of men at Martigny the poor lady might have been carried on some twenty miles, in the cooler evening, to the head of the lake, and so have been got into the steamer; but she was too exhausted to be borne beyond the inn, and there she had to remain until joined by relatives from Frankfort. . . .

## IV

### 1846

SOME sketches from the life in his pleasantest vein now claim to be taken from the same series of letters; and I will prefix one or two less important notices, for the most part personal also, that have characteristic mention of his opinions in them:—"I am very sorry to hear of Haydon's death. If any subscription be proposed, put me down for five pounds." An unfortunate son of Leigh Hunt died also just at this time, and I preserve the allusion to him for the opportunity of explaining it. "I quite shuddered at John Hunt's having applied to that generous duke. It went against the grain with me, sorely, after the story of the two hundred pounds. I don't know what I should have done, if I had been Hunt." The duke was the late Duke of Devonshire; and the story was this. During the delay of the promised production of Leigh Hunt's first play, he asked the duke for £200 as a loan for two years; and the duke replied by taking the money himself to Hunt's house in Edwardes Square. On the last day of the second year within which repayment was promised, Hunt sent back the £200; and was startled, the morning after, by another visit from the duke, who pressed upon him its reacceptance as a gift. He added that there would be no obligation, for he was himself Hunt's debtor. He was ill when he asked for the loan, and it had done him good to comply with the request. Never but once before had borrowed money ever come back to him, and he should always retain the sense of pleasure which its return had occasioned. "He remained grateful." It is a charming story, and hard to say who shows in it to the greatest advantage, Hunt or the duke. . . .

[In another letter] ". . . There are two old ladies (English) living here who may serve me for a few lines of gossip—as I have intended they should, over and over again, but I have always forgotten it. There were originally four old ladies, sisters, but two of them have faded away in the course of eighteen years, and withered by the side of John Kemble in the cemetery. They are very little and very skinny; and each of them wears a row of false curls, like little rolling-pins, so low upon her brow, that there is no forehead; nothing above the eyebrows but a deep horizontal wrinkle, and then the curls. They live upon some small annuity. For thirteen years they have wanted very much to move to Italy, as the eldest old lady says the climate of this part of Switzerland doesn't agree with her, and preys upon her spirits; but they have never been able to go, because of the difficulty of moving 'the books.' This tremendous library belonged once upon a time to the father of these old ladies, and comprises about fifty volumes. I have never been able to see what they are, because one of the old ladies always sits before them; but they look, outside, like very old backgammon boards. The two deceased sisters died in the firm persuasion that this precious property could never be got over the Simplon without some gigantic effort to which the united family was unequal. The two remaining sisters live, and will die also, in the same belief. I met the eldest (evidently drooping) yesterday, and recommended her to try Genoa. She looked shrewdly at the snow that closes up the mountain prospect just now, and said when the spring was quite set in, and the avalanches were down, and the passes well open, she would certainly try that place, if they could devise any plan, in the course of the winter, for moving 'the books.' The whole library will be sold by auction here, when they are both dead, for about a napoleon; and some young woman will carry it home in two journeys with a basket.'

The last letter sent me before he fell upon his self-appointed task for Christmas, contained a delightful account of the trip to the Great St. Bernard. It was dated on 6 September.

"The weather obstinately clearing, we started off last Tuesday for the Great St. Bernard, returning here on Friday afternoon. The party consisted of eleven people and two servants—Haldimand, Mr. and Mrs. Cerjat and one daughter, Mr. and Mrs. Watson, two Ladies Taylor, Kate, Georgy, and I. We were wonderfully unanimous and cheerful; went away from here by the steamer; found at its destination a whole omnibus provided by the Brave (who went on in advance everywhere); rode therein to Bex; found two large carriages ready to take us to Martigny; slept there; and proceeded up the mountain on mules next day. Although the St. Bernard convent is, as I dare say you know, the highest inhabited spot but one in the world, the ascent is extremely gradual and uncommonly easy: really presenting no difficulties at all until within the last league, when the ascent, lying through a place called the valley of desolation, is very awful and tremendous, and the road is rendered toilsome by scattered rocks and melting snow. The convent is a most extraordinary place, full of great vaulted passages, divided from each other with iron gratings; and presenting a series of the most astonishing little dormitories, where the windows are so small (on account of the cold and snow), that it is as much as one can do to get one's head out of them. Here we slept: supping, thirty strong, in a rambling room with a great wood-fire in it set apart for that purpose; with a grim monk, in a high black sugar-loaf hat with a great knob at the top of it, carving the dishes. At five o'clock in the morning the chapel bell rang in the dismallest way for matins: and I, lying in bed close to the chapel, and being awakened by the solemn organ and the chaunting, thought for a moment I had died in the night and passed into the unknown world.

"I wish to God you could see that place. A great hollow on the top of a range of dreadful mountains, fenced in by riven rocks of every shape and colour: and in the midst, a black lake, with phantom clouds perpetually stalking over it. Peaks, and points, and plains of eternal ice and snow, bounding the view, and shutting out the world on every side: the lake reflecting nothing: and no human figure in the scene. The air so fine, that it is difficult to breathe without feeling out of breath; and the cold so exquisitely thin and sharp that it is not to be described. Nothing of life or living interest in the picture, but the grey dull walls of the convent. No vegetation of any sort or kind. Nothing growing, nothing stirring. Everything iron-bound, and frozen up. Beside the convent, in a little outhouse with a grated iron door which you may unbolt for yourself, are the bodies of people found in the snow who have never been claimed and are withering away—not laid down, or stretched out, but standing up, in corners and against walls; some erect and horribly human, with distinct expressions on the faces; some sunk down on their knees; some dropping over on one side; some tumbled down altogether, and presenting a heap of skulls and fibrous dust. There is no other decay in that atmosphere; and there they remain during the short days and the long nights, the only human company out of doors, withering away by grains, and holding ghastly possession of the mountain where they died.

"It is the most distinct and individual place I have seen, even in this transcendent country. But, for the Saint Bernard holy fathers and convent in themselves, I am sorry to say that they are a piece of as sheer humbug as we ever learnt to believe in, in our young days. Trashy French sentiment and the dogs (of which, by the by, there are only three remaining) have done it all. They are a lazy set of fellows; not over fond of going out themselves; employing servants to clear the road (which has not been important or much used as a pass these hundred years); rich; and driving a good trade in Innkeeping: the convent being a common tavern in everything but the sign. No charge is made for their hospitality, to be sure; but you are shown to a box in the chapel, where everybody puts in more than could, with any show of face, be charged for the entertainment; and from this the establishment derives a right good income. As to the self-sacrifice of living up there, they are obliged to go there young, it is true, to be inured to the climate: but it is an infinitely more exciting and various life than any other convent can offer; with constant change and company through the whole summer; with a hospital for invalids down in the valley, which affords another change; and with an annual begging-journey to Geneva and this place and all the places round for one brother or other, which affords further change. The brother who carved at our supper could speak some English, and had just had *Pickwick* given him!—what a humbug he will think me when he tries to understand it! If I had had any other book of mine with me, I would have given it him, that I might have had some chance of being intelligible. . . ."

*          *          *          *

[After working for some time at Lausanne, Dickens proceeded to Geneva.]

He found it to be a very good place; pleasantly reporting himself as quite dismayed at first by the sight of gas in it, and as trembling at the noise in its streets, which he pronounced to be fully equal to the uproar of Richmond in Surrey; but deriving from it some sort of benefit both in health and in writing. So far his trip had been successful, though he had to leave the place hurriedly to welcome his English visitors to Rosemont.

One social and very novel experience he had in his hotel, however, the night before he left, which may be told before he hastens back to Lausanne; for it could hardly now offend anyone even if the names were given. "And now, sir, I will describe, modestly, tamely, literally, the visit to the small select circle which I promised should make your hair stand on end. In our hotel were a Mother and a Daughter, who came to the Peschiere shortly before we left it, and who have a deep admiration for your humble servant the inimitable B. They are both very clever. Daughter, extremely well-informed in languages living and dead, books, and gossip; very pretty; with two little children, and not yet five and twenty. Mother, plump, fresh, and rosy; matronly, both full of spirits and good looks. Nothing would serve them but we *must* dine with them; and accordingly, on Friday at six, we went down to their room. I knew them to be rather odd. For instance, I have known the Mother, *full dressed*, walk alone through the streets of Genoa, the squalid Italian by-streets, to the Governor's soirée; and announce herself at the palace of state, by knocking at the door. I have also met the Daughter full dressed, without any cap or bonnet, walking a mile to the opera, with all sorts of jingling jewels about her, beside a sedan chair in which sat enthroned her mama. Consequently, I was not surprised at such little sparkles in the conversation (from the young lady) as 'Oh God what a sermon we had here last Sunday!' 'And did you ever read such infernal trash as Mrs. Gore's?'—and the like. Still, but for Kate and Georgy (who were decidedly in the way, as we agreed afterwards), I should have thought it all very funny; and, as it was, I threw the ball back again, was mighty free and easy, made some rather broad jokes, and was highly applauded. 'You smoke, don't you?' said the young lady, in a pause of this kind of conversation. 'Yes,' I said, 'I generally take a cigar after dinner when I am alone.' 'I'll give you a good 'un,' said she, 'when we go upstairs.' Well sir, in due course we went upstairs, and there we were joined by an American lady residing in the same hotel, who looked like what we call in old England 'a reg'lar Bunter'—fluffy face (rouged); considerable development of figure; one groggy eye; blue satin dress made low with short sleeves, and shoes of the same. Also a daughter; face likewise fluffy; figure likewise developed; dress likewise low, with short sleeves, and shoes of the same; and one eye not yet actually groggy, but going to be. American lady married at sixteen; American daughter sixteen now, often mistaken for sisters, etc.

When that was over, the younger of our entertainers brought out a cigar box, and gave me a cigar, made of negrohead she said, which would quell an elephant in six whiffs. The box was full of cigarettes— good large ones, made of pretty strong tobacco; I always smoke them here, and used to smoke them at Genoa, and I knew them well. When I lighted my cigar, Daughter lighted hers at mine; leaned against the mantelpiece, in conversation with me; put out her stomach, folded her arms, and with her pretty face cocked up sideways and her cigarette smoking away like a Manchester cotton mill, laughed, and talked, and smoked, in the most gentlemanly manner I ever beheld. Mother immediately lighted her cigar; American lady immediately lighted hers; and in five minutes the room was a cloud of smoke, with us four in the centre pulling away bravely, while American lady related stories of her 'Hookah' upstairs, and described different kinds of pipes. But even this was not all. For presently two Frenchmen came in, with whom, and the American lady, Daughter sat down to whist. The Frenchmen smoked of course (they were really modest gentlemen and seemed dismayed), and Daughter played for the next hour or two with a cigar continually in her mouth—never out of it. She certainly smoked six or eight. Mother gave in soon—I think she only did it out of vanity. American lady had been smoking all the morning. I took no more; and Daughter and the Frenchmen had it all to themselves.

"Conceive this in a great hotel, with not only their own servants, but half a dozen waiters coming constantly in and out! I showed no atom of surprise, but I never *was* so surprised, so ridiculously taken aback, in my life; for in all my experience of 'ladies' of one kind and another, I never saw a woman—not a basket woman or a gipsy— smoke, before!" He lived to have larger and wider experience, but there was enough to startle as well as amuse him in the scene described.

But now Saturday is come; he has hurried back for the friends who are on their way to his cottage; and on his arrival, even before they have appeared, he writes to tell me his better news of himself and his work.

"In the breathless interval" (Rosemont, 3 October) "between our return from Geneva and the arrival of the Talfourds (expected in an hour or two), I cannot do better than write to you. For I think you will be well pleased if I anticipate my promise, and Monday, at the same time. I have been greatly better at Geneva, though I am still made uneasy by occasional giddiness and headache: attributable, I have not the least doubt, to the absence of streets. There is an idea here, too, that people are occasionally made despondent and sluggish in their spirits by this great mass of still water, Lake Leman. At any rate I have been very uncomfortable: at any rate I am, I hope, greatly better: and (lastly) at any rate I hope and trust, *now*, the Christmas book will come in due course!! I have had three very good days' work at Geneva, and I trust I may finish the second part (the third is the shortest) by this day week. Whenever I finish it, I will send you the first two together. I do not think they can begin to illustrate it, until the third arrives; for it is a single-minded story, as it were, and an artist should know the end: which I don't think very likely, unless he reads it." Then, after relating a superhuman effort he was making to lodge his visitors in his doll's house ("I didn't like the idea of turning them out at night. It is so dark in these lanes and groves, when the moon's not bright"), he sketched for me what he possibly might, and really did, accomplish. He would by great effort finish the small book on the 20th; would fly to Geneva for a week to work a little at *Dombey*, if he felt "pretty sound;" in any case would finish his number three by the 10th of November; and on that day would start for Paris: "so that, instead of resting unprofitably here, I shall be using my interval of idleness to make the journey and get into a new house, and shall hope so to put a pinch of salt on the tail of the sliding number in advance. . . . I am horrified at the idea of getting the blues (and bloodshots) again." Though I did not then know how gravely ill he had been, I was fain to remind him that it was bad economy to make business out of rest itself; but I received prompt confirmation that all was falling out as he wished. The Talfourds stayed two days: "and I think they were very happy. He was in his best aspect; the manner so well known to us, not the less lovable for being laughable; and if you could have seen him going round and round the coach that brought them, as a preliminary to paying the *voiturier* to whom he couldn't speak, in a currency he didn't understand, you never would have forgotten it." His friends left Lausanne on the 5th; and five days later he sent me two-thirds of the manuscript of his Christmas book.

\*     \*     \*     \*

## V

### THREE MONTHS IN PARIS

#### 1846-7

HE had begun his third number of *Dombey* on 26 October, on the 4th of the following month he was half through it, on the 7th he was in "the agonies" of its last chapter, and on the 9th, one day before that proposed for its completion, all was done. This was marvellously rapid work, after what else he had undergone; but within a week, Monday the 16th being the day for departure, they were to strike their tents, and troubled and sad were the few days thus left him for preparation and farewell. He included in his leave-taking his deaf, dumb, and blind friends; and, to use his own homely phrase, was yet more terribly "down in the mouth" at taking leave of his hearing.

speaking, and seeing friends. "I shall see you soon, please God, and that sets all to rights. But I don't believe there are many dots on the map of the world where we shall have left such affectionate remembrances behind us, as in Lausanne. It was quite miserable this last night, when we left them at Haldimand's."

He shall himself describe how they travelled post to Paris, occupying five days. "We got through the journey charmingly, though not quite so quickly as we hoped. The children as good as usual, and even Skittles jolly to the last. That name has long superseded Sampson Brass, by the by. I call him so, from something skittle-playing and public-housey in his countenance. We have been up at five every morning, and on the road before seven. We were three carriages: a sort of waggon, with a cabriolet attached, for the luggage; a ramshackle villainous old swing upon wheels (hired at Geneva), for the children; and for ourselves, that travelling chariot which I was so kind as to bring here for sale. It was very cold indeed crossing the Jura—nothing but fog and frost; but when we were out of Switzerland and across the French frontier, it became warmer, and continued so. We stopped at between six and seven each evening; had two rather queer inns, wild French country inns; but the rest good. They were three hours and a half examining the luggage at the frontier custom-house—atop of a mountain, in a hard and biting frost; where Anne and Roche had sharp work I assure you, and the latter insisted on volunteering the most astonishing and unnecessary lies about my books, for the mere pleasure of deceiving the officials. When we were out of the mountain country, we came at a good pace, but were a day late in getting to our hotel here."

They were in Paris when that was written; at the Hôtel Brighton; which they had reached in the evening of Friday, 20 November.

No man enjoyed brief residence in a hotel more than Dickens, but "several tons of luggage, other tons of servants, and other tons of children" are not desirable accompaniments to this kind of life; and his first day in Paris did not close before he had offered for an "eligible mansion." That same Saturday night he took a "colossal" walk about the city, of which the brilliancy and brightness almost frightened him; and among other things that attracted his notice was "rather a good book announced in a bookseller's window as *Les Mystères de Londres par Sir Trollopp*. Do you know him?" A countryman better known had given him earlier greeting. "The first man who took hold of me in the street, immediately outside this door, was Bruffum in his check trousers, and without the proper number of buttons on his shirt, who was going away this morning, he told me, but coming back in two months, when we would go and dine—at some place known to him and fame."

Next day he took another long walk about the streets, and lost himself fifty times. This was Sunday, and he hardly knew what to say of it, as he saw it there and then. The bitter observance of that day he always sharply resisted, believing a little rational enjoyment to be not opposed to either rest or religion; but here was another matter. "The dirty churches, and the clattering carts and waggons, and the open shops (I don't think I passed fifty shut up, in all my strollings in and out), and the work-a-day dresses and drudgeries, are not comfortable. Open theatres and so forth I am well used to, of course, by this time; but so much toil and sweat on what one would like to see, apart from religious observances, a sensible holiday, is painful."

The date of his letter was 22 November, and it had three post-scripts. The first, "Monday afternoon," told me a house was taken; that, unless the agreement should break off or any unforeseen fight between Roche and the agent ("a French Mrs. Gamp"), I was to address him at No. 48 Rue de Courcelles, Faubourg, St. Honoré; and that he would merely then advert to the premises as in his belief the "most ridiculous, extraordinary, unparalleled, and preposterous" in the whole world; being something between a baby-house, a "shades," a haunted castle, and a mad kind of clock. "They belong to a Marquis Castellan, and you will be ready to die of laughing when you go over them." The second P.S. declared that his lips should be sealed till I beheld for myself. "By Heaven it is not to be imagined by the mind of man!" The third P.S. closed the letter. "One room is a tent. Another room is a grove. Another room is a scene at the Victoria. The upstairs rooms are like fanlights over street-doors. The nurseries—but no, no, no, no more! . . ."

His following letter nevertheless sent more, even in the form of an additional protestation that never till I saw it should the place be described. "I will merely observe that it is fifty yards long, and eighteen feet high, and that the bedrooms are exactly like opera-boxes. It has its little courtyard and garden, and porter's house and cordon to open the door, and so forth; and is a Paris mansion in little. There is a gleam of reason in the drawing-room. Being a gentleman's house, and not one furnished to let, it has some very curious things in it; some of the oddest things you ever beheld in your life; and an infinity of easy chairs and sofas. . . . Bad weather. It is snowing hard. There is not a door or window here—but that's nothing! there's not a door or window in all Paris—that shuts; not a chink in all the billions of trillions of chinks in the city that can be stopped to keep the wind out. And the cold!—but you shall judge for yourself; and also of this preposterous dining-room. The invention, sir, of Henry Bulwer, who when he had executed it (he used to live here), got frightened at what he had done, as well he might, and went away. . . . The Brave called me aside on Saturday night, and showed me an improvement he had effected in the decorative way. 'Which,' he said, 'will very much s'prise Mis'r Fors'er when he come.' You are to be deluded into the belief that there is a perspective of chambers twenty miles in length, opening from the drawing-room. . . ."

I had frequent report of his progress with his famous fifth number, on the completion of which I was to join him. The day at one time seemed doubtful. "It would be miserable to have to work while you were here. Still I make such sudden starts, and am so possessed of what I am going to do, that the fear may prove to be quite groundless, and if any alteration would trouble you, let the 13th stand at all hazards." The cold he described as so intense, and the price of fuel so enormous, that though the house was not half warmed ("as you'll say, when you feel it"), it cost him very near a pound a day. Begging-letter writers had found out "Monsieur Dickens, le romancier célèbre," and waylaid him at the door and in the street as numerously as in London: their distinguishing peculiarity being that they were nearly all of them "Chevaliers de la Garde Impériale de sa Majesté Napoléon le Grand," and that their letters bore immense seals with coats of arms as large as five-shilling pieces. His friends the Watsons passed New Year's Day with him on their way to Rockingham from Lausanne, leaving that country covered with snow and the Bise blowing cruelly over it, but describing it as nothing to the cold of Paris. On the day that closed the old year he had gone into the Morgue and seen an old man with grey head lying there. "It seemed the strangest thing in the world that it should have been necessary to take any trouble to stop such a feeble, spent, exhausted morsel of life. It was just dusk, when I went in; the place was empty; and he lay there, all alone, like an impersonation of the wintry eighteen hundred and forty-six. . . . I find I am getting inimitable, so I'll stop."

The time for my visit [to him at Paris] having come, I had grateful proof of the minute and thoughtful provision characteristic of him in everything. Dinner had been ordered to the second at Boulogne, a place in the *malle-poste* taken, and these and other services announced in a letter, which, by way of doing its part also in the kindly work of preparation, broke out into French. He never spoke that language very well, his accent being somehow defective; but he practised himself into writing it with remarkable ease and fluency. "I have written to the Hôtel des Bains at Boulogne to send on to Calais and take your place in the *malle-poste*. . . . Of course you know that you'll be assailed with frightful shouts all along the two lines of ropes, from all the touters in Boulogne, and of course you'll pass on like the princess who went up the mountain after the talking bird; but don't forget quietly to single out the Hôtel des Bains commissionaire. The following circumstances will then occur. My experience is more recent than yours, and I will throw them into a dramatic form. . . . You are filtered into the little office, where there are some soldiers; and a gentleman with a black beard and a pen and ink sitting behind a counter. *Barbe Noire* (to the lord of L. I. F.). Monsieur, votre passeport. *Monsieur*. Monsieur, le voici! *Barbe Noire*. Où allez-vous, monsieur? *Monsieur*. Monsieur, je vais à Paris. *Barbe Noire*. Quand allez-vous partir, monsieur? *Monsieur*. Monsieur, je vais partir aujourd'hui. Avec la malle-poste. *Barbe Noire*. C'est bien. (To Gendarme.) Laissez sortir monsieur! *Gendarme*. Par ici, monsieur, s'il vous plaît. Le gendarme

ouvert une très petite porte. Monsieur se trouve subitement entouré
de tous les gamins, agents, commissionnaires, porteurs, et polissons,
en général, de Boulogne, qui s'élancent sur lui, en poussant des cris
épouvantables. Monsieur est, pour le moment, tout-à-fait effrayé,
bouleversé. Mais monsieur reprend ses forces et dit, de haute voix:
'Le Commissionnaire de l'Hôtel des Bains!' *Un petit homme* (s'avan-
çant rapidement, et en souriant doucement). Me voici, monsieur.
Monsieur Fors Tair, n'est-ce pas? . . . Alors . . . Alors monsieur se
promène à l'Hôtel des Bains, où monsieur trouvera qu'un petit salon
particulier, en haut, est déjà préparé pour sa réception, et que son
dîner est déjà commandé, grace aux soins du brave Courier, *a midi
et demi.* . . . Monsieur mangera son dîner près du feu, avec beaucoup
de plaisir, et il boirera de vin rouge à la santé de Monsieur de Boze, et
sa famille intéressante et aimable. La malle-poste arrivera au bureau
de la poste aux lettres à deux heures ou peut-être un peu plus tard.
Mais monsieur chargera le commissionnaire d'y l'accompagner de
bonne heure, car c'est beaucoup mieux de l'attendre que de la perdre.
La malle-poste arrivée, monsieur prendra sa place, aussi comfortable-
ment qu'il le pourra, et il y restera jusqu'à son arrivée au bureau de
la poste aux lettres à Paris. Parceque, le convoi (*train*) n'est pas
l'affaire de monsieur, qui gardera sa place dans la malle-poste, sur
le chemin de fer, et après le chemin de fer, jusqu'il se trouve à la basse-
cour du bureau de la poste aux lettres à Paris, où il trouvera une voi-
ture qui a été dépêché de la Rue de Courcelles, quarante-huit. Mais
monsieur aura la bonté d'observer—Si le convoi arriverait à Amiens
après le départ du convoi à minuit, il faudrait y rester jusqu'à
l'arrivée d'un autre convoi à trois heures moins un quart. En attendant, monsieur peut rester au buffet (*refreshment room*), où l'on peut
toujours trouver un bon feu, et du café chaud, et de très bonnes choses
à boire et à manger, pendant toute la nuit.—Est-ce que monsieur
comprend parfaitement toutes ces règles?—Vive le Roi des Français!
Roi de la nation la plus grande, et la plus noble, et la plus extra-
ordinairement merveilleuse, du monde! A bas les Anglais!

"CHARLES DICKENS,

"Français naturalisé, et Citoyen de Paris."

We passed a fortnight together, and crowded into it more than
might seem possible to such a narrow space. One day we visited in the
Rue du Bac the sick and ailing Chateaubriand, whom we thought
like Basil Montagu; found ourselves at the other extreme of opinion
in the sculpture-room of David d'Angers; and closed that day at the
house of Victor Hugo, by whom Dickens was received with infinite
courtesy and grace. The great writer then occupied a floor in a noble
corner-house in the Place Royale, the old quarter of Ninon l'Enclos
and the people of the Regency, of whom the gorgeous tapestries, the
painted ceilings, the wonderful carvings and old golden furniture,
including a canopy of state out of some palace of the middle age,
quaintly and grandly reminded us. He was, himself, however, the best

thing we saw; and I find it difficult to associate the attitudes and aspect
in which the world has lately wondered at him, with the sober grace
and self-possessed quiet gravity of that night of twenty-five years ago.
Just then Louis Philippe had ennobled him, but the man's nature
was written noble. Rather under the middle size, of compact close-
buttoned-up figure, with ample dark hair falling loosely over his
close-shaven face, I never saw upon any features so keenly intellectual
such a soft and sweet gentility, and certainly never heard the French
language spoken with the picturesque distinctness given to it by
Victor Hugo. He talked of his childhood in Spain, and of his father
having been Governor of the Tagus in Napoleon's wars; spoke warmly
of the English people and their literature; declared his preference for
melody and simplicity over the music then fashionable at the Con-
servatoire; referred kindly to Ponsard, laughed at the actors who had
murdered his tragedy at the Odéon, and sympathised with the
dramatic venture of Dumas. To Dickens he addressed very charming
flattery, in the best taste; and my friend long remembered the enjoyment of that evening. . . .

Our last talk before I quitted Paris, after dinner at the Embassy,
was of the danger underlying all this, and of the signs also visible
everywhere of the Napoleon-worship which the Orleanists themselves
had most favoured. Accident brought Dickens to England a fortnight
later, when again we met together, at Gore House, the self-contained
reticent man whose doubtful inheritance was thus rapidly preparing
to fall to him.

The accident was the having underwritten his number of *Dombey*
by two pages, which there was not time to supply otherwise than by
coming to London to write them. This was done accordingly; but
another, greater trouble followed. He had hardly returned to Paris
when his eldest son, whom I had brought to England with me and
placed in the house of Doctor Major, then headmaster of King's
College School, was attacked by scarlet fever; and this closed prematurely Dickens's residence in Paris. But though he and his wife at
once came over, and were followed after some days by the children
and their aunt, the isolation of the little invalid could not so soon be
broken through. His father at last saw him, nearly a month before
the rest, in a lodging in Albany Street, where his grandmother, Mrs.
Hogarth, had devoted herself to the charge of him; and an incident
of the visit, which amused us all very much, will not unfitly introduce
the subject that waits me in my next chapter.

An elderly charwoman employed about the place had shown so
much sympathy in the family trouble, that Mrs. Hogarth specially
told her of the approaching visit, and who it was that was coming
to the sick-room. "Lawk ma'am!" she said. "Is the young gentleman
upstairs the son of the man that put together *Dombey*?" Reassured
upon this point, she explained her question by declaring that she
never thought there was a man that *could* have put together *Dombey*.
Being pressed further as to what her notion was of this mystery of a

*Dombey* (for it was known she could not read), it turned out that she lodged at a snuff-shop kept by a person named Douglas, where there were several other lodgers; and that on the first Monday of every month there was a Tea, and the landlord read the month's number of *Dombey*, those only of the lodgers who subscribed to the tea partaking of that luxury, but all having the benefit of the reading; and the impression produced on the old charwoman revealed itself in the remark with which she closed her account of it. "Lawk ma'am! I thought that three or four men must have put together *Dombey*!" Dickens thought there was something of a compliment in this, and was not ungrateful.

# BOOK SIXTH

## AT THE SUMMIT

### 1847-52. ÆT. 35-40

## SPLENDID STROLLING

### 1847–52

DEVONSHIRE TERRACE remaining still in possession of Sir James
Duke, a house was taken in Chester Place, Regent's Park, where, on
18 April, Dickens's fifth son, to whom he gave the name of Sydney
Smith Haldimand, was born. Exactly a month before, he had attended
the funeral at Highgate of his publisher Mr. William Hall, his old
regard for whom had survived the recent temporary cloud, and with
whom he had the association as well of his first success, as of much
kindly intercourse not forgotten at this sad time. Of the summer
months that followed, the greater part was passed by him at Brighton
or Broadstairs; and the chief employment of his leisure, in the
intervals of *Dombey*, was the management of an enterprise originating
in the success of our private play, of which the design was to benefit
a great man of letters.

The purpose and name had hardly been announced, when, with the
statesman-like attention to literature and its followers for which Lord
John Russell has been eccentric among English politicians, a civil-
list pension of two hundred a year was granted to Leigh Hunt; but
though this modified our plan so far as to strike out of it performances
meant to be given in London, so much was still thought necessary
as might clear off past liabilities, and enable a delightful writer better
to enjoy the easier future that had at last been opened to him. Reserving therefore anything realised beyond a certain sum for a dramatic
author of merit, Mr. John Poole, to whom help had become also
important, it was proposed to give, on Leigh Hunt's behalf, two
representations of Ben Jonson's comedy, one at Manchester and the
other at Liverpool, to be varied by different farces in each place; and
with a prologue of Talfourd's which Dickens was to deliver in Manchester, while a similar address by Sir Edward Bulwer Lytton was
to be spoken by me in Liverpool. Among the artists and writers
associated in the scheme were Mr. Frank Stone, Mr. Augustus Egg,
Mr. John Leech, and Mr. George Cruikshank; Mr. Douglas Jerrold,
Mr. Mark Lemon, Mr. Dudley Costello, and Mr. George Henry
Lewes; the general management and supreme control being given to
Dickens.

Leading men in both cities contributed largely to the design, and
my friend Mr. Alexander Ireland of Manchester has lately sent me
some letters not more characteristic of the energy of Dickens in regard

to it than of the eagerness of everyone addressed to give what help they could. Making personal mention of his fellow-sharers in the enterprise he describes the troop, in one of those letters, as "the most easily governable company of actors on earth"; and to this he had doubtless brought them, but not very easily. One or two of his managerial troubles at rehearsals remain on record in letters to myself, and may give amusement. Comedy and farces are referred to indiscriminately, but the farces were the most recurring plague. "Good Heaven! I find that A. hasn't twelve words, and I am in hourly expectation of rebellion!"—"You were right about the green baize, that it would certainly muffle the voices; and some of our actors, by Jove, haven't too much of that commodity at the best."—"B. shocked me so much the other night by a restless, stupid movement of his hands in his first scene with you, that I took a turn of an hour with him yesterday morning, and I hope quieted his nerves a little." —"I made a desperate effort to get C. to give up his part. Yet in spite of all the trouble he gives me I am sorry for him, he is so evidently hurt by his own sense of not doing well. He clutched the part, however, tenaciously; and three weary times we dragged through it last night."—"That infernal E. forgets everything."—"I plainly see that F. when nervous, which he is sure to be, loses his memory. Moreover, his asides are inaudible, even at Miss Kelly's; and as regularly as I stop him to say them again, he exclaims (with a face of agony) that 'he'll speak loud on the night,' as if anybody ever did without doing it always!"—"G. not born for it at all, and too innately conceited, I much fear, to do anything well. I thought him better last night, but I would as soon laugh at a kitchen poker."—"Fancy H., ten days after the casting of that farce, wanting F.'s part therein! Having himself an excellent old man in it already, and a quite admirable part in the other farce." From which it will appear that my friend's office was not a sinecure, and that he was not, as few amateur-managers have ever been, without the experiences of Peter Quince. Fewer still, I suspect, have fought through them with such perfect success, for the company turned out at last would have done credit to any enterprise. They deserved the term applied to them by Maclise, who had invented it first for Macready, on his being driven to "star" in the provinces when his managements in London closed. They were "splendid strollers."

On Monday, 26 July, we played at Manchester, and on Wednesday the 28th at Liverpool; the comedy being followed on the first night by *A Good Night's Rest* and *Turning the Tables*, and on the second by *Comfortable Lodgings, or Paris in* 1750; and the receipts being, on the first night £440 12s., and on the second, £463 8s. 6d. But though the married members of the company who took their wives defrayed that part of the cost, and every one who acted paid three pounds ten to the benefit fund for his hotel charges, the expenses were necessarily so great that the profit was reduced to four hundred guineas, and handsomely as this realised the design, expectations had been raised to five hundred. There was just that shade of disappointment, therefore, when, shortly after we came back and Dickens had returned to Broadstairs, I was startled by a letter from him. On 3 August he had written: "All well. Children" (who had been going through whooping cough) "immensely improved. Business arising out of the late blaze of triumph, worse than ever." Then came what startled me, the very next day. As if his business were not enough, it had occurred to him that he might add the much longed-for hundred pounds to the benefit fund by a little *jeu d'esprit* in form of a history of the trip, to be published with illustrations from the artists; and his notion was to write it in the character of Mrs. Gamp. It was to be, in the phraseology of that notorious woman, a new "Piljians Projiss"; and was to bear upon the title-page its description as an Account of a late Expedition into the North, for an Amateur Theatrical Benefit, written by Mrs. Gamp (who was an eyewitness), Inscribed to Mrs. Harris, Edited by Charles Dickens, and published, with illustrations on wood by so and so in aid of the benefit fund. "What do you think of this idea for it? The argument would be, that Mrs. Gamp, being on the eve of an excursion to Margate as a relief from her professional fatigues, comes to the knowledge of the intended excursion of our party; hears that several of the ladies concerned are in an interesting situation; and decides to accompany the party unbeknown, in a second-class carriage—'in case.' There, she finds a gentleman from the Strand in a checked suit, who is going down with the wigs"—the theatrical hairdresser employed on these occasions, Mr. Wilson, had eccentric points of character that were a fund of infinite mirth to Dickens—"and to his politeness Mrs. Gamp is indebted for much support and countenance during the excursion. She will describe the whole thing in her own manner: sitting, in each place of performance, in the orchestra, next the gentleman who plays the kettle-drums. She gives her critical opinion of Ben Jonson as a literary character, and refers to the different members of the party, in the course of her description of the trip: having always an invincible animosity towards Jerrold, for Caudle reasons. She addresses herself, generally, to Mrs. Harris, to whom the book is dedicated—but is discursive. Amount of matter, half a sheet of *Dombey*: may be a page or so more, but not less." Alas! it never arrived at even that small size, but perished prematurely, as I feared it would, from failure of the artists to furnish needful nourishment. Of course it could not live alone. Without suitable illustration it must have lost its point and pleasantry. "Mac will make a little garland of the ladies for the title-page. Egg and Stone will themselves originate something fanciful, and I will settle with Cruikshank and Leech. I have no doubt the little thing will be droll and attractive." So it certainly would have been, if the Thanes of art had not fallen from him; but on their desertion it had to be abandoned after the first few pages were written. They were placed at my disposal then; and, though the little jest had lost much of its flavour now, I cannot find it in my heart to omit them here. There are so many friends of Mrs. Gamp who will rejoice at this unexpected visit from her!

## "I. Mrs Gamp's Account of her Connexion with this Affair

"Which Mrs. Harris's own words to me, was these: 'Sairey Gamp,' she says, 'why not go to Margate? Srimps,' says that dear creetur, 'is to your liking, Sairey; why not go to Margate for a week, bring your constitootion up with srimps, and come back to them loving arts as knows and wallies of you, blooming? Sairey,' Mrs. Harris says, 'you are but poorly. Don't denige it, Mrs. Gamp, for books is in your looks. You must have rest. Your mind,' she says, 'is too strong for you; it gets you down and treads upon you, Sairey. It is useless to disguige the fact—the blade is a wearing out the sheets.' 'Mrs Harris,' I says to her, 'I could not undertake to say, and I will not deceive you ma'am, that I am the woman I could wish to be. The time of worrit as I had with Mrs. Colliber, the baker's lady, which was so bad in her mind with her first, that she would not so much as look at bottled stout, and kept to gruel through the month, has agued me, Mrs. Harris. But ma'am,' I says to her, 'talk not of Margate, for if I do go anywheres, it is elsewheres and not there.' 'Sairey,' says Mrs. Harris, solemn, 'whence this mystery? If I have ever deceived the hardest-working, soberest, and best of women, which her name is well beknown is S. Gamp Midwife Kingsgate Street High Holborn, mention it. If not,' says Mrs. Harris, with the tears a standing in her eyes, 'reweal your intentions.' 'Yes, Mrs. Harris,' I says, 'I will. Well I knows you Mrs. Harris; well you knows me; well we both knows wot the characters of one another is. Mrs. Harris then,' I says. 'I *have* heard as there *is* a expedition going down to Manjestir and Liverpool, a play-acting. If I goes anywheres for change it is along with that.' Mrs Harris clasps her hands, and drops into a chair, as if her time was come—which I know'd it couldn't be, by rights, for six weeks odd. 'And have I lived to hear,' she says, 'of Sairey Gamp, as always kept herself respectable, in company with play-actors!' 'Mrs. Harris,' I says to her, 'be not alarmed—not reg'lar play-actors—hammertoors.' 'Thank Evans!' says Mrs. Harris, and bustiges into a flood of tears.

"When the sweet creetur had compoged hersef (which a sip of brandy and warm water, and sugared pleasant, with a little nutmeg did it), I proceeds in these words. 'Mrs Harris, I am told as these Hammertoors are litter'ry and artistickle.' 'Sairey,' says that best of wimmin, with a shiver and a slight relasp, 'go on, it might be worse.' 'I likewise hears,' I says to her, 'that they're agoin play-acting, for the benefit of two litter'ry men; one as has had his wrongs a long time ago, and has got his rights at last, and one as has made a many people merry in his time, but is very dull and sick and lonely his own sef, indeed.' 'Sairey,' says Mrs. Harris, 'you're an Inglish woman, and that's no business of you'rn.'

" 'No, Mrs. Harris,' I says, 'that's very true; I hope I knows my dooty and my country. But,' I says, 'I am informed as there is Ladies in this party, and that half a dozen of 'em if not more, is in various stages of a interesting state. Mrs. Harris, you and me well knows what Ingeins often does. If I accompanies this expedition, unbeknown and second cladge, may I not combine my calling, with change of air, and prove a service to my feller creeturs?' 'Sairey,' was Mrs. Harris's reply, 'you was born to be a blessing to your sex, and bring 'em through it. Good go with you! But keep your distance till called in, Lord bless you Mrs. Gamp; for people is known by the company they keeps, and litterary and artistickle society might be the ruin of you before you was aware, with your best customers, both sick and monthly, if they took a pride in themselves."

## "II. MRS. GAMP IS DESCRIPTIVE

"The number of the cab had a seven in it I think, and a ought I know—and if this should meet his eye (which it was a black 'un, new done, that he saw with; the other was tied up), I give him a warning that he'd better take that umbreller and patten to the Hackney Coach Office before he repents it. He was a young man in a weskit with sleeves to it and strings behind, and needn't flatter himsef with a suppogition of escape, as I gave this description of him to the Police the moment I found he had drove off with my property; and if he thinks there an't laws enough he's much mistook—I tell him that.

"I do assure you, Mrs. Harris, when I stood in the railways office that morning with my bundle on my arm and one patten in my hand, you might have knocked me down with a feather, far less pork-mangers which was a lumping against me, continual and sewere all round. I was drove about like a brute animal and almost worrited into fits, when a gentleman with a large shirt-collar and a hook nose, and a eye like one of Mr. Sweedlepipes's hawks, and long locks of hair, and wiskers that I wouldn't have round no lady as I was engaged to meet suddenly a turning round a corner, for any sum of money you could offer me, says, laughing, 'Halloa, Mrs. Gamp, what are *you* up to!' I didn't know him from a man (except by his clothes); but I says faintly, 'If you're a Christian man, show me where to get a second-cladge ticket for Manjestir, and have me put in a carriage, or I shall drop!' Which he kindly did, in a cheerful kind of a way, skipping about in the strangest manner as ever I see, making all kinds of actions and looking and vinking at me from under the brim of his hat (which was a good deal turned up), to that extent, that I should have thought he meant something but for being so flurried as not to have no thoughts at all until I was put into a carriage along with a individgle—the politest as ever I did see—in a shepherd's plaid suit with a long gold watch-guard hanging round his neck, and his hand a trembling through nervousness worse than a aspian leaf.

" 'I'm wery appy, ma'am,' he says—the politest vice as ever I heerd!—'to go down with a lady belonging to our party.'

" 'Our party, sir!' I says.

" 'Yes, ma'am,' he says, 'I'm Mr. Wilson. I'm going down with the wigs.'

"Mrs. Harris, wen he said he was agoing down with the wigs, such was my state of confugion and worrit that I thought he must be connected with the Government in some ways or another, but directly moment he explains himsef, for he says:

" 'There's not a theatre in London worth mentioning that I don't attend punctually. There's five-and-twenty wigs in these boxes, ma'am,' he says, a pinting towards a heap of luggage, 'as was worn at the Queen's Fancy Ball. There's a black wig, ma'am,' he says, 'as was worn by Garrick; there's a red one, ma'am,' he says, 'as was worn by Kean; there's a brown one, ma'am,' he says, 'as was worn by Kemble; there's a yellow one, ma'am,' he says, 'as was made for Cooke; there's a grey one, ma'am,' he says, 'as I measured Mr. Young for, myself; and there's a white one, ma'am, that Mr. Macready went mad in. There's a flaxen one as was got up express for Jenny Lind the night she came out at the Italian Opera. It was very much applauded was that wig, ma'am, through the evening. It had a great reception. The audience broke out the moment they see it.'

" 'Are you in Mr. Sweedlepipes's line, sir?' I says.

" 'Which is that, ma'am?' he says—the softest and genteelest vice I ever heerd, I do declare, Mrs. Harris!

" 'Hair-dressing,' I says.

" 'Yes, ma'am,' he replies, 'I have that honour. Do you see this ma'am?' he says, holding up his right hand.

" 'I never see such a trembling,' I says to him. And I never did!

" 'All along of Her Majesty's Costume Ball, ma'am,' he says. 'The excitement did it. Two hundred and fifty-seven ladies of the first rank and fashion had their heads got up on that occasion by this hand and my t'other one. I was at it eight-and-forty hours on my feet ma'am, without rest. It was a Powder ball, ma'am. We have a Powder piece at Liverpool. Have I not the pleasure,' he says, looking at me curious, 'of addressing Mrs. Gamp?'

" 'Gamp I am, sir,' I replies. 'Both by name and natur.'

" 'Would you like to see your beeographer's moustache and wiskers ma'am?' he says. 'I've got 'em in this box.'

" 'Drat my beeograffer, sir,' I says, 'he has given me no region to wish to know anythink about him.'

" 'Oh, Missus Gamp, I ask your parden'—I never see such a polite man, Mrs. Harris! 'P'raps,' he says, 'if you're not of the party, yo don't know who it was that assisted you into this carriage!'

" 'No, sir,' I says, 'I don't, indeed.'

" 'Why, ma'am,' he says, a wisperin', 'that was George, ma'am.'

" 'What George, sir? I don't know no George,' says I.

" 'The great George, ma'am,' says he. 'The Crookshanks.'

"If you'll believe me, Mrs. Harris, I turns my head, and see th wery man a making picturs of me on his thumb nail, at the winder! while another of 'em—a tall, slim, melancolly gent, with dark hair and a bage vice—looks over his shoulder, with his head o' one side as if he understood the subject, and coolly says, '*I*'ve draw'd her several times—in *Punch*,' he says too! The owdacious wretch!

" 'Which I never touches, Mr. Wilson,' I remarks out loud—I couldn't have helped it, Mrs. Harris, if you had took my life for it!—'which I never touches, Mr. Wilson, on account of the lemon!'

" 'Hush!' says Mr. Wilson, 'There he is!'

"I only see a fat gentleman with curly black hair and a merry face, a standing on the platform rubbing his two hands over one another, as if he was washing of 'em, and shaking his head and shoulders wery much; and I was a wondering wot Mr. Wilson meant, wen he says 'There's Dougladge, Mrs. Gamp!' he says. 'There's him as wrote the life of Mrs. Caudle!'

"Mrs. Harris, wen I see that little willain bodily before me, it give me such a turn that I was all in a tremble. If I hadn't lost my umbreller in the cab, I must have done him a injury with it! Oh the bragian little traitor! right among the ladies, Mrs. Harris; looking his wickedest and deceitfullest of eyes while he was a talking to 'em; laughing at his own jokes as loud as you please; holding his hat in one hand to cool his-sef, and tossing back his iron-grey mop of a head of hair with the other, as if it was so much shavings—there, Mrs. Harris, I see him gettin encouragement from the pretty delooded creeturs, which never know'd that sweet saint, Mrs. C., as I did, and being treated with as much confidence as if he'd never wiolated none of the domestic ties, and never showed up nothing! Oh the aggrawation of that Dougladge! Mrs. Harris, if I hadn't apologiged to Mr. Wilson, and put a little bottle to my lips which was in my pocket for the journey, and which it is very rare indeed I have about me, I could not have abared the sight of him—there, Mrs. Harris! I could not!—I must have tore him, or have give way and fainted.

"While the bell was a ringing, and the luggage of the hammer-toors in great confusion—all a litter'ry indeed—was handled up, Mr. Wilson demeens his-sef politer than ever. 'That,' he says, 'Mrs. Gamp,' a pinting to a officer-looking gentleman, that a lady with a little basket was a taking care on, 'is another of our party. He's a author too—continivally going up the walley of the Muses, Mrs. Gamp. There,' he says, alluding to a fine looking, portly gentleman, with a face like a amiable full moon, and a short mild gent, with a pleasant smile, 'is two more of our astists, Mrs. G., well beknowed at the Royal Academy, as sure as stones is stones, and eggs is eggs. This resolute gent,' he says, 'a coming along here as is aperrently going to take the railways by storm—him with the tight legs, and his weskit very much buttoned, and his mouth very much shut, and his coat a flying open, and his heels a-giving it to the platform, is a cricket and beeograffer, and our principal tragesian.' 'But who,' says I, when the bell had left off, and the train had begun to move, 'who,

Mr. Wilson, is the wild gent in the prespiration, that's been a-tearing up and down all this time with a great box of papers under his arm, a-talking to everybody wery indistinct, and exciting of himself dreadful?' 'Why?' says Mr. Wilson, with a smile. 'Because, sir,' I says, 'he's being left behind.' 'Good God!' cries Mr. Wilson, turning pale and putting out his head, 'it's *your* beeograffer—the Manager—and he has got the money, Mrs. Gamp!' Hous'ever, someone chucked him into the train and we went off. At the first shreek of the whistle, Mrs. Harris, I turned white, for I had took notice of some of them dear creeturs as was the cause of my being in company, and I know'd the danger that—but Mr. Wilson, which is a married man, puts his hand on mine, and says, 'Mrs. Gamp, calm yourself; it's only the Ingein.' "

Of those of the party with whom these humorous liberties were taken, there are only two now living to complain of their friendly caricaturist; and Mr. Cruikshank will perhaps join me in a frank forgiveness not the less heartily for the kind words about himself that reached me from Broadstairs not many days after Mrs. Gamp. "At Canterbury yesterday" (2 September) "I bought George Cruikshank's *Bottle.* I think it very powerful indeed; the two last plates most admirable, except that the boy and girl in the very last are too young, and the girl more like a circus phenomenon than that no-phenomenon she is intended to represent. I question, however, whether anybody else living could have done it so well. There is a woman in the last plate but one, garrulous about the murder, with a child in her arms, that is as good as Hogarth. Also, the man who is stooping down, looking at the body. The philosophy of the thing, as a great lesson, I think all wrong; because to be striking, and original too, the drinking should have begun in sorrow, or poverty, or ignorance—the three things in which, in its awful aspect, it *does* begin. The design would then have been a double-handed sword—but too 'radical' for good old George, I suppose."

The same letter made mention of other matters of interest. His accounts for the first half-year of *Dombey* were so much in excess of what had been expected from the new publishing arrangements, that from this date all embarrassments connected with money were brought to a close. His future profits varied of course with his varying sales, but there was always enough, and savings were now to begin. "The profits of the half-year are brilliant. Deducting the hundred pounds a month paid six times, I have still to receive two thousand, two hundred and twenty pounds, which I think is tidy. Don't you? . . ."

Devonshire Terrace meanwhile had been quitted by his tenant; and coming up joyfully himself to take possession, he brought for completion in his old home an important chapter of *Dombey.* On the way he lost his portmanteau, but "Thank God! the MS. of the chapter wasn't in it. Whenever I travel, and have anything of that valuable article, I always carry it in my pocket." He had begun at this time to find difficulties in writing at Broadstairs, of which he told me on his return. "Vagrant music is getting to that height here, and is so impossible to be escaped from, that I fear Broadstairs and I must part company in time to come. Unless it pours of rain, I cannot write half-an-hour without the most excruciating organs, fiddles, bells, or glee-singers. There is a violin of the most torturing kind under the window now (time, ten in the morning) and an Italian box of music on the steps—both in full blast." He closed with a mention of improvements in the Margate theatre since his memorable last visit. In the past two years it had been managed by a son of the great comedian, Dowton, with whose name it is pleasant to connect this note. "We went to the manager's benefit on Wednesday" (10 September): "*As You Like It* really very well done, and a most excellent house. Mr Dowton delivered a sensible and modest kind of speech on the occasion, setting forth his conviction that a means of instruction and entertainment possessing such a literature as the stage in England, could not pass away; and that what inspired great minds, and delighted great men, two thousand years ago, and did the same in Shakespeare's day, must have within itself a principle of life superior to the whim and fashion of the hour. And with that, and with cheers, he retired. He really seems a most respectable man, and he has cleared out this dust-hole of a theatre into something like decency." . . .

## II

### SEASIDE HOLIDAYS

#### 1848-51

THE portion of Dickens's life over which his adventures of strolling extended was in other respects not without interest; and this chapter will deal with some of his seaside holidays before I pass to the publication in 1848 of the story of *The Haunted Man*, and to the establishment in 1850 of the Periodical which had been in his thoughts for half a dozen years before, and has had foreshadowings nearly as frequent in my pages.

Among the incidents of 1848 before the holiday season came, were the dethronement of Louis Philippe, and birth of the second French republic: on which I ventured to predict that a Gore House friend of ours, and *his* friend, would in three days be on the scene of action. The three days passed, and I had this letter. "Mardi, Février 29, 1848. MON CHER. Vous êtes homme de la plus grande pénétration! Ah, mon Dieu, que vous êtes absolument magnifique! Vous prévoyez presque toutes les choses qui vont arriver; et aux choses qui viennent

335*

d'arriver vous êtes merveilleusement au-fait. Ah, cher enfant, quelle idée sublime vous vous aviez à la tête quand vous prévîtes si clairement que M. le Comte Alfred d'Orsay se rendrait au pays de sa naissance! Quel magicien! Mais—c'est tout égal, mais—il n'est pas parti. Il reste à Gore House, où, avant-hier, il y avait un grand dîner à tout le monde. Mais quel homme, quel ange, néanmoins! Mon Ami, je trouve que j'aime tant la République, qu'il me faut renoncer ma langue et écrire seulement le langage de la République de France— langage des Dieux et des Anges—langage, en un mot, des Français! Hier au soir je rencontrai à l'Athenæum Monsieur Mack Leese, qui me dit que MM. les Commissionnaires des Beaux Arts lui avaient écrit, par leur secrétaire, un billet de remerciements à propos de son tableau dans la Chambre des Députés, et qu'ils lui avaient prié de faire l'autre tableau en fresque, dont on y a besoin. Ce qu'il a promis. Voici des nouvelles pour les champs de Lincoln's Inn! Vive la gloire de France! Vive la République! Vive le Peuple! Plus de Royauté! Plus de Bourbons! Plus de Guizot! Mort aux traîtres! Faisons couler le sang pour la liberté, la justice, la cause populaire! Jusqu'à cinq heures et demie, adieu, mon brave! Recevez l'assurance de ma considération distinguée, et croyez-moi, concitoyen! votre tout dévoué, Citoyen Charles Dickens." I proved to be not quite so wrong, nevertheless, as my friend supposed.

Somewhat earlier than usual this summer, on the close of the Shakespeare House performances, he tried Broadstairs once more, having no important writing in hand: but in the brief interval before leaving he saw a thing of celebrity in those days, the Chinese junk; and I had all the details in so good a description that I could not resist the temptation of using some parts of it at the time. "Drive down to the Blackwall railway," he wrote to me, "and for a matter of eighteen-pence you are at the Chinese Empire in no time. In half a score of minutes, the tiles and chimney-pots, backs of squalid houses, frowsy pieces of waste ground, narrow courts and streets, swamps, ditches, masts of ships, gardens of duckweed, and unwholesome little bowers of scarlet beans, whirl away in a flying dream, and nothing is left but China. How the flowery region ever came into this latitude and longitude is the first thing one asks; and it is not certainly the least of the marvel. As Aladdin's palace was transported hither and thither by the rubbing of a lamp, so the crew of Chinamen aboard the *Keying* devoutly believed that their good ship would turn up, quite safe, at the desired port, if they only tied red rags enough upon the mast, rudder, and cable. Somehow they did not succeed. Perhaps they ran short of rag; at any rate they hadn't enough on board to keep them above water; and to the bottom they would undoubtedly have gone but for the skill and coolness of a dozen English sailors, who brought them over the ocean in safety. Well, if there be any one thing in the world that this extraordinary craft is not at all like, that thing is a ship of any kind. So narrow, so long, so grotesque; so low in the middle, so high at each end, like a China pen-tray; with no rigging, with nowhere to go to aloft; with mats for sails, great warped cigars for masts, gaudy dragons and sea-monsters disporting themselves from stem to stern, and *on* the stern a gigantic cock of impossible aspect, defying the world (as well he may) to produce his equal—it would look more at home at the top of a public building, or at the top of a mountain, or in an avenue of trees, or down in a mine, than afloat on the water. As for the Chinese lounging on the deck, the most extravagant imagination would never dare to suppose them to be mariners. Imagine a ship's crew, without a profile among them, in gauze pinafores and plaited hair; wearing stiff clogs a quarter of a foot thick in the sole; and lying at night in little scented boxes, like back-gammon men or chess-pieces, or mother-of-pearl counters! But by Jove! even this is nothing to your surprise when you go down into the cabin. There you get a torture of perplexity. As, what became of all those lanterns hanging to the roof when the Junk was out at sea? Whether they dangled there, banging and beating against each other, like so many jesters' baubles? Whether the idol Chin Tee, of the eighteen arms, enshrined in a celestial Punch's Show, in the place of honour, ever tumbled out in heavy weather? Whether the incense and the joss-stick still burnt before her, with a faint perfume and a little thread of smoke, while the mighty waves were roaring all around? Whether that preposterous tissue-paper umbrella in the corner was always spread, as being a convenient maritime instrument for walking about the decks with in a storm? Whether all the cool and shiny little chairs and tables were continually sliding about and bruising each other, and if not why not? Whether anybody on the voyage ever read those two books printed in characters like bird-cages and fly-traps? Whether the Mandrin passenger, He Sing, who had never been ten miles from home in his life before, lying sick in a bamboo couch in a private china closet of his own (where he is now perpetually writing autographs for inquisitive barbarians), ever began to doubt the potency of the Goddess of the Sea, whose counterfeit presentment, like a flowery monthly nurse, occupies the sailors' joss-house in the second gallery? Whether it is possible that the said Mandarin, or the artist of the ship, Sam Sing, Esquire, R.A. of Canton, *can* ever go ashore without a walking-staff of cinnamon, agreeably to the usage of their likenesses in British tea-shops? Above all, whether the hoarse old ocean could ever have been seriously in earnest with this floating toy-shop; or had merely played with it in lightness of spirit—roughly, but meaning no harm—as the bull did with another kind of china-shop on St. Patrick's Day in the morning." . . .

Other letters of the summer from Broadstairs will complete what he wrote from the same place last year on Mr. Cruikshank's efforts in the cause of temperance, and will enable me to say, what I know he wished to be remembered in his story, that there was no subject on which through his whole life he felt more strongly than this. No man advocated temperance, even as far as possible its legislative enforcement, with greater earnestness; but he made important reservations. Not thinking drunkenness to be a vice inborn, or incident to the poor more than to other people, he never would agree that the existence of a gin-shop was the alpha and omega of it. Believing it to be *the* "national horror," he also believed that many operative causes had to do with having made it so; and his objection to the temperance agitation was that these were left out of account altogether. He thought the gin-shop not fairly to be rendered the exclusive object of attack until, in connection with the classes who mostly made it their resort, the temptations that led to it, physical and moral, should have been more bravely dealt with. Among the former he counted foul smells, disgusting habitations, bad workshop-customs, scarcity of light, air, and water, in short the absence of all easy means of decency and health; and among the latter, the mental weariness and languor so induced, the desire of wholesome relaxation, the craving for *some* stimulus and excitement, not less needful than the sun itself to lives so passed, and last, and inclusive of all the rest, ignorance, and the want of rational mental training generally applied. This was consistently Dickens's "platform" throughout the years he was known to me; and holding it to be within the reach as well as the scope of legislation, which even our political magnates have been discovering lately, he thought intemperance to be but the one result that, out of all of those arising from the absence of legislation, was the most wretched. For him, drunkenness had a teeming and reproachful history anterior to the drunken stage; and he thought it the first duty of the moralist bent upon annihilating the gin-shop, to "strike deep and spare not" at those previous remediable evils. Certainly this was not the way of Mr. Cruikshank, any more than it is that of the many excellent people who take part in temperance agitations. His former tale of the *Bottle*, as told by his admirable pencil, was that of a decent working man, father of a boy and a girl, living in comfort and good esteem until near the middle age, when happening unluckily to have a goose for dinner one day in the bosom of his thriving family, he jocularly sends out for a bottle of gin, persuades his wife, until then a picture of neatness, and good housewifery, to take a little drop after the stuffing, and the whole family from that moment drink themselves to destruction. The sequel, of which Dickens now wrote to me, traced the lives of the boy and girl after the wretched deaths of their drunken parents, through gin-shop, beer-shop, and dancing-rooms, up to their trial for robbery: when the boy is convicted, dying aboard the hulks; and the girl desolate and mad after her acquittal, flings herself from London Bridge into the night-darkened river.

"I think," said Dickens, "the power of that closing scene quite extraordinary. It haunts the remembrance like an awful reality. It is full of passion and terror, and I doubt very much whether any hand but his could so have rendered it. There are other fine things too. The death-bed scene on board the hulks; the convict who is composing the face, and the other who is drawing the screen round the bed's head; seem to me masterpieces worthy of the greatest painter. The reality of the place and the fidelity with which every minute object illustrative of it is presented, are surprising. I think myself no bad judge of this feature, and it is remarkable throughout. In the trial scene at the Old Bailey, the eye may wander round the Court, and observe everything that is a part of the place. The very light and atmosphere are faithfully reproduced. So, in the gin-shop and the beer-shop. An inferior hand would indicate a fragment of the fact, and slur it over; but here every shred is honestly made out. The man behind the bar in the gin-shop, is as real as the convicts at the hulks, or the barristers round the table in the Old Bailey. I found it quite curious, as I closed the book, to recall the number of faces, I had seen of individual identity, and to think what a chance they have of living, as the Spanish friar said to Wilkie, when the living have passed away. But it only makes more exasperating to me the obstinate one-sidedness of the thing. When a man shows so forcibly the side of the medal on which the people in their faults and crimes are stamped, he is the more bound to help us to a glance at that other side on which the faults and vices of the governments placed over the people are not less gravely impressed."

This led to some remark on Hogarth's method in such matters, and I am glad to be able to preserve a masterly criticism of that great Englishman, by a writer who closely resembled him in genius; as another generation will be probably more apt than our own to discover. "Hogarth avoided the Drunkard's Progress, I conceive, precisely because the causes of drunkenness among the poor were so numerous and widely spread, and lurked so sorrowfully deep and far down in all human misery, neglect, and despair, that even *his* pencil could not bring them fairly and justly into the light. It was never his plan to be content with only showing the effect. In the death of the miser-father, his shoes new-soled with the binding of his Bible, before the young Rake begins his career; in the worldly father, listless daughter, impoverished young lord, and crafty lawyer, of the first plate of Marriage-à-la-mode; in the detestable advances through the stages of Cruelty; and in the progress downward of Thomas Idle; you see the effects indeed, but also the causes. He was never disposed to spare the kind of drunkenness that was of more 'respectable' engenderment, as one sees in his Midnight Modern Conversation, the election plates, and crowds of stupid aldermen and other guzzlers. But after one immortal journey down Gin Lane, he turned away in pity and sorrow—perhaps in hope of better things, one day, from better laws and schools and poor men's homes—and went back no more. The scene of Gin Lane, you know, is that just cleared away for the extension of Oxford Street, which we were looking at the other day; and I think it a remarkable trait of Hogarth's picture, that, while it exhibits drunkenness in the most appalling forms, it also forces on attention a most neglected wretched neighbourhood, and an unwholesome, indecent abject condition of life that might be put as frontispiece to our sanitary report of a hundred years later date. I have always myself thought the purpose of this fine piece to be not adequately stated even by Charles Lamb. 'The very houses seem absolutely reeling' it is true; but beside that wonderful picture of what follows intoxication, we have indication quite as powerful of what leads to it among the neglected classes. There is no evidence that any of the actors in the dreary scene have ever been much better than we see them there. The best are pawning the commonest necessaries, and tools of their trades; and the worst are homeless vagrants who give us no clue to their having been otherwise in bygone days. All are living and dying miserably. Nobody is interfering for prevention or for cure, in the generation going out before us, or the generation coming in. The beadle is the only sober man in the composition except the pawnbroker, and he is mightily indifferent to the orphan-child crying beside its parent's coffin. The little charity-girls are not so well taught or looked after, but that they can take to dram-drinking already. The church indeed is very prominent and handsome; but as, quite passive in the picture, it coldly surveys these things in progress under shadow of its tower, I cannot but bethink me that it was not until this year of grace 1848 that a Bishop of London first came out respecting something wrong in poor men's social accommodations, and I am confirmed in my suspicions that Hogarth had many meanings which have not grown obsolete in a century." . . .

Of what otherwise occupied him at Broadstairs in 1848 there is not much to mention until the close of his holiday. He used to say that he never went for more than a couple of days from his own home without something befalling him that never happened to anyone else, and his Broadstairs adventure of the present summer verged closer on tragedy than comedy. Returning there one day in August after bringing up his boys to school, it had been arranged that his wife should meet him at Margate; but he had walked impatiently far beyond the place for meeting when at last he caught sight of her, not in a small chaise but in a large carriage and pair followed by an excited crowd, and with the youth that should have been driving the little pony bruised and bandaged on the box behind the two prancing horses. "You may faintly imagine my amazement at encountering this carriage, and the strange people, and Kate, and the crowd, and the bandaged one, and all the rest of it." And then in a line or two I had the story. "At the top of a steep hill on the road, with a ditch on each side, the pony bolted, whereupon what does John do but jump out! He says he was thrown out, but it cannot be. The reins immediately became entangled in the wheels, and away went the pony down the hill madly, with Kate inside rending the Isle of Thanet with her screams. The accident might have been a fearful one, if the pony had not, thank Heaven, on getting to the bottom, pitched over the side; breaking the shaft and cutting her hind legs, but in the most extraordinary manner smashing her own way apart. She tumbled down, a bundle of legs with her head tucked underneath, and left the chaise standing on the bank! A Captain Devaynes and his wife where passing in their carriage at the moment, saw the accident with no power of preventing it, got Kate out, laid her on the grass, and behaved with infinite kindness. All's well that ends well, and I think she's really none the worse for the fright. John is in bed a good deal bruised, but without any broken bone, and likely soon to come right; though for the present plastered all over, and, like Squeers, a brown-paper parcel chock-full of nothing but groans. The women generally have no sympathy for him whatever, and the nurse says, with indignation, How could he go and leave a unprotected female in the shay!" . . .

Not till the close of September I heard of work intruding itself, in a letter twitting me for a broken promise in not joining him: "We are reasonably jolly, but rurally so; going to bed o' nights at ten, and bathing o' mornings at half-past seven; and not drugging ourselves with those dirty and spoiled waters of Lethe that flow round the base of the great pyramid." Then, after mention of the friends who had left him, Sheriff Gordon, the Leeches, Lemon, Egg and Stone: "reflection and pensiveness are coming. I have NOT

> '—seen Fancy write
> With a pencil of light
> On the blotter so solid, commanding the sea!'

but I shouldn't wonder if she were to do it, one of these days. Dim visions of divers things are floating around me; and I must go to work, head foremost, when I get home. I am glad, after all, that I have not been at it here, for I am all the better for my idleness, no doubt. . . . Roche was very ill last night, and looks like one with his face turned to the other world, this morning. When *are* you coming? Oh what days and nights there have been here, this week past!" . . .

His first seaside holiday in 1849 was at Brighton, where he passed some weeks in February; and not, I am bound to add, without the *un*usual adventure to signalise his visit. He had not been a week in his lodgings, where Leech and his wife joined him, when both his landlord and the daughter of his landlord went raving mad, and the lodgers were driven away to the Bedford Hotel. "If you could have heard the cursing and crying of the two; could have seen the physician and nurse quoited out into the passage by the madman at the hazard of their lives; could have seen Leech and me flying to the doctor's rescue; could have seen our wives pulling us back; could have seen the M.D. faint with fear; could have seen three other M.D.'s come to his aid; with an atmosphere of Mrs. Gamp's strait-waistcoats, struggling friends and servants, surrounding the whole; you would have said it was quite worthy of me, and quite in keeping with my usual proceedings." The letter ended with a word on what then his thoughts were full of, but for which no name had yet been found.

"A sea-fog to-day, but yesterday inexpressibly delicious. My mind running, like a high sea, on names—not satisfied yet, though." When he next wrote from the seaside, in the beginning of July, he had found the name; had started his book; and was "rushing to Broadstairs" to write the fourth number of *David Copperfield*.

In this came the childish experiences which had left so deep an impression upon him, and over which he had some difficulty in throwing the needful disguises. "Fourteen miles to-day in the country," he had written to me on 21 June, "revolving number four!" Still he did not quite see his way. Three days later he wrote: "On leaving you last night, I found myself summoned on a special jury in the Queen's Bench to-day. I have taken no notice of the document, and hourly expect to be dragged forth to a dungeon for contempt of court. I think I should rather like it. It might help me with a new notion or two in my difficulties. Meanwhile I shall take a stroll to-night in the green fields from seven to ten if you feel inclined to join." . . .

He had taken a house at Bonchurch, attracted there by the friend who had made it a place of interest for him during the last few years, the Rev. James White, with whose name and its associations my mind connects inseparably many of Dickens's happiest hours. To pay him fitting tribute would not be easy, if here it were called for. In the kindly shrewd Scotch face, a keen sensitiveness to pleasure and pain was the first thing that struck any common observer. Cheerfulness and gloom coursed over it so rapidly that no one could question the tale they told. But the relish of his life had outlived its more than usual share of sorrows; and quaint sly humour, love of jest and merriment, capital knowledge of books and sagacious quips at men, made his companionship delightful. Like his life, his genius was made up of alternations of mirth and melancholy. He would be immersed, at one time, in those darkest Scottish annals from which he drew his tragedies; and overflowing, at another, into Sir Frizzle Pumpkin's exuberant farce. The tragic histories may probably perish with the actor's perishable art; but three little abstracts of history written at a later time in prose, with a sunny clearness of narration and a glow of picturesque interest to my knowledge unequalled in books of such small pretension, will find, I hope, a lasting place in literature. They are filled with felicities of phrase, with breadth of understanding and judgment, with manful honesty, quiet sagacity, and a constant cheerful piety, valuable for all and priceless for the young. Another word I permit myself to add. With Dickens, White was popular supremely for his eager good fellowship; and few men brought him more of what he always liked to conceive. But he brought nothing so good as his wife. "He is excellent, but she is better," is the pithy remark of his first Bonchurch letter; and the true affection and respect that followed is happily still borne her by his daughters. . . .

After a few more days I heard of progress with his writing in spite

Certainly nobody in Ballard's. We are in the part, which is the house next door to the hotel itself, that we once had for three years running, and just as quiet and snug now as it was then. I don't think I shall return before the 20th or so, when the number is done; but I *may*, in some inconstant freak, run up to you before. Preliminary despatches and advices shall be forwarded in any case to the fragrant neighbourhood of Clare Market and the Portugal Street burying-ground." Such was his polite designation of my whereabouts: for which nevertheless he had secret likings. "On the Portsmouth railway, coming here, encountered Kenyon. On the ditto ditto at Reigate, encountered young Dilke, and took him in tow to Canterbury. On the ditto ditto at ditto (meaning Reigate), encountered Fox, M.P. for Oldham, and his daughter. All within an hour. Young Dilke great about the proposed Exposition under the direction of H.R.H. Prince Albert, and evincing, very pleasantly to me, unbounded faith in our old friend his father." There was one more letter, taking a rather gloomy view of public affairs in connection with an inflated pastoral from Doctor Wiseman "given out of the Flaminian Gate," and speaking dolefully of some family matters; which was subscribed, each word forming a separate line, "Yours Despondently, And Disgustedly, Wilkins Micawber."

His visit to the little watering-place in the following year was signalised by his completion of the most famous of his novels, and his letters otherwise were occupied by elaborate managerial preparation for the private performances at Knebworth. But again the plague of itinerant music flung him into such fevers of irritation, that he finally resolved against any renewed attempt to carry on important work here; and the summer of 1851, when he was busy with miscellaneous writing only, was the last of his regular residences in the place. He then let his London house for the brief remainder of its term; running away at the end of May, when some grave family sorrows had befallen him, from the crowds and excitements of the Great Exhibition; and I will only add generally of these seaside residences that his reading was considerable and very various at such intervals of labour. One of them, as I remember, took in all the minor tales as well as the plays of Voltaire, several of the novels (old favourites with him) of Paul de Kock, Ruskin's *Lamps of Architecture*, and a surprising number of books of African and other travel for which he had insatiable relish: but there was never much notice of his reading in his letters. "By the by, I observe, reading that wonderful book the *French Revolution* again for the 500th time, that Carlyle, who knows everything, don't know what Mumbo Jumbo is. It is not an Idol. It is a secret preserved among the men of certain African tribes, and never revealed by any of them, for the punishment of their women. Mumbo Jumbo comes in hideous form out of the forest, or the mud, or the river, or where not, and flogs some woman who has been backbiting, or scolding, or with some other domestic mischief disturbing the general peace. Carlyle's seems to confound him with the common Fetish; but he is quite another thing. He is a disguised man; and all about him is a freemasons' secret *among the men*."—"I finished the *Scarlet Letter* yesterday. It falls off sadly after that fine opening scene. The psychological part of the story is very much overdone, and not truly done I think. Their suddenness of meeting and agreeing to go away together after all those years, is very poor. Mr. Chillingworth ditto. The child out of nature altogether. And Mr. Dimmisdale certainly never could have begotten her." In Mr. Hawthorne's earlier books he had taken especial pleasure; his *Mosses from and Old Manse* having been the first book he placed in my hands on his return from America, with reiterated injunctions to read it. . . .

## III

### CHRISTMAS BOOKS CLOSED AND "HOUSEHOLD WORDS" BEGUN

#### 1848–50

IT has been seen that his fancy for his Christmas book of 1848 first arose to him at Lausanne in the summer of 1846, and that, after writing its opening pages in the autumn of the following year, he laid it aside under the pressure of his *Dombey*. These lines were in the letter that closed his 1848 Broadstairs holiday. "At last I am a mentally matooring of the Christmas book—or, as poor Macrone used to write, 'booke,' 'boke,' 'buke,' etc." It was the first labour to which he applied himself at his return.

In London it soon came to maturity; was published duly as *The Haunted Man, or the Ghost's Bargain*; sold largely, beginning with a subscription of twenty thousand; and had a great success on the Adelphi stage, to which it was rather cleverly adapted by Lemon. He had placed on its title-page originally four lines from Tennyson's *Departure*.

> And o'er the hills, and far away
> Beyond their utmost purple rim,
> Beyond the night, across the day,
> Thro' all the world IT followed him;

but they were less applicable to the close than to the opening of the tale, and were dropped before publication. . . .

The design for his much-thought-of new Periodical was still "dim," as we have seen, when the first cogitation of it at Bonchurch occupied him; but the expediency of making it clearer came soon after with a visit from Mr. Evans, who brought his half-year's accounts of sales, and some small disappointment for him in those of

*Copperfield.* "The accounts are rather shy, after *Dombey*, and what you said comes true after all. I am not sorry I cannot bring myself to care much for what opinions people may form; and I have a strong belief, that, if any of my books are read years hence, *Dombey* will be remembered as among the best of them: but passing influences are important for the time, and as *Chuzzlewit* with its small sale sent me up, *Dombey's* large sale has tumbled me down. Not very much, however, in real truth. These accounts only include the first three numbers, have of course been burdened with all the heavy expenses of number one, and ought not in reason to be complained of. But it is clear to me that the Periodical must be set a-going in the spring; and I have already been busy, at odd half-hours, in shadowing forth a name and an idea. Evans says they have but one opinion repeated to them of *Copperfield*, and they feel very confident about it. A steady twenty-five thousand, which it is now on the verge of, will do very well. The back numbers are always going off. Read the enclosed." . . .

The week before he left Bonchurch I again had news of the old and often recurring fancy. "The old notion of the Periodical, which had been agitating itself in my mind for so long, I really think is at last gradually growing into form." . . . It was to be a weekly miscellany of general literature; and its stated objects were to be, to contribute to the entertainment and instruction of all classes of readers, and to help in the discussion of the more important social questions of the time: It was to comprise short stories by others as well as himself; matters of passing interest in the liveliest form that could be given to them; subjects suggested by books that might most be attracting attention; and poetry in every number if possible, but in any case something of romantic fancy. This was to be a cardinal point. There was to be no more utilitarian spirit; with all familiar things, but especially those repellent on the surface, something was to be connected that should be fanciful or kindly; and the hardest workers were to be taught that their lot is not necessarily excluded from the sympathies and graces of imagination. This was all finally settled by the close of 1849, when a general announcement of the intended adventure was made. There remained only a title and an assistant-editor; and I am happy now to remember that for the latter important duty Mr. Wills was chosen at my suggestion. He discharged its duties with admirable patience and ability for twenty years, and Dickens's later life had no more intimate friend.

The title took some time and occupied many letters. One of the first thought-of has now the curious interest of having fore-shadowed, by the motto proposed to accompany it, the title of the series of *All the Year Round* which he was led to substitute for the older series in 1859. "THE ROBIN. With this motto from Goldsmith. *The redbreast, celebrated for its affection to mankind, continues with us, the year round.*" That however was rejected. Then came: "MANKIND. This I think very good." It followed the other nevertheless. After it came: "And here a strange idea, but with decided advantages. 'CHARLES DICKENS.

A weekly journal designed for the instruction and entertainment of all classes of readers. CONDUCTED BY HIMSELF.'" Still something was wanting in that also. Next day there arrived: "I really think if there *be* anything wanting in the other name, that this is very pretty, and just supplies it. THE HOUSEHOLD VOICE. I have thought of many others, as—THE HOUSEHOLD GUEST. THE HOUSEHOLD FACE. THE COMRADE. THE MICROSCOPE. THE HIGHWAY OF LIFE. THE LEVER. THE ROLLING YEARS. THE HOLLY TREE (with two lines from Southey for a motto). EVERYTHING. But I rather think the VOICE is it." It was near indeed; but the following day came, "HOUSEHOLD WORDS. This is a very pretty name": and the choice was made.

The first number appeared on Saturday, 30 March, 1850, and contained among other things the beginning of a story by a very original writer, Mrs. Gaskell, for whose powers he had a high admiration, and with whom he had friendly intercourse during many years. Other opportunities will arise for mention of those with whom this new labour brought him into personal communication, but I may at once say that of all the writers, before unknown, whom his journal helped to make familiar to a wide world of readers, he had the strongest personal interest in Mr. Sala, and placed at once in the highest rank his capabilities of help in such an enterprise. An illustrative trait of what I have named as its cardinal point to him will fitly close my account of its establishment. Its first number, still unpublished, had not seemed to him quite to fulfil his promise, "tenderly to cherish the light of fancy inherent in all breasts"; and, as soon as he received the proof of the second, I heard from him. "Looking over the suggested contents of number two at breakfast this morning" (Brighton: 14 March, 1850) "I felt an uneasy sense of there being a want of something tender, which would apply to some universal household knowledge. Coming down in the railroad the other night (always a wonderfully suggestive place to me when I am alone) I was looking at the stars, and revolving a little idea about them. Putting now these two things together, I wrote the enclosed little paper, straightway; and should like you to read it before you send it to the printers (it will not take you five minutes), and let me have a proof by return." This was the child's "dream of a star," which opened his second number; it appears among his reprinted pieces. . . .

His sister Fanny and himself, he told me long before this paper was written, used to wander at night about a churchyard near their house, looking up at the stars; and her early death, of which I am shortly to speak, had vividly reawakened all the childish associations which made her memory dear to him.

## IV

1850–2

IN the year of the establishment of *Household Words* Dickens re-sumed what I have called his splendid strolling on behalf of a scheme for the advantage of men of letters, to which a great brother-author had given the sanction of his genius and name. In November 1850, in the hall of Lord Lytton's old family seat in Knebworth Park, there were three private performances by the original actors in Ben Jonson's *Every Man in His Humour*, of which all the circumstances and surroundings were very brilliant; some of the gentlemen of the country played both in comedy and farces; our generous host was profuse of all noble encouragement; and amid the general pleasure and excitement hopes rose high. Recent experience had shown what the public interest in this kind of amusement might place within reach of its providers; and there came to be discussed the possibility of making permanent such help as had been afforded to fellow writers, by means of an endowment that should not be mere charity, but should combine something of both pension-list and college-lectureship, without the drawbacks of either. It was not enough considered that schemes for self-help, to be successful, require from those they are meant to benefit, not only a general assent to their desirability, but zealous co-operation. Too readily assuming what should have had more thorough investigation, the enterprise was set on foot, and the "Guild of Literature and Art" originated at Knebworth. A five-act comedy was to be written by Sir Edward Lytton; and, when a certain sum of money had been obtained by public representations of it, the details of the scheme were to be drawn up, and appeal made to those whom it addressed more especially. In a very few months everything was ready, except a farce which Dickens was to have written to follow the comedy, and which unexpected cares of management and preparation were held to absolve him from. There were other reasons. "I have written the first scene," he told me (23 March, 1851), "and it has droll points in it, 'more farcical points than you commonly find in farces.' really better. Yet I am constantly striving, for my reputation's sake, to get into it a meaning that is impossible in a farce; constantly thinking of it, therefore, against the grain; and constantly impressed with a con-viction that I could never act in it myself with that wild abandon-ment which can alone carry a farce off. Wherefore I have confessed to Bulwer Lytton and asked for absolution.' There was substituted a new farce of Lemon's, to which, however, Dickens soon contributed so many jokes and so much Gampish and other fun of his own, that it came to be in effect a joint piece of authorship; and Gabblewigg, which the manager took to himself, was one of those personation parts requiring five or six changes of face, voice, and gait in the course of it, from which, as we have seen, he derived all the early theatrical ambition that the elder Mathews had awakened in him. "You have no idea," he continued, "of the immensity of the work as the time advances, for the Duke even throws the whole of the audience on us, or he would get (he says) into all manner of scrapes."

"The Duke" was the Duke of Devonshire, of whose love of letters and interest for men of that calling I have given one of the many instances that adorned a life which alone perhaps in England was genuinely and completely that of the Grand Seigneur. Well-read and very accomplished, he had the pleasing manners which proceed from a kind nature; and splendid in his mode of living beyond any other English noble, his magnificence, by the ease and elegance that accompanied it, was relieved from all offence of ostentation. He had offered his house in Piccadilly for the first representations, and in his princely way discharged all the expenses attending them. A movable theatre was built and set up in the great drawing-room, the library was turned into a green-room, and here Lytton's comedy was presented. . . .

The design nevertheless did not prosper, and both the great writers who had associated themselves with it are now passed away. Since it first was mentioned on this page, Lord Lytton has himself been borne to the Abbey where Dickens is laid, and which never opened to receive a more varied genius, a more gallant spirit, a man more constant to his friends, more true to any cause he represented, or whose name will hereafter be found entitled to a more honoured place in the history of his time. The Guild design failed because the support indispensable to success was not, as Dickens too sanguinely hoped, given to it by literary men themselves. . . .

## V

EXCEPTING always the haunts and associations of his childhood, Dickens had no particular sentiment of locality, and any special regard for houses he had lived in was not a thing noticeable in him. But he cared most for Devonshire Terrace, perhaps for the bit of ground attached to it; and it was with regret he suddenly discovered, at the close of 1847, that he should have to resign it "next Lady Day three years. I had thought the lease two years more." To that brief remaining time belong some incidents of which I have still to give account; and I connect them with the house in which he lived during the progress of what is generally thought his greatest book, and of what I think were his happiest years.

We had never had such intimate confidences as in the interval since his return from Paris; but these have been used in my narrative of the childhood and boyish experiences, and what remain are incidental only. Of the fragment of autobiography there also given, the origin has been told: but the intention of leaving such a record had been also in his mind at an earlier date; and it was the very depth of our interest in the opening of his fragment that led to the larger design in which it became absorbed. "I hardly know why I write this," was his own comment on one of his personal revelations, "but the more than friendship which has grown between us seems to force it on me in my present mood. We shall speak of it all, you and I, Heaven grant, wisely and wonderingly many and many a time in after years. In the meanwhile I am more at rest for having opened all my heart and mind to you. . . . This day eleven years, poor dear Mary died." That was written on 7 May, 1848. . . .

In all the later part of the year Dickens's thoughts were turning much to the form his next book should assume. A suggestion that he should write it in the first person, by way of change, had been thrown out by me, which he took at once very gravely; and this, with other things, though as yet not dreaming of any public use of his early personal trials, conspired to bring about the resolve to use them. His determination once taken, with what a singular truthfulness he contrived to blend the fact with the fiction may be shown by a small occurrence of this time. It has been inferred, from the vividness of the boy-impressions of Yarmouth in David's earliest experiences, that the place must have been familiar to his own boyhood: but the truth was that at the close of 1848 he first saw that celebrated seaport.

One of its earlier months had been signalised by an adventure in which Leech, Lemon, and myself took part with him, when, obtaining horses from Salisbury, we passed the whole of a March day in riding over every part of the Plain; visiting Stonehenge, and exploring Hazlitt's "hut" at Winterslow, birthplace of some of his finest essays; altogether with so brilliant a success that now (13 November) he proposed to "repeat the Salisbury Plain idea in a new direction in midwinter, to wit, Blackgang Chine in the Isle of Wight, with dark winter cliffs and roaring oceans." But mid-winter brought with it too much dreariness of its own, to render these stormy accompaniments to it very palatable; and on the last day of the year he bethought him "it would be better to make an outburst to some old cathedral city we don't know, and what do you say to Norwich and Stanfield Hall?" Thither accordingly the three friends went, illness at the last disabling me; and of the result I heard (12 January, 1849) that Stanfield Hall, the scene of a recent frightful tragedy, had nothing attractive unless the term might be applied to "a murderous look that seemed to invite such a crime. We arrived," continued Dickens, "between the Hall and Potass farm, as the search was going on for the pistol in a manner so consummately stupid, that there was nothing on earth to prevent any of Rush's labourers from accepting five pounds from Rush junior to find the weapon and give it to him. Norwich, a disappointment" (one pleasant face "transformeth a city," but he was unable yet to connect it with our delightful friend Elwin); "all save its place of execution, which we found fit for a gigantic scoundrel's exit. But the success of the trip, for me, was to come. Yarmouth, sir, where we went afterwards, is the strangest place in the wide world: one hundred and forty-six miles of hill-less marsh between it and London. More when we meet. I shall certainly try my hand at it." He made it the home of his "little Em'ly."

Everything now was taking that direction with him; and soon, to give his own account of it, his mind was upon names "running like a high sea." Four days after the date of the last-quoted letter ("all over happily, thank God, by four o'clock this morning") there came the birth of his eighth child and sixth son; whom at first he meant to call by Oliver Goldsmith's name, but settled afterwards into that of Henry Fielding; and to whom that early friend Ainsworth who had first made us known to each other, welcome and pleasant companion always, was asked to be godfather. Telling me of the change in the name of the little fellow, which he had made in a kind of homage to the style of work he was now so bent on beginning, he added, "What should you think of this for a notion of a character? 'Yes, that is very true; but now, *What's his motive?*' I fancy I could make something like it into a kind of amusing and more innocent Pecksniff. 'Well now, yes—no doubt that was a fine thing to do! But now, stop a moment, let us see—*What's his motive?*'" Here again was but one of the many outward signs of fancy and fertility that accompanied the outset of all his more important books; though, as in their cases also, other moods of the mind incident to such beginnings were less favourable. "Deepest despondency, as usual, in commencing, besets me;" is the opening of the letter in which he speaks of what of course was always one of his first anxieties, the selection of a name. In this particular instance he had been undergoing doubts and misgivings to more than the usual degree. It was not until 23 February he got to anything like the shape of a feasible title. "I should like to know how the enclosed (one of those I have been thinking of) strikes you, on a first acquaintance with it. It is odd, I think, and new: but it may have A's. difficulty of being 'too comic, my boy.' I suppose I should have to add, though, by way of motto, 'And in short it led to the very Mag's Diversions. *Old Saying.*' Or would it be better, there being equal authority for either, 'And in short they all played Mag's Diversions. *Old Saying*'?"

"*Mag's Diversions.*

Being the personal history of
MR. THOMAS MAG THE YOUNGER,
Of Blunderstone House."

This was hardly satisfactory, I thought; and it soon became apparent that he thought so too, although within the next three days I had it in three other forms. "*Mag's Diversions*, being the Personal History, Adventures, Experience, and Observation of Mr. David Mag the Younger, of Blunderstone House." The second omitted Adventures, and called his hero Mr. David Mag the Younger, of Copperfield House. The third made nearer approach to what the destinies were leading him to, and transformed Mr. David Mag into Mr. David Copperfield the Younger and his great-aunt Margaret; retaining still as his leading title, *Mag's Diversions*. It is singular that it should never have occurred to him, while the name was thus strangely as by accident bringing itself together, that the initials were but his own reversed. He was much startled when I pointed this out, and protested it was just in keeping with the fates and chances which were always befalling him. "Why else," he said, "should I so obstinately have kept to that name when once it turned up?"

It was quite true that he did so, as I had curious proof following close upon the heels of his third proposal. "I wish," he wrote on 25 February, "you would look over carefully the titles now enclosed, and tell me to which you most incline. You will see that they give up *Mag* altogether, and refer exclusively to one name—that which I last sent you. I doubt whether I could, on the whole, get a better name.

"1. *The Copperfield Disclosures.* Being the personal history, experience, and observation, of Mr. David Copperfield the Younger, of Blunderstone House.

"2. *The Copperfield Records.* Being the personal history, experience, and observation, of Mr. David Copperfield the Younger, of Copperfield Cottage.

"3. *The Last Living Speech and Confession of David Copperfield, Junior,* of Blunderstone Lodge, who was never executed at the Old Bailey, being his personal history found among his papers.

"4. *The Copperfield Survey of the World as it Rolled.* Being the personal history, experience, and observation of David Copperfield the Younger, of Blunderstone Rookery.

"5. *The Last Will and Testament of Mr. David Copperfield.* Being his personal history left as a legacy.

"6. *Copperfield, Complete.* Being the whole personal history and experience of Mr. David Copperfield of Blunderstone House, which he never meant to be published on any account.

Or, the opening words of No. 6 might be *Copperfield's Entire;* and *The Copperfield Confessions* might open Nos. 1 and 2. NOW, WHAT SAY YOU?"

What I said is to be inferred from what he wrote back on the 28th. "The *Survey* has been my favourite from the first. Kate picked it out from the rest, without my saying anything about it, Georgy too. You hit upon it, on the first glance. Therefore I have no doubt that it is indisputably the best title; and I will stick to it." There was a change nevertheless. His completion of the second chapter defined to himself, more clearly than before, the character of the book; and the propriety of rejecting everything not strictly personal from the name given to it. The words proposed, therefore, became ultimately these only: "The Personal History, Adventures, Experience, and Observation of David Copperfield the Younger, of Blunderstone Rookery, which he never meant to be published on any account." And the letter which told me that with this name it was finally to be launched on 1 May, told me also (19 April) the difficulties that still beset him at the opening. "My hand is out in the matter of *Copperfield*. To-day and yesterday I have done nothing. Though I know what I want to do, I am lumbering on like a stage-waggon. I can't even dine at the Temple to-day, I feel it so important to stick at it this evening, and make some head. I am quite aground; quite a literary Benedict, as he appeared when his heels wouldn't stay upon the carpet; and the long Copperfieldian perspective looks snowy and thick, this fine morning." The allusion was to a dinner at his house the night before; when not only Rogers had to be borne out, having fallen sick at the table, but, as we rose soon after to quit the dining-room, Mr. Jules Benedict had quite suddenly followed the poet's lead, and fallen prostrate on the carpet in the midst of us. Amid the general consternation there seemed a want of proper attendance on the sick: the distinguished musician faring in this respect hardly so well as the famous bard, by whose protracted sufferings in the library, whither he had been removed, the sanitary help available on the establishment was still absorbed: and as Dickens had been eloquent during dinner on the atrocities of a pauper-farming case at Tooting which was then exciting a fury of indignation, Fonblanque now declared him to be no better himself than a second Drouet, reducing his guests to a lamentable state by the food he had given them, and aggravating their sad condition by absence of all proper nursing. The joke was well kept up by Quin and Edwin Landseer, Lord Strangford joining in with a tragic sympathy for his friend the poet; and the banquet so dolefully interrupted ended in uproarious mirth. For nothing really serious had happened. Benedict went laughing away with his wife, and I helped Rogers on with his over-shoes for his usual night-walk home. "Do you know how many waistcoats I wear?" asked the poet of me, as I was doing him this service. I professed my inability to guess. "Five" he said: "and here they are!" Upon which he opened them, in the manner of the grave-digger in *Hamlet*, and showed me every one. That dinner was in the April 1849. . . .

The month of May was that of the start of *David Copperfield*, and to one more dinner (on the 12th) I may especially refer for those who were present at it. Carlyle and Mrs. Carlyle came, Thackeray and Rogers, Mrs. Gaskell and Kenyon, Jerrold and Hablot Browne, with Mr. and Mrs. Tagart; and it was a delight to see the enjoyment of Dickens at Carlyle's laughing reply to questions about his health, that he was, in the language of Mr. Peggotty's housekeeper, a lorn lone creature and everything went contrary with him. Things were not likely to go better, I thought, as I saw the great writer—kindest as well as wisest of men, but not very patient under sentimental philosophies—seated next the good Mr. Tagart, who soon was heard launching at him various metaphysical questions in regard to heaven and such like; and the relief was great when Thackeray introduced, with quaint whimsicality, a story which he and I had just heard Macready relate in talking to us about his boyish days, of a country actor who had supported himself for six months on his judicious treatment of the "tag" to the *Castle Spectre*. In the original it stands that you are to do away with suspicion, banish vile mistrust, and, almost in the words we had just heard from the minister to the philosopher, "Believe there is a heaven, nor doubt that heaven is just!" in place of which Macready's friend, observing that the drop fell for the most part quite coldly, substituted one night the more telling appeal, "And give us your Applause, for *that* is ALWAYS JUST!" which brought down the house with rapture. . . .

Some incidents that belong specially to the three years that closed his residence in the home thus associated with not the least interesting part of his career, will further show what now were his occupations and ways of life. In the summer of 1849 he came up from Broadstairs to attend a Mansion House dinner, which the lord mayor of that day had been moved by a laudable ambition to give to " literature and art," which he supposed would be adequately represented by the Royal Academy, the contributors to *Punch*, Dickens, and one or two newspaper men. On the whole the result was not cheering; the worthy chief magistrate, no doubt quite undesignedly, expressing too much surprise at the unaccustomed faces around him to be altogether complimentary. In general (this was the tone) we are in the habit of having princes, dukes, ministers, and what not for our guests, but what a delight, all the greater for being unusual, to see gentlemen like you! In other words, what could possibly be pleasanter than for people satiated with greatness to get for a while by way of change into the butler's pantry? This in substance was Dickens's account to me next day, and his reason for having been very careful in his acknowledgment of the toast of "The Novelists." He was nettled not a little therefore by a jesting allusion to himself in the *Daily News* in connection with the proceedings, and asked me to forward a remonstrance. Having a strong dislike to all such displays of sensitiveness, I suppressed the letter; but it is perhaps worth printing now. Its date is Broadstairs, Wednesday, 11 July, 1849. "I have no other interest in, or concern with, a most facetious article on last Saturday's dinner at the Mansion House, which appeared in your paper of yesterday, and found its way here to-day, than that it misrepresents me in what I said on the occasion. If you should not think it at all damaging to the wit of that satire to state what I did say, I shall be much obliged to you. It was this. . . . That I considered the compliment of a recognition of Literature by the citizens of London the more acceptable to us because it was unusual in that hall, and likely to be an advantage and benefit to them in proportion as it became in future less unusual. That, on behalf of the novelists, I accepted the tribute as an appropriate one; inasmuch as we had sometimes reason to hope that our imaginary worlds afforded an occasional refuge to men busily engaged in the toils of life, from which they came forth none the worse to a renewal of its strivings; and certainly that the chief magistrate of the greatest city in the world might be fitly regarded as the representative of that class of our readers."

Of an incident towards the close of the year, though it had important practical results, brief mention will here suffice. We saw the Mannings executed on the walls of Horsemonger Lane Gaol; and with the letter which Dickens wrote next day to *The Times* descriptive of what we had witnessed on that memorable morning, there began an active agitation against public executions which never ceased until the salutary change was effected which has worked so well. . . .

The chief occupation of the past and present year, *David Copperfield*, will have a section to itself, and in this may be touched but lightly. Once fairly in it, the story bore him irresistibly along; certainly with less trouble to himself in the composition, beyond that ardent sympathy with the creatures of the fancy which always made so absolutely real to him their sufferings or sorrows; and he was probably never less harassed by interruptions or breaks in his invention. His principal hesitation occurred in connection with the child-wife Dora, who had become a great favourite as he went on; and it was shortly after her fate had been decided, in the early autumn of 1850, but before she breathed her last, that a third daughter was born to him, to whom he gave his dying little heroine's name. On these and other points, without forestalling what waits to be said of the composition of this fine story, a few illustrative words from his letters will properly find a place here. "*Copperfield* half done," he wrote of the second number on 6 June. "I feel, thank God, quite confident in the story. I have a move in it ready for this month; another for next; and another for the next." "I think it is necessary" (15 November) "to decide against the special pleader. Your reasons quite suffice. I am not sure but that the banking house might do. I will consider it in a walk." "Banking business impracticable" (17 November) "on account of the confinement: which would stop the story, I foresee. I have taken, for the present at all events, the proctor. I am wonderfully in harness, and nothing galls or frets." "*Copperfield* done" (20 November) "after two days' very hard work indeed; and I think a smashing number. His first dissipation I hope will be found worthy of attention, as a piece of grotesque truth." "I feel a great hope" (23 January, 1850) "that I shall be remembered by little Em'ly, a good many years to come." "I begin to have my doubts of being able to join you" (20 February), "for *Copperfield* runs high, and must be done to-morrow. But I'll do it if possible, and strain every nerve. Some beautiful comic love, I hope, in the number." "Still undecided about Dora" (7 May), "but MUST decide to-day." "I have been" (Tuesday, 20 August) "very hard at work these three days, and have still Dora to kill. But with good luck, I may do it to-morrow. Obliged to go to Shepherd's Bush to-day, and can consequently do little this morning. Am eschewing all sorts of things that present themselves to my fancy—coming in such crowds!" "Work in a very decent state of advancement" (13 August) "domesticity notwithstanding. I hope I shall have a splendid number. I feel the story to its minutest point." "Mrs. Micawber is still" (15 August), "I regret to say, in *statu quo*. Ever yours, WILKINS MICAWBER." The little girl was born the next day, the 16th, and received the name of Dora Annie. The most part of what remained of the year was passed away from home.

The year following did not open with favourable omen, both the child and its mother having severe illness. The former rallied, however, and "little Dora is getting on bravely, thank God!" was his bulletin of the early part of February. Soon after, it was resolved to make trial of Great Malvern for Mrs. Dickens; and lodgings were taken there in March, Dickens and her sister accompanying her, and the children being left in London. "It is a most beautiful place," he wrote to me (15 March). "O Heaven, to meet the Cold Waterers (as I did this morning when I went out for a shower-bath) dashing down the hills, with severe expressions on their countenances, like men doing matches and not exactly winning! Then, a young lady in a grey polka going *up* the hills, regardless of legs; and meeting a young gentleman (a bad case, I should say) with a light black silk cap on under his hat, and the pimples of I don't know how many douches under that. Likewise an old man who ran over a milk-child, rather than stop!—with no neckcloth, on principle; and with his mouth wide open to catch the morning air." He had to return to London after the middle of March, for business connected with a charitable Home established at Shepherd's Bush by Miss Coutts in the benevolent hope of rescuing fallen women by testing their fitness for emigration, frequently mentioned in his letters, and which largely and regularly occupied his time for several years. On this occasion his stay was prolonged by the illness of his father, whose health had been failing latterly and graver symptoms were now spoken of. "I saw my poor father twice yesterday," he wrote to me on the 27th, "the second time between ten and eleven at night. In the morning I thought him not so well. At night, as well as anyone in such a situation could be." Next day he was so much better that his son went back to Malvern: but the end came suddenly. We were expecting him at Knebworth, and I supposed that some accident had detained him in Malvern; but at my return this letter waited me. "Devonshire Terrace, Monday, thirty-first of March, 1851. . . . My poor father died this morning at five and twenty minutes to six. They had sent for me to Malvern, but I passed John on the railway. . . . Arrived at eleven last night, and was in Keppel Street at a quarter past eleven. He did not know me, nor anyone. He began to sink at about noon yesterday, and never rallied afterwards. I remained there until he died—O so quietly. . . . I hardly know what to do. I am going up to Highgate to get the ground. Perhaps you may like to go, and I should like it if you do. I will not leave here before two o'clock, but I must go down to Malvern again, at night. . . ." Mr. John Dickens was laid in Highgate Cemetery on 5 April; and the stone placed over him by the son who has made his name a famous one in England, bore tribute to his "zealous, useful, cheerful spirit." What more is to be said of him will be most becomingly said in speaking of *David Copperfield*. While the book was in course of being written, all that had been best in him came more and more vividly back to its author's memory; as time wore on, nothing else was remembered; and five years before his own death, after using in one of his letters to me a phrase rather out of the common with him, this was added: "I find this looks like my poor father, whom I regard as a better man the longer I live."

He was at this time under promise to take the chair at the General Theatrical Fund on 14 April. Great efforts were made to relieve him from the promise; but such special importance was attached to his being present, and the Fund so sorely then required help, that, no change of day being found possible for the actors who desired to attend, he yielded to the pressure put upon him; of which the result was to throw upon me a sad responsibility. The reader will understand why, even at this distance of time, my allusion to it is brief.

The train from Malvern brought him up only five minutes short of the hour appointed for the dinner, and we first met that day at the London Tavern. I never heard him to greater advantage than in the speech that followed. His liking for this Fund was the fact of its not confining its benefits to any special or exclusive body of actors, but opening them undoubtingly to all; and he gave a description of the kind of actor, going down to the infinitesimally small, not omitted from such kind help, which had a half-pathetic humour in it that makes it charming still. "In our Fund," he said, "the word exclusiveness is not known. We include every actor, whether he be Hamlet or Benedict: the ghost, the bandit, or the court physician; or, in his one person, the whole king's army. He may do the light business, or the heavy, or the comic, or the eccentric. He may be the captain who courts the young lady, whose uncle still unaccountably persists in dressing himself in a costume one hundred years older than his time. Or he may be the young lady's brother in the white gloves and inexpressibles, whose duty in the family appears to be to listen to the female members of it whenever they sing, and to shake hands with everybody between all the verses. Or he may be the baron who gives the fête, and who sits uneasily on the sofa under a canopy with the baroness while the fête is going on. Or he may be the peasant at the fête who comes on to the stage to swell the drinking chorus, and who, it may be observed, always turns his glass upside down before he begins to drink out of it. Or he may be the clown who takes away the doorstep of the house where the evening party is going on. Or he may be the gentleman who issues out of the house on the false alarm, and is precipitated into the area. Or, if an actress, she may be the fairy who resides for ever in a revolving star with an occasional visit to a bower or a palace. Or again, if an actor, he may be the armed head of the witch's cauldron; or even that extraordinary witch concerning whom I have observed in country places, that he is much less like the notion formed from the description of Hopkins than the Malcolm or Donalbain of the previous scenes. This society, in short, says, 'Be you what you may, be you actor or actress, be your path in your profession never so high or never so low, never so haughty or never so humble, we offer you the means of doing good to yourselves, and of doing good to your brethren.' "

Half an hour before he rose to speak I had been called out of the room. It was the servant from Devonshire Terrace to tell me his child Dora was suddenly dead. She had not been strong from her birth; but there was just at this time no cause for special fear, when unexpected convulsions came, and the frail little life passed away. My decision had to be formed at once; and I satisfied myself that it would be best to permit his part of the proceedings to close before the truth was told to him. But as he went on, after the sentences I have quoted, to speak of actors having to come from scenes and sickness, of suffering, aye, even of death itself, to play their parts before us, my part was very difficult. "Yet how often is it with all of us," he proceeded to say, and I remember to this hour with what anguish I listened to words that had for myself alone, in all the crowded room, their full significance: "how often is it with all of us, that in our several spheres we have to do violence to our feelings, and to hide our hearts in carrying on this fight of life, if we would bravely discharge in it our duties and responsibilities." In the disclosure that followed when he left the chair, Mr. Lemon, who was present, assisted me; and I left this good friend with him next day, when I went myself to Malvern and brought back Mrs. Dickens and her sister. The little child lies in a grave at Highgate near that of Mr. and Mrs. John Dickens; and on the stone which covers her is now written also her father's name, and those of two of her brothers.

One more public discussion he took part in, before quitting London for the rest of the summer; and what he said (it was a meeting, with Lord Carlisle in the chair, in aid of Sanitary reform) very pregnantly illustrates what was remarked by me on a former page. He declared his belief that neither education nor religion could do anything really useful in social improvement until the way had been paved for their ministrations by cleanliness and decency. He spoke warmly of the services of Lord Ashley in connection with ragged schools, but he put the case of a miserable child tempted into one of those schools out of the noisome places in which his life was passed, and he asked what a few hours' teaching could effect against the ever-renewed lesson of a whole existence. "But give him, and his, a glimpse of heaven through a little of its light and air; give them water; help them to be clean; lighten the heavy atmosphere in which their spirits flag, and which makes them the callous things they are; take the body of the dead relative from the room where the living live with it, and where such loathsome familiarity deprives death itself of awe; and then, but not before, they will be brought willingly to hear of Him whose thoughts were so much with the wretched, and who had compassion for all human sorrow." He closed by proposing Lord Ashley's health as having preferred the higher ambition of labouring for the poor to that of pursuing the career open to him in the service of the State; and as having also had "the courage on all occasions to face the cant which is the worst and commonest of all, the cant about the cant of philanthropy." Lord Shaftesbury first dined with him in the following year at Tavistock House.

Shortly after the Sanitary meeting, came the first Guild performances, and then Dickens left Devonshire Terrace, never to return to it. With intervals of absence, chiefly at the Guild representations, he stayed in his favourite Fort House by the sea until October, when he took possession of Tavistock House. . . .

It was not until the end of November, when he had settled himself

The House in Devonshire Terrace where Charles Dickens wrote "David Copperfield" and Other Works.

in his new London abode, that the book was begun (and as generally happened with the more important incidents of his life, though always accidentally, begun on a Friday); but precedence is due, before anything more is said of *Bleak House*, to what remains to be said of *Copperfield*.

It was the last book written in Devonshire Terrace; and on the page opposite is engraved a drawing by Maclise of this house where so many of Dickens's masterpieces were composed, done on the first anniversary of the day when his daughter Kate was born.

# VI

## "DAVID COPPERFIELD"

### 1850

DICKENS never stood so high in reputation as at the completion of *Copperfield*. From the first it had surpassed in popularity, though not in sale, all his previous books excepting *Pickwick*. "You gratify me more than I can tell you," he wrote to Lytton, "by what you say about *Copperfield*, because I hope myself that some heretofore deficient qualities are there." If the power was not greater than in *Chuzzlewit*, the subject had more attractiveness; there was more variety of incident, with a freer play of character; and there was withal a suspicion, which though general and vague had sharpened interest not a little, that underneath the fiction lay something of the author's life. How much was not known by the world until he had passed away. When engaged upon its close he had written thus (21 October, 1850): "I am within three pages of the shore; and am strangely divided, as usual in such cases, between sorrow and joy. Oh, my dear Forster, if I were to say half of what *Copperfield* makes me feel to-night, how strangely, even to you, I should be turned inside-out! I seem to be sending some part of myself into the Shadowy World."

To be acquainted with English literature is to know that into its most famous prose fiction autobiography has entered largely in disguise, and that the characters most familiar to us in the English novel had originals in actual life. Smollett never wrote a story that was not in some degree a recollection of his own adventures; and Fielding, who put something of his wife into all his heroines, had been as fortunate in finding, not Trulliber only, but Parson Adams himself, among his living experiences. To come later down, there was hardly anyone ever known to Scott of whom his memory had not treasured up something to give minuter reality to the people of his fancy; and we know exactly whom to look for in Dandie Dinmont and Jonathan Oldbuck, in the office of Alan Fairford and the sick-room of Crystal Croftangry. We are to observe also that it is never anything complete that is thus taken from life by a genuine writer, but only leading traits, or such as may give greater finish; that the fine artist will embody in his portraiture of one person his experiences of fifty; and that this would have been Fielding's answer to Trulliber if he had objected to the pigsty, and to Adams if he had sought to make a case of scandal out of the affair in Mrs. Slipslop's bedroom. Such questioning befell Dickens repeatedly in the course of his writings, where he freely followed, as we have seen, the method thus common to the masters in his art; but there was an instance of alleged wrong in the course of *Copperfield* where he felt his vindication to be hardly complete, and what he did thereupon was characteristic.

"I have had the queerest adventure this morning," he wrote (28 December, 1849) on the eve of his tenth number, "the receipt of the enclosed from Miss Moucher! It is serio-comic, but there is no doubt one is wrong in being tempted to such a use of power." Thinking a grotesque little oddity among his acquaintance to be safe from recognition he had done what Smollett did sometimes, but never Fielding, and given way, in the first outburst of fun that had broken out around the fancy, to the temptation of copying too closely peculiarities of figure and face amounting in effect to deformity. He was shocked at discovering the pain he had given, and a copy is before me of the assurances by way of reply which he at once sent to the complainant. That he was grieved and surprised beyond measure. That he had not intended her altogether. That all his characters, being made up out of many people, were composite, and never individual. That the chair (for table) and other matters were undoubtedly from her, but that other traits were not hers at all; and that in Miss Moucher's "Ain't I volatile " his friends had quite cor-rectly recognised the favourite utterance of a different person. That he felt nevertheless he had done wrong, and would now do anything to repair it. That he had intended to employ the character in an unpleasant way, but he would, whatever the risk or inconvenience, change it all, so that nothing but an agreeable impression should be left. The reader will remember how this was managed, and that the thirty-second chapter went far to undo what the twenty-second had done. . . .

In the book that followed *Copperfield*, characters appeared having resemblances in manner and speech to distinguished writers too vivid to be mistaken by their personal friends. To Lawrence Boythorn, under whom Landor figured, no objection was made; but Harold Skimpole, recognisable for Leigh Hunt, led to much remark; the difference being, that ludicrous traits were employed in the first to enrich without impairing an attractive person in the tale, whereas to the last was assigned a part in the plot which no fascinating foibles or gaieties of speech could redeem from contempt. Though a want of consideration was thus shown to the friend whom the character would be likely to recall to many readers, it is nevertheless very certain that the intention of Dickens was not at first, or at any time, an unkind one. He erred from thoughtlessness only. What led him to the subject at all, he has himself stated. Hunt's philosophy of moneyed obligations, always, though loudly, half jocosely proclaimed, and his ostentatious wilfulness in the humouring of that or any other theme on which he cared for the time to expatiate, had so often seemed to Dickens to be whimsical and attractive, that, wanting an "airy quality" for the man he invented, this of Hunt occurred to him; and "partly for that reason, and partly, he has since often grieved to think, for the pleasure it afforded to find a delightful manner reproducing itself under his hand, he yielded to the temptation of too often making the character speak like his old friend." This apology was made after Hunt's death,* and mentioned a revision of the first sketch, so as to render it less like, at the suggestion of two other friends of Hunt. The friends were Procter (Barry Cornwall) and myself; the feeling having been mine from the first that the likeness was too like. Procter did not immediately think so, but a little reflection brought him to that opinion. "You will see from the enclosed," Dickens wrote (17 March, 1852), "that Procter is much of my mind. I will nevertheless go through the character again in the course of the afternoon, and soften down words here and there." But before the day closed Procter had again written to him, and next morning this was the result. "I have again gone over every part of it very carefully, and I think I have made it much less like. I have also changed Leonard to Harold. I have no right to give Hunt pain, and I am so bent upon not doing it that I wish you would look at all the proof once more, and indicate any particular place in which you feel it particularly like. Whereupon I will alter the place."

Upon the whole the alterations were considerable, but the radical wrong remained. The pleasant sparkling airy talk, which could not be mistaken, identified with odious qualities a friend only known to the writer by attractive ones; and for this there was no excuse. Perhaps the only person acquainted with the original who failed to recognise the copy, was the original himself (a common case); but good-natured friends in time told Hunt everything, and painful explanations followed, where nothing was possible to Dickens but what amounted to a friendly evasion of the points really at issue. The time for redress had gone. I yet well remember with what eager earnestness, on one of these occasions, he strove to set Hunt up again in his own esteem. "Separate in your own mind," he said to him, "what you see of yourself from what other people tell you that they see. As it has given you so much pain, I take it at its worst, and say I am deeply sorry, and that I feel I did wrong in doing it. I should otherwise have taken it at its best, and ridden off upon what I strongly feel to be the truth, that there is nothing in it that *should*

* In a paper in *All the Year Round.*

have given you pain. Everyone in writing must speak from points of his experience, and so I of mine with you but when I have felt it was going too close I stopped myself, and the most blotted parts of my MS. are those in which I have been striving hard to make the impression I was writing from, *un*like you. The diary-writing I took from Haydon, not from you. I now first learn from yourself that you ever set anything to music, and I could not have copied *that* from you. The character is not you, for there are traits in it common to fifty thousand people besides, and I did not fancy you would ever recognise it. Under similar disguises my own father and mother are in my books, and you might as well see your likeness in Micawber." The distinction is that the foibles of Mr. Micawber and of Mrs. Nickleby, however laughable, make neither of them in speech or character less lovable; and that this is not to be said of Skimpole's. The kindly or unkindly impression makes all the difference where liberties are taken with a friend; and even this entirely favourable condition will not excuse the practice to many, where near relatives are concerned.

For what formerly was said of the Micawber resemblances, Dickens has been sharply criticised; and in like manner it was thought objectionable in Scott that for the closing scenes of Crystal Croftangry he should have found the original of his fretful patient at the death-bed of his own father. Lockhart, who tells us this, adds with a sad significance that he himself lived to see the curtain fall at Abbotsford upon even such another scene. But to no purpose will such objections still be made. All great novelists will continue to use their experiences of nature and fact, whencesoever derivable; and a remark made to Lockhart by Scott himself suggests their vindication. "If a man will paint from nature, he will be most likely to interest and amuse those who are daily looking at it."

The Micawber offence otherwise was not grave. We have seen in what way Dickens was moved or inspired by the rough lessons of his boyhood, and the groundwork of the character was then undoubtedly laid; but the rhetorical exuberance impressed itself upon him later, and from this, as it expanded and developed in a thousand amusing ways, the full-length figure took its great charm. Better illustration of it could not perhaps be given than by passages from letters of Dickens, written long before Micawber was thought of, in which this peculiarity of his father found frequent and always agreeable expression. Several such have been given in this work from time to time, and one or two more may here be added. It is proper to preface them by saying that no one could know the elder Dickens without secretly liking him the better for these flourishes of speech, which adapted themselves so readily to his gloom as well as to his cheerfulness, that it was difficult not to fancy they had helped him considerably in both, and had rendered more tolerable to him, if also more possible, the shade and sunshine of his chequered life. "If you should have an opportunity, *pendente lite*, as my father would observe—indeed did on some memorable ancient occasions when he informed me that the ban-dogs would shortly have him at bay"—Dickens wrote in December 1847. "I have a letter from my father" (May 1841) "lamenting the fine weather, invoking congenial tempests, and informing me that it will not be possible for him to stay more than another year in Devonshire, as he must then proceed to Paris to consolidate Augustus's French." "There has arrived," he writes from the Peschiere in September 1844, "a characteristic letter for Kate from my father. He dates it Manchester, and says he has reason to believe that he will be in town with the pheasants, on or about the first of October. He has been with Fanny in the Isle of Man for nearly two months finding there, as he goes on to observe, troops of friends, and every description of continental luxury at a cheap rate." Describing in the same year the departure from Genoa of an English physician and acquaintance, he adds: "We are very sorry to lose the benefit of his advice—or, as my father would say, to be deprived, to a certain extent, of the concomitant advantages, whatever they may be, resulting from his medical skill, such as it is, and his professional attendance, in so far as it may be so considered." Thus also it delighted Dickens to remember that it was of one of his connections his father wrote a celebrated sentence; "And I must express my tendency to believe that his longevity is (to say the least of it) extremely problematical": and that it was to another, who had been insisting somewhat obtrusively on dissenting and nonconformist superiorities, he addressed words which deserve to be no less celebrated; "The Supreme Being must be an entirely different individual from what I have every reason to believe Him to be, if He would care in the least for the society of your relations." There was a laugh in the enjoyment of all this, no doubt, but with it much personal fondness; and the feeling of the creator of Micawber, as he thus humoured and remembered the foibles of his original, found its counterpart in that of his readers for the creation itself, as its part was played out in the story. Nobody likes Micawber less for his follies; and Dickens liked his father more, the more he recalled his whimsical qualities. "The longer I live, the better man I think him," he exclaimed afterwards. The fact and the fancy had united whatever was most grateful to him in both.

It is a tribute to the generally healthful and manly tone of the story of *Copperfield* that such should be the outcome of the eccentricities of this leading personage in it; and the superiority in this respect of Micawber over Skimpole is one of the many indications of the inferiority of *Bleak House* to its predecessor. With leading resemblances that make it difficult to say which character best represents the principle or no principle of impecuniosity, there cannot be any doubt which has the advantage in moral and intellectual development. It is genuine humour against personal satire. Between the worldly circumstances of the two, there is nothing to choose; but as to everything else it is the difference between shabbiness and greatness. Skimpole's sunny talk might be expected to please as much as Micawber's

gorgeous speech, the design of both being to take the edge off poverty
But in the one we have no relief from attendant meanness or distress,
and we drop down from the airiest fancies into sordidness and pain;
whereas in the other nothing pitiful or merely selfish ever touches us.
At its lowest depth of what is worst, we never doubt that something
better must turn up; and of a man who sells his bedstead that he may
entertain his friend, we altogether refuse to think nothing but badly.
This is throughout the free and cheery style of *Copperfield*. The
masterpieces of Dickens's humour are not in it; but he has nowhere
given such variety of play to his invention, and the book is un-
approached among his writings for its completeness of effect and
uniform pleasantness of tone.

What has to be said hereafter of those writings generally, will
properly restrict what is said here, as in previous instances, mainly to
personal illustration. The *Copperfield* disclosures formerly made will
for ever connect the book with the author's individual story; but too
much has been assumed, from those revelations, of a full identity of
Dickens with his hero, and of a supposed intention that his own
character as well as parts of his career should be expressed in the
narrative. It is right to warn the reader as to this. He can judge for
himself how far the childish experiences are likely to have given the
turn to Dickens's genius; whether their bitterness had so burnt into
his nature, as, in the hatred of oppression, the revolt against abuse
of power, and the war with injustice under every form displayed in
his earliest books, to have reproduced itself only; and to what extent
mere compassion for his own childhood may account for the strange
fascination always exerted over him by child-suffering and sorrow.
But, many as are the resemblances in Copperfield's adventures to
portions of those of Dickens, and often as reflections occur to David
which no one intimate with Dickens could fail to recognise as but the
reproduction of his, it would be the greatest mistake to imagine anything like a complete identity of the fictitious novelist with the real
one, beyond the Hungerford scenes; or to suppose that the youth,
who then received his first harsh schooling in life, came out of it as
little harmed or hardened as David did. The language of the fiction
reflects only faintly the narrative of the actual fact; and the man
whose character it helped to form was expressed not less faintly in
the impulsive impressionable youth, incapable of resisting the leading
of others, and only disciplined into self-control by the later griefs
of his entrance into manhood. Here was but another proof how
thoroughly Dickens understood his calling, and that to weave fact
with fiction unskilfully would be only to make truth less true.

The character of the hero of the novel finds indeed his right place
in the story he is supposed to tell, rather by unlikeness than by
likeness to Dickens, even where intentional resemblance might seem
to be prominent. Take autobiography as a design to show that any
man's life may be as a mirror of existence to all men, and the
individual career becomes altogether secondary to the variety of

experiences received and rendered back in it. This particular form in imaginative literature has too often led to the indulgence of mental analysis, metaphysics, and sentiment, all in excess but Dickens was carried safely over these allurements by a healthy judgment and sleepless creative fancy; and even the method of his narrative is more simple here than it generally is in his books. His imaginative growths have less luxuriance of underwood, and the crowds of external images always rising so vividly before him are more within control.

Consider Copperfield thus in his proper place in the story, and sequence as well as connection will be given to the varieties of its childish adventure. The first warm nest of love in which his vain fond mother, and her quaint kind servant, cherish him; the quick-following contrast of hard dependence and servile treatment; the escape from that premature and dwarfed maturity by natural relapse into a more perfect childhood; the then leisurely growth of emotions and faculties into manhood; these are component parts of a character consistently drawn. The sum of its achievement is to be a successful cultivation of letters; and often as such imaginary discipline has been the theme of fiction, there are not many happier conceptions of it. The ideal and real parts of the boy's nature receive development in the proportions which contribute best to the end desired; the readiness for impulsive attachments that had put him into the leading of others, has underneath it a base of truthfulness on which at last he rests in safety; the practical man is the outcome of the fanciful youth; and a more than equivalent for the graces of his visionary days, is found in the active sympathies that life has opened to him. Many experiences have come within its range, and his heart has had room for all. Our interest in him cannot but be increased by knowing how much he expresses of what the author had himself gone through; but David includes far less than this, and infinitely more.

That the incidents arise easily, and to the very end connect themselves naturally and unobtrusively with the characters of which they are apart, is to be said perhaps more truly of this than of any other of Dickens's novels. There is a profusion of distinct and distinguishable people, and a prodigal wealth of detail; but unity of drift or purpose is apparent always, and the tone is uniformly right. By the course of the events we learn the value of self-denial and patience, quiet endurance of unavoidable ills, strenuous effort against ills remediable; and everything in the fortunes of the actors warns us, to strengthen our generous emotions and to guard the purities of home. It is easy thus to account for the supreme popularity of *Copperfield*, without the addition that it can hardly have had a reader, man or lad, who did not discover that he was something of a Copperfield himself. Childhood and youth live again for all of us in its marvellous boy-experiences. Mr. Micawber's presence must not prevent my saying that it does not take the lead of the other novels in humorous creation; but in the use of humour to bring out prominently the ludicrous in any object or incident without excluding or weakening its most enchanting sentiment, it stands decidedly first. It is the perfection of English mirth. We are apt to resent the exhibition of too much goodness, but it is here so qualified by oddity as to become not merely palatable but attractive; and even pathos is heightened by what in other hands would only make it comical. That there are also faults in the book is certain, but none that are incompatible with the most masterly qualities; and a book becomes everlasting by the fact, not that faults are not in it, but that genius nevertheless is there.

Of its method, and its author's generally, in the delineation of character, something will have to be said on a later page. The author's own favourite people in it, I think, were the Peggotty group; and perhaps he was not far wrong. It has been their fate, as with all the leading figures of his invention, to pass their names into the language, and become types; and he has nowhere given happier embodiment to that purity of homely goodness, which, by the kindly and all-reconciling influences of humour, may exalt into comeliness and even grandeur the clumsiest forms of humanity. What has been indicated in the style of the book as its greatest charm is here felt most strongly. The ludicrous so helps the pathos, and the humour so uplifts and refines the sentiment, that mere rude affection and simple manliness in these Yarmouth boatmen, passed through the fires of unmerited suffering and heroic endurance, take forms half-chivalrous, half-sublime. It is one of the cants of critical superiority to make supercilious mention of the serious passages in this great writer; but the storm and shipwreck at the close of *Copperfield*, when the body of the seducer is flung dead upon the shore amid the ruins of the home he has wasted and by the side of the man whose heart he has broken, the one as unconscious of what he had failed to reach as the other of what he has perished to save, is a description that may compare with the most impressive in the language. And to those who, knowing Dickens best, know what realities his books were to him, the expression of his sense of suffering in composing such passages, will have in it not a grain of pretence or affectation. "I have been tremendously at work these two days" (15 September), "eight hours at a stretch yesterday, and six hours and a half to-day, with the Ham and Steerforth chapter, which has completely knocked me over—utterly defeated me." . . .

Of the heroines who divide so equally between them the impulse, easily swayed, not disloyal but sorely distracted affections of the hero, the spoilt foolishness and tenderness of the loving little child-wife, Dora, is more attractive than the too unfailing wisdom and self-sacrificing goodness of the angel-wife, Agnes. The scenes of the courtship and housekeeping are matchless; and the glimpses of Doctors' Commons, opening those views, by Mr. Spenlow, of man's vanity of expectation and inconsistency of conduct in neglecting the sacred duty of making a will, on which he largely moralises the day before he dies intestate, form a background highly appropriate to

David's domesticities. This was among the reproductions of personal experience in the book; but it was a sadder knowledge that came with the conviction some years later, that David's contrasts in his earliest married life between his happiness enjoyed and his happiness once anticipated, the "vague unhappy loss or want of something" of which he so frequently complains, reflected also a personal experience which had not been supplied in fact so successfully as in fiction.

# BOOK SEVENTH

## CONTINENT REVISITED

### 1852-6. ÆT. 40-43

# I

## "BLEAK HOUSE" AND "HARD TIMES"

### 1852–6

THESE books were written between 1851 and 1854, when for a portion of the time the author was living abroad; and, reserving to another section the home life that filled the same interval, some account of both novels will be given here. *Little Dorrit*, though begun in Paris, was not finished until some time after the continental residence had closed, and belongs therefore to a later division. *David Copperfield* had been written between the opening of 1849 and October 1850, its publication covering that time; and its sale, which has since taken the lead of all his books but *Pickwick*, never then exceeding twenty-five thousand. But though it remained thus steady for the time, the popularity of the book added largely to the sale of its successor. *Bleak House* was begun in his new abode of Tavistock House at the end of November 1851; was carried on, amid the excitements of the Guild performances, through the following year; was finished at Boulogne in the August of 1853; and was dedicated to "his friends and companions in the Guild of Literature and Art." *Hard Times* was planned and begun in the winter of 1853, amid the busy preparation of Christmas theatricals for his children to be presently described; was finished at Boulogne in the summer of 1854; and was dedicated to Carlyle.

The autobiographical form of *Copperfield* was in some respect continued in *Bleak House* by means of extracts from the personal relation of its heroine. But the distinction between the narrative of David and the diary of Esther, like that between Micawber and Skimpole, marks the superiority of the first to its successor. . . .

What in one sense is a merit, however, may in others be a defect, and this book has suffered by the very completeness with which its Chancery moral is worked out. The didactic in Dickens's earlier novels derived its strength from being merely incidental to interest of a higher and more permanent kind, and not in a small degree from the playful sportiveness and fancy that lighted up its graver illustrations. Here it is of sterner stuff, too little relieved, and all-pervading. The fog so marvellously painted in the opening chapter has hardly cleared away when there arises, in *Jarndyce v. Jarndyce*, as bad an atmosphere to breathe in; and thenceforward to the end, clinging round the people of the story as they come or go, in dreary mist or in heavy cloud, it is rarely absent. Dickens has himself described his purpose to have been to dwell on the romantic side of familiar things. But it is the romance of discontent and misery, with a very restless dissatisfied moral, and is too much brought about by agencies disagreeable and sordid. The Guppys, Weevles, Snagsbys, Chadbands, Krooks, and Smallweeds, even the Kenges, Vholeses, and Tulkinghorns, are much too real to be pleasant; and the necessity becomes urgent for the reliefs and contrasts of a finer humanity. These last are not wanting; yet it must be said that we hardly escape, even with them, into the old freedom and freshness of the author's imaginative worlds, and that the too conscious unconsciousness of Esther flings something of a shade on the radiant goodness of John Jarndyce himself. Nevertheless there are very fine delineations in the story. The crazed little Chancery lunatic, Miss Flite; the loud-voiced tender-souled Chancery victim, Gridley; the poor good-hearted youth, Richard, broken up in life and character by the suspense of the Chancery suit on whose success he is to "begin the world," believing himself to be saving money when he is stopped from squandering it, and thinking that having saved it he is entitled to fling it away; trooper George, with the Bagnets and their household, where the most ludicrous points are more forcible for the pathetic touches underlying them: the Jellyby interior, and its philanthropic strong-minded mistress, placid and smiling amid a household muddle out-muddling Chancery itself; the model of deportment, Turveydrop the elder, whose relations to the young people, whom he so superbly patronises by being dependent on them for everything, touch de-lightfully some subtle points of truth; the inscrutable Tulkinghorn, and the immortal Bucket; all these, and especially the last, have been added by this book to the list of people more intimately and permanently known to us than the scores of actual familiar acquaint-ance whom we see around us living and dying. . . .

. . . Dickens was encouraged and strengthened in his design of assailing Chancery abuses and delays by receiving, a few days after the appearance of his first number, a striking pamphlet on the subject containing details so apposite that he took from them, without change in any material point, the memorable case related in his fifteenth chapter. Anyone who examines the tract will see how exactly true is the reference to it made by Dickens in his preface. "The case of Gridley is in no essential altered from one of actual occurrence, made public by a disinterested person who was professionally acquainted with the whole of the monstrous wrong from beginning to end." The suit, of which all particulars are given, affected a single farm, in value not more than £1200, but all that its owner possessed in the world, against which a bill had been filed for a £300 legacy left in the will bequeathing the farm. In reality there was only one defendant, but in the bill, by the rule of the Court, there were seventeen; and, after two years had been occupied over the seventeen answers, everything had to begin over again because an eighteenth had been accidentally omitted. "What a mockery of justice this is," says Mr. Challinor, "the facts speak for themselves, and I can personally vouch for their accuracy. The costs already incurred in reference to this £300 legacy are not less than from £800 to £900, and the parties are no forwarder. Already near five years have passed by, and the plaintiff would be glad to give up his chance of the legacy if he could escape from his liability to costs, while the defendants who own the little farm left by the testator, have scarce any other prospect before them than ruin."

## II

### HOME INCIDENTS

#### 1853-4-5

THE first number of *Bleak House* had appeared in March 1852, and its sale was mentioned in the same letter from Tavistock House (7 March) which told of his troubles in the tale at its outset, and of other anxieties incident to the common lot and inseparable equally from its joys and sorrows, through which his life was passing at the time. "My Highgate journey yesterday was a sad one. Sad to think how all journeys tend that way. I went up to the cemetery to look for a piece of ground. In no hope of a Government bill, and in a foolish dislike to leaving the little child shut up in a vault there, I think of pitching a tent under the sky. . . . Nothing has taken place here: but I believe, every hour, that it must next hour. Wild ideas are upon me of going to Paris—Rouen—Switzerland—somewhere—and writing the remaining two-thirds of the next No. aloft in some queer inn room. I have been hanging over it, and have got restless. Want a change I think. Stupid. We were at 30,000 when I last heard. . . . I am sorry to say that after all kinds of evasions, I am obliged to dine at Lansdowne House to-morrow. But maybe the affair will come off to-night and give me an excuse! I enclose proofs of No. 2. Browne has done Skimpole, and helped to make him singularly unlike the great original. Look it over, and say what occurs to you. . . . Don't you think Mrs. Gaskell charming? With one ill-considered thing that looks like a want of natural perception, I think it masterly." His last allusion is to the story by a delightful writer then appearing in *Household Words*; and of the others it only needs to say that the family affair which might have excused his absence at the Lansdowne dinner did not come off until four days later. On 13 March his last child was born; and the boy, his seventh son, bears his godfather's distinguished name, Edward Bulwer Lytton.

The inability to "grind sparks out of this dull blade," as he characterised his present labour at *Bleak House*, still fretting him, he struck out a scheme for Paris. "I could not get to Switzerland very well at this time of year. The Jura would be covered with snow. And if I went to Geneva I don't know where I might *not* go to." It ended at last in a flight to Dover; but he found time before he left, amid many occupations and some anxieties, for a good-natured journey to Walworth to see a youth rehearse who was supposed to have talents for the stage, and he was able to gladden Mr. Toole's friends by thinking favourably of his chances of success. "I remember what I once myself wanted in that way," he said, "and I should like to serve him." . . .

Before the year closed, the time to which his publishing arrangements with Messrs. Bradbury and Evans were limited had expired, but at his suggestion the fourth share in such books as he might write, which they had now received for eight years, was continued to them on the understanding that the publishers' percentage should no longer be charged in the partnership accounts, and with a power reserved to himself to withdraw when he pleased. In the new year his first adventure was an ovation in Birmingham, where a silver-gilt salver and a diamond ring were presented to him, as well for eloquent service specially rendered to the Institution, as in general testimony of "varied literary acquirements, genial philosophy, and high moral teaching." A great banquet followed on Twelfth Night, made memorable by an offer to give a couple of readings from his books at the following Christmas, in aid of the new Midland Institute. It might seem to have been drawn from him as a grateful return for the enthusiastic greeting of his entertainers, but it was in his mind before he left London. It was his first formal undertaking to read in public.

His eldest son had now left Eton, and the boy's wishes pointing at the time to a mercantile career, he was sent to Leipzig for completion of his education. At this date it seemed to me that the overstrain of attempting too much, brought upon him by the necessities of his weekly periodical, became first apparent in Dickens. Not unfrequently a complaint strange upon his lips fell from him. " Hypochondriacal whisperings tell me that I am rather overworked. The spring does not seem to fly back again directly, as it always did when I put my own work aside, and had nothing else to do. Yet I have everything to keep me going with a brave heart, Heaven knows !" Courage and hopefulness he might well derive from the increasing sale of *Bleak House*, which had risen to nearly forty thousand; but he could no longer bear easily what he carried so lightly of old, and enjoyments with work, were too much for him. "What with *Bleak House* and *Household Words* and *Child's History*" (he dictated from week to week the papers which formed that little book, and cannot be said to have quite hit the mark with it), "and Miss Coutts's Home, and the invitations to feasts and festivals, I really feel as if my head would split like a fired shell if I remained here." He tried Brighton first, but did not find it answer and returned. A few days of unalloyed enjoyment were afterwards given to the visit of his excellent American friend Felton; and on 13 June he was again in Boulogne, thanking heaven for escape from a breakdown. "If I had substituted anybody's knowledge of myself for my own, and lingered in London, I never could have got through." . . .

He completed *Bleak House* by the third week of August, and it was resolved to celebrate the event by a two months' trip to Italy, in company with Mr. Wilkie Collins and Mr. Augustus Egg. The start was to be made from Boulogne in the middle of October, when he would send his family home; and he described the intervening weeks as a fearful "reaction and prostration of laziness" only broken by the *Child's History*. At the end of September he wrote: "I finished the little *History* yesterday, and am trying to think of something for the Christmas number. After which I shall knock off; having had quite enough to do, small as it would have seemed to me at any other time, since I finished *Bleak House*." He added, a week before his departure: "I get letters from Genoa and Lausanne as if I were going to stay in each place at least a month. If I were to measure my deserts by people's remembrance of me, I should be a prodigy of intolerability. Have recovered my Italian, which I had all but forgotten, and am one entire and perfect chrysolite of idleness."

From this trip, of which the incidents have an interest independent of my ordinary narrative, Dickens was home again in the middle of December 1853, and kept his promise to his Birmingham friends by reading in their Town Hall his *Christmas Carol* on the 27th, and his *Cricket on the Hearth* on the 29th. The enthusiasm was great, and he consented to read his *Carol* a second time, on Friday the 30th, if seats were reserved for working men at prices within their means. The result was an addition of between four and five hundred pounds to the funds for establishment of the new Institute; and a prettily worked flower-basket in silver, presented to Mrs. Dickens, commemorated these first public readings "to nearly six thousand people," and the design they had generously helped. Other applications then followed to such extent that limits to compliance had to be put. . . . He nevertheless soon found the question rising again with the same importunity; his own position to it being always that of a man assenting against his will that it should rest in abeyance. But nothing further was resolved on yet. The readings mentioned came off as promised, in aid of public objects; and besides others two years later for the family of a friend, he had given the like liberal help to institutes in Folkestone, Chatham, and again in Birmingham, Peterborough, Sheffield, Coventry, and Edinburgh, before the question settled itself finally in the announcement for paid public readings issued by him in 1858. . . .

Then came the beginning of *Nobody's Fault*, as *Little Dorrit* continued to be called by him up to the eve of its publication; a flight to Folkestone, to help his sluggish fancy; and his return to London in October, to preside at a dinner to Thackeray on his going to lecture in America. . . .

Dickens went to Paris early in October, and at its close was brought again to London by the sudden death of a friend, much deplored by himself, and still more so by a distinguished lady who had his loyal service at all times. An incident before his return to France is worth brief relation. He had sallied out for one of his night walks, full of thoughts of his story, one wintry rainy evening (8 November), and "pulled himself up," outside the door of Whitechapel Workhouse, at a strange sight which arrested him there. Against the dreary enclosure of the house were leaning, in the midst of the down-pouring rain and storm, what seemed to be seven heaps of rags "dumb, wet, silent horrors," he described them, "sphinxes set up against that dead wall, and no one likely to be at the pains of solving them until the General Overthrow." He sent in his card to the Master. Against him there was no ground of complaint; he gave prompt personal attention; but the casual ward was full, and there was no help. The rag-heaps were all girls, and Dickens gave each a shilling. One girl, "twenty or so," had been without food a day and night. "Look at me," she said, as she clutched the shilling, and without thanks shuffled off. So with the rest. There was not a single "thank you." A crowd meanwhile, only less poor than these objects of misery, had gathered round the scene; but though they saw the seven shillings given away they asked for no relief to themselves, they recognised in their sad wild way the other greater wretchedness, and made room in silence for Dickens to walk on.

Not more tolerant of the way in which laws meant to be most humane are too often administered in England, he left in a day or two to resume his *Little Dorrit* in Paris. But before his life there is described, some sketches from his holiday trip to Italy with Mr. Wilkie Collins and Mr. Augustus Egg, and from his three summer visits to Boulogne, claim to themselves two intervening chapters.

# III

## IN SWITZERLAND AND ITALY

### 1853

BEFORE October closed, the travellers had reached Genoa, having been thirty-one consecutive hours on the road from Milan. They arrived in somewhat damaged condition, and took up their lodging in the top rooms of the Croce di Malta, "overlooking the port and sea pleasantly and airily enough, but it was no joke to get so high, and the apartment is rather vast and faded." The warmth of personal greeting that here awaited Dickens was given no less to the friends who accompanied him, and though the reader may not share in such private confidences as would show the sensation created by his reappearance, and the jovial hours that were passed among old associates, he will perhaps be interested to know how far the intervening years had changed the aspect of things and places made pleasantly familiar to us in his former letters. The voyage thence to Naples, written from the latter place, is too capital a description to be lost. The steamer in which they embarked was "the new express English ship," but they found her to be already more than full of passengers from Marseilles (among them an old friend, Sir Emerson Tennent, with his family), and everything in confusion. There were no places at the captain's table, dinner had to be taken on deck, no berth or sleeping accommodation was available, and heavy first-class fares had to be paid. Thus they made their way to Leghorn, where worse awaited them. The authorities proved to be not favourable to the "crack" English-officered vessel (she had just been started for the India mail); and her papers not being examined in time, it was too late to steam away again that day, and she had to lie all night long off the lighthouse. "The scene on board beggars description. Ladies on the tables; gentlemen under the tables; bedroom appliances not usually beheld in public airing themselves in positions where soup-tureens had been lately developing themselves; and ladies and gentlemen lying indiscriminately on the open deck, arranged like spoons on a sideboard. No mattresses, no blankets, nothing. Towards midnight attempts were made, by means of awning and flags, to make this latter scene remotely approach an Australian encampment; and we three (Collins, Egg, and self) lay together on the bare planks covered with our coats. We were all gradually dozing off, when a perfectly tropical rain fell, and in a moment drowned the whole ship. The rest of the night we passed upon the stairs, with an immense jumble of men and women. When anybody came up for any purpose we all fell down, and when anybody came down we all fell up again. Still, the good-humour in the English part of the passengers was quite extraordinary. . . . There were excellent officers aboard, and, in the morning, the first mate lent me his cabin to wash in—which I afterwards lent to Egg and Collins. Then we, the Emerson Tennents, the captain, the doctor, and the second officer, went off on a jaunt together to Pisa, as the ship was to lie all day at Leghorn. The captain was a capital fellow, but I led him, facetiously, such a life the whole day, that I got most things altered at night. Emerson Tennent's son, with the greatest amiability, insisted on turning out of his stateroom for me, and I got a good bed there. The store-room down by the hold was opened for Collins and Egg; and they slept with the moist sugar, the cheese in cut, the spices, the cruets, the apples and pears, in a perfect chandler's shop—in company with what a friend of ours would call a hold gent, who had been so horribly wet through overnight that his condition frightened the authorities; a cat; and the steward, who dozed in an armchair, and all-night-long fell head foremost, once every five minutes, on Egg, who slept on the counter or dresser. Last night, I had the steward's own cabin, opening on deck, all to myself. It had been previously occupied by some desolate lady who went ashore at Civita Vecchia. There was little or no sea, thank Heaven, all the trip; but the rain was heavier than any I have ever seen, and the lightning very constant and vivid. We were, with the crew—some 200 people—provided with boats, at the utmost stretch, for one hundred perhaps. I could not help thinking what would happen if we met with any accident: the crew being chiefly Maltese, and evidently fellows who would cut off alone in the largest boat, on the least alarm; the speed very high; and the running, thro' all the narrow rocky channels. Thank God, however, here we are."

A whimsical postscript closed the amusing narrative. "We towed from Civita Vecchia, the entire Greek navy, I believe; consisting of a little brig-of-war with no guns, fitted as a steamer, but disabled by having burnt the bottoms of her boilers out, in her first run. She was just big enough to carry the captain and a crew of six or so; but the captain was so covered with buttons and gold that there never would have been room for him on board to put those valuables away, if he hadn't worn them—which he consequently did, all night. Whenever anything was wanted to be done, as slackening the tow-rope or anything of that sort, our officers roared at this miserable potentate, in violent English, through a speaking trumpet; of which he couldn't have understood a word in the most favourable circumstances. So he did all the wrong things first, and the right thing always last. The absence of any knowledge of anything but English on the part of the officers and stewards was most ridiculous. I met an Italian gentleman on the cabin steps yesterday morning, vainly endeavouring to explain that he wanted a cup of tea for his sick wife. And when we were coming out of the harbour at Genoa, and it was necessary to order away that boat of music you remember, the chief officer (called 'aft' for the purpose, as 'knowing something of Italian') delivered himself in this explicit and clear Italian to the principal performer—'Now Signora, if you don't sheer off you'll be run down, so you had better trice up that guitar of yours and put about.'"

At Naples some days were passed very merrily; going up Vesuvius and into the buried cities, with Layard who had joined them, and with the Tennents. Here a small adventure befell Dickens specially, in itself extremely unimportant, but told by him with delightful humour in a letter to his sister-in-law. The old idle Frenchman, to whom all things are possible, with his snuff-box and dusty umbrella and all the delicate and kindly observation, would have enchanted Leigh Hunt, and made his way to the heart of Charles Lamb. After mentioning Mr. Lowther, then English chargé d'affaires in Naples, as a very agreeable fellow who had been at the Rockingham play, he alludes to a meeting at his house. "We had an exceedingly pleasant dinner of eight, preparatory to which I was near having the ridiculous adventure of not being able to find the house and coming back dinnerless. I went in an open carriage from the hotel in all state, and the coachman to my surprise pulled up at the end of the Chiaja. 'Behold the house,' says he, 'of Il Signor Larthoor!'—at the same time pointing with his whip into the seventh heaven where the early stars were shining. 'But the Signor Larthorr,' says I, 'lives at Pausilippo.' 'It is true,' says the coachman (still pointing to the evening star), 'but he lives high up the Salita Sant' Antonio where no carriage ever yet ascended, and that is the house' (evening star as aforesaid), 'and one must go on foot. Behold the Salita Sant' Antonio!' I went up it, a mile and a half I should think. I got into the strangest places among the wildest Neapolitans; kitchens, washing-places, archways, stables, vineyards; was baited by dogs, and answered, in profoundly unintelligible language, from behind lonely locked doors in cracked female voices, quaking with fear; but could hear of no such Englishman, nor any Englishman. By and by, I came upon a polentashop in the clouds, where an old Frenchman with an umbrella like a faded tropical leaf (it had not rained in Naples for six weeks) was staring at nothing at all, with a snuff-box in his hand. To him I appealed, concerning the Signor Larthoor. 'Sir,' said he, with the sweetest politeness, 'can you speak French?' 'Sir,' said I, 'a little.' 'Sir,' said he, 'I presume the Signor Loothere'—you will observe that he changed the name according to the custom of his country—'is an Englishman?' I admitted that he was the victim of circumstances and had that misfortune. 'Sir,' said he, 'one word more. *Has* he a servant with a wooden leg?' 'Great heaven, sir,' said I, 'how do I know? I should think not, but it is possible.' 'It is always,' said the Frenchman, 'possible. Almost all the things of the world are always possible.' 'Sir,' said I—you may imagine my condition and dismal sense of my own absurdity by this time—'that is true.' He then took an immense pinch of snuff, wiped the dust off his umbrella, led me to an arch commanding a wonderful view of the Bay of Naples, and pointed deep into the earth from which I had mounted. 'Below there, near the lamp, one finds an Englishman with a servant with a wooden leg. It is always possible that he is the Signor Loothere.' I had been asked at six o'clock, and it was now getting on for seven. I went back in a state of perspiration and misery not to be described, and without the faintest hope of finding the spot. But as I was going farther down to the lamp, I saw the strangest staircase up a dark corner, with a man in a white waistcoat (evidently hired) standing on the top of it fuming. I dashed in at a venture, found it was the house, made the most of the whole story, and achieved much popularity. The best of it was that as nobody ever did find the place, Lowther had put a servant at the bottom of the Salita to wait for an English gentleman'; but the servant (as he presently pleaded), deceived by the moustache, had allowed the English gentleman to pass unchallenged."

From Naples they went to Rome, where they found Lockhart, "fearfully weak and broken, yet hopeful of himself too" (he died the following year); smoked and drank punch with David Roberts, then painting every day with Louis Haghe in St. Peter's; and took the old walks. The Coliseum, Appian Way, and Streets of Tombs, seemed desolate and grand as ever; but generally, Dickens adds, "I discovered the Roman antiquities to be *smaller* than my imagination in nine years had made them. The Electric Telegraph now goes like a sunbeam through the cruel old heart of the Coliseum—a suggestive thing to think about, I fancied. The Pantheon I thought even nobler than of yore." The amusements were of course an attraction; and nothing at the Opera amused the party of three English more, than another party of four Americans who sat behind them in the pit. "All the seats are numbered arm-chairs, and you buy your number at the pay-place, and go to it with the easiest direction on the ticket itself. We were early, and the four places of the Americans were on the next row behind us—all together. After looking about them for some time, and seeing the greater part of the seats empty (because the audience generally wait in a caffè which is part of the theatre), one of them said 'Waal I dunno—I expect we ain't no call to set so nigh to one another neither—will you scatter Kernel, will you scatter sir?'—Upon this the Kernel 'scattered' some twenty benches off; and they distributed themselves (for no earthly reason apparently but to get rid of one another) all over the pit. As soon as the overture began, in came the audience in a mass. Then the people who had got the numbers into which they had 'scattered,' had to get them out; and as they understood nothing that was said to them, and could make no reply but 'A-mericani,' you may imagine the number of cocked hats it took to dislodge them. At last they were all got back into their right places, except one. About an hour afterwards when Moses (*Moses in Egypt* was the opera) was invoking the darkness, and there was a dead silence all over the house, unwonted sounds of disturbance broke out from a distant corner of the pit, and here and there a beard got up to look. 'What is it neow, sir?' said one of the Americans to another; 'some person seems to be getting along, again streeem.' 'Waal sir' he replied 'I dunno. But I xpect 'tis the Kernel sir, a holdin on.' So it was. The Kernel was ignominiously escorted back to his right place, not in the least disconcerted, and in perfectly good spirits and temper." The opera was excellently done, and the price of the stalls one and threepence English. At Milan, on the other hand, the Scala was fallen from its old estate, dirty, gloomy, dull, and the performance execrable.

Another theatre of the smallest pretension Dickens sought out with avidity in Rome, and eagerly enjoyed. He had heard it said in his old time in Genoa that the finest Marionetti were here; and now, after great difficulty, he discovered the company in a sort of stable attached to a decayed palace. "It was a wet night, and there was no audience but a party of French officers and ourselves. We all sat together. I never saw anything more amazing than the performance—altogether only an hour long, but managed by as many as ten people, for we saw them all go behind, at the ringing of a bell. The

saving of a young lady by a good fairy from the machinations of an
enchanter, coupled with the comic business of her servant Pulcinella
(the Roman Punch) formed the plot of the first piece. A scolding old
peasant woman, who always leaned forward to scold and put her
hands in the pockets of her apron, was incredibly natural. Pulcinella,
so airy, so merry, so life-like, so graceful, he was irresistible. To see
him carrying an umbrella over his mistress's head in a storm, talking
to a prodigious giant whom he met in the forest, and going to bed
with a pony, were things never to be forgotten. And so delicate are
the hands of the people who move them, that every puppet was an
Italian, and did exactly what an Italian does. It he pointed at any
object, if he saluted anybody, if he laughed, if he cried, he did it as
never Englishman did it since Britain first at Heaven's command
arose—arose—arose, etc. There was a ballet afterwards, on the same
scale, and we came away really quite enchanted with the delicate
drollery of the thing. French officers more than ditto." . . .

From Rome they posted to Florence, and the last place visited
was Turin, where the travellers arrived on 5 December. . . .

# IV

## THREE SUMMERS AT BOULOGNE

### 1853, 1854, *and* 1856

DICKENS was in Boulogne, in 1853, from the middle of June to the
end of September, and for the next three months, as we have seen,
was in Switzerland and Italy. In the following year he went again
to Boulogne in June, and stayed, after finishing *Hard Times*, until
far into October. In February of 1855 he was for a fortnight in Paris
with Mr. Wilkie Collins; not taking up his more prolonged residence
there until the winter. From November 1855 to the end of April 1856
he made the French capital his home, working at *Little Dorrit* during
all those months. Then, after a month's interval in Dover and London, he took up his third summer residence in Boulogne, whither his
younger children had gone direct from Paris; and stayed until
September, finishing *Little Dorrit* in London in the spring of 1857.

Of the first of these visits, a few lively notes of humour and character out of his letters will tell the story sufficiently. The second and
third had points of more attractiveness. Those were the years of the
French-English alliance, of the great exposition of English paintings,
of the return of the troops from the Crimea, and of the visit of the
Prince Consort to the Emperor; such interest as Dickens took in
these several matters appearing in his letters with the usual vividness,
and the story of his continental life coming out with amusing dis-

tinctness in the successive pictures they paint with so much warmth
and colour. Another chapter will be given to Paris. This deals only
with Boulogne.

For his first summer residence, in June 1853, he had taken a house
on the high ground near the Calais road; an odd French place with
the strangest little rooms and halls, but standing in the midst of a
large garden, with wood and waterfall, a conservatory opening on a
great bank of roses, and paths and gates on one side to the ramparts,
on the other to the sea. Above all there was a capital proprietor and
landlord, by whom the cost of keeping up gardens and wood (which
he called a forest) was defrayed, while he gave his tenant the whole
range of both and all the flowers for nothing, sold him the garden
produce as it was wanted, and kept a cow on the estate to supply
the family milk. . . .

Then came a letter with his description of his landlord, lightly
sketched by him in print as M. Loyal-Devasseur, but here filled in
with the most attractive touches his loving hand could give. "But
the landlord —M. Beaucourt—is wonderful. Everybody here has two
surnames (I cannot conceive why), and M. Beaucourt, as he is always
called, is by rights M. Beaucourt-Mutuel. He is a portly jolly fellow
with a fine open face; lives on the hill behind, just outside the top
of the garden; and was a linen draper in the town, where he still has
a shop, but is supposed to have mortgaged his business and to be in
difficulties—all along of this place, which he has planted with his
own hands; which he cultivates all day; and which he never on any
consideration speaks of but as "the property." He is extraordinarily
popular in Boulogne (the people in the shops invariably brightening
up at the mention of his name, and congratulating us on being his
tenants), and really seems to deserve it. He is such a liberal fellow
that I can't bear to ask him for anything, since he instantly supplies
it whatever it is. The things he has done in respect of unreasonable
bedsteads and washing-stands, I blush to think of. I observed the
other day in one of the side gardens—there are gardens at each side
of the house too—a place where I thought the Comic Countryman"
(a name he was giving just then to his youngest boy) "must infallibly
trip over, and make a little descent of a dozen feet. So I said 'M.
Beaucourt'—who instantly pulled off his cap and stood bareheaded—
'there are some spare pieces of wood lying by the cow-house, if you
would have the kindness to have one laid across here I think it would
be safer.' 'Ah, mon Dieu sir,' said M. Beaucourt, 'it must be iron.
This is not a portion of the property where you would like to see
wood.' 'But iron is so expensive,' said I, 'and it really is not worth
while——' 'Sir, pardon me a thousand times,' said M. Beaucourt,
'it shall be iron. Assuredly and perfectly it shall be iron.' 'Then M.
Beaucourt,' said I, 'I shall be glad to pay a moiety of the cost.' 'Sir,'
said M. Beaucourt, 'Never!' Then to change the subject, he slided
from his firmness and gravity into a graceful conversational tone,
and said, 'In the moonlight last night, the flowers on the property

appeared, O heaven, to be *bathing themselves in the sky*. You like the property?' 'M. Beaucourt,' said I, 'I am enchanted with it; I am more than satisfied with everything.' 'And I sir,' said M. Beaucourt, laying his cap upon his breast, and kissing his hand —'I equally!' Yesterday two blacksmiths came for a day's work, and put up a good solid handsome bit of iron-railing, mortised into the stone parapet. . . . If the extraordinary things in the house defy description, the amazing phenomena in the gardens never could have been dreamed of by anybody but a Frenchman bent upon one idea. Besides a portrait of the house in the dining-room, there is a plan of the property in the hall. It looks about the size of Ireland; and to every one of the extraordinary objects there is a reference with some portentous name. There are fifty-one such references, including the Cottage of Tom Thumb, the Bridge of Austerlitz, the Bridge of Jena, the Hermitage, the Bower of the Old Guard, the Labyrinth (I have no idea which is which); and there is guidance to every room in the house, as if it were a place on that stupendous scale that without such a clue you must infallibly lose your way, and perhaps perish of starvation between bedroom and bedroom.''

On 3 July there came a fresh trait of the good fellow of a landlord. "Fancy what Beaucourt told me last night. When he 'conceived the inspiration' of planting the property ten years ago, he went over to England to buy the trees, took a small cottage in the market-gardens at Putney, lived there three months, held a symposium every night attended by the principal gardeners of Fulham, Putney, Kew, and Hammersmith (which he calls Hamsterdam), and wound up with a supper at which the market-gardeners rose, clinked their glasses, and exclaimed with one accord (I quote him exactly) VIVE BEAUCOURT! He was a captain in the National Guard, and Cavaignac his general. Brave Capitaine Beaucourt! said Cavaignac, you must receive a decoration. My General, said Beaucourt, No! It is enough for me that I have done my duty. I go to lay the first stone of a house upon a Property I have—that house shall be my decoration. (Regard that house!)" Addition to the picture came in a letter of 24 July; with a droll glimpse of Shakespeare at the theatre, and of the Saturday's pig-market. . . .

"We went to the theatre last night, to see the *Midsummer Night's Dream*—of the Opéra Comique. It is a beautiful little theatre now, with a very good company; and the nonsense of the piece was done with a sense quite confounding in that connection. Willy Am Shay Kes Peer; Sirzhon Foll Stayffe; Lor Lattimeer; and that celebrated Maid of Honour to Queen Elizabeth, Meees Oleeveeir—were the principal characters.

"Outside the old town, an army of workmen are (and have been for a week or so, already) employed upon an immense building which I supposed might be a Fort, or a Monastery, or a Barrack, or other something designed to last for ages. I find it is for the annual fair, which begins on the 5th of August and lasts a fortnight. Almost every Sunday we have a fête, where there is dancing in the open air, and where immense men with prodigious beards revolve on little wooden horses like Italian irons, in what we islanders call a round-about, by the hour together. But really the good humour and cheerfulness are very delightful. Among the other sights of the place, there is a pig-market every Saturday, perfectly insupportable in its absurdity. An excited French peasant, male or female, with a determined young pig, is the most amazing spectacle. I saw a little Drama enacted yesterday week, the drollery of which was perfect. *Dram. Pers.* 1. A pretty young woman with short petticoats and trim blue stockings, riding a donkey with two baskets and a pig in each. 2. An ancient farmer in a blouse, driving four pigs, his four in hand, with an enormous whip—and being drawn against walls and into smoking shops by any one of the four. 3. A cart, with an old pig (manacled) looking out of it, and terrifying six hundred and fifty young pigs in the market by his terrific grunts. 4. Collector of Octroi in an immense cocked hat, with a stream of young pigs running, night and day, between his military boots and rendering accounts impossible. 5. Inimitable, confronted by a radiation of elderly pigs, fastened each by one leg to a bunch of stakes in the ground. 6. John Edmund Reade, poet, expressing eternal devotion to and admiration of Landor, unconscious of approaching pig recently escaped from barrow. 7. Priests, peasants, soldiers, etc." . . .

When leaving Paris for his third visit to Boulogne, at the beginning of June 1856, he had not written a word of the ninth number of his new book, and did not expect for another month to "see land from the running sea of *Little Dorrit*." He had resumed the house he first occupied, the cottage or villa "des Moulineaux," and after dawdling about his garden for a few days with surprising industry in a French farmer garb of blue blouse, leathern belt, and military cap, which he had mounted as "the only one for complete comfort," he wrote to me that he was getting "Now to work again—to work! The story lies before me, I hope, strong and clear. Not to be easily told; but nothing of that sort is to be easily done that *I* know of." At work it became his habit to sit late, and then, putting off his usual walk until night, to lie down among the roses reading until after tea ("middle-aged Love in a blouse and belt"), when he went down to the pier. . . .

His own household had got into a small war, of which the commander-in-chief was his man-servant "French," the bulk of the forces engaged being his children, and the invaders two cats. Business brought him to London on the hostilities breaking out, and on his return after a few days the story of the war was told. "Dick," it should be said, was a canary very dear both to Dickens and his eldest daughter, who had so tamed to her loving hand its wild little heart that it was become the most docile of companions. "The only thing new in this garden is that war is raging against two particularly tigerish and fearful cats (from the mill, I suppose), which are always glaring in dark corners, after our wonderful little Dick. Keeping the

house open at all points, it is impossible to shut them out, and they
hide themselves in the most terrific manner: hanging themselves up
behind draperies, like bats, and tumbling out in the dead of night
with frightful caterwaulings. Hereupon French borrows Beaucourt's
gun, loads the same to the muzzle, discharges it twice in vain and
throws himself over with the recoil, exactly like a clown. But at last
(while I was in town) he aims at the more amiable cat of the two,
and shoots that animal dead. Insufferably elated by this victory, he
is now engaged from morning to night in hiding behind bushes to get
aim at the other. He does nothing else whatever. All the boys
encourage him and watch for the enemy—on whose appearance they
give an alarm which immediately serves as a warning to the creature,
who runs away. They are at this moment (ready dressed for church)
all lying on their stomachs in various parts of the garden. Horrible
whistles give notice to the gun what point it is to approach. I am
afraid to go out, lest I should be shot. Mr. Plornish says his prayers
at night in a whisper, lest the cat should overhear him and take
offence. The tradesmen cry out as they come up the avenue, 'Me
voici! C'est moi - boulanger—ne tirez pas, Monsieur Franche!' It is
like living in a state of siege; and the wonderful manner in which the
cat preserves the character of being the only person not much put
out by the intensity of this monomania, is most ridiculous." (6 July.)
. . . "About four pounds of powder and half a ton of shot have
been" (13 July) "fired off at the cat (and the public in general) during
the week. The finest thing is that immediately after I have heard
the noble sportsman blazing away at her in the garden in front, I
look out of my room door into the drawing-room, and am pretty sure
to see her coming in after the birds, in the calmest manner, by the
back window Intelligence has been brought to me from a source on
which I can rely, that French has newly conceived the atrocious project of tempting her into the coach-house by meat and kindness, and
there, from an elevated portmanteau, blowing her head off. This I
mean sternly to interdict, and to do so to-day as a work of piety." . . .

An epidemic broke out in the town, affecting the children of several
families known to Dickens, among them that of his friend Mr.
Gilbert A'Beckett; who, upon arriving from Paris, and finding a
favourite little son stricken dangerously, sank himself under an illness
from which he had been suffering, and died two days after the boy.
"He had for three days shown symptoms of rallying, and we had
some hope of his recovery, but he sank and died, and never even
knew that the child had gone before him. A sad, sad story." Dickens
meanwhile had sent his own children home with his wife, and the
rest soon followed. Poor M. Beaucourt was inconsolable. "The desolation of the place is wretched. When Mamey and Katey went, Beaucourt came in and wept. He really is almost broken-hearted about it.
He had planted all manner of flowers for next month, and had thrown
down the spade and left off weeding the garden, so that it looks something like a dreary bird-cage with all manner of grasses and chick-

weeds sticking through the bars and lying in the sand. 'Such a loss too,' he says, 'for Monsieur Dickens!' Then he looks in at the kitchen window (which seems to be his only relief), and sighs himself up the hill home." . . .

The interval of residence in Paris between these two last visits to Boulogne is now to be described.

## V

### RESIDENCE IN PARIS

### 1855–6

IN Paris Dickens's life was passed among artists, and in the exercise of his own art. His associates were writers, painters, actors, or musicians, and when he wanted relief from any strain of work he found it at the theatre. The years since his last residence in the great city had made him better known, and the increased attentions pleased him. He had to help in preparing for a translation of his books into French; and this, with continued labour at the story he had in hand, occupied him as long as he remained. It will be all best told by extracts from his letters; in which the people he met, the theatres he visited, and the incidents, public or private, that seemed to him worthy of mention, reappear with the old force and liveliness.

Nor is anything better worth preserving from them than choice bits of description of an actor or a drama, for this perishable enjoyment has only so much as may survive out of such recollections to witness for itself to another generation; and an unusually high place may be challenged for the subtlety and delicacy of what is said in these letters of things theatrical, when the writer was especially attracted by a performer or a play. Frédéric Lemaître has never had a higher tribute than Dickens paid to him during his few days' earlier stay at Paris in the spring.

"Incomparably the finest acting I ever saw, I saw last night at the Ambigu. They have revived that old piece, once immensely popular in London under the name of *Thirty Years of a Gambler's Life*. Old Lemaître plays his famous character, and never did I see anything, in art, so exaltedly horrible and awful. In the earlier acts he was so well made up, and so light and active, that he really looked sufficiently young. But in the last two, when he had grown old and miserable, he did the finest things, I really believe, that are within the power of acting. Two or three times a great cry of horror went all round the house. When he met, in the inn yard, the traveller whom he murders, and first saw his money, the manner in which the crime came into his head—and eyes—was as truthful as it was terrific." . . .

That was at the close of February. In October, Dickens's longer residence began. He betook himself with his family, after two unsuccessful attempts in the new region of the Rue Balzac and Rue Lord Byron, to an apartment in the Avenue des Champs Elysées. Over him was an English bachelor with an establishment consisting of an English groom and five English horses. "The concierge and his wife told us that his name was *Six*, which drove me nearly mad until we discovered it to be *Sykes*." . . .

At the first play he went to, the performance was stopped while the news of the last Crimean engagement, just issued in a supplement to the *Moniteur*, was read from the stage. "It made not the faintest effect upon the audience; and even the hired claqueurs, who had been absurdly loud during the piece, seemed to consider the war not at all within their contract, and were as stagnant as ditch-water. The theatre was full. It is quite impossible to see such apathy, and suppose the war to be popular, whatever may be asserted to the contrary." . . .

A piece of honest farce is a relief. "An uncommonly droll piece with an original comic idea in it has been in course of representation here. It is called *Les Cheveux de ma Femme*. A man who is dotingly fond of his wife, and who wishes to know whether she loved anybody else before they were married, cuts off a lock of her hair by stealth, and takes it to a great mesmeriser, who submits it to a clairvoyante who never was wrong. It is discovered that the owner of this hair has been up to the most frightful dissipations, insomuch that the clairvoyante can't mention half of them. The distracted husband goes home to reproach his wife, and she then reveals that she wears a wig, and takes it off." . . .

At the house of that great artist, Madame Viardot, the sister of Malibran, Dickens dined to meet George Sand, that lady having appointed the day and hour for the interesting festival, which came off duly on 10 January. "I suppose it to be impossible to imagine anybody more unlike my preconceptions than the illustrious Sand. Just the kind of woman in appearance whom you might suppose to be the Queen's monthly nurse. Chubby, matronly, swarthy, black-eyed. Nothing of the blue-stocking about her, except a little final way of settling all your opinions with hers, which I take to have been acquired in the country, where she lives, and in the domination of a small circle. A singularly ordinary woman in appearance and manner. The dinner was very good and remarkably unpretending. Ourselves, Madame and her son, the Scheffers, the Sartorises, and some Lady somebody (from the Crimea last) who wore a species of paletot, and smoked. The Viardots have a house away in the new part of Paris, which looks exactly as if they had moved into it last week and were going away next. Notwithstanding which, they had lived in it eight years. The opera the very last thing on earth you would associate with the family. Piano not even opened. Her husband is an extremely good fellow, and she is as natural as it is possible to be."

337

Dickens was hardly the man to take fair measure of Madame Dudevant in meeting her thus. He was not familiar with her writings, and had no very special liking for such of them as he knew. But no disappointment, nothing but amazement, awaited him at a dinner that followed soon after. Emile de Girardin gave a banquet in his honour. His description of it, which he declares to be strictly prosaic, sounds a little Oriental, but not inappropriately so. "No man unacquainted with my determination never to embellish or fancify such accounts, could believe in the description I shall let off when we meet, of dining at Emile Girardin's—of the three gorgeous drawing-rooms with ten thousand wax candles in golden sconces, terminating in a dining-room of unprecedented magnificence with two enormous transparent plate-glass doors in it, looking (across an ante-chamber full of clean plates) straight into the kitchen, with the cooks in their white paper caps dishing the dinner. From his seat in the midst of the table, the host (like a Giant in a Fairy story) beholds the kitchen, and the snow-white tables, and the profound order and silence there prevailing. Forth from the plate-glass doors issues the Banquet—the most wonderful feast ever tasted by mortal: at the present price of Truffles, that article alone costing (for eight people) at least five pounds. On the table are ground glass jugs of peculiar construction, laden with the finest growth of Champagne and the coolest ice. With the third course is issued Port Wine (previously unheard of in a good state on this continent), which would fetch two guineas a bottle at any sale. The dinner done, Oriental flowers in vases of golden cobweb are placed upon the board. With the ice is issued Brandy, buried for 100 years. To that succeeds Coffee, brought by the brother of one of the convives from the remotest East, in exchange for an equal quantity of Californian gold dust. The company being returned to the drawing-room—tables roll in by unseen agency, laden with Cigarettes from the Hareem of the Sultan, and with cool drinks in which the flavour of the Lemon arrived yesterday from Algeria, struggles voluptuously with the delicate Orange arrived this morning from Lisbon. That period past, and the guests reposing on Divans worked with many-coloured blossoms, big table rolls in, heavy with massive furniture of silver, and breathing incense in the form of a little present of Tea direct from China—table and all, I believe; but cannot swear to it, and am resolved to be prosaic. All this time the host perpetually repeats 'Ce petit dîner-ci n'est que pour faire la connaissance de Monsieur Dickens; il ne compte pas; ce n'est rien.' And even now I have forgotten to set down half of it—in particular the item of a far larger plum pudding than ever was seen in England at Christmas time, served with a celestial sauce in colour like the orange blossom, and in substance like the blossom powdered and bathed in dew, and called in the carte (carte in a gold frame like a little fish-slice to be handed about) 'Hommage à l'illustre écrivain d'Angleterre.' That illustrious man staggered out at the last drawing-room door, speechless with wonder, finally; and even at that moment his host, holding to his lips a chalice set with precious stones and containing nectar distilled from the air that blew over the fields of beans in bloom for fifteen summers, remarked 'Le dîner que nous avons eu, mon cher, n'est rien—il ne compte pas—il a été tout-à-fait en famille—il faut dîner (en vérité, dîner) bientôt. Au plaisir! Au revoir! Au dîner!' "

The second dinner came, wonderful as the first; among the company were Regnier, Jules Sandeau, and the new Director of the Français; and his host again played Lucullus in the same style, with success even more consummate. The only absolutely new incident however was that "After dinner he asked me if I would come into another room and smoke a cigar? and on my saying Yes, coolly opened a drawer, containing about 5000 inestimable cigars in prodigious bundles—just as the Captain of the Robbers in *Ali Baba* might have gone to a corner of the cave for bales of brocade. A little man dined who was blacking shoes 8 years ago, and is now enormously rich—the richest man in Paris—having ascended with rapidity up the usual ladder of the Bourse. By merely observing that perhaps he might come down again, I clouded so many faces as to render it very clear to me that *everybody present* was at the same game for some stake or other!" He returned to that subject in a letter a few days later. "If you were to see the steps of the Bourse at about 4 in the afternoon, and the crowd of blouses and patches among the speculators there assembled, all howling and haggard with speculation, you would stand aghast at the consideration of what must be going on. Concierges and people like that perpetually blow their brains out, or fly into the Seine, 'à cause des pertes sur la Bourse.' I hardly ever take up a French paper without lighting on such a paragraph. On the other hand, thoroughbred horses without end, and red velvet carriages with white kid harness on jet black horses, go by here all day long; and the pedestrians who turn to look at them, laugh, and say, 'C'est la Bourse!' Such crashes must be staved off every week as have not been seen since Law's time." . . .

Before Dickens left Paris in May he had completed the arrangements for a published translation of all his books, and had sent over two descriptions that the reader most anxious to follow him to a new scene would perhaps be sorry to lose. A Duchess was murdered in the Champs Elysées. "The murder over the way (the third or fourth event of that nature in the Champs Elysées since we have been here) seems to disclose the strangest state of things. The Duchess who is murdered lived alone in a great house which was always shut up, and passed her time entirely in the dark. In a little lodge outside lived a coachman (the murderer), and there had been a long succession of coachmen who had been unable to stay there, and upon whom, whenever they asked for their wages, she plunged out with an immense knife, by way of an immediate settlement. The coachman never had anything to do, for the coach hadn't been driven out for years; neither would she ever allow the horses to be taken out for exercise. Between the lodge and the house, is a miserable bit of garden, all overgrown with long rank grass, weeds, and nettles; and in this, the horses used to be taken out to swim—in a dead green vegetable sea, up to their haunches. On the day of the murder there was a great crowd, of course; and in the midst of it up comes the Duke her husband (from whom she was separated), and rings at the gate. The police open the grate. 'C'est vrai donc,' says the Duke, 'que Madame la Duchesse n'est plus?'—'C'est trop vrai, Monseigneur.'—'Tant mieux,' says the Duke, and walks off deliberately, to the great satisfaction of the assemblage.''

The second description relates an occurrence in England of only three years' previous date, belonging to that wildly improbable class of realities which Dickens always held, with Fielding, to be (properly) closed to fiction. Only, he would add, critics should not be so eager to assume that what had never happened to themselves could not, by any human possibility, ever be supposed to have happened to anybody else. "B. was with me the other day, and, among other things that he told me, described an extraordinary adventure in his life, at a place not a thousand miles from my 'property' at Gadshill, three years ago. He lived at the tavern and was sketching one day when an open carriage came by with a gentleman and lady in it. He was sitting in the same place working at the same sketch, next day, when it came by again. So, another day, when the gentleman got out and introduced himself. Fond of art; lived at the great house yonder, which perhaps he knew; was an Oxford man and a Devonshire squire, but not resident on his estate, for domestic reasons; would be glad to see him to dinner to-morrow. He went, and found among other things a very fine library. 'At your disposition,' said the Squire, to whom he had now described himself and his pursuits. 'Use it for your writing and drawing. Nobody else uses it.' He stayed in the house *six months*. The lady was a mistress, aged five-and-twenty, and very beautiful, drinking her life away. The Squire was drunken, and utterly depraved and wicked; but an excellent scholar, an admirable linguist, and a great theologian. Two other mad visitors stayed the six months. One, a man well known in Paris here, who goes about the world with a crimson silk stocking in his breast pocket, containing a tooth-brush and an immense quantity of ready money. The other, a college chum of the Squire's, now ruined; with an insatiate thirst for drink; who constantly got up in the middle of the night, crept down to the dining-room, and emptied all the decanters. . . . B. stayed on in the place, under a sort of devilish fascination to discover what might come of it. . . . Tea or coffee never seen in the house, and very seldom water. Beer, champagne, and brandy, were the three drinkables. Breakfast: leg of mutton, champagne, beer, and brandy. Lunch: shoulder of mutton, champagne, beer, and brandy. Dinner: every conceivable dish (Squire's income, £7000 a year), champagne, beer, and brandy. The Squire had married a woman of the town from whom he was now separated, but by whom he had a daughter. The mother, to spite the father, had bred the daughter in every conceivable vice. Daughter, then 13, came from school once a month. Intensely coarse in talk, and always drunk. As they drove about the country in two open carriages, the drunken mistress would be perpetually tumbling out of one, and the drunken daughter perpetually tumbling out of the other. At last the drunken mistress drank her stomach away, and began to die on the sofa. Got worse and worse, and was always raving about Somebody's where she had once been a lodger, and perpetually shrieking that she would cut somebody else's heart out. At last she died on the sofa, and, after the funeral, the party broke up. A few months ago, B. met the man with the crimson silk stocking at Brighton, who told him that the Squire was dead 'of a broken heart'; that the chum was dead of delirium tremens; and that the daughter was heiress to the fortune. He told me all this, which I fully believe to be true, without any embellishment—just in the off-hand way in which I have told it to you."

Dickens left Paris at the end of April, and, after the summer in Boulogne, which has been described, passed the winter in London, giving to his theatrical enterprise nearly all the time that *Little Dorrit* did not claim from him. His book was finished in the following spring; was inscribed to Clarkson Stanfield; and now claims to have something said about it. The theatrical enterprise to be at the same time related, with what it led to, will be found to open a new phase in the life of Dickens.

# BOOK EIGHTH

## PUBLIC READER

### 1856–67. ÆT. 44–55

# I

## "LITTLE DORRIT," AND A LAZY TOUR

### 1855-7

BETWEEN *Hard Times* and *Little Dorrit*, Dickens's principal literary work had been the contribution to *Household Words* of two tales for Christmas (1854 and 1855) which his readings afterwards made widely popular, the Story of Richard Doubledick,* and Boots at the Holly Tree Inn. In the latter was related, with a charming naturalness and spirit, the elopement, to get married at Gretna Green, of two little children of the mature respective ages of eight and seven. At Christmas 1855 came out the first number of *Little Dorrit*, and in April 1857 the last. . . .

The first number appeared in December 1855, and on its sale there was an exultant note. *"Little Dorrit* has beaten even *Bleak House* out of the field. It is a most tremendous start, and I am overjoyed at it"; to which he added, writing from Paris on the 6th of the month following, "You know that they had sold 35,000 of number two on new years' day." He was still in Paris on the day of the appearance of that portion of the tale by which it will always be most vividly remembered, and thus wrote on 30 January, 1856: "I have a grim pleasure upon me to-night in thinking that the Circumlocution Office sees the light, and in wondering what effect it will make. But my head really stings with the visions of the book, and I am going, as we French say, to disembarrass it by plunging out into some of the strange places I glide into of nights in these latitudes." The Circumlocution heroes led to the Society scenes, the Hampton Court dowager-sketches, and Mr. Gowan; all parts of one satire levelled against prevailing political and social vices. Aim had been taken, in the course of it, at some living originals, disguised sufficiently from recognition

---

* The framework for this sketch was a graphic description, also done by Dickens, of the celebrated Charity at Rochester founded in the sixteenth century by Richard Watts, "for six poor travellers, who, not being Rogues or Proctors, may receive gratis for one night, lodging, entertainment, and fourpence each." A quaint monument to Watts is the most prominent object on the wall of the south-west transept of the cathedral, and underneath it is now placed a brass thus inscribed: "CHARLES DICKENS. Born at Portsmouth, seventh of February 1812. Died at Gadshill Place by Rochester, ninth of June 1870. Buried in Westminster Abbey. To connect his memory with the scenes in which his earliest and his latest years were passed, and with the associations of Rochester Cathedral and its neighbourhood which extended over all his life, this Tablet, with the sanction of the Dean and Chapter, is placed by his Executors."

to enable him to make his thrust more sure; but there was one exception self-revealed. "I had the general idea," he wrote while engaged on the sixth number, "of the Society business before the Sadleir affair, but I shaped Mr. Merdle himself out of that precious rascality. Society, the Circumlocution Office, and Mr. Gowan, are of course three parts of one idea and design. Mr. Merdle's complaint, which you will find in the end to be fraud and forgery, came into my mind as the last drop in the silver cream-jug on Hampstead Heath. I shall beg, when you have read the present number, to inquire whether you consider 'Bar' an instance, in reference to K F, of a suggested likeness in not many touches?" The likeness no one could mistake; and, though that particular Bar has since been moved into a higher and happier sphere, Westminster Hall is in no danger of losing "the insinuating Jury-droop, and persuasive double eye-glass," by which this keen observer could express a type of character in half a dozen words.

Of the other portions of the book that had a strong personal interest for him I have spoken on a former page, and I will now only add an allusion of his own. "There are some things in Flora in number seven that seem to me to be extraordinarily droll, with something serious at the bottom of them after all. Ah, well! was there *not* something very serious in it once? I am glad to think of being in the country with the long summer mornings as I approach number ten, where I have finally resolved to make Dorrit rich. It should be a very fine point in the story. . . . Nothing in Flora made me laugh so much as the confusion of ideas between gout flying upwards, and its soaring with Mr. F. to another sphere" (7 April). . . .

Shortly after the date of his letter he was in London on business connected with the purchase of Gadshill Place, and he went over to the Borough to see what traces were left of the prison of which his first impression was taken in his boyhood, which had played so important a part in this latest novel, and every brick and stone of which he had been able to rebuild in his book by the mere vividness of his marvellous memory. "Went to the Borough yesterday morning before going to Gadshill, to see if I could find any ruins of the Marshalsea. Found a great part of the original building—now 'Marshalsea Place.' Found the rooms that have been in my mind's eye in the story. Found, nursing a very big boy, a very small boy, who, seeing me standing on the Marshalsea pavement, looking about, told me how it all used to be. God knows how he learned it (for he was a world too young to know anything about it), but he was right enough. . . . There is a room there—still standing, to my amazement—that I think of taking! It is the room through which the ever-memorable signers of Captain Porter's petition filed off in my boyhood." "The spikes are gone, and the wall is lowered, and anybody can go out now who likes to go, and is not bed-ridden; and I said to the boy, 'Who lives there?' and he said, 'Jack Pithick.'

'Who is Jack Pithick?' I asked him. And he said, 'Joe Pithick's uncle.' " . . .

His book was finished soon after at Gadshill Place, to be presently described, which he had purchased the previous year, and taken possession of in February; subscribing himself, in the letter announcing the fact, as "the Kentish Freeholder on his native heath, his name Protection." The new abode occupied him in various ways in the early part of the summer; and Hans Andersen the Dane had just arrived upon a visit to him there, when Douglas Jerrold's unexpected death befell. It was a shock to everyone, and an especial grief to Dickens. Jerrold's wit, and the bright shrewd intellect that had so many triumphs, need no celebration from me; but the keenest of satirists was one of the kindliest of men, and Dickens had a fondness for Jerrold as genuine as his admiration for him. . . .

A plan for a theatrical performance and a reading by Dickens, on behalf of Jerrold's dependent, was carried to its close with vigour, promptitude, and success. In addition to the performances named, there were others in the country also organised by Dickens, in which he took active personal part; and the result did not fall short of his expectations. The sum was invested ultimately for our friend's unmarried daughter, who now receives, under direction of the Court of Chancery, the income of it until lately paid by myself, the last surviving trustee.

So passed the greater part of the summer, and when the country performances were over at the end of August I had this intimation. "I have arranged with Collins that he and I will start next Monday on a ten or twelve days' expedition to out-of-the-way places, to do (in inns and coast-corners) a little tour in search of an article and in avoidance of railroads. I must get a good name for it, and I propose it in five articles, one for the beginning of every number in the October part." Next day: "Our decision is for a foray upon the fells of Cumberland; I having discovered in the books some promising moors and bleak places thereabout." Into the lake-country they went accordingly; and The Lazy Tour of Two Idle Apprentices, contributed to *Household Words*, related the trip. But his letters had descriptive touches, and some whimsical experiences, not in the published account.

Looking over the *Beauties of England and Wales* before he left London, his ambition was fired by mention of Carrick Fell, "a gloomy old mountain 1500 feet high," which he secretly resolved to go up. "We came straight to it yesterday" (9 September). "Nobody goes up. Guides have forgotten it. Master of a little inn, excellent north-countryman, volunteered. Went up, in a tremendous rain. C. D. beat Mr. Porter (name of landlord) in half a mile. Mr. P. done up in no time. Three nevertheless went on. Mr. P. again leading; C. D. and C." (Mr. Wilkie Collins "following. Rain terrific, black mists, darkness of night. Mr. P. agitated. C. D. confident. C. (a long way down in perspective) submissive. All wet through. No poles. Not so much as a walking-stick in the party. Reach the summit at about one in the day. Dead darkness as of night. Mr. P. (excellent fellow to the last) uneasy. C. D. produces compass from pocket. Mr. P. reassured. Farm-house where dog-cart was left, N.N.W. Mr. P. complimentary. Descent commenced. C. D. with compass triumphant, until compass, with the heat and wet of C. D.'s pocket, breaks. Mr. P. (who never had a compass), inconsolable, confesses he has not been on Carrick Fell for twenty years, and he don't know the way down. Darker and darker. Nobody discernible, two yards off, by the other two. Mr. P. makes suggestions, but not way. It becomes clear to C. D. and to C. that Mr. P. is going round and round the mountain, and never coming down. Mr. P. sits on angular granite, and says he is 'just fairly doon.' C. D. revives Mr. P. with laughter, the only restorative in the company. Mr. P. again complimentary. Descent tried once more. Mr. P. worse and worse. Council of war. Proposals from C. D. to go 'slap down.' Seconded by C. Mr. P. objects, on account of precipice called The Black Arches, and terror of the countryside. More wandering. Mr. P. terror-stricken, but game. Watercourse, thundering and roaring, reached. C. D. suggests that it must run to the river, and had best be followed, subject to all gymnastic hazards. Mr. P. opposes, but gives in. Watercourse followed accordingly. Leaps, splashes, and tumbles, for two hours. C. lost. C. D. whoops. Cries for assistance, from behind. C. D. returns. C. with horribly sprained ankle, lying in rivulet!"

All the danger was over when Dickens sent his description; but great had been the trouble in binding up the sufferer's ankle and getting him painfully on, shoving, shouldering, carrying alternately, till terra firma was reached. "We got down at last in the wildest place, preposterously out of the course; and, propping up C. against stones, sent Mr. P. to the other side of Cumberland for dog-cart, so got back to his inn, and changed. Shoe or stocking on the bad foot out of the question. Foot bundled up in a flannel waistcoat. C. D. carrying. C. melodramatically (Wardour to the life!) everywhere; into and out of carriages; up and down stairs; to bed; every step. And so to Wigton, got doctor, and here we are!! A pretty business, we flatter ourselves!" . . .

On their way home the friends were at Doncaster, and this was Dickens's first experience of the St. Leger and its saturnalia. His companion had by this time so far recovered as to be able, doubled-up, to walk with a thick stick; in which condition, "being exactly like the gouty admiral in a comedy I have given him that name." The impressions received from the race-week were not favourable. It was noise and turmoil all day long, and a gathering of vagabonds from all parts of the racing earth. Every bad face that had ever caught wickedness from an innocent horse had its representative in the streets; and as Dickens, like Gulliver looking down upon his fellow-men after coming from the horse-country, looked down into Doncaster High Street from his inn-window, he seemed to see everywhere a then notorious personage who had just poisoned his betting-companion. "Everywhere I see the late Mr. Palmer with his betting-book in his hand. Mr. Palmer sits next me at the theatre; Mr. Palmer goes before me down the street; Mr. Palmer follows me into the chemist's shop where I go to buy rose-water after breakfast, and says to the chemist 'Give us soom sal volatile or soom damned thing o' that soort, in wather—my head's bad!' And I look at the back of his bad head repeated in long, long lines on the race course, and in the betting-stand and outside the betting-rooms in the town, and I vow to God that I can see nothing in it but cruelty, covetousness, calculation, insensibility, and low wickedness."

Even a half-appalling kind of luck was not absent from my friend's experiences at the race course, when, what he called a "wonderful, paralysing, coincidence" befell him. He bought the card; facetiously wrote down three names for the winners of the three chief races (never in his life having heard or thought of any of the horses, except that the winner of the Derby, who proved to be nowhere, had been mentioned to him); "and, if you can believe it without your hair standing on end, those three races were won, one after another, by those three horses!!!" That was the St. Leger Day, of which he also thought it noticeable, that, though the losses were enormous, nobody had won, for there was nothing but grinding of teeth and blaspheming of ill-luck. Nor had matters mended on the Cup-day, after which celebration "a groaning phantom " lay in the doorway of his bedroom and howled all night. The landlord came up in the morning to apologise, "and said it was a gentleman who had lost £1500 or £2000; and he had drunk a deal afterwards; and then they put him to bed, and then he—took the 'orrors, and got up, and yelled till morning." Dickens might well believe, as he declared at the end of his letter, that if a boy with any good in him, but with a dawning propensity to sporting and betting, were but brought to the Doncaster races soon enough, it would cure him.

## II

### WHAT HAPPENED AT THIS TIME

#### 1857–8

AN unsettled feeling greatly in excess of what was usual with Dickens, more or less observable since his first residence at Boulogne, became at this time almost habitual, and the satisfactions which home should have supplied, and which indeed were essential requirements of his nature, he had failed to find in his home. He had not the alternative that under this disappointment some can discover in what is called society. It did not suit him, and he set no store by it. No man was better fitted to adorn any circle he entered, but beyond that of friends and equals he rarely passed. He would take as much pains to keep out of the houses of the great as others take to get into them. Not always wisely, it may be admitted. Mere contempt for toadyism and flunkeyism was not at all times the prevailing motive with him which he supposed it to be. Beneath his horror of those vices of Englishmen in his own rank of life, there was a still stronger resentment at the social inequalities that engender them, of which he was not so conscious and to which he owned less freely. Not the less it served secretly to justify what he might otherwise have had no mind to. To say he was not a gentleman would be as true as to say he was not a writer; but if anyone should assert his occasional preference for what was even beneath his level over that which was above it, this would be difficult of disproof. It was among those defects of temperament for which his early trials and his early successes were accountable in perhaps equal measure. He was sensitive in a passionate degree to praise and blame, which yet he made for the most part a point of pride to assume indifference to; the inequalities of rank which he secretly resented took more galling as well as glaring prominence from the contrast of the necessities he had gone through with the fame that had come to him; and when the forces he most affected to despise assumed the form of barriers he could not easily overlap, he was led to appear frequently intolerant (for he very seldom was really so) in opinions and language. His early sufferings brought with them the healing powers of energy, will, and persistence, and taught him the inexpressible value of a determined resolve to live down difficulties; but the habit, in small as in great things, of renunciation and self-sacrifice, they did not teach; and, by his sudden leap into a world-wide popularity and influence, he became master of everything that might seem to be attainable in life, before he had mastered what a man must undergo to be equal to its hardest trials.

Nothing of all this has yet presented itself to notice, except in occasional forms of restlessness and desire of change of place, which were themselves, when his books were in progress, so incident as well to the active requirements of his fancy as to call, thus far, for no other explanation. Up to the date of the completion of *Copperfield* he had felt himself to be in possession of an all-sufficient resource. Against whatever might befall he had a set-off in his imaginative creations, a compensation derived from his art that never failed him, because there he was supreme. It was the world he could bend to his will, and make subserve to all his desires. He had otherwise, underneath his exterior of a singular precision, method, and strictly orderly arrangement in all things, and notwithstanding a temperament to which home and home interests were really a necessity, something in common with those eager, impetuous, somewhat overbearing natures, that rush at existence without heeding the cost of it, and are not more ready to accept and make the most of its enjoyments than to be easily and quickly overthrown by its burdens. But the world he had called into being had thus far borne him safely through these perils. He had his own creations always by his side. They were living, speaking companions. With them only he was everywhere thoroughly identified. He laughed and wept with them; was as much elated by their fun as cast down by their grief; and brought to the consideration of them a belief in their reality as well as in the influences they were meant to exercise, which in every circumstance sustained him.

It was during the composition of *Little Dorrit* that I think he first felt a certain strain upon his invention which brought with it other misgivings. In a modified form this was present during the later portions of *Bleak House*, of which not a few of the defects might be traced to the acting excitements amid which it was written; but the succeeding book made it plainer to him; and it is remarkable that in the interval between them he resorted for the first and only time in his life to a practice, which he abandoned at the close of his next and last story published in the twenty-number form, of putting down written "Memoranda" of suggestions for characters or incidents by way of resource to him in his writing. Never before had his teeming fancy seemed to want such help; the need being less to contribute to its fulness than to check its overflowing; but it is another proof that he had been secretly bringing before himself, at least, the possibility that what had ever been his great support might some day desert him. It was strange that he should have had such doubt, and he would hardly have confessed it openly; but apart from that wonderful world of his books, the range of his thoughts was not always proportioned to the width and largeness of his nature. His ordinary circle of activity, whether in likings or thinkings, was full of such surprising animation, that one was apt to believe it more comprehensive than it really was; and again and again, when a wide horizon might seem to be ahead of him he would pull up suddenly and stop short, as though nothing lay beyond. For the time, though each had its term and change, he was very much a man of one idea, each having its turn of absolute predominance; and this was one of the secrets of the thoroughness with which everything he took in hand was done. As to the matter of his writings, the actual truth was that his creative genius never really failed him. Not a few of his inventions of character and humour, up to the very close of his life, his Marigolds, Lirripers, Gargerys, Pips, Sapseas and many others, were as fresh and fine as in his greatest day. He had however lost the free and fertile method of the earlier time. He could no longer fill a wide-spread canvas with the same facility and certainty as of old; and he had frequently a quite unfounded apprehension of some possible breakdown, of which the end might be at any moment beginning. There came accordingly, from time to time, intervals of unusual impatience and restlessness, strange to me in connection with his home; his old pursuits were too often laid aside for other excitements and occupations; he joined a public political agitation, set on foot by administrative reformers; he got up various quasi-public private theatricals, in which he took the leading place; and though it was but part of his always generous devotion in any friendly duty to organise the series of performances on his friend Jerrold's death, yet the eagerness with which he flung himself into them, so arranging them as to assume an amount of labour in acting and travelling that might have appalled an experienced comedian, and carrying them on week after week unceasingly in London and the provinces, expressed but the craving which still had possession of him to get by some means at some change that should make existence easier. What was highest in his nature had ceased for the time to be highest in his life, and he had put himself at the mercy of lower accidents and conditions. The mere effect of the strolling wandering ways into which this acting led him could not be other than unfavourable. But remonstrance as yet was unavailing.

To one very earnestly made in the early autumn of 1857, in which opportunity was taken to compare his recent rush up Carrick Fell to his rush into other difficulties, here was the reply. "Too late to say, put the curb on, and don't rush at hills—the wrong man to say it to. I have now no relief but in action. I am become incapable of rest. I am quite confident I should rust, break, and die, if I spared myself. Much better to die, doing. What I am in that way, nature made me first, and my way of life has of late, alas! confirmed. I must accept the drawback—since it is one—with the powers I have; and I must hold upon the tenure prescribed to me." Something of the same sad feeling, it is right to say, had been expressed from time to time, in connection also with home dissatisfactions and misgivings, through the three years preceding; but I attributed it to other causes, and gave little attention to it. During his absences abroad for the greater part of 1854, '55, and '56, while the elder of his children were growing out of childhood, and his books were less easy to him than in his earlier manhood, evidences presented themselves in his letters of the old "unhappy loss or want of something" to which he had given a pervading prominence in *Copperfield*. In the first of those years he made express allusion to the kind of experience which had been one of his descriptions in that favourite book, and, mentioning the drawbacks of his present life, had first identified it with his own: "the so happy and yet so unhappy existence which seeks its realities in unrealities, and finds its dangerous comfort in a perpetual escape from the disappointment of heart around it."

Later in the same year he thus wrote from Boulogne: "I have had dreadful thoughts of getting away somewhere altogether by myself. If I could have managed it, I think possibly I might have gone to the Pyreennees (you know what I mean that word for, so I won't rewrite it) for six months! I have put the idea into the perspective of six months, but have not abandoned it. I have visions of living for half a year or so, in all sorts of inaccessible places, and opening a new book therein. A floating idea of going up above the snow-line in

Switzerland, and living in some astonishing convent, hovers about me. If *Household Words* could be got into a good train, in short, I don't know in what strange place, or at what remote elevation above the level of the sea, I might fall to work next. *Restlessness*, you will say. Whatever it is, it is always driving me, and I cannot help it. I have rested nine or ten weeks, and sometimes feel as if it had been a year—though I had the strangest nervous miseries before I stopped. If I couldn't walk fast and far, I should just explode and perish." Again, four months later he wrote: "You will hear of me in Paris, probably next Sunday, and I *may* go on to Bordeaux. Have general ideas of emigrating in the summer to the mountain-ground between France and Spain. Am altogether in a dishevelled state of mind—motes of new books in the dirty air, miseries of older growth, threatening to close upon me. Why is it, that as with poor David, a sense comes always crushing on me now, when I fall into low spirits, as of one happiness I have missed in life, and one friend and companion I have never made?"

Early in 1856 (20 January) the notion revisited him of writing a book on solitude. "Again I am beset by my former notions of a book whereof the whole story shall be on the top of the Great St. Bernard. As I accept and reject ideas for *Little Dorrit*, it perpetually comes back to me. Two or three years hence, perhaps you'll find me living with the Monks and the Dogs a whole winter—among the blinding snows that fall about that monastery. I have a serious idea that I shall do it, if I live." He was at this date in Paris; and during the visit to him of Macready in the following April, the self-revelations were resumed. The great actor was then living in retirement at Sherborne, to which he had gone on quitting the stage; and Dickens gave favourable report of his enjoyment of the change to his little holiday at Paris....

It would be unjust and uncandid not to admit that these and other similar passages in the letters that extended over the years while he lived abroad, had served in some degree as a preparation for what came after his return to England in the following year. It came with a great shock nevertheless; because it told plainly what before had never been avowed, but only hinted at more or less obscurely. The opening reference is to the reply which had been made to a previous expression of his wish for some confidences as in the old time. I give only what is strictly necessary to account for what followed, and even this with deep reluctance. "Your letter of yesterday was so kind and hearty, and sounded so gently the many chords we have touched together, that I cannot leave it unanswered, though I have not much (to any purpose) to say. My reference to 'confidences' was merely to the relief of saying a word of what has long been pent up in my mind. Poor Catherine and I are not made for each other, and there is no help for it. It is not only that she makes me uneasy and unhappy, but that I make her so too—and much more so. She is exactly what you know, in the way of being amiable and complying; but we are strangely ill-assorted for the bond there is between us. God knows she would have been a thousand times happier if she had married another kind of man, and that her avoidance of this destiny would have been at least equally good for us both. I am often cut to the heart by thinking what a pity it is, for her own sake, that I ever fell in her way; and if I were sick or disabled to-morrow, I know how sorry she would be, and how deeply grieved myself, to think how we had lost each other. But exactly the same incompatibility would arise, the moment I was well again; and nothing on earth could make her understand me, or suit us to each other. Her temperament will not go with mine. It mattered not so much when we had only ourselves to consider, but reasons have been growing since which make it all but hopeless that we should even try to struggle on. What is now befalling me I have seen steadily coming, ever since the days you remember when Mary was born; and I know too well that you cannot, and no one can, help me. Why I have even written I hardly know; but it is a miserable sort of comfort that you should be clearly aware how matters stand. The mere mention of the fact, without any complaint or blame of any sort, is a relief to my present state of spirits—and I can get this only from you, because I can speak of it to no one else." In the same tone was his rejoinder to my reply. "To the most part of what you say— Amen! You are not so tolerant as perhaps you might be of the wayward and unsettled feeling which is part (I suppose) of the tenure on which one holds an imaginative life, and which I have, as you ought to know well, often only kept down by riding over it like a dragoon— but let that go by. I make no maudlin complaint. I agree with you as to the very possible incidents, even not less bearable than mine, that might and must often occur to the married condition when it is entered into very young. I am always deeply sensible of the wonderful exercise I have of life and its highest sensations, and have said to myself for years, and have honestly and truly felt, This is the drawback to such a career, and is not to be complained of. I say it and feel it now as strongly as ever I did; and, as I told you in my last, I do not with that view put all this forward. But the years have not made it easier to bear for either of us; and, for her sake as well as mine, the wish will force itself upon me that something might be done. I know too well it is impossible. There is the fact, and that is all one can say. Nor are you to suppose that I disguise from myself what might be urged on the other side. I claim no immunity from blame. There is plenty of fault on my side, I dare say, in the way of a thousand uncertainties, caprices, and difficulties of disposition; but only one thing will alter all that, and that is, the end which alters everything."

It will not seem to most people that there was anything here which in happier circumstances might not have been susceptible of considerate adjustment; but all the circumstances were unfavourable, and the moderate middle course which the admissions in that letter might wisely have prompted and wholly justified, was unfortunately not taken. Compare what before was said of his temperament, with what is there said by himself of its defects, and the explanation will not be difficult. Every counteracting influence against the one idea which now predominated over him had been so weakened as to be almost powerless. His elder children were no longer children; his books had lost for the time the importance they formerly had over every other consideration in his life; and he had not in himself the resource that such a man, judging him from the surface, might be expected to have had. Not his genius only, but his whole nature, was too exclusively made up of sympathy for, and with, the real in its most intense form, to be sufficiently provided against failure in the realities around him. There was for him no " city of the mind " against outward ills, for inner consolation and shelter. It was in and from the actual he still stretched forward to find the freedom and satisfaction of an ideal, and by his very attempts to escape the world he was driven back into the thick of it. But what he would have sought there, it supplies to none; and to get the infinite out of anything so finite, has broken many a stout heart.

At the close of that last letter from Gadshill (5 September) was this question—"What do you think of my paying for this place, by reviving that old idea of some readings from my books. I am strongly tempted. Think of it." The reasons against it had great force, and took, in my judgment, greater from the time at which it was again proposed. The old ground of opposition remained. It was a substitution of lower for higher aims; a change to commonplace from more elevated pursuits; and it had so much of the character of a public exhibition for money as to raise, in the question of respect for his calling as a writer, a question also of respect for himself as a gentleman. This opinion, now strongly reiterated, was referred ultimately to two distinguished ladies of his acquaintance, who decided against it. Yet not without such momentary misgiving in the direction of "the stage," as pointed strongly to the danger, which, by those who took the opposite view, was most of all thought incident to the particular time of the proposal. It might be a wild exaggeration to fear that he was in danger of being led to adopt the stage as a calling, but he was certainly about to place himself within reach of not a few of its drawbacks and disadvantages. To the full extent he perhaps did not himself know, how much his eager present wish to become a public reader was but the outcome of the restless domestic discontents of the last four years; and that to indulge it, and the unsettled habits inseparable from it, was to abandon every hope of resettling his disordered home. There is nothing, in its application to so divine a genius as Shakespeare, more affecting than his expressed dislike to a profession, which, in the jealous self-watchfulness of his noble nature, he feared might hurt his mind. The long subsequent line of actors, admirable in private as in public life, and all the gentle and generous associations of the histrionic art, have not weakened the testimony of its greatest name against its less favourable influences; against the laxity of habits it may encourage; and its public manners, bred of public means, not always compatible with home felicities and duties. But, freely open as Dickens was to counsel in regard of his books, he was, for reasons formerly stated, less accessible to it on points of personal conduct; and when he had neither self-distrust nor self-denial to hold him back, he would push persistently forward to whatever object he had in view.

An occurrence of the time hastened the decision in this case. An enterprise had been set on foot for establishment of a hospital for sick children; a large old-fashioned mansion in Great Ormond Street, with spacious garden, had been fitted up with more than thirty beds; during the four or five years of its existence, outdoor and indoor relief had been afforded by it to nearly fifty thousand children, of whom thirty thousand were under five years of age; but, want of funds having threatened to arrest the merciful work, it was resolved to try a public dinner by way of charitable appeal, and for president the happy choice was made of one who had enchanted everybody with the joys and sorrows of little children. Dickens threw himself into the service heart and soul. There was a simple pathos in his address from the chair quite startling in its effect at such a meeting; and he probably never moved any audience so much as by the strong personal feeling with which he referred to the sacrifices made for the Hospital by the very poor themselves: from whom a subscription of fifty pounds, contributed in single pennies, had come to the treasurer during almost every year it had been open. The whole speech, indeed, is the best of the kind spoken by him; and two little pictures from it, one of the misery he had witnessed, the other of the remedy he had found, should not be absent from the picture of his own life.

"Some years ago, being in Scotland, I went with one of the most humane members of the most humane of professions, on a morning tour among some of the worst lodged inhabitants of the old town of Edinburgh. In the closes and wynds of that picturesque place (I am sorry to remind you what fast friends picturesqueness and typhus often are), we saw more poverty and sickness in an hour than many people would believe in, in a life. Our way lay from one to another of the most wretched dwellings, reeking with horrible odours; shut out from the sky and from the air, mere pits and dens. In a room in one of these places, where there was an empty porridge-pot on the cold hearth, a ragged woman and some ragged children crouching on the bare ground near it—and, I remember as I speak, where the very light, refracted from a high damp-stained wall outside, came in trembling, as if the fever which had shaken everything else had shaken even it—there lay, in an old egg-box which the mother had begged from a shop, a little feeble, wan, sick child. With his little wasted face, and his little hot worn hands folded over his breast, and his little bright attentive eyes, I can see him now, as I have seen him for several years, looking steadily at us. There he lay in his small frail box, which was not at all a bad emblem of the small body from which he was slowly parting—there he lay, quite quiet, quite patient, saying never a word. He seldom cried, the mother said; he seldom complained; 'he lay there, seemin' to woonder what it was a' aboot.' God knows, I thought, as I stood looking at him, he had his reasons for wondering. . . . Many a poor child, sick and neglected, I have seen since that time in London; many have I also seen most affectionately tended, in unwholesome houses and hard circumstances where recovery was impossible: but at all such times I have seen my little drooping friend in his egg-box, and he has always addressed his dumb wonder to me what it meant, and why, in the name of a gracious God, such things should be! . . . But, ladies and gentlemen," Dickens added, "such things need NOT be, and will not be, if this company, which is a drop of the life-blood of the great compassionate public heart, will only accept the means of rescue and prevention which it is mine to offer. Within a quarter of a mile of this place where I speak, stands a once courtly old house, where blooming children were born, and grew up to be men and women, and married, and brought their own blooming children back to patter up the old oak staircase which stood but the other day, and to wonder at the old oak carvings on the chimney-pieces. In the airy wards into which the old state drawing-rooms and family bedchambers of that house are now converted, are lodged such small patients that the attendant nurses look like reclaimed giantesses, and the kind medical practitioner like an amiable Christian ogre. Grouped about the little low tables in the centre of the rooms, are such tiny convalescents that they seem to be playing at having been ill. On the doll's beds are such diminutive creatures that each poor sufferer is supplied with its trays of toys: and, looking round, you may see how the little tired flushed cheek has toppled over half the brute creation on its way into the ark ; or how one little dimpled arm has mowed down (as I saw myself) the whole tin soldiery of Europe. On the walls of these rooms are graceful, pleasant, bright, childish pictures. At the beds' heads, hang representations of the figure of Him who was once a child Himself, and a poor one. But alas! reckoning up the number of beds that are there, the visitor to this Child's Hospital will find himself perforce obliged to stop at very little over thirty; and will learn, with sorrow and surprise, that even that small number, so forlornly, so miserably diminutive compared with this vast London, cannot possibly be maintained unless the Hospital be made better known. I limit myself to saying better known, because I will not believe that in a Christian community of fathers and mothers, and brothers and sisters, it can fail, being better known, to be well and richly endowed." It was a brave and true prediction. The Child's Hospital has never since known want. That night alone added greatly more than three thousand pounds to its funds, and Dickens put the crown to his good work by reading on its behalf, shortly afterwards, his *Christmas Carol*; when the sum realised, and the urgent demand that followed for a repetition of the pleasure given by the reading, bore down further opposition to the project of his engaging publicly in such readings for himself.

The Child's Hospital night was 9 February, its reading was appointed for 15 April, and, nearly a month before, renewed efforts at remonstrance had been made. "Your view of the reading matter," Dickens replied, "I still think is unconsciously taken from your own particular point. You don't seem to me to get out of yourself in considering it. A word more upon it. You are not to think I have made up my mind. If I had, why should I not say so? I find very great difficulty in doing so because of what you urge, because I know the question to be a balance of doubts, and because I most honestly feel in my innermost heart, in this matter (as in all others for years and years), the honour of the calling by which I have always stood most conscientiously. But do you quite consider that the public exhibition of oneself takes place equally, whosoever may get the money? And have you any idea that at this moment—this very time—half the public at least supposes me to be paid? My dear F., out of the twenty or five-and-twenty letters a week that I get about readings, twenty will ask at what price, or on what terms, it can be done. The only exceptions, in truth, are when the correspondent is a clergyman, or a banker, or the member for the place in question. Why at this very time half Scotland believes that I am paid for going to Edinburgh!—Here is Greenock writes to me, and asks could it be done for a hundred pounds? There is Aberdeen writes, and states the capacity of its hall, and says, though far less profitable than the very large hall in Edinburgh, is it not enough to come on for? W. answers such letters continually. (—At this place enter Beale. He called here yesterday morning, and then wrote to ask if I would see him to-day. I replied 'Yes,' so here he came in. With long preface called to know whether it was possible to arrange anything in the way of readings for this autumn—say six months. Large capital at command. Could produce partners, in such an enterprise, also with large capital. Represented such. Returns would be enormous. Would I name a sum? a minimum sum that I required to have, in any case? Would I look at it as a Fortune, and in no other point of view? I shook my head, and said, my tongue was tied on the subject for the present; I might be more communicative at another time. Exit Beale in confusion and disappointment.)—You will be happy to hear that at one on Friday, the Lord Provost, Dean of Guild, Magistrates, and Council of the ancient city of Edinburgh will wait (in procession) on their brother freeman, at the Music Hall, to give him hospitable welcome. Their brother freeman has been cursing their stars and his own, ever since the solemn notification to this effect." But very grateful, when it came, was the enthusiasm of the greeting, and welcome the gift of the silver wassail-bowl which followed the reading of the *Carol*. "I had no opportunity of asking anyone's advice in Edinburgh," he wrote on his return. "The crowd was too enormous, and the excitement in it much too great. But my determination is all but taken. I must do *something*, or I shall wear my heart away. I can see no better thing to do that is half so hopeful in itself, or half so well suited to my restless state."

What is pointed at in those last words had been taken as a ground of objection, and thus he turned it into an argument the other way. During all these months many sorrowful misunderstandings had continued in his home, and the relief sought from the misery had but the effect of making desperate any hope of a better understanding. "It becomes necessary," he wrote at the end of March, "with a view to the arrangements that would have to be begun next month if I decided on the readings, to consider and settle the question of the Plunge. Quite dismiss from your mind any reference whatever to present circumstances, at home. Nothing can put *them* right, until we are all dead and buried and risen. It is not, with me, a matter of will or trial, or sufferance, or good humour, or making the best of it, or making the worst of it, any longer. It is all despairingly over. Have no lingering hope of, or for, me in this association. A dismal failure has to be borne, and there an end. Will you then try to think of this reading project (as I do) apart from all personal likings and dislikings, and solely with a view to its effect on that particular relation (personally affectionate and like no other man's) which subsists between me and the public? I want your most careful consideration. If you would like, when you have gone over it in your mind, to discuss the matter with me and Arthur Smith (who would manage the whole of the Business, which I should never touch); we will make an appointment. But I ought to add that Arthur Smith plainly says, 'Of the immense return in money, I have no doubt. Of the Dash into the new position, however, I am not so good a judge.' I enclose you a rough note of my project, as it stands in my mind."

Mr. Arthur Smith, a man possessed of many qualities that justified the confidence Dickens placed in him, might not have been a good judge of the "Dash" into the new position, but no man knew better every disadvantage incident to it, or was less likely to be disconcerted by any. His exact fitness to manage the scheme successfully, made him an unsafe counsellor respecting it. Within a week from this time the reading for the Charity was to be given. "They have let," Dickens wrote on 9 April, "five hundred stalls for the Hospital night; and as people come every day for more, and it is out of the question to make more, they cannot be restrained at St. Martin's Hall from taking down names for other readings." This closed the attempt at further objection. Exactly a fortnight after the reading for the children's hospital, on Thursday, 29 April, came the first public reading, for his own benefit; and before the next month was over, this launch into a new life had been followed by a change in his old home. Thenceforward he and his wife lived apart. The eldest son went with his mother, Dickens at once giving effect to her expressed wish in this respect; and the other children remained with himself, their intercourse with Mrs. Dickens being left entirely to themselves. It was thus far an arrangement of a strictly private nature, and no decent person could have had excuse for regarding it in any other light, if pubic attention had not been unexpectedly invited to it by a printed statement in *Household Words*. Dickens was stung into this by some miserable gossip at which in ordinary circumstances no man would more determinedly have been silent; but he had now publicly to show himself, at stated times, as a public entertainer, and this, with his name even so aspersed, he found to be impossible. All he would concede to my strenuous resistance against such a publication, was an offer to suppress it, if, upon reference to the opinion of a certain distinguished man (still living), that opinion should prove to be in agreement with mine. Unhappily it fell in with his own, and the publication went on. It was followed by another statement, a letter subscribed with his name, which got into print without his sanction; nothing publicly being known of it (I was not among those who had read it privately) until it appeared in the *New York Tribune*. It had been addressed and given to Mr. Arthur Smith as an authority for correction of false rumours and scandals, and Mr. Smith had given a copy of it, with like intention, to the *Tribune* correspondent in London. Its writer referred to it always afterwards as his "violated letter."

The course taken by the author of this book at the time of these occurrences, will not be departed from here. Such illustration of grave defects in Dickens's character as the passage in his life affords, I have not shrunk from placing side by side with such excuses in regard to it as he had unquestionable right to claim should be put forward also. How far what remained of his story took tone or colour from it, and especially from the altered career on which at the same time he entered, will thus be sufficiently explained; and with anything else the public have nothing to do.

## III

### GADSHILL PLACE

#### 1856–70

"I was better pleased with Gadshill Place last Saturday," he wrote to me from Paris on 13 February, 1856, "on going down there, even than I had prepared myself to be. The country, against every disadvantage of season, is beautiful; and the house is so old-fashioned, cheerful, and comfortable, that it is really pleasant to look at. The good old Rector now there, has lived in it six and twenty years, so I have not the heart to turn him out. He is to remain till Lady Day next year, when I shall go in, please God; make my alterations; furnish the house; and keep it for myself that summer." Returning to England through the Kentish country with Mr. Wilkie Collins in July, other advantages occurred to him. "A railroad opened from Rochester to Maidstone, which connects Gadshill at once with the whole sea coast, is certainly an addition to the place, and an enhancement of its value. By and by we shall have the London, Chatham and Dover, too; and that will bring it within an hour of Canterbury and an hour and a half of Dover. I am glad to hear of your having been in the neighbourhood. There is no healthier (marshes avoided), and none in my eyes more beautiful. One of these days I shall show you some places up the Medway with which you will be charmed."

The association with his youthful fancy that first made the place attractive to him has been told; and it was with wonder he had heard one day, from his friend and fellow-worker at *Household Words*, Mr. W. H. Wills, that not only was the house for sale to which he had so often looked wistfully, but that the lady chiefly interested as its owner had been long known and much esteemed by himself. Such curious chances led Dickens to the saying he so frequently repeated about the smallness of the world; but the close relation often found thus existing between things and persons far apart, suggests not so much the smallness of the world as the possible importance of the least things done in it, and is better explained by the grander teaching of Carlyle, that causes and effects, connecting every man and thing with every other, extend through all space and time.

It was at the close of 1855 the negotiation for its purchase began. "They wouldn't," he wrote (25 November), "take £1700 for the Gadshill property, but 'finally' wanted £1800. I have finally offered £1750. It will require an expenditure of about £300 more before yielding £100 a year." The usual discovery of course awaited him that this first estimate would have to be increased threefold. "The changes absolutely necessary" (9 February, 1856) "will take a thousand pounds; which sum I am always resolving to squeeze out of this, grind out of that, and wring out of the other; this, that, and the other generally all three declining to come up to the scratch for the purpose." "This day," he wrote on 14 March, "I have paid the purchase-money for Gadshill Place. After drawing the cheque (1790) I turned round to give it to Wills, and said, 'Now isn't it an extraordinary thing—look at the Day—Friday! I have been nearly drawing it half a dozen times when the lawyers have not been ready, and here it comes round upon a Friday as a matter of course.' " He had no thought at this time of reserving the place wholly for himself, or of making it his own residence except at intervals of summer. He looked upon it as an investment only. "You will hardly know Gadshill again," he wrote in January 1858, "I am improving it so much— yet I have no interest in the place." But continued ownership brought increased liking; he took more and more interest in his own improvements, which were just the kind of occasional occupation and resource his life most wanted in its next seven or eight years; and any further idea of letting it he soon abandoned altogether. It only once passed out of his possession thus, for four months in 1859; in the following year, on the sale of Tavistock House, he transferred to it his books and pictures and choicer furniture; and thenceforward, varied only by houses taken from time to time for the London season, he made it his permanent family abode. Now and then, even during those years, he would talk of selling it; and on his final return from America, when he had sent the last of his sons out into the world, he really might have sold it if he could then have found a house in London suitable to him, and such as he could purchase. But in this he failed; secretly to his own satisfaction, as I believe; and thereupon, in that last autumn of his life, he projected and carried out his most costly addition to Gadshill. Already of course more money had been spent upon it than his first intention in buying it would have justified. He had so enlarged the accommodation, improved the grounds and offices, and added to the land, that, taking also into account this closing outlay, the reserved price placed upon the whole after his death more than quadrupled what he had given in 1856, for the house, shrubbery, and twenty years' lease of a meadow field. It was then purchased, and is now inhabited, by his eldest son.

Its position has been described, and a history of Rochester published a hundred years ago quaintly mentions the principal interest of the locality. "Near the twenty-seventh stone from London is Gadshill, supposed to have been the scene of the robbery mentioned by Shakespeare in his play of *Henry IV*.; there being reason to think also that it was Sir John Falstaff, of truly comic memory, who under the name of Oldcastle inhabited Cooling Castle, of which the ruins are in the neighbourhood. A small distance to the left appears on an eminence the Hermitage, the seat of the late Sir Francis Head, Bart.; and close to the road, on a small ascent, is a neat building lately erected by Mr. Day. In descending Strood Hill is a fine prospect of Strood, Rochester, and Chatham, which three towns form a continued street extending above two miles in length." It had been supposed that "the neat building lately erected by Mr. Day" was that which the great novelist made famous; but Gadshill Place had no existence until eight years after the date of the history. The good rector who so long lived in it told me, in 1859, that it had been built eighty years before by a well-known character in those parts, one Stevens, grandfather-in-law of Henslow the Cambridge professor of botany. Stevens, who could only with much difficulty manage to write his name, had begun life as ostler at an inn; had become husband to the landlord's widow; then a brewer; and finally, as he subscribed himself on one occasion, "mare" of Rochester. Afterwards the house was inhabited by Mr. Lynn (from some of the members of whose family Dickens made his purchase; and, before the Rev. Mr. Hindle became its tenant it was inhabited by a Macaroni parson named Townshend, whose horses the Prince Regent bought, throwing into the bargain a box of much desired cigars. Altogether the place had notable associations even apart from those which have connected it with the masterpieces of English humour. "THIS HOUSE, GADSHILL PLACE, stands on the summit of Shakespeare's Gadshill, ever memorable for its association with Sir John Falstaff in his noble fancy. *But, my lads, my lads, to-morrow morning, by four o'clock, early at Gadshill! there are pilgrims going to Canterbury with rich offerings, and traders riding to London with fat purses; I have vizards for you all; you have horses for yourselves.*" Illuminated by Mr. Owen Jones, and placed in a frame on the first-floor landing, these words were the greeting of the new tenant to his visitors. It was his first act of ownership. . . .

On abandoning his notion, after the American readings, of exchanging Gadshill for London, a new staircase was put up from the hill; a parquet floor laid on the first landing; and a conservatory built, opening into both drawing-room and dining-room, "glass and iron," as he described it, "brilliant but expensive, with foundations as of an ancient Roman work of horrible solidity." This last addition had long been an object of desire with him; though he would hardly even now have given himself the indulgence but for the golden shower from America. He saw it first in a completed state on the Sunday before his death, when his younger daughter was on a visit to him. "Well, Katey," he said to her, "now you see POSITIVELY the last improvement at Gadshill"; and everyone laughed at the joke against himself. The success of the new conservatory was unquestionable. It was the remark of all around him that he was certainly, from this last of his improvements, drawing more enjoyment than from any of its predecessors, when the scene for ever closed.

Of the course of his daily life in the country there is not much to be said. Perhaps there was never a man who changed places so much and habits so little. He was always methodical and regular; and passed his life from day to day, divided for the most part between working and walking, the same wherever he was. The only exception was when special or infrequent visitors were with him. When such friends as Longfellow and his daughters, or Charles Eliot Norton and his wife, came, or when Mr. Fields brought his wife and Professor Lowell's daughter, or when he received other Americans to whom he owed special courtesy, he would compress into infinitely few days an enormous amount of sight-seeing and country enjoyment, castles, cathedrals, and fortified lines, lunches and picnics among cherry orchards and hop-gardens, excursions to Canterbury or Maidstone and their beautiful neighbourhoods, Druid Stone and Blue Bell Hill. "All the neighbouring country that could be shown in so short a time," he wrote of the Longfellow visit, "they saw. I turned out a couple of postilions in the old red jackets of the old red royal Dover road for our ride, and it was like a holiday ride in England fifty years ago." For Lord Lytton he did the same, for the Emerson

Tennents, for Mr. Layard and Mr. Helps, for Lady Molesworth and the Higginses (Jacob Omnium), and such other less frequent visitors.

Excepting on such particular occasions however, and not always even then, his mornings were reserved wholly to himself; and he would generally preface his morning work (such was his love of order in everything around him) by seeing that all was in its place in the several rooms, visiting also the dogs, stables, and kitchen garden, and closing, unless the weather was very bad indeed, with a turn or two round the meadow before settling to his desk. His dogs were a great enjoyment to him; and, with his high road traversed as frequently as any in England by tramps and wayfarers of a singularly undesirable description, they were also a necessity. There were always two, of the mastiff kind, but latterly the number increased. His own favourite was Turk, a noble animal, full of affection and intelligence, whose death by a railway accident, shortly after the Staplehurst catastrophe, caused him great grief. Turk's sole companion up to that date was Linda, puppy of a great St. Bernard brought over by Mr. Albert Smith, and grown into a superbly beautiful creature. After Turk there was an interval of an Irish dog, Sultan, given by Mr. Percy Fitzgerald; a cross between a St. Bernard and a bloodhound, built and coloured like a lioness and of splendid proportions, but of such indomitably aggressive propensities, that, after breaking his kennel-chain and nearly devouring a luckless little sister of one of the servants, he had to be killed. Dickens always protested that Sultan was a Fenian, for that no dog, not a secretly sworn member of that body, would ever have made such a point, muzzled as he was, of rushing at and bearing down with fury anything in scarlet with the remotest resemblance to a British uniform. Sultan's successor was Don, presented by Mr. Frederick Lehmann, a grand Newfoundland brought over very young, who with Linda became parent to a couple of Newfoundlands, that were still gambolling about their master, huge, though hardly out of puppydom, when they lost him. He had given to one of them the name of Bumble, from having observed, as he described it, "a peculiarly pompous and overbearing manner he had of appearing to mount guard over the yard when he was an absolute infant." Bumble was often in scrapes. Describing to Mr. Fields a drought in the summer of 1868, when their poor supply of ponds and surface wells had become waterless, he wrote: "I do not let the great dogs swim in the canal, because the people have to drink of it. But when they get into the Medway, it is hard to get them out again. The other day Bumble (the son, Newfoundland dog) got into difficulties among some floating timber, and became frightened. Don (the father) was standing by me, shaking off the wet and looking on carelessly, when all of a sudden he perceived something amiss, and went in with a bound and brought Bumble out by the ear. The scientific way in which he towed him along was charming." . . .

Round Cobham, skirting the park and village, and passing the

Leather Bottle famous in the page of *Pickwick*, was a favourite walk with Dickens. By Rochester and the Medway, to the Chatham Lines, was another. He would turn out of Rochester High Street through The Vines (where some old buildings, from one of which called Restoration House he took Satis House for *Great Expectations*, had a curious attraction for him), would pass round by Fort Pitt, and coming back by Frindsbury would bring himself by some cross fields again into the high road. Or, taking the other side, he would walk through the marshes to Gravesend, return by Chalk church, and stop always to have greeting with a comical old monk who for some incomprehensible reason sits carved in stone, cross-legged with a jovial pot, over the porch of that sacred edifice. To another drearier churchyard, itself forming part of the marshes beyond the Medway, he often took friends to show them the dozen small tombstones of various sizes adapted to the respective ages of a dozen small children of one family which he made part of his story of *Great Expectations*, though, with the reserves always necessary in copying nature not to overstep her modesty by copying too closely, he makes the number that appalled little Pip not more than half the reality. About the whole of this Cooling churchyard, indeed, and the neighbouring castle ruins, there was a weird strangeness that made it one of his attractive walks in the late year or winter, when from Higham he could get to it across country over the stubble fields; and, for a shorter summer walk, he was not less fond of going round the village of Shorn and sitting on a hot afternoon in its pretty shaded churchyard. But, on the whole, though Maidstone had also much that attracted him to its neighbourhood, the Cobham neighbourhood was certainly that which he had greatest pleasure in; and he would have taken oftener than he did the walk through Cobham park and woods, which was the last he enjoyed before his life suddenly closed upon him, but that here he did not like his dogs to follow.

Don now has his home with Lord Darnley, and Linda lies under one of the cedars at Gadshill.

## IV

### 1858-9

DICKENS gave his paid public readings successively, with not long intervals, at four several dates; in 1858–9, in 1861–3, in 1866–7, and in 1868–70; the first series under Mr. Arthur Smith's management, the second under Mr. Headland's, and the third and fourth, in America as well as before and after it, under that of Mr. George Dolby, who, excepting in America, acted for the Messrs. Chappell. The references in the present chapter are to the first series only.

It began with sixteen nights at St. Martin's Hall, the first on 29 April, the last on 22 July, 1858; and there was afterwards a provincial tour of eighty-seven readings, beginning at Clifton on 2 August, ending at Brighton on 13 November, and taking in Ireland and Scotland as well as the principal English cities to which were added, in London, three Christmas readings, three in January, with two in the following month; and, in the provinces in the month of October, fourteen, beginning at Ipswich and Norwich, taking in Cambridge and Oxford, and closing with Birmingham and Cheltenham. The series had comprised altogether 125 readings when it ended on 27 October, 1859; and without the touches of character and interest afforded by his letters written while thus employed, the picture of the man would not be complete.

Here was one day's work at the opening which will show something of the fatigue they involved even at their outset. "On Friday we came from Shrewsbury to Chester; saw all right for the evening; and then went to Liverpool. Came back from Liverpool and read at Chester. Left Chester at 11 at night, after the reading, and went to London. Got to Tavistock House at 5 a.m. on Saturday, left it at a quarter past 10 that morning, and came down here" (Gadshill. 15 August, 1858).

The "greatest personal affection and respect" had greeted him everywhere. Nothing could have been "more strongly marked or warmly expressed"; and the readings had "gone" quite wonderfully. What in this respect had most impressed him, at the outset of his adventures, was Exeter. "I think they were the finest audience I ever read to; I don't think I ever read in some respects so well; and I never beheld anything like the personal affection which they poured out upon me at the end. I shall always look back upon it with pleasure." He often lost his voice in these early days, having still to acquire the art of husbanding it; and in the trial to recover it would again waste its power. "I think I sang half the Irish melodies to myself as I walked about, to test it."

An audience of two thousand three hundred people (the largest he had had) greeted him at Liverpool on his way to Dublin, and, besides the tickets sold, more than two hundred pounds in money was taken at the doors. This taxed his business staff a little. "They turned away hundreds, sold all the books, rolled on the ground of my room knee-deep in checks, and made a perfect pantomime of the whole thing." (20 August.) He had to repeat the reading thrice.

It was the first time he had seen Ireland, and Dublin greatly surprised him by appearing to be so much larger and more populous than he had supposed. He found it to have altogether an unexpectedly thriving look, being pretty nigh as big, he first thought, as Paris; of which some places in it, such as the quays on the river, reminded him. Half the first day he was there, he took to explore it; walking till tired, and then hiring a car. "Power, dressed for the character of Tedy the Tiler, drove me: in a suit of patches, and with his hat unbrushed for twenty years. Wonderfully pleasant, light, intelligent, and careless." A letter to his eldest daughter makes humorous addition. "The man who drove our jaunting car yesterday hadn't a piece in his coat as big as a penny roll . . . but he was remarkably intelligent and agreeable, with something to say about everything. When we got into the Phœnix Park, he looked round him as if it were his own, and said 'THAT'S a Park sir, av ye plase!' I complimented it, and he said 'Gintlemen tills me as they iv bin, sir, over Europe and never see a Park aqualling ov it. Yander's the Vice-regal Lodge, sir; in thim two corners lives the two Sicretaries, wishing I was thim sir. There's air here, sir, av yer plase! There's scenery here sir! There's mountains thim sir!'" The number of common people he saw in his drive, also "riding about in cars as hard as they could split," brought to his recollection a more distant scene, and but for the dresses he could have thought himself on the Toledo at Naples.

In respect of the number of his audience, and their reception of him, Dublin was one of his marked successes. He came to have some doubt of their capacity of receiving the pathetic, but of their quickness as to the humorous there could be no question, any more than of their heartiness. He got on wonderfully well with the Dublin people and the Irish girls outdid the American in one particular. He wrote to his sister-in-law. "Every night since I have been in Ireland, they have beguiled my dresser out of the bouquet from my coat; and yesterday morning, as I had showered the leaves from my geranium in reading *Little Dombey*, they mounted the platform after I was gone, and picked them all up as a keepsake." The Boots at Morrison's expressed the general feeling in a patriotic point of view. "He was waiting for me at the hotel door last night. 'Whaat sart of a hoose sur?' he asked me. 'Capital.' 'The Lard be praised fur the 'onor o' Dooblin!'" Within the hotel, on getting up next morning, he had a dialogue with a smaller resident, landlord's son he supposed, a little boy of the ripe age of six, which he presented, in his letter to his sister-in-law, as a colloquy between Old England and Young Ireland inadequately reported for want of the "imitation" it required for its full effect. "I am sitting on the sofa, writing, and find him sitting beside me.

"*Old England*. Holloa old chap.

"*Young Ireland*. Hal—loo!

"*Old England* (in his delightful way). What a nice old fellow you are. I am very fond of little boys.

"*Young Ireland*. Air yes? Ye'r right.

"*Old England*. What do you learn, old fellow?

"*Young Ireland* (very intent on Old England, and always childish except in his brogue). I lairn wureds of three sillibils—and wureds of two sillibils—and wureds of one sillibil.

"*Old England* (cheerfully). Get out, you humbug! You learn only words of one syllable.

"*Young Ireland* (laughs heartily). You may say that it is mostly wureds of one sillibil.

"*Old England*. Can you write?

"*Young Ireland*. Not yet, Things comes by deegrays.

"*Old England*. Can you cipher?

"*Young Ireland* (very quickly). Whaat's that?

"*Old England*. Can you make figures?

"*Young Ireland*. I can make a nought, which is not asy, being roond.

"*Old England*. I say, old boy! Wasn't it you I saw on Sunday morning in the hall, in a soldier's cap? You know!—In a soldier's cap?

"*Young Ireland* (cogitating deeply). Was it a very good cap?

"*Old England*. Yes.

"*Young Ireland*. Did it fit ankommon?

"*Old England*. Yes.

"*Young Ireland*. Dat was me!"

The last night in Dublin was an extraordinary scene. "You can hardly imagine it. All the way from the hotel to the Rotunda (a mile), I had to contend against the stream of people who were turned away. When I got there, they had broken the glass in the pay-boxes, and were offering £5 freely for a stall. Half of my platform had to be taken down, and people heaped in among the ruins. You never saw such a scene." "Ladies stood all night with their chins against my platform," he wrote to his daughter. "Other ladies sat all night upon my steps. We turned away people enough to make immense houses for a week." But he would not return after his other Irish engagements. "I have positively said No. The work is too hard. It is not like doing it in one easy room, and always the same room. With a different place every night, and a different audience with its own peculiarity every night, it is a tremendous strain . . . I seem to be always either in a railway carriage or reading, or going to bed; and I get so knocked up whenever I have a minute to remember it, that then I go to bed as a matter of course."

Belfast he liked quite as much as Dublin in another way. "A fine place with a rough people; everything looking prosperous; the railway ride from Dublin quite amazing in the order, neatness, and cleanness of all you see; every cottage looking as if it had been whitewashed the day before; and many with charming gardens, prettily kept with bright flowers." The success, too, was quite as great. "Enormous audiences. We turn away half the town. I think them a better audience on the whole than Dublin; and the personal affection is something overwhelming. I wish you and the dear girls" (he is writing to his sister-in-law) "could have seen the people look at me in the street; or heard them ask me, as I hurried to the hotel after the reading last night, to 'do me the honour to shake hands Misther Dickens and God bless you sir; not ounly for the light you've been to me this night, but for the light you've been in mee house sir (and God love your face!) this many a year!'" He had never seen men "go in to cry so undisguisedly," as they did at the Belfast *Dombey* reading; "and as to the *Boots* and *Mrs. Gamp* it was just one roar with me and them. For they made me laugh so, that sometimes I *could not* compose my face to go on." His greatest trial in this way however was a little later at Harrogate—"the queerest place, with the strangest people in it, leading the oddest lives of dancing, newspaper-reading, and tables d'hôte"—where he noticed, at the same reading, embodiments respectively of the tears and laughter to which he has moved his fellow-creatures so largely. "There was one gentleman at the *Little Dombey* yesterday morning" (he is still writing to his sister-in-law) "who exhibited—or rather concealed—the profoundest grief. After crying a good deal without hiding it, he covered his face with both his hands and laid it down on the back of the seat before him, and really shook with emotion. He was not in mourning, but I supposed him to have lost some child in old time. . . . There was a remarkably good fellow too, of thirty or so, who found something so very ludicrous in Toots that he *could not* compose himself at all, but laughed until he sat wiping his eyes with his handkerchief; and whenever he felt Toots coming again, he began to laugh and wipe his eyes afresh; and when Toots came once more, he gave a kind of cry, as if it were too much for him. It was uncommonly droll, and made me laugh heartily."

At Harrogate he read twice on one day (a Saturday), and had to engage a special engine to take him back that night to York, which, having reached at one o'clock in the morning, he had to leave, because of Sunday restrictions on travel, the same morning at half-past four, to enable him to fulfil a Monday's reading at Scarborough. Such fatigues became matters of course; but their effect, not noted at the time, was grave. Here again he was greatly touched by the personal greeting. "I was brought very near to what I sometimes dream may be my Fame," he wrote to me in October from York, "when a lady whose face I had never seen stopped me yesterday in the street, and said to me, *Mr. Dickens, will you let me touch the hand that has filled my house with many friends.*" . . .

The reception that awaited him at Manchester had very special warmth in it, occasioned by an adverse tone taken in the comment of one of the Manchester daily papers on the letter which by a breach of confidence had been then recently printed. "My violated letter" Dickens always called it (*ante*, 600). "When I came to Manchester on Saturday I found seven hundred stalls taken! When I went into the room at night 2500 people had paid, and more were being turned away from every door. The welcome they gave me was astounding in its affectionate recognition of the late trouble, and fairly for once unmanned me. I never saw such a sight or heard such a sound. When they had thoroughly done it, they settled down t oenjoy themselves; and certainly did enjoy themselves most heartily to the last minute." Nor, for the rest of his English tour, in any of the towns that remained, had he reason to complain of any want of hearty greeting. At Sheffield great crowds in excess of the places came. At Leeds the hall overflowed in half an hour. At Hull the vast concourse had to be addressed by Mr. Smith on the gallery stairs, and additional readings had to be given, day and night, "for the people out of town and for the people in town."

The net profit to himself, thus far, had been upwards of three hundred pounds a week; but this was nothing to the success in Scotland, where his profit in a week, with all expenses paid, was five hundred pounds. The pleasure was enhanced, too, by the presence of his two daughters, who had joined him over the Border. At first the look of Edinburgh was not promising. "We began with, for us, a poor room. . . . But the effect of that reading (it was the *Chimes*) was immense; and on the next night, for *Little Dombey*, we had a full room. It is our greatest triumph everywhere. Next night (*Poor Traveller, Boots,* and *Gamp*) we turned away hundreds upon hundreds of people; and last night, for the *Carol,* in spite of advertisements in the morning that the tickets were gone, the people had to be got in through such a crowd as rendered it a work of the utmost difficulty to keep an alley into the room. They were seated about me on the platform, put into the doorway of the waiting-room, squeezed into every conceivable place, and a multitude turned away once more. I think I am better pleased with what was done in Edinburgh than with what has been done anywhere, almost. It was so completely taken by storm, and carried in spite of itself. Mary and Katey have been infinitely pleased and interested with Edinburgh. We are just going to sit down to dinner and therefore I cut my missive short. Travelling, dinner, reading, and everything else, come crowding together into this strange life."

Then came Dundee: "An odd place," he wrote, "like Wapping, with high rugged hills behind it. We had the strangest journey here— bits of sea, and bits of railroad, alternately; which carried my mind back to travelling in America. The room is an immense new one, belonging to Lord Kinnaird, and Lord Panmure, and some others of that sort. It looks something between the Crystal Palace and Westminster Hall (I can't imagine who wants it in this place), and has never been tried yet for speaking in. Quite disinterestedly of course, I hope it will succeed." The people he thought, in respect of taste and intelligence, below any other of his Scotch audiences, but they woke up surprisingly, and the rest of his Caledonian tour was a succession of triumphs. "At Aberdeen we were crammed to the street twice in one day. At Perth (where I thought when I arrived, there literally could be nobody to come) the gentlefolk came posting in from thirty miles round, and the whole town came besides, and filled an immense hall. They were as full of perception, fire, and enthusiasm as any people I have seen. At Glasgow, where I read three evenings and one morning, we took the prodigiously large sum of six hundred pounds! And this at the Manchester prices, which are lower than St. Martin's Hall. As to the effect—I wish you could have seen them after Lilian died in the *Chimes*, or when Scrooge woke in the *Carol* and talked to the boy outside the window. And at the end of *Dombey* yesterday afternoon, in the cold light of day, they all got up, after a short pause, gentle and simple, and thundered and waved their hats with such astonishing heartiness and fondness that, for the first time in all my public career, they took me completely off my legs, and I saw the whole eighteen hundred of them reel to one side as if a shock from without had shaken the hall. Notwithstanding which, I must confess to you, I am very anxious to get to the end of my readings, and to be at home again, and able to sit down and think in my own study. There has been only one thing quite without alloy. The dear girls have enjoyed themselves immensely, and their trip with me has been a great success."

The subjects of his readings during this first circuit were the *Carol*, the *Chimes*, the *Trial in Pickwick*, the chapters containing *Paul Dombey*, *Boots at the Holly Tree Inn*, the *Poor Traveller* (Captain Doubledick), and *Mrs. Gamp*: to which he continued to restrict himself through the supplementary nights that closed in the autumn of 1859. Of these the most successful in their uniform effect upon his audiences were undoubtedly the *Carol*, the *Pickwick* scene, *Mrs. Gamp*, and the *Dombey*—the quickness, variety, and completeness of his assumption of character, having greatest scope in these. Here, I think, more than in the pathos or graver level passages, his strength lay; but this is entitled to no weight other than as an individual opinion, and his audiences gave him many reasons for thinking differently. . . .

## V

IN the interval before the close of the first circuit of readings, painful personal disputes arising out of the occurrences of the previous year were settled by the discontinuance of *Household Words*, and the establishment in its place of *All the Year Round*. The disputes turned upon matters of feeling exclusively, and involved no charge on either side that would render any detailed reference here other than gravely out of place. The question into which the difference ultimately resolved itself was that of the respective rights of the parties as proprietors of *Household Words*; and this, upon a bill filed in Chancery, was settled by a winding-up order, under which the property was sold. It was bought by Dickens, who, even before the sale, exactly fulfilling a previous announcement of the proposed discontinuance of the existing periodical and establishment of another in its place, precisely similar but under a different title, had started *All the Year Round*. It was to be regretted perhaps that he should have thought it necessary to move at all, but he moved strictly within his rights.

To the publishers first associated with his great success in literature, Messrs. Chapman and Hall, he now returned for the issue of the remainder of his books; of which he always in future reserved the copyrights, making each the subject of such arrangement as for the time might seem to him desirable. In this he was met by no difficulty; and indeed it will be only proper to add, that, in any points affecting his relations with those concerned in the production of his books, though his resentments were easily and quickly roused, they were never very lasting. The only fair rule therefore was, in a memoir of his life, to confine the mention of such things to what was strictly necessary to explain its narrative. This accordingly has been done; and, in the several disagreements it has been necessary to advert to, I cannot charge myself with having in a single instance overstepped the rule. Objection has been made to my revival of the early differences with Mr. Bentley. But silence respecting them was incompatible with what absolutely required to be said, if the picture of Dickens in his most interesting time, at the outset of his career in letters, was not to be omitted altogether; and, suppressing everything of mere temper that gathered round the dispute, use was made of those letters only containing the young writer's urgent appeal to be absolved, rightly or wrongly, from engagements he had too precipitately entered into. Wrongly, some might say, because the law was undoubtedly on Mr. Bentley's side; but all subsequent reflection has confirmed the view I was led strongly to take at the time, that in the facts there had come to be involved what the law could not afford to overlook, and that the sale of brain-work can never be adjusted by agreement with the same exactness and certainty as that of ordinary goods and chattels. Quitting the subject once for all with this remark, it is not less incumbent on me to say that there was no stage of the dispute in which Mr. Bentley, holding as strongly the other view, might not think it to have sufficient justification; and certainly in later years there was no absence of friendly feeling on the part of Dickens to his old publisher. This already has been mentioned; and on the occasion of Hans Andersen's recent visit to Gadshill, Mr. Bentley was invited to meet the celebrated Dane. Nor should I omit to say, that, in the year to which this narrative has now arrived, his prompt compliance with an intercession made to him for a common friend pleased Dickens greatly.

At the opening of 1859, bent upon such a successor to *Household Words* as should carry on the associations connected with its name, Dickens was deep in search of a title to give expression to them. "My determination to settle the title arises out of my knowledge that I shall never be able to do anything for the work until it has a fixed name; also out of my observation that the same odd feeling affects everybody else." He had proposed to himself a title that, as in *Household Words*, might be capable of illustration by a line from Shakespeare; and alighting upon that wherein poor Henry the Sixth is fain to solace his captivity by the fancy, that, like birds encaged he might soothe himself for loss of liberty "at last by notes of household harmony," he for the time forgot that this might hardly be accepted as a happy comment on the occurrences out of which the supposed necessity had arisen of replacing the old by a new household friend. "Don't you think," he wrote on 24 January, "this is a good name and quotation? I have been quite delighted to get hold of it for our title.

### "HOUSEHOLD HARMONY.

#### 'At last by notes of Household Harmony.'—*Shakespeare*."

He was at first reluctant even to admit the objection when stated to him. "I am afraid we must not be too particular about the possibility of personal references and applications: otherwise it is manifest that I never can write another book. I could not invent a story of any sort, it is quite plain, incapable of being twisted into some such nonsensical shape. It would be wholly impossible to turn one through half a dozen chapters." Of course he yielded, nevertheless; and much consideration followed over sundry other titles submitted. Reviving none of those formerly rejected, here were a few of these now rejected in their turn. THE HEARTH. THE FORGE. THE CRUCIBLE. THE ANVIL

OF THE TIME. CHARLES DICKENS'S OWN. SEASONABLE LEAVES.
EVERGREEN LEAVES. HOME. HOME-MUSIC. CHANGE. TIME AND
TIDE. TWOPENCE. ENGLISH BELLS. WEEKLY BELLS. THE ROCKET.
GOOD HUMOUR. Still the great want was the line adaptable from
Shakespeare, which at last exultingly he sent on 28 January. "I am
dining early, before reading, and write literally with my mouth full.
But I have just hit upon a name that I think really an admirable
one—especially with the quotation *before* it, in the place where our
present *H. W.* quotation stands.

" ' The story of our lives, from year to year.'—*Shakespeare*.

ALL THE YEAR ROUND.

A weekly journal conducted by Charles Dickens."

With the same resolution and energy other things necessary to the
adventure were as promptly done. "I have taken the new office,"
he wrote from Tavistock House on 21 February; "have got workmen
in; have ordered the paper; settled with the printer; and am getting
an immense system of advertising ready. Blow to be struck on the
12th of March. . . . Meantime I cannot please myself with the
opening of my story" (the *Tale of Two Cities*, which *All the Year
Round* was to start with), "and cannot in the least settle at it or take
to it. . . . I wish you would come and look at what I flatter myself
is a rather ingenious account to which I have turned the Stanfield
scenery here." He had placed the *Lighthouse* scene in a single frame;
had divided the scene of the *Frozen Deep* into two subjects, a British
man-of-war and an Arctic sea, which he had also framed; and the
schoolroom that had been the theatre was now hung with sea-pieces
by a great painter of the sea. To believe them to have been but the
amusement of a few mornings was difficult indeed. Seen from the
due distance there was nothing wanting to the most masterly and
elaborate art.

The first number of *All the Year Round* appeared on 30 April, and
the result of the first quarter's accounts of the sale will tell everything that needs to be said of a success that went on without inter-
mission to the close. "A word before I go back to Gadshill," he wrote
from Tavistock House in July, "which I know you will be glad to
receive. So well has *All the Year Round* gone that it was yesterday
able to repay me, with five per cent. interest, all the money I
advanced for its establishment (paper, print etc. all paid, down to the
last number), and yet to leave a good £500 balance at the banker's!"
Beside the opening of his *Tale of Two Cities* its first number had contained another piece of his writing, the "Poor Man and his Beer";
as to which an interesting note has been sent me. The Rev. T. B.
Lawes, of Rothamsted, St. Albans, had been associated upon a
sanitary commission with Mr. Henry Austin, Dickens's brother-in-
law and counsellor in regard to all such matters in his own houses,

or in the houses of the poor; and this connection led to Dickens's knowledge of a club that Mr. Lawes had established at Rothamsted, which he became eager to recommend as an example to other country neighbourhoods. The club had been set on foot to enable the agricultural labourers of the parish to have their beer and pipes independent of the public-house; and the description of it, says Mr. Lawes, "was the occupation of a drive between this place (Rothamsted) and London, twenty-five miles, Mr. Dickens refusing the offer of a bed, and saying that he could arrange his ideas on the journey. In the course of our conversation I mentioned that the labourers were very jealous of the small tradesmen, blacksmiths and others, holding allotment-gardens; but that the latter did so indirectly by paying higher rents to the labourers for a share. This circumstance is not forgotten in the verses on the Blacksmith in the same number, composed by Mr. Dickens and repeated to me while he was walking about, and which close the mention of his gains with allusion to

> A share (concealed) in the poor man's field,
> Which adds to the poor man's store."

It is pleasant to be able to add that the club was still flourishing when I received Mr. Lawes's letter, on 18 December, 1871.

The periodical thus established was in all respects, save one, so exactly the counterpart of what it replaced, that a mention of this point of difference is the only description of it called for. Besides his own three-volume stories of the *Tale of Two Cities* and *Great Expectations*, Dickens admitted into it other stories of the same length by writers of character and name, of which the authorship was avowed. It published tales of varied merit and success by Mr. Edmund Yates, Mr. Percy Fitzgerald, and Mr. Charles Lever. Mr. Wilkie Collins contributed to it his *Woman in White*, *No Name*, and *Moonstone*, the first of which had a pre-eminent success; Mr. Reade his *Hard Cash*; and Lord Lytton his *Strange Story*. Conferring about the latter Dickens passed a week at Knebworth, accompanied by his daughter and sister-in-law, in the summer of 1861, as soon as he had closed *Great Expectations*; and there met Mr. Arthur Helps, with whom and Lord Orford he visited the so-called "Hermit" near Stevenage, whom he described as Mr. Mopes in *Tom Tiddler's Ground*. With his great brother-artist he thoroughly enjoyed himself, as he invariably did; and reported him as "in better health and spirits than I have seen him in, in all these years—a little weird occasionally regarding magic and spirits, but always fair and frank under opposition. He was brilliantly talkative, anecdotical, and droll; he looked young and well; laughed heartily; and enjoyed with great zest some games we played. In his artist-character and talk, he was full of interest and matter, saying the subtlest and finest things—but that he never fails in. I enjoyed myself immensely, as we all did."

In *All the Year Round*, as in its predecessor, the tales for Christmas were of course continued, but with a surprisingly increased popularity; and Dickens never had such sale for any of his writings as for his Christmas pieces in the latter periodical. It had reached before he died, to nearly three hundred thousand. The first was called the *Haunted House*, and had a small mention of a true occurrence in his boyhood which is not included in the bitter record on a former page. "I was taken home, and there was debt at home as well as death, and we had a sale there. My own little bed was so superciliously looked upon by a power unknown to me hazily called The Trade, that a brass coal-scuttle, a roasting-jack, and a bird-cage were obliged to be put into it to make a lot of it, and then it went for a song. So I heard mentioned, and I wondered what song, and thought what a dismal song it must have been to sing!" The other subjects will have mention in another chapter. . . .

The *Uncommercial Traveller* papers, his two serial stories, and his Christmas tales, were all the contributions of any importance made by Dickens to *All the Year Round*; but he reprinted in it, on the completion of his first story, a short tale called *Hunted Down*, written for a newspaper in America called the *New York Ledger*. . . .

## VI

### SECOND SERIES OF READINGS

### 1861-3

AT the end of the first year of residence at Gadshill it was the remark of Dickens that nothing had gratified him so much as the confidence with which his poorer neighbours treated him. He had tested generally their worth and good conduct, and they had been encouraged in any illness or trouble to resort to him for help. There was pleasant indication of the feeling thus awakened, when, in the summer of 1860, his younger daughter Kate was married to Charles Alston Collins, brother of the novelist, and younger son of the painter and academician, who might have found, if spared to witness that summer morning scene, subjects not unworthy of his delightful pencil in many a rustic group near Gadshill. All the villagers had turned out in honour of Dickens, and the carriages could hardly get to and from the little church for the succession of triumphal arches they had to pass through. It was quite unexpected by him; and when the *feu de joie* of the blacksmith in the lane, whose enthusiasm had smuggled a couple of small cannon into his forge, exploded upon him at the return, I doubt if the shyest of men was ever so taken aback at an ovation. . . .

The first portion of this second series was planned by Mr. Arthur

Smith, but he only superintended the six readings in London which opened it. These were the first at St. James's Hall (St. Martin's Hall having been burnt since the last readings there), and were given in March and April 1861. "We are all well here and flourishing," he wrote to me from Gadshill on 28 April. "On the 18th I finished the readings as I purposed. We had between seventy and eighty pounds *in the stalls*, which, at four shillings apiece, is something quite unprecedented in these times. . . . The result of the six was, that, after paying a large staff of men and all other charges, and Arthur Smith's ten per cent. on the receipts, and replacing everything destroyed in the fire at St. Martin's Hall (including all our tickets, country baggage, check-boxes, books, and a quantity of gas-fittings and what not), I got upwards of £500. A very great result. We certainly might have gone on through the season, but I am heartily glad to be concentrated on my story."

It had been part of his plan that the provincial readings should not begin until a certain interval after the close of his story of *Great Expectations*. They were delayed accordingly until 28 October, from which date, when they opened at Norwich, they went on with the Christmas intervals to be presently named to 30 January, 1862, when they closed at Chester. Kept within England and Scotland, they took in the border town of Berwick, and, besides the Scotch cities, comprised the contrasts and varieties of Norwich and Lancaster, Bury St. Edmunds and Cheltenham, Carlisle and Hastings, Plymouth and Birmingham, Canterbury and Torquay, Preston and Ipswich, Manchester and Brighton, Colchester and Dover, Newcastle and Chester. They were followed by ten readings at the St. James's Hall, between 13 March and 27 June, 1862; and by four at Paris in January 1863, given at the Embassy in aid of the British Charitable Fund. The second series had thus in the number of the readings nearly equalled the first, when it closed at London in June 1863 with thirteen readings in the Hanover Square Rooms; and it is exclusively the subject of such illustrations or references as this chapter will supply.

On *Great Expectations* closing in June 1861, Bulwer Lytton, at Dickens's earnest wish, took his place in *All the Year Round* with the *Strange Story*; and he then indulged himself in idleness for a little while. "The subsidence of those distressing pains in my face the moment I had done my work, made me resolve to do nothing in that way for some time if I could help it." But his "doing nothing" was seldom more than a figure of speech, and what it meant in this case was soon told. "Every day for two or three hours, I practise my new readings, and (except in my office work) do nothing else. With great pains I have made a continuous narrative out of *Copperfield*, that I think will reward the exertion it is likely to cost me. Unless I am much mistaken, it will be very valuable in London. I have also done Nicholas Nickleby at the Yorkshire school, and hope I have got something droll out of Squeers, John Browdie, & Co. Also, the Bastille prisoner from the *Tale of Two Cities*. Also, the Dwarf from

one of our Christmas numbers." Only the first two were added to the
list for the present circuit. . . .

His mention of Newcastle, which he had taken on his way to
Edinburgh, reading two nights there, should be given. "At Newcastle,
against the very heavy expenses, I made more than a hundred guineas
profit. A finer audience there is not in England, and I suppose them to
be a specially earnest people; for, while they can laugh till they shake
the roof, they have a very unusual sympathy with what is pathetic
or passionate. An extraordinary thing occurred on the second night.
The room was tremendously crowded and my gas-apparatus fell down.
There was a terrible wave among the people for an instant, and God
knows what destruction of life a rush to the stairs would have caused.
Fortunately a lady in the front of the stalls ran out towards me,
exactly in a place where I knew that the whole hall could see her. So
I addressed her, laughing, and half-asked and half-ordered her to sit
down again; and, in a moment, it was all over. But the men in attendance had such a fearful sense of what might have happened (besides
the real danger of Fire) that they positively shook the boards I
stood on, with their trembling, when they came up to put things
right. I am proud to record that the gasman's sentiment, as delivered
afterwards, was, 'The more you want of the master, the more you'll
find in him.' With which complimentary homage, and with the wind
blowing so that I can hardly hear myself write, I conclude." . . .

Two brief extracts from letters will sufficiently describe the
London readings. "The money returns have been quite astounding.
Think of £190 a night! The effect of *Copperfield* exceeds all the expectations which its success in the country led me to form. It seems to
take people entirely by surprise. If this is not new to you, I have not
a word of news. The rain that raineth every day seems to have washed
news away or got it under water." That was in April. In June he
wrote: "I finished my readings on Friday night to an enormous hall—
nearly £200. The success has been throughout complete. It seems
almost suicidal to leave off with the town so full, but I don't like to
depart from my public pledge. A man from Australia is in London
ready to pay £10,000 for eight months there. If——" It was an If
that troubled him for some time, and led to agitating discussion. . . .
It closed at once when he clearly saw that to take any of his family
with him, and make satisfactory arrangements for the rest during
such an absence, would be impossible. By this time also he began to
find his way to the new story, and better hopes and spirits had
returned. . . .

## VII

THE sudden death of Thackeray on the Christmas eve of 1863 was a painful shock to Dickens. It would not become me to speak, when he has himself spoken, of his relations with so great a writer and so old a friend.

"I saw him first, nearly twenty-eight years ago, when he proposed to become the illustrator of my earliest book. I saw him last, shortly before Christmas, at the Athenæum Club, when he told me that he had been in bed three days ... and that he had it in his mind to try a new remedy which he laughingly described. He was cheerful, and looked very bright. In the night of that day week, he died. The long interval between these two periods is marked in my remembrance of him by many occasions when he was extremely humorous, when he was irresistibly extravagant, when he was softened and serious, when he was charming with children. . . . No one can be surer than I, of the greatness and goodness of his heart. . . . In no place should I take it upon myself at this time to discourse of his books, of his refined knowledge of character, of his subtle acquaintance with the weaknesses of human nature, of his delightful playfulness as an essayist, of his quaint and touching ballads, of his mastery over the English language. . . . But before me lies all that he had written of his latest story . . . and the pain I have felt in perusing it has not been deeper than the conviction that he was in the healthiest vigour of his powers when he worked on this last labour. . . . The last words he corrected in print were ' And my heart throbbed with an exquisite bliss.' God grant that on that Christmas Eve when he laid his head back on his pillow and threw up his arms as he had been wont to do when very weary, some consciousness of duty done, and of Christian hope throughout life humbly cherished, may have caused his own heart so to throb, when he passed away to his Redeemer's rest. He was found peacefully lying as above described, composed, undisturbed, and to all appearance asleep." *

Other griefs were with Dickens at this time, and close upon them came the too certain evidence that his own health was yielding to the overstrain which had been placed upon it by the occurrences and anxieties of the few preceding years. His mother, whose infirm health had been tending for more than two years to the close, died in September 1863; and on his own birthday in the following February

* From the *Cornhill Magazine* for February 1864.

he had tidings of the death of his second son Walter, on the last day of the old year, in the officers' hospital at Calcutta; to which he had been sent up invalided from his station, on his way home. He was a lieutenant in the 26th Native Infantry regiment, and had been doing duty with the 42nd Highlanders. . . .

The old year ended and the new one opened sadly enough. The death of Leech in November affected Dickens very much, and a severe attack of illness in February put a broad mark between his past life and what remained to him of the future. The lameness now began in his left foot which never afterwards wholly left him, which was attended by great suffering, and which baffled experienced physicians. He had persisted in his ordinary exercise during heavy snowstorms, and to the last he had the fancy that the illness was merely local. But that this was an error is now certain; and it is more than probable that if the nervous danger and disturbance it implied had been correctly appreciated at the time, its warning might have been of priceless value to Dickens. Unhappily he never thought of husbanding his strength except for the purpose of making fresh demands upon it, and it was for this he took a brief holiday in France during the summer. "Before I went away," he wrote to his daughter, "I had certainly worked myself into a damaged state. But the moment I got away, I began, thank God, to get well. I hope to profit by this experience, and to make future dashes from my desk before I want them." At his return he was in the terrible railway accident at Staplehurst, on a day which proved afterwards more fatal to him; and it was with shaken nerves but unsubdued energy he resumed the labour to be presently described. He was beset by nervous apprehensions which the accident had caused to himself, not lessened by his generous anxiety to assuage the severer sufferings inflicted by it on others; his foot also troubled him more or less throughout the autumn; and that he should nevertheless have determined, on the close of his book, to undertake a series of readings involving greater strain and fatigue than any hitherto, was a startling circumstance. He had perhaps become conscious, without owning it even to himself, that for exertion of this kind the time left him was short; but, whatever pressed him on, his task of the next three years, self-imposed, was to make the most money in the shortest time without any regard to the physical labour to be undergone. The very letter announcing his new engagement shows how entirely unfit he was to enter upon it.

"For some time," he wrote at the end of February 1866, "I have been very unwell. F. B. wrote me word that with such a pulse as I described, an examination of the heart was absolutely necessary. 'Want of muscular power in the heart,' B. said. 'Only remarkable irritability of the heart,' said Doctor Brinton of Brook Street, who had been called into consultation. I was not disconcerted; for I knew well beforehand that the effect could not possibly be without the one cause at the bottom of it, of some degeneration of some function of the heart. Of course I am not so foolish as to suppose that all my work can have been achieved without *some* penalty, and I have noticed for some time a decided change in my buoyancy and hopefulness—in other words, in my usual 'tone.' But tonics have already brought me round. So I have accepted an offer, from Chappells of Bond Street, of £50 a night for thirty nights to read 'in England, Ireland, Scotland, or Paris'; they undertaking all the business, paying all personal expenses, travelling and otherwise, of myself, John" (his office servant) "and my gasman; and making what they can of it. . . ."

The success everywhere went far beyond even the former successes. A single night at Manchester, when eight hundred stalls were let, two thousand five hundred and sixty-five people admitted, and the receipts amounted to more than three hundred pounds, was followed in nearly the same proportion by all the greater towns; and on 20 April the outlay for the entire venture was paid, leaving all that remained, to the middle of the month of June, sheer profit. . . .

One memorable evening he had passed at my house in the interval, when he saw Mrs. Carlyle for the last time. Her sudden death followed shortly after, and near the close of April he had thus written to me from Liverpool. "It was a terrible shock to me, and poor dear Carlyle has been in my mind ever since. How often I have thought of the unfinished novel. No one now to finish it. None of the writing women come near her at all." This was an allusion to what had passed at their meeting. It was on 2 April, the day when Mr. Carlyle had delivered his inaugural address as Lord Rector of Edinburgh University, and a couple of ardent words from Professor Tyndall had told her of the triumph just before dinner. She came to us flourishing the telegram in her hand, and the radiance of her enjoyment of it was upon her all the night. Among other things she gave Dickens the subject for a novel, from what she had herself observed at the outside of a house in her street; of which the various incidents were drawn from the condition of its blinds and curtains, the costumes visible at its windows, the cabs at its door, its visitors admitted or rejected, its articles of furniture delivered or carried away; and the subtle serious humour of it all, the truth in trifling bits of character, and the gradual progress into a half-romantic interest, had enchanted the skilled novelist. She was well into the second volume of her small romance before she left, being as far as her observation then had taken her; but in a few days exciting incidents were expected, the denouement could not be far off, and Dickens was to have it when they met again. Yet it was to something far other than this amusing little fancy his thoughts had carried him, when he wrote of no one being capable to finish what she might have begun. In greater things this was still more true. None could doubt it who had come within the fascinating influence of that sweet and noble nature. With some of the highest gifts of intellect, and the charm of a most varied knowledge of books and things, there was something " beyond, beyond." No one who knew Mrs. Carlyle could replace her loss when she had passed away.

The same letter which told of his uninterrupted success to the last, told me also that he had a heavy cold upon him, and was "very tired and depressed." Some weeks before the first batch of readings closed, Messrs. Chappell had already tempted him with an offer for fifty more nights to begin at Christmas, for which he meant, as he then said, to ask them seventy pounds a night. "It would be unreasonable to ask anything now on the ground of the extent of the late success, but I am bound to look to myself for the future. The Chappells are speculators, though of the worthiest and most honourable kind. They make some bad speculations, and have made a very good one in this case, and will set this against those. I told them when we agreed: 'I offer these thirty readings to you at fifty pounds a night, because I know perfectly well beforehand that no one in your business has the least idea of their real worth, and I wish to prove it.' The sum taken is £4720." The result of the fresh negotiation, though not completed until the beginning of August, may be at once described. "Chappell instantly accepts my proposal of forty nights at sixty pounds a night, and every conceivable and inconceivable expense paid. To make an even sum, I have made it forty-two nights for £2500. So I shall now try to discover a Christmas number [he means the subject for one], and shall, please Heaven, be quit of the whole series of readings so as to get to work on a new story for our proposed new series of *All the Year Round* early in the spring. The readings begin probably with the New Year." These were fair designs, but the fairest are the sport of circumstance, and though the subject for Christmas was found, the new series of *All the Year Round* never had a new story from its founder. With whatever consequence to himself the strong tide of the readings was to sweep on to its full. The American war had ceased, and the first renewed offers from the States had been made and rejected. Hovering over all, too, were other sterner dispositions. "I think," he wrote in September, "there is some strange influence in the atmosphere. Twice last week I was seized in a most distressing manner—apparently in the heart; but, I am persuaded, only in the nervous system."

In the midst of his ovations such checks had not been wanting. "The police reported officially," he wrote to his daughter from Liverpool on 14 April, "that three thousand people were turned away from the hall last night. . . . Except that I can *not* sleep, I really think myself in very much better training than I had anticipated. A dozen oysters and a little champagne between the parts every night, seem to constitute the best restorative I have ever yet tried." "Such a prodigious demonstration last night at Manchester," he wrote to the same correspondent twelve days later, "that I was obliged (contrary to my principle in such cases) to go back. I am very tired to-day; for it would be of itself very hard work in that immense place, if there were not to be added eighty miles of railway and late hours to boot." "It has been very heavy work," he wrote to his sister-in-law on 11 May from Clifton, "getting up at 6.30 each morning after a heavy night, and I am not at all well to-day. We had a tremendous hall at Birmingham last night, £230 odd, 2,100 people; and I made a most ridiculous mistake. Had *Nickleby* on my list to finish with, instead of *Trial*. Read *Nickleby* with great go, *and the people remained*. Went back again at 10 o'clock, and explained the accident: but said if they liked I would give them the *Trial*. They *did* like;—and I had another half-hour of it, in that enormous place. . . . I have so severe a pain in the ball of my left eye that it makes it hard for me to do anything after 100 miles' shaking since breakfast. My cold is no better, nor my hand either." It was his left eye, it will be noted, as it was his left foot and hand; the irritability or faintness of heart was also of course on the left side; and it was on the same left side he felt most of the effect of the railway accident.

Everything was done to make easier the labour of travel, but nothing could materially abate either the absolute physical exhaustion, or the nervous strain. "We arrived here," he wrote from Aberdeen (16 May), "safe and sound between 3 and 4 this morning. There was a compartment for the men, and a charming room for ourselves furnished with sofas and easy chairs. We had also a pantry and washing-stand. This carriage is to go about with us." Two days later he wrote from Glasgow. "We halted at Perth yesterday, and got a lovely walk there. Until then I had been in a condition the reverse of flourishing; half strangled with my cold, and dyspeptically gloomy and dull; but, as I feel much more like myself this morning, we are going to get some fresh air aboard a steamer on the Clyde." The last letter during his country travel was from Portsmouth on 24 May, and contained these words: "You need have no fear about America."

\*          \*          \*          \*

The letter which told me of the close of his English readings [in the following year] had in it no word of the further enterprise, yet it seemed to be in some sort a preparation for it. "Last Monday evening" (14 May) "I finished the 50 readings with great success. You have no idea how I have worked at them. Finding it necessary, as their reputation widened, that they should be better than at first, I have *learnt them all*, so as to have no mechanical drawback in looking after the words. I have tested all the serious passion in them by everything I know; made the humorous points much more humorous; corrected my utterance of certain words; cultivated a self-possession not to be disturbed; and made myself master of the situation. Finishing with *Dombey* (which I had not read for a long time), I learnt that, like the rest; and did it to myself, often twice a day, with exactly the same pains as at night, over and over and over again. . . ." Six days later brought his reply to a remark, that no degree of excellence to which he might have brought his readings could reconcile me to what there was little doubt would soon be pressed upon him. "It is curious" (20 May) "that you should touch the American subject, because I must confess that my mind is in a most disturbed state about it. That the people there have set themselves on having the readings, there is no question. Every mail brings me proposals, and the number of Americans at St. James's Hall has been surprising. A certain Mr. Grau, who took Ristori out, and is highly responsible, wrote to me by the last mail (for the second time) saying that if I would give him a word of encouragement he would come over immediately and arrange on the boldest terms for any number I chose, and would deposit a large sum of money at Coutts's. Mr. Fields writes to me on behalf of a committee of private gentlemen at Boston who wished for the credit of getting me out, who desired to hear the readings and did not want profit, and would put down as a guarantee £10,000—also to be banked here. Every American speculator who comes to London repairs straight to Dolby, with similar proposals. And, thus excited, Chappells, the moment this last series was over, proposed to treat for America!" Upon the mere question of these various offers he had little difficulty in making up his mind. If he went at all, he would go on his own account, making no compact with anyone. Whether he should go at all, was what he had to determine.

One thing with his usual sagacity he saw clearly enough. He must make up his mind quickly. "The Presidential election would be in the autumn of next year. They are a people whom a fancy does not hold long. They are bent upon my reading there, and they believe (on no foundation whatever) that I am going to read there. If I ever go, the time would be when the Christmas number goes to press. . . ."

Then there came that which should have availed to dissuade, far more than any of the arguments which continued to express my objection to the enterprise. "I am laid up," he wrote on 6 August, "with another attack in my foot, and was on the sofa all last night in tortures. I cannot bear to have the fomentations taken off for a moment. I was so ill with it on Sunday, and it looked so fierce, that I came up to Henry Thompson. He has gone into the case heartily, and says that there is no doubt the complaint originates in the action of the shoe, in walking, on an enlargement in the nature of a bunion. Erysipelas has supervened upon the injury; and the object is to avoid a gathering, and to stay the erysipelas where it is. Meantime I am on my back and chafing. . . . I didn't improve my foot by going down to Liverpool to see Dolby off, but I have little doubt of its yielding to treatment, and repose." A few days later he was chafing still; the accomplished surgeon he consulted having dropped other hints that somewhat troubled him. "I could not walk a quarter of a mile to-night for £500. I make out so many reasons against supposing it to be gouty that I really do not think it is."

So momentous in my judgment were the consequences of the American journey to him that it seemed right to preface thus much of the inducements and temptations that led to it. My own part in the discussion was that of steady dissuasion throughout: though this might perhaps have been less persistent if I could have reconciled myself to the belief, which I never at any time did, that public readings were a worthy employment for a man of his genius. But it had by this time become clear to me that nothing could stay the enterprise. . . .

The remaining time was given to preparations; on 2 November there was a Farewell Banquet in the Freemasons' Hall over which Lord Lytton presided; and on the 9th Dickens sailed for Boston.

# BOOK NINTH

## AMERICA REVISITED

1867–8.  ÆT. 55–6

# I

## 1867

IT is the intention of this and the following chapter to narrate the incidents of the visit to America in Dickens's own language, and in that only. They will consist almost exclusively of extracts from his letters written home, to members of his family and to myself.

On the night of Tuesday, 19 November, he arrived at Boston, where he took up his residence at the Parker House Hotel; and his first letter (21st) stated that the tickets for the first four readings, all to that time issued, had been sold immediately on their becoming saleable. "An immense train of people waited in the freezing street for twelve hours, and passed into the office in their turns, as at a French theatre. The receipts already taken for these nights exceed our calculation by more than £250." Up to the last moment, he had not been able to clear off wholly a shade of misgiving that some of the old grudges might make themselves felt; but from the instant of his setting foot in Boston not a vestige of such fear remained. The greeting was to the full as extraordinary as that of twenty-five years before, and was given now, as then, to the man who had made himself the most popular writer in the country. . . .

He had written, the day before he left, that he was making a clear profit of thirteen hundred pounds English a week, even allowing seven dollars to the pound; but words were added having no good omen in them, that the weather was taking a turn of even unusual severity, and that he found the climate, in the suddenness of its changes, "and the wide leaps they take," excessively trying. "The work is of course rather trying too; but the sound position that everything must be subservient to it enables me to keep aloof from invitations. To-morrow," ran the close of the letter, "we move to New York. We cannot beat the speculators in our tickets. We sell no more than six to any one person for the course of four readings; but these speculators, who sell at greatly increased prices and make large profits, will employ any number of men to buy. One of the chief of them—now living in this house, in order that he may move as we move!—can put on 50 people in any place we go to; and thus he gets 300 tickets into his own hands." Almost while Dickens was writing these words an eyewitness was describing to a Philadelphia paper the sale of the New York tickets. The pay-place was to open at nine on a Wednesday morning, and at midnight of Tuesday a long line of speculators were assembled in queue; at two in the morning a few honest buyers had begun to arrive; at five there were, of all classes, two lines of not less than 800 each; at eight there were at least 5000 persons in the two lines; at nine each line was more than three-quarters of a mile in length, and neither became sensibly shorter during the whole morning. "The tickets for the course were all sold before noon. Members of families relieved each other in the queues; waiters flew across the streets and squares from the neighbouring restaurant, to serve parties who were taking their breakfast in the open December air; while excited men offered five and ten dollars for the mere permission to exchange places with other persons standing nearer the head of the line!"

The effect of the reading in New York corresponded with this marvellous preparation, and Dickens characterised his audience as an unexpected support to him; in its appreciation quick and unfailing, and highly demonstrative in its satisfactions. On 11 December he wrote to his daughter: ". . . We have not yet had in it less than £430 per night, allowing for the depreciated currency! I send £3000 to England by this packet. From all parts of the States, applications and offers continually come in. We go to Boston next Saturday for two more readings, and come back here on Christmas Day for four more. I am not yet bound to go elsewhere, except three times, each time for two nights, to Philadelphia; thinking it wisest to keep free for the largest places. I have had an action brought against me by a man who considered himself injured (and really may have been) in the matter of his tickets. Personal service being necessary, I was politely waited on by a marshal for that purpose; whom I received with the greatest courtesy, apparently very much to his amazement. The action was handsomely withdrawn next day, and the plaintiff paid his own costs. . . ."

The time had now come when the course his readings were to take independently of the two leading cities must be settled, and the general tour made out. His agents' original plan was that they should be in New York every week. "But I say No. By the 10th of January I shall have read to 35,000 people in that city alone. Put the readings out of the reach of all the people behind them, for the time. It is that one of the popular peculiarities which I most particularly notice, that they must not have a thing too easily. Nothing in the country lasts long; and a thing is prized the more, the less easy it is made. Reflecting therefore that I shall want to close, in April, with farewell readings here and in New York, I am convinced that the crush and pressure upon these necessary to their adequate success is only to be got by absence; and that the best thing I can do is not to give either city as much reading as it wants now, but to be independent of both while both are most enthusiastic. . . ."

An incident at Boston should have mention before he resumes his readings in New York. In the interval since he was first in America, the Harvard professor of chemistry, Dr. Webster, whom he had at that visit met among the honoured men who held chairs in their Cambridge University, had been hanged for the murder, committed in his laboratory in the college, of a friend who had lent him money, portions of whose body lay concealed under the lid of the lecture-room table where the murderer continued to meet his students. "Being in Cambridge," Dickens wrote to Lord Lytton, "I thought I would go over the Medical School, and see the exact localities where Professor Webster did that amazing murder, and worked so hard to rid himself of the body of the murdered man. (I find there is of course no rational doubt that the Professor was always a secretly cruel man.) They were horribly grim, private, cold, and quiet; the identical furnace smelling fearfully (some anatomical broth in it I suppose) as if the body were still there; jars of pieces of sour mortality standing about, like the forty robbers in *Ali Baba* after being scalded to death; and bodies near us ready to be carried in to next morning's lecture. At the house where I afterwards dined I heard an amazing and fearful story; told by one who had been at a dinner-party of ten or a dozen, at Webster's, less than a year before the murder. They began rather uncomfortably, in consequence of one of the guests (the victim of an instinctive antipathy) starting up with the sweat pouring down his face, and crying out, 'O Heaven! There's a cat somewhere in the room!' The cat was found and ejected, but they didn't get on very well. Left with their wine, they were getting on a little better; when Webster suddenly told the servants to turn the gas off and bring in that bowl of burning minerals which he had prepared, in order that the company might see how ghastly they looked by its weird light. All this was done, and every man was looking, horror-stricken, at his neighbour; when Webster was seen bending over the bowl with a rope round his neck, holding up the end of the rope, with his head on one side and his tongue lolled out, to represent a hanged man!"

Dickens read at Boston on 23 and 24 December, and on Christmas Day travelled back to New York where he was to read on the 26th. The last words written before he left were of illness. "The low action of the heart, or whatever it is, has inconvenienced me greatly this last week. On Monday night, after the reading, I was laid upon a bed, in a very faint and shady state; and on the Tuesday I did not get up till the afternoon." But what in reality was less grave took outwardly the form of a greater distress; and the effects of the cold which had struck him in travelling to Boston, as yet not known to his English friends, appear most to have alarmed those about him. I depart from my rule in this narrative, otherwise strictly observed, in singling out one of those friends for mention by name; but a business connection with the readings, as well as untiring offices of personal kindness and sympathy, threw Mr. Fields into closer relations with Dickens from arrival to departure, than any other person had; and his description of the condition of health in which Dickens now quitted Boston and went through the rest of the labour he had undertaken, will be a sad though fit prelude to what the following chapter has to tell. "He went from Boston to New York carrying with him a severe catarrh contracted in our climate. He was quite ill from the effects of the disease; but he fought courageously against them. . . . His spirit was wonderful, and, although he lost all appetite and could partake of very little food, he was always cheerful and ready for his work when the evening came round. A dinner was tendered to him by some of his literary friends in Boston; but he was so ill the day before that the banquet had to be given up. The strain upon his strength and nerves was very great during all the months he remained, and only a man of iron will could have accomplished what he did. He was accustomed to talk and write a good deal about eating and drinking, but I have rarely seen a man eat and drink less. He liked to dilate in imagination over the brewing of a bowl of punch, but when the punch was ready he drank less of it than anyone who might be present. It was the sentiment of the thing and not the thing itself that engaged his attention. I scarcely saw him eat a hearty meal during his whole stay. Both at Parker's hotel in Boston, and at the Westminster in New York, everything was arranged by the proprietors for his comfort, and tempting dishes to pique his invalid appetite were sent up at different hours of the day; but the influenza had seized him with masterful power, and held the strong man down till he left the country."

When he arrived in New York on the evening of Christmas Day he found a letter from his daughter. Answering her next day he told her: "I wanted it much, for I had a frightful cold (English colds are nothing to those of this country) and was very miserable. . . . It is a bad country to be unwell and travelling in. You are one of, say, a hundred people in a heated car with a great stove in it, all the little windows being closed; and the bumping and banging about are indescribable, the atmosphere detestable, the ordinary motion all but intolerable." The following day this addition was made to the letter. "I managed to read last night, but it was as much as I could do. To-day I am so very unwell that I have sent for a doctor. He has just been, and is in doubt whether I shall not have to stop reading for a while."

His stronger will prevailed, and he went on without stopping. On the last day of the year he announced to us that though he had been very low he was getting right again; that in a couple of days he should have accomplished a fourth of the entire readings; and that the first month of the new year would see him through Philadelphia and Baltimore, as well as through two more nights in Boston. He also prepared his English friends for the startling intelligence they might shortly expect, of four readings coming off in a church, before an audience of two thousand people accommodated in pews, and with himself emerging from a vestry.

## II

### JANUARY TO APRIL

#### 1868

THE reading on 3 January closed a fourth of the entire series, and on that day Dickens wrote of the trouble brought on them by the "speculators," which to some extent had affected unfavourably the three previous nights in New York. When adventurers bought up the best places, the public resented it by refusing the worst; to prevent it by first helping themselves, being the last thing they ever thought of doing. "We try to withhold the best seats from the speculators, but the unaccountable thing is that the great mass of the public buy of them (prefer it), and the rest of the public are injured if we have not got those very seats to sell them. We have now a travelling staff of six men, in spite of which Dolby, who is leaving me to-day to sell tickets in Philadelphia to-morrow morning, will no doubt get into a tempest of difficulties. Of course also, in such a matter, as many obstacles as possible are thrown in an Englishman's way; and he may himself be a little injudicious into the bargain. Last night, for instance, he met one of the ' ushers ' (who show people to their seats) coming in with one of our men. It is against orders that anyone employed in front should go out during the reading, and he took this man to task in the British manner. Instantly, the free and independent usher put on his hat and walked off. Seeing which, all the other free and independent ushers (some twenty in number) put on *their* hats and walked off; leaving us absolutely devoid and destitute of a staff for to-night. One has since been improvised: but itwas a small matter to raise a stir and ill-will about, especially as one of our men was equally in fault; and really there is little to be done at night. American people are so accustomed to take care of themselves, that one of these immense audiences will fall into their places with an ease amazing to a frequenter of St. James's Hall; and the certainty with which they are all in, before I go on, is a very acceptable mark of respect. Our great labour is outside; and we have been obliged to bring our staff up to six, besides a boy or two, by employment of a regular additional clerk, a Bostonian. The speculators buying the front seats (we have found instances of this being done by merchants in good position) the public won't have the back seats; return their tickets; write and print volumes on the subject; and deter others from coming. You are not to suppose that this prevails to any great extent, as our lowest house here has been £300; but it does hit us. There is no doubt about it. Fortunately I saw the danger when the trouble began, and changed the list at the right time. . . . You may get an idea of the staff's work, by what is in hand now. They are preparing, numbering, and stamping, 6000 tickets for Philadelphia, and 8000 tickets for Brooklyn. The moment those are done, another 8000 tickets will be wanted for Baltimore, and probably another 6000 for Washington; and all this in addition to the correspondence, advertisements, accounts, travelling, and the nightly business of the readings four times a week. . . . I cannot get rid of this intolerable cold! My landlord invented for me a drink of brandy, rum, and snow, called it a 'Rocky Mountain Sneezer,' and said it was to put down all less effectual sneezing; but it has not yet had the effect. Did I tell you that the favourite drink before you get up is an Eye-opener? There has been another fall of snow, succeeded by a heavy thaw."

The day after (the 4th) he went back to Boston, and next day wrote to me: "I am to read here on Monday and Tuesday, return to New York on Wednesday, and finish there (except the farewells in April) on Thursday and Friday. The New York reading of *Doctor Marigold* made really a tremendous hit. The people doubted at first, having evidently not the least idea what could be done with it, and broke out at last into a perfect chorus of delight. At the end they made a great shout, and gave a rush towards the platform as if they were going to carry me off. It puts a strong additional arrow into my quiver. Another extraordinary success has been *Nickleby* and *Boots at the Holly Tree* (appreciated here in Boston, by the by, even more than *Copperfield*); and think of our last New York night bringing £500 English into the house, after making more than the necessary deduction for the present price of gold! The manager is always going about with an immense bundle that looks like a sofa-cushion, but is in reality paper-money, and it had risen to the proportions of a sofa on the morning he left for Philadelphia. Well, the work is hard, the climate is hard, the life is hard: but so far the gain is enormous. My cold steadily refuses to stir an inch. It distresses me greatly at times, though it is always good enough to leave me for the needful two hours. I have tried allopathy, homœopathy, cold things, warm things, sweet things, bitter things, stimulants, narcotics, all with the same result. Nothing will touch it."

In the same letter, light was thrown on the ecclesiastical mystery. "At Brooklyn I am going to read in Mr. Ward Beecher's chapel: the only building there available for the purpose. You must understand that Brooklyn is a kind of sleeping-place for New York, and is supposed to be a great place in the money way. We let the seats pew by pew! the pulpit is taken down for my screen and gas! and I appear out of the vestry in canonical form! These ecclesiastical entertainments come off on the evenings of the 16th, 17th, 20th, and 21st of the present month." His first letter after returning to New York (9 January) made additions to the Brooklyn picture. "Each evening an enormous ferry-boat will convey me and my state-carriage (not to mention half a dozen wagons and any number of people and a few score of horses) across the river to Brooklyn, and will bring me back again. The sale of tickets there was an amazing scene. The noble army of speculators are now furnished (this is literally true, and I am quite serious) each man with a straw mattress, a little bag of bread and meat, two blankets, and a bottle of whisky. With this outfit, *they lie down in line on the pavement* the whole of the night before the tickets are sold: generally taking up their position at about 10. It being severely cold at Brooklyn, they made an immense bonfire in the street—a narrow street of wooden houses—which the police turned out to extinguish. A general fight then took place; from which the people farthest off in the line rushed bleeding when they saw any chance of ousting others nearer the door, put their mattresses in the spots so gained, and held on by the iron rails. At 8 in the morning Dolby appeared with the tickets in a portmanteau. He was immediately saluted with a roar of Halloa! Dolby! Dolby! So Charley has let you have the carriage, has he, Dolby? How is he, Dolby? Don't drop the tickets, Dolby! Look alive, Dolby, etc., in the midst of which he proceeded to business, and concluded (as usual) by giving universal dissatisfaction. He is now going off upon a little journey to look over the ground and cut back again. This little journey (to Chicago) is twelve hundred miles on end, by railway, besides the back again!" It might tax the Englishman, but was nothing to the native American. It was part of his New York landlord's ordinary life in a week, Dickens told me, to go to Chicago and look at his theatre there on a Monday; to pelt back to Boston and look at his theatre there on a Thursday; and to come rushing to New York on a Friday, to apostrophise his enormous ballet. . . .

His testimony as to improved social habits and ways was expressed very decidedly. "I think it reasonable to expect that as I go westward, I shall find the old manners going on before me, and may tread upon their skirts mayhap. But so far, I have had no more intrusion or boredom than I have when I lead the same life in England. I write this in an immense hotel, but I am as much at peace in my own rooms, and am left as wholly undisturbed, as if I were at the Station Hotel in York. I have now read in New York city to 40,000 people, and am quite as well known in the streets there as I am in London. People will turn back, turn again and face me, and have a look at me, or will say to one another, 'Look here! Dickens coming!' But no one ever stops me or addresses me. Sitting reading in the carriage outside the New York post office while one of the staff was stamping the letters inside, I became conscious that a few people who had been looking at the turn-out had discovered me within. On my peeping out good-humouredly, one of them (I should say a merchant's book-keeper) stepped up to the door, took off his hat, and said in a frank way: 'Mr. Dickens, I should very much like to have the honour of shaking hands with you'—and, that done, presented two others. Nothing could be more quiet or less intrusive. In the railways cars, if I see anybody who clearly wants to speak to me, I usually anticipate the wish by speaking myself. If I am standing on the brake outside (to avoid the intolerable stove), people getting down will say with a smile: 'As I am taking my departure, Mr. Dickens, and can't trouble you for more than a moment, I should like to take you by the hand, sir.' And so we shake hands and go our ways. . . . Of course many of my impressions come through the readings. Thus I find the people lighter and more humorous than formerly; and there must be a great deal of innocent imagination among every class, or they never could pet with such extraordinary pleasure as they do, the Boots's story of the elopement of the two little children. They seem to see the children; and the women set up a shrill undercurrent of half-pity and half-pleasure that is quite affecting. To-night's reading is my 26th; but as all the Philadelphia tickets for four more are sold, as well as four at Brooklyn, you must assume that I am at—say—my 35th reading. I have remitted to Coutts's in English gold £10,000 odd; and I roughly calculate that on this number Dolby will have another thousand pounds profit to pay me. These figures are of course between ourselves, at present; but are they not magnificent? . . ."

Then came, as ever, the constant shadow that still attended him, the slave in the chariot of his triumph. "The work is very severe. There is now no chance of my being rid of this American catarrh until I embark for England. It is very distressing. It likewise happens, not seldom, that I am so dead beat when I come off that they lay me down on a sofa after I have been washed and dressed, and I lie there, extremely faint, for a quarter of an hour. In that time I rally and come right." One week later from New York, where he had become due on the 16th for the first of his four Brooklyn readings, he wrote to his sister-in-law. "My cold sticks to me, and I can scarcely exaggerate what I undergo from sleeplessness. I rarely take any breakfast but an egg and a cup of tea—not even toast or bread and butter. My small dinner at 3, and a little quail or some such light thing when I come home at night, is my daily fare; and at the hall I have established the custom of taking an egg beaten up in sherry before going in, and another between the parts, which I think pulls me up. . . .

Baltimore and Washington were the cities in which he was now, on quitting New York, to read for the first time; and as to the latter some doubts arose. He was at Philadelphia on 23 January, when he wrote: "The worst of it is, that everybody one advises with has a monomania respecting Chicago. 'Good heavens, sir,' the great Philadelphia authority said to me this morning, 'if you don't read in Chicago the people will go into fits!' Well, I answered, I would rather they went into fits than I did. But he didn't seem to see it at all." . . .

To myself he wrote from Philadelphia, beginning with a thank Heaven that he had struck off Canada and the West, for he found the wear and tear "enormous." "Dolby decided that the croakers were wrong about Washington, and went on: the rather as his raised prices, which he put finally at three dollars each, gave satisfaction. Fields is so confident about Boston, that my remaining list includes, in all, 14 more readings there. I don't know how many more we might not have had here (where I have had attentions otherwise that have been very grateful to me), if we had chosen. Tickets are now being resold at ten dollars each. At Baltimore I had a charming little theatre, and a very apprehensive impulsive audience. It is remarkable to see how the Ghost of Slavery haunts the town; and how the shambling, untidy, evasive, and postponing Irrepressible proceeds about his free work, going round and round it, instead of at it. The melancholy absurdity of giving these people votes, at any rate at present, would glare at one out of every roll of their eyes, chuckle in their mouths, and bump in their heads, if one did not see (as one cannot help seeing in the country) that their enfranchisement is a mere party trick to get votes. Being at the Penitentiary the other day (this, while we mention votes), and looking over the books, I noticed that almost every man had been 'pardoned' a day or two before his time was up. Why? Because if he had served his time out, he would have been *ipso facto* disfranchised. So, this form of pardon is gone through to save his vote; and as every officer of the prison holds his place only in right of his party, of course his hopeful clients vote for the party that has let them out! When I read in Mr. Beecher's church at Brooklyn, we found the trustees had suppressed the fact that a certain upper gallery holding 150 was 'the Coloured Gallery.' On the first night not a soul could be induced to enter it; and it was not until it became known next day that I was certainly not going to read there more than four times, that we managed to fill it. One night at New York, on our second or third row, there were two well-dressed women with a tinge of colour—I should say, not even quadroons. But the holder of one ticket who found his seat to be next them, demanded of Dolby 'What he meant by fixing him next to those two Gord darmed cusses of niggers?' and insisted on being supplied with another good place. Dolby firmly replied that he was perfectly certain Mr. Dickens would not recognise such an objection on any account, but he could have his money back if he chose. Which, after some squabbling, he had. In a comic scene in the New York Circus one night, when I was looking on, four white people sat down upon a form in a barber's shop to be shaved. A coloured man came as the fifth customer, and the four immediately ran away. This was much laughed at and applauded. In the Baltimore Penitentiary, the white prisoners dine on one side of the room, the coloured prisoners on the other; and no one has the slightest idea of mixing them. But it is indubitably the fact that exhalations not the most agreeable arise from a number of coloured people got together, and I was obliged to beat a quick retreat from their dormitory. I strongly believe that they will die out of this country fast. It seems, looking at them, so manifestly absurd to suppose it possible that they can ever hold their own against a restless, shifty, striving, stronger race."

On 4 February he wrote to me from Washington: It will be no violation of the rule of avoiding private detail if the very interesting close of his letter is given. Its anecdote of President Lincoln was repeatedly told by Dickens after his return, and I am under no necessity to withhold from it the authority of Mr. Sumner's name. "I am going to-morrow to see the President, who has sent to me twice. I dined with Charles Sumner last Sunday, against my rule; and as I had stipulated for no party, Mr. Secretary Stanton was the only other guest, besides his own secretary. Stanton is a man with a very remarkable memory, and extraordinarily familiar with my books. . . . He and Sumner having been the first two public men at the dying President's bedside, and having remained with him until he breathed his last, we fell into a very interesting conversation after dinner, when, each of them giving his own narrative separately, the usual discrepancies about details of time were observable. Then Mr. Stanton told me a curious little story which will form the remainder of this short letter.

"On the afternoon of the day on which the President was shot, there was a cabinet council at which he presided. Mr. Stanton, being at the time commander-in-chief of the Northern troops that were concentrated about here, arrived rather late. Indeed they were waiting for him, and on his entering the room the President broke off in something he was saying, and remarked: 'Let us proceed to business, gentlemen.' Mr. Stanton then noticed, with great surprise, that the President sat with an air of dignity in his chair instead of lolling about it in the most ungainly attitudes, as his invariable custom was; and that instead of telling irrelevant or questionable stories, he was grave and calm, and quite a different man. Mr. Stanton, on leaving the council with the Attorney-General, said to him, 'That is the most satisfactory cabinet meeting I have attended for many a long day! What an extraordinary change in Mr. Lincoln!' The Attorney-General replied, 'We all saw it, before you came in. While we were waiting for you, he said, with his chin down on his breast, "Gentlemen, something very extraordinary is going to happen, and that very soon." ' To which the Attorney-General had observed, 'Something good, sir, I hope?' when the President answered very gravely: 'I don't know; I don't know. But it will happen, and shortly too!' As they were all impressed by his manner, the Attorney-General took him up again: 'Have you received any information, sir, not yet disclosed to us?' 'No,' answered the President: 'but I have had a dream. And I have now had the same dream three times. Once, on the night preceding the Battle of Bull Run. Once, on the night preceding' such another (naming a battle also not favourable to the North). His chin sank on his breast again, and he sat reflecting. 'Might one ask the nature of this dream, sir?' said the Attorney-General. 'Well,' replied the President, without lifting his head or changing his attitude, 'I am on a great broad rolling river—and I am in a boat—and I drift—and I drift!—but this is not business'— suddenly raising his face and looking round the table as Mr. Stanton entered, 'let us proceed to business, gentlemen.' Mr. Stanton and the Attorney-General said, as they walked on together, it would be curious to notice whether anything ensued on this; and they agreed to notice. He was shot that night." . . .

Dickens's last letter from America was written to his daughter Mary from Boston on 9 April, the day before his sixth and last farewell night. "I not only read last Friday when I was doubtful of being able to do so, but read as I never did before, and astonished the audience quite as much as myself. You never saw or heard such a scene of excitement. Longfellow and all the Cambridge men have urged me to give in. I have been very near doing so, but feel stronger to-day. I cannot tell whether the catarrh may have done me any lasting injury in the lungs or other breathing organs, until I shall have rested and got home. I hope and believe not. Consider the weather! There have been two snowstorms since I wrote last, and to-day the town is blotted out in a ceaseless whirl of snow and wind. Dolby is as tender as a woman, and as watchful as a doctor. He never leaves me during the reading, now, but sits at the side of the platform, and keeps his eye upon me all the time. Ditto George the gasman, steadiest and most reliable man I ever employed. . . ."

In New York, where there were five farewell nights, three thousand two hundred and ninety-eight dollars were the receipts of the last, on 20 April; those of the last at Boston, on the 8th, having been three thousand four hundred and fifty-six dollars. But, on earlier nights in the same cities respectively, these sums also had been reached; and indeed, making allowance for an exceptional night here and there, the receipts varied so wonderfully little, that a mention of the highest average returns from other places will give no exaggerated impression of the ordinary receipts throughout, excluding fractions of dollars, the lowest were New Bedford ($1640), Rochester ($1906), Springfield ($1970), and Providence ($2140). Albany and Worcester averaged something less than $2400; while Hartford, Buffalo, Baltimore, Syracuse, Newhaven, and Portland rose to $2600. Washington's last night was $2610, no night there having less than $2500. Philadelphia exceeded Washington by $300, and Brooklyn went ahead of Philadelphia by $200. The amount taken at the four Brooklyn readings was 11,128 dollars.

The New York public dinner was given at Delmonico's, the hosts were more than two hundred, and the chair was taken by Mr. Horace Greeley. Dickens attended with great difficulty, and spoke in pain. But he used the occasion to bear his testimony to the changes of twenty-five years; the rise of vast new cities; growth in the graces and amenities of life; much improvement in the press, essential to every other advance; and changes in himself leading to opinions more deliberately formed. He promised his kindly entertainers that no copy of his *Notes* or his *Chuzzlewit*, should in future be issued by him without accompanying mention of the changes to which he had referred that night; of the politeness, delicacy, sweet temper, hospitality, and consideration in all ways for which he had to thank them; and of his gratitude for the respect shown, during all his visit, to the privacy enforced upon him by the nature of his work and the condition of his health.

He had to leave the room before the proceedings were over. On the following Monday he read to his last American audience, telling them at the close that he hoped often to recall them, equally by his winter fire and in the green summer weather, and never as a mere public audience but as a host of personal friends. He sailed two days later in the *Russia*, and reached England in the first week of May 1868.

# BOOK TENTH

## SUMMING UP

1868–70.  ÆT.  56–8

# I

## LAST READINGS

### 1868–70

FAVOURABLE weather helped Dickens pleasantly home. He had profited greatly by the sea voyage, perhaps more greatly by its repose; and on 25 May he described himself to his Boston friends as brown beyond belief, and causing the greatest disappointment in all quarters by looking so well. "My doctor was quite broken down in spirits on seeing me for the first time last Saturday. *Good Lord ! seven years younger !* said the doctor, recoiling." That he gave all the credit to "those fine days at sea," and none to the rest from such labours as he had passed through, the close of the letter too sadly showed. "We are already settling—think of this! the details of my farewell course of readings."

Even on his way out to America that enterprise was in hand. From Halifax he had written to me: "I told the Chappells that when I got back to England, I would have a series of farewell readings in town and country; and then read No More. They at once offer in writing to pay all expenses whatever, to pay the ten per cent. for management, and to pay me, for a series of 75, six thousand pounds." The terms were raised and settled before the first Boston readings closed. The number was to be a hundred: and the payment, over and above expenses and percentage, eight thousand pounds. Such a temptation undoubtedly was great; and though it was a fatal mistake which Dickens committed in yielding to it, it was not an ignoble one. He did it under no excitement from the American gains, of which he knew nothing when he pledged himself to the enterprise. No man could care essentially less for mere money than he did. But the necessary provision for many sons was a constant anxiety; he was proud of what the readings had done to abridge this care; and the very strain of them under which it seems that his health had first given way, and which he always steadily refused to connect especially with them, had also broken the old confidence of being at all times available for his higher pursuit. What affected his health only he would not regard as part of the question either way. That was to be borne as the lot more or less of all men; and the more thorough he could make his feeling of independence, and of ability to rest, by what was now in hand, the better his final chances of a perfect recovery would be. That was the spirit in which he entered on this last engagement. It was an opportunity offered for making a particular work really

complete before he should abandon it for ever. Something of it will
not be indiscernible even in the summary of his past acquisitions,
which with a pardonable exultation he now sent me.

"We had great difficulty in getting our American accounts squared
to the point of ascertaining what Dolby's commission amounted to
in English money. After all, we were obliged to call in the aid of a
money-changer, to determine what he should pay as his share of the
average loss of conversion into gold. With this deduction made, I
think his commission (I have not the figures at hand) was £2888;
Ticknor and Fields had a commission of £1000, besides 5 per cent.
on all Boston receipts. The expenses in America to the day of our
sailing were 38,949 dollars;—roughly 39,000 dollars, or £13,000.
The preliminary expenses were £614. The average price of gold was
nearly 40 per cent. and yet my profit was within a hundred or so of
£20,000. Supposing me to have got through the present engagement
in good health, I shall have made by the readings, *in two years*,
£33,000 that is to say: £13,000 received from the Chappells, and
£20,000 from America. What I had made by them before, I could
only ascertain by a long examination of Coutts's books. I should
say, certainly not less than £10,000: for I remember that I made
half that money in the first town and country campaign with poor
Arthur Smith. These figures are of course between ourselves; but
don't you think them rather remarkable? The Chappell bargain
began with £50 a night and everything paid; then became £60; and
now rises to £80." . . .

He had scarcely begun these last readings than he was beset by a
misgiving, that, for a success large enough to repay Messrs. Chappell's liberality, the enterprise would require a new excitement to
carry him over the old ground; and it was while engaged in Manchester and Liverpool at the outset of October that this announcement came. "I have made a short reading of the murder in *Oliver
Twist*. I cannot make up my mind, however, whether to do it or not.
I have no doubt that I could perfectly petrify an audience by carrying out the notion I have of the way of rendering it. But whether the
impression would not be so horrible as to keep them away another
time, is what I cannot satisfy myself upon. What do you think?
It is in three short parts: 1. Where Fagin sets Noah Claypole on to
watch Nancy. 2. The scene on London Bridge. 3. Where Fagin rouses
Claypole from his sleep to tell his perverted story to Sikes: and the
Murder, and the Murderer's sense of being haunted. I have adapted
and cut about the text with great care, and it is very powerful. I have
to-day referred the book and the question to the Chappells as so
largely interested." I had a strong dislike to this proposal, less perhaps on the ground which ought to have been taken of the physical
exertion it would involve, than because such a subject seemed to be
altogether out of the province of reading; and it was resolved, that,
before doing it, trial should be made to a limited private audience in
St. James's Hall. . . . "We might have agreed," he wrote, "to

differ about it very well, because we only wanted to find out the truth if we could, and because it was quite understood that I wanted to leave behind me the recollection of something very passionate and dramatic, done with simple means, if the art would justify the theme." Apart from mere personal considerations, the whole question lay in these last words. It was impossible for me to admit that the effect to be produced was legitimate, or such as it was desirable to associate with the recollection of his readings. . . .

The second portion of the enterprise opened with the New Year; and the *Sikes and Nancy* scenes, everywhere his prominent subject, exacted the most terrible physical exertion from him. In January he was at Clifton, where he had given, he told his sister-in-law, "by far the best Murder yet done"; while at the same date he wrote to his daughter: "At Clifton on Monday night we had a contagion of fainting; and yet the place was not hot. I should think we had from a dozen to twenty ladies taken out stiff and rigid, at various times! It became quite ridiculous." He was afterwards at Cheltenham. "Macready is of opinion that the Murder is two Macbeths. He declares that he heard every word of the reading, but I doubt it. Alas! he is sadly infirm." On the 27th he wrote to his daughter from Torquay that the place into which they had put him to read, and where a pantomine had been played the night before, was something between a Methodist chapel, a theatre, a circus, a riding-school, and a cowhouse. That day he wrote to me from Bath: "Landor's ghost goes along the silent streets here before me. . . . The place looks to me like a cemetery which the Dead have succeeded in rising and taking. Having built streets of their old gravestones, they wander about scantly trying to 'look alive.' A dead failure."

In the second week of February he was in London, under engagement to return to Scotland (which he had just left) after the usual weekly reading at St. James's Hall, when there was a sudden interruption. "My foot has turned lame again!" was his announcement to me on the 15th. . . .

A few days' rest again brought so much relief, that, against the urgent entreaties of members of his family as well as other friends, he was in the railway carriage bound for Edinburgh on the morning of 20 February, accompanied by Mr. Chappell himself. "I came down lazily on a sofa," he wrote to me from Edinburgh next day, "hardly changing my position the whole way. The railway authorities had done all sorts of things, and I was more comfortable than on the sofa at the hotel. The foot gave me no uneasiness, and has been quiet and steady all night." He was nevertheless under the necessity, two days later, of consulting Mr. Syme; and he told his daughter that this great authority had warned him against over-fatigue in the readings, and given him some slight remedies, but otherwise reported him in "just perfectly splendid condition." . . .

The whole of that March month he went on with the scenes from *Oliver Twist.* "The foot goes famously," he wrote to his daughter.

"I feel the fatigue in it (four Murders in one week) but not overmuch It merely aches at night, and so does the other, sympathetically, I suppose." . . . The end was near. A public dinner had been given him in Liverpool on 10 April, with Lord Dufferin in the chair, and a reading was due from him in Preston on the 22nd of that month. But on Sunday the 18th we had ill report of him from Chester, and on the 21st he wrote from Blackpool to his sister-in-law: "I have come to this Sea-Beach Hotel (charming) for a day's rest. I am much better than I was on Sunday; but shall want careful looking to, to get through the readings. My weakness and deadness are all on the left side; and if I don't look at anything I try to touch with my left hand, I don't know where it is. I am in (secret) consultation with Frank Beard who says that I have given him indisputable evidences of overwork which he could wish to treat immediately; and so I have telegraphed for him. I have had a delicious walk by the sea to-day, and I sleep soundly, and have picked up amazingly in appetite. My foot is greatly better too, and I wear my own boot." Next day was appointed for the reading at Preston; and from that place he wrote to me, while waiting the arrival of Mr. Beard: "Don't say anything about it, but the tremendous, severe nature of this work is a little shaking me. At Chester last Sunday I found myself extremely giddy, and extremely uncertain of my sense of touch, both in the left leg and the left hand and arms. . . . Don't say anything in the Gad's direction about my being a little out of sorts. I have broached the matter of course; but very lightly. Indeed there is no reason for broaching it otherwise."

Even to the close of that letter he had buoyed himself up with the hope that he might yet be "coached" and that the readings need not be discontinued. But Mr. Beard stopped them at once, and brought his patient to London. On Friday morning the 23rd, the same envelope brought me a note from himself to say that he was well enough, but tired; in perfectly good spirits, not at all uneasy, and writing this himself that I should have it under his own hand; with a note from his eldest son to say that his father appeared to him to be very ill, and that a consultation had been appointed with Sir Thomas Watson. . . .

## II

### LAST BOOK

#### 1869-70

THE last book undertaken by Dickens was to be published in illustrated monthly numbers, of the old form, but to close with the twelfth.* It closed, unfinished, with the sixth number, which was itself underwritten by two pages.

His first fancy for the tale was expressed in a letter in the middle of July. "What should you think of the idea of a story beginning in this way?—Two people, boy and girl, or very young, going apart from one another, pledged to be married after many years—at the end of the book. The interest to arise out of the tracing of their separate ways, and the impossibility of telling what will be done with that impending fate." This was laid aside; but it left a marked trace on the story as afterwards designed, in the position of Edwin Drood and his betrothed.

I first heard of the later design in a letter dated "Friday the 6th of August 1869," in which after speaking, with the usual unstinted praise he bestowed always on what moved him in others, of a little tale he had received for his journal, he spoke of the change that had occurred to him for the new tale by himself. "I laid aside the fancy I told you of, and have a very curious and new idea for my new story. Not a communicable idea (or the interest of the book would be gone) but a very strong one, though difficult to work." The story, I learnt immediately afterward, was to be that of the murder of a nephew by his uncle; the originality of which was to consist in the review of the murderer's career by himself at the close, when its temptations were to be dwelt upon as if, not he the culprit, but some other man, were the tempted. The last chapters were to be written in the condem ned cell, to which his wickedness, all elaborately elicited from him

* In drawing the agreement for the publication, Mr. Ouvry had, by Dickens's wish, inserted a clause thought to be altogether needless, but found to be sadly pertinent. It was the first time such a clause had been inserted in one of his agreements. "That if the said Charles Dickens shall die during the composition of the said work of the *Mystery of Edwin Drood*, or shall otherwise become incapable of completing the said work for publication in twelve monthly numbers as agreed, it shall be referred to John Forster, Esq., one of Her Majesty's Commissioners in Lunacy, or in the case of his death, incapacity, or refusal to act, then to such person as shall be named by Her Majesty's Attorney-General for the time being, to determine the amount which shall be repaid by the said Charles Dickens, his executors or administrators, to the said Frederic Chapman as a fair compensation for so much of the said work as shall not have been completed for publication." The sum to be paid at once for 25,000 copies was £7500; publisher and author sharing equally in the profit of all sales beyond that impression. . . .

as if told of another, had brought him. Discovery by the murderer of the utter needlessness of the murder for its object, was to follow hard upon commission of the deed; but all discovery of the murderer was to be baffled till towards the close, when, by means of a gold ring which had resisted the corrosive effects of the lime into which he had thrown the body, not only the person murdered was to be identified but the locality of the crime and the man who committed it. So much was told to me before any of the book was written; and it will be recollected that the ring, taken by Drood to be given to his betrothed only if their engagement went on, was brought away with him from their last interview. Rosa was to marry Tartar, and Crisparkle the sister of Landless, who was himself, I think, to have perished in assisting Tartar finally to unmask and seize the murderer.

Nothing had been written, however, of the main parts of the design excepting what is found in the published numbers; there was no hint or preparation for the sequel in any notes of chapters in advance; and there remained not even what he had himself so sadly written of the book by Thackeray also interrupted by death. The evidence of matured designs never to be accomplished, intentions planned never to be executed, roads of thought marked out never to be traversed, goals shining in the distance never to be reached, was wanting here. It was all a blank. Enough had been completed nevertheless to give promise of a much greater book than its immediate predecessor. "I hope his book is finished," wrote Longfellow when the news of his death was flashed to America. "It is certainly one of his most beautiful works, if not the most beautiful of all. It would be too sad to think the pen had fallen from his hand, and left it incomplete." Some of its characters are touched with subtlety, and in its descriptions his imaginative power was at its best. Not a line was wanting to the reality, in the most minute local detail, of places the most widely contrasted; and we saw with equal vividness the lazy cathedral town and the lurid opium-eater's den. Something like the old lightness and buoyancy of animal spirits gave a new freshness to the humour; the scenes of the child-heroine and her luckless betrothed had both novelty and nicety of character in them; and Mr. Grewgious in chambers with his clerk and the two waiters, the conceited fool Sapsea, and the blustering philanthropist Honeythunder, were first-rate comedy. Miss Twinkleton was of the family of Miss La Creevy; and the lodging-house keeper, Miss Billickin, though she gave Miss Twinkleton but a sorry account of her blood, had that of Mrs. Todgers in her veins. "I was put in early life to a very genteel boarding-school, the mistress being no less a lady than yourself, of about your own age, or it may be some years younger, and a poorness of blood flowed from the table which has run through my life." Was ever anything better said of a school-fare of starved gentility?

The last page of *Edwin Drood* was written in the Chalet in the afternoon of his last day of consciousness. The MS. more startlingly showed him how unsettled the habit he most prized had become, in the clashing of old and new pursuits. "When I had written" (22 December, 1869) "and, as I thought, disposed of the first two Numbers of my story, Clowes informed me to my horror that they were, together, *twelve printed pages too short!!!* Consequently I had to transpose a chapter from number two to number one, and remodel number two altogether! This was the more unlucky, that it came upon me at the time when I was obliged to leave the book, in order to get up the readings" (the additional twelve for which Sir Thomas Watson's consent had been obtained); "quite gone out of my mind since I left them off. However, I turned to it and got it done, and both numbers are now in type. Charles Collins has designed an excellent cover." It was his wish that his son-in-law should have illustrated the story; but this not being practicable, upon an opinion expressed by Mr. Millais which the result thoroughly justified, choice was made of Mr. S. L. Fildes.

---

This reference to the last effort of Dickens's genius had been written as it thus stands when a discovery of some interest was made by the writer. Within the leaves of one of Dickens's other manuscripts were found some detached slips of his writing, on paper only half the size of that used for the tale, so cramped, underlined, and blotted as to be nearly illegible, which on close inspection proved to be a scene in which Sapsea the auctioneer is introduced as the principal figure, among a group of characters new to the story. The explanation of it perhaps is, that having become a little nervous about the course of the tale, from a fear that he might have plunged too soon into the incidents leading on to the catastrophe, such as the Datchery assumption in the fifth number (a misgiving he had certainly expressed to his sister-in-law), it had occurred to him to open some fresh veins of character incidental to the interest, though not directly part of it, and so to handle them in connection with Sapsea as a little to suspend the final development even while assisting to strengthen it. Before beginning any number of a serial, he used, as we have seen in former instances, to plan briefly what he intended to put into it chapter by chapter; and his first number-plan of *Drood* had the following: "Mr. Sapsea. Old Tory jackass. Connect Jasper with him. (He will want a solemn donkey by and by)": which was effected by bringing together both Durdles and Jasper, for connection with Sapsea, in the matter of the epitaph for Mrs. Sapsea's tomb. The scene now discovered might in this view have been designed to strengthen and carry forward that element in the tale; and otherwise it very sufficiently expresses itself. It would supply an answer, if such were needed, to those who have asserted that the hopeless decadence of Dickens as a writer had set in before his death. Among the lines last written by him, these are the very last we can ever hope to receive; and they seem to me a delightful specimen of the power possessed by him in his prime, and the rarest which any novelist can have, of revealing a character, by a touch. Here are a couple of people, Kimber and Peartree, not known to us before, whom we read off thoroughly in a dozen words; and as to Sapsea himself, auctioneer and Mayor of Cloisterham, we are face to face with what before we only dimly realised, and we see the solemn jackass, in his business pulpit, playing off the airs of Mr. Dean in his Cathedral pulpit, with Cloisterham laughing at the impostor.

### HOW MR. SAPSEA CEASED TO BE A MEMBER OF THE EIGHT CLUB
#### Told by himself

"Wishing to take the air, I proceeded by a circuitous route to the club, it being our weekly night of meeting. I found that we mustered our full strength. We were enrolled under the denomination of the Eight Club. We were eight in number; we met at eight o'clock during eight months of the year; we played eight games of four-handed cribbage, at eightpence the game; our frugal supper was composed of eight rolls, eight mutton chops, eight pork sausages, eight baked potatoes, eight marrow-bones, with eight toasts, and eight bottles of ale. There may, or may not, be a certain harmony of colour in the ruling idea of this (to adopt a phrase of our lively neighbours) reunion. It was a little idea of mine.

"A somewhat popular member of the Eight Club was a member by the name of Kimber. By profession, a dancing-master. A common-place, hopeful sort of man, wholly destitute of dignity or knowledge of the world.

"As I entered the Club-room, Kimber was making the remark: 'And he still half-believes him to be very high in the Church.'

"In the act of hanging up my hat on the eighth peg by the door, I caught Kimber's visual ray. He lowered it, and passed a remark on the next change of the moon. I did not take particular notice of this at the moment, because the world was often pleased to be a little shy of ecclesiastical topics in my presence. For I felt that I was picked out (though perhaps only through a coincidence) to a certain extent to represent what I call our glorious constitution in Church and State. The phrase may be objected to by captious minds; but I own to it as mine. I threw it off in argument some little time back. I said; 'OUR GLORIOUS CONSTITUTION in CHURCH and STATE.'

"Another member of the Eight Club was Peartree; also member of the Royal College of Surgeons. Mr. Peartree is not accountable to me for his opinions, and I say no more of them here than that he attends the poor gratis whenever they want him, and is not the parish doctor. Mr. Peartree may justify it to the grasp of *his* mind thus to do his republican utmost to bring an appointed officer into contempt. Suffice it that Mr. Peartree can never justify it to the grasp of *mine*.

"Between Peartree and Kimber there was a sickly sort of feeble-minded alliance. It came under my particular notice when I sold off Kimber by auction. (Goods taken in execution.) He was a widower in a white under-waistcoat, and slight shoes with bows, and had two daughters not ill-looking. Indeed the reverse. Both daughters taught dancing in scholastic establishments for Young Ladies—had done so at Mrs. Sapsea's; nay, Twinkleton's—and both, in giving lessons, presented the unwomanly spectacle of having little fiddles tucked under their chins. In spite of which, the younger one might, if I am correctly informed—I will raise the veil so far as to say I KNOW she might—have soared for life from this degrading taint, but for having the class of mind allotted to what I call the common herd, and being so incredibly devoid of veneration as to become painfully ludicrous.

"When I sold off Kimber without reserve, Peartree (as poor as he can hold together) had several prime household lots knocked down to him. I am not to be blinded; and of course it was as plain to me what he was going to do with them; as it was that he was a brown hulking sort of revolutionary subject who had been in India with the soldiers, and ought (for the sake of society) to have his neck broke. I saw the lots shortly afterwards in Kimber's lodgings—through the window—and I easily made out that there had been a sneaking pretence of lending them till better times. A man with a smaller knowledge of the world than myself might have been led to suspect that Kimber had held back money from his creditors, and fraudulently bought the goods. But, besides that I knew for certain he had no money. I knew that this would involve a species of forethought not to be made compatible with the frivolity of a caperer, inoculating other people with capering, for his bread.

"As it was the first time I had seen either of those two since the sale, I kept myself in what I call Abeyance. When selling him up, I had delivered a few remarks—shall I say a little homily?—concerning Kimber, which the world did regard as more than usually worth notice. I had come up into my pulpit, it was said, uncommonly like—and a murmur of recognition had repeated his (I will not name whose) title, before I spoke. I had then gone on to say that all present would find, in the first page of the catalogue that was lying before them, in the last paragraph before the first lot, the following words: 'Sold in pursuance of a writ of execution issued by a creditor.' I had then proceeded to remind my friends, that however frivolous, not to say contemptible, the business by which a man got his goods together, still his goods were as dear to him, and as cheap to society (if sold without reserve), as though his pursuits had been of a character that would bear serious contemplation. I had then divided my text (if I may be allowed so to call it) into three heads: firstly, Sold; secondly, In pursuance of a writ of execution; thirdly, Issued by a creditor; with a few moral reflections on each, and winding up with, 'Now to the first lot' in a manner that was complimented when I afterwards mingled with my hearers.

"So, not being certain on what terms I and Kimber stood, I was grave, I was chilling. Kimber, however, moving to me, I moved to Kimber. (I was the creditor who had isssued the writ. Not that it matters.)

"'I was alluding Mr. Sapsea,' said Kimber, 'to a stranger who entered into conversation with me in the street as I came to the Club. He had been speaking to you just before, it seemed, by the church-yard; and though you had told him who you were, I could hardly persuade him that you were not high in the Church.'

"'Idiot!' said Peartree.

"'Ass!' said Kimber.

"'Idiot and Ass!' said the other five members.

"'Idiot and Ass, gentlemen,' I remonstrated, looking around me, 'are strong expressions to apply to a young man of good appearance and address.' My generosity was roused; I own it.

"'You'll admit that he must be a Fool,' said Peartree.

"'You can't deny that he must be a Blockhead,' said Kimber.

"Their tone of disgust amounted to being offensive. Why should the young man be so calumniated? What had he done? He had only made an innocent and natural mistake. I controlled my generous indignation, and said so.

"'Natural?' repeated Kimber. '*He's* a Natural!'

"The remaining six members of the Eight Club laughed unanimously. It stung me. It was a scornful laugh. My anger was roused in behalf of an absent, friendless stranger. I rose (for I had been sitting down).

"'Gentlemen,' I said with dignity, 'I will not remain one of this Club allowing opprobrium to be cast on an unoffending person in his absence. I will not so violate what I call the sacred rites of hospitality. Gentlemen, until you know how to behave yourselves better, I leave you. Gentlemen, until then I withdraw, from this place of meeting, whatever personal qualifications I may have brought into it. Gentlemen, until then you cease to be the Eight Club, and must make the best you can of becoming the Seven.'

"I put on my hat and retired. As I went downstairs I distinctly heard them give a suppressed cheer. Such is the power of demeanour and knowledge of mankind. I had forced it out of them.

"II

"Whom should I meet in the street, within a few yards of the door of the inn where the Club was held, but the selfsame young man whose cause I had felt it my duty so warmly—and I will add so disinterestedly—to take up.

" 'Is it Mr. Sapsea,' he said doubtfully, 'or is it——'

" 'It is Mr. Sapsea,' I replied.

" 'Pardon me, Mr. Sapsea; you appear warm, sir.'

" 'I have been warm,' I said, 'and on your account.' Having stated the circumstances at some length (my generosity almost overpowered him), I asked him his name.

" 'Mr. Sapsea,' he answered, looking down, 'your penetration is so acute, your glance into the souls of your fellow men is so penetrating, that if I was hardy enough to deny that my name is Poker, what would it avail me?'

"I don't know that I had quite exactly made out to a fraction that his name was Poker, but I daresay I had been pretty near doing it.

" 'Well, well,' said I, trying to put him at his ease by nodding my head in a soothing way. 'Your name is Poker, and there is no harm in being named Poker.'

" 'Oh Mr. Sapsea!' cried the young man, in a very well-behaved manner. 'Bless you for those words!' He then, as if ashamed of having given way to his feelings, looked down again.

" 'Come, Poker,' said I, 'let me hear more about you. Tell me. Where are you going to, Poker? and where do you come from?'

" 'Ah Mr. Sapsea!' exclaimed the young man. 'Disguise from you is impossible. You know already that I come from somewhere, and am going somewhere else, if I was to deny it, what would it avail me?'

" 'Then don't deny it,' was my remark.

" 'Or,' pursued Poker, in a kind of despondent rapture, 'or if I was to deny that I came to this town to see and hear you, sir, what would it avail me? Or if I was to deny——' "

The fragment ends there, and the hand that could alone have completed it is at rest for ever.

———————

Some personal characteristics remain for illustration before the end is briefly told.

## III

OBJECTION has been taken to this biography as likely to disappoint its readers in not making them "talk to Dickens as Boswell makes them talk to Johnson." But where will the blame lie if a man takes up *Pickwick* and is disappointed to find that he is not reading *Rasselas*? A book must be judged for what it aims to be, and not for what it cannot by possibility be. I suppose so remarkable an author as Dickens hardly ever lived who carried so little of authorship into ordinary social intercourse. Potent as the sway of his writings was over him, it expressed itself in other ways. Traces or triumphs of literary labour, displays of conversational or other personal predominance, were no part of the influence he exerted over friends. To them he was only the pleasantest of companions, with whom they forgot that he had ever written anything, and felt only the charm which a nature of such capacity for supreme enjoyment causes everyone around it to enjoy. His talk was unaffected and natural, never bookish in the smallest degree. He was quite up to the average of well-read men; but as there was no ostentation of it in his writing, so neither was there in his conversation. This was so attractive because so keenly observant, and lighted up with so many touches of humorous fancy; but, with every possible thing to give relish to it, there were not many things to bring away. . . .

A dislike of all display was rooted in him; and his objection to posthumous honours, illustrated by the instructions in his will, was very strikingly expressed two years before his death, when Mr. Thomas Fairbairn asked his help to a proposed recognition of Rajah Brooke's services by a memorial in Westminster Abbey. "I am very strongly impelled" (24 June, 1868) "to comply with any request of yours. But these posthumous honours of committee, subscriptions, and Westminster Abbey are so profoundly unsatisfactory in my eyes that—plainly—I would rather have nothing to do with them in any case. My daughter and her aunt unite with me in kindest regards to Mrs. Fairbairn, and I hope you will believe in the possession of mine until I am quietly buried without any memorial but such as I have set up in my lifetime." Asked a year later (August 1869) to say something on the inauguration of Leigh Hunt's bust at his grave in Kensal Green, he told the committee that he had a very strong objection to speech-making beside graves. "I do not expect or wish my feelings in this wise to guide other men; still, it is so serious with me, and the idea of ever being the subject of such a ceremony myself is so repugnant to my soul, that I must decline to officiate."

His aversion to every form of what is called patronage of literature was part of the same feeling. A few months earlier he had received an application for support to such a scheme from a person assuming a title to which he had no pretension, but which appeared to sanction the request. "I beg to be excused," was his reply, "from complying with the request you do me the honour to prefer, simply because I hold the opinion that there is a great deal too much patronage in England. The better the design, the less (as I think) should it seek such adventitious aid, and the more composedly should it rest on its own merits." This was the belief Southey held: it extended to the support by way of patronage given by such societies as the Literary Fund, which Southey also strongly resisted; and it survived the failure of the Guild whereby it was hoped to establish a system of self-help, under which men engaged in literary pursuits might be as proud to receive as to give. Though there was no project of his life into which he flung himself with greater eagerness than the Guild, it was not taken up by the class it was meant to benefit, and every renewed exertion more largely added to the failure. There is no room in these pages for the story, which will add its chapter some day to the vanity of human wishes; but a passage from a letter to Bulwer Lytton at its outset will be some measure of the height from which the writer fell, when all hope for what he had so set his heart upon ceased. "I do devoutly believe that this plan carried by the support which I trust will be given to it, will change the status of the literary man in England, and make a revolution in his position which no government, no power on earth but his own, could ever effect. I have implicit confidence in the scheme—so splendidly begun—if we carry it out with a steadfast energy. I have a strong conviction that we hold in our hands the peace and honour of men of letters for centuries to come, and that you are destined to be their best and most enduring benefactor. . . . Oh what a procession of new years may walk out of all this for the class we belong to, after we are dust."

These views about patronage did not make him more indulgent to the clamour with which it is so often invoked for the ridiculously small. "You read that life of Clare?" he wrote (15 August, 1865). "Did you ever see such preposterous exaggeration of small claims? And isn't it expressive, the perpetual prating of him in the book as *the Poet*? So another Incompetent used to write to the Literary Fund when I was on the committee: 'This leaves the Poet at his divine mission in a corner of the single room. The Poet's father is wiping his spectacles. The Poet's mother is weaving.'—Yah!" . . .

Of his ordinary habits of activity I have spoken, and they were doubtless carried too far. In youth it was all well, but he did not make allowance for years. This has had abundant illustration, but will admit of a few words more. To all men who do much, rule and order are essential; method in everything was Dickens's peculiarity;

and between breakfast and luncheon, with rare exceptions, was his time of work. But his daily walks were less of rule than of enjoyment and necessity. In the midst of his writings they were indispensable, and especially, as it has often been shown, at night. Mr. Sala is an authority on London streets, and, in the eloquent and generous tribute he was among the first to offer to his memory, has described himself encountering Dickens in the oddest places and most inclement weather, in Ratcliffe Highway, on Haverstock Hill, on Camberwell Green, in Gray's Inn Lane, in the Wandsworth Road, at Hammersmith Broadway, in Norton Folgate, and at Kensal New Town. "A hansom whirled you by the Bell and Horns at Brompton, and there he was striding, as with seven-league boots, seemingly in the direction of North End, Fulham. The Metropolitan Railway sent you forth at Lisson Grove, and you met him plodding speedily towards the Yorkshire Stingo. He was to be met rapidly skirting the grim brick wall of the prison in Coldbath Fields, or trudging along the Seven Sisters Road at Holloway, or bearing, under a steady press of sail, underneath Highgate Archway, or pursuing the even tenor of his way up the Vauxhall Bridge Road." But he was equally at home in the intricate byways of narrow streets as in the lengthy thoroughfares. Wherever there was "matter to be heard and learned," in back streets behind Holborn, in Borough courts and passages, in City wharfs or alleys, about the poorer lodging-houses, in prisons, workhouses, ragged-schools, police-courts, rag-shops, chandlers' shops, and all sorts of markets for the poor he carried his keen observation and untiring study. . .

Agreeable pleasantries might be cited from his letters. "An old priest" (he wrote from France in 1862), "the express image of Frédéric Lemaître got up for the part, and very cross with the toothache, told me in a railway carriage the other day, that we had no antiquities in heretical England. 'None at all,' I said. 'You have some ships, however?' 'Yes; a few.' 'Are they strong?' 'Well,' said I, 'your trade is spiritual, my father: ask the ghost of Nelson.' A French captain who was in the carriage was immensely delighted with this small joke. I met him at Calais yesterday going somewhere with a detachment; and he said—Pardon! But he had been so limited as to suppose an Englishman incapable of that bonhommie!" In humouring a joke he was excellent, both in letters and talk; and for this kind of enjoyment his least important little notes are often worth preserving. Take one small instance. So freely had he admired a tale told by his friend and solicitor Mr. Frederic Ouvry, that he had to reply to a humorous proposal for publication of it, in his own manner, in his own periodical. "Your modesty is equal to your merit. . . . I think your way of describing that rustic courtship in middle life, quite matchless. . . . A cheque for £1000 is lying with the publisher. We would willingly make it more, but that we find our law charges so exceedingly heavy." His letters have also examples now and then of what he called his conversational triumphs. "I have distinguished myself"

(28 April, 1861) "in two respects lately. I took a young lady, unknown, down to dinner, and, talking to her about the Bishop of Durham's Nepotism in the matter of Mr. Cheese, I found she was Mrs. Cheese. And I expatiated to the member for Marylebone, Lord Fermoy, generally conceiving him to be an Irish member, on the contemptible character of the Marylebone constituency and Marylebone representation." . . .

# BOOK ELEVENTH

## THE CLOSE

### 1870. ÆT. 58

# I

1869–70

THE summer and autumn of 1869 were passed quietly at Gadshill.
He received there, in June, the American friends to whom he had
been most indebted for unwearying domestic kindness at his most
trying time in the States. In August, he was at the dinner of the International boat race; and, in a speech that might have gone far to reconcile the victors to changing places with the vanquished, gave the
healths of the Harvard and the Oxford crews. He went to Birmingham,
in September, to fulfil a promise that he would open the session of the
Institute; and there, after telling his audience that his invention, such
as it was, never would have served him as it had done, but for the
habit of commonplace, patient, drudging attention, he declared his
political creed to be infinitesimal faith in the people governing and
illimitable faith in the People governed. In such engagements as these,
with nothing of the kind of strain he had most to dread, there was
hardly more movement or change than was necessary to his enjoyment of rest.

He had been able to show Mr. Fields something of the interest of
London as well as of his Kentish home. He went over its General Post
Office with him, took him among its cheap theatres and poor lodging-
houses, and piloted him by night through its most notorious thieves'
quarter. Its localities that are pleasantest to a lover of books, such as
Johnson's Bolt Court and Goldsmith's Temple Chambers, he explored
with him; and, at his visitor's special request, mounted a staircase he
had not ascended for more than thirty years, to show the chamber
in Furnival's Inn where the first page of *Pickwick* was written. One
more book, unfinished, was to close what that famous book began;
and the original of the scene of its opening chapter, the opium-eater's
den, was the last place visited. "In a miserable court at night," says
Mr. Fields, "we found a haggard old woman blowing at a kind of pipe
made of an old ink-bottle; and the words that Dickens puts into the
mouth of this wretched creature in *Edwin Drood*, we heard her croon
as we leaned over the tattered bed in which she was lying." . . .

He finished his first number of *Edwin Drood* in the third week of
October, and on the 26th read it at my house with great spirit. A few
nights before we had seen together at the Olympic a little drama
taken from his *Copperfield*, which he sat out with more than patience,
even with something of enjoyment; and another pleasure was given

him that night by its author, Mr. Halliday, who brought into the box another dramatist, Mr. Robertson, to whom Dickens, who then first saw him, said that to himself the charm of his little comedies was "their unassuming form," which had so happily shown that "real wit could afford to put off any airs of pretension to it." He was at Gadshill till the close of the year; coming up for a few special occasions, such as Procter's eighty-second birthday; and at my house on New Year's Eve he read to us a fresh number of his *Edwin Drood*. Yet these very last days of December had not been without a reminder of the grave warnings of April. The pains in somewhat modified form had returned in both his left hand and his left foot a few days before we met; and they were troubling him still on that day. But he made so light of them himself; so little thought of connecting them with the uncertainties of touch and tread of which they were really part; and read with such an overflow of humour Mr. Honeythunder's boisterous philanthropy; that there was no room, then, for anything but enjoyment. His only allusion to an effect from his illness was his mention of a now invincible dislike which he had to railway travel. This had decided him to take a London house for the twelve last readings in the early months of 1870, and he had become Mr. Milner Gibson's tenant at 5 Hyde Park Place.

St. James's Hall was to be the scene of these readings, and they were to occupy the interval from 11 January to 15 March; two being given in each week to the close of January, and the remaining eight on each of the eight Tuesdays following. Nothing was said of any kind of apprehension as the time approached; but, with a curious absence of the sense of danger, there was certainly both distrust and fear. Sufficient precaution was supposed to have been taken by arrangement for the presence, at each reading, of his friend and medical attendant, Mr. F. C. Beard; but this resolved itself, not into any measure of safety, the case admitting of none short of stopping the reading altogether, but simply into ascertainment of the exact amount of strain and pressure, which, with every fresh exertion, he was placing on those vessels of the brain where the Preston trouble too surely had revealed that danger lay. No supposed force in reserve, no dominant strength of will, can turn aside the penalties sternly exacted for disregard of such laws of life as were here plainly overlooked; and though no one may say that it was not already too late for any but the fatal issue, there will be no presumption in believing that life might yet have been for some time prolonged if these readings could have been stopped.

"I am a little shaken," he wrote on 9 January, "by my journey to Birmingham to give away the Institution's prizes on Twelfth Night, but I am in good heart; and, notwithstanding Lowe's worrying scheme for collecting a year's taxes in a lump, which they tell me is damaging books, pictures, music, and theatres beyond precedent, our 'let' at St. James's Hall is enormous." He opened with *Copperfield* and the *Pickwick Trial*; and I may briefly mention, from the notes taken by

Mr. Beard and placed at my disposal, at what cost of exertion to himself he gratified the crowded audiences that then and to the close made these evenings memorable. His ordinary pulse on the first night was at 72; but never on any subsequent night was lower than 82, and had risen on the later nights to more than 100. After *Copperfield* on the first night it went up to 96, and after *Marigold* on the second to 99; but on the first night of the *Sikes and Nancy* scenes (Friday, 21 January) it went from 80 to 112, and on the second night (1 February) to 118. From this, through the six remaining nights, it never was lower than 110 after the first piece read; and after the third and fourth readings of the *Oliver Twist* scenes it rose, from 90 to 124 on 15 February, and from 94 to 120 on 8 March; on the former occasion, after twenty minutes' rest, falling to 98, and on the latter, after fifteen minutes' rest, falling to 82. His ordinary pulse on entering the room, during these last six nights, was more than once over 100, and never lower than 84; from which it rose, after *Nickleby* on 22 February, to 112. On 8 February, when he read *Dombey*, it had risen from 91 to 114; on 1 March, after *Copperfield*, it rose from 100 to 124; and when he entered the room on the last night it was at 108, having risen only two beats more when the reading was done. The pieces on this occasion were the *Christmas Carol*, followed by the *Pickwick Trial*; and probably in all his life he never read so well. On his return from the States, where he had to address his effects to audiences composed of immense numbers of people, a certain loss of refinement had been observable; but the old delicacy was now again delightfully manifest and a subdued tone, as well in the humorous as the serious portions, gave something to all the reading as of a quiet sadness of farewell. The charm of this was at its height when he shut the volume of *Pickwick* and spoke in his own person. He said that for fifteen years he had been reading his own books to audiences whose sensitive and kindly recognition of them had given him instruction and enjoyment in his art such as few men could have had; but that he nevertheless thought it well now to retire upon older associations, and in future to devote himself exclusively to the calling which had first made him known. "In but two short weeks from this time I hope that you may enter, in your own homes, on a new series of readings at which my assistance will be indispensable; but from these garish lights I vanish now for evermore, with a heartfelt, grateful, respectful, affectionate farewell." The brief hush of silence as he moved from the platform; and the prolonged tumult of sound that followed suddenly, stayed him, and again for another moment brought him back; will not be forgotten by any present.

Little remains to be told that has not in it almost unmixed pain and sorrow. Hardly a day passed, while the readings went on or after they closed, unvisited by some effect or other of the disastrous excitement shown by the notes of Mr. Beard. On 23 January, when for the last time he met Carlyle, he came to us with his left hand in a sling; on 7 February, when he passed with us his last birthday, and on the

25th, when he read the third number of his novel, the hand was still swollen and painful; and on 21 March, when he read admirably his fourth number, he told us that as he came along, walking up the length of Oxford Street, the same incident had recurred as on the day of a former dinner with us, and he had not been able to read, all the way, more than the right-hand half of the names over the shops. Yet he had the old fixed persuasion that this was rather the effect of a medicine he had been taking than of any grave cause, and he still strongly believed his other troubles to be exclusively local. Eight days later he wrote: "My uneasiness and hemorrhage, after having quite left me, as I supposed, has come back with an aggravated irritability that it has not yet displayed. You have no idea what a state I am in to-day from a sudden violent rush of it; and yet it has not the slightest effect on my general health that I know of." This was a disorder which troubled him in his earlier life; and during the last five years, in his intervals of suffering from other causes, it had from time to time taken aggravated form.

His last public appearances were in April. On the 5th he took the chair for the newsvendors, whom he helped with a genial address in which even his apology for little speaking overflowed with irrepressible humour. He would try, he said, like Falstaff, "but with a modification almost as large as himself," less to speak himself than to be the cause of speaking in others. "Much in this manner they exhibit at the door of a snuff-shop the effigy of a Highlander with an empty mull in his hand, who, apparently having taken all the snuff he can carry, and discharged all the sneezes of which he is capable, politely invites his friends and patrons to step in and try what they can do in the same line." On the 30th of the same month he returned thanks for "Literature" at the Royal Academy dinner. . . .

We met for the last time on Sunday, 22 May, when I dined with him in Hyde Park Place. The death of Mr. Lemon, of which he heard that day, had led his thoughts to the crowd of friendly companions in letters and art who had so fallen from the ranks since we played Ben Jonson together that we were left almost alone. "And none beyond his sixtieth year," he said, "very few even fifty." It is no good to talk of it, I suggested. "We shall not think of it the less," was his reply; and an illustration much to the point was before us, afforded by an incident deserving remembrance in this story. Not many weeks before, a correspondent had written to him from Liverpool describing himself as a self-raised man, attributing his prosperous career to what Dickens's writings had taught him at its outset of the wisdom of kindness, and sympathy for others; and asking pardon for the liberty he took in hoping that he might be permitted to offer some acknowledgment of what not only had cheered and stimulated him through all his life, but had contributed so much to the success of it. The letter enclosed £500. Dickens was greatly touched by this; and told the writer, in sending back his cheque, that he would certainly have taken it if he had not been, though not a man of fortune, a prosperous man himself; but that the letter, and the spirit of its offer, had so gratified him, that if the writer pleased to send him any small memorial of it in another form he would gladly receive it. The memorial soon came. A richly worked basket of silver, inscribed "from one who has been cheered and stimulated by Mr. Dickens's writings, and held the author among his first remembrances when he became prosperous," was accompanied by an extremely handsome silver centrepiece for the table, of which the design was four figures representing the Seasons. But the kindly donor shrank from sending Winter to one whom he would fain connect with none save the brighter and milder days, and he had struck the fourth figure from the design. "I never look at it," said Dickens, "that I don't think most of the Winter." The gift had yet too surely foreshadowed the truth, for the winter was never to come to him.

A matter discussed that day with Mr. Ouvry was briefly resumed in a note of 29 May, the last I ever received from him; which followed me to Exeter, and closed thus. "You and I can speak of it at Gads by and by. Foot no worse. But no better." The old trouble was upon him when we parted, and this must have been nearly the last note written before he quitted London. He was at Gadshill on 30 May; and I heard no more until the telegram reached me at Launceston on the night of 9 June, which told me that the "by and by" was not to come in this world.

The few days at Gadshill had been given wholly to work on his novel. He had been easier in his foot and hand; and though he was suffering severely from the local hemorrhage before named, he made no complaint of illness. But there was observed in him a very unusual appearance of fatigue. "He seemed very weary." He was out with his dogs for the last time on Monday, 6 June, when he walked with his letters into Rochester. On Tuesday the 7th, after his daughter Mary had left on a visit to her sister Kate, not finding himself equal to much fatigue, he drove to Cobham Wood with his sister-in-law, there dismissed the carriage, and walked round the park and back. He returned in time to put up in his new conservatory some Chinese lanterns sent from London that afternoon; and the whole of the evening, he sat with Miss Hogarth in the dining-room that he might see their effect when lighted. More than once he then expressed his satisfaction at having finally abandoned all intention of exchanging Gadshill for London; and this he had done more impressively some days before. While he lived, he said, he should wish his name to be more and more associated with the place; and he had a notion that when he died he should like to lie in the little graveyard belonging to the Cathedral at the foot of the Castle wall.

On 8 June he passed all the day writing in the Chalet. He came over for luncheon; and, much against his usual custom, returned to his desk. In the sentences he was then writing, he imagines such a brilliant morning as had risen with that 8 June shining on the old city of Rochester. He sees in surpassing beauty, with the lusty ivy gleaming in the sun, and the rich trees waving in the balmy air, its antiquities and its ruins; its Cathedral and Castle. But his fancy, then, is not with the stern dead forms of either; but with that which makes warm the cold stone tombs of centuries, and lights them up with flecks of brightness, "fluttering there like wings." To him, on that sunny summer morning, the changes of glorious light from moving boughs, the songs of birds, the scents from garden, woods, and fields, have penetrated into the Cathedral, have subdued its earthy odour, and are preaching the Resurrection and the Life.

He was late in leaving the Chalet; but before dinner, which was ordered at six o'clock with the intention of walking afterwards in the lanes, he wrote some letters, among them one to his friend Mr. Charles Kent appointing to see him in London next day; and dinner was begun before Miss Hogarth saw, with alarm, a singular expression of trouble and pain in his face. "For an hour," he then told her, "he had been very ill"; but he wished dinner to go on. These were the only really coherent words uttered by him. They were followed by some, that fell from him disconnectedly, of quite other matters; of an approaching sale at a neighbour's house, of whether Macready's son was with his father at Cheltenham, and of his own intention to go immediately to London; but at these latter he had risen, and his sister-in-law's help alone prevented him from falling where he stood. Her effort was then to get him on the sofa, but after a slight struggle he sank heavily on his left side. "On the ground" were the last words he spoke. It was now a little over ten minutes past six o'clock. His two daughters came that night with Mr. F. Beard, who had also been telegraphed for, and whom they met at the station. His eldest son arrived early next morning, and was joined in the evening (too late) by his younger son from Cambridge. All possible medical aid had been summoned. The surgeon of the neighbourhood was there from the first, and a physician from London was in attendance as well as Mr. Beard. But human help was unavailing. There was effusion on the brain; and though stertorous breathing continued all night, and until ten minutes past six o'clock on the evening of Thursday, 9 June, there had never been a gleam of hope during the twenty-four hours. He had lived four months beyond his 58th year.

## II

### 1870

THE excitement and sorrow at his death are within the memory of all. Before the news of it even reached the remoter parts of England, it had been flashed across Europe; was known in the distant continents of India, Australia, and America; and not in English-speaking communities only, but in every country of the civilised earth, had awakened grief and sympathy. In his own land it was as if a personal bereavement had befallen everyone. Her Majesty the Queen telegraphed from Balmoral "her deepest regret at the sad news of Charles Dickens's death"; and this was the sentiment alike of all classes of her people. There was not an English journal that did not give it touching and noble utterance; and *The Times* took the lead in suggesting that the only fit resting-place for the remains of a man so dear to England was the Abbey in which the most illustrious Englishmen are laid.

With the expression thus given to a general wish, the Dean of Westminster lost no time in showing ready compliance; and on the morning of the day when it appeared was in communication with the family and the executors. The public homage of a burial in the Abbey had to be reconciled with his own instructions to be privately buried without previous announcement of time or place, and without monument or memorial. He would himself have preferred to lie in the small graveyard under Rochester Castle wall, or in the little churches of Cobham or Shorne; but all these were found to be closed; and the desire of the Dean and Chapter of Rochester to lay him in their Cathedral had been entertained, when the Dean of Westminster's request, and the considerate kindness of his generous assurance that there should be only such ceremonial as would strictly obey all injunctions of privacy, made it a grateful duty to accept that offer. The spot already had been chosen by the Dean; and before midday on the following morning, Tuesday, 14 June, with knowledge of those only who took part in the burial, all was done. The solemnity had not lost by the simplicity. Nothing so grand or so touching could have accompanied it, as the stillness and the silence of the vast cathedral. Then, later in the day and all the following day, came unbidden mourners in such crowds, that the Dean had to request permission to keep open the grave until Thursday; but after it was closed they did not cease to come, and "all day long," Doctor Stanley wrote on the 17th, "there was a constant pressure to the spot, and many flowers were strewn upon it by unknown hands, many tears shed from unknown eyes." He alluded to this in the impressive funeral discourse delivered by him in the Abbey on the morning of Sunday the 19th, pointing to the fresh flowers that then had been newly thrown (as they still are thrown, in this fourth year after the death), and saying that "the spot would thenceforward be a sacred one with both the New World and the Old, as that of the representative of the literature, not of this island only, but of all who speak our English tongue." The stone placed upon it is inscribed

CHARLES DICKENS

BORN FEBRUARY THE SEVENTH, 1812

DIED JUNE THE NINTH, 1870

The highest associations of both the arts he loved surround him where he lies. Next to him is RICHARD CUMBERLAND. Mrs. PRITCHARD's monument looks down upon him, and immediately behind is DAVID GARRICK's. Nor is the actor's delightful art more worthily represented than the nobler genius of the author. Facing the grave, and on its left and right, are the monuments of CHAUCER, SHAKESPEARE, and DRYDEN, the three immortals who did most to create and settle the language to which CHARLES DICKENS has given another undying name.

# APPENDIX

## THE WILL OF CHARLES DICKENS

"I, CHARLES DICKENS, of Gadshill Place, Higham in the county of Kent, hereby revoke all my former Wills and Codicils and declare this to be my last Will and Testament. I give the sum of £1000 free of legacy duty to Miss Ellen Lawless Ternan, late of Houghton Place, Ampthill Square, in the county of Middlesex. I GIVE the sum of £19 19 0 to my faithful servant Mrs. Anne Cornelius. I GIVE the sum of £19 19 0 to the daughter and only child of the said Mrs. Anne Cornelius. I GIVE the sum of £19 19 0 to each and every domestic servant, male and female, who shall be in my employment at the time of my decease, and shall have been in my employment for a not less period of time than one year. I GIVE the sum of £1000 free of legacy duty to my daughter Mary Dickens. I also give to my said daughter an annuity of £300 a year, during her life, if she shall so long continue unmarried; such annuity to be considered as accruing from day to day, but to be payable half-yearly, the first of such half-yearly payments to be made at the expiration of six months next after my decease. If my said daughter Mary shall marry, such annuity shall cease; and in that case, but in that case only, my said daughter shall share with my other children in the provision hereinafter made for them. I GIVE to my dear sister-in-law Georgina Hogarth the sum of £8000 free of legacy duty. I also give to the said Georgina Hogarth all my personal jewellery not hereinafter mentioned, and all the little familiar objects from my writing-table and my room, and she will know what to do with those things. I ALSO GIVE to the said Georgina Hogarth all my private papers whatsoever and wheresoever, and I leave her my grateful blessing as the best and truest friend man ever had. I GIVE to my eldest son Charles my library of printed books, and my engravings and prints; and I also give to my son Charles the silver salver presented to me at Birmingham, and the silver cup presented to me at Edinburgh, and my shirt studs, shirt pins, and sleeve buttons. AND I BEQUEATH unto my said son Charles and my son Henry Fielding Dickens, the sum of £8000 upon trust to invest the same, and from time to time to vary the investments thereof, and to pay the annual income thereof to my wife during her life, and after her decease the said sum of £8000 and the investments thereof shall be in trust for my children (but subject as to my daughter Mary to the proviso hereinbefore contained) who being a son or sons shall have attained or shall attain the age of twenty-one years, or being a daughter or daughters shall have attained or shall attain that age

669

or be previously married, in equal shares if more than one. I GIVE my watch (the gold repeater presented to me at Coventry), and I give the chains and seals and all appendages I have worn with it, to my dear and trusty friend John Forster, of Palace Gate House, Kensington, in the county of Middlesex aforesaid; and I also give to the said John Forster such manuscripts of my published works as may be in my possession at the time of my decease. AND I DEVISE AND BEQUEATH all my real and personal estate (except such as is vested in me as a trustee or mortgagee) unto the said Georgina Hogarth and the said John Forster, their heirs, executors, administrators, and assigns respectively, upon trust that they the said Georgina Hogarth and John Forster, or the survivor of them or the executors or administrators of such survivor, do and shall, at their, his, or her uncontrolled and irresponsible direction, either proceed to an immediate sale or conversion into money of the said real and personal estate (including my copyrights), or defer and postpone any sale or conversion into money, till such time or times as they, he, or she shall think fit, and in the meantime may manage and let the said real and personal estate (including my copyrights), in such manner in all respects as I myself could do, if I were living and acting therein; it being my intention that the trustees or trustee for the time being of this my Will shall have the fullest power over the said real and personal estate which I can give to them, him, or her. AND I DECLARE that, until the said real and personal estate shall be sold and converted into money, the rents and annual income thereof respectively shall be paid and applied to the person or persons in the manner and for the purposes to whom and for which the annual income of the monies to arise from the sale or conversion thereof into money would be payable or applicable under this my Will in case the same were sold or converted into money. AND I DECLARE that my real estate shall for the purposes of this my Will be considered as converted into personalty upon my decease. AND I DECLARE that the said trustees or trustee for the time being, do and shall, with and out of the monies which shall come to their, his, or her hands, under or by virtue of this my Will and the trusts thereof pay my just debts, funeral and testamentary expenses, and legacies. AND I DECLARE that the said trust funds or so much thereof as shall remain after answering the purposes aforesaid, and the annual income thereof, shall be in trust for all my children (but subject as to my daughter Mary to the proviso hereinbefore contained), who being a son or sons shall have attained or shall attain the age of twenty-one years, and being a daughter or daughters shall have attained or shall attain that age or be previously married, in equal shares if more than one. PROVIDED ALWAYS, that, as regards my copyrights and the produce and profits thereof, my said daughter Mary, notwithstanding the proviso hereinbefore contained with reference to her, shall share with my other children therein whether she be married or not. AND I DEVISE the estates vested in me at my decease as a trustee or mortgagee unto the use of the said Georgina

Hogarth and John Forster, their heirs and assigns, upon the trusts and subject to the equities affecting the same respectively. AND I APPOINT the said GEORGINA HOGARTH and JOHN FORSTER executrix and executor of this my Will, and GUARDIANS of the persons of my children during their respective minorities. AND LASTLY, as I have now set down the form of words which my legal advisers assure me are necessary to the plain objects of this my Will, I solemnly enjoin my dear children always to remember how much they owe to the said Georgina Hogarth, and never to be wanting in a grateful and affectionate attachment to her, for they know well that she has been, through all the stages of their growth and progress, their ever useful self-denying and devoted friend. AND I DESIRE here simply to record the fact that my wife, since our separation by consent, has been in the receipt from me of an annual income of £600, while all the great charges of a numerous and expensive family have devolved wholly upon myself. I emphatically direct that I be buried in an inexpensive, unostentatious, and strictly private manner; that no public announcement be made of the time or place of my burial; that at the utmost not more than three plain mourning coaches be employed; and that those who attend my funeral wear no scarf, cloak, black bow, long hat-band, or other such revolting absurdity. I DIRECT that my name be inscribed in plain English letters on my tomb, without the addition of 'Mr.' or 'Esquire.' I conjure my friends on no account to make me the subject of any monument, memorial, or testimonial whatever. I rest my claims to the remembrance of my country upon my published works, and to the remembrance of my friends upon their experience of me in addition thereto. I commit my soul to the mercy of God through our Lord and Saviour Jesus Christ, and I exhort my dear children humbly to try to guide themselves by the teaching of the New Testament in its broad spirit, and to put no faith in any man's narrow construction of its letter here or there. IN WITNESS whereof I the said Charles Dickens, the testator, have to this my last Will and Testament set my hand this 12th day of May in the year of our Lord 1869.

"CHARLES DICKENS.

"Signed published and declared by the above-named Charles Dickens the testator as and for his last Will and Testament in the presence of us (present together at the same time) who in his presence at his request and in the presence of each other have hereunto subscribed our names as witnesses.

"G. HOLSWORTH,
"26 Wellington Street, Strand.

"HENRY WALKER,
"26 Wellington Street, Strand.

"I, CHARLES DICKENS of Gadshill Place near Rochester in the county of Kent Esquire declare this to be a Codicil to my last Will and Testament which Will bears date the 12th day of May 1869. I GIVE to my son Charles Dickens the younger all my share and interest in the weekly journal called *All the Year Round*, which is now conducted under Articles of Partnership made between me and William Henry Wills and the said Charles Dickens the younger, and all my share and interest in the stereotypes stock and other effects belonging to the said partnership, he defraying my share of all debts and liabilities of the said partnership which may be outstanding at the time of my decease, and in all other respects I confirm my said Will. IN WITNESS whereof I have hereunto set my hand the 2nd day of June in the year of our Lord 1870.

"CHARLES DICKENS.

"Signed and declared by the said CHARLES DICKENS, the testator as and for a Codicil to his Will in the presence of us present at the same time who at his request in his presence and in the presence of each other hereunto subscribe our names as witnesses.

"G. HOLSWORTH,
"26 Wellington Street, Strand.

"H. WALKER,
"26 Wellington Street, Strand."

The real and personal estate—taking the property bequeathed by the last codicil at a valuation of something less than two years' purchase; and of course before payment of the legacies, the (inconsiderable) debts, and the testamentary and other expenses,—amounted as nearly as may be calculated, to £93,000.

*Made and Printed in Great Britain by*
*Hazell, Watson & Viney, Ltd., London and Aylesbury*